19/20

SLC

Irregular Armed Forces and Their Role in Politics and State Formation

Existing models of state formation are derived primarily from early Western European experience and are misleading when applied to those nation-states struggling to consolidate their dominion in the present period. They also oversimplify aspects of the Western European experience itself. In this volume, scholars of politics and state formation focusing on a variety of countries and time periods suggest that the early Western European model of armies' waging war on behalf of sovereign states does not hold universally. In particular, the importance of "irregular" armed forces – militias, guerrillas, paramilitaries, mercenaries, bandits, vigilantes, police, and so on – has been seriously neglected in the literature on this subject.

The case studies in this book suggest, among other things, that the creation of the nation-state as a secure political entity rests as much on "irregular" as regular armed forces. In many parts of the world, the state's legitimacy has been extraordinarily difficult to achieve, constantly eroding or under challenge by irregular armed forces within a country's borders. No account of modern state formation can be considered complete without attending to these irregular forces.

Professor Diane E. Davis is Associate Professor of Political Sociology at the Massachusetts Institute of Technology. She has been the recipient of major fellowships from groups such as the Mellon Foundation, the Ford Foundation, and the MacArthur Foundation, and she has edited the research annual *Political Power and Social Theory* for ten years. She is the author of *Urban Leviathan: Mexico City in the Twentieth Century* (1994).

Professor Anthony W. Pereira is Associate Professor in the Department of Political Science at Tulane University. His research interests include social movements, state formation, and judicial politics in Latin America. He is the author of *The End of the Peasantry: The Emergence of the Rural Labor Movement in Northeast Brazil, 1961–1988* (1997).

Irregular Armed Forces and Their Role in Politics and State Formation

Edited by

DIANE E. DAVIS
Massachusetts Institute of Technology

ANTHONY W. PEREIRA
Tulane University

CAMBRIDGE
UNIVERSITY PRESS

PUBLISHED BY THE PRESS SYNDICATE OF THE UNIVERSITY OF CAMBRIDGE
The Pitt Building, Trumpington Street, Cambridge, United Kingdom

CAMBRIDGE UNIVERSITY PRESS
The Edinburgh Building, Cambridge CB2 2RU, UK
40 West 20th Street, New York, NY 10011-4211, USA
477 Williamstown Road, Port Melbourne, VIC 3207, Australia
Ruiz de Alarcón 13, 28014 Madrid, Spain
Dock House, The Waterfront, Cape Town 8001, South Africa

http://www.cambridge.org

First published 2003

Printed in the United States of America

Typeface Sabon 10/12 pt.   *System* QuarkXPress [BTS]

A catalog record for this book is available from the British Library.

Library of Congress Cataloging in Publication data
Irregular armed forces and their role in politics and state formation / edited by Diane E.
Davis, Anthony W. Pereira.
     p. cm.
Includes bibliographical references and index.
   ISBN 0-521-81277-1
     1. Civil-military relations.   2. Armed Forces – Political activity.   3. State, The.
   I. Davis, Diane E.   II. Pereira, Anthony W.
JF195 .I77 2002
322'.5 – dc21

2002017392

ISBN   0 521 81277 1   hardback

Contents

Contributors

Achilles Batalas
New School for Social Research

Richard Franklin Bensel
Cornell University

Susan M. Browne
New School for Social Research

Alec Campbell
Colby College

Miguel Angel Centeno
Princeton University

Diane E. Davis
Massachusetts Institute of Technology

Eiko Ikegami
New School for Social Research

Laura Kalmanowiecki
Rowan University

Anthony W. Pereira
Tulane University

Anne Raffin
National University of Singapore

William Reno
Northwestern University

Mauricio Romero
Universidad Nacional de Colombia

Ian Roxborough
State University of New York at Stony Brook

Charles Tilly
Columbia University

Lizabeth Zack
Rhodes College

Irregular Armed Forces and Their Role in Politics
and State Formation

INTRODUCTION

I

Contemporary Challenges and Historical Reflections on the Study of Militaries, States, and Politics

Diane E. Davis

War-Making in the New Millennium

The post–Cold War era ushered in a new wave of optimism about an end to world wars and a possible reduction in global-scale violence. As the new millennium loomed large, heightened expectations about world peace and global political stability captured the imagination of those who scarcely a decade earlier concerned themselves primarily with war-making among superpowers and their satellites. Shifting rhetorics and rising expectations were further fueled by the so-called third wave of democracy that continued materializing in the post-1989 world. As democratization and globalization reached ever further corners of the globe, long-standing claims of political scientists that democracies do not fight each other took on greater significance. For many security analysts, new forms of regional and international economic cooperation between countries committed to a common project of liberalization also promised to reduce the likelihood of widespread global conflict.

But now, from the vantage point of a new millennium, and in a post-9/11 world, initial optimism seems muted. Few would counsel that the threat of armed conflict is on the wane, at least insofar as violence and armed coercion still continue as facts of life. Even as a tentative peace settles in among previously contending geopolitical superpowers struggling over spheres of influence, those countries and regions that lay in the interstices of this larger power structure – and whose fates not that long ago seemed overdetermined by the economic or political competition between Cold War antagonists – are beginning to implode with greater frequency. This is especially the case in countries where liberalization of the economy has proceeded more rapidly than the expansion of citizenship rights and the consolidation of newly democratic institutions. In those places with particularly vulnerable political and economic conditions, the strong arm of the state is directed inwardly as much as outwardly, as is increasingly evident

3

in Central and East Europe, Latin America, Africa, Central and East Asia, and the Middle East. In many of these locations, specialized paramilitary forces and police now replace the national military on the front lines of violent conflict, while citizens arm themselves both offensively and defensively as vigilante groups, militias, terrorists, and even mafia organizations seeking to counteract or bypass the state's claim on a monopoly of legitimate force. These developments not only suggest that further study of the origins and larger political impacts of these new patterns of armed force might take us far in explaining the potential obstacles to world peace, and even the erosion of democracy and citizenship rights in the contemporary era; they also shed light on a potential paradox that few were prepared to consider during the celebratory dawn of the initial post–Cold War euphoria: as the probability of world war diminishes, the likelihood of "internal" war and subnational violence may be increasing, at least for certain countries of the world.

What seems to have changed, in short, is not the likelihood of militarized coercion and armed conflict so much as its character and scope. In those regions of the world where violence seems most prevalent, the predominant forms of war-making and the means of coercion appear markedly different than in the immediate past; and with the terrain of experience shifting so dramatically, old theories and long-standing analytic points of entry must be called into question, even if the persistence of conflict is not. Today we see a large number of armed conflicts in which the main protagonists comprise not nationally conscripted standing armies waging war in the name of sovereign nations but states acting against their own peoples. We also see popularly constituted or clandestine armed forces who frequently act on behalf of subnational groups (often defined in terms of ethnicity, language, region, or religion) and whose claims to national sovereignty themselves are problematic. What seems to be most under contention, then, are not the interstate hegemonies or globally contested geopolitical balances of power that led to large-scale wars in previous decades, but the legitimacy, power, and reach of national states, especially as seen from the point of view of those populations contained within their own territorial jurisdictions.

The stakes and terms of these conflicts also are different than they were when nations primarily fought each other. Many of these more "irregular" armed forces – ranging in form from paramilitaries and the police to vigilantes, terrorists, and militias – derive their charge and calling from civil society; and if they do answer to the state in some fashion, it is generally not to the national executive or the military defense establishment but to locally organized law enforcement agencies (as in the case of police) or more clandestine security apparatuses (as with specialized paramilitary forces). These latter agencies may be closely articulated with the national executive and national defense ministries, to be sure. But historically, police, militias, and paramilitary personnel have operated under different organizational, political, and disciplinary dynamics than have conventional armed forces. Moreover, to the extent that many of these alternative armed forces comprise previous military personnel, especially in the context of the transition from authoritarian rule, they may carry with them traditions, techniques, and networks (not to mention arms) that still link them to national defense ministries although they are formally separate from national armed forces. As such, their relationships to the military, the state, and even civil society may differ in ways that are not well articulated in the conventional literature on armed forces.

The military as a key national institution is not about to disappear; nor in all probability will the nation-state and interstate or international conflicts, including those in which nations cooperate regionally or globally to fight against particular regimes. But developments in recent years, especially when compared to the period starting with World War I to the end of the Cold War in 1989, do suggest a fundamental transformation in what we have generally considered war-making, and in the types of coercive violence being deployed by citizens and the state.[1] To the extent that so many different forms and agents of internally directed violence now seem to proliferate, it is time to reexamine conventional views about warfare, armed force, and their larger implications. We must be prepared to consider the possibility that nation-states, in addition to losing their monopoly over the means of coercion, may also be in the position of losing the incentives, will, or means to establish universal social contracts with their own peoples, as occurred during the nineteenth and twentieth centuries when national governments conscripted citizens to fight on their behalf.[2]

Reconsidering the War-Making–State-Making Nexus

Our collective aim in this volume is to examine alternative or "irregular"[3] agents of militarized coercion and armed struggle, to consider the extent to which their activities – both in form and impact – parallel those of conventional armed forces, and to assess the theoretical and practical implications of this knowledge for the study of national politics and state formation. Among the issues that concern us here are whether the apparent pervasiveness of irregular armed force in the contemporary period necessarily entails a rethinking of the literature on war-making, especially the relationship between war-making and state-making or national political development. Should we assume that the predominance of armed veteran groups, police, militia, paramilitary, and a variety of other subnational forces in the front lines of violent coercion is really as new as it may appear, both in given countries or across the board? Or, is it just that methodological blinders and prevailing theoretical frameworks – as opposed to substantively "real" transformations – have discouraged us from examining them with a sharpened comparative and historical eye?

Scholars have been slow to tackle these questions or to examine conscientiously the relationship between irregular armed force, state-building, and national political development. For decades, the most popular theoretical guides to war-making and state-making among political scientists, sociologists, and historians analyzed the relationship between standing armies and the development of state structures and capacities, with the actions of conscripted military personnel whose role is to defend national sovereignty vis-à-vis foreign or external aggressors serving as the main empirical point of departure. Most of this literature identified the nation-state as the key unit of analysis, while conventional organizations for warfare were considered the primary mode of militarized conflict. These assumptions were evident not just in the seminal writings of historians and sociologists like Charles Tilly (1990) and Michael Mann (1988), who constructed many of their arguments about military power and state formation on the basis of propositions about militaries and states drawn from classic works by Max Weber, who himself was most interested in the rise of national states and interstate conflict during the early modern era. The failure to transcend the confines of the nation-state or to examine nonconventional military forces also held true in most of the political science literature, in which scholars crafted arguments about the relationships between militaries and national states for the purposes of supplanting larger claims about international systems of states, Cold War balances of power, and the likelihood of democracy or authoritarianism (with a leading concern in the latter studies being the extent to which the state is subject to civilian or military rule) in Africa, Latin America, and East Asia as their nations sought to modernize both politically and economically.

To be sure, despite their firm theoretical grounding in the early modern experience of mainly European nation-states, most of the originating arguments about military power and states were judged to be so powerful and compelling that they also enjoyed much contemporary regard, and were frequently utilized to explain late twentieth-century forms of political development in a variety of comparative contexts. As such, it is not that scholars have completely failed to think comparatively and historically about armed force and national politics or state formation. Writings by Charles Tilly (in *Bringing the State Back In*, 1985) and Peter Evans (*Embedded Autonomy*, 1995) are exemplary in these regards, as is recent work by Robert Bates (2001). While the former authors are well known among sociologists for developing the notion of protection rackets and focusing on predatory states that exploit their own peoples through military rule and other coercive techniques, Bates has posed new and intriguing questions about the impact of the global political economy on late-developing states' predatory relationships vis-à-vis their own populations. In the process he has raised the possibility that recent transformations in the global political economy may have fundamentally altered the long-standing connections between war-making, state-making, and the rise of democratic institutions that prevailed in the nineteenth and twentieth centuries, in no small part by reinforcing warlord-type politics in regions of the world like Africa. In these regards, he comes close to suggesting a historical convergence between the premodern and postmodern eras or, perhaps better said, between early and late developers.

Despite their application to a more contemporary period, however, and the comparative-historical advances contained in these studies, most writings on the present period still tended to use conventional armed force as their key frame of reference, looking for the ways that patterns of political and economic development might disrupt their dynamics rather than vice versa, as we do here. It is no real surprise, then, that much of the available literature on the topic does not easily transfer to the globalized, early twenty-first-century world where the nation-state is ever more called into question and where violence and armed coercion continue even in the face of democratic inroads. One of our aims here is to continue with Bates's formulation and to analyze what is similar and what is different across these comparative and historical contexts. To what extent do the models that emerged out of close examination of much earlier historical experiences hold up in new or different contexts? What modifications might be necessary to account for new patterns of internally as well as externally directed warfare and the wide range of armed forces now active in regions and nations around the world? And what are the implications of any such modifications for our theoretical and practical understanding of politics and coercive forces in both the past and the present?

To be entirely fair, a focus on nonconventional militaries organized locally, as mercenaries or other forms of paramilitary armed brigands, is not completely absent in the literature. Charles Tilly, whose own contribution in the first section of this volume sets the framework for the studies that follow, has underscored elsewhere that most of the original writings about war-making and state-making were built on the assumption that subnational coercion and the use of "irregular" armed force were necessary to the consolidation of national states in the first place. He and others have shown that the putative national states of the early modern era used irregular forces to reinforce conscription patterns, to form standing armies, to continue interstate war-making, and thus to further extend and reinforce citizenship rights, all in ways that buttressed national state institutions and capacities. But this narrative is generally reproduced in the context of conventional war-making–state-making dynamics, with a focus on the militarized conditions under which national states form, expand their institutional reach, and become legitimate, and with an analytical focus on the outcome of these processes. One consequence is that nation-states and conventional war-making organizations have remained the central subject of study in the literature, while the focus on irregular forces, generally speaking, as well as subnational domains of political organization, has dropped out of the picture unless the premodern period remains of interest. A second consequence is that scholars armed with this framework tend to gravitate toward the study of times and places most likely to parallel conditions present in the early modern era that inspired the argument in the first place. This explains the preoccupation with Western Europe and the study of interstate rivalries in this part of the globe during the period of the world wars, as well as the continued focus on those countries of the world not yet considered "modern," like Africa, Asia, and Latin America.

Our practical aim in this edited volume is to reintroduce studies of irregular or nonconventional armed forces to the literature on politics and state formation, to do so with an expanded focus that includes countries and time periods routinely ignored in this literature, and to do so with an eye to subnational as well as transnational politics and coercive actors. The collection comprises both historical and contemporary case studies as well as theoretically informed essays that examine a wide variety of experiences in which armed forces other than national militaries representing sovereign national powers in interstate conflicts are the subject of study. In presenting these cases and theorizing their implications, we stand on the shoulders of several recent authors in the fields of political science and sociology who have made significant gains in these regards already. In addition to Robert Bates, whose *Prosperity and Violence* (2001) has been noted earlier, they include Margaret Levi (1997) and Mark Osiel (1999), whose recent books have taken the field in entirely new directions by focusing on how preparation for war, either in the form of conscription or military training, establishes and sometimes transforms the social contract between the governing and the governed. We also turn for inspiration to Theda Skocpol's pioneering work, *Protecting Soldiers and Mothers* (1992), whose focus on postwar dynamics sustained a larger argument about the impact of veterans organizations and claims for veterans' pensions on the formation of the U.S. welfare state. In this edited volume we continue in the spirit of innovation embodied in these leading works, but we try to expand our framework and analytic scope even more to include a far wider set of countries, armed forces, and historical time periods in the mix. We accomplish this in four specific ways.

First, we include essays that analyze the interaction between war-making and state-making in countries where the coercive arm of the state and the activities of national militaries are internally as well as externally directed, such that agents of the state search for enemies within their own borders and/or repressively police their own populations. Second, we showcase the work of authors who focus their attention on a variety of armed personnel, including militias, paramilitaries, and police, as well as demobilized militaries, including veterans. Third, rather than focusing only on the nation-state as the principal source of coercive capacity, both regular and irregular, internally directed or not, we also examine armed forces active or convened on behalf of local states and imperial states, seeking to understand the ways that the activities of locally or globally constituted armed forces also contribute to national state formation and political developments, both domestic and international. Last, we make a deliberate effort to transcend the constraining assumptions drawn from work on authoritarian versus democratic regime types by rejecting the popular epistemological premise that irregular armed forces and internally directed coercive agents are analytically or theoretically relevant only in authoritarian countries. As such, we include studies of irregular armed forces across a variety of comparative and historical contexts, democratic or not.

Given the book's originating concern with the present period, it may seem counterintuitive to be raising questions and offering case studies that span the centuries and all parts of the globe, as we do here. The essays in this book focus on countries in Africa, Latin America, and Asia as well as France, Greece, Japan, and the United States, and they treat periods as early as the fourteenth century and as late as the newly crowned twenty-first century. Yet the selection of these widely divergent cases and sweeping time periods is purposeful and grounded in careful attention to the importance of history and method. It allows us to ask similar questions about earlier historical cases and the present, and to look for parallels or differences either in terms of the nature of the armed forces involved or the domains in which these conflicts have unfolded. Together, this methodological framing should provide the tools and materials to understand the dynamics of militarized coercion and politics in the contemporary world, even as they may also shed new practical and theoretical light on the past.

Transcending Past Assumptions

What guides do we use to recast our understanding of the relationships between militaries, state formation, and national politics as well as to establish our own comparative and historical points of entry? Perhaps the best point of departure is the literature itself, which can be evaluated for its internal logic as well as for its capacity to account for contemporary and historical developments in the world of states and wars. In addition to the classic literature on war-making and state formation by Tilly and Mann and to the newest variations on these themes in the work of Bates, Skocpol, Levi, and Osiel, noted earlier, there exists a substantial body of literature on the military, state power, and national political development formulated by political scientists, historians, and strategic defense specialists of the Cold War era that must be considered. Its authors have paid considerable attention to the ways that levels of economic development, the organizational power of the national state, and the absence of democracy can affect a country's capacity institutionally to subordinate the military to civilian rulers, and vice versa (see, e.g., Huntington 1959: esp. 80–85; Vagts 1973;

Rouquié 1987; Remmer 1989). To the extent that this literature laid much of the groundwork for contemporary knowledge of the relationship between armed forces and political development, it is worth reviewing here in order to assess what must be salvaged or discarded to make sense of the present.

Historically, this field developed around three "generations" of scholars, each attentive to pressing contemporary questions, but all preoccupied with the relationships between militaries and democracy or regime type more than state formation. The first generation of scholarship was organized in the 1960s around modernization theory. Its authors were concerned with how former colonies in Africa, Asia, and Latin America could achieve political "development," and they identified military professionalization and civilian control of the military as essential to the modern democratic project. In the 1970s, a second generation of scholars, reacting to the wave of military regimes that appeared in the late 1960s and early 1970s, replaced the optimistic teleology of modernization theory. These social scientists were divided into two camps. One camp applauded military intervention, seeing the military as a middle-class institution that could control popular "disorder" and usher in political modernization; the other condemned military intervention, attributing it to dependent capitalist development and superpower clientelism reflecting Cold War antagonisms. Most recently, a third generation, responding to the collapse or negotiated transition of many military-based authoritarian regimes, sought to explain why such political transitions occurred, and what role miltaries should play if new democracies are to be consolidated.

We find three blind spots in this literature, each of which sustains our current effort to seek a new analytic framework. The first blind spot, alluded to already, results from the use of broadly defined regime type as the central axis of comparison, a strategy that has meant that most scholars have failed to examine commonalities across political systems or differences within them. All three generations of scholars have assumed that significant differences in military actions and power are best captured in a regime-type trichotomy (democracy-authoritarianism-totalitarianism). Within this formulation, democracies are characterized by civilian control of the military, which authoritarian regimes lack (Finer 1982; Perlmutter 1982; Wolpin 1986; Maniruzzaman 1987; Lopez and Stohl 1989). In democracies, for example, the military is assumed to be institutionally subordinated to the state, and thus is neither a significant nor a threatening political actor in government and society. In authoritarian regimes, in contrast, the military often shares power with the state, which means it can politically influence state actions and oppress civil society, although perhaps not completely. In totalitarian regimes, the military is assumed to dominate the state and terrorize society in despotic ways that limit political opposition and curtail political freedom on all levels.

Armed with this framework, scholars interested in the military's role and impact on society, politics, or state power turned most of their attention to authoritarian and totalitarian regimes. Again, their studies have specified the features that distinguish these types of regimes from each other and from democracies, rather than the historically produced commonalities across them. Most important, perhaps, owing to these assumptions scholars failed to explore systematically those variations in the military's character and political capacity that occurred even within democracies, because in this regime type the "problem" of the military was assumed to be nonexistent. To be sure, some scholars have questioned both the assumption that the military's power and political influence in the state correlate strictly with regime type and the extent to which the military's role or influence in democracies is politically unproblematic. This approach is perhaps best demonstrated by recent studies on the varying forms of military power within countries now shedding authoritarianism and embracing democracy (Stepan 1988; Aguero 1992; McSherry 1992; Zaverucha 1993; Acuña and Smulovitz 1996; Pion-Berlin 1997). Nevertheless, even these newer studies are based on the assumption that once democratization is formally on the political agenda, formerly authoritarian countries will institutionalize an effective separation of military and state power, and thus the "military question" is no longer problematic. It is presumed that once such a separation is implemented, discussion of political stability or democratic consolidation can move on to other concerns.

A closer look at the evidence, however, as well as the articles presented in this book, suggests that it is important to examine the historically constituted differences in the nature of the military or other armed forces and their popular legitimacy among similar regime types, even and especially within democracies. Much is lost in the study of both new and old democracies, for example, if we fail to recognize that countries may have had similar or dissimilar histories of military autonomy and development, and that these historical patterns have had important impacts on the institutional and ideological contours of democratic states and their national politics. In this volume, this point is made in Susan Browne's examination of the postcolonial United States, Richard Bensel's discussion of the post–Civil War era, and Lizabeth Zack's discussion of the Third Republic in France. All three articles underscore that even in old democracies like France and the United States what we call militarized forces – ranging from militias to veterans to police – possess varying degrees of popular legitimacy and, as such, have differentially affected internal political developments.

A second assumption in the existing literature on the military and politics is that the military is a relatively centralized and homogeneous national institution established in the service of the national state (Huntington 1962; Finer 1982; Perlmutter 1982; Clapham and Philip 1985; Maniruzziman 1987; Im 1987). In contrast, we argue the importance of seeing military forces as networks of persons in different institutional and regional loci, which furthermore can be crosscut by transnational, ethnic, linguistic, religious, and other local or individual pressures. To be sure, we are not the first to identify heterogeneity within the military. Yet most studies of divisions within the military have generally been limited to political ideology, as in discussions of hard-liners and soft-liners, anticommunists, nationalists, and so on (see, e.g., Loveman and Davies 1978; Handelman and Sanders 1981; Potash and Lewis 1983; Stepan 1988). Obviously there are exceptions, for example, in studies of tribal conflict within African militaries (Luckman 1971) and in those which examine the impact of transnational relations on domestic militaries (Powell 1965; Fitch 1979; Petras 1987; Tilly 1990). Still, even in these writings national borders are taken as fixed and the potential problem of disintegration of either national states or their militaries has not been well theorized, perhaps because it has happened only rarely until recently.

As some of the cases presented in this book demonstrate, however, there may be internal divisions within militaries. In Bensel's discussion of the post–Civil War era in the United States, internal divisions were based on regional allegiance. They may also be based on consciously formulated distinctions between formal and "irregular" armies, as Achilles Batalas shows in his study of Greece. There may even be divisions in terms of the jurisdictional levels on which military personnel are formally organized or substantively active (i.e., the city or the region or the subnational state versus the nation). All of these can both result from and influence long-term patterns of national politics and state formation. The latter point is made especially clear in Laura Kalmanowiecki's discussion of the military-police nexus in Argentina, and the ways the expansion of relatively repressive police forces across Argentine national territory results from an articulation with the national military and the federal government, a dynamic that in turn helped sustain military rule in the nation as a whole.

Just as it is necessary to look at intranational overlaps and distinctions in the military and between the military and other coercive forces like the police or militias, it is also important to examine the military as an institution comprising individuals whose routine practices and social relations can transcend state borders even when not engaged in active war-making. William Reno's discussion of warlords in Africa and their capacities to sustain state power violently rests on an understanding of the cross-border relations they establish with other warlord and tribal constituencies as much as the alliances they establish with forces contained within their own formal territorial boundaries. In a similar vein, Anne Raffin's discussion of the transnational linkages between military-led youth activities in France and Indochina also shows that common military practices joined youth populations together even across national borders and in ways that buttressed colonial power in the short-term even as they sustained anticolonial practices in the long-term. Her study is particularly compelling because it also shows how certain military practices were used to transcend key ethnic and linguistic differences even within Indochina, a finding that stands in stark contrast to the conventional way of analyzing ethnicity and militarization, in which militarized action or armed forces are invoked in the service of protecting or preserving ethnic difference.

The third limitation in most of the existing literature on militaries, states, and politics stems from the widely accepted notion that the military is first and foremost an elite-led institution, the main raison d'être of which is to guarantee *external* security and whose character and contours are the product of elite bargaining at the national political level. Yet the military's power and activities as well as its impact on politics are not merely products of elite negotiations and bargains, nor are they solely associated with the active war projects of the national armed forces convened for the purpose of fighting external wars. Indeed, the Mexican government's decision to use the military for civilian policing in its capital city and the Colombian government's announcement that it would "subcontract" units of its armed forces to private oil companies seeking protection for their property both suggest that militaries can be transformed within their statutory roles and in articulation with civil society in ways that most earlier studies have not considered. It is important to challenge the elite-centrism of studies of the military and politics, however, not just because it blinds us to the wide range of activities in which military personnel can be involved, but also because it fuels the tendency for most scholars to focus on the national armed forces, their high-ranking officers, and their centralized and elite-led infrastructure (chain of command, defense ministries, military academies). One unfortunate by-product is that scholars often fail to examine the ways in which the military rank and file may articulate (or not) with the rest of civil society rather than the military leadership. This possibility is further raised in Susan Browne's discussion of Shays's rebels, who as veterans forged common ties with other family farmers that often distanced them from the military leadership. It also plays a role in Ian Roxborough's study of the contemporary U.S. military rank and file, whose estrangement from the rest of civil society is suggested to have an impact on both the strategies of the military leadership and their potential impact on national politics.

An equally distorting by-product of the elite-centered emphasis on a centralized military leadership answerable to national defense ministries is that scholars rarely examine the wide variety of diverse social and political and even economic institutions in which military personnel or other "armed forces" play a part. These include intelligence agencies, militia, paramilitary forces, police, and even veterans associations; and they often entail an understanding of the ways that these forces contribute to the development of welfare-state programs and policies, a point introduced by both Alec Campbell in his comparative-historical study of veterans and Eiko Ikegami in her examination of the Japanese military's role in the transformation of proprietary relationships and the state-market nexus. In order to understand the role and larger significance of armed forces, then, "unpacking" the military as an institution is absolutely necessary. In this book we do so by examining a broad range of professional activities and institutions – including police, militias, and paramilitaries – that have come to articulate with or be dominated by the military and military personnel. As we shift our focus beyond regime type, the military elite, and the major military institutions, and examine conditions internal as much as external to the nation-state, we are able to identify several social, cultural, and economic articulations that affect positively or negatively the likelihood that the military or other equally significant armed forces will be actively involved in politics, even as they influence the form and character of the state as well as vice versa. Among the factors that have been particularly significant in the essays in this volume are: the extent of popularity (or distrust) of certain military personnel and institutions, perceptions that are often historically constructed, sometimes imposed by defeat or victory in war; the ways that military personnel are (or are not) integrated into the economy, party politics, and social relations, both before and after formal demilitarization or demobilization; and the ways in which military personnel articulate (or not) with other "armed forces," mainly paramilitaries, militias, and police, often to the point of competing to control the means of violence, often in ways that threaten the viability if not the legitimacy of the national state.

Notes on Terminology

In a book that seeks to move beyond the constraining grammar of regime type and analyze the relationship between armed forces and state formation and political developments more broadly understood, a few words about definitions and an explanation of terminology are in order before moving on to the contents of the volume. After all, in many ways there is great elective affinity between all three of the terms we use as we assess the relationship between armed forces and politics: regime type, state forms, political development. In fact, regime type is considered by many to represent a particular state form, and both state form and regime type can tell us much about long-*durée* patterns of political development. Rather than laying out an overly formalized or rigid definition of these terms a priori, however, it is preferable to elucidate what is at stake in emphasizing one set of terms over another, and to do so by sharing the historical and analytic logic behind this book's emphasis on state formation and political development rather than regime type.

Much of the originating concern with regime type in the fields of political science and sociology owes its origins to discussions about the social construction of political systems that dominated these two academic disciplines in the immediate post–World War II period in the modern West, before the preoccupation with the late industrializing, so-called Third World captured attention. Starting in the 1950s, social and political theorists as diverse as Hannah Arendt (1948), Seymour Martin Lipset (1959), and Barrington Moore (1966) were all concerned with democracies and dictatorships, be they communist or fascist. Although they may have disagreed about the origins of these different political regime types, or even the key features that distinguished them from each other, most shared the idea that political systems could be understood in terms of democratic versus nondemocratic ideologies and institutions (i.e., guaranteeing private property rights and forms of political participation in the case of democracies). The popularity of modernization theory reinforced the disciplinary preoccupation with democracies and the conditions that made them more likely, although the emphasis shifted as much to individual characteristics and levels of income as to the stability of political institutions and the coercive power of states as prefiguring the democratic option over others.

All this began to change in the 1970s, however, in part because of Theda Skocpol. Her *States and Social Revolutions* (1979) was conceived in part as a theoretical and methodological repudiation of Barrington Moore's *Social Origins of Dictatorship and Democracy* (1966); and she not only challenged his emphasis on class relations as opposed to state actions and geopolitical military relations, but also his efforts to methodologically distinguish among regime types in political terms. For Skocpol, what was most interesting was not that France, Russia, and China may have taken different political routes to the modern world (i.e., democratic versus communist), as Moore contended, but that out of each ideologically distinct revolution came relatively common state structures – that is, similar patterns of state formation. And with Skocpol's critique, analysis of state formation and the common organizational and institutional features of modern states began to preoccupy scholars as much as regime type. Concurrent work by Charles Tilly on European state formation (1975; 1990) reinforced this trend and the growing concern with explaining how and why the modern state emerged in the centralized form and character that it did, such that even now, scholars are still debating state formation.

This is not to say that, after Tilly and Skocpol, scholars totally ignored questions about the social construction of democracies or that they abandoned all their inquiries into regime types. Recent scholarship on transitions from authoritarian rule, by Guillermo O'Donnell and Philippe Schmitter (1986), among numerous others, has preoccupied political scientists and sociologists for more than a decade now. But much of this work has concerned itself with problems inherent in state forms and political systems, having to do with the delegitimization of party politics and the overbureaucratization of the state, and not with the ideological content of the regime. Yet even for those modernization theorists or political-economic scholars of the newly industrializing world for whom the presence or absence of democracy was still a larger concern, the study of state forms and state structures gained popularity, and these themes soon began to challenge the overwhelming concern with questions about democracy or its absence that had dominated the writings of political scientists in the 1960s and 1970s. As one example, Guillermo O'Donnell's own seminal book, *Bureaucratic-Authoritarianism* (1973), made some headway in these regards, moving both political scientists and sociologists away from their preoccupation with classifying countries in terms of the formally democratic workings of their political systems or the political ideology of governance, and examining instead the centralized structure and power of the state itself.

Of course, O'Donnell's study of bureaucratic authoritarianism was also informed by a concern with flawed democracies and their replacement by military regimes even as it did turn greater attention to states and not just regime types. In his recent writings on the (un)rule of law in Latin America, O'Donnell and his associates have carried this concern even further, arguing that changes of regime types, even from authoritarian to democratic, have failed to solve the fundamental problems of weak Latin American states. As a result, over the past decade or two we have started to see scholars in various disciplines ranging from sociology to political science to anthropology concerning themselves with state formation and with the ways in which existent *structures* of political participation and state decision making are as central as ideology or democratic-nondemocratic regime type to the fate and nature of contemporary political development. This trend has been all but set in stone with the global popularity of political liberalization, because most scholars now work under the assumption that there is widespread civilian commitment to democratic ideals. Indeed, even scholars whose main concern has long been the study of democratization or democratic transition have found themselves increasingly distanced from the concepts and categories that prevailed when regime type was the principal analytic point of entry. If anything, their starting point seems to be the ways in which formal democracy (read regime type) fails to engender substantive democracy, and the concern is less with the advent or consolidation of democratic regimes and more with the institutional and legal practices that make democracy work on the ground. Accordingly, the research questions now most in play in both political science and sociology have to do with which other social, cultural, geographic, or even economic patterns or practices, independent of citizens' normative allegiance to democracy, will most color the nature and character of modern states, most of which are now formally democratic but only some of which have extended the citizenship rights, legal guarantees, and participatory political practices anticipated by citizens living within their borders. It is in the context of these paradigm shifts and real-world political transformations, then, that we pose our questions about armed forces and politics without linking them to regime type.

To be sure, in recent years many, many scholars have moved away from studying states and have instead cast their eyes on civil society and the growing importance of citizens in politics. Recent writings by Andrew Arato and Jean Cohen, especially their book *Civil Society and Political Theory* (1992), as well as the growing popularity of recent works by internationally eminent scholars like Jürgen Habermas and Alain Touraine, were significant in contributing to this shift in emphasis, which is linked in no small part to a normative assessment of the state as a negative force that colonizes civil society. With this new analytic point of entry fully entrenched in the academic horizon, we see considerable preoccupation with so-called new ways of doing politics, generally exemplified through social movement activism and the reinvigoration of civil society. Yet precisely because this shift in emphasis is so pervasive scholars have been less likely to raise questions about regime type per se (because social movements have been active in democratic and nondemocratic regimes), or even about state formation (because social movements have been as likely to emerge in countries with centralized as opposed to decentralized states), and more likely to concern themselves with general claims about political development, broadly understood. Accordingly, at least from our vantage point, even the newfound emphasis on civil society in many of the social sciences is quite consistent with our larger concern with political developments that are not necessarily reducible to regime types or the formal presence or absence of democracy.

Granted, the notion of political development is less specific as a subject of study than regime type or even state form; and in that sense we may court the disaster of imprecision if explaining political development, so to speak, is our sole aim. Still, our equal concern with state formation, a term that refers broadly to the development of state institutions and the variation in the specific institutional forms of the state (i.e., centralized versus decentralized) or its capacities, as well as the different ways in which parties or interest groups articulate with states, attests to our aims to achieve a more exacting understanding of political trajectories among states. Thus, if we consider political development and even state forms as terms that help us move beyond the constraining assumptions about military behavior associated with certain political ideologies or predefined political regime types, and look at the structure and character of state institutions as well as civil society in understanding the actions and impacts of armed forces, then this terminology may in fact liberate us from overly restrictive assumptions about when, how, and why armed forces matter even as it leads us to new hypotheses and a new analytic framing of the problem. That, essentially, is our aim.

Analytic Structure and Theoretical Aims of the Book

This book is divided into three main sections, organized in terms of their focused treatment of different dimensions of the relationship between armed forces and political development. Overall, the argument is that irregular armed forces have been central protagonists in processes of state formation and political development in a wide variety of countries, modern or not, democratic or otherwise; but that the paths taken differ with respect to (1) how they articulate with conventional armed forces; (2) at what level of the state (local, regional, national, or transnational) these armed forces are most salient; and (3) in combination with which class or social forces in civil society they most wield their power or articulate their aims.

The book begins in Part I with a section titled "The Basic Framework and Beyond: Mobilization, Demobilization, and National State Formation," which includes four essays by leading scholars of state formation and/or militaries who collectively lay out the general analytic contours of the book, albeit with focused arguments. Unlike the contributions in the following two parts of the book, which are primarily case studies that examine one or two countries in a single time period, each of these initial essays takes a broad comparative and/or historical sweep, examining numerous countries or spanning multiple time periods. The section begins with a chapter by Charles Tilly prepared especially for this volume, titled "Armed Force, Regimes, and Contention in Europe since 1650." Tilly is considered by many to be the foremost living theorist of the relationship between war-making and state-making, as well as a scholar whose knowledge and expertise in European studies of the subject is matched by no other. In this essay, Tilly offers an overview of his seminal argument about war-making and state-making, drawn partially from his book on the subject, *Coercion, Capital, and European States* (1990), but also supplemented by more recent research on a stunning array of times and places through which he has added several new dimensions to his argument, including a concern with shifting regimes and even their democratic potential in the early modern era. It may be somewhat paradoxical that as many of the rest of the volume's contributors purposely move away from discussing democracy or regime type per se and focus instead on state formation, Tilly himself finds it valuable to reintroduce questions about regimes and their characteristics in his work, especially in the context of a historical framing known best for the attention paid just to state forms. The result, we hope, is not only to establish the analytic and theoretical importance of the interrelationship between patterns of state formation and regime types, but also to consider the latter not as an ideological shorthand for a state's democratic or nondemocratic character, as was the case in most of the literature up until now, but as a more precise way of studying state forms, which Tilly identifies as ranging from sovereign city-states to confederated provinces, free cities, peripheral provinces, territories or principalities, autocratic monarchies, and constitutional monarchies.

The next chapter, "Limited War and Limited States" by Miguel Centeno, takes long-standing arguments about war-making and state-making formulated by Tilly and others and applies them to a region of the world underexamined in this literature, Latin America, where external war-making has been neither as frequent nor as comprehensive as in Europe, the context for much of this theorizing. Centeno's piece draws impressively on the study of a wide variety of Latin American countries, compares this region with other parts of the world, and assesses the patterns of war-making in these divergent contexts to arrive at some generalizations about the predominant character and extent of war-making in the Latin American continent. By raising questions about the predominance of what he calls partial war, and theorizing that certain patterns of "limited" war-making impacted state formation in Latin America to produce a slightly different pattern than is evident in Europe, Centeno establishes the analytic importance of acknowledging but also recasting the original literature on war-making and state-making, the defining theme and aim of the book. His chapter is followed by Alec Campbell's "Where Do All the Soldiers Go? Veterans and the Politics of Demobilization," which carries the revisionist sentiment one step further by introducing the importance of looking not just at war-making and mobilization for war but also at demobilization and the aftermath of war, much as did Skocpol in *Protecting Soldiers and Mothers*, only in a much wider comparative and historical framing. One of the key challenges that any state faces, Campbell argues, is what to do with soldiers who have been armed and trained, but now must return to civilian life. Through analysis of contexts as diverse as the ancient Roman Republic, nineteenth-century Europe, and twentieth-century Europe and the United States, Campbell argues that the ways in which states manage demobilization establishes a wide variety of political outcomes, ranging from the granting of citizenship rights to the formation of welfare states. War, in short, is not just something to be made; it also has to be ended. And, in modern times at least, when strong and centralized state apparatuses have already been relatively well established, it may be at the home front that the longer-range political implications of ending wars may be most influential and most deeply cast.

Eiko Ikegami's "Military Mobilization and the Transformation of Property Relationships: Wars That Defined the Japanese Style of Capitalism" builds on the contributions of all three of the preceding chapters by examining both mobilization *and* demobilization as well as by looking at the economics and the politics of war. With respect to the latter, in fact, Ikegami's essay inverts the originating concerns that Tilly established in *Coercion, Capital, and European States* by examining how mobilization and demobilization for war affected capitalism and proprietary relations, and not just vice versa. In analytical terms, then, Ikegami forges new theoretical ground that is left relatively unexplored in the contributions by Tilly, Centeno, and Campbell, although it is nonetheless marshaled for the purposes of answering similar questions about war-making and state-making. Through detailed historical analysis of several centuries of Japanese history, starting with the Tokugawa shogunate and extending up through the post-1945 period, her article demonstrates the ways that mobilizing for war and accommodating the end of war significantly altered what Ikegami terms property relationships, or the access to and control of various "possessive" resources, including the skills, legitimacy, and social identities associated with being able to pay for and fight in wars. Her quintessentially historical argument is that war transformed these property relationships sequentially, in ways that not only affected later prospects of waging and mobilizing for war but also contributed to the formation of certain patterns of state-market interaction. As such, while one of the explicit objectives of this article is to link war-making to the formation of a peculiarly Japanese form of capitalism, Ikegami's emphasis on state-market relations in the constitution of this unique form of capitalism also makes this an argument about the militarized origins of what might be considered the Japanese welfare state.

In the second part of the book, titled "Deconstructing Armed Forces: From Militaries to Militias, Paramilitaries, Police, and Veterans," we turn more directly to focused case studies, although the main purpose of this section is to introduce the reader to a wide variety of irregular armed forces that have existed over time and place, to examine similarities and differences in their manner of operation, and to focus on the ways in which these different kinds of armed forces have fundamentally contributed to patterns of state formation and trajectories of national politics. In this section themes of both mobilization and demobilization continue to be relevant, with the articles examining a variety of circumstances in which veterans, militias, paramilitaries, and police – sometimes employed by the state and sometimes acting against it, sometimes connected to the military and sometimes not – have affected state formation and national politics.

Using cases as diverse as the United States in the eighteenth and nineteenth centuries, Greece in the twentieth century, war-torn Columbia in the present period, and Argentina during the initial period of its modern state formation in the early twentieth century, the authors included in Part II collectively make the case that it would be difficult to understand national patterns of politics or state formation if conventional armed forces were the only point of departure. In so doing, these chapters offer a somewhat different accounting for the relationship between armed forces and state formation not just because they highlight the ways in which militia, paramilitary, police, and veteran activities were absolutely central in determining the actual form and reach of the state, whether that form be centralized (Argentina), decentralized (the United States), or some contested combination of elements that fundamentally limited state power (Greece) or produced total state breakdown (Colombia). These chapters are also significant to the larger aims of the volume because many of them conceptualize irregular armed forces as linked to civil society and its concerns as much as to the state. This becomes theoretically significant when, in comparing across the chapters in Part II, it is made evident that those irregular armed forces whose principal point of reference is civil society and not the state – as in the U.S. case – were those most likely to sustain the development of decentralized rather than centralized state forms.

The discussion begins with a chapter by Achilles Batalas, "Send a Thief to Catch a Thief: State-Building and the Employment of Irregular Military Formations in Mid-Nineteenth-Century Greece," which examines the Greek state's reliance on a nonprofessional military force in its efforts to wage war. In his examination of these "irregular" forces, understood primarily as brigands or bandits, Batalas argues that Greek state formation can be characterized as a case of "inverse racketeering," to the extent the state became the client and not the supplier of protection against internal and external adversaries. By turning Tilly's argument upside down, so to speak, Batalas opens a new line of analysis into the ways that irregular armed forces may have participated in similar activities organized around similar aims as the professional military of the Greek state but whose distinct and relatively independent location in civil society significantly altered the character of their relationship to the state and their impact on state formation. Questions of demobilization also figure as central in this account, particularly to the extent that the demands for employment advanced by these irregular forces became a key political liability for the Greek state. One by-product was the development of new forms of paramilitary organizations; another was the imposition of new forms of taxation to pay for sustained demobilization. Both processes strengthened the state, even as they never resolved the state's incapacity to eliminate irregular troops and thus maintain a full monopoly over the means of coercion.

Mauricio Romero's "Reform and Reaction: Paramilitary Groups in Contemporary Colombia" gives evidence of similar dynamics at play in the contemporary Colombian case, where paramilitary forces linked to regional elites have become central protagonists in a protracted armed struggle that has undermined the Colombian state's capacity to monopolize the means of coercion. In contrast to Batalas's chapter, which focuses on irregular armed forces as a distinct social group, in Romero's chapter the analytic point of departure is regional elites who deploy paramilitary forces against the central state in an effort to protect their own economic and political interests. One by-product is a state of near civil war in Colombia, where no single (or centralized) state authority has acquired the legitimate claim to rule the entire national territory. Complicating matters for the central government is the fact that the country appears divided into three distinct regions where elites and their paramilitaries fight between themselves, with guerrilla armies, and with the national state, creating an environment of intense conflict and everyday violence that threatens to undermine both regime stability and the nation's democratic prospects. What makes the Romero chapter particularly striking – if not paradoxical – is his claim that recent efforts at state-political decentralization implemented in the late 1980s precisely to facilitate Colombia's democratic transition toward a more liberalized state and economy have contributed to the regional violence and the internal breakdown of the state, by unleashing broader competition for local offices and thus increasing elites' interests in maintaining coercive forces at the subnational level.

The next chapter, Laura Kalmanowiecki's "Policing the People, Building the State: The Police-Military Nexus in Argentina, 1880–1945," also examines Latin America but focuses on a different case in a much earlier time period. In many ways, the story Kalmanowiecki tells for Argentina also sheds light on the contemporary problems in Colombia, to the extent that it demonstrates what made it possible to consolidate successfully the process of modern state-building in such a way that the same point of anarchy would not be reached as occurred in Colombia. Kalmanowiecki shows that in Argentina the state relied on the police to reach down into civil society deeply enough to control local populations who threatened the federal government's plans for a centralized national state. The police, acting as a coercive force with formal autonomy from the military but not from the national state, and with a "legitimate" institutional mandate to operate in cities and localities across the provinces throughout the country, slowly expanded its reach across national territory. Through an examination of the ways that police activities developed and were organized for the purposes of fighting an "internal war" against radicals and communists defined as enemies of the state, ultimately in collaboration with the military, Kalmanowiecki builds on many of the insights about war-making and state-making offered by Tilly as well as on Centeno's argument about the weakness of the Latin American state in the absence of massive or more "total" external war-making. Yet it is by virtue of her recognition that it takes different types of armed forces to fight internal as opposed to external wars that Kalmanowiecki links the activities of the Argentine police to a highly contested process of state formation.

The problem of expanding the territorial or institutional reach of the national state and the extent to which this is violently contested by both regular and irregular armed forces also are at the heart of the subsequent chapters in Part II, both of which focus on the United States. Susan Browne's "War-Making and U.S. State Formation: Mobilization, Demobilization, and the Inherent Ambiguities of Federalism" focuses on a period of American history that is rarely examined in the literature on war-making and state-making: the period immediately following U.S. independence from Britain. With a focus on Shays's Rebellion, Browne argues that much of the political contestation in the newly independent colonies after the War of Independence could be traced to problems associated with demobilization from war. She suggests that the new U.S. government was unwilling or unable to respond to the land and tax demands of veterans of the independence war, among which Shays's rebels were the most vocal and organized. As such, Browne's argument builds on some of the insights offered in the Campbell chapter; but it goes beyond them by linking veterans' claims not just to state formation and consolidation broadly understood but also to ongoing political struggles within Massachusetts and between Massachusetts and Confederation-based political leaders over the organizational character of the state, especially its extent of centralization or decentralization.

Browne's chapter not only brings a discussion of war-making and state-making to a country context and time period that have been almost completely ignored in most studies of these themes, but also offers an argument for one of the most problematic, well-studied, and controversial aspects of American exceptionalism: the uniquely decentralized federalist form of the American state. According to Browne, Shays's rebels allied with Confederation military personnel in order to get support for their claims for veterans benefits, while pitting themselves against the elite power structures in the Boston-dominated Massachusetts state government, which were more concerned about keeping state fiscal solvency than spending on veterans pensions. One by-product of this political controversy, which reached the point of armed rebellion among Shays's men (most of them armed veterans), was the formation of the national constitution in which local states' rights were guaranteed but cast within the context of a still powerful national state structure.

The final chapter of Part II, Richard Bensel's "Politics Is Thicker Than Blood: Union and Confederate Veterans in the U.S. House of Representatives in the Late Nineteenth Century," looks at the longer-term consequences of this unique form of American political development. Like Browne, Bensel is concerned with the scope, composition, and reach of the national state, but he focuses on a much later period, following the Civil War; and rather than examining rebel militia, as does Browne, Bensel focuses on conventional political actors and structures. Specifically, he examines the political composition of Congress and how the election of veterans who fought against each other in the war affected the development of party politics and state policy at the end of the nineteenth century. By examining the aftermath of the Civil War, Bensel's article underscores the importance of conflict in U.S. national political development, but rather than focusing on the actual period of strife and military mobilization, as does Romero, for example, Bensel, like Campbell and Browne, concerns himself with the period of demobilization and postwar reconstruction. Specifically, he studies the regional identities and political loyalties forged during the Civil War, the extent to which they persisted among veterans elected to Congress, and how they were translated into state structures even after the formal end of war-making.

As such, rather than examining veterans from only the perspective of demands advanced purely from the domain of civil society, as do Campbell and even Ikegami, Bensel examines veterans' direct political involvement in the postwar state and policy-making through their involvement in the party system and the various congressional committees that served as a central source of postwar policy-making and state activity. While Bensel discusses questions of pensions and other issues that generally concern veterans, his main point is that we cannot understand how and why the U.S. national state responded with the social or welfare-state policies that it finally implemented without an understanding of the ways that veterans themselves were brought into the structures of the state. As such, this chapter stands as an analytic corrective to other accounts in the volume that tend to pose questions about veterans' impact mainly in terms of a state-civil society divide, rather than through a focus on the mediating political institutions and practices that transcend and even unite these two domains.

In Part III, "Not Just the Nation-State: Examining the Local, Regional, and International Nexus of Armed Force and State Formation," we continue with a focus on some of the irregular armed forces examined earlier, but cast our eye more directly to the problem of different jurisdictional levels of the state and the impact of armed forces organized either subnationally or transnationally on national state formation. The first chapter in this part, "The *Police Municipale* and the Formation of the French State" by Lizabeth Zack, echoes the focus of the Kalmanowiecki article on the Argentine police by taking as its central point of entry the problematic institutional and coercive relationships between police and the state. In this historical study of the period from the late nineteenth to early twentieth century, Zack examines the tensions between local and national police forces in France and the ways that ongoing conflicts between these two sets of authorities molded the process of French national state formation in a key historical juncture leading to the Third Republic. Like Kalmanowiecki and even Browne, Zack is interested in the tension-filled relations between those who controlled the means of violence on both local and national levels. But in contrast to the U.S. and Argentine cases, Zack argues that in the French case it was local police linked to the local state – not militias that grounded their authority and identities in civil society or police linked directly to a national military – who served as the greatest challenge to the national state.

This chapter proceeds under the assumption that most studies of the highly centralized French state fail to acknowledge the contested character of this outcome, by virtue of the fact that they cite the French Revolution, a subsequent set of institutional reforms, and deeply embedded traditions in the postrevolutionary political culture as unproblematically sustaining extensive state centralization. Zack, in contrast, suggests that if we examine patterns of control over the means of coercion on the municipal as well as federal levels, we see an altogether different picture. Municipal police in certain key cities, regions, and colonial outposts of France at times were relatively powerful enough to challenge the monopoly of coercive power on the national level; and they frequently did so in ways that challenged the political aims and objectives of the national state, primarily by sustaining the local hegemony of opposition political forces who did not share the central state's aims. Moreover, it was precisely the existence or potential threat of decentralized state powers who controlled their own means of coercion that spurred the French state to work so actively to centralize its coercive power through the creation of a Federal police that served to disempower local police forces. It was the contested nature of the state's organizational control over armed forces, in short, that produced the highly centralized French state and that, by virtue of its successes in centralizing control of a wide variety of armed forces, may even have helped craft twentieth-century France's semi-militarized democracy.

The next chapter, Anne Raffin's "Domestic Militarization in a Transnational Perspective: Patriotic and Militaristic Youth Mobilization in France and Indochina, 1940–1945," extends the focus on France directly into the period of militarized democracy, perhaps best exemplified in the World War II period at a time when generals and military forces sought to influence politics and civil society both at home and abroad. This chapter breaks from many of the previous essays in its explicit focus on formal military personnel convened in the service of national sovereignty and defense. Yet unlike most studies of this kind, and in keeping with one of the main objectives of this volume, the Raffin chapter explores the activities and larger political impact of the French military forces through examination of their nonmilitary – or, better said, paramilitary – activities, themselves directed and generated from civil society. Moreover, like the other authors in Part III, Raffin examines these paramilitary activities on more than just the level of the nation-state; but rather than turning to subnational patterns and considering how they articulate with the national state, as do Zack and Browne, Raffin examines transnational patterns of paramilitary activities and their impact on state formation in both France and Indochina. The chapter focuses on the authorities' use of paramilitary and sporting youth organizations to build and channel conservative and patriotic feelings toward the Vichyist regime and its ideology both in France and abroad in its colonies. In addition to illuminating the subtle and civil-society-based ways that

France's governing officials and its military personnel legitimized the French national state and its political projects, this chapter shows how these patterns initially sustained colonial rule even as they later laid the seeds for its overthrow by nationalist forces in Indochina. As such, these patriotic, paramilitary practices contributed not just to colonial state formation, in both the core and the metropole, they also served to challenge the legitimacy of both states in subsequent time periods.

Raffin's chapter is followed by William Reno's "The Changing Nature of Warfare and the Absence of State-Building in West Africa." This chapter, which focuses comparatively on Nigeria, Liberia, and Sierra Leone, combines into one piece many of the divergent questions and themes in the volume. With the exception of Romero's discussion of Colombia, it is one of the few that directly examines the relationship between armed force and state formation with a focus on the present period, and with a closer examination of the types of violent conflict and militarized coercion that inspired this volume in the first place. Reno's piece accomplishes several important things. First, he introduces yet a new form of irregular armed force, what he calls a warlord, or those elites that sustain their hold over the national state and formal territory through the use of predatory force generated within and against civil society. Warlords can work for or against the national state; but, unlike a more "conventional" military regime, a warlord regime would most likely sustain its power by fomenting war and conflict among its own peoples. This divide-and-conquer strategy has particularly brutal consequences, to be sure; but it allows a lock on state power, especially when it is sustained by tribal or subnational ethnic political identities that can transcend regions and national borders. The latter point not only highlights the analytic importance of using a transnational framework when examining armed force and state formation, a theme also pursued by Raffin; it further underscores the historical specificity of the African experience and those of other states formed in the twentieth century. Because many of these states emerged in the context of postcolonial or Cold War bargains and compromises, their borders were often imposed arbitrarily. As such, the prospects for successful national state formation without coercive force were already limited. Combine that difficult situation with a civil society torn by ethnic difference and an economic environment of great scarcity, one of the few ways for states to consolidate themselves has been through predatory or warlord politics.

Reno establishes and deepens this general argument in two important ways. First, he offers a comparative analysis of three different African regimes and, in the process, examines the historical conditions that made some more or less likely to consolidate their states through violent predation. Second, he examines the role that international peace-keeping forces can and have played in the process. Although this second aspect of the narrative is not his central point of entry, it does force the reader to consider that when Reno refers to the "changing nature of warfare," he has in mind the transnational dimensions of foreign intervention as much as internal practices within African states. In a world where international peace-keeping forces have become much more prevalent, and where the appropriateness and larger impact of these so-called peace-keepers is still under question from the point of view of both sending and receiving nations, Reno suggests that only under certain conditions can they positively affect the internal actions and alliances of some of the world's most coercive armed forces, both warlords and their military state enemies.

In light of Reno's treatment of international peace-keeping forces, it is appropriate that the volume closes with a chapter by Ian Roxborough, titled "The Ghost of Vietnam: America Confronts the New World Disorder" in which we are given an explanation for the character and dynamics of U.S. military involvement abroad. Roxborough takes as his point of departure the challenge of irregular warfare, beginning with Vietnam, through the development of what he calls a new American "way of war" in the decade following the Cold War, and up to the recent challenges implied by a possible "global war against terrorism." He examines the changes in military strategies and actions, both here and abroad, and discusses their implications both for external war-making and domestic political developments, including increased domestic security operation. One of his concerns is the impact of these developments on civilian-military relations.

In many ways, the Roxborough chapter brings us full circle from where we began with Tilly, because it links state-military and military–civil society relations to the practices of war, and does so through an eminently historical analysis. Roxborough argues that the legacies of the Cold War and the military's efforts to find or cultivate new enemies in a post–Cold War world, who now may be identified within rather than outside our national borders, could lead to the military's estrangement from civil society. The historical legacies of the Vietnam era, in particular, may contribute to these developments, not just because they tend to remind military personnel of the antimilitaristic sentiments that used to prevail in civil society when body counts were high, and by so doing they hold the potential to set the military and civil society further apart; but also because the military has established limits on the ways in which the military can make war externally, and imposed these limits on civilian politicians. These two developments are interrelated to the extent that in order to keep from becoming further estranged from a civil society that may find itself with a Vietnam-era antimilitary sentiment if civilian casualties accelerate in any armed foreign conflict, the military continues to insist on fighting wars only in which they can brandish powerful and technically sophisticated weapons without engaging too many ground troops. This set of circumstances directly affects what types of wars will be waged, with whom, and over what.

First conceived months before the NATO-led operation in Yugoslavia, Roxborough's initial argument that the U.S. military will only support what he calls "standoff precision strike warfare" continued to ring true as the U.S. muddled through the Kosovo crisis seemingly paralyzed over the issue of whether to send ground troops even as it was criticized for using precision bombing that harmed as many civilians and Kosovo refugees as Serbian soldiers and policemen. It has taken on further urgency in the post-9/11 world as terrorists continue to challenge the American military to wage a new type of war. Now, as this volume goes to print and we have a new administration in Washington embroiled in a battle with "irregular" armed forces in Afghanistan, it remains to be seen where the U.S. military leadership will go – and with what types of weapons – and what civil society will or will not support for its troops.

Thinking Ahead

So where does all this leave us? Several general observations inspired by the Roxborough chapter and the arguments of the other contributors are worth sharing before closing. Most have to do with what we do and do not know, and what we still need to find out. One observation, as expected, is that there is sufficient evidence that military activities themselves and patterns of state formation are both intricately linked to the embeddedness of armed forces in civil society. Whether or not armed forces are defined traditionally as military personnel or in broader terms so as to encompass paramilitaries, police, militia, and even veterans, the extent to which they are able to draw on the support and sympathies of citizens around them will directly affect their sense of self as well as the ways in which they undertake coercive activities on behalf of the state. Accordingly, in the upcoming chapters and in future work we must pay closer attention to the civil societies in which militaries or armed (and disarmed) forces are embedded, and be prepared to theorize the historical conditions under which certain social or civil contexts affect the use and character of armed force as well as its articulation with either local or national authorities.

Second, we must be prepared to theorize the differences among a wide variety of armed forces, not just with respect to their roles in national politics and state formation as we do here, but also on a much more fundamental conceptual basis. For example, should national militaries be considered more autonomous from civil society and more articulated with the state than militias or police or paramilitaries or veterans? Under what conditions and why; and with what clear implications for more macrosociological theorizing about political and social change? Moreover, would all forms of armed forces answer to the same authorities and rules of law, so to speak; or will some find themselves linked more to informal structures of power and authority in civil society, and as such see their charge not so much in terms of rule of law or national governance but in terms of social "security" and/or grass-roots politics? To date, almost all discussion of these questions has revolved around a focus on national military forces and whether they in theory or in practice are considered autonomous from or beholden to national authorities and the constitutional limitations established on military action. These questions, moreover, have been answered primarily through studies of war-making, coups d'etat, or military rule in which military leaders and the rank and file are conceptualized as institutionally distinct from civil society and placed in an orbit of constitutionally mandated national authority. Yet as noted earlier, not only are these assumptions questionable in certain national contexts, they seem far off the mark when examining nonmilitary armed forces like the police or militias or paramilitaries or veterans. And this raises the metatheoretical possibility that some of these forces might be more conceptually understandable as situated in civil society rather than in the state sphere. If so, how do we understand their social, political, or nationalist allegiances, their relationship to the rule of law, and their impact on national politics and state formation?

Third, we must be prepared to disaggregate levels of the state with the same care and precision that we use when we distinguish among different forms of armed forces, and conceptually to link these two sets of concerns together if necessary. One of the clearest observations that can be drawn from the chapters in this volume is that state formation is not necessarily something that occurs only on the national level; "local" states, or state apparatuses whose dominion may be much more circumscribed than the federal or national state (i.e., city or regional governing structures), often rely on the same sets of concerns about mobilizing and demobilizing coercive forces as national states. After all, as Charles Tilly always admonishes and Max Weber has so well demonstrated, all state formation was in essence "local" at one time; and it was only through constant competition and interaction with other "local" state powers that previously independent, decentralized structures of governance ultimately became subsumed under or joined with what we have come to know as national states, whose distinguishing claim to fame is generally control over a much larger territory. Yet, even scholars who acknowledge this historical dynamic often forget that empowered and institutionally autonomous local states, especially in modern times, can coexist with national states. They are not always subsumed in them; and, in fact, depending on the form and character of national state formation, it can be the constant give-and-take of local and national states – conceptualized in Susan Browne's argument as the "inherent ambiguities of federalism" in the context of U.S. political development and state formation – that defines the contours of a particular political system. Accordingly, one future line of inquiry would be to examine the coexistence of different levels of the state, and of different armed forces linked to these different levels of the state (i.e., police at the local and military at the national), and to theorize the larger implications of these tensions and interrelationships for both local and national state formation and political development.

To the extent that we are prepared to recognize that certain types of armed forces have more political power and are differentially embedded in civil society when they are organized on the local as opposed to the regional, national, or transnational levels, this new line of inquiry can also lead us to yet another theme that emerges in the upcoming chapters, which is the impact of coexisting state structures and coercive forces on the character of a political system, be it a democracy or something else. Although our initial aim was to move away from the strict understanding of regime type, which posited a particular set of relations between civilian and military power for democracies and nondemocracies, it is nonetheless clear that we can still say something about democracies – how they differ from each other or even parallel nondemocracies – if we also seek to integrate our understanding of regime type with state form, an aim that is not so distant from what Thomas Ertman has tried to do in his recent book, *Birth of the Leviathan: Building States and Regimes in Medieval and Early Modern Europe*. Yet to do so for the periods most under study here, which is to say throughout most of the nineteenth century and up to the present, *after* the so-called birth of the archetypal leviathan form of the national state decades before, it is helpful to deconstruct the state into its local and national components and to understand the role played by armed forces on both levels. Indeed, both France and the United States are democracies, but in the former case the organization of coercive forces on the municipal level ultimately was subsumed into the nation, whereas in the latter an uneasy tension between local authority and national authority was established and still exists. Accordingly, the "state infrastructures" of these two democracies differ considerably, such that decisions about both war-making and a wide variety of national policies, not to mention the role of localities in national policy-making, also differ considerably.

Likewise, both Colombia and Argentina are two countries where formal democracy has advanced slowly and in a similarly elusive fashion, but where the relative power of local authorities in the national political system differs considerably, largely because in the former case local and regional authorities have managed to marshal their own alternative coercive forces, whereas in the latter the coercive arm of the national state has tended to reach directly down to localities, and still does in many ways. This line of reasoning not only allows us to understand the differences between these two countries, rather than lumping them together as prototypically semi-authoritarian regimes, or countries similarly in transition to democracy; it also allows us to differentiate among them with respect to what Miguel Centeno calls their weak or limited states. Both sets of information give us much more fuel for theorizing processes and patterns of state formation or disintegration, not to mention the degrees of centralization of authority or the everyday use of violence, two sets of concerns that are increasingly conceived as obstacles to basic citizenship rights and are themselves a major component in understanding a country's general democratic potential.

Armed with this new way of thinking about states, patterns of coercion, and citizenship rights as understood both locally and nationally, moreover, we may even be able to ask new questions about the similarities across democratic and nondemocratic states, as would be evident in a comparison of the common patterns of centralization of coercive forces in both France and Argentina, two countries that are rarely compared in terms of larger political trajectories, democratic and otherwise. But let us leave further discussion of rights and democracy as linked to coercive power to Anthony Pereira, who offers concluding remarks about these and other issues that will further tie together the contributions in this volume.

Most of the chapters in this book were prepared for a year-long Sawyer Seminar on the Military, Politics, and Society in Comparative and Historical Perspective funded by the Andrew W. Mellon Foundation and hosted at the New School for Social Research from September 1997 through June 1998. We thank the Mellon Foundation, and especially Harriet Zuckerman, for seminar support in a multiplicity of ways, from funding our working group to supporting doctoral students affiliated with the seminar. We also thank Louise Tilly for her energies in conceptualizing the original proposal and organizing the seminar, as well as the numerous speakers and participants who shared their time and thoughts during the seminar. In addition to all the contributors to this volume, we thank our editor at Cambridge University Press, Lew Bateman, and the general participants and presenters in the original Sawyer Seminar. Principal among the latter whom we would like to acknowledge are Andrew Arato, Robert Barros, Douglas Chalmers, Paul Chevigny, Michael Desch, Louis Goodman, Michael Robert Lucas, Patrice McSherry, Paolo Mesquita Neto, James Nolt, Marifeli Perez-Stable, David Plotke, Deborah Poole, Andrew Schlewitz, and Mark von Hagen.

Notes

1. For more on these transformations, see Charles Tilly's "State-Incited Violence, 1900–1999" and the debate between him and Harriet Friedmann, Michael Barnett, and Timothy Wickham Crowley, all in Diane E. Davis and Howard Kimeldorf, eds., *Political Power and Social Theory*, vol. 9 (1995).
2. This breach with society has become so dire that scholars such as the military historian Caleb Carr have begun to label as terrorist those states that engage in warfare against their rebellious citizens. For more, see his *The Lessons of Terror: A History of Warfare against Civilians: Why It Has Always Failed and Why It Will Fail Again* (2002).

3. In this text "irregular" armed forces are those coercive actors and institutions we have broadly defined as falling outside the conventional category of uniformed standing armed forces fighting external aggressors in the name of national sovereignty.

References

Acuña, Carlos, and Catalina Smulovitz. 1996. "Adjusting the Armed Forces to Democracy: Successes, Failures, and Ambiguities in the Southern Cone," in Elizabeth Jelin and Eric Hershberg, eds., *Constructing Democracy: Human Rights, Citizenship and Society in Latin America*, 13–38. Boulder: Westview.

Aguero, Felipe. 1992. "The Military and the Limits to Democratization in South America," in Scott Mainwaring, Guillermo O'Donnell, and J. Samuel Valenzuela, eds., *Issues in Democratic Consolidation*, 153–198. Notre Dame: University of Notre Dame Press.

Al-Khalil, Samir. 1989. *Republic of Fear*. New York: Pantheon Books.

Arato, Andrew, and Jean L. Cohen. 1992. *Civil Society and Political Theory*. Cambridge, Mass.: MIT Press.

Arendt, Hannah. 1948. *The Origins of Totalitarianism*. New York: Harvest/HBJ.

Bates, Robert. 2001. *Prosperity and Violence: The Political Economy of Development*. New York: W. W. Norton.

Cammack, Paul, David Pool, and William Tordoff. 1993. "The Military in Africa, Latin America and the Middle East," in *Third World Politics: A Comparative Introduction*, 133–169. 2nd ed. Baltimore: Johns Hopkins University Press.

Carr, Caleb. 2002. *The Lessons of Terror: A History of Warfare against Civilians: Why It Has Always Failed and Why It Will Fail Again*. New York: Random House.

Clapham, Christopher, and George Philip. 1985. *The Political Dilemmas of Military Regimes*. Totowa, N.J.: Barnes and Noble.

Eboe, Hutchful. 1986. "The Modern State and Violence: The Peripheral Situation," *International Journal of the Sociology of Law* 14: 153–178.

Ertman, Thomas. 1997. *Birth of the Leviathan: Building States and Regimes in Medieval and Early Modern Europe*. Cambridge: Cambridge University Press.

Evans, Peter. 1995. *Embedded Autonomy: States and Industrial Transformation*. Princeton: Princeton University Press.

Finer, Samuel E. 1982. "The Morphology of Military Regimes," in Roman Kolkowicz and Andrezej Korbonski, eds., *Soldiers, Peasants, and Bureaucrats*, 281–309. London: Allen and Unwin.

Fitch, John Samuel. 1977. *The Military Coup d'Etat as a Political Process*. Baltimore: Johns Hopkins University Press.

1979. "The Political Impact of U.S. Military Aid to Latin America," *Armed Forces in Society* 5, 3: 360–386.

Handelman, Howard, and Thomas Sanders, eds. 1981. *Military Government and the Movement toward Democracy in South America*. Bloomington: Indiana University Press.

Huntington, Samuel. 1959. *The Soldier and the State: The Theory and Politics of Civil Military Relations*. Cambridge, Mass.: Harvard University Press.

ed. 1962. *Changing Patterns of Military Politics*. New York: Free Press.

1968. *Political Order in Changing Societies*. New Haven: Yale University Press.

Huntington, Samuel, and Andrew Goodpaster. 1977. *Civil-Military Relations*. Washington, D.C.: American Enterprise Institute for Public Policy Research.

Im, Hyung Baeg. 1987. "The Rise of Bureaucratic Authoritarianism in South Korea," *World Politics* 39, 2: 231–257.

Levi, Margaret. 1997. *Consent, Dissent, and Patriotism*. Cambridge: Cambridge University Press.

Linz, Juan. 1975. "Totalitarian and Authoritarian Regimes," in Fred Greenstein and Nelson Polsby, eds., *Handbook of Political Science*, 175–411. Reading, Mass.: Addison-Wesley.

Linz, Juan, and Alfred Stepan. 1966a. *Problems of Democratic Transition and Consolidation*. Baltimore: Johns Hopkins University Press.

1966b. "Toward Consolidated Democracies," *Journal of Democracy* 7, 2: 14–33.

Lipset, Seymour Martin. 1959. *Political Man*. Garden City, N.J.: Doubleday.

Lopez, George, and Michael Stohl, eds. 1989. *Dependence, Development, and State Repression*. New York: Greenwood Press.

Loveman, Brian, and Thomas Davies. 1978. *The Politics of Anti-Politics: The Military in Latin America*. Lincoln: University of Nebraska Press.

Lowenthal, Abraham F. 1974. "Armies and Politics in Latin America," *World Politic* 27, 1: 107–130.

Luckman, Robin. 1971. *The Nigerian Military: A Sociological Analysis of Authority and Revolt, 1960–67*. Cambridge: Cambridge University Press.

Mainwaring, Scott, Guillermo O'Donnell, and J. Samuel Valenzuela, eds. 1992. *Issues in Democratic Consolidation*. Notre Dame: University of Notre Dame Press.

Maniruzzaman, Talukdar. 1987. *Military Withdrawal from Politics*. Cambridge, Mass.: Ballinger.

Mann, Michael. 1988. *States, War, and Capitalism*. Oxford: Blackwell.

1993. *The Sources of Social Power. II. The Rise of Classes and Nation-States, 1760–1914*. Cambridge: Cambridge University Press.

McSherry, J. Patrice. 1992. "Military Power, Impunity and State-Society Changes in Latin America," *Canadian Journal of Political Science* 15, 3: 463–488.

Moore, Barrington, Jr. 1966. *The Social Origins of Dictatorship and Democracy*. Boston: Beacon Press.

O'Donnell, Guillermo. 1973. *Modernization and Bureaucratic-Authoritarianism*. Berkeley: University of California Press.

1999. "Polyarchies and the (Un)Rule of Law in Latin America," in Juan E. Mendez, Guillermo O'Donnell, and Paulo Sergio Pinheiro, eds., *The (Un)Rule of Law and the Underprivileged in Latin America*, 303–337. South Bend: University of Notre Dame Press.

O'Donnell, Guillermo, and Philippe Schmitter, eds. 1986. *Transitions from Authoritarian Rule*. Baltimore: Johns Hopkins University Press.

Osiel, Mark J. 1999. *Obeying Orders: Atrocity, Military Discipline, and the Law of War*. New Brunswick, N.J.: Transaction.

Pereira, Anthony W., and Diane E. Davis. 2000. *Violence, Coercion, and Rights in Contemporary Latin America*. 2 Vols. Beverly Hills: Sage. Special issue of *Latin American Perspectives*.

Perlmutter, Amos. 1982. "Civil-Military Relations in Praetorian States," in Roman Kolkowicz and Andrezej Korbonski, eds., *Soldiers, Peasants, and Bureaucrats*, 310–331. London: Allen and Unwin.

Petras, James. 1987. "State Terror in the Americas: Political Economy of State Terror: Chile, El Salvador, and Brazil," *Crime and Social Justice* 27–28: 88–109.

Pion-Berlin, David. 1993. "Military Autonomy and Emerging Democracies in South America," *Comparative Politics* 25, 1: 83–102.

Potash, Robert, and Paul Lewis. 1983. "The Right and Military Rule, 1955–1983," in Sandra McGee Deutsch and Ronald Dolkart, eds., *The Argentine Right: Its History and Intellectual Origins, 1910 to the Present*, 147–180. Wilmington: Scholarly Resources.

Powell, John Duncan. 1965. "Military Assistance and Militarism in Latin America," *Western Political Quarterly* 18: 382–392.

Remmer, Karen. 1989. *Military Rule in Latin America*. Boston: Unwin Hyman.

Rodríguez, Linda Alexander, ed. 1994. *Rank and Privilege: The Military and Society in Latin America*. Wilmington: Scholarly Resources.

Rouquié, Alain. 1987. *The Military and the State in Latin America*. Berkeley: University of California Press. Translation by Paul E. Signmund of *L'etat militaire en Amerique latine* (Paris: Editions du Seuil, 1982).

Rowe, Peter J., and Christopher J. Whelan. 1985. *Military Intervention in Democratic Societies*. London: Croom Helm.

Salomon, Albert. 1942. "The Spirit of the Soldier and Nazi Militarism," *Social Research* 9, 1: 82–103.

Schmitter, Philippe, ed. 1973. *Military Rule in Latin America: Function, Consequence, and Perspectives*. Beverly Hills: Sage.

Skocpol, Theda. 1979. *States and Social Revolutions: A Comparative Analysis of France, China and Russia*. Cambridge, Mass.: Harvard University Press.

1992. *Protecting Soldiers and Mothers: The Political Origins of Social Policy*. Cambridge, Mass.: Belknap Press of Harvard University.

Stepan, Alfred. 1971. *The Military in Politics: Changing Patterns in Brazil*. Princeton: Princeton University Press.

1988. *Rethinking Military Politics: Brazil and the Southern Cone*. Princeton: Princeton University Press.

Tilly, Charles, ed. 1975. *The Formation of National States in Western Europe*. Princeton: Princeton University Press.

1985. "War Making and State Making as Organized Crime," in Peter B. Evans, Dietrich Rueschemeyer, and Theda Skocpol, *Bringing the State Back In*, 169–191. Cambridge: Cambridge University Press.

1990. *Coercion, Capital, and European States, AD 990–1992*. Cambridge, Mass.: Blackwell.

Tilly, Charles, Louise Tilly, and Richard Tilly. 1976. *The Rebellious Century: 1830–1930*. Cambridge, Mass.: Harvard University Press.

Vagts, Alfred. 1959 [1973]. *A History of Militarism*. New York: Free Press.

Wolpin, Miles. 1986. "State Terrorism and Repression in the Third World," in George Lopez and Michael Stohl, eds., *Government Violence and Repression*, 97–164. Westport, Conn.: Greenwood.

Zaverucha, Jorge. 1993. "The Degree of Military Political Autonomy during the Spanish Argentine and Brazilian Transitions," *Journal of Latin American Studies* 25, 2: 283–300.

PART I

THE BASIC FRAMEWORK AND BEYOND

Mobilization, Demobilization, and
National State Formation

2

Armed Force, Regimes, and Contention in Europe since 1650

Charles Tilly

Contention and Democratization in Nineteenth-Century Switzerland

As seen in the vivid light cast by French and British examples, Switzerland followed an astonishing path to partial democracy during the nineteenth century. Long a scattering of belligerent fiefs within successive German empires, most Swiss areas acquired de facto independence at the Peace of Basel (1499) and de jure recognition as a federation at the Peace of Westphalia (1648). Until the very end of the eighteenth century the federation remained no more than a loose alliance of thirteen jealously sovereign cantons with strong ties to allied territories of Geneva, Grisons (Graubünden), and Valais, plus subject territories (e.g., Vaud, Lugano, Bellinzona, and Valtellina) of their component units. From the sixteenth to eighteenth century, Switzerland withdrew almost entirely from war on its own account, but provided crack mercenary troops to much of Europe. During that period, Switzerland's politics operated chiefly at the local and cantonal levels: outward-looking efforts to hold off other powers, inward-looking efforts to deal with – or defend – enormous disparities and particularities of privilege.

Conquered by Napoleon (with some assistance from Swiss revolutionaries) in 1798, then given new constitutions that year and in 1803, the Swiss adopted a much more centralized form of government with a national assembly, official multilingualism, and relative equality among cantons. Despite some territorial adjustments, the basic governmental form survived Napoleon's defeat. After 1830 Switzerland became a temporary home for many exiled revolutionaries (e.g., Mazzini and Weitling), who collaborated with Swiss radicals in calling for reform. Historians of the 1830s speak of a Regeneration Movement pursued by means of "publicity, clubs, and

I wrote this chapter while a Fellow at the Center for Advanced Study in the Behavioral Sciences, supported by National Science Foundation Grant SBR-9601236. For criticism of earlier drafts I am grateful to Ronald Aminzade, Doug McAdam, and Sidney Tarrow.

37

mass marches" (Nabholz et al. 1938: 2:406). With France's July 1830 revolution, anticlericalism became more salient in Swiss radicalism. Nevertheless, the new constitutions enacted in that mobilization stressed liberty and fraternity far more than equality. We might call the resulting regimes constitutional oligarchies.

From the early nineteenth century, Switzerland's already extensive rural textile industry and crafts began to urbanize and capitalize, which spurred disproportionate population growth in existing urban regions. With a Protestant majority concentrated in the richer, more urbanized cantons, an approximate political split – Protestant-liberal-radical versus Catholic-conservative – became salient in Swiss politics. On the average, predominantly Catholic cantons lay in the country's central, higher-altitude, more rural areas. In regions dominated by conservative cities (e.g., Basel), the countryside (widely industrialized during the eighteenth century, but suffering contraction in cottage industry during the early nineteenth) often supported liberal or radical programs.

The political problem became acute because national alignments of the mid-1840s pitted twelve richer and predominantly liberal-Protestant cantons against ten poorer, predominantly conservative-Catholic cantons in a diet where each canton had a single vote. Thus liberals deployed the rhetoric of national patriotism and majority rule while conservatives countered with cantonal rights and defense of religious traditions.

From 1830 to 1848, republicans and radicals repeatedly formed military bands (often called free corps, or *Freischaren*) and attempted to take over particular cantonal capitals by force of arms. Such bands failed in Lucerne (1841), but brought new administrations to power in Lausanne (1847), Geneva (1847), and Neuchâtel (1848). The largest military engagement took place in 1847. The federal diet ordered dissolution of the league (*Sonderbund*) formed for mutual defense by Catholic cantons Lucerne, Uri, Schwyz, Unterwalden, Zug, Fribourg, and Valais two years earlier; when the Catholic cantons refused, the diet sent an army to Fribourg (whose forces capitulated without serious fighting), then Lucerne (where a short battle occurred). The Sonderbund had about 79,000 men under arms, the federation some 99,000. After two more weeks of skirmishing and cleaning up, the Sonderbund War ended with twenty-four dead among the Catholic forces and seventy-four dead among the attackers. The Sonderbund's defeat consolidated the dominance of liberals in Switzerland as a whole and led to the adoption of a cautiously liberal constitution (with many features modeled on the U.S. Constitution) in 1848.

A last ricochet of the 1847–1848 military struggles occurred in 1856: forces loyal to the king of Prussia (effectively, but not formally, displaced from shared sovereignty in Neuchâtel by the republican coup of 1848) seized military control of part of Neuchâtel's cantonal capital only to be displaced almost immediately by the cantonal militia. Prussia's threats to invade Switzerland only incited other European powers to hold Prussia in check. From that point on, the limited republican constitution applied to all of the Swiss Federation. Between 1849 and 1870, furthermore, the Swiss cantons terminated their profitable centuries-old export of mercenary units for military service elsewhere.

Whatever else we say about the Swiss itinerary toward democracy, it certainly passed through intense popular struggle, including extensive military action. The same process that produced a higher-capacity central government, furthermore, also created Switzerland's restricted but genuine democracy: as compared with what went before, relatively broad and equal citizenship, binding consultation of citizens, and substantial protection of citizens from arbitrary action by governmental agents. As compared with late nineteenth-century French or British models of democracy, however, the Swiss federal system looks extraordinarily heterogeneous: a distinctive constitution and citizenship for each canton, multiple authorities and compacts, a surprising combination of exclusiveness with the capacity to create particular niches for newly accepted political actors. Through all subsequent constitutional changes, those residues of Swiss political history have persisted. They continue to exercise profound effects on social movements and other forms of contentious politics within Switzerland (Giugni and Passy 1997; Kriesi 1981; Kriesi et al. 1995).

Drawing on a lifetime of comparisons between French and British experiences, this dense essay clears ground for a more general explanation of variation in the impact of regimes on contention, and vice versa, over Europe as a whole since 1650. Differences among Swiss, British, French, Dutch, Iberian, and other European experiences with regime change and contention set challenging empirical, conceptual, and theoretical problems. Considering the great variety of European trajectories, how can we possibly pinpoint important similarities and differences in the interplay among changes in social environments, alterations in governmental forms, histories of contentious politics, and approaches to (or retreats from) democracy? How can we single out the effects of varying patterns of military activity? What concepts will help discipline those comparisons and single out significant causal mechanisms? To what extent can we identify recurrent cause-effect relationships that operated throughout the range of European history since 1650? This chapter's task is to lay out tools for pursuit of those questions.

The tools are chiefly conceptual – lots of definitions and schemata, no systematic presentation of evidence, no more than preliminary statement of causal propositions. They make it possible to talk cogently about causal interactions among three complex clusters of processes:

1. Alterations and differences in politically significant social environments of different European regions, defined chiefly in terms of coercion, capital, and connection.

2. Change and variation in the organizations and practices of political regimes, seen particularly in terms of differing governmental capacities and degrees of protected consultation for populations subject to those regimes – with special reference to the processes by which undemocratic regimes became more democratic.
3. Fluctuation, transformation, and variety in forms and intensities of contentious politics, conceived of especially in terms of their degree of localism, particularism, and directness of claim making.

In each of the three cases, let us seek first to identify the relevant field of variation, then to identify empirical and causal regularities within that field, finally to link change and variation in that regard to change and variation in each of the other clusters. But, to head off likely misunderstandings of so grandiloquent a program, let me immediately post two warnings.

First, social processes are coherent and explicable, but very complex – more like undersea life than planetary motion. They do not lend themselves to universal explanations involving two or three variables. Rather than general laws of political change, contention, or democracy, we should search for robust but partial causal mechanisms of relatively broad scope that recur in different sequences and different contexts with different outcomes on the large scale (see Hedström and Swedberg 1998). I have no hope or desire to promulgate a singular model of contention or democratization, much less to specify necessary or sufficient conditions for their appearance. I want instead to show something quite different: once we make due allowance for variation in sequences, environments, and initial conditions some of the same causal mechanisms that recurred significantly in European experience with variable outcomes depending on context, conjunction, and sequence also help explain patterns of contention and democratization outside of Europe. We should be astonished to find whole sequences or structures that we notice within Europe repeating themselves outside of Europe. If we have done an astute analysis of European political change, however, we should have some hope of identifying similar causal mechanisms operating elsewhere.

Second, the chapter's argument repeatedly performs an intellectual dance step we might describe as Two Splits and a Lump. At first encounter with an analytical problem it introduces lists of elements, significant distinctions, and minute formulations concerning covariation of elements. Then it turns around abruptly and adopts a much simpler formulation as a tool for historical analysis. It performs that disconcerting reel in order to acknowledge the subject's complexity, to make connections with readers who are chiefly interested in applying its conclusions elsewhere than in European history, to prepare other readers for qualifications and distinctions when explanation requires them, yet to render a narrative of three and one-half centuries manageable.

Polities and Political Identities

As no more than a point of departure, my argument assumes existence of an identifiable government and a polity organized around it. Figure 2.1 presents a crude, static model of government and polity. The government consists of an organization exercising control over concentrated means of coercive within recognized territorial limits. We call the organization a state if the organization is distinct from kinship groups, its means of coercion are enduring and extensive, the territories are relatively large, the organization enjoys priority over other organizations within those territories, and similar organizations nearby act to reinforce its authority. The polity attached to a particular government includes rulers, governmental agents, and other organized actors having some standing with respect to the government.

Organized actors vary in the extent to which they have routine access to agents, resources, and services under the government's control. As a first rough cut we can distinguish rulers; agents of the government; members of the polity enjoying routine access to the government; challengers outside the polity, constituted actors lacking routine access; and outside actors (such as other governments, international organizations, and external allies of

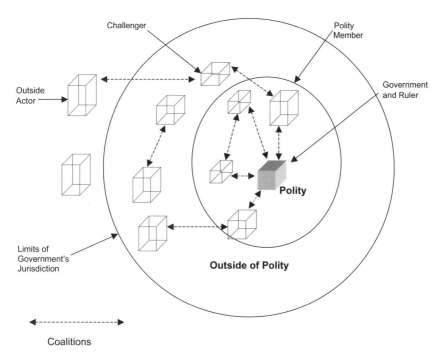

FIGURE 2.1. A static polity model

dissidents) that sometimes intervene in the polity's operation. All of these actors rest to some degree on social construction in the sense that people put organizational effort into creating coherent performances, separating the identities involved (e.g., as peasants, as members of a given community, or as followers of a certain leader) from other identities, and display signs of common membership. Nevertheless, the public identities of organized actors vary between two very different extremes: embedded identities figure widely in social life outside of public politics (as member of X family or inhabitant of hamlet Y are likely to do in complex rural communities), whereas detached identities appear almost exclusively in public politics (as is generally the case with such labels as Whig or Dissenter).

Embedded and detached identities imply not only significantly different forms of contentious politics but also contrasting processes of social construction. To the extent that embedded identities prevail in contention, transitions from daily routines to collective claim-making (e.g., as regular participants in a local market gang up on a price-gouging merchant) occur easily, but claims ordinarily remain local, particular, and short-lived whereas large-scale coordination of collective action faces serious obstacles. To the extent that detached identities prevail, specialized political entrepreneurs and organizations gain importance, transitions between explicitly political and nonpolitical interactions become more dramatic, and sustained, standardized large-scale making of claims increases in feasibility.

A liberal-to-radical Western tradition (e.g., Boggs 1997) has often identified a "public sphere" or "civil society" mediating between routine social life and public politics. Public opinion, organized preferences, trust, and collective commitment to change are supposed to form chiefly in that intermediate area, with social movements often regarded as the twentieth century's quintessential participants in relevant interactions and debates. The more vigorous, extensive, and autonomous that public sphere, runs a characteristic argument, the stronger the foundations of democracy. No agreement has emerged concerning the actual groups, social relations, or activities that constitute the public sphere or civil society (Ahrne 1996; Bratton 1989; Cohen and Arato 1992; Diamond 1997; Fatton 1992; Gellner 1994; Mamdani 1996; Mastnak 1990; Minkoff 1997; Seligman 1992; Somers 1993). Analysts also divide sharply as to whether civil society makes a difference to democracy through its production of shared attitudes, values, understandings, and practices that then permeate public politics or through its operation as an institutional constraint on professional politicians.

Within the polity model, a plausible site for the processes analysts have located in the public sphere or civil society would be in relations among constituted actors, both polity members and challengers. In addition to the coalitions already represented in Figure 2.1, an elaborated version of the diagram might then display opinion-forming interactions among all non-state actors that actually communicate with each other. Those interactions would then differ significantly among polities, depending on the distribution of constituted actors along the continuum from embedded to detached identities. We will, in fact, discover different interactions, and different political consequences of interactions, in polities whose principal actors bear strongly embedded identities, other polities whose principal actors deploy detached identities, and still other polities that lie between the two extremes. While avoiding reification of public sphere or civil society, I will borrow the insight that routine relations among constituted political actors, broadly defined, significantly affect prospects for democracy.

As we proceed to real political change and its explanation, of course, we will have to modify any such model and set it into motion: convert sharp boundaries into gradients, recognize strong differences among the relations of polity members to their governments, represent the continuous, contingent jockeying for position that occurs in any polity, unpack governments into their many levels, units, and agents, allow for the many forms of control over governments. For the moment, nevertheless, let us lump instead of splitting; a static polity model calls attention to the political context within which contentious claims emerge.

Coercion, Capital, and Connection

Regimes are to polities as fish species are to all fish. Regimes designate variable organizations of polities: more or less inclusive, more or less centralized, more or less unequal, and so on. Three variable elements of regimes' social environments strongly affect their organization. Let us call those three elements coercion, capital, and connection.

Coercion includes all concerted means of action that commonly cause loss or damage to the persons or possessions of social actors. We stress means such as weapons, armed forces, prisons, damaging information, and organized routines for imposing sanctions. Accumulation of such means within a given polity varies in principle from nonexistent (0) to huge (1), with low accumulation signifying that over a specified population the total volume of such means is small, high accumulation signifying that the population contains extensive coercive means. Concentration of coercive means likewise varies from trivial (0) to total (1), with low concentration signifying that whatever means exist disperse across the population, high accumulation signifying that all coercive means – however extensive – come close to forming a single clump under one agent's control. These distinctions define a two-dimensional space, whose four corners we might label anarchy, petty tyranny, guerrilla, and Leviathan. Figure 2.2's first panel represents that two-dimensional space.

The organization of coercion helps define the nature of a regime. In the lower left-hand corner of our diagram (anarchy) all regimes are insubstantial, whereas in the upper right-hand corner (Leviathan) all regimes are

A. COERCION

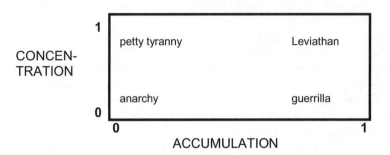

B. CAPITAL

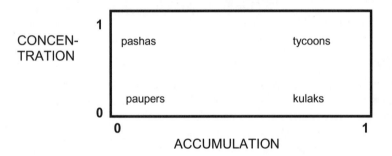

C. CONNECTION

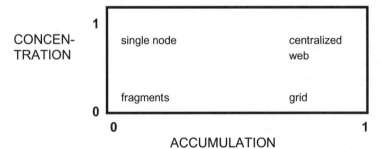

FIGURE 2.2. Coercion, capital, and connection

formidable. But because no government ever gains control of all the coercive means within its territory, the organization of coercion constitutes not only a feature of regimes but also part of each regime's immediate environment. All other things equal, for example, regimes in circumstances of high coercive accumulation and low coercive concentration (guerrilla) spend a good deal of their effort fighting off, repressing, evading, or making deals with violent entrepreneurs who are operating within the regime's territory but outside the government. Southern Italian regimes long operated in just such circumstances.

Capital refers to tangible, transferable resources that in combination with effort can produce increases in use value, plus enforceable claims on such resources. As with coercion, accumulation of capital varies in principle from nonexistent (o) to huge (1). Capital's concentration likewise varies from trivial (o) to total (1). The resulting two-dimensional space (panel B of Figure 2.2) contains corners we can call paupers, pashas, kulaks, and tycoons. In the case of pashas, for example, the total population in question has accumulated little capital, but a large share of what capital exists lies under the control of a few wealthy figures. In the idealized case of kulaks, relatively little concentration of capital obtains, but households all have substantial capital of their own.

In Europe since 1650, the organization of capital in a region shaped the region's regimes in several different ways: by determining the prominence of capitalists and cities as presences with which agents of government had to contend; by affecting the extent and form of resources that were available for governmental activities such as war, infrastructural investment, or enrichment of rulers; by affecting relations of nongovernmental activity (e.g., industrial production, trade, agriculture, migration) within the government's jurisdiction to activities outside that jurisdiction. Kulaks present very different problems and opportunities to aspiring rulers from the combination of pashas with impoverished shepherds or serfs.

By connection I mean relations among social sites (persons, groups, structures, or positions) that promote their taking account of each other. Connection's local organization varies as dramatically as do the structures of coercion and capital. Connections can take the form of shared religion or ethnicity, trading ties, work-generated solidarities, communities of taste, and much more. Accumulation in this regard varies in principle from a nonexistent o (every person an isolate, and no collective structures at all) to an overwhelming 1 (vast collective organization, including ties of every person to every other one). But concentration likewise occurs: from an even dispersion of relations across all social sites (o) to binding of everyone and everything that is connected at all into a single centralized system (1). Panel C represents variations in connection as one more two-dimensional space. Names for the four corners of this space are fragments, single node, grid, and centralized web.

How does connection impinge on regimes? First, it confronts agents of government with varying cleavages and solidarities inside the government's subject population – for example, the presence or absence of large religious, linguistic, racial, ethnic, or cultural minorities. Second, it affects the degree to which members of the subject population maintain strong relations with persons, groups, or organizations outside the government's own territory. Third, it influences the ease with which (and the means by which) governmental agents incorporate members of the subject population into the governmental structure. A fragmented population faces high costs of communication and resistance on a large scale but also presents formidable coordination costs to its government. In contrast, a population that resembles an evenly and intensely connected grid combines lower communication and resistance costs with vulnerability to observation and infiltration by governmental agents.

Over time and space, coercion, capital, and connection covary to some degree; as great chunks of accumulated coercion form, so in general do clumps of accumulated capital and webs of accumulated connection. Yet, in European experience as a whole, plenty of independent variation occurred in these regards: regions, periods, and structures combining high capital concentration with relatively little coercion, others combining extensive connection with little capital accumulation, and so on. A quarter century ago, the great Norwegian political analyst Stein Rokkan sketched "conceptual maps" of Europe to capture crucial geopolitical dimensions of variation in state formation. His maps excluded Russia and the Ottoman Empire, but they captured important patterns in the rest of Europe. Figure 2.3 presents one of Rokkan's more compact conceptual maps. It suggests three crucial insights:

1. Over the long sweep of history the continent's regimes varied significantly along an east-west axis differentiating the commercial-urban belt between central Italy and southern England from its more agrarian and landlord-dominated flanks.
2. Another north-south axis defined increasingly strong influence of international churches – notably the Roman Catholic Church – with proximity to the Mediterranean; on the whole Reformation-based state churches, which prevailed toward the north, fostered national unification, whereas strong relations with Rome hindered it.
3. Nevertheless over recent centuries regimes in these different regions underwent common experiences and mutual influences that pushed them toward increasing similarity in organization and operation.

As a consequence, east-west and north-south differences have attenuated without by any means disappearing. Rokkan himself looked backward, concentrating on origins of twentieth-century variation: why Scandinavian regimes resemble each other while differing so greatly from Mediterranean

	Distal Empire-Nations: Seaward	Proximal Empire-Nations: Seaward	Central City-State Europe	Proximal Empire-Nations: Landward	Distal Empire-Nations: Landward
PROTESTANT	Norway	Denmark	Hanse Germany	Prussia	Sweden
MIXED	Britain	France	Low Countries Rhineland Switzerland		
CATHOLIC	Portugal	Aragon-Castile: Spain	Italy	Bavaria Austria	Poland Hungary

FIGURE 2.3. Stein Rokkan's conceptual map of Europe. *Source:* Adapted from Rokkan 1975: 586.

regimes, and so on. He searched the past for "variables" that would explain differences in the present. But we can invert Rokkan's retrospective proce- dure, refining his conceptual maps to explain transformation of European governmental forms and their geographical distribution after 1650.

When we do so, some quibbles with Rokkan's formulation immediately come to mind. Whether we label Britain as more "distal" – less well connected with the central city-state band of Europe – than France, for example, depends heavily on what date we choose for the comparison. Britain remained relatively peripheral vis-à-vis France at the time of the Norman Conquest in 1066, but by 1650 the difference had vanished. Rokkan's omission of territories that became Russia and the Ottoman Empire hides the great influence of Muscovites, Vikings, Mongols, and other invaders on politics in the continent's eastern half, not to mention the significance of Orthodoxy, Islam, and Byzantine Christianity as organizing principles in European state formation. To ignore the profound influence of Muslim empires around the Mediterranean is to distort the political history of Iberia. As I can testify from many conversations with him on these matters, Rokkan would have been the first to recognize these limita- tions of his scheme, then to propose modifications that would take them into account. The Rokkanian scheme cannot serve us as a precise map. It nevertheless distills an important insight: the clustering of different sorts of state-forming conditions in different regions of Europe.

For our base line of 1650, we can easily translate Stein Rokkan's insight into the language of coercion, capital, and connection. On his east-west axis, the main differences concern the relative predominance of coercion and capital: landlord-controlled coercive means relatively powerful at the "distal" peripheries; merchant-organized capital relatively powerful in city- state Europe; and more equal combinations of coercion and capital along the flanks of the city-state region. The chief qualifications we require come from recognition that by 1650 the icy fingers of capital had long since gripped not only the central city-state band from Amsterdam to Venice but also the coastal regions of the Baltic, the North Sea, the British Isles, France, Iberia, and the Ottoman Empire.

With regard to connection and the north-south axis, we need a little more caution. Rokkan stressed the relative predominance of Catholic and Protestant religions, but other distinctions also require attention: not only other religious entities and identities such as Islam and Orthodoxy but also connections mediated by kinship, trading systems, linguistic pools, crafts, and membership in overarching political structures such as the Holy Roman Empire. As of the twelfth century, after all, the Hohenstaufen Empire ran from what are now the Netherlands and Denmark down through Sicily; such previous imperial connections left traces in the seventeenth century. Connection rose not only from north to south but also from periphery to center. With that qualification, Rokkan's formulation holds for 1650: on the whole, people toward the south and closer to the central city-state band connected more intensely with various long-distance networks that facilitated distant people's taking serious account of each other. This does not mean, of course, that they lived in sunny harmony.

How Social Environments Shaped Regimes

As of 1650, how did the geography of coercion, capital, and connection affect the character of regimes? No large European regime of that time greatly resembled a twentieth-century state; none exercised anything like routine twentieth-century state controls over resources, activities, and populations within its nominal territories, and none afforded anything like the extent of popular participation in national affairs that became commonplace after 1900. But prevailing combinations of coercion, capital, and connection in a region significantly affected the character of that region's regimes. In general, state capacity ran higher at intermediate levels of coercion, capital, and connection. Let us simplify again by reading "high" or "low" from the diagonals of our coercion, capital, and connection diagrams. That means multiplying accumulation by concentration and temporarily disregarding the difference between them. At very low levels of any (and especially all) of them, would-be rulers lacked the means to assemble organizations that could control resources and activities within their claimed territories; petty, fluctuating tyrannies characterized such marginal regions in the Europe of 1650. Much of the interior Balkans, buffer areas between the Russian and Ottoman empires, high mountain valleys, and pastoral islands such as Corsica and Sardinia conformed to this pattern.

Very high values on just one of the elements – coercion, capital, or connection – likewise blocked the creation of high-capacity governments; high accumulations and concentrations of coercion, as in Poland of the time, yielded war-making magnates who bowed reluctantly to central control and interfered incessantly in each other's regional rule. Disproportionate strength of capital yielded merchant-dominated political structures with great propensities to factionalism – although the case of the Dutch Republic shows that merchant oligarchies were also capable of fierce, if intermittent, coordination in warfare. In the absence of equivalent coercion and capital, extensive connection typically meant that local people had the means of escape from or resistance to the exactions of would-be state builders, as when persecuted Protestants received aid from their co-religionists elsewhere.

Intermediate and relatively equal levels of coercion, capital, and connection facilitated the creation of governmental capacity through synergy. Creators of effective states used their coercive means to draw resources from their capitalists in exchange for protection of commerce. But they also employed moderately centralized webs of connection to integrate subject

populations into their state enterprises through stable indirect rule.
Although Scandinavian, Burgundian, Habsburg, Ottoman, and North
Italian rulers had at various times over the two previous centuries made
partially successful attempts to create stable state capacity, by 1650 the two
leading exemplars were no doubt France and Britain.

Until the nineteenth century, Europe's large states worked their will on
subject populations chiefly through indirect rule; they empowered established, relatively autonomous local and regional authorities to collect taxes,
gather troops, administer justice, and maintain order on their behalf
without dispatching central agents for local or regional administration more
than intermittently. Rulers ruled directly in their capitals, indirectly elsewhere. Such an arrangement reduced the cost and personnel of government from the center's perspective, but it also set stringent limits on the
resources central authorities could extract from their nominal jurisdictions, reduced the amount of standardized control those authorities could
exert over activities within remote regions, promoted or tolerated the
formation of variable rights and obligations connecting different clusters
of subjects to agents of the central power, and augmented the influence
of privileged intermediaries. European colonizers exported a very similar
system to conquered territories outside of Europe. As Mahmood Mamdani
sums up for Africa:

Debated as alternative modes of controlling natives in the early colonial period,
direct and indirect rule actually evolved into complementary ways of native control.
Direct rule was the form of urban civil power. It was about the exclusion of natives
from civil freedoms guaranteed to citizens in civil society. Indirect rule, however,
signified a rural tribal authority. It was about incorporating natives into a state-
enforced customary order. Reformulated, direct and indirect rule are better understood as variants of despotism: the former centralized, the latter decentralized.
(Mamdani 1996: 18)

Although European "natives" sometimes belonged to the same broad linguistic and cultural groups as their rulers, the partition between direct and
indirect rule operated quite similarly within the colonizer's own continent.

More so than in European-conquered regions of Africa, however,
European indirect rule resulted from the interaction of top-down and
bottom-up politics. From the top, expanding states selectively incorporated
constituted leaders and their followers into state structures while granting
retention of previously existing rights and customs. From the bottom, constituted political actors bargained for particular rights as the price of peace
when they could not fight off their would-be conquerors. Thus even
centralizing Britain and France fashioned special systems of rule for such
territories as Ireland, Scotland, Brittany, and Franche-Comté.

Since 1650, accumulations and concentrations of coercion, capital, and
connection have all increased enormously in Europe as a whole. Although

the formation of standing armies, police forces, and weapons of mass destruction certainly register great expansions of coercive means, the sensational growth has occurred on the side of capital; as measured by total wealth, current income, productive plant, or domination of production and distribution, capital's influence over European life has multiplied (Bairoch 1976; Bairoch and Lévy-Leboyer 1981; de Vries 1984; Dodgshon 1987; Hohenberg and Lees 1985; Kellenbenz 1976). Connection has altered in a more mixed fashion: on one side an undoubted multiplication of connections among Europeans by means of political organization, commercial ties, and improved means of communication; on the other, undermining of transnational trade diasporas, linguistic networks, and crafts in favor of segmentation of social life within a limited number of well-bordered, increasingly monolingual states. Until the recent past, the net effect of changes in coercion, capital, and connection has been to make the particular state to which European citizens were attached more and more salient in all varieties of contentious politics. Even today, great debates surround the question of whether the European Community, international agencies such as the World Bank, and the globalization of capital are eroding the autonomous powers of established European states (see, e.g., Tilly et al. 1995; Wiener 1998).

Military Organization and Regime Change

Up to the nineteenth century, war and preparation for war played a large part in the formation of European states. War operated in contradictory fashion, creating similarities in state organization as it created dissimilarities in international power (Blockmans 1996; Blockmans and Genet 1993; Blockmans and Tilly 1994; Burke 1997; Koch 1993; Mann 1986, 1993; Porter 1994; Rasler and Thompson 1990; Spruyt 1994; Thomson 1994; 't Hart 1993; Tilly 1992, 1993). Most weak-state trajectories that might eventually have led to democratization sputtered out either because the ruling dynasties failed to produce viable heirs or because more powerful states conquered and incorporated them. Even where the physical environment provided some protection against outside political predators, as in Switzerland, defensive or offensive preparations generally left large traces in political organization. Swiss military forces, indeed, figured importantly in European warfare on their own account well into the sixteenth century, then as formidable mercenaries until the end of the eighteenth. They left behind them, among other things, strong ties between (male) military service and (male) citizenship at the cantonal level.

Aside from its notorious death, destruction, and wasted resources, the trouble with war was that it gave advantages to those political officials and entrepreneurs who could commandeer and discipline the means of military action: men, arms, transportation, food, clothing, military expertise, and money to buy them. Despite such counterexamples as Switzerland, Hesse, and the Dutch Republic, on the whole states based on large territories and populations did better in military competition than their small neighbors; in fact, they often gobbled up or subordinated those neighbors. France absorbed Franche-Comté; the English conquered Wales; the expanding Russian Empire incorporated dozens of previously autonomous but militarily weak political entities. For such smaller states, outside connections mattered greatly; links established by trade, dynastic solidarity, and religion increased the likelihood that powerful outsiders would intervene to stop the dissolution of a militarily vulnerable state.

Characteristic procedures for creation of military forces varied by era and region. Averaging brutally over Europe as a whole, we can impose a chronology something like this:

- Before 1300 or so, rulers drew armed forces from retainers, vassals, and militias who owed them personal service, but only in specified numbers, forms, seasons, and circumstances. Beyond those contractual limits, rulers had only their personal retinues to defend them.
- Between roughly 1300 and 1700, these older forms of military levy lost ground as contractor-supplied mercenaries became increasingly central to European warfare, peaking in the Thirty Years War (1618–1648). Even militia levies, as in Switzerland, fell under increasingly professional discipline. In the same process, tax farmers and other fiscal contractors who could raise money for warfare quickly acquired greater and greater power within European regimes. Military entrepreneurs and their forces similarly posed growing threats to the very regimes they served, because they enjoyed considerable autonomy from rulers and could either switch sides or refuse to fight when treated unsatisfactorily.
- Quite variably and through extensive struggle, after 1700 war-making powers shifted toward the formation of standing armies drawn from their domestic populations, thus absorbing military organization much more directly and durably into central state structures (Lynn 1990, 1993; Thomson 1994). Although partly autonomous financiers continued to organize much of the fiscal preparation for war, increasingly regimes internalized the fiscal apparatus, building bulky administrative structures for customs, excise, direct taxes, and other sources of money to finance war. In the longer run, dependence on the state-controlled fiscal apparatus reduced political autonomy of the military. How this process worked and how far it went in a particular regime strongly affected the extent and character of democratization.
- Over the long-run process, war-driven conquest and consolidation reduced the number of at least nominally autonomous political units in Europe from thousands at the first millennium of the Christian era to thirty-odd at the second millennium.

- Creation of large-scale centralized control over means of war expanded state capacity in general, usually at the expense of protected consultation. But most weak states disappeared. As a result, far more long-term trajectories of European regimes resembled our strong-state cartoon than our weak-state cartoon. When we search for special characteristics of those few trajectories that led to early and general democratization, we are mainly picking our way among strong-state trajectories.

The relative weights of coercion, capital, and connection in a region and era, however, strongly affected how these state-forming processes operated, and with what organizational consequences. Regarding intersections of coercion and capital, we can distinguish among three stylized paths of change: coercion-intensive, capital-intensive, and capitalized coercion. Coercion-intensive state formation, which occurred in regions where autonomous holders of coercion such as troop-raising large landlords predominated in the absence of powerful cities and capitalists, involved rule by means of those coercion-wielding intermediaries as in Russia, Poland, and Castile. Coercion-intensive states had military advantages so long as most wars were being fought by militias and feudal levies, but they lost out in naval warfare, in the rental of mercenaries, and in the purchase of heavy military equipment.

Capital-intensive state formation, the characteristic process of what Stein Rokkan called city-state Europe, depended heavily on cities and capitalists, as in the Dutch and Venetian republics. Militias, freebooters, mercenaries, and convertible fleets gave city-states substantial advantages in defensive actions, maritime warfare, and acquisition of military means on international markets. But states following this trajectory remained vulnerable to fragmentation, to merchants' pursuit of their parochial interests, and to land warfare against large standing armies.

State formation through capitalized coercion resulted from the conjunction between substantial concentrations of coercion and capital, such that rulers (as in England and France) could play each against the other and acquire war-making resources from both sides. In the creation of effective military power, states that could draw on capitalized coercion eventually prevailed over those following coercion-intensive and capital-intensive trajectories. Through conquest and emulation, their forms of organization then became the dominant European models of state structure. As a consequence, many a European area that entered the sixteenth century on a well-defined coercion-intensive or capital-intensive path entered the twentieth century under a regime centering on capitalized coercion.

Connection modified effects of capital and coercion without fundamentally altering them. Between 1450 and 1700 Europe underwent enormous struggles over proper relations between state attachments and religious identities: expulsions and forced conversions of Muslims and Jews in Iberia, reform movements, Protestant breakaways, and outright creations of state-based Protestant churches in the rest of Catholic Europe, intermittent armed conflict between Protestants and Catholics in France, Britain, Switzerland, the Netherlands, and elsewhere. Although war between the expanding Ottomans and their Christian neighbors always had religious overtones, these conflicts had relatively little impact within Orthodox and Ottoman Europe. Ottoman obliteration of the Byzantine Empire during the fifteenth century, however, freed Orthodox hierarchies to cluster around protective states. As Rokkan's conceptual maps indicated, those struggles generally fortified state capacity to the degree that they established the independence of national churches from Rome and Constantinople-Istanbul.

Between the treaties of Westphalia (1648) and the French Revolution of 1789–1799, state churches and statist churches continued to support the expansion of state capacity in much of Europe. Despite their nominal Catholicism, for example, France, Portugal, and Spain all expelled the Rome-oriented Jesuit order during the eighteenth century. Where sub-divisions of a state adhered officially to different faiths (as in the Swiss confederation) religious cleavage inhibited that expansion.

A great shift in the salience of connection, however, occurred with the French Revolution; partly as a result of French conquests in the name of captive nations, common ethnic origin – nationality – acquired unprece-dented importance as a basis for state formation. On one side, rulers who already controlled a state organized state-led nationalism, promoting the predominance of a single cultural complex including language, festivals, costumes, historical accounts of national origins, and sometimes religious traditions. On the other side, cultural minorities within empires and large states organized state-seeking nationalism, demanding political autonomy on the grounds that they constituted distinctive peoples. The nineteenth-century unifications of Germany and Italy combined state-led with state-seeking nationalisms. As they picked apart the multicultural Ottoman Empire, European powers encouraged state-seeking nationalism on the part of Greeks, Albanians, and many others.

In almost every such process, rival claimants arose who demanded recog-nition as leaders either of the same putative nationalities or of other nation-alities whose rights recognition of the first claimant would trample. That cycle of claim and counterclaim continues into our day. It added to coercion-intensive, capital-intensive, and capitalized-coercion trajectories alike regular creation and imposition of the routines, understandings, and obligations of nationality.

Any of these paths entailed extensive demands on subject populations for the means of war. (Partial exceptions occurred where international trade or tribute from colonies provided state revenues. But, as the experiences of Spain and Portugal illustrate, that form of financing for war made rulers vulnerable both to interruptions of revenue flows and to pressures from international bankers who supplied them with short-term credit.) Subject populations most often responded with evasion, rebellion, or intermittent compliance. Where rulers succeeded in overcoming those obstacles, they always engaged in bargaining with brokers, with groups yielding the crucial resources, or with both at once. Bargains established mutual rights and obligations between subjects and state agents, for example, by defining legitimate and illegitimate procedures for conscription or taxation.

Where state capacity increased significantly, that expansion made control over the state an increasing advantage for whoever had it, hence an increasing object of struggle. Sometimes contention over state apparatus, personnel, and action had the effect of establishing citizenship, broadening it, equalizing it, creating mechanisms of binding consultation, and expanding protection for citizens. In those rare cases, the spiral of militarization and struggle promoted democratization.

Region by region, ghosts of regimes that had prevailed in a given part of Europe haunted later regimes in the same regions (Downing 1992; Ertman 1997). Two different mechanisms produced that effect: borrowing of visible organizational models for political work, shaping of political regimes by social relations that outlasted them. Iberia provides striking examples of the two mechanisms at work. Christian rulers from the Iberian North accomplished the centuries-long expulsion of Muslim rulers from the peninsula largely by licensing municipalities and freebooting horsemen to raise their own military forces in exchange for booty and extensive, autonomous but royally sanctioned political rights. The creation of government as federations of chartered nobles and municipalities rightfully exercising licensed violence and fiscal privileges then became a standard Iberian model and the fundamental structures of parliaments in the peninsula. But it also established relations between aristocrats and plebeians – the latter liable to regionally based taxation, forced labor, and military service not as horsemen (*caballeros*) but as foot-soldiers (*peones*) – that survived the centuries. When newly crowned emperor Charles V put down Castile's rebellion of the Holy League (or Comuneros) in 1520, he cemented the settlement by ceding fiscal, administrative, and representative advantages to the very municipalities whose militias had constituted the rebellion's most effective fighting forces.

In a superb synthesis of scattered research on popular participation in European contentious politics between 1500 and 1700, Wayne te Brake (1998) has mapped the great variety of regimes that existed north of the Balkans and west of Russia. Figure 2.4 sums up his mapping. The "late medieval composite state" itself designates a wide variety of structures from small to large and from urban leagues to dynastic tyrannies. Almost all, te Brake rightly insists, involved diverse organizational components, multiple layers of sovereignty, and contingent, contested relations among their elements. Te Brake argues strongly (and again rightly) against the teleological idea that as of either 1500 or 1700 all states were converging on a single

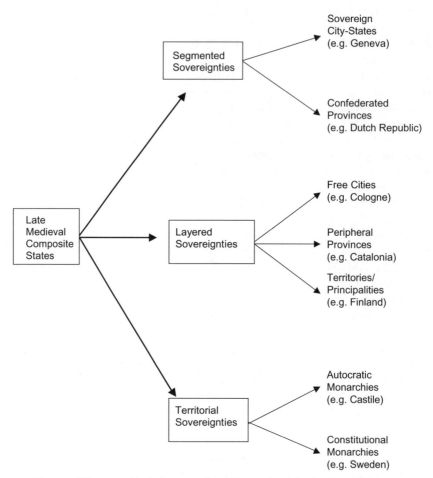

FIGURE 2.4. Wayne te Brake's map of regime trajectories in Europe, 1500–1700. *Source:* Adapted from te Brake 1998: 184–186.

type of presumably modern state. On the contrary, he shows, struggles of the sixteenth and seventeenth centuries shaped new sorts of states, quite different from each other, that persisted well into the following century. These diverse trajectories laid down distinctive institutional and cultural materials in different parts of Europe.

Because they are necessarily particular, these influences of previous regimes do not lend themselves to the same simple schematization as coercion, capital, and connection. Nevertheless, one general feature of historical influence deserves our attention. The major empires that impinged on European territory all left indelible marks on the continent's political life. The Roman Empire and its successors, right through the Habsburgs, provided a legacy of Roman law, Romance languages, municipal autonomy, and regional military organization that shaped subsequent state formation throughout the continent's western half. Nomadic invaders such as Mongols and Turks repeatedly swept in from the Eurasian steppe to create empires in Europe's southeastern third; their tribute-taking institutions, subordination of sedentary cultivators, impaling of enemies, and reliance on episodic terror to keep urban populations in check marked subsequent regimes within their zones of influence. The wide incorporation of southern European territory in Islamic empires (notably including the Ottomans, for all the ultimate origins of their founders in the steppe) established procedures for attaching chartered religious, ethnic, and commercial minorities to culturally distinct regimes; they also provided institutionalized connections to the long-dominant trading system that linked the Middle East, East Africa, India, China, and Southeast Asia (Abu-Lughod 1989; Chaudhuri 1990). Byzantine, Bulgarian, and other more fleeting empires likewise left institutions, languages, and ties among dispersed peoples in their wake. These were the connections and cultural materials with which later creators of political systems had to work.

Regional variation in the accumulation and concentration of coercion, capital, and connection, then, strongly affected the sorts of governmental institutions that formed in different parts of Europe through the centuries, but the prior impact of certain kinds of regime in a region constrained what kinds of regimes formed later. Adjacent governments consequently tended to form similar sorts of relations with their subject populations as well as with other governments, and to reinforce each other in doing so.

So far we have concentrated on change and variation in (1) politically relevant social environments, (2) regimes, (3) interactions between them. In order to bring the analysis of contention more directly into the discussion, we have to stop splitting for a while and undertake some more lumping. The remainder of this chapter takes social environments for granted, introduces a simple model of politics, then incorporates contentious politics into that model.

The word "claims" resonates across my analysis of contention. It refers to interactions in which one party acts (however successfully or ineffectually) to elicit responses from another party. Typical claim-making verbs include request, propose, demand, command, beseech, beg, implore, petition, solicit, attack, bribe, entice, require, expel, chase, massacre, and confront. Contentious politics, then, refers to collective making of claims on others, which, if realized, would affect those others' interests, when at least one of the parties (including third parties) is a government. The definition excludes quite a bit of political life, for example, gathering to plan, to celebrate, to persuade, or to exercise routine political rights and obligations; such actions join contentious politics only when they include explicit claims on others and affect relations of people to governments. Contentious

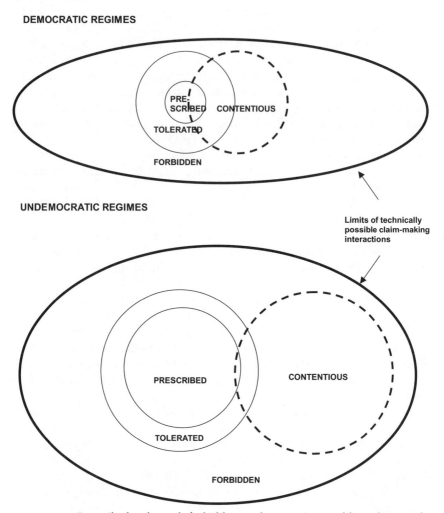

FIGURE 2.5. Prescribed, tolerated, forbidden, and contentious public politics under democratic and undemocratic regimes

politics includes, however, wars, revolutions, social movements, rallies, terrorist actions, many strikes, collective attacks on officials or public properties, and a wide variety of other concerted actions, just so long as participants make fairly definite interest-affecting claims on others and at least one government is somehow involved as claimant, object of claims, arbiter, monitor, guarantor, or partisan in some other regard.

Routine, institutionalized politics often includes circumscribed forms of contention, thus defined: legal proceedings, parliamentary debates, contested elections, humble petitions, and more. Figure 2.5 schematizes the problem and frames some preliminary hypotheses concerning differences between relatively democratic and undemocratic regimes. In both kinds of regimes, authorities prescribe a certain number of political performances such as payment of taxes and military service; authorities offer both positive and negative incentives for meeting those political obligations. They also tolerate a range of performances outside the prescribed zone, for example, by allowing leaders of established churches to take positions on current political issues or by declining to intervene in local struggles over control of turf. Within limits of their capacity, they typically forbid a considerably larger array of technically possible ways of making claims, for example, assassination and mass religious ecstasy. Contentious claim-making can, in principle, coincide with prescribed means, as when challengers disrupt public ceremonies. It can coincide with tolerated means, as when legal public meetings entertain seditious demands. Or it can enter the terrain of forbidden means, as when challengers of the established order take up armed attacks on public officials.

Politics in general centers on two kinds of interactions: between agents of government and other actors, between other actors when governments figure as significant third parties. Most politics consists of performances in the sense that previously established scripts exist for the relevant interactions, however much participants improvise in their enactment of those scripts. Here we concentrate on collective, public performances, both contentious and otherwise, treating the give-and-take of small-scale patron-client relations, politicians' individual efforts at mutual influence, private deal-making, and routine governmental administration as essential background, but not as our major object of analysis.

All these points are matters of definition. The scheme also incorporates four hypotheses for verification and modification in further research:

1. Technically possible claim-making interactions cover a wider range in undemocratic regimes, both because experience with democracy systematically unfits the subject population for many damaging and high-risk forms of claim-making and because, on the average, democratic regimes rest on states and economies that have installed greater uniformity in social structure within their territories.

2. For essentially the same reasons, contentious claim-making includes a wider range of performances in undemocratic regimes than in democratic regimes.

3. Democratic regimes impose a smaller ratio of prescribed to tolerated political performances, so that a considerable portion of democratic public politics takes place in forms and settings that state agents authorize and monitor but do not prescribe. Undemocratic regimes prescribe and forbid more performances, leaving only narrow ranges of toleration. (The hypothesis, as we will soon see, makes more sense for high-capacity than for low-capacity states.)

4. Under democratic regimes, contentious politics greatly overlaps prescribed and tolerated forms of political performance. Under undemocratic regimes, in contrast, contentious claim-making rarely enters
the prescribed sphere (and there chiefly as subversion or covert
protest) while extending farther into forbidden performances than
under democracies.

Democratic regimes, runs the main argument, draw contention toward
their prescribed and tolerated performances, whereas undemocratic regimes
generally make sure that prescribed performances – the great bulk of routine
public politics – stay away from contested claims. Prescribed and tolerated
forms of contention often figure in my analysis as contexts, counterparts,
and even objects of more unruly actions. The analysis stresses, however,
contentious action that is public, repeated, organized, but not prescribed
by the governments in question – not routine voting or exchanges of favors
in patron-client networks, but gathering visibly to demand, complain,
attack, affirm, oppose, support, block, resist, and so on through the lexicon
of claim-making verbs. Each of the relevant verbs entails a relation between
claimants and objects of claims, rather than the single-minded attitude,
mentality, or state of consciousness implied by such words as "protest" and
"rebellion." I stress nonprescribed contentious relations out of a belief that
they play crucial – and usually underestimated – parts in the formation of
democracy.

Democracy? Here I adopt a relational definition. It lies halfway between
two other competing conceptual traditions: substantive and constitutional.
Substantive definitions of democracy stress outcomes such as equity, justice,
community, and satisfaction of needs. Constitutional definitions stress
legally prescribed arrangements such as contested elections, representative
parliaments, and independent judiciaries. A relational definition highlights
interactions between citizens and their governments. It requires a substantial government that enforces rights and obligations of citizenship. Although
the content of citizenship often varies by age, gender, and other social
characteristics, citizenship in general identifies a set of mutual, binding
rights and obligations linking governmental agents directly to whole categories of people defined by their attachment to a given government. In
relational terms, a regime is democratic in so far as it installs: broad citizenship; equal citizenship; binding consultation of citizens with respect to
governmental personnel, resources, and policies; and protection of citizens,
especially members of minorities, from arbitrary action by governmental
agents.

In this view, a regime may be democratic without providing well-being
to all its citizens, much less all people subject to its influence. A regime may
also be undemocratic despite having all the constitutional consultative
apparatus of functioning democracies, simply because it does not protect

its citizens from arbitrary action by state agents or because rich and powerful persons subvert ostensibly binding consultation of citizens. By these standards, no regime in the world has ever been fully democratic. All have operated somewhere on the plane between full democracy at one extreme, and narrow, unequal, or nonexistent citizenship; no governmental consultation of the subject population; and no protection from arbitrary governmental agents, at the other.

The bulk of historical polities have not featured citizenship in any strong sense of the word. Constituted political actors have enjoyed (or suffered from) variable relations to governments and each other, but most regimes have not established general categories of the population defined exclusively by the rights and obligations that tie them to governmental agents. Instead, custom, compact, and conquest have typically created particular relations between existing groups and governments: patron-client chains, purchased immunities, customary tributes, recognitions of communal peculiarities, treaty-based rights of appeal, and so on. Relatively embedded identities have predominated over the course of political history.

Each element of democracy – breadth, equality, consultation, and protection – is a citizenship-tinged special case of a more general element that varies among polities:

1. Breadth of polity membership: what proportion of a government's subject population belongs to constituted actors that are polity members?
2. Equality of polity membership: how similar is the access to governmental agents, resources, and services available to constituted polity members?
3. Consultation of polity members: to what extent do existing polity members exercise collective control over governmental agents, services, and resources?
4. Protection of polity members: how extensive are constraints on arbitrary action by rulers and governmental agents?

Only where breadth, equality, consultation, and protection couple with categorical establishment of rights and obligations – that is, with citizenship – can we reasonably characterize a regime as democratic. Although we will often explore breadth, equality, consultation, and protection separately, for the sake of setting our problem, it helps to lump them, to combine them into a single index of protected consultation, high being relatively democratic, low being undemocratic. Imagine each of them as running from 0 (e.g., no protection whatsoever) to 1 (e.g., full protection of all citizens). Then imagine a multiple: breadth × equality × consultation × protection = extent of protected consultation. The multiple's range runs in principle from 0 (no breadth, equality, consultation, or protection whatsoever) to 1 (full breadth, equality, consultation, and protection). Near the bottom of this range we would find seventeenth-century Russia, near its top the Netherlands after World War II.

Effective democratization depends not only on the presence of protected consultation at the small scale but also on the capacity of governments to sustain breadth, equality, consultation, and protection. Governmental capacity is the actual impact of action by governmental agents on activities and resources within the government's jurisdiction, relative to some standard of quality and efficiency. (Eventually any full analysis of these processes must distinguish two aspects of governmental capacity, the top-down extractive and coercive ability that Michael Mann calls "despotic power" and the collective ability to change things that Mann calls "infra-structural power," but it will simplify the work at hand to blur Mann's distinction.) As with protected consultation, we can imagine governmental capacity as ranging in principle from 0 (no impact whatsoever) to 1 (when they occur, governmental actions completely control relevant activities and resources). Effective democratization only occurs above some combined threshold of governmental capacity and protected consultation.

Figure 2.6 schematizes the argument. At low levels of governmental capacity and protected consultation, no citizenship worthy of the name exists. Instead, fragmented tyranny prevails, with warlords, landlords, bandits, priests, merchants, and/or heads of kinship groups competing with each other and exercising hegemony on a small scale. The zone of citizenship lies at the other end, where some minimum degrees of govern-mental capacity and protected consultation coexist. Citizenship, according to the scheme, varies within limits set by three extremes: (A) relatively low levels of protected consultation combined with very high state capacity, which more or less describes totalitarian citizenship; (B) relatively low state capacity with very extensive protected consultation, which more or less describes limited citizenship; and (C) extensive protected consultation in company with high state capacity, which more or less describes an idealized welfare-state citizenship.

Only those cases closer to extremes B and C qualify as democratic. The diagram's curved diagonal arrow accordingly represents the main line (although, of course, not the actual historical trajectory) of democratiza-tion. Its downward slope toward the upper right incorporates the hypoth-esis that very high levels of governmental capacity actually bar effective democratization because they increase incentives and abilities of govern-mental agents and their closest allies to intervene on behalf of their own interests instead of providing effective consultation or protection. Thus the argument built into the diagram implies that conflict between the many and the few increases with rising state capacity, that at the extreme citizenship based on vast state powers begins to contradict protected consultation among citizens.

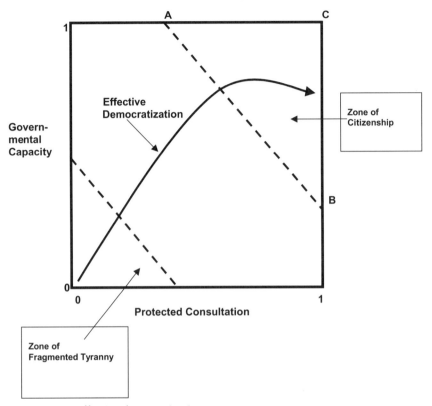

FIGURE 2.6. Effective democratization

Figure 2.7 sketches two idealized paths out of fragmented tyranny into democracy, taking only central states into account. The "strong state" path involves early increases of governmental capacity, often at the expense of whatever protected consultation existed in previous regimes. Later we see expansion of protected consultation as struggle produces broadening and equalization of access to state agents, services, and resources while binding consultation and protection generalize. In such historical experiences, goes the hypothesis, even the resulting democratic state bears distinct marks of its authoritarian history in the form of centralized institutions and serious constraints on the range of tolerated political performances.

Russia and Prussia stand as exemplars of the strong-state path to citizenship and democracy. The weak-state trajectory entails elaboration of protected consultation – relatively broad and equal access to the state, binding consultation, and creation of protections from arbitrary state action – before any great expansion of state capacity. Here again we expect to see

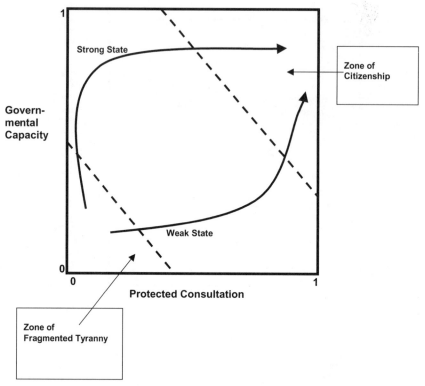

FIGURE 2.7. Strong-state versus weak-state paths to democracy

residues of previous history in the workings of democracy and citizenship, with greater restraints on the state's power of intervention in local affairs and greater accommodation of difference. In this case Switzerland will serve as a model.

Even where they eventuated in democracy, most European experiences lay between the two idealized trajectories and followed more irregular paths. In Great Britain, for example, eighteenth-century wars and colonial expansion built up a strong central-state apparatus amid local autonomies that had previously been vested in landlords, magistrates, municipalities, and (especially after 1689) elements of the Anglican Church. In the Low Countries, municipal oligarchies predominated until French conquests under the Revolution and Napoleon established centralized regimes that endured into the nineteenth century. In Scandinavia, the Protestant Reformation promoted alliances between war-making rulers and state-serving pastors in the construction of relatively high-capacity states, but (especially in Norway and Sweden) peasants acquired corporate representation in return for provision of military service. Russia went from tribute-taking regimes leaving great autonomy to landlords and warlords to extensive incorporation of landlords and bureaucrats into a repressive administrative hierarchy. Both the Balkans and much of Iberia featured sharp alternations between imperial expansion and petty tyrannies, with effects on democratic politics that endure today. In short, strong-state and weak-state paths to democracy present cartoons of limiting cases.

Along either of these idealized trajectories, democracy builds on citizenship but does not exhaust it. Indeed, most Western states created some forms of citizenship after 1800, but over most of that period the citizenship in question was too narrow, too unequal, too nonconsultative and/or too unprotective to qualify their regimes as democratic. Take the regimes we loosely call "totalitarian": they typically combined high governmental capacity with relatively broad and equal citizenship, but afforded neither binding consultation nor extensive protection from arbitrary action by agents. Some monarchies maintained narrow, unequal citizenship while consulting the happy few who enjoyed citizenship and protecting them from arbitrary action by governmental agents; those regimes thereby qualified as oligarchies. In searching for democratic regimes, we can take relatively high governmental capacity for granted because it is a necessary condition for strong consultation and protection. We will recognize a high-capacity regime as democratic when it installs not only citizenship in general, but broad citizenship, relatively equal citizenship, strong consultation of citizens, and significant protection of citizens from arbitrary action by governmental agents.

Both consultation and protection require further stipulations. Although many rulers have claimed to embody their people's will, only states that have created concrete preference-communicating institutions have installed binding, effective consultation. In the West, representative assemblies, contested elections, referenda, petitions, courts, and public meetings of the empowered figure most prominently among such institutions. Whether opinion polls, discussions in mass media, or special-interest networks qualify in fact or in principle remains highly controversial; to the extent that governmental agents routinely alter their performances in response to these forms of consultation, however, we should no doubt include them among the instruments of democracy – with due regard to their frequently antidemocratic effects on breadth, equality, and protection.

On the side of protection, democracies typically guarantee zones of toleration for speech, belief, assembly, association, and public identity, despite generally imposing some cultural standards for participation in the polity; a regime that prescribes certain forms of speech, belief, assembly, association, and public identity while banning all other forms may maintain broad, equal citizenship and a degree of consultation, but it slides away from democracy toward populist authoritarianism. Some of democracy's most acute dilemmas concern the ways in which supporting one actor's preferred cultural patterns threatens another actor's well-being or survival: is it consistent with democracy, for example, to impose a majority culture's norms with regard to familial, sexual, or conflict-settlement behavior on minorities that have nurtured contrary norms? High-capacity states run the risk not only of compromising democracy by diverting state resources to influential polity members but also of imposing debilitating demands on culturally distinct minorities.

The place of brokerage in contention illustrates a similar interplay of political culture, state capacity, and democracy. People live their lives within historically accumulated and historically modified cultural complexes containing cosmologies, discourses, categories, sets of meanings, and allowable social relations. Those cultural complexes constrain social life by channeling the social interactions of which people can readily conceive, collective understandings concerning the propriety and likely consequences of those interactions, routines and connections that facilitate such interactions, and collectively available stories that people use to interpret past, present, and future interactions. Every social world beyond a very small scale contains multiple cultural complexes of this sort, some overlapping and some segregated from each other. Cultural brokers – either simultaneous members of two or more cultural complexes or knowledgeable mediators among them – play critical roles in organizing communication and mobility among cultural complexes. Thus bilingual travel agents often become significant figures in today's immigrant communities; they acquire influence outside by claiming successfully to speak for those communities. Historically, Europe's priests, landlords, merchants, and schoolteachers often played similar roles as cultural brokers.

The very general phenomenon of cultural brokerage has a political version. Each government selects and creates a limited cultural complex as the medium of its official business. To the extent that the government is powerful and attractive, its limited cultural complex informs claim-making throughout its polity. Nationalist governments aggressively pursue programs to impose a single cultural standard on public life, but all governments do some thinning and standardizing of cultural complexes within their own spheres (Scott 1998). Separatists, in contrast, defend threatened cultural complexes from obliteration by officially imposed cultural forms. Hence a discrepancy (and sometimes intense conflict) occurs between cultural complexes prevailing in zones strongly influenced by government and zones in which people live out other parts of their lives. It has become a cliché of academic and cinematic writing, for example, to dramatize contrasts between the stylized culture of Louis XIV's courtiers and grim living conditions in the seventeenth-century French countryside.

We can distinguish five stylized responses of governments to incompatibilities between their official cultural complexes and those that pervade all or some of their subject populations: (1) ignore, (2) repress, (3) segregate,

(4) incorporate, (5) create an unacknowledged set of accommodations. Response Number 1 happens chiefly in low-capacity states; its operation in high-capacity states requires a paradoxical deliberate organization of ignorance. Number 2 is the standard strategy of state-led nationalism. Numbers 3, 4, and 5 constitute variants on the same strategy, the establishment of a modus vivendi with populations that retain some sort of relation to centers of power but also maintain their own distinct cultural complexes. In all three variants of the accommodative strategy, cultural brokers play crucial parts as simultaneous interpreters. As brokers do in a wide variety of settings, governmental or otherwise, they typically acquire power and access to resources in the process, and therefore acquire an interest in maintaining existing relations between the distinct populations they represent and central authorities.

All other things equal, increasing state capacity enhances the salience of brokerage, while democratization diminishes it. Why? At least up to the point where state capacity begins to destroy or assimilate all nonstate cultural complexes, increasing state capacity sharpens the discrepancy between the state sphere and other spheres of life while augmenting the significance of state actions for the lives of all people within the state's jurisdiction. Hence brokers who bridge the gap between public and private spheres gain prominence as mediators and interlocutors. But democratization moves all persons and politically constituted actors closer toward having their own established means of access to state services, resources, and personnel, a process that diminishes the leverage brokers wield. Established rights and obligations of citizenship substitute for brokerage.

To be sure, in a world of ever-incomplete democracy brokerage never disappears. As we will see abundantly later on, every democratic social movement features intermediate figures who claim to speak for aggrieved populations but in the face of those populations also claim privileged access to circles of power; indeed radical members of their followings often accuse such brokers of selling out to the establishment. Immigrants in pursuit of citizenship frequently rely on longer-term immigrants as their guides and intermediaries. Political parties themselves often employ favor dispensers who garner votes for their candidates. Yet such temporary brokers occupy much less significant places in the contentious politics of their time than do the religious leaders, tribal chiefs, party patrons, and regional princes who figure centrally in less democratic versions of high-capacity politics.

Figure 2.8 summarizes the joint effect of democratization and increasing state capacity on the salience of brokerage, arguing that brokerage reaches its peak in circumstances of little democracy and high state capacity. If correct, this argument has deep significance for the character, trajectories, and dynamics of contentious politics – notably for the centrality of brokers as initiators, interlocutors, and negotiators of contested claims. In a strong-state path to democratization, for example, we should find brokers first

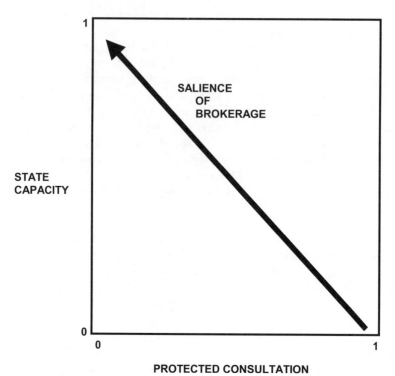

FIGURE 2.8. Salience of brokerage in popular politics as a function of state capacity and protected consultation

increasing greatly in political activity as state capacity increases, then fading away dramatically with the move of a high-capacity state toward protected consultation.

Political culture matters in another way. In the corner of our two-dimensional space that contains effective democratic regimes, previous historical experience has laid down a set of models, understandings, and practices concerning such matters as how to conduct a contested election. Once Britain, France, and other major countries had created procedures for routine electoral consultation, their examples shaped later innovations. This political culture of democracy limits options for newcomers both because it offers templates for the construction of new regimes and because it affects the likelihood that existing power holders – democratic or not – will recognize a new regime as democratic.

Over the long run of human history, must regimes have been undemocratic; democratic regimes are rare, contingent, recent creations. Partial democracies have, it is true, formed intermittently at a local scale – for example, in villages ruled by councils incorporating most heads of house-

hold. At the scale of a city-state, a warlord's domain, or a regional federation, forms of government have run from dynastic hegemony to oligarchy,
with narrow, unequal citizenship or none at all, little or no binding consultation, and uncertain protection from arbitrary governmental action.

Before the nineteenth century, as we have seen, large states and empires
generally managed by means of indirect rule: systems in which the central
power received tribute, cooperation, and guarantees of compliance on
the part of subject populations from regional power holders who enjoyed
great autonomy within their own domains. Up to the French Revolution
of 1789–99, ecclesiastical, noble, judicial, and even fiscal intermediaries –
political and cultural brokers – who continued to evade or resist central
control played significant parts in the government of France. The great
regional power exercised by British justices of the peace exemplifies the persistence of indirect rule into the politics of nineteenth-century Great Britain.
Seen from the bottom, such systems often imposed tyranny on ordinary
people. Seen from the top, however, they lacked capacity; intermediaries
supplied resources, but they also set stringent limits to rulers' ability to
govern or transform the world within their presumed jurisdictions.

Under systems of indirect rule, bicultural and bipolitical brokers maintain and profit from crucial links between ruling classes and the subject
population. The subject population typically organizes its relations to rulers
around distinctive, manifestly subordinate identities: as commoners in relation to nobles, as members of tolerated religious minorities in relation to
followers of the state religion, as tribal clusters in relation to ostensibly
national populations, and so on.

Only the nineteenth century brought Europe widespread adoption of
direct rule, creation of structures extending governmental communication
and control continuously from central institutions to individual localities
or even to households, and back again. Even then, direct rule ranged from
the unitary hierarchies of centralized monarchy to the segmentation of
federalism. On a large scale, direct rule made substantial citizenship, and
therefore democracy, possible. Possible, but not likely, much less inevitable:
instruments of direct rule have sustained many oligarchies, some auto-
cracies, a number of party- and army-controlled states, and a few fascist
tyrannies. Even in the era of direct rule most polities have remained far
from democratic.

In France and Britain, nevertheless, installation of direct rule eventually
promoted democratization. In both countries, eighteenth-century expansion
of military activities greatly increased the state's demand for money,
supplies, manpower, and popular compliance. Increased state demands,
however, also generated resistance, often including resistance by segments
of the ruling classes – major members, that is, of the polity – who found
their privileges and identities threatened. Responding to, suppressing,
bypassing, or bargaining with elite and popular resistance all involved state

agents in creation of new forms of organization, new connections with subject populations, and new understandings concerning rights and obligations binding states and their subjects. In the process, intermediaries such as priests and landlords lost some of their own power and autonomy.

These organizational innovations moved both French and British states toward direct rule, toward creation of citizenship, and toward elements of democracy. What is more, political leaders and organizers in the two countries eyed each other uneasily across the Channel, sometimes borrowing institutions such as the lobby and the meeting (both terms carried intact from English into French), sometimes deliberately fashioning alternatives to their neighbors' practices, as when French revolutionaries of 1848 eliminated their equivalent of the House of Lords and adopted near-manhood suffrage.

Beyond these very general common properties, France and Britain followed rather different trajectories, even after 1650: through outright revolution on the French side, through a series of challenges, rebellions, standoffs, negotiations, and (especially if we include Ireland) near-revolutions on the British side. That contrast offers a splendid opportunity for explanation. An effective explanation of similarities and differences in French and British experiences with democratizaiton will offer a valuable entrée into comparing the democratizing experiences of France and Britain with those of other European countries that democratized later, differently, or not at all.

My long-term aim is to trace causal connections between (1) national histories of contentious politics and (2) a polity's changing position in a terrain one edge of which touches high governmental capacity, broad citizenship, equal citizenship, strong consultation, and significant protection, while the opposite edge features a weak state, nonexistent citizenship, unequal access to the state, no consultation of people subject to a state's jurisdiction, and no protection against arbitrary governmental action. We must trace those causal connections, however, within significant limits set by the path-dependent histories of different European regions. Democratic arrangements that emerged in one country or another bore strong marks of earlier political struggles in the same countries.

Some episodes of contention actually promoted democracy in two different ways: first, they induced power holders to make direct concessions such as broadening the franchise. Second, struggles often generated innovations – special-interest associations, nonmilitary policing, claim-making forms such as the demonstration, governmental surveillance or public opinion, and more – that in turn had the (often unintended) effect of broadening citizenship, equalizing it, expanding consultation, or increasing protection from arbitrary government action. Democracy, in short, often advanced as a by-product of struggles in which no party was explicitly demanding democracy as such. Any struggle that, on balance, fortified citizenship, broadened it, equalized it, strengthened consultation, and/or increased protection of citizens had such an effect.

Like lepidopterists who net a trembling butterfly, let us seize that observation, dissect it, and examine its implications for the analysis of contentious politics. Different sorts of political regimes emerge from long-term struggles centering on means of production, coercion, and affiliation. Those struggles form governments and collective actors sustaining variable relations to the government and to each other – that is, polities. The same process creates standard forms of political communication and control that are prescribed, ratified, rewarded, or at least tolerated by governmental authorities – routine politics. Contentious politics – public, collective claim-making by politically constituted actors that bears on interests of other actors, including the government – comes into being as a penumbra of routine politics. Having emerged, however, it transforms the character of routine politics.

Sometimes contentious claims divert government-prescribed means such as regular elections toward conflict-filled ends. Sometimes they take place in the zone of tolerated means, as when assemblies of dissidents adopt the same organizational forms as their conformist counterparts. Often, however, contentious politics involves means that the government has forbidden, such as armed attacks on authorities and their symbols. The proximity of contentious politics to the forms, issues, and personnel of routine politics varies with circumstances and type of regime. Loosely knit empires, for example, host a wide variety of local struggles in which representatives of central authority intervene only intermittently if at all, whereas high-capacity democracies draw contenders and conflicts of all sorts into their own orbits.

In all regimes, nevertheless, contentious politics reshapes routine non-contentious politics and relations among political actors; at a minimum, acts of repression and intervention by central authorities divert resources and alter the organization of power even when power holders thereby hold off challenges to their advantages. Installation of effective political policing, for example, alters governmental organization and routine politics as it limits the maneuverability of dissidents. Contentious politics provides the primary site of political innovation, experimentation, and bottom-up signaling. It sometimes issues in tyranny, anarchy, or deadlock, but under rare circumstances it yields moves toward democracy. Our challenge is to survey a wide range of changing regimes, examine their characteristic contentious politics, then specify how, when, and where struggle promotes net movement toward broad, equal citizenship with binding consultation and widespread protection from arbitrary action by governmental agents.

Being more numerous, more widely spread in time and space, and less well connected to each other than their democratic counterparts are, nondemocratic regimes necessarily vary in political life far more than democratic regimes do. Europe's nondemocratic regimes range from vast nomadic empires such as those the Mongols ran to tightly controlled city-states such as the Vatican. Each form of rule generates its own qualities of politics, contentious or otherwise. On the average, nevertheless, by definition nondemocratic regimes feature narrower polity membership, more unequal access among polity members, weaker consultation, and fewer protections from arbitrary governmental action than do democratic regimes.

We can clarify the implications of those on-the-average conditions by turning to the idea of contentious repertoires. A repertoire of contention is a set of established performances by means of which contenders in a given polity make claims on each other – emphatically including claims on or by governmental agents. Strictly speaking, repertoires link pairs of interacting parties, for example, unionized workers and corporate managers. For convenience, nevertheless, we can sum up interactions over all pairs in a polity, calling all currently available performances part of a national repertoire. The British national repertoire of the 1990s includes, among other performances, demonstrations, creation of special-purpose associations, public meetings, petition drives, appeals to mass media, and lobbying. It does not include the collective seizures of high-priced grain, donkeying of non-conforming workers, tearing down of dishonored houses, forcible expulsions of tax collectors, invasions of fenced commons, or shaming ceremonies that conveyed collective claims repeatedly in Great Britain two hundred years earlier.

Two strands of history intertwine in the evolution of contentious repertoires. One of them accumulates the experiences and interactions of potential collective actors outside of open contention: day-to-day relations of masters with journeymen, of landlords with peasants, of merchants with their customers, of party leaders with constituents, of constables with people who live in their jurisdictions, of neighbors with each other. These relations establish understandings, solidarities, hostilities, interests, shared memories, collective identities, and specific social ties that are available as materials of contentious politics. But involvement in collective contention itself lays down a record and memory of interaction and innovation; people learn collectively that certain forms of claim-making are possible, feasible, costly, efficacious, ineffectual, destructive, dangerous, or gratifying. The course of struggle itself confirms some known ways of making claims, generates some new ones, and eliminates others. Through the interplay of everyday interaction and intermittent struggle, contentious repertoires evolve.

Let us begin with a classificatory approach, simply associating types of contention with types of regime. We can think of repertoires as varying along three dimensions: (1) particularism: how specifically the forms of claim-making in question attach to certain localities, groups, or issues; (2) scale: how many clusters of people who are readily distinguishable in routine social life participate in the making of claims; (3) mediation: the degree to which the communication of claims depends on privileged intermediaries, as opposed to direct confrontation with objects of claims. On the whole, contentious politics that builds on embedded identities features relatively particular and small-scale repertoires while bifurcating between direct confrontation (often violent) on a local scale and mediation by established authorities on the larger scale. Contentious politics building on detached identities more regularly involved modular, generalized forms of claim-making, large-scale coordination, and reliance on specialized representatives or political entrepreneurs.

What do these dimensions imply for differences between democratic and nondemocratic contention? Here is a gross generalization for later refinement; on the whole, contentious repertoires of nondemocratic polities feature:

- more particular, small-scale, and mediated forms of claim-making;
- more violent competition between similar groups;
- more direct action against renegades, moral reprobates, and agents of central authority;
- more clandestine retaliatory damage;
- more concerted resistance to outside threats;
- more localized action;
- closer ties to embedded identities; and
- more variation in cultural content

than apply in democratic polities. These features recur in nondemocratic polities because, on the average, governments have lower capacity, governmental claims on subjects occur more episodically and brutally, governmental repression is more selective, erratic, and violent, fewer contenders have routine noncontentious means of making claims on governmental agents, and political power is more fragmented. Later we will have to qualify such gross generalizations by examining, for example, contention in nondemocratic polities that center on high-capacity government.

Democratic polities, in contrast, create contentious repertoires that more often:

- include modular forms of claim-making that transfer easily among populations, localities, and issues;
- operate on a large scale, involving multiple populations and localities simultaneously;
- involve direct claims on regional or national power holders instead of passing through honored brokers;
- depend on extensive organization and preparation rather than springing from noncontentious daily routines such as marketing, working, drinking, or attending religious services;

- activate collective identities broader than or separate from those that inform routine social relations, for example, workers in general rather than a machinist in this particular shop;
- broadcast capacity, threat, and/or intentions to act – both individual and collective – rather than immediately engaging the actions in question;
- involve displays of the worthiness, unity, numbers, and commitment both of direct participants and of the populations they claim to represent; and
- target regional or national power holders, including agents of national governments.

Democratic repertoires rely on cumulation, coordination, and communication among multiple actors and events much more so than do nondemocratic repertoires. Because they rely so heavily on cumulation, coordination, and communication, indeed, critics of existing democracies properly complain that normal democratic procedures offer great advantages to classes and clusters whose routine social life gives them access to centralized organizations, that the poor and marginal therefore regularly lose out in standard democratic struggles for power, that the apparatus of democratic politics imposes uniformity on culturally and organizationally diverse populations, that particularity and difference therefore lose some of their public means for self-expression as democracy advances.

What implications do these static contrasts between nondemocratic and democratic contention have for the dynamics of contentious politics? Three implications stand out. First, because a larger share of contention in nondemocratic polities takes place at a distance from the state, rhythms and trajectories of nondemocratic contention depend more heavily on fluctuations in local and regional circumstances, whereas in democratic polities national and international political-economic fluctuations predominate; as democratization proceeds, therefore, the rhythms of contention become more highly coordinated at a national scale and more closely dependent on governmental action.

Second, in nondemocratic polities ordinary sequences of claim-making depend relatively little on realignments within the polity and greatly on realignments and responses of local and regional actors; only in cases where national economic crisis (e.g., famine or disaster) or massive governmental action (e.g., warfare, dynastic struggle, or rapid augmentation of taxes) intervenes simultaneously across the jurisdiction are parallel sequences of action across the polity likely to occur. Within democratic polities, in contrast, interplay among government, polity members, and challengers combines with coordination among challengers to favor generalization of political interaction's forms across all of a polity's many niches.

Third, in the repertoires of nondemocratic polities standard sequences of action crystallize as a function of local or regional histories and cultures, with only attenuated effects of politics in national centers. Routines for sanctioning nonconforming workers, forcing stored grain into a local market, or sabotaging an effort at tax collection unfold locally, within channels set by local knowledge and localized social relations. Only rarely – typically in response to such major national cleavages as dynastic succession struggles or to major threats from rulers such as military mobilization or suppression of religious sects – do local people employ those performances in coordinated action against regional and national authorities. Contentious performances of democratic repertoires, in contrast, generally cluster adjacent to the routines of politics as usual: elections, parliamentary deliberations, governmental pronouncements, and so on. Their sequences interact with those of politics at usual, and at times merge with politics as usual. Thus social movements acquire the power to influence conventional politics by broadcasting the identities of challengers, publicizing defective governmental performance, and announcing programs that deserve attention. In the same process, they lose the power to make revolutions.

A finer analysis would, of course, qualify these generalizations, for example, by noting that in nondemocratic regimes protected sites and authorized assemblies (e.g., mosques, markets, public holidays) often provide occasions for claim-making and criticism, whereas in democratic regimes challengers generally enjoy more liberty in the timing and sites of their action. We will also start making distinctions, notably between low-capacity and high-capacity nondemocratic regimes. To judge from the experience of state socialism, for example, in high-capacity nondemocratic regimes the very operation of the state typically promotes the formation of clandestine networks of cooperation, influence, and mutual aid without which major governmental activities would collapse, and without which ordinary people would lack goods, services, information, or ability to nudge agents of the state. Those same networks become major channels of contentious politics when a split in leadership or an externally generated crisis facilitates action against agents of the state. That sort of political process looks very different from contentious politics at the peripheries of empires or in wealthy city-states.

Contention in democratic polities reflects a political system shaped by repeated mobilization of excluded groups demanding places in the system of power. Such mobilizations permit outsiders or previously unrecognized actors to make known their presence, their identities, their programs, and their capacity to act collectively in ways that could disrupt the existing power structure. They therefore give established polity members incentives and opportunities to recognize outsiders, fight them, repress them, ally with them, absorb them, bargain with them, or buy them off before they have carried out promised or threatened actions. Electoral campaigns and social-movement politics epitomize activation of democratic repertoires.

These characteristics of democratic repertoires create ambivalent relations between social-movement politics and prescribed democratic procedures such as voting, paying taxes, and honoring national symbols. On one side, established holders of power, who have less strenuous and visible ways of working their will, generally condemn and denigrate attention-getting actions of social-movement activists, except when those power holders seek allies against other members of the establishment. On the other side, social-movement activists can best demonstrate their potential impact on politics as usual by innovating at the edge, or just beyond the edge, of established legal means. Instead of assassinating rulers or blowing up parliaments, they ostentatiously refuse conscription, boycott or disrupt elections, desecrate public ceremonies, block streets, burn national flags, shout outrageous slogans, withhold their taxes, or stage enormous marches. Because even those marginal tactics evoke disapproval from members of the establishment, social movement activists and organizations that move toward accommodation with the existing polity ordinarily moderate their tactics, only to face accusations from within their own ranks that they are selling out the cause.

As a consequence of this intimate interdependence between prescribed and forbidden means of political expression, democracies that lay down precise procedures for electoral participation and access to governmental services characteristically leave vague and contested the boundaries of acceptable speech, assembly, association, and assertion of collective identity. As another consequence, public performances of social-movement politics almost always involve prior negotiation among activists, allies, journalists, police, and public authorities, each estimating and negotiating how others will act. Such performances, indeed, regularly eschew violent direct action in favor of demonstrating the potential of disciplined social-movement activists for forceful action if authorities or other power holders fail to meet their demands. More generally, democratic contention differs from nondemocratic contention, on the average, by calling up a politics of anticipation, oriented to how various weighty actors might act, could act, will act, or deliberately threaten to act.

This chapter's arguments therefore propose partial answers to a series of questions concerning the interplay of military activity, regimes, contention, and democratization:

- What accounts for variation in the sorts of regimes that prevailed in different parts of Europe at various times since 1650? Distinctive histories of contention interacted with alterations of coercion, capital, and connection to shape Europe's political regimes.
- What caused the forms and intensities of popular contention to vary and change over the same period? In particular, how did characteristics of regimes and of contentious politics interact? Alterations in governmental capacity and protected consultation, on one side, occurred in tight interdependence with shifts in the actors and repertoires of collective contention, on the other.

- Under what conditions, how, and why did the interaction between exist-ing regimes and their contentious politics promote democratization? Expansion of state activities, containment of military involvement in politics, reduction of political and cultural brokerage, and sustained mobilization of excluded but essential segments of the population interact to make democratic programs more attractive and feasible as provisional settlements – but in very different patterns according to the priority of state capacity and protected consultation.
- How did democratization affect the character of popular contention? On the whole, it moved contentious claim-making closer to routine politics, reduced the role of established intermediaries, increased the salience of specialized political entrepreneurs, and promoted modular, organiza-tionally connected forms of large-scale claim-making.
- What part did military organization and activity play in these dynamic processes? The ways that rulers brought military power under their control in different parts of Europe strongly influenced the forms of governmental organization that emerged in their territories. Top-down attempts to acquire military means repeatedly generated popular resis-tance, which in turn created governmental structure through repression and bargaining. In those regimes that moved toward democracy through revolution, conquest, or colonization, military control figured directly in democratization, whereas in those where expansion of oligarchic institutions constituted the main path toward democracy, military conflict among the principal parties, defeat of national military forces in international war, and extraction of military means from the subject population all frequently generated opportunities for democratization. To the extent that military forces retained autonomous political power, however, that power impeded democratization.

Such schematic questions and answers invite us to a dialectic of theory and evidence. If they make sense, they should allow us to identify common properties and systematic variation in the tangled histories of different European regions. The optimal results of such an inquiry will not be general laws of contention and democratization but strong causal analogies. Such causal analogies will allow us to explain how different initial conditions, different historical paths, and different environments produce varying con-catenations and sequences of similar causal mechanisms, thus generating distinctive histories of democratization and contention.

References

Abu-Lughod, Janet. 1989. *Before European Hegemony*. New York: Oxford University Press.
Ahrne, Göran. 1996. "Civil Society and Civil Organizations," *Organization* 3: 109–120.

Bairoch, Paul. 1976. "Europe's Gross National Product, 1800–1975," *Journal of European Economic History* 5: 273–340.

1988. *Cities and Economic Development*. Chicago: University of Chicago Press.

Bairoch, Paul, and Maurice Lévy-Leboyer. 1981. *Disparities in Economic Development since the Industrial Revolution*. London: Macmillan.

Barber, Benjamin. 1974. *The Death of Communal Liberty: The History of Freedom in a Swiss Mountain Canton*. Princeton: Princeton University Press.

Bermeo, Nancy. 1997. "The Power of the People." Working paper 1997/97. Madrid: Instituto Juan March de Estudios e Investigaciones.

Blickle, Peter. 1988. *Unruhen in der ständischen Gesellschaft, 1300–1800*. Enzyklopädie Deutscher Geschichte, vol. 1. Munich: Oldenbourg.

Blockmans, Wim P. 1996. "The Growth of Nations and States in Europe before 1800," *European Review* 4: 241–251.

Blockmans, Wim P., and Jean-Philippe Genet, eds. 1993. *Visions sur le développement des états européens. Théories et historiographies de l'état moderne*. Rome: Ecole Française de Rome.

Blockmans, Wim P., and Charles Tilly, eds. 1994. *Cities and the Rise of States in Europe*. Boulder: Westview.

Boggs, Carl. 1997. "The Great Retreat: Decline of the Public Sphere in Late Twentieth-Century America," *Theory and Society* 26: 741–780.

Bonjour, Edgar. 1948. *Die Gründung des schweizerischen Bundesstaates*. Basel: Benno Schwabe.

Bonjour, Edgar, H. S. Offler, and G. R. Potter. 1952. *A Short History of Switzerland*. Oxford: Clarendon Press.

Bratton, Michael. 1989. "Beyond the State: Civil Society and Associational Life in Africa," *World Politics* 41: 407–430.

Braun, Rudolf. 1965. *Sozialer und kultureller Wandel in einem ländlichen Industriegebiet*. Zurich: Rentsch.

Burke, Victor Lee. 1997. *The Clash of Civilizations. War-Making and State Formation in Europe*. Cambridge: Polity.

Casparis, John. 1982. "The Swiss Mercenary System: Labor Emigration from the Semi-Periphery," *Review* 5: 593–642.

Chaudhuri, K. N. 1990. *Asia before Europe: Economy and Civilisation of the Indian Ocean from the Rise of Islam to 1750*. Cambridge: Cambridge University Press.

Clark, Samuel. 1995. *State and Status: The Rise of the State and Aristocratic Power in Western Europe*. Montreal: McGill-Queen's University Press.

Cohen, Jean L., and Andrew Arato. 1992. *Civil Society and Political Theory*. Cambridge, Mass.: MIT Press.

Craig, Gordon A. 1988. *The Triumph of Liberalism. Zürich in the Golden Age, 1830–1869*. New York: Scribner's.

Creveld, Martin van. 1989. *Technology and War From 2000 B.C. to the Present*. New York: Free Press.

1991. *The Transformation of War*. New York: Free Press.

Cruz, Rafael. 1992–1993. "La lógica de la guerra. Ejército, estado y revolución en la España contemporánea," *Studia Historica-Historia Contemporánea* 10–11: 207–222.

de Vries, Jan. 1976. *The Economy of Europe in an Age of Crisis, 1600–1750*. Cambridge: Cambridge University Press.

1984. *European Urbanization, 1500–1800.* Cambridge, Mass.: Harvard University Press.

Dewald, Jonathan. 1996. *The European Nobility, 1400–1800.* Cambridge: Cambridge University Press.

Diamond, Larry. 1997. "Civil Society and the Development of Democracy." Working paper 1997/101. Madrid: Instituto Juan March de Estudios e Investigaciones.

Dodgshon, Robert A. 1987. *The European Past: Social Evolution and Spatial Order.* London: Macmillan.

Downing, Brian M. 1992. *The Military Revolution and Political Change: Origins of Democracy and Autocracy in Early Modern Europe.* Princeton: Princeton University Press.

Ertman, Thomas. 1997. *Birth of the Leviathan: Building States and Regimes in Medieval and Early Modern Europe.* Cambridge: Cambridge University Press.

Fatton, Robert. 1992. *Predatory Rule: State and Civil Society in Africa.* Boulder: Lynne Rienner.

Gellner, Ernest. 1994. *Conditions of Liberty: Civil Society and Its Rivals.* London: Allen Lane/Penguin Press.

Gerstenberger, Heide. 1990. *Die subjektlose Gewalt. Theorie der Entstehung bürgerlicher Staatsgewalt.* Münster: Westfälisches Dampfboot.

Gilliard, Charles. 1955. *A History of Switzerland.* London: George Allen & Unwin.

Giugni, Marco, and Florence Passy. 1997. *Histoires de mobilisation politique en Suisse. De la contestation à l'intégration.* Paris: L'Harmattan.

Gorski, Philip S. 1993. "The Protestant Ethic Revisited: Disciplinary Revolution and State Formation in Holland and Prussia," *American Journal of Sociology* 99: 265–316.

Gran, Thorvald. 1994. *The State in the Modernization Process: The Case of Norway, 1850–1970.* Oslo: Ad Notam Gyldendal.

Gruner, Erich. 1968. *Die Arbeiter in der Schweiz im 19. Jahrhundert.* Bern: Francke.

Gustafsson, Harald. 1994. *Political Interaction in the Old Regime: Central Power and Local Society in the Eighteenth-Century Nordic States.* Lund: Studentlitteratur.

Hedström, Peter, and Richard Swedberg, eds. 1998. *Social Mechanisms: An Analytical Approach to Social Theory.* Cambridge: Cambridge University Press.

Henshall, Nicholas. 1992. *The Myth of Absolutism: Change and Continuity in Early Modern European Monarchy.* London: Longman.

Hoffman, Philip T., and Kathryn Norberg, eds. 1994. *Fiscal Crises, Liberty, and Representative Government, 1450–1789.* Stanford: Stanford University Press.

Hohenberg, Paul M., and Lynn Hollen Lees. 1985. *The Making of Urban Europe, 1000–1950.* Cambridge, Mass.: Harvard University Press.

Kellenbenz, Hermann. 1976. *The Rise of the European Economy: An Economic History of Continental Europe from the Fifteenth Century.* London: Weidenfeld and Nicolson.

Kiser, Edgar, and Yoram Barzel. 1991. "The Origins of Democracy in England," *Rationality and Society* 3: 396–422.

Kishlansky, Mark. 1996. *A Monarchy Transformed: Britain, 1603–1714.* London: Allen Lane/Penguin Press.

Koch, Koen. 1993. *Over Staat en Statenvorming.* Leiden: DSWO Press.

Kohn, Hans. 1956. *Nationalism and Liberty: The Swiss Example*. London: George Allen & Unwin.

Kriesi, Hanspeter. 1981. *Politische Aktivierung in der Schweiz, 1945–1978*. Diessenhofen: Verlag Ruegger.

Kriesi, Hanspeter, Ruud Koopmans, Jan Willem Duyvendak, and Marco Giugni. 1995. *New Social Movements in Western Europe: A Comparative Analysis*. Minneapolis: University of Minnesota Press.

Lynn, John, ed. 1990. *Tools of War: Instruments, Ideas, and Institutions of Warfare, 1445–1871*. Urbana: University of Illinois Press.

    ed. 1993. *Feeding Mars: Logistics in Western Warfare from the Middle Ages to the Present*. Boulder: Westview.

Mamdani, Mahmood. 1996. *Citizen and Subject: Contemporary Africa and the Legacy of Late Colonialism*. Princeton: Princeton University Press.

Mann, Michael. 1986, 1993. *The Sources of Social Power. Vol. 1: A History of Power from the Beginning to A.D. 1760. Vol. 2: The Rise of Classes and Nation-States, 1760–1914*. Cambridge: Cambridge University Press.

Martínez Dorado, Gloria. 1993. "La formación del Estado y la acción colectiva en España: 1808–1845," *Historia Social* 15: 101–118.

Mastnak, Tomaz. 1990. "Civil Society in Slovenia: From Opposition to Power," *Studies in Comparative Communism* 23: 305–317.

Minkoff, Debra C. 1997. "Producing Social Capital: National Social Movements and Civil Society," *American Behavioral Scientist* 40: 606–619.

Nabholz, Hans, Leonhard von Muralt, Richard Feller, and Edgar Bonjour. 1938. *Geschichte der Schweiz*. 2 vols. Zurich: Schulthess.

Porter, Bruce. 1994. *War and the Rise of the State*. New York: Free Press.

Pounds, N. J. G. 1990. *An Historical Geography of Europe*. Cambridge: Cambridge University Press.

Powers, James F. 1988. *A Society Organized for War: The Iberian Municipal Militias in the Central Middle Ages, 1000–1284*. Berkeley: University of California Press.

Pro Ruiz, Juan. 1992. *Estado, geometría y propriedad. Les orígenes del catastro en España, 1715–1941*. Madrid: Ministerio de Economia y Hacienda.

Raeff, Marc. 1983. *The Well-Ordered Police State: Social and Institutional Change through Law in the Germanies and Russia, 1600–1800*. New Haven: Yale University Press.

Rasler, Karen A., and William R. Thompson. 1990. *War and State Making: The Shaping of the Global Powers*. Boston: Unwin Hyman.

Rokkan, Stein. 1975. "Dimensions of State Formation and Nation-Building: A Possible Paradigm for Research on Variations within Europe," in Charles Tilly, ed., *The Formation of National States in Western Europe*, 562–600. Princeton: Princeton University Press.

Scott, James C. 1998. *Seeing like a State*. New Haven: Yale University Press.

Seligman, Adam. 1992. *The Idea of Civil Society*. New York: Free Press.

Somers, Margaret R. 1993. "Citizenship and the Place of the Public Sphere: Law, Community, and Political Culture in the Transition to Democracy," *American Sociological Review* 58: 587–620.

Spruyt, Hendrik. 1994. *The Sovereign State and Its Competitors. An Analysis of Systems Change*. Princeton: Princeton University Press.

te Brake, Wayne. 1998. *Shaping History. Ordinary People in European Politics, 1500–1700.* Berkeley: University of California Press.

't Hart, Marjolein. 1993. *The Making of a Bourgeois State: War, Politics and Finance during the Dutch Revolt.* Manchester: Manchester University Press.

Thomson, Janice E. 1994. *Mercenaries, Pirates, and Sovereigns: State-Building and Extraterritorial Violence in Early Modern Europe.* Princeton: Princeton University Press.

Tilly, Charles. 1986. *The Contentious French.* Cambridge, Mass.: Harvard University Press.

1992. *Coercion, Capital, and European States, A.D. 990–1990.* Rev. ed. Oxford: Blackwell.

1993. *European Revolutions, 1492–1992.* Oxford: Blackwell.

1995a. *Popular Contention in Great Britain, 1758–1834.* Cambridge, Mass.: Harvard University Press.

ed. 1995b. *Citizenship, Identity, and Social History.* Cambridge: Cambridge University Press.

1998. *Durable Inequality.* Berkeley: University of California Press.

Tilly, Charles, Louise A. Tilly, and Richard Tilly. 1975. *The Rebellious Century, 1830–1930.* Cambridge, Mass.: Harvard University Press.

Tilly, Charles, et al. 1995. "Globalization Threatens Labor's Rights," *International Labor and Working Class History* 47: 1–23. Responses from Immanuel Wallerstein, Aristide Zolberg, Eric Hobsbawm, and Lourdes Benería, followed by Tilly's reply, 24–55.

Wiener, Antje. 1998. *"European" Citizenship Practice: Building Institutions of a Non-State.* Lanham, Md.: Rowman & Littlefield.

3

Limited War and Limited States

Miguel Angel Centeno

All peaceful states may be alike, but warring states each fight in their own way. Wars reflect the political and social idiosyncrasies of the states that fight them. The structures and habits of political life obviously help shape the manner in which a society practices war. Consider the contrast between the hoplite armies of the Greek city-states and those of imperial Persia. The first was characterized by individual prowess woven into a powerful strategic weapon by the discipline of shared citizenship and constant training. The other, while physically impressive, was often rotten at the core and unable to withstand adversity. A millennium later, Machiavelli despondently compared the mercenary armies of the Italian city-states with those larger and more homegrown varieties that appeared to enjoy an unbeatable advantage on the battlefield. In the 1790s, the French Revolution gave birth to the first true national army of citizens, which militarily and politically transformed the rest of Europe. The world wars of the twentieth century may be seen as products and producers of the contemporary regulatory welfare state. In short, armies reflect their societies and help in turn to shape them through their demands and socializing influences. We are, at least partly, how we fight.

This essay argues that the particular form of interstate warfare seen in Latin America is closely related to the social, fiscal, and political bases of these states. Latin American states do not appear to have enjoyed the structural boosts offered by warfare, nor have they been able to practice the kind of war seen in Western Europe or North America. My argument is openly and explicitly circular. Not only did wars produce *limited* states in Latin America, but also these states could not but fight *limited* wars. That is, states in Latin America have had and continue to have severe limitations on the types of wars they may engage in, while these wars never develop into the kind of struggles that produce more powerful states.

To understand what I mean by limited war, first consider a definition of contemporary *total* war. This form of conflict may be said to have begun with the military revolution of the seventeenth century, to have achieved new levels of destruction and social consequences with the French Revolution and the Napoleonic Wars, to have developed into their modern counterparts beginning with the Crimean War and the U.S. Civil War, and to have culminated in World Wars I and II. Total wars may be characterized by increasing lethalness of the battlefield; the expansion of the killing zone to include not only hundreds of miles of front lines but also civilian targets; association with a form of moral or ideological crusade, which contributes to the demonization of the enemy; the involvement of significant parts of the population either in direct combat or in support roles; and the militarization of society in which social institutions are increasingly oriented toward military success and judged on their contribution to a war effort.

Such efforts require that states be therefore able to amass and concentrate large amounts of men and matériel in a relatively short time; be able to expand their efforts across hundreds if not thousands of miles; prescribe some form of coherent ideological message, and convince significant numbers of the population to accept direct military authority over their lives; and transform their societies to be able to meet these challenges.

These same efforts are associated with particular forms of institutional residue that these wars leave behind them. Wars help build the institutional basis of the modern state by requiring a degree of organization and efficiency that only new political structures could provide; they are the great stimulus for state-building. The effects of total war include increased state capacity to extract resources; centralization of power in national capitals and the gradual disappearance of regional loyalties or identities; stronger emotional links between the population and both a set of state institutions and the often abstract notion of a nation, which these are meant to represent; and a qualitative shift in the relationship of the individual to these institutions, which may be summarized as the transition from subject to citizen.

Total wars produce richer, more powerful states, with more intimate connections to the bulk of the populations within their territories. Note that none of these characteristics implies a particular form of regime. They describe a degree of relationship between a set of institutions and the populace that lives under them, not the manner in which the latter participate in their own governance. Both totalitarian and democratic regimes may be able to mobilize their populations and resources in ways unavailable to limited authoritarian regimes that avoid the politicization of the population in any way.

Limited wars, on the other hand, involve short overall duration of conflict with isolated moments of ferocity; are restricted to few and small geographical areas; are between states with shared ideological or cultural profiles and originate in economic or frontier clashes; are fought by either professional mercenary armies, or those made up of small numbers of draftees from lower classes; and may be practically ignored by the typical civilian. They do not require dramatic fiscal or personal sacrifices or states able to impose these. Most important, they do not require the political or military mobilization of the society except (and not always) in the euphoric initial moments. Because of these limited needs, such conflicts leave little of the historical legacy associated with total wars. The streets are not full of veterans, the state is not a postbellic leviathan, and economic wealth is barely touched by fiscal authorities. Life goes on much as before.

The variation in institutional outcomes from limited war is much greater than in the case of total war. We can, however, safely predict some general patterns. Limited wars are likely to leave some form of fiscal or debt crisis if states fail to adjust to the extra expenditures; support the development of a professionalized military with little popular participation, and possibly even resentment from civilians who have not participated in the struggle; lead to the alienation from patriotic symbols as gains from war will be limited and some element of disenchantment arises; and possibly produce economic downturns resulting from shifts in resources or breaks with global market. The most generalizable trend may be that limited wars rarely leave positive institutional legacies and often have costs long after their conclusion.

States that have historically fought limited wars may also, in time, find it practically impossible to consider fighting total wars. As the technological, social, economic, and organizational demands of total war have increased, those states that have not participated in any of its previous stages would require an even more traumatic transformation than usual to participate in such conflicts. In societies where military service has never been institutionalized, the removal of entire cohorts is inconceivable. In economies where the ability of the state to enforce its tax laws has always been constrained, the ability of central authorities to pay for or borrow the goods of war may be severely constrained. Moreover, by having avoided previous ideological mobilizations, states that have avoided holocausts may lack the historical memories required for mobilization. They may lack what we could call the "cultural repertoires" of war. Patriotic calls may sound shallower than in other societies and calls for sacrifice may go unheeded.

The Latin American experience has been largely defined by this limited war pattern. The number and intensity of wars fought on the continent has been relatively limited, and their effects have been much less than what have been seen in North America and Western Europe. The capacity of contemporary Latin American states to wage war continues to be severely limited. Latin America thus occupies a unique geopolitical position. Its state system is not much younger than Europe's (say the 160 years separating Westphalia from the independence wars). Until the 1950s it was the only independent geopolitical unit outside of Europe. Yet it has had a vastly different international experience and has produced something of a hybrid state. While possessing much of the institutional apparatus of the European state, it often acts more like its African counterparts. Some of the Latin American paradox may be explained by its particular history (or nonhistory) of conflict.

How Much War?

Since independence in the early nineteenth century, the continent has been relatively free of major international conflict. Even if we include civil wars, Latin America has enjoyed relative peace. Outside of the cases of Paraguay, Mexico, and Colombia, no country has suffered a large number of deaths during *conventional* warfare. When compared with any other region, Latin America stands out for the general absence of organized slaughter. Southeast and South Asia, the Middle East, and, most of all, Europe have had much bloodier historical experiences. On a per capita basis, the nations of Europe and North America, for example, have had over 86 times the number of men in their armed forces, have killed proportionally 123 times as many people, and at nearly 40 times the rate per month at war. Even Africa, which has a much shorter period of independence, has witnessed more international conflicts. Latin America has not only been peaceful, but has also lived with relatively low levels of militarization: both the organization of society for the production of violence and the mobilization of resources for potential use in warfare have been less than elsewhere (Best 1989: 13). Note that this pattern holds for both the nineteenth and the twentieth centuries, but is obviously more pronounced in the latter.[1] The one exception is that Latin American wars in the nineteenth century appear to have been relatively deadlier, but this is mostly a reflection of the Paraguayan deaths during the War of the Triple Alliance, about which there remains some debate. The important point is not that Latin Americans have not tried to kill each other (they have), but that they have generally not attempted to organize their societies with such a goal in mind.

If we look at the individual wars, we note that they are geographically and historically concentrated. The vast number and by far the most significant occurred in the nineteenth century. Following the Wars of Independence of 1810–1825, these wars were largely "land grabs" by more powerful neighbors seeking to increase their access to resources. None of the international wars experienced by Latin America has featured ideological, nationalistic, or ethnic hatreds that were so much a part of the history of other parts of the globe. The wars have also tended to be concentrated in two regions: the La Plata basin shared by Brazil, Paraguay, Uruguay, and Argentina and the mid-Pacific littoral where Bolivia, Peru, and Chile meet. Two other wars deserve mention: the U.S. war against Mexico of 1846 and the Chaco War between Paraguay and Bolivia in 1932. Other disputes have flared from time to time (the most prominent being between Peru and

Ecuador), but these have not involved large numbers of men or lengthy periods of conflict.

Wars Building States

If Latin America has been largely spared the bloodbath of conventional war, has peace also exacted a cost? Has Latin America missed the crucial institutional stimuli of war? I have divided this discussion into two roughly equivalent halves: one dealing with "physical" changes in the state and the other with "ideological" transformations. These two measures of a contemporary "war-made" state, taxation and conscription, appear to be positively correlated. If we understand conscription to be yet another form of state power, then it makes sense that it would be positively correlated with taxation. If, on the other hand, it also serves as an indication of links between the state and its population, then we have the potentially paradoxical situation of state power associated with popular participation. From the point of view of this chapter, the most relevant point may be that Latin America consistently reports low values for both measures.

State Capacity

This form of change is most associated with the work of Charles Tilly. The key to this process is what Finer (1975) calls the "extraction-coercion cycle." On the one hand, wars force states to penetrate their societies in increasingly complex forms in order to obtain resources. On the other hand, the new form of the post-Westphalian state is particularly well suited to the organizational task of managing this penetration and channeling the resources thus obtained into "productive" violence directed at some external enemy. The military revolution thus served as "a crucible of modernization that helped melt the institutions of medieval government into new political forms" (Porter 1994: 9) The increasing costs of war and the organizational metamorphosis this required are at the heart of the rise of the absolutist state in Europe (Anderson 1974). Thus, wars both build and are an expression of political power.

As part of the increased administrative efficiency, wars also encourage the centralization of power and authority. Wars pushed power toward the center. The process by which a state acquires monopoly over violence in its territory is often dependent on the conduct of armed conflict with other states. War provided both the incentive *and* the means with which the central power was able to dominate. Both the increase in the administrative capacity of the state and the growing centralization contributed to what Michael Mann (1988) has called infrastructural power: the capacity to penetrate civil society and to implement logistically political decisions throughout the realm. The occasion of war provides the administrative order that is able to extract resources from the society. This administrative order can then be used against internal or external powers, providing success and even more resources.

Why, in Latin America, was war never able to break the "disastrous equilibrium" between a variety of powers? I believe that the answer lies in the relatively limited level of military organization involved in the Wars of Independence. This is not to deny the violence and destruction that these caused. However, while the wars *weakened* the colonial order, they did not kill it. The armed effort was small enough so as not to require the militarization of society throughout the continent. Certainly in comparison with the equivalent wars in European history (e.g., the Thirty Years' War), the independence conflicts left a much more limited institutional legacy. Moreover, the wars left not proto-absolutist states able to impose their control over their newly territorially defined nations but a variety of military groups able to resist any attempts to monopolize authority. This initial failure meant that subsequent conflicts were not usually fought between institutional kernels of states that could use them to grow, but between embryonic governments that were overwhelmed by the effort.

What were the effects of the limited wars of nineteenth-century Latin America on the fiscal capacity of the state? Simply put, they were practically nil. Instead of a state built on "blood and iron," they constructed a constantly bankrupt beggar made of blood and debt (Centeno 1997). The easy availability of external financing allowed the state the luxury of not coming into conflict with those social sectors that possessed the required resources. Whether through loans or through the sale of a commodity, the Latin American state was able to escape the need to force itself on society. When such loans were not forthcoming, the state either relied on customs (not requiring an extensive administrative commitment) or simply institutionally ceased to play a major role in society.

The evidence for centralization is more ambiguous. The case of Argentina is particularly interesting in this regard. Its first experience with war (against Brazil in the 1820s) accompanied the disintegration of the country as a coherent political unit. The next thirty years of civil wars failed to produce a replacement for that state. But, one could argue that the War of the Triple Alliance did help seal the unity created by Mitre and his successors. Chile might serve as a better example of the "early modern European" model. Certainly both wars against Peru and Bolivia helped consolidate the Chilean nation-state. The Mexican case may represent another "positive" example in that both the war against the French in the 1860s and the Revolution in the 1910s helped consolidate the authority of subsequent regimes.

Terms of Citizenship

If wars are responsible for increasing the "infrastructural" power of the state, they may do so at the expense of "despotic" power. That is, the greater capacity provided by military expansion also requires greater support and participation from the population. Conscription and citizenship are two sides of the same coin. The "proletarization" of the military gives the state a large capacity for violence, but it also arms the populace. One could see this as a form of political barter: in exchange for the right to participate in war, citizens were rewarded with greater rights and more welfare services.

Whereas the political consolidation discussed earlier occurred during the sixteenth to mid-eighteenth centuries in Europe, the nationalist "by-product" of war developed in the nineteenth. According to Ardant (1975) the pressure to extend the suffrage, increase national consciousness, give representation to the working classes, and generally draw the population into political life came to an important degree from the fiscal demands of the great military and administrative machines brought into being by the Napoleonic Wars. The fifty years before World War I represent both the peak of industrial development and the creation of "nations at arms." "Conscription, compulsory education and the right to vote formed three pillars of the democratic state" (Kiernan 1973: 141). Armies also served to teach discipline, obedience, and order (Howard 1976: 56). Thus armies and war produced a population that participated much more in the creation of a political order, *but* was also much more trained to obey the dictates of that order.

Military activity and/or preparation may have also encouraged greater *social* equality (Mann 1992). Since antiquity, armies have provided outstanding opportunities for social mobility. Andreski (1971) notes a relationship between popular participation in military conflict and social leveling or equality. Napoleon's marshals are not the first or last example of humble births leading to prestige and wealth via the battlefield. Certainly, central efforts to monopolize violence weakened or at least transformed the power of aristocracies, whether in France and Britain or Russia and Germany. According to Ralston, European-style armies functioned as agents of social mobility in Egypt and Japan in the nineteenth century. In the latter case, the first official reference to the rights of the people occurred in military context: the equality of samurai and commoners to render military service to the emperor (Bendix 1978).

Military service may have also improved health and longevity. The first social welfare measures appear to have been associated with the care of veterans (e.g., the first Hôtel Royal des Invalides founded in 1670). More recent work has established a similar link in the United States (Skocpol 1993). Public welfare also had its uses. According to Howard (1976, 1984) much of the effort in post-1870 education and public health was intended to produce new generations physically and intellectually prepared for war. Welfare measures could also be seen as part of the exchange process between the population and the newly powerful state: "Conscription and Bismarck's welfare program were two sides of the same flag: one showed the young man how powerful was the State and how limitless its claim on him, the other showed him how much the State could do for him" (Kiernan 1973: 147).

Although it is risky to generalize about the relationship between citizenship and military service, one could see armies as providing modern nation-states with a relatively disciplined and well-educated population ready and able to work in the new industrial order. But such a population now also has immediate access to the means of violence and offers the state a resource that the latter needs. This forms the basis for a new political contract. Conscription and mass armies also helped revolutionize the nature of the violence involved in military conflict. The new types of wars temporarily transformed "wolf packs" into coherent and obedient organizations (Howard 1976).

The Latin American states were never strong enough to demand and enforce even the limited full conscription seen in the United States during the Civil War or after 1870 throughout Europe. Latin American countries did formally create universal conscription laws in the late nineteenth and early twentieth centuries, but the actual numbers involved were relatively minuscule. Consistently through the nineteenth and twentieth centuries, the Latin American countries have had a much lower percentage of their populations under arms than their European or North American equivalents. While conscription was socially regressive in all societies, in Latin America it largely remained a limited phenomenon.

Most important, there was never the perceived need for the kind of social upheaval implied by mass armies. The state did not need the population, as soldiers or even as future workers, and thus could afford to exclude it. Moreover, the types of wars that were fought were limited enough to be paid for by resources available to the states, thereby not requiring the redesigning of a social contract. The state and dominant elites in almost all these countries also appeared to prefer passive populations. A too active or fervent sense of nationhood could actually backfire and create conditions inimical to continued elite domination. The key issue here is that the perceived enemy (from the point of view of the "commanding heights") was internal – the poor, the Indian, the black – rather than external. Following that logic, to arm the populace to fight a different national elite with whom one shared ideological, cultural, and economic interests was sheer insanity. Conversely, because there was little reason to fear that congruent elites would also choose to commit political suicide by creating a mass army, there was no need to mobilize the population. Obviously there were exceptions to these rules. Brazil, for example, armed freed slaves to fight the Paraguayans, and the othering of neighbors as more "poor, Indian, or black" went on in many conflicts. As a general rule, however, Latin American elites felt much less confident in their abilities to control an armed population than did their European counterparts.

Wars also encourage a different attitude toward the state – one based on collective identity. The link between military conflict and national loyalty is well known (Smith 1981). Nothing unites a nation behind a faltering leader as a war. Although there remains considerable debate about the relationship between "nations" defined by common ethnic characteristics and "states" defined by some legal existence, one could argue that for much of the nineteenth century the state created nationalism and not vice versa (Hobsbawm 1991). One mechanism by which it did so was the army and military activity. Armies and the experience of war helped create a unified identity that could obscure domestic divisions. Experience in the military increased the scope of what Mann (1992) calls discursive literacy: the set of nationalist assumptions and myths that contribute toward the creation of a national identity. Wars may have been the key to the creation of "imagined communities" (Anderson 1983). Through the absorption of elements of the newly arising bourgeoisie and petit-bourgeoisie, armies may also have encouraged class cohesion during critical periods of early industrialization (Best 1989; Mann 1992). Under these circumstances armies and war helped transform class societies into armed nations. According to Palmer (1959), war and military experience also helped break down provincial allegiances and networks and replace these with ones more centered on a national community.

Did armies and war propagate the idea of a nation in Latin America? Did these serve as "institutions of popular education"? Given the reputation for "nationalism" (often ill-defined) of Latin American countries, one sees little evidence of the kind of mass identification evident in Europe or the United States. Independence wars did provide some of the mythology on which so much of modern nationalism depends. But Latin America lacks the ubiquitous monuments to "our glorious dead" that are such a common part of the landscape in Europe and the United States. The prototypical "man on horseback" in a central plaza is usually a general or an independence hero, and not the "everyman" honored in North American and European military legends. With few exceptions (e.g., Paraguay, Nicaragua) the continent does not have a tradition of a nation discovering its collective identity through war. The memory of both victory and defeat seems to play a major role in the definition of various national identities, but war does not appear to have served as the "social glue" that helped to define and unify a society (Centeno 1999).

In general, then, war did not provide the support for the institutionalization of political authority we have seen in the Western European and North American cases. War was too infrequent and limited an enterprise to have this effect. Limited war may be said to have even contributed to the relatively isolated state that remains the Latin American norm – lacking a set of institutional capillaries that link it to the population at large. Peace may also have contributed to the relative social isolation of the military and its concentration on internal enemies. In a separate analysis of the professional journals of the military in a variety of countries, the absence of concern with geopolitical and strategic planning is striking (Centeno 2001).

The military was less concerned with defeating its neighbors than with developing its organizational structure and, after World War II, with meeting the internal enemy. If it did not serve as a "school for the nation," it should not be surprising that it saw itself as a "guardian" of that nation which it barely understood and with which it had limited contact. There is a yet unexplored causal link between the relative peace enjoyed by the continent and the particular form of professionalization followed by its military. Deprived of a need to study or develop battle tactics, the military defined new missions of social strategies. The same process may be seen in post–Cold War NATO countries as vast institutions seek a new mission with which to justify themselves. Latin America may provide an object lesson in the danger of maintaining a superfluous armed force.

Capacity for War

If wars made for a very different type of state in Latin America, how do we account for the fact that states appear to have made little war? In other essays I have discussed a variety of possibly important factors, including a common culture, geographical constraints, the guarantees provided by the British and American *pax imperium*, and diplomatic dynamics. I have argued, however, that in order to understand the relative absence of war and the limits on those that have occurred we have to understand the limits under which the Latin American states operate. That is, rare and limited war was to be expected in a region of states without the capacity to fight any other kind of wars.

We may begin with a rough measure of state capacity to engage in war: its ability to tax its own population in order to pay for military adventures. Despite Latin American states' reputation for dominating economies, in the past thirty years Latin American states have *not* taxed their populations at levels approaching those of Western Europe and the United States. If we consider that ability to tax is also representative of a state's capacity to penetrate and impose its will on a society, the likelihood of a Latin American state being able to impose draconian measures is severely limited. Contemporary examples of interstate war such as the Falklands/Malvinas War and the Ecuador-Peru border conflict indicate that this is still the case.

Because they have limited access to fiscal revenues, Latin American countries can spend much less on creating the type of military apparatus necessary for contemporary warfare. Some countries have devoted a comparable degree of attention to their militaries (as measured by percentage of GDP). Note, however, that given the relatively small size of their economies, the amount of moneys available for their armed forces has remained severely limited. In publications such as the Jane's *Annuals*, the detailed description of the weaponry and technology available to the Latin American militaries makes it clear that these are incapable of fighting for prolonged periods in any broad front. Simply put, wars cost money and the Latin American militaries have not had access to the massive infusion of resources required to equip themselves for anything but the most limited border clashes or police actions.

There is a parallel situation if we look at the forces available to use this equipment. Latin America has traditionally employed a much smaller percentage of its population in its military. Even Chile in the 1980s, with its armed forces enjoying the full support of the government, with a significant historical adversary (Peru), and with a long tradition of military prowess, had an army of only 57,000 men – hardly enough to mount even a limited defense of the national territory. No matter the sophistication of equipment, war requires men (the gender specificity is especially relevant for Latin America) to physically move into and hold territory. The Latin American militaries simply do not have the human resources to fulfill even the most basic missions. Perhaps equally important, relatively small parts of the population have been exposed to a martial culture and there may be subsequently less inherent support for such adventures.

There are, of course, exceptions to these trends. The three most salient would be the War of the Triple Alliance in the nineteenth century, the civil wars of Central America of the 1960s–1980s, and the post-1959 Cuban state. The incredibly violent civil wars of Mexico, Colombia, or Central America in the 1920s and 1930s (to mention a few) could be others, but I would argue that these are not examples of the kind of *state-sponsored* war that is under discussion here.

Paraguay has suffered the most from conventional war, having been defeated in both the Triple Alliance and Chaco conflicts. The first experience was perhaps the closest equivalent to the Polish fate seen in Latin America, and it led to the practical disappearance of the Paraguayan state until the twentieth century. The Lopez regime did produce a war-oriented state with the kind of internal control and social penetration associated with the European cases. The war was fought by practically the entire population and exhausted the entire country's resources. It came as close as any war in postindependence Latin America to a scorched-earth policy and was arguably an originator of the "total war" seen later (although it has never been recognized as such and has received little notice from military historians). For Brazil, the war also required considerable sacrifice in terms of resources and manpower. Argentina, however, largely retreated from active participation once the cost became clear, and Uruguay was largely irrelevant after the initial conflict. The war did provide Mitre with the opportunity to destroy the last major regional threat to central authority and it helped consolidate a sense of Brazilian identity in the southern third of that country. One could even argue that the war did require the mobilization or militarization of a whole region. But given that Paraguay was eliminated as a player within the geopolitical region, this militarization never became institutionalized. The war did not last long enough to leave the kind of political and social residue we see in nineteenth-century Europe.

In the Central America of the past three decades, we have also seen a militarization of society and an often violent intrusion of the state into everyday life. I would argue, however, that these cases represent important deviations from the Western European norm. First and perhaps most important is the role played by the United States as financier and organizer of last resort. I have not been able to locate evidence on the extent to which the Salvadoran or Guatemalan upper classes, for example, financed the protection of their position (aside from the employment of private gangs). Second, the wars did little to unify their countries; instead of obscuring internal divisions through the demonization of an enemy, the wars exacerbated these divisions. Finally, they certainly did not contribute to the economic well-being of the governments or their societies as a whole. As in the other cases, some argument might be made that they did in fact help establish the domination of centralized political authority, but even that may be debatable.

Perhaps the most interesting exception to the overall trend is contemporary Cuba, which has twice been able to operate in a strategic theater thousands of miles from its home base and has deployed significant numbers of men and used a large amount of sophisticated equipment. But Cuba is precisely the exception that proves the rule as it has achieved a permanent mobilization of society that is alien to the Latin American political tradition. This pattern may offer the best clue for explaining the relative peace on the continent. Total wars require mobilization, which in turn requires some degree of integration and even inclusion. As has become increasingly obvious in the 1990s, the "permanent state of war" under which Cuba lives may also be critical to the preservation of state power, to the centralization of its authority, and to its ability to mobilize the population. Please note that none of this necessarily implies democratic participation, but it does involve the creation of equal societies not yet seen anywhere on the continent.

Contemporary Cuba also differs from the other Latin American countries in having developed a conflictive international discourse. One could argue that the conflict with the United States is at the very heart of the political project of the Cuban Revolution. Preliminary results from a longer research project would indicate that this has not occurred in other countries on the continent. If we analyze newspaper accounts of major patriotic feast days, we note the absence of *revanchiste* myths (with some exceptions in the Andes). In Latin America there are few of the racial or ethnic demonizations common to total war. Perhaps the most important reason for the absence of war is that it was not part of a political repertoire available to states. That is, precisely because of the "long peace," by the early twentieth century war was no longer a part of the political vocabulary of either the populations or their respective governments. In such an atmosphere, the kind of jingoistic mobilization and militarization required by total war would be practically impossible. Note, for example, that despite the early euphoria that accompanied the Argentinean invasion of the Falklands/Malvinas, the population soon tired of the affair and accepted defeat with remarkable ease. Latin American states and their populations do not appear to have had the historically forged institutional or political appetite for the type of organizational insanity of modern war.

Conclusions

This chapter has argued three major points. First, wars have had limited effects in Latin America since they have rarely required the kind of mobilization that leaves institutional residues. Wars did not lead to wider definitions of citizenship, produce more powerful states, or help consolidate national identity. Second, partly as a result of this experience, Latin American states have had limited organizational and political capacities to wage war. Given their resource and manpower endowments, Latin American countries have not been able to pursue "total war" strategies. Finally, perhaps the most important cause and product of these two trends have been the limited integration of Latin American society and the development of militaries whose professional gaze is largely turned inward. This last point may be worth noting as it would suggest that the benefits of modern states may have even more severe costs than had previously been considered.

Note

1. Details may be found in *Blood and Debt: State and Nation Making in Latin America* (University Park: Pennsylvania State University Press, 2002).

References

Anderson, Benedict. 1993. *Imagined Communities*. London: Verso.
Anderson, P. 1974. *The Lineages of the Absolutist State*. Norfolk: Verso.
Andreski, S. 1971. *Military Organization and Society*. Berkeley: University of California Press.
Ardant, Gabriel. 1975. "Financial Policy and Economic Infrastructure of Modern States and Nations," in Charles Tilly, ed., *The Formation of National States in Western Europe*. Princeton: Princeton University Press.
Bendix, Reinhard. 1978. *Kings or People*. Berkeley: University of California Press.
Best, Geoffrey. 1988. Introduction to M. S. Anderson, *War and Society in Europe of the Old Regime, 1618–1789*. New York: St. Martin's Press.

1989. "The Militarization of European Society, 1870–1914," in John Gillis, ed., *The Militarization of the Western World*. New Brunswick: Rutgers University Press.

Centeno, Miguel Angel. 1997. "Blood and Debt: War and Taxation in Latin America," *American Journal of Sociology* 102, 6: 1565–1606.

1999. "'Wars and Memories': Symbols of State Nationalism in Latin America," *European Journal of Latin American and Caribbean Studies* 66 (July): 75–106.

2001. "Explaining the Long Peace: The Latin American Model," in Daniel Chirot, ed., *Ethnopolitical Warfare*. Washington, D.C.: American Psychological Association.

Finer, Samuel. 1975. "State and Nation-Building in Europe: The Role of the Military," in Charles Tilly, ed., *The Formation of National States in Western Europe*. Princeton: Princeton University Press.

Hobsbawm, E. J. 1991. *Nations and Nationalism*. London: Verso.

Howard, Michael. 1976. *War in European History*. Oxford: Oxford University Press.

1984. *The Causes of War*. Cambridge, Mass.: Harvard University Press.

Kiernan, V. G. 1973. "Conscription and Society in Europe before the War of 1914–1918," in M. R. D. Foot, ed., *War and Society*. London: Elek Books.

Mann, Michael. 1986. *The Sources of Social Power: A History of Power from the Beginning to A. D. 1760*. Vol. 1. Cambridge: Cambridge University Press.

1988. *States, War and Capitalism*. Oxford: Blackwell.

1992. *The Sources of Social Power: The Rise of Classes and Nation-States, 1760 to 1914*. Vol. 2. Cambridge: Cambridge University Press.

Palmer, R. 1959. *The Age of Democratic Revolutions*. Princeton: Princeton University Press.

Porter, Bruce. 1994. *War and the Rise of the State: The Military Foundations of Modern Politics*. New York: Free Press.

Ralston, David. 1990. *Importing the European Army: The Introduction of European Military Techniques and Institutions into the Extra-European World, 1600–1914*. Chicago: University of Chicago Press.

Skocpol, Theda. 1993. *Protecting Soldiers and Mothers*. Cambridge, Mass.: Belknap Press.

Smith, Anthony D. 1981. "War and Ethnicity: The Role of Warfare in the Formation, Self Images and Cohesion of Ethnic Communities," *Ethnic and Racial Studies* 4, 4: 375–397.

Tilly, Charles. 1975. "Reflections on the History of European State-Making," in Charles Tilly, ed., *The Formation of National States in Western Europe*. Princeton: Princeton University Press.

1985. "War Making and State Making as Organized Crime," in Peter Evans et al. eds., *Bringing the State Back In*. Cambridge: Cambridge University Press.

1992. *Coercion, Capital, and European States, AD 990–1992*. Cambridge, Mass.: Blackwell.

4

Where Do All the Soldiers Go?

Veterans and the Politics of Demobilization

Alec Campbell

The positive relationship between war and state formation in Europe has been well established (Finer 1975; Mann 1988, 1993; Tilly 1990; Porter 1994). Its logic is contained in the "extraction-coercion cycle" discussed by Finer. States use coercion to extract military resources – men, money, and matériel – which increase their coercive powers for later rounds of extraction. States grew around the need to organize both coercion (armies and their supply) and extraction (taxation, requisition, conscription). Through this process, war served as a mechanism of natural selection for the hundreds of statelike entities in fifteenth-century Europe. Those states adapting in ways that allowed them to ride the upward spiral of the coercion-extraction cycle have survived; the rest have been swallowed up.

This model of state formation emphasizes mobilization (extraction in preparation for war) over demobilization. To a degree this is justified. Mobilization is a risky proposition from the perspective of states and ruling classes, in part because the extraction of men, money, and matériel can engender resistance from subjects (Tilly 1990: 99–103). One way of reducing effective resistance is to monopolize the means of coercion. Thus, Tilly argues that disarming subjects was central to the process of state formation. States monopolized the use of force by building up "fearsome coercive means of their own as they deprived civilian populations to access to those means" by making it "criminal, unpopular, and impractical for most of their citizens to bear arms" (Tilly 1990: 70).

Paradoxically, this preference for disarmament fetters the development of coercive power because mobilizing men into the military necessarily implies arming some subjects. Retrieving weapons (re-disarmament) and breaking up armies after the war are the basic problems of demobilization. Whatever it was that rulers feared subjects might have done with the weapons taken away in the processes described by Tilly, they can now do with weapons provided by the state itself. Expanding military power and the disarmament of subjects are inherently contradictory aims.

One solution to the paradox is selective mobilization. European feudal and absolutist states built armies composed of foreigners and/or subjects with limited social attachments – those men Wellington called "the scum of the earth." Selective mobilization uses labor markets to solve the demobilization problem. These soldiers served on a cash basis. Pay them, and they usually went away. However, this mobilization strategy is limited by its tremendous expense. In military competition, where, ceteris paribus, larger armies are better armies, labor costs can quickly spiral out of control. Moreover, mercenaries and "scum" lack internal motivation in battle and sometimes run away if given the chance.

The cheap alternative to expensive labor markets is ideology. Troops fighting for causes are often willing to fight – and die – cheaply. Here, soldiers are conscripted by states into immense low-cost armies on the basis of national citizenship. Of course, asking people to do their duty as citizens is much easier if they have citizenship rights. Without them potential soldiers may refuse to serve, or revolt after induction. Conscription solves the problem of cost but sacrifices disarmament. It is no surprise then that political demands for citizenship rights – including the franchise and the social citizenship rights of the welfare state – have often been linked to military service (Therborn 1977; Mann 1993: 499–502; Tilly 1990: 83).

But wars are national crises, and the citizenship rights due as payment for wartime sacrifice are often deferred to the end of the war (Mann 1988: 158). After all, if the war is lost, citizenship gains are meaningless. The end of war is the end of the crisis, and the promised citizenship rights can become a point of contention between rulers and ruled. In these postwar conflicts between rulers and ruled, veterans can and have played a crucial and even decisive role. In this chapter I examine the problem of demobilization, and the ways in which attempts at solving it have affected state development. In brief, I argue that demobilization is a moment of potential crisis that different states have managed differently with different consequences. I also argue that veterans are the unique element in this moment of crisis and that their actions have often determined its outcome.

Demobilization, Veterans, and Political Struggle in Ancient Rome

Like Europe in the nineteenth and twentieth centuries, Rome raised citizen armies and a brief discussion of its repeated demobilization (and mobilization) crises is useful. Military service was required of citizens in the Roman Republic. This duty was particularly burdensome for plebeians who frequently returned from war only to find their crops failed or destroyed. This forced them to borrow, which created debts leading to impoverishment or imprisonment. On several occasions the plebeians refused to serve in the military until their demands for political representation and debt relief had been met (Mann 1993: 252; Livy 1971: esp. 129–30; Brunt 1971: 52).

More of a strike than a revolt, plebeians could link their class-based political demands to citizenship and military mobilization because the state and
the patrician ruling class had no alternative to their service. Unfortunately,
the need was episodic and the patricians repeatedly abrogated their concessions once the crisis had passed. It took several such military strikes for
the plebeians to gain permanent redress of their grievances.

The extension of political rights did not permanently solve the plebeian's
problems, which worsened with the expansion of Roman territory and
military needs. Perry Anderson points to this process:

> Constant conscription had steadily weakened and reduced the whole small-holder
> class as such: but its economic aspirations lived on and now found expression in
> the mounting pressures from the time of Marius onwards for allocations of land to
> discharged veterans – the bitter survivors of the military duties that lay so heavily
> on the Roman peasantry. . . . To have paid them bounties on discharge would have
> meant taxing the possessing classes, however slightly, and this the ruling aristocracy
> refused to consider. The result was to create an inherent tendency within the later
> Republican armies to a deflection of military loyalty away from the state, towards
> successful generals who could guarantee their soldiers plunder or donatives by their
> personal power. (Anderson 1974: 69–70)

This is the essence of the demobilization problem. The difficulty was not
getting soldiers but getting rid of them.

Rome eventually solved this problem in the transition from republic to
empire. Augustus provided "allotments of land for the thousands of soldiers demobilized after the civil wars, financing many of them out of his
personal fortune." The empire disenfranchised the possessing classes
who had earlier opposed the taxation needed to pay bounties and pensions.
Eventually, veterans received "regular cash bounties on discharge, worth
thirteen years' wages paid out of a specially created military treasury
financed by modest sales and inheritance taxes on the propertied classes of
Italy." These measures brought a renewed discipline and loyalty to the army
but "did little to improve the social situation of the peasantry as a whole."
They did "effectively pacify the demands of the critical minority of the
peasant class in arms, the key section of the rural population." Thus
the political problem of the peasantry was "solved" through the pacification
of veterans who demobilized peacefully under Augustus because they were
paid (Anderson 1974: 71).

Several aspects of the Roman example deserve special mention. First, the
"private" relationship of borrower and lender was displaced into the public
arena of state policy through military service and citizenship. The impoverished plebeians demanded their political rights as citizens because they
had served in the military. Second, war is good (politically) for lower classes
if the state needs them for military service. Third, wartime gains were not
permanent. Once the threat had passed, and soldiers demobilized, plebeians

repeatedly lost what they had gained. Fourth, although the root political problem involved class relations, the solution was in terms of army and veterans. The state pacified the army and its veterans through the extension of social citizenship in the form of pensions and land.

Between the citizen armies of the Roman Republic and the conscripted armies of the past 150 years, states relied on relatively small, selectively mobilized noncitizen armies to solve the demobilization problem. This prevented the deflection of lower-class political demands onto military service and citizenship because their military service was not needed. This was possible only because armies were comparatively small. At the height of the empire, Roman legions numbered in the area of 450,000 standing troops (Anderson 1974: 85). In contrast, feudal armies rarely exceeded 10,000 short-term troops. Later, absolutist states created much larger armies but there was still no obligation to serve on the basis of citizenship. Armies were the personal possession of the monarch and there was little sense that the people owed military service to the state.

Warfare through the Nineteenth Century

Revolutionary France revived the citizen army through the *levée en mass*. Important as this was, it did not herald a return to citizen armies across Europe, or even in France. While Napoleon relied on ideology to raise some of his troops, he also relied on markets – only half the troops in the *grand armée* were Frenchmen (McNeill 1982: 200). European rulers saw the mass army as a dangerous instrument. After 1815 the preference for disarmament seen by Tilly reasserted itself and "all regimes backed away from the citizen army, frightened by the notion of placing arms in the hands of a free people" (Mann 1993: 427; Kiernan 1973: 43). Mass armies of conscripted citizens would not become the norm for another forty-five years, when industrialization made their benefits significantly more important than their political costs.

Prior to industrialization, the availability of equipment limited the size of armies.[1] Industrialization removed this limitation. Unheard of numbers of troops could be equipped with modern arms and an essentially limitless supply of ammunition. At the same time, railroad systems allowed the delivery of both armies and their supplies over long distances in almost any kind of weather, and the telegraph ensured reliable and instantaneous communications.

Naturally, the ability to equip, transport, and communicate with large numbers of soldiers is only useful if large numbers of soldiers are available. Transforming industrial strength into military strength requires massive armies to haul the nation's industrial might onto the battlefield. Before 1850 European militarism was characterized by moderately sized standing armies composed of long-service professional troops led by an officer corps of

aristocratic amateurs. There were few organized reserve forces. With industrialization, the military advantages of mass armies began to outweigh
their potential problems. Any state that tamed conscription would wield a
decisive military instrument. After 1850, first in Prussia, and then across
the continent, conscript armies composed of enormous numbers of short-
term conscripted soldiers backed by massive reserves and led by long-service
professional officers began to appear.

Any thought that smaller industrially equipped but selectively mobilized
armies could compete with the mass army was removed by quick Prussian
victories over Austrian and French professional armies in 1866 and 1871
(Vagts 1959: 207–209; Preston, Roland, and Wise 1991: 222–225).

Obviously mass mobilization was the basis of Moltke's success. His victories had
been won by getting Prussian armies into motion before their opponents were ready.
Speed, mass and momentum, in turn depended on skillful use of railroads to assemble and deploy troops and their equipment. Numbers required an army of conscripts
reinforced in time of war by reservists. Since conscripts were paid the merest pittance, a conscript army was also the only way European governments could afford
to field a force big enough for the first critical encounters of this new style of war.
Simultaneously, machinery for the mass production of small arms had made the cost
of equipping vast citizen armies affordable. Every continental European army therefore sought to imitate the Prussians in the decades that followed. (McNeill 1982:
253)

Conscription and reserve forces were the only solution to the cost of massive
industrial armies. While conscription solved the financial problem of the
mass army, rulers still faced its political consequences. It meant arming the
very segments of the population re-disarmed after 1815. But there was little
choice. After the Prussian demonstrations of the superiority of mass armies,
states and ruling classes everywhere could either retain a professional army
and risk external military defeat, or conscript a mass army and face internal revolt. All continental powers moved toward conscription. Along with
armies of citizen conscripts came the possibility of a Roman-style displacement of domestic political grievances through military service and/or
veterans' status.

One way to tame the conscript army was to make the people somewhat
more free. Thus, "while the Prussians were perfecting their mass army,
always in fear of its democratic potentialities, the French military under
Napoleon III were preparing their professional army, likewise in fear of
evoking mass discontent." After defeats in 1866 and 1871, both Austria
and France were "compelled to make concessions to popular elements
while enrolling them for war" and both "proceeded to make constitutional
reforms within. Napoleon moving step after step in the direction of a parliamentary regime as the price of an army reform bill . . ." (Vagts 1959:
207–208). Later, other countries including Canada, Italy, and England

extended the franchise either in anticipation of, or response to, the mobilization of troops for World War I (Therborn 1977). Some countries, like the Roman Empire, created extensive benefit systems and social privileges for veterans (Mann 1993: 499–503; Orloff and Skocpol 1984; Orloff 1993; Skocpol 1992).

In the event, these concessions proved sufficient and conscription was not the political powder keg that rulers feared. Indeed, Mann argues that at this time "commanders were actually tightening military organization over their soldiers, reducing their ability to identify themselves as citizens or as members of classes" and strengthening the established order (Mann 1993: 428). In other words, military service created an opportunity for ideological intervention by the state in which basic training could replace church, pub, village square, and union hall as primary locations for the formation of consciousness, and the nation could replace class as the primary axis of consciousness. In addition, conscription, though broader than selective mobilization, did have some flexibility. Many countries did not draft everyone eligible for service. Germany, for example, only called up about half of those eligible for service. However, if conscription did not have the political effects feared by ruling classes, war did.

Total Warfare in the Twentieth Century

The mobilization wars of 1866 and 1871 were over before nations could organize their industrial might to support the continuing war effort. The call-up obviously affected the lives of those called, but for civilians war was largely a spectator event. The total wars of the twentieth century were different. Beyond conscription and reserve call-ups, they required total mobilization of national productive capacity to sustain armies in the field. Such wars are won on farms and in mines and mills as much as on the battlefield.

Workers and farmers have a double importance in total war, as soldiers and as producers. On the one hand, the working class and the peasantry provide the majority of soldiers. At the same time, the production of workers and farmers is crucial to the prosecution of the war. This duality gives workers political leverage but also carries the seeds of division. Roman plebeians became soldiers and then returned to their farms as a group. Total war divides the working class; some become soldiers, while others remain workers.

For those workers not serving in the military, war initially creates favorable economic conditions. Labor supply tightens, unemployment falls, and demand increases, all because the state is now supporting millions of unproductive soldiers and demanding increased production of all sorts of war materials. These conditions make war a politically opportune moment for labor and other oppressed groups; there is no better time to pursue class

TABLE 4.1. *Approximate Union Densities of Major European Powers in 1914, 1920, and 1925*

Country	1914	1920	1925	Absolute Change 1914–1920	Absolute Change 1920–1925	Absolute Change 1914–1925
Austria	7	51	42	44	−9	35
Belgium	10	48	34	38	−14	24
Britain	23	45	30	22	−15	7
Denmark	23	48	36	25	−12	13
France	8	10	8	2	−2	0
Germany	17	53	28	36	−25	11
Holland	17	36	25	19	−11	8
Italy	10	45	0	35	−45	−10
Norway	10	20	14	10	−6	4
Spain	3	15	14	12	−1	11
Sweden	10	28	29	18	1	19
United States	10	17	10	7	−7	0

Source: Mann 1995: table 1, p. 20.

interests. As the war lengthens, economic conditions deteriorate, real wages decline, and food supplies decrease, further spurring the working class to act in its own interests.

If labor pressed these advantages fully through strikes or other job actions, the war effort could be seriously hindered. Put differently, no nation can successfully fight international military and domestic class wars simultaneously. Thus, the successful prosecution of total war requires class compromise in the national interest: *burgfrieden* in Germany, *union sacrée* in France, and the no-strike pledge in the United States. The state often engineers this compromise through corporatist institutions with representatives of labor, capital, and the state. In this compromise the working class typically sacrifices the right to strike and often the right to change jobs freely in exchange for freedom to organize and promises of postwar social and political changes (Mann 1988: 158). In many cases, the U.S. and Britain in particular, state involvement in capital-labor relations and economic policy was in itself viewed as a victory by labor, which hoped to continue state intervention after the war. During World War I workers everywhere were asked to sacrifice their short-term class interests. The gains for labor were primarily in the form of greater trade-union rights, which produced the dramatic increases in unionization seen in Table 4.1.

As war lengthens, the initial patriotic enthusiasm wears off, casualties mount, prices rise, shortages develop, and morale falls. By 1916 all countries engaged in World War I were experiencing problems on the home front

including pressure for a negotiated settlement. By 1917 increased restlessness among both workers and troops led to increased strike activity in
Britain and France and mutinies among French and Russian troops. In this
climate some governments had to extend additional concessions to workers
to maintain class compromise. In England, the government promised
fundamental postwar reconstruction symbolized by Lloyd George's slogan
"a land fit for heroes to live in" (Marwick 1965: 239; Ward 1975: 22). The
German government made vague promises of a "new orientation" after the
war (Diehl 1994: 8).

Demobilization and Class Struggle

Although total war tends to improve the position of working-class organizations, there is no guarantee that wartime gains can be carried forward
into the postwar period. The end of war eliminates the necessity of class
compromise, and in postwar periods internal conflict is reborn as workers
and others attempt to consolidate their gains while ruling classes attempt
to reinstate the prewar status quo. Governments have often proved unreli-
able allies for unions hoping for the continuation of wartime intervention
in capital-labor relations. This was evident when plebeians, having taken
up arms to defend Rome, saw their gains disappear along with the military
crisis. After World Wars I and II, all of the major powers saw tremendous
internal conflict. This conflict was particularly intense after World War
I with fascist revolution in Italy, Communist revolution in Russia and
Hungary, civil war in Germany, a major strike wave in Britain, and major
strikes and the Red Scare in the United States. Table 4.1 reveals the imper-
manence of wartime gains. Between 1920 and 1925, union density declined
in every country except Sweden.

Although the pattern of wartime gains and postwar losses is reminiscent
of Rome, the politics are very different. Plebeians needed the army to organize, but modern workers have had socialist parties and trade unions. On
the other hand, the plebeians all served together but the double burden of
the modern working class divides it during war. Thus, the displacement
of civilian (class based) political goals onto citizenship through military
service is made difficult because some have soldiered, while others remained
in factories and on farms. These different experiences may lead to different
postwar goals and interests. Thus, the presence of soldiers and veterans
makes postwar political struggles unique. At war's end veterans are an
armed and potentially organizable group related to but different from the
working class.

Several things differentiate workers from soldiers in the postwar period.
First, because their previous "occupation" was separate from the "normal"
workings of civil society, the function of soldiering is made redundant (for
the vast majority of troops) at the end of the war. This separates workers

from soldiers but also implies that the separation is characteristic of the postwar moment. Workers can organize, be defeated, and organize again because workers are continuously produced by industrial society. Soldiers are not. If they are not organized in the postwar moment, they will tend to drift back into civil society and lose the potential for a unique veterans' consciousness with broad political impact. Second, soldiers are neither productive workers nor profit takers. Soldiering is an endeavor outside the class system. Among other things, this makes soldiers' relationship to both the working and capitalist classes unclear. Third, soldiers share what Oliver Wendell Holmes called "the incommunicable experience of war." It is a defining moment for many of those who participate in it. This commonality can be the basis of organization and collective action.

I believe that these millions of men returning from war, many without strong ties to class organizations and without any objective class location, are a wild card in postwar class struggles. They may participate in class struggles, but if they do, their role is indeterminate because of the wartime separation of workers and soldiers. Thus, from a working-class perspective, industrial war is a double-edged sword. It revives the citizen army but eliminates the organic connection of workers and soldiers in that army, and creates the possibility that soldiers can use the leverage of military service separate from the working class.

The political consciousness of veterans and soldiers is indeterminate. There is no meaning *inherent* in the soldier's experience. Soldiers share in an experience, but that experience must be interpreted if it is to have political consequences. Just as workers have been organized as Catholic, socialist, communist, and Peronist, or, have remained unorganized, so too veterans have been organized as fascists, pacifists, and communists. Objective circumstances limit, but only limit, postwar possibilities for soldiers. Thus, the political potential of veterans must be realized by active organization, which includes an interpretation of their experiences. In the absence of organization they will not participate as veterans. If organized, they may ally with workers, capitalists, or nationalists, but they are a force uniquely present in the typically conflictual demobilization period.

In the brief comparative discussion that follows, I show that veterans were a central element in postwar political struggles. I am more interested in the fact that soldiers played an independent role in these struggles than with the specific nature of that role. For now, my limited aim is to establish that veterans mattered. I then look more extensively at how they came to matter in the U.S. case.

Russia
The Russian case is unique in four ways. First, Russia relied more than any other country on the military to maintain domestic order. Second, Russia was defeated before 1918. Third, defeat led to (or was caused by) the almost

complete dissolution of the army – the primary instrument of domestic coercion. Fourth, Russia's economy was simply inadequate for the demands of World War I; it was never able to adequately supply its army (Kolko 1994: 140–146). As a result, in Russia soldiers did not merely join the revolution; they frequently led it.

What role did soldiers and veterans play in the Russian Revolution? Broadly speaking, an active one. Skocpol argues that after the defeat of the 1917 offensive, "the dissolution of the army and the deepening of agrarian revolt became intertwined. Former soldiers returned to the villages to join in, and often lead, the land seizures" (Skocpol 1979: 136). Kolko also argues for the centrality of soldiers. "But action among the soldiers was significant ultimately because it paralleled and then interacted with activities among workers in cities and the peasantry, for they shared fundamental problems and some crucial social attributes" (Kolko 1994: 144). Evidence of both the importance and uniqueness of soldiers' experiences is evident in the fact that the Bolsheviks organized soldiers separately from workers. This reveals that even an organization with a class-based political analysis could not assign class positions to soldiers.

Hungary

The situation in Hungary was very similar to that in Russia.[2] As in Russia, the army disintegrated and soldiers returned to form soviets in association with workers and peasants. As in Russia, the monarchy was replaced by a social democratic government. As in Russia, communists organized workers' and soldiers' councils. As in Russia, the separate organization of soldiers by communists indicates the autonomy and centrality of veterans and soldiers in postwar conflict. Unlike Russia, the communist revolution failed, but soldiers did play an independent role in the political struggles of the period.

Germany

Nowhere were veterans and soldiers more important than in postwar Germany.[3] Unique among European nations, Germany had a large (close to three million members) politically important veterans' organization before World War I. The Kyffhauser Bund was explicitly supportive of the existing regime and consequently antisocialist. The Bund excluded social democrats, and in response social democratic unions excluded members of veterans' organizations. During the war both the Kyffhauser Bund and the social democrats attempted to organize veterans.

After the armistice, Germany imploded into civil war. Veterans supported both sides. As in Russia and Hungary, communists organized veterans into their own soldiers' councils. On the right, soldiers were organized (largely by the army itself) into paramilitary *Freikorps*. The social democratic government, in conjunction with the army, used these right-wing veterans to put down the communist-led revolt in late 1918 and early 1919. When the immediate postwar crisis passed, the social democrats eliminated their veterans' organizations, returning to a more normal class ideology. However, right-wing veterans remained organized as veterans.

Because almost all men of a certain age served in the military, German veterans' political attitudes in the Weimar Republic could not be significantly different from those of the average male citizen. The veteran *was* the average male citizen. However, *organized* veterans were almost uniformly opposed to the existence of the republic and their organizations were at the center of the antirepublican opposition. To the extent that soldiers retained a separate consciousness, it was right-wing and antirepublican.

Between 1923 and 1926 veterans' organizations were transformed into antirepublican political organizations. As a part of this transformation, they began to allow nonveterans into their ranks. While this meant that they were no longer strictly veterans' organizations, they continued to be led by veterans and were still largely composed of veterans, many of whose identities were forged in the *Freikorps*. The Nazi Party was one such organization. It was not a veterans' organization per se but was rooted in the veterans' experience and drew a disproportionate number of its early members and leadership from among veterans.

In Germany then, veterans played an important role, both in the immediate postwar struggles and in the longer opposition to the republic, which ultimately led to Nazism. The veterans' organizations and their progeny were the core of the opposition to Weimar.

Italy

Opposition to the war by Italian socialists made socialist organization of veterans difficult.[4] At the same time, Italian unions grew dramatically during the war. In the period just after the war, the possibility of socialist or communist revolution was apparent. In 1919 and 1920 the militant actions of the working class had led to very real gains, including increases in real wages over their prewar levels and the eight-hour day. In this period it looked very much like the Italian working class would be able to consolidate its wartime gains.

Despite this apparent progress, Italy became the first fascist country in Europe. Although not a veterans' organization, the Italian fascists drew heavily from World War I veterans. In 1921, 57 percent of the rank-and-file membership had been in the military, many of them in the elite units. Beginning in 1921, the fascists began a violent campaign against the left, attacking union halls and smashing socialist party offices. In that year alone the fascists wrecked some hundred or so premises belonging to the urban and rural unions or socialists (Kolko 1994: 167). As in Germany, the fascists were in the beginning, and at their core, a veterans' organization.

England

In England many veterans joined the British Legion, but this organization was almost entirely apolitical.[5] The Legion dedicated itself to self-help efforts and worked quite diligently to avoid politics. In the postwar strike wave, socialists and communists attempted to organize soldiers but were not particularly effective. Why there was no role for veterans in England cannot be answered here. It appears that England's lack of preparedness for the war, however, created problems early on in the war as massive numbers of wounded were repatriated to England. In response to this crisis, English parties were organizing veterans well before demobilization. I suspect that British parties were able to continue this activity into the postwar period, which helped to direct veterans toward already existing political identities.

France

French veterans resembled the English in that they never played the decisive role in politics that they did in Russia, Hungary, Italy, and Germany.[6] For the most part, veterans' organizations reflected the political division evident in civil society. Unlike England, no single veterans' organization was dominant in the interwar period. As in Italy and Germany, the French fascist leagues in the 1930s were composed largely of veterans. Unlike Germany and Italy, these were not the dominant veterans' organizations in the country. The two largest organizations were right and center-right, each with just under 1 million members. The socialist veterans' organization had about 100,000 members and the communists a mere 5,000 (Soucy 1975: 70). In addition, there was a Catholic veterans' organization and some special organizations of war-wounded.

These brief descriptions are intended to establish demobilization as a special kind of political time and highlight the importance of veterans in it. Everywhere that communists and socialists were active, they organized soldiers separately. This is an important recognition of the role of veterans in these struggles, coming as it does from groups that believed class struggle to be the motor of history. Clearly, they felt they had no choice but to organize this massive nonclass element of society. Similarly, everywhere that fascism took root, veterans of the Great War were at its core.

Just as important as veterans' organization is their nonorganization. English and French veterans were not particularly important in postwar class struggles, nor were they a significant element in interwar politics. Thus, the organization of veterans is a contingent event. Demobilized soldiers are a potentially decisive political force but their potential can go unrealized. An adequate theory must account for both organization (and nonorganization) and its direction. That theory must wait. In the final section of this chapter I turn to the most successful group of veterans to come out of World War I, with the hope that this more detailed case study will be a first step toward a general theory of veterans and demobilization.

American Soldiers after World War I

American veterans are particularly interesting because their actions belie simple macrolevel explanations. For example, in Europe it looks as though veterans' action is a simple consequence of victory. Veterans organized in Germany, Hungary, and Russia, which lost, and not in England and France, which won. Italy is problematic: although in the winning alliance, it lost most of its battles and failed to achieve any of its war objectives. From this perspective it is often viewed as a loser in the war. On this basis, we would expect American veterans to be like the French and English, but they are not. America can only be seen as a winner and yet its veterans organized. One might also think that socialist opposition to the war was the key to later veterans' organization but socialists supported the war in Germany and opposed it in Italy and yet both countries produced right-wing veterans.

If comparative conditions don't explain American veterans' organization, then perhaps uniquely American conditions will. However, American military and political conditions were opposed to veterans' organization. First, U.S. involvement was brief. Few troops arrived in France before the spring of 1918 and *nearly one-half of the 4 million Americans mobilized never even left the United States.* Moreover, American troops missed the horrors of the Great War. Just over 116,000 Americans were killed in battle but this pales in comparison to the 1.8 million Germans, 1.3 million French, 1.2 million Austro-Hungarians, and three-quarters of a million Britons who died. Given this limited involvement one might expect that American soldiers would, like their French and English counterparts, simply drift back to the civilian life they had so recently left.

Second, the domestic political context within which American veterans had to organize was hostile to the project. True, the United States had a tradition of veterans' organization and veterans' benefits (see Browne, Chapter 9, and Bensel, Chapter 10, in this volume), but this tradition could not be exploited because the public perception of a close association between the corruption of patronage politics and veterans' organizations and benefits had created "negative feedbacks" in the political culture. Ann Orloff and Theda Skocpol describe the ways in which these feedbacks served to undermine the development of social provision in the Progressive Era (Orloff and Skocpol 1984; Orloff 1993; Skocpol 1992). It seems reasonable that the public that refused to support extensions of social provisions because of memories of Civil War excesses would be inhospitable to a new veterans' organization, particularly one which was discussing a "bonus" in early 1919. Indeed as early as April 7, 1919, the *New York Times* was warning that "what the Grand Army of the Republic was as a political force in the twenty-five years immediately following the Civil War, the new solider organization promises to be in the future politics of the nation."

But despite socialist opposition, victory, late entry, limited casualties, and an inhospitable political culture, American soldiers did organize. By the end of 1919, the American Legion had nearly a million members, which translates into one of every four men who had served in the military during the war. The impact of this massive new voluntary association was immediately felt in politics and state budgets.

As in other countries, U.S. demobilization from World War I was typified by political crisis. Table 4.1 shows that U.S. trade unions made dramatic gains during World War I. Between 1919 and 1921 capital and labor fought an intense battle over the permanence of these gains. This battle produced memorable conflicts such as the Seattle general strike, the Boston police strike, the national steel strike, and the West Virginia coal field wars, all of which ended in labor defeats.

This postwar explosion in working-class activism was embedded in a more general nativist, antiradical witch hunt known as the Red Scare in which radicals were harassed and deported and labor activists were painted as radicals regardless of their political associations. Although the first stirrings of Legion organization predate the Red Scare it is clear that the soldiers' actions in Russia and Germany motivated the organizers of the American Legion. Thus, an early historian of the Legion argues that after the Armistice:

Talk of the Bolshevik revolution was in the air, of the German soldiers' rising against their generals, of French mutinies. American bankers and businessmen who visited Europe returned filled with anxiety. What would be the attitude of returning troops? Might they join hands with the I.W.W. who were creating disturbances on the West Coast and threatening to spread the trouble through the East? Would the soldiers upset things? (Duffield 1931: 5)

According to another official Legion history, "A safe and sound organization of veterans might be the best insurance against their [Soviet ideas] spread. This concern about a condition then generally covered by the term Bolshevism was to be voiced frequently during the formative period of the Legion" (Jones 1946: 45; see also Gray 1948: 53; Wecter 1944: 428–429; Severo and Milford 1989: 244; Minot 1962: 38).

Born amid postwar conflict and sired by a concern with radicalism among soldiers, it is no surprise that the Legion was fanatically antiradical. In May 1919 the Legion's first U.S. caucus passed a resolution asking that Congress "pass a bill for immediately deporting every one of those Bolshevik or IWW's." Throughout the nation, Legionnaires "made unalterable opposition to all Bolshevistic, Anarchistic, Nihilistic, I.W.W. or Soviet forms of government their first priority" (Pencak 1989: 60, 149). By July 1919 the *American Legion Weekly* was featuring articles decrying the Red

menace written by Seattle mayor Ole Hanson. At its first convention
(November 1919), the Legion ordered local posts to "organize immediately
for the purpose of meeting the insidious propaganda of Bolshevism,
I.W.W.ism, radicalism, and all other anti-Americanism" (Duffield 1931:
166). A passage entitled "Why the American Legion" from the first
"history" of the Legion, published in mid-1919 illustrates the Legion's
concern with Bolshevism.

There is a wolf at the gates of civilized Europe. If he gets inside nothing can stop
him from ravishing us. This war has bound us so closely to Europe that we are, in
a sense, one and the same. He who strikes our brother strikes us, even though he
be so far away that the distance is measured by an ocean. We must get over the idea
that distance makes a difference. The Atlantic ocean has just been crossed in sixteen
hours. Remember, thought travels even faster. The wolf that I mentioned is a Mad
Thought. He is Bolshevism. (Wheat 1919: 181)

The Legion did not stop at statements. It committed itself to action,
resolving to ask local posts to cooperate with authorities in the "suppression of riots and mob violence" where "anarchistic and un-American
groups" were involved. Their enthusiastic response included hundreds of
mobbings, kidnappings, and intimidations according to the newly formed
American Civil Liberties Union (ACLU). Because labor activism and
radicalism were linked, local posts broke strikes in Omaha, Oakland,
Denver, Youngstown, Kansas, New York City, various towns in West
Virginia, Boston, and other places. Taken together, "Mob incidents against
Socialists involving Legionnaires, when added to those against the IWW,
Non-Partisan League, and others were so numerous that the ACLU
despaired of counting them." The ACLU called the Legion "the most
active agency in intolerance and repression in the United States," a dubious
honor given the rebirth of the Ku Klux Klan in the same period (Pencak
1989: 74, 150–154; Duffield 1931: 166–169; Jones 1946: 195–197).

The Legion took a different view. As National Commander Franklin
D'Olier stated in 1919, "during these days of unrest and readjustment, the
American Legion and the stand of the ex-serviceman for law and order is
the greatest insurance policy our nation could possibly have" (Pencak 1989:
156). Although labor and the left were quickly defeated, National Commander Alvin Owsley revealed the distance the Legion was willing to travel
in a 1923 interview:

If ever needed, the American Legion stands ready to protect our country's institutions and ideals as the Fascisti dealt with the destructionists who menaced Italy!
. . . the American Legion is fighting every element that threatens our democratic government – Soviets, anarchists, IWW, revolutionary socialists and every other
red. . . . Do not forget that the Fascisti are to Italy what the American Legion is
to the United States. (Hapgood 1927)

Owsley then "went so far as to say that the Legion would take over the
government to counter subversive or Communist groups if they managed

to gain undue influence." Commander John McQuigg reiterated the Legion's admiration for Mussolini, calling the Italian Fascists the "Legionnaires of Italy." As late as 1930 the Legion invited Mussolini to speak at its annual convention (Pencak 1989: 21).

Veterans and American State Formation

I began this chapter with a discussion of state formation and I want now to show how the American Legion grew out of and contributed to distinctive aspects of U.S. state formation. In the first place the Legion remained central to the American anticommunist movement for the next fifty years. Thus its organizers achieved their intended effect, which was to create a bastion of right-wing sentiment in the thousands of American Legion posts in cities and towns across the country. Explanations of American exceptionalism often look to long-term structural features of American life like liberalism or immigration, which covertly undermine socialism in America. The Legion may prove to be a more direct explanation. Here is an organization with hundreds of thousands of members spanning the country that actively opposed all left-wing ideologies and organizations by participating in two massive state-led antiradical inquisitions after each of the centuries world wars.

The Legion also affected the development of the American welfare state. Through the 1920s the Legion gained such tremendous political power "that more than one observer remarked that its capture of Congress was complete" (Mack 1989; Schriftgiesser 1951: 49). The Legion used this power to build an enviable system of welfare benefits for veterans, which accounted for up to one-half of all federal nonmilitary expenditures (roughly similar to the numbers reported by Bensel for Civil War veterans in chapter 10 in this volume). By 1930 the Legion had successfully lobbied for health care, civil service hiring preferences, and disability insurance. In cross-national perspective these benefits were unrivaled. Thus in 1932 the United States, with 325 thousand dead and wounded, spent over $860 million on veterans' benefits, while England, France, Germany, and Italy together spent around $830 million, despite having over 16 million dead and wounded (Powell 1932: 265). Thus through the 1920s the American government was simultaneously backing away from the Progressive Era's ideas of a general welfare state in favor of corporate-led welfare capitalism while recreating and even expanding the veterans' welfare system of the post–Civil War period.

One benefit deserves special mention because it embodies the division between workers and soldiers created by the production needs of total warfare. Almost as soon as the war ended veterans were calling for a "bonus" – essentially a lump-sum payment in appreciation for their service as veterans. The Legion was initially opposed to the bonus, which it viewed as a payment for patriotism – a duty of citizenship, not a market

TABLE 4.2. *Military Personnel of the Major Powers in 1910*

	Population (Millions)	Military Personnel (Thousands)	Military Personnel as % of Population
Austria	28.57	247	0.86
Great Britain	35.79	372	1.04
France	39.61	650	1.65
Germany	64.93	680	1.05
United States	92.51	139	0.15

Source: Mann 1993: 803–810.

relationship. But by 1921 the Legion was supporting what it called "adjusted compensation." The Legion reasoned that while a bonus was illegitimate, soldiers were entitled to an adjustment to their wartime wages because wartime economic conditions had raised the wages of those (possibly slackers) who had not served. This heightens the separation of workers and soldiers. As we have seen total war requires both workers and soldiers. Governments actively discourage the enlistment of skilled workers, and wartime propaganda often emphasizes the unity of workers and soldiers. This unity in the war effort can lead to unity in postwar politics. Adjusted compensation emphasized the differences between workers and soldiers and undermined the potential political alliance between them.

So far I have described the consequences of the American veterans' organization on state formation, but their organization is itself a consequence of unique features of American state formation. Although the United States conforms to the general relationship of state growth around increasing rounds of extraction-coercion, the quality of the relationship could not be more different. European states grew up in an environment of interstate military competition surrounded by hostile neighbors. In this environment "A Regime that did not pay close attention [to militarism and warfare] and was not modernizing its military would not survive long" (Mann 1993: 412–413). This does not apply to the United States, whose history is characterized by haphazard military organization. Each American war increased the size of the military and the state, but both were puny compared with European armies and states. Table 4.2 shows the United States had by far the largest population and by far the smallest military of any major power prior to World War I. Most important, the transition to massive conscript armies in Europe was safely ignored by the United States.

This low level of military development had an unexpected consequence in the latter half of the century. European armies had always served to repress domestic discontent (Mann 1993: 403; Tilly 1986) but the U.S. Army was too small, too scattered, and too busy exterminating Native Americans to do so. This became evident during the great railroad strike of 1877. In response, business interests sought not the expansion of the U.S. Army, but the reorganization of state militia or National Guard units for whom strike duty was a central activity. The Guard was financed, equipped, and, to a significant degree, staffed by businessmen (Riker 1957: chapter 4; Derthick 1965: chapter 2; Depuy 1971: chapter 10; Montgomery 1993: 95–96). The creation of these local level military forces was only possible because the United States had not participated in the disarmament process described by Tilly. Early democracy made an armed populace less of a threat.

A second consequence of the low level of state-sponsored militarism was the preparedness movement, which arose between the beginning of World War I in 1914 and American entry in 1917. The most important of these movements was the Plattsburg Military Training Camps. These were essentially reserve officer training organized by civilians for themselves. Although they had the blessing and assistance of the U.S. Army, they were civilian organizations.

Both the National Guard and the preparedness movement represent a civilianization of militarism. Functions that in Europe were tightly controlled by the state and its military were left to civilians in America. What is particularly important is that members of both the National Guard and the Plattsburg movement were central to the organization of the American Legion in 1919. Nearly half of the very earliest organizers had participated in the Plattsburg camps.[7] Information on the National Guard participation is more difficult to gather but it appears that Guardsmen were also significantly overrepresented among Legion organizers. Thus the nature of American militarism, which is a distinctive feature of American state formation, led the Legion's organizers first to the Guard and preparedness and later to the Legion.

Conclusions

Discussions of state formation have looked at war but have omitted what is perhaps the most difficult political period in war: demobilization. In this chapter I have argued that demobilization is a unique kind of political time in which social struggles including but not limited to those between workers and capital are particularly likely. An adequate understanding of these struggles requires a recognition of the role of soldiers in political struggle. The role of soldiers becomes potentially decisive when states must override their natural inclination toward disarmament in the interests of mobilizing sufficient numbers of soldiers. States may conscript soldiers to fight foreign enemies, but in so doing they simultaneously arm a potential internal opposition.

Total war creates a conflict between class interests and citizenship duties. Workers' strength is naturally increased by labor shortages and increased demand. This makes war an excellent time to strike. On the other hand, citizenship duties require the setting aside of class differences in the effort to win the war. In ancient Rome plebeians drafted into the army were able to use their military labor (the labor of citizenship) to make demands on the state. But the natural unity of workers and soldiers that we found in Rome is shattered in industrial war when some citizens become soldiers, while others remain as workers.

This is particularly important during the demobilization period when class compromise is no longer necessary, and labor and capital fight over the permanence of wartime gains. In this struggle soldiers are the X factor. They have come largely from working-class and farming backgrounds, but war has removed them from their own class origins and provided them with an alternative – an "incommunicable" set of formative experiences. In the postwar period soldiers can ally with workers, with capital or they can make no alliance at all. Whoever manages to organize soldiers to their side in postwar struggles gains a tremendous advantage. This is the unique feature of the demobilization period. In Russia, Germany, Italy, and the United States, the side that organized soldiers managed to control the outcome of the demobilization period.

In my examination of the United States I showed how veterans acted and how they came to be organized as they were. In the United States the combination of early democracy with low levels of militarism encouraged and allowed the development of a private militarism for some citizens. It was precisely this segment of the population which was poised to organize soldiers during the demobilization crisis following World War I. In this way the pattern of state formation that preceded the demobilization period figured in how demobilization politics were played out.

Demobilization is not only a consequence but also a cause of variation in state formation and development. Clearly, demobilization was involved in the development of both communism and fascism. But the effects of demobilization need not be so dramatic, nor are they restricted to regime type. The nature of demobilization from both world wars has had significant impact on the development of the American welfare system. From the Veterans Administration hospitals to the GI bill, the United States has consistently focused welfare benefits on veterans. In the same period in Britain demobilization led to the development of a more general welfare system for all citizens. This was undoubtedly due in part to the colonization of a part of the state (the Veterans Administration) by organized veterans of World War I; in contrast, British veterans of the earlier conflict had not organized politically.

In conclusion I think the relationship between war and state formation outlined by Tilly and others is largely accurate but I do think we need to balance the emphasis of raising and using troops with some attention to how states rid themselves of unwanted troops. Put differently, how do states demobilize an armed citizenry at the end of war? The history of the twentieth century reveals that this is at least as difficult as raising troops in the first place.

Notes

1. In 1810 French production for Napoleon's armies peaked at 97,000 guns per year. At this rate, it would have taken 60 years to supply the French army in World War I.
2. My discussion of Hungary relies on Kolko 1994: 157–160.
3. This discussion relies upon Diehl 1975, 1993: chapter 1; Kolko 1994: 146–156; Moore 1978: chapters 8 and 9; and Waite 1953.
4. This section relies on Elazar 1993; Ledeen 1975; and Kolko 1994: 161–168.
5. This section relies on Ward 1975.
6. This discussion relies upon Soucy 1975.
7. Plattsburg participants were less than 1% of all veterans.

References

Anderson, Perry. 1974. *Passages from Antiquity to Feudalism.* London: Verso.

Brunt, P. A. 1971. *Social Conflicts in the Roman Republic.* New York: W. W. Norton.

Depuy, R. Ernest. 1971. *The National Guard: A Compact History.* New York: Hawthorn.

Derthick, Martha. 1965. *The National Guard in Politics.* Cambridge, Mass.: Harvard University Press.

Diehl, James M. 1975. "Veterans' Politics under Three Flags," in Stephen Ward, ed., *The War Generation,* 135–186. Port Washington, N.Y.: Kennikat.

———. 1993. *The Thanks of the Fatherland: German Veterans after the Second World War.* Chapel Hill: University of North Carolina Press.

Duffield, Marcus. 1931. *King Legion.* New York: Jonathan Cape and Harrison Smith.

Elazar, Dahlia Sabina. 1993. "The Making of Italian Fascism: The Seizure of Power, 1919–1922." Ph.D. dissertation, University of California, Los Angeles.

Finer, Samuel. 1975. "State- and Nation-Building in Europe: The Role of the Military," in Charles Tilly, ed., *The Formation of National States in Western Europe,* 84–163. Princeton: Princeton University Press.

Gray, Justin. 1948. *Inside Story of the Legion.* New York: Boni and Gaer.

Hapgood, Norman. 1927. *Professional Patriots.* New York: Boni.

Jones, Richard S. 1946. *A History of the American Legion.* New York: Bobbs-Merrill.

Kiernan, V. G. 1973. "Conscription and Society in Europe before the War of 1914–18," in M. D. R. Foote, ed., *War and Society,* 41–58. New York: Harper and Row.

Kolko, Gabriel. 1994. *Century of War.* New York: New Press.

Ledeen, Michael A. 1975. "War as a Style of Life," in Stephen Ward, ed., *The War Generation,* 104–134. Port Washington, N.Y.: Kennikat.

Livy. 1971. *The Early History of Rome*. London: Penguin.

Mack, Charles S. 1989. *Lobbying and Government Relations: A Guide for Executives*. New York: Quorum Books.

Mann, Michael. 1988. *States, War and Capitalism*. Oxford: Blackwell.

1993. *Sources of Social Power*. Vol. 2: *The Rise of Classes and Nation-States, 1760–1914*. Cambridge: Cambridge University Press.

1995. "Sources of Variation in Working Class Movements in Twentieth-Century Europe," *New Left Review* 212: 14–54.

Marwick, Arthur. 1965. *The Deluge: British Society and the First World War*. New York: Norton.

McNeill, William H. 1982. *The Pursuit of Power*. Chicago: University of Chicago.

Minot, Rodney. 1962. *Peerless Patriots: Organized Veterans and the Spirit of Americanism*. Washington, D.C.: Public Affairs Press.

Montgomery, David. 1993. *Citizen Worker: The Experience of Workers in the United States with Democracy and the Free Market during the Nineteenth Century*. Cambridge: Cambridge University Press.

Moore, Barrington. 1978. *Injustice: The Social Bases of Obedience and Revolt*. White Plains, N.Y.: Sharpe.

Orloff, Ann Shola. 1993. *The Politics of Pensions: A Comparative Analysis of Britain, Canada, and the United States, 1880–1940*. Madison: University of Wisconson.

Orloff, Ann Shola, and Theda Skocpol. 1984. "Why Not Equal Protection?: Explaining the Politics of Public Social Spending in Britain, 1900–1911, and the United States, 1880–1920," *American Sociological Review* 49: 726–750.

Pencak, William. 1989. *For God and Country*. Boston: Northeastern University Press.

Porter, Bruce D. 1994. *War and the Rise of the State*. New York: Free Press.

Powell, Talcott. 1932. *Tattered Banners*. New York: Harcourt.

Preston, Richard A., Alex Roland, and Sydney F. Wise. 1991. *Men in Arms: A History of Warfare and Its Interrelationships with Western Society*. 5th ed. Fort Worth: Holt, Rinehart and Winston.

Riker, William H. 1957. *Soldiers of the States*. Washington, D.C.: Public Affairs Press.

Schriftgeisser, Karl. 1951. *The Lobbyists: The Art and Business of Influencing Lawmakers*. Boston: Little, Brown.

Severo, Richard, and Lewis Milford. 1989. *The Wages of War: When America's Soldiers Came Home from Valley Forge to Vietnam*. New York: Simon and Schuster.

Skocpol, Theda. 1979. *States and Social Revolutions*. Cambridge: Cambridge University Press.

1992. *Protecting Soldiers and Mothers*. Cambridge, Mass.: Belknap.

Soucy, Robert. 1975. "Veterans Politics between the Wars," in Stephen Ward, ed., *The War Generation*, 59–103. Port Washington, N.Y.: Kennikat.

Therborn, Goran. 1977. "The Rule of Capital and the Rise of Democracy," *New Left Review*, no. 103: 3–41.

Tilly, Charles. 1986. *The Contentious French*. Cambridge, Mass.: Belknap.

1990. *Coercion, Capital, and European States, AD 990–1990*. Cambridge, Mass.: Blackwell.

Vagts, Alfred. 1959. *A History of Militarism: Civilian and Military*. New York: Free Press.

Ward, Stephen R. 1975. "Land Fit for Heroes Lost," in Stephen Ward, ed., *The War Generation*, 10–37. Port Washington, N.Y.: Kennikat.

Wecter, Dixon. 1944. *When Johnny Comes Marching Home*. Cambridge, Mass.: Riverside Press.

Wheat, George. S. 1919. *The Story of the American Legion*. New York: G. P. Putnam's Sons.

5

Military Mobilization and the Transformation of Property Relationships

Wars That Defined the Japanese Style of Capitalism

Eiko Ikegami

In this chapter, I would like to shed new light on the social consequences of military involvement from an insufficiently explored perspective – namely, the impact of waging war on the transformation of possessiveness in social relationships. Conceptualizing the influence of wars as a bridge between a theory of state formation and a theory of property relationships, I start my discussion by redefining the notion of property sociologically as a nexus of social relationships rather than a thing "out-there." I argue that the waging of wars often decisively influenced the style of capitalism in a society. After presenting my theoretical argument on property as the embodiment of social relationships, I examine a case from Japanese history in which the historical experiences of preparing for and engaging in three wars have changed "property relationships." This historical process of changing property relationships, I believe, shaped a distinctive style of capitalism in Japan.

Wars are projects that require the most forceful mobilization of human capacities and material resources. The preparation for and prosecution of war frequently restrict or override individuals' control over their possessive resources. War redistributes goods and services and reorganizes the flow of material resources for military purposes in ways that affect existing property relationships. The outcome of a war – victory, defeat, or stalemate – may also bring about the reorganization of property relationships and may redefine new categories of property rights. For example, the compulsory recruitment of soldiers through conscription restricts, in the most profound manner, persons' proprietorship of their own bodies. On the other hand, a person's surrender of physical property to the cause of a war is sometimes offset by material, political, or economic gains in other categories of ownership. Historians and sociologists have pointed to the close relationship between the rise of national armies and the emergence of universal suffrage in various societies and the introduction of such welfare entitlements as Social Security payments or national health insurance. In this way, the mobilization of one kind of resource may be compensated for by another kind of possessive entitlement that results in the redistribution of possessive resources. I call such a socially negotiated relational pattern of access to and control of various possessive resources a "property relationship" in this chapter. War affects the social redistribution of ownership, not only in terms of property in the strict sense but often through simultaneous alterations in the many forms and levels of property relationships.

To be sure, the following analysis of the role of military preparation and activity in the development of property relationships should not be misunderstood as implying that wars always drive social changes in property rights and proprietorship. In addition, I do not regard all significant transitions in property relationships solely as by-products of wars and military adventures. Often, changes in property relationships were triggered not by extreme effects of military mobilization but by more peaceful social and economic factors. At times, however, wars do introduce significant discontinuities into existing patterns of property relationship, which in turn define the "character" of capitalism in society.

The effects of military involvement on conceptions, relations, and definitions of possession are complex and multifaceted; moreover, they differ across various societies in different historical periods and in different institutional contexts. This chapter illustrates this process of transformation with historical examples drawn from three different phases of Japanese history: the period around the time of pacification under the Tokugawa shoguns (the late sixteenth through the early seventeenth century); the era of modern state formation, beginning around 1868 in response to Western military pressure; and the period of the Second World War and its aftermath. Assessment of the reorganization of possessive relationships resulting from the impact of war offers us a fresh perspective on the social processes that helped to form various types of capitalist societies in the contemporary world. I propose to demonstrate that the emergence of the distinctive style of postwar Japanese capitalism cannot be elucidated without an understanding of Japan's experiences with war, in both its preparation and its actual conduct.

Japan's trajectory of long-term social development and state formation was closely linked to wars and military activity. For example, the formation of the Tokugawa state (1603) was the final product of the reorganization of the samurai's national hierarchies through continuous civil wars among the warlords.[1] The subsequent evolution of the modern Japanese state and economy, however, was also closely bound to military interests and activity. Western imperialism in its nineteenth-century form prompted the most recent phase of Japanese nation-building. The regime that emerged as a result of the collapse of the Tokugawa shogunate and the Meiji Restoration (1868) was motivated to build a strong state in response to constant threats from the Western powers. This drive made Japan the first non-Western industrialized military power by the turn of the twentieth century. Finally, Japan's entry into World War II, culminating in disastrous defeat in 1945, provided the direct impetus for restructuring the country's political economy. The three historical examples that I examine here illustrate three variations on the institutional mechanisms of change as well as the effects of militarization on property relationships.

A Theory of State and a Theory of Property

Over the past three decades, the literature of comparative state formation has been enriched by several noteworthy reexaminations of the effects of military preparation and waging war on the varied routes and structures of state formation (Tilly 1975; Finer 1975; Mann 1986, 1988; Brewer 1985; Downing 1992; Ertman 1997). These scholars have advanced wide-ranging explanations of the varieties of political regimes and administrative infrastructures that characterize modern states. The challenges posed by a series of European wars led to recognizably modern forms of concentrated bureaucracy in England and Western Europe in the seventeenth and eighteenth centuries. Although analysts of comparative state formation differ in their methods of assessing the political transformations of the European states, they agree in emphasizing the role of military conflict in refining political organizations and institutions. Wars required intensive commitment of resources, leading to structural innovations in the interest of greater military efficiency. As Charles Tilly puts it, "war made the state and the state made war."[2] This development in the literature of comparative state formation, together with the parallel interest of Theda Skocpol and others in "bringing the state back in" to the social sciences, has stimulated fresh and dynamic inquiries into the organizational-structural and developmental variations of modern states.

Investigations of the institutional effects of war have revitalized studies of long-term state development because they illuminate a particular aspect of historical innovation and discontinuity. Long-term social changes cannot usually be articulated solely as the natural results of inch-by-inch increments of social change. Focusing on the various economic and social effects of war has allowed for a fuller exposition of radical changes in the structures of European states that could not be achieved by traditional methods of class-based or conventional liberal analysis.[3]

The present chapter examines the assumption that the impact of war on long-term social development can shed light on a different area of radical historical *discontinuity*. The prosecution of war and military preparation have often stimulated the simultaneous renegotiation of relations regarding access to and control over possessive resources in a given society. But, although the relationship between military involvement and state structures has received extensive discussion in the literature, the rise of capitalism, which is another key factor in the creation of the modern world, has been analyzed primarily in the context of economic history, a field dominated by narratives of *continuity.* I argue that the emergence of modern property relationships cannot be understood simply as auxiliary outgrowths of economic developments. This thesis is likely to provoke an immediate critical reaction because the emergence of legal definitions of private-property ownership is commonly regarded as an aspect of the development of capitalism and the rise of liberal politics. The right to hold private property is considered a symbol of the political triumph of a capitalist class, which in turn laid the foundations of modern liberal conceptions of citizenship and democracy.

Yet economic historians have shown that the rise of property rights and market economy in European history was not a "natural" outcome of economic growth. North and Thomas (1973), by focusing on the state's role in the protection of property rights and the enforcement of contracts, illustrated that efficient economic organization hinged upon the state's involvement in institution-building that significantly reduced the costs of transaction. North considered that "it is the state that specifies the property right structure" (North 1981: 17; North and Thomas 1973). Thus, a theory of the state and a theory of property rights have to be interconnected as the building blocks for understanding the patterns of economic development.[4]

North's two sets of explanatory models, a theory of state and a theory of property rights, bring us to an intersection with the theme I am investigating here. If we juxtapose the insight of North and the sociological theories of state formation and military (á la Charles Tilly), a missing piece for the theoretical bridge is a connection between wars and property rights. If military mobilization can change the structure of the state and sometimes even trigger and structure state formation, property rights and other economic institutions that were hinged upon the state's infrastructural initiatives may be also influenced by waging wars. From this orientation, I claim that the experience of waging wars and the pattern of military mobilization often significantly influence the style of capitalism in a host-society in which the pattern of property relationships played a significant role; however, I would also like to expand and redefine the notion of property because "possessive" qualities in society change and transform significantly throughout history.

Japan offers useful illustrative case studies for my purpose. For one thing, postwar Japanese capitalism is known for its distinctive style. Although Japan's economic growth in the postwar period certainly derived from an American-style competitive market economy, it is nonetheless supplemented by, socially integrated with, and coordinated through a set of idiosyncratic redistributive mechanisms. There is presently a strong popular sentiment in favor of a just redistribution of economic resources and benefits. I should explain that my use of the term *redistribution* is not confined to such direct functions of the state as welfare programs and progressive taxation. I include the combination of socially embedded aspects of corporate operations under redistribution as well as state provisions for the transfer of wealth. Both sets of factors are involved in the emergence of specific styles of Japanese capitalism. In particular, the postwar Japanese approach to the management of large corporations has appeared to outside observers to be the direct antithesis of contemporary Wall Street's "cowboy capitalism." A brief example will suffice. In the typical large Japanese corporation, it is unclear in practice whether the company's stockholders really "own" and control the firm. Although Japanese corporations are legally defined as entities owned by their stockholders, the combination of low reliance on the open market for obtaining capital, high rate of stable shareholders who are affiliated companies, and high reliance on long-term credit gives management a relatively free hand vis-à-vis the short-term profit interests of individual floating stockholders. In addition, the Japanese corporation's distinctive style of eliciting loyalty from employees through a system of guaranteed long-term employment and company-based labor unions has also generated the belief that a company belongs to all its members, including its employees. (Much has been written concerning the peculiar pseudoegalitarianism of the Japanese corporation; I therefore dispense with further discussion of it at this point.)

As a consequence, until the recent economic recession that has significantly undermined the Japanese style of corporate management, it was often the case that the management of the firm, the long-term employees, and the stockholders together claimed certain rights of shared proprietorship in the company. The large corporations' version of company welfare and their relatively stable guarantees of job security thus made up in part for the Japanese state welfare system. In other words, postwar Japanese capitalism has emphasized a shared and relational approach to the possessive resources of a capitalist society. As a result, it has nurtured a strong ideology of egalitarianism through several decades of remarkable economic growth since the 1950s.

At first glance, this characteristic feature of Japanese capitalism may appear to reflect little more than a supposed traditional cultural preference for familial and communal values. A closer examination of the history of Japanese social relations, however, indicates that an egalitarian approach to management is a relative latecomer to Japanese business culture. The Japanese pattern is also different from those that dominate other Asian societies. For example, family-owned businesses in China and Korea favor elitist styles of management; in addition, the owners of these companies have real control over their corporations. These considerations prompt us to explore the historical origins of the egalitarian attitudes that characterize the operational style of capitalism in postwar Japan.

To be sure, an investigation of the emergence of the Japanese form of capitalism involves a number of historical contingencies, domestic as well as international. A full exploration of all these factors is outside the scope of this short essay. But by focusing on the interaction between military involvements and changing property relationships, I hope to illuminate a relatively unexplored aspect of the historical development of Japanese capitalism.

Property as the Embodiment of Social Relationships

Before proceeding with a historical analysis, however, I first redefine the notion of property in sociological terms. For my present purposes, the political theory of C. B. Macpherson offers some useful insights into the many layers and multidimensional meanings of the term "property." Macpherson observed that the right of possession is basic to an adequate understanding of the rise of liberal democratic thought. He attempted to restore the complexity of the term "property" by examining early modern liberal theories of property rights. Macpherson maintained that the protection of individuals' property with regard to their persons and goods – in other words, the "possessive" quality of individualism – is basic to liberal political theory in British thinkers from Hobbes to Locke. In Macpherson's own words, "The individual, it is thought, is free inasmuch as he is proprietor of his person and capacities." Parallel to this sense of personal proprietorship was a cultural emerging property, a new conception of the individual. Macpherson termed this emerging property "possessive individualism." The "possessive quality" of human nature thus became important for Macpherson's normative theory of liberalism.[5] If we take Macpherson's thesis seriously, as I believe it deserves to be taken, changes in property relationships may have implications not only for the domains of economics and politics, but also for democracy, freedom, and citizenship.

Although the concepts of property and proprietorship play important positive roles in Macpherson's liberal political theory, he also opposed narrow capitalist definitions of property.[6]

The difficulty is that the individual property right which liberal theory has inferred from the nature of man is . . . too narrow. What is needed is to broaden it. . . . [Property], although it must always be an individual right, need not be confined, as liberal theory has confined it, to a right to exclude others from the use or benefit of some thing, but may equally be an individual right not to be excluded by others from the use or benefit of some thing.

In the spirit of Macpherson, I use the term "property" broadly in this chapter in order to emphasize the fact that there are and have been many possible ways of conceptualizing and enacting property rights and proprietorship.[7] The prevailing contemporary conception of private property tends to focus narrowly on the right to exercise exclusive control over an objectively specified resource. This understanding of property, which is predicated on liberal market assumptions, is a historically specific notion that became *normative* by excluding other definitions of property. This prevailing conception does not mean that property exists exclusively *in reality* as control of specific resources, either in past societies or in the modern market economy.

As is well known to students of medieval European or Japanese feudalism, feudal property relationships were characterized by multiple layers of rights over landed properties shared by a number of different agents. Anthropologists are familiar with various forms of communal ownership in preindustrial non-Western societies. Although the right to ownership of private property is often conventionally described as foundational to modern capitalist civilization, in reality modern industrial societies have never recognized the right to private property as exclusive. For example, the owner of a hog farm that produces offensive odors strong enough to disturb the neighbors may be obliged to accept local regulations on the use of his own property. Although the owners of certain materials used in industry may retain the right to use or sell them, the owners may be forbidden to dispose of the waste products in ways that are toxic to the environment. Furthermore, control of property operates on several different levels; the rights of use, consumption, trade, or disposal of property can be shared by different proprietors. Rights are also subject to different types of regulation. The rights to a specific good can be divided and controlled in different ways, as is reflected in the evolution of patent and copyright law. Even in the market operations of modern liberal societies, the exclusivity of private property is guaranteed only within strictly delimited contexts. This multidimensional and multilayered nature of property makes the trading and reorganizing of various kinds of property rights possible.

Consequently, I propose to redefine the term "property" in three respects for the purposes of sociological analysis. First, instead of conceptualizing property as a thing or object "out there," I propose to redefine property as the nexus of relationships that are embodied in rights and enacted through social interactions. In this usage, "property relationship" refers to a set of social agreements (or lack thereof) regarding the control of various social resources. The second point is related to the first: I emphasize actual enactments of control and access rather than static legal definitions of property ownership. The third point concerns the proprietorship of the human body and human capacities. Human capacities, without any doubt, are critical factors in economic development. In a postindustrial age, in particular with the rise of cyberspace and biotech industries, assets of modern corporations moved from actual physical properties to nonmaterial technologies, and knowledge that were ultimately held in the form of human capital (Blair and Kochan 2000). Although such a shift in properties was obvious for modern economists, human capacities, in particular those represented by the physicality of human lives, were a critical necessity in military and economic activities. I regard the proprietorship of human physical capacities and mental skills as an important dimension of property relationships. The term "property" in this chapter, then, denotes control over and access to various possessive resources in this broader sense of the term. These resources include material goods and artifacts, landed wealth, knowledge, skills, and entitlements, as well as proprietorship of a person's own body and associated capacities. Given this definition, I am concerned with *the effects of wars on the reorganization of relationships that redistribute access to and control of various forms of resources among different social actors.*

The necessity of the mobilization and subsequent redistribution of possessive resources are two closely connected yet categorically distinct mechanisms through which military involvements affect property relationships. Preparation for and prosecution of war require the effective mobilization of people, materials, and fiscal resources – all of which impact existing property relationships. Military mobilization and the waging of war have often forcefully introduced discontinuities and innovations into power relationships on the homefront, thus restructuring the entire landscape of property and proprietorship. In the following review of three critical phases of Japanese social developments, note that military involvement played a central role in the transformation of proprietorship in very different ways.

Tokugawa State Formation, "Sword-Hunting," and Changes in Property Relationships

In the course of the past five centuries, Japan experienced three distinct phases of the concentration of coercive force. In each case, there were complex mechanisms of mobilization and redistribution at work that radically altered property relationships on many different levels. Although I focus my analysis on the third stage – Japan's involvement in the Second World War – I begin my exposition with earlier historical periods because these preliminary phases of economic growth have also conditioned the development of Japanese capitalism.

The Tokugawa Shogunate

After more than a century of continuous wars among regional warlords (*daimyo*), the Tokugawa family pacified the country with an allied army of daimyo troops. The result was the establishment of the Tokugawa shogunate (1603–1867). Japan's pacification under the Tokugawa shoguns was a classic case of state formation in which the regime's complete monopoly of armed violence created a new form of political dominance. This statement, however, does not apply to the military struggles among the samurai themselves for reconstituting their national hierarchy. Behind the triumphs on the battlefield, the rulers of the unification period succeeded in disarming the nonsamurai population through a series of edicts that embodied a policy called "sword hunting." This phase of sword-hunting represented a shift in the distribution of military force by forbidding the nonsamurai population to bear arms. As long as the samurai were fighting among themselves, it was impossible to draw a strict line of demarcation between the armed warrior elite and the agricultural population. In this sense, Perry Anderson's idiosyncratic definition of the absolutist state as a redeployed form of feudalism is applicable to the Tokugawa shogunate because the shoguns established a politically redeployed form of domination. They did this in order to subordinate the peasantry so that the samurai could continue to extract revenue from the agricultural population. This political reconstitution was so successful that the Tokugawa state retained its neofeudal structure for the next two and a half centuries. As a result, while the European states experienced a number of organizational developments with the rise of a capitalist economy in the seventeenth and eighteenth centuries, Japan remained neofeudal. This situation led to the evolution of a number of distinctive characteristics in Japanese property relationships.

Various changes in Tokugawa property relationships resulted from the formation of a distinctively military state. The most obvious modification occurred in the redistribution of the ownership and control of landed wealth. Before the unification of Japan around 1600 under the Tokugawa, the samurai were in essence landed military lords whose primary interest was to increase their wealth by extending their land holdings. They lived on their own estates for the most part and defended their economic interests with their own armed forces. The political and economic power of the samurai was vested in their self-equipped private armies. Their power was derived from this possessive quality, a kind of proprietorship based on the firm conviction that the individual warrior did not simply own his landed estate and military force but also his body and destiny. The medieval samurai might choose to become the vassal of an overlord, but his submission was voluntary, with a view to his personal interest. The medieval samurai's clear sense of self-possession, of ownership of his person and assets, resembled the "possessive individualism" that Macpherson has described. After the pacification of Japan under the Tokugawa shoguns, however, the political and economic basis of the samurai vassals' possessive independence was seriously undermined. The vassal samurai were forced to live in the castle cities of their masters, the daimyo lords, and were excluded from direct supervision of their lands and agricultural production. Many vassal samurai received no income apart from a semihereditary stipend paid by their overlords. The samurai no longer exercised actual control over their landed properties. An individual samurai vassal might have a more secure economic base under the shogunate compared with the situation of his grandfather in the conflict-ridden medieval period, but he would lose his economic and political independence vis-à-vis his daimyo lord. The samurai were also no longer feudal lords in the medieval style, living in physical proximity to their possessions and thus able to supervise production and subordinate unruly peasants. Thus, Tokugawa Japan did not develop an elitist and aristocratic notion of property holding.

If the samurai did not actually "own" the land, were the farmers, no longer concerned with samurai living in their villages, regarded as the owners of landed properties? Under the Tokugawa system, the nonsamurai farmers' accumulation of wealth, as well as their private control over their wealth, was in practice relatively unrestricted by the samurai authorities. Yet, given the largely feudal character of the political framework of the Tokugawa state, landownership on the part of nonsamurai farmers was a dubious notion. To be sure, farmers from the commoner class were able in practice to have relatively free access to and control over their own landed wealth as long as they paid their taxes to the samurai. The farmers were also able to make independent decisions regarding agricultural production. On the other hand, however, the nonsamurai farmers' control of landed wealth was not conceived in terms of Western legal definitions of private property. As a result of the shoguns' policy of demilitarization during the pacification of Japan, the nonsamurai classes (farmers, craftsmen, and merchants) were formally defined as hereditary subordinates ruled by the samurai hierarchies. Furthermore, under the Tokugawa system, the agricultural communities (*mura*) were collectively responsible for taxes owed to the samurai authorities. This provision also meant that the use of landed properties was not simply a private matter but a public and communal concern. The strong sense of communal solidarity in the agricultural villages and the villages' practices of property control also hindered the development of a conception of private property as exclusive possession of a resource. Thus the combination of the samurai's feudal privileges over land as well as the villagers' reluctance to identify land as private property meant that Tokugawa property relationships did not favor the evolution of legally defined notions of landownership as exclusive rights over private property. Rather, a number of different social actors had access to and control over various layers of benefits associated with a given piece of land. *In essence, the distinctive path of military* conquest and state formation in Tokugawa Japan restructured a preexisting pattern of property relationships; the resulting new system obscured who actually "owned" pieces of property.

In the second half of the Tokugawa period, the Japanese economy developed national networks of market exchanges that led to the appearance of capitalist features in market operations. In the Tokugawa market economy, therefore, the ownership of private property was honored in actual practice but not defined legally. The trading and sales of commodities as well as properties were conducted through a highly developed system of customary rules. In addition, the Japanese economic system failed to develop a concept of private landed property that empowered property holders. The ownership of private property in Japan was perceived as a privilege rather than a right.

Furthermore, the members of the samurai elite were forbidden to participate in business enterprises. In contrast to their Japanese counterparts, the British landed elite were able to initiate the first moves toward proto-industrialization and rural commercialization by enclosing their landed property in order to use the land more profitably. They therefore developed a strong possessive sense of property. In Japan, the Tokugawa samurai could not have the same elitist sense of possession that their medieval ancestors had had regarding their feudal estates, nor could they term themselves the first generation of entrepreneurs.

The pacification of Japan and the establishment of a stable political system also altered possessive relationships in terms of physical force and political autonomy. The disarmed commoners were understood as having a nonautonomous social existence – even though they were often, in fact, contentious social actors. Under the *pax Tokugawa*, the Japanese commoners no longer had the "burden" of self-defense as they were in theory "protected" by the shogunate. Commoners were also not affected by mobilization for war because military duties were defined as the exclusive privilege of the samurai class. The ruling ideology of the Tokugawa regime held that once the farmers had dutifully paid their grain taxes, "nothing [was] more peaceful than a farmer's life." But, on the other hand, the end of the period of civil war also deprived the nonsamurai farmers of opportunities for political independence and upward mobility within the class system. The fact that they had no military obligations was understood symbolically as implying that they had no control over their bodies or their other life circumstances. In contrast, even though the Tokugawa samurai's social and economic life became more and more dependent on the state, with the symbolic qualification that they were warriors who would voluntarily risk their lives on the battlefield if necessary, as a status group the samurai were still considered autonomous political and moral actors. For example, Tokugawa law defined *hara-kiri*, or ritual suicide, as a privileged form of the death penalty reserved for individual samurai. Ritual suicide symbolized the political fact that the samurai "owned" his own body; hence, his life, honor, and moral judgment were under his own control. In contrast, commoners were simply beheaded, flogged, or tattooed under criminal punishment. These penalties represented the fact that commoners were not regarded as "owning" their bodies. In other words, instead of acquiring a sense of physical safety and protection associated with their disarmament, Tokugawa commoners were perceived as losing their full possessiveness in terms of their corporal and political autonomy.

The military pacification of Japan at the turn of the seventeenth century thus ushered in a number of ramifications for the subsequent reorganization of property relationships. Two specific aspects of change in Japanese property relationships should be summarized here. First, the notion of private property was obscured even though the transition to a capitalist market economy was well underway under the Tokugawa shogunate. The theoretical foundations of individual political rights and moral responsibilities that were associated with the Western liberal notion of private property did not develop indigenous counterparts in Japan. The second point concerns the symbolic political significance of military obligations and physical possessiveness. Under the Tokugawa shogunate, military activity was closely connected to the samurai's class privilege and political power. This connection fostered the belief among the commoner classes that they were exempt from military duties. The peasantry assumed that, in an exchange for their political and economic subordination to the samurai class, they were exempted from submitting their physical property to the requirement of military duties. All in all, the complexities of Japanese property relationships thus created a situation in which the rights and responsibilities associated with property ownership lacked conceptual clarity as well as legal definition.

Nation-Building under the Meiji Restoration and the Construction of a National Army

After the collapse of the Tokugawa shogunate, Japan rapidly implemented a process of modern nation-building under the symbolic leadership of the Meiji emperor (1867–1912). The Meiji government began by abolishing the socioeconomic and political privileges of the samurai class, namely its exclusive right to bear arms, hold office, and receive hereditary stipends. By 1900 Japan was already equipped with a modern constitution; a parliamentary system; an updated judicial system, with a modern national and local bureaucracy; mandated universal education; a national standing army; a national taxation system; and legally defined private ownership of land. This political transformation was amazingly rapid, given that none of these institutions associated with modern states existed in Japan prior to 1868.

Social scientists have been accustomed to view the achievements of the Meiji Regime as the results of a "revolution from above," that is, as the forceful implementation of political reforms initiated by a segment of the former samurai class. Although this overall picture is for the most part valid, we should not neglect the fact that the radical reforms imposed from above encountered serious initial opposition from the general population. After all, if the Meiji reform was no more than a process of modernization from the top down, given the supposed national propensity for collaboration, then the question arises as to why the elitist oligarchy incorporated many liberal institutions at the time that it drafted the first constitution. The necessity of mobilizing a reluctant population of eligible males for military preparation played a critical role in this process.

During the period immediately preceding the Meiji Restoration, Japan was subject to constant pressures from Western imperial powers. Japanese observers witnessed China, a country that their intellectuals had long admired as the center of civilization, falling into a disgraceful condition of partial colonization. The obsolescence of the samurai's military skills and equipment in the face of Western technology was obvious. The shogunate's collapse was triggered by the growing recognition that the outdated Tokugawa system could never effectively oppose the West. After 1868 the construction of an effective modern state that could hold its own against Western imperialism became the central mandate of the new regime. During the transition period, the newly emerging Meiji state had the pressing internal task of recruiting the support of the citizenry for the creation of a national standing army, along with other aspects of modern nation-building. In order to achieve its goals, the new regime had to mobilize people along two fronts: given the immaturity of its industrial and commercial base in the late 1860s, the Meiji government had to secure and increase its tax revenue primarily from the agricultural sector; and the abolition of the samurai class meant that any national army would have to rely on conscription for its manpower. Both burdens – higher taxes and liability to conscription – fell disproportionately on the agrarian population.

At this point, the confused relationship between ownership of property and military obligations posed a significant obstacle for the Meiji regime. To begin with, the peasants, who had been accustomed to leave military matters in the hands of the samurai, felt that soldiery was none of their business. The taxes that they had paid under the shogunate had been regarded as purchasing a kind of exemption from armed service. Because the taxes imposed on the farming population were never lowered under the Meiji regime, peasant families did not feel any moral obligation to send off their able-bodied menfolk to additional military duties. The disillusioned farmers in various regions of Japan began to organize protests against the new regime. Most of their grievances had to do with land tax reform, military conscription, and public education.

The Meiji government thus recognized the need for a reliable standing military force capable of handling internal insurrection as well as external threats from the Western powers. The 1872 imperial decree instituting conscription used quasi-democratic rhetoric to persuade the population to think of military service as a patriotic duty: "Now the samurai's stipends are decreased and they are allowed to lay down their swords; people from all four status groups are gaining the rights of freedom. . . . If the country were overwhelmed by a disaster, however, all people would be affected in part. Therefore, people should know that their fundamental protection against personal disaster lies in defending the country against catastrophe." The new government discovered, however, that the peasants were not easily persuaded. A poorly worded passage in the 1872 decree, which described military duty as analogous to *ketsuzei*, or blood tax, touched off a series of so-called *ketsuzei ikki*, or blood tax revolts. Many parents interpreted the decree to mean that the government would extract their sons' blood as a new form of tax. Many people also availed themselves of a variety of exemptions in order to keep their sons at home, or encouraged their sons to leave home. In 1881 the minister of defense reported a figure of 10,360 draft dodgers. Thus, in order to overcome the peasants' lack of enthusiasm for military service, the army increasingly made use of democratic rhetoric that emphasized the egalitarian nature of conscription.

The complexity of the situation lies in the fact that not only the construction of a strong army depended on the cooperation of the largest segment of the population – the peasantry – but that all kinds of modernization programs were financially dependent on tax revenue from the agrarian population. In fact, because Japan's industrial base was still underdeveloped, the only source of tax revenue that the government could hope to increase was the agricultural sector. After 1872 the Meiji regime accelerated efforts to implement a tax reform project (*chiso kaisei*) that involved a land survey and official assessments of land prices as the basis for calculating individual tax schedules. This land tax reform was intended to resolve the complicated property relationships in the agrarian communities that dated back to the Tokugawa period. Identification of taxpayers was an important step toward increasing tax revenue as well as normalizing the status of landholdings as legally defined private property. The farmers, however, feared that the Meiji land survey would lead to further tax increases. The result was a series of rural revolts: 56 in 1873, 21 in 1874, 19 in 1875, 28 in 1876, and 48 in 1877. The most extensive revolt, affecting four provinces, took place in December 1876. About 57,000 peasants were eventually arrested for participating in the uprising. These peasant revolts forced the government to institute significant reductions in national and local tax rates. Furthermore, the introduction of incidental inflationary economic measures that helped to raise the price of rice reduced the burden of cash tax payments. The combination of economic inflation and the government's willingness to compromise led to the successful completion of the land survey and tax reform. The abolition of feudal land tenure and the concept of land as private property were firmly institutionalized in the course of this process.

The Meiji government did succeed in obtaining a significant increase in land tax revenue from the agricultural population. In 1870 the government received 8,220,000 yen from taxes on land. After the tax reform in 1873, the land tax revenue rose sharply to 60,600,000 yen – 90 percent of the total tax revenue and 70 percent of the government's total income. It was only in 1896 that income from land taxes fell to less than half of the total tax revenue of the Meiji government. These figures indicate that modern notions of private landed property did not arise in Japan as an extension

of indigenous capitalist development. The necessity of military mobilization, supported by a modern bureaucracy and system of tax collection,
became a critical ingredient in the development of newer conceptions of
private property.

The normalization of private properties and the introduction of universal conscription inevitably altered the possessive quality of Japanese citizens. Farmers who owned land and paid taxes on it had an understandable
desire to be more active participants in the political process. Even those
who did not have much in the way of material properties increased their
political proprietorship because they were willing to serve in the army as
"able bodies." The newly extended concept of proprietorship provided
the basis of modern notions of citizenship and political participation. The
Freedom and People's Rights Movement (*jiyu minken undo*, which reached
its peak between 1874 and 1881) worked for the establishment of a constitutional polity and a parliamentary system. Its leaders proudly claimed
that the people of Japan were qualified to be full participants in the political process. One popular petition to the government included the following statement:

Although the people have spirit and energy, unless the state gives them proper outlets
for their energy, their sincere and loyal spirit will be wasted. As we witness the deterioration of the state's finances, we the people can only deplore the situation. We
cannot do anything to change it. Knowing that the revision of the unequal treaties
with the West [an urgent political issue considered to be the most visible symbol of
the Western imperial dominance over Japan] is not yet realized, we can only feel a
sense of intolerable national humiliation. . . . [W]hy not let the people participate in
politics on an equal basis and allow them to debate the future of our nation and
our fiscal system?

Japan's first modern constitution (1889) codified the civic rights of imperial subjects, including freedom of speech and religion, property rights, and
political participation through a parliamentary system. The constitution
was the final result of the Meiji oligarchy's willingness to compromise with
intense popular sentiment. The oligarchs were obliged to include generous
provisions of liberal human rights in the constitution, even though its
assertion of the emperor's divinity was less than ideal from a modern
democratic standpoint.[8]

World War II and the Creation of Postwar Japanese Capitalism

Social scientists usually regard the prewar Japanese state as a strong regime
that forcefully imposed economic modernization on the country. Although,
as with any stereotype, this view contains a grain of truth,[9] this top-down
pattern should not be understood to mean that the Meiji state attempted
to regulate the dynamic activities of its economy in detail. The regime's
initiatives for economic growth (*shokusan kogyo*) were mostly institutional,

in order to create social infrastructures conducive to the stable operation of modern capitalism. In terms of *regulating* its already lively areas of economic activities, however, the Meiji government's style was surprisingly liberal – somewhat comparable with that of the British. For example, because the Japanese banking industry was only lightly regulated, the number of banks, both large and small, mushroomed. In 1901 the total number of Japanese banks reached 1,867.

Prior to World War I the Japanese economy had a well-developed competitive infrastructure of capital markets, including commercial banks, savings banks, national banks, banks for long-term credit, and a variety of insurance companies, together with a small but lively market for stocks and bonds. This young and relatively unregulated capitalist economy was animated by a competitive entrepreneurial spirit. World War I benefited the Japanese economy because its heavy industries were important suppliers to the European belligerents. The earliest version of so-called lifelong employment, or job security, first emerged during this period because of the shortage of skilled labor to meet the expanding industrial demand. This practice was not widespread at first and applied only to blue-collar rather than white-collar workers. Company welfare as such, a symbol of the stability of the large postwar Japanese corporation, had not yet been introduced. The competitive capitalists of the World War I period preferred to take risks with flexible labor relations in order to maximize their profits. At the same time, during the first two decades of the twentieth century, Japan further extended the suffrage, and parliamentary partisan politics acquired a solid institutional form. Yet, the majority of party politicians were seen as the allies of capitalists who did not like the government's regulations on economic transactions.

This brief outline of the development of Japanese capitalism and democratic institutions may lead to the question as to why the Japanese version of capitalism did not move in the direction of the American form. The evolution of capitalism in Japan is a complex multicausal process that cannot be reduced to a single factor. In my opinion, however, the simultaneous institutional changes in various levels of property relationships during the period preceding World War II played a critical role in formulating the pattern of postwar Japanese capitalism. In fact, there was a clear aspect of continuity between the social structure of wartime economy and that of postwar Japanese capitalism in many levels as it is shown in Table 5.1.[10] Of course, the forceful wartime economic regulation did not abruptly start in the late 1930s. Some historical contingencies must be acknowledged.

After the Great Depression of 1929, popular political feeling became more and more critical of the alliance that was thought to exist between the Japanese *zaibatsu* (business conglomerates) and parliamentary politicians. Because of its nonrestrictive economic policies in the earlier phase of

TABLE 5.1. *The Wartime Mobilization as the Platform for the Postwar Japanese System*

	Prewar	Wartime	Postwar
The Japanese style of management	Not yet clearly developed	A platform for the present style formulated	Institutionalized in the high-growth period
Employment	Higher rate of turnover among blue collars	Long-term commitment encouraged	Institutionalization of lifetime employment in big corporations
Pay scale	Meritocratic pay scale	Wage control law of 1939 encouraged seniority pay scale	Seniority pay scale became common
Labor union	Labor not highly organized, yet many labor disputes	Unions break up; company-based "Patriotic Industrial Association" institutionalized including blue and white collars	Company-based unions including blue and white collars institutionalized
Corporate governance	Stockholders owned the corporation; high rate of dividend	Stockholders' control over management decreased; the rate of dividend regulated	Management largely autonomous from stock holders
Source of capital for corporations	Stock market + bonds form 87% of capital source in 1931	Loans became 77% of capital source in 1944; the decline of stock market	Bank loans driving force of growth, as 80% of capital source in 1964
Number of commercial banks	500 in early 1930	61 in 1945 control by MOF	About 60 until 1990s; collaboration with and protection by the government
Personal savings rate	6% of personal income in 1930	30% in 1940	20% in 1960
Health insurance	Very limited	Expanded to cover many	Universal public health plan
Social Security	None	Started in 1944	Expanded to cover all citizens

	Prewar	Wartime	Postwar
Taxation	Decentralized; indirect tax	Centralized; direct; withholding	Centralized; direct; withholding
Agriculture	Highly contentious tenant farmers	Tenant farmers' rights protected for maximizing food production	GHQ's land reform: land distributed to tenant farmers Rice price control
	No subsidies	Food price control	Small independent farmers support the LDP
Bureaucractic control over industries	Limited industrial policies	Increased bureaucratic power through wartime regulation; the infamous "administrative guidance" emerged	Less affected by the GHQ's purge than politicians and business leaders

industrialization, early twentieth-century Japanese capitalism was dominated by the *zaibatsu*. The resulting sharp economic stratification and the perceived alliance between the *zaibatsu* and party politicians led to social unrest. In reaction, the army in particular made itself a symbol of popular egalitarianism. By expanding the draft system, advocating universal conscription, and opposing exemptions for the wealthy or otherwise privileged, the Japanese military had always taken a populist line. To be sure, universal conscription did not mean that all qualified males were actually drafted – the army chiefs of staff preferred to have a relatively small but well-trained standing army whose size was limited by budgetary constraints. With regard to the *zaibatsu*, most were not severely affected by the Depression, while ordinary citizens, especially the peasants, were considerably worse off. Taking advantage of popular anti-*zaibatsu* and antiparliamentary sentiment, the so-called progressive "reformists" (*shin kanryô* or *kakushin kanryô*) became a prominent force in the national bureaucracy in the early 1930s. The reformists were by and large not militarists, but idealistic young technocrats who supported state interventions in market activities. They were influenced by a variety of international trends ranging from Marxist and Nazi corporatism to Roosevelt's New Deal. The *kakushin kanryô* played a critical role, however, in moving Japanese institutional arrangements in the direction of the wartime system because they were allied with the army, which was dissatisfied with the dominance of party politicians in parliamentary politics.

The idealism of the reformists was the force behind the institutionalization of the Japanese public health insurance system (Law of National Health Insurance, 1938) and Social Security (Law of Workers' Pensions, 1941). The agricultural sector was the most prominent focus of interventionist reform. The rights of tenant cultivators were protected through various measures intended to achieve maximum food production. These social policies were legitimated by the then politically persuasive argument that they would guarantee able-bodied youths capable of defending the country in the event of war. In this way, the reformists' concern for social reform and the interests of the military were closely related. The army in fact had good reasons to support populist policies, not only from rational arguments regarding the strengthening of Japan's fighting capacity but also from the ideological standpoint that they had held for decades.

In order to understand the alliance of the military and progressive reformist bureaucrats, at this point it is useful to look at the actual figures of personnel recruited for the Japanese armed forces. The Meiji army began on a very modest scale, with 2,300 soldiers in 1873. The number increased very gradually, reaching 50,000 men around 1900. During this period, draft exemptions for the wealthy were largely abolished. The military advocated an egalitarian view of military service as a basic duty of citizenship. Partly because of budgetary limitations, the Japanese army in its early form was a small standing force consisting of draftees rather than volunteers. The men received intensive military training after induction. The scale of mobilization increased rapidly in the late 1930s, however, after Japan invaded China. As a result, the Japanese army expanded exponentially, calling up 6 million soldiers during the Second World War. Unlike the United States Army, which consisted of almost 40 percent volunteers during the Second World War, the Japanese army by 1941 consisted almost entirely of draftees. The high rate of forced mobilization through conscription, which affected about 80 percent of the qualified male age group during the war, compelled the government to introduce a number of egalitarian policies in order to make the sacrifices of wartime more acceptable.

In the late 1930s and 1940s, the Japanese government implemented a number of drastic policies that remolded the socioeconomic system in order to prepare the country for war. The enactment of the Law of Total National Mobilization in 1938 represented this change. The impact of these radical changes brought about the prototypical social system that is now often referred to as the Japanese System.

As the reader will observe from Table 5.1, there are notable discontinuities between the prewar and wartime systems in various areas of the Japanese political economy. In contrast, we find notable institutional continuities between those of the wartime and postwar Japanese capitalism. The four major characteristics of the so-called Japanese style of corporate management – lifelong employment; pay scale and promotion on the basis of seniority; company-based unions; and reliance on bank loans rather than the stock market as the major source of capital – resulted at least in part from wartime regulations. For example, the 1937 law of dividend regulation restricted the shareholders' right to receive a high dividend rate. A 1939 law that controlled pay scales led to the introduction of a pay scale differentiated by seniority. The rapid increase of labor disputes in 1937 induced the government to institute a system of company-based unions called "Patriotic Industrial Associations." These unions encouraged labor to cooperate with management for the sake of increasing productive output. Because these company-based associations organized both blue-collar and white-collar workers under one umbrella, they helped to generate a sense of community among employees. In the area of finance, the number of commercial banks indicated most clearly the impact of wartime regulations. During the prewar period, even after the significant decrease by the Great Depression, the number of Japanese commercial banks still totaled about five hundred in early 1930. By 1945, however, the number of Japanese commercial banks was reduced to sixty-one under the strict control by the Ministry of Finance. It must be noted that until recently, the number of Japanese commercial banks stayed around sixty.

These wartime government restrictions on free capitalist activities were coupled with redistributive policies in the areas of health insurance, social security, and agricultural subsidies, as indicated in Table 5.1. The tenant farmers' rights over the land that they farmed were expanded, while the landowners' control of agricultural land was restricted in order to guarantee adequate food production.

Of course, this does not mean that there were no signs of institutional developments anticipating the characteristics of the postwar system before the late 1930s and 1940s. For example, some large firms instituted a limited form of long-term employment during the prewar period in direct response to the labor shortage rather than to legal pressure. In general, however, the components of the Japanese system included in Table 5.1 reinforce each other. For example, the shift of capital from the stock market to loans and the resulting decrease in the stockholders' control over corporate management facilitated the development of communitarian features in Japanese corporations. In addition, a high rate of personal savings became a major feature of Japanese capitalism after the war and was a critical factor in the emergence of strong banks within the new financial system. The decentralized Japanese tax system was reorganized into a heavily centralized system that relied on direct withholding taxes, a move that strengthened the fiscal power of the central bureaucracy. In this way, the *simultaneous* introduction of the full complement of wartime institutions enabled the emergence of many characteristics that we now associate with Japanese capitalism.

The most important characteristic of the wartime system was *shared* control of properties. It was not only the legally defined owner of private properties but rather a number of different social actors who sought access to the benefits produced by the properties. To be sure, this shared access was not confined to multiple holders of rights claiming benefits from a single source of property – for example, a private business corporation. It was a system derived from a kind of social contract that covered the relations of the entire society in order to turn it into an efficient war machine. Not only the workers in the industrial sector but also the peasants received benefits in the form of increased tenant rights over the land that they were cultivating. The state, of course, received benefits in the form of mobilizing soldiers as well as the loyalty of the population but was also able to maximize industrial output for the war effort. The war mobilization system of this era thus wiped out nascent capitalism and decreased the culture of possessive individualism in Macpherson's sense. Assertions of autonomy and claims based upon possessive ownership did not harmonize with the spirit of the time, which favored communal dilution of property holders' rights. In this sense, the wartime reformulation of Japanese economic institutions was reminiscent of the communalistic traditions of property relationships under the Tokugawa shoguns.

Although Japan's wartime political economy was dismantled after 1945, significant continuities remained. The dissolution of the Japanese army and the introduction of Western-style democracy revived the tradition of political association activities in Japan, which became one of the foundations of postwar Japanese civil society. The revival of civil society did not by itself, however, bring about a return to the prewar style of free capitalism. Rather, the prior development of wartime institutions provided the institutional field a subsequent period of rapid economic growth. The following important factors characterized this new situation.

1. Unlike politicians or members of the business elite who were purged by the General Headquarters (GHQ), the Japanese national bureaucracy was almost untouched by the American army of occupation. The relatively intact bureaucracy thus provided an organizational base for institutional continuity between the wartime and postwar periods. Because the GHQ staff could not directly oversee the detailed administration of a ruined non-Western society with a complex institutional structure, it also had to rely on the existing bureaucratic arms in order to "remold" Japan.
2. The GHQ was eager to dismantle the political structures of Japan, but did not have a clear understanding of the country's economic and financial policies. The personnel structure of the Ministry of Finance in particular was unaffected by the GHQ. This decision allowed for continuity in the areas of taxation and basic financial policy and

provided a critical institutional environment within which postwar market organizations could reemerge. The progressive policies modeled on the New Deal – such as land reform – that were introduced by the GHQ did not conflict with the egalitarian orientation of Japanese politics that was already developing during the war. Rather, these policies assisted the further development of egalitarian tendencies but this time under the label of "democracy."

3. The scarcity of all kinds of resources, including food, raw materials, and capital, immediately after the war required governmental regulation and redistribution. These measures were necessary in order to guarantee basic survival for a traumatized population.

4. Once institutionalized, the wartime system developed and operated according to its own dynamics. Because the GHQ did not do away with the critical economic and social institutional arrangements that had first been introduced during the war (e.g., financial market structures, corporate governance, welfare policies, agricultural subsidies, and land policies), they continued to support a distinctive style of capitalism that came to maturity only in the postwar era.

The progressive political reforms under the GHQ in fact enhanced the institutional infrastructures that were responsible for the development of the egalitarian elements in Japanese capitalism. The land reforms transferred ownership to the tenant farmers who were actually working the land. The prewar live-in and absentee landowners who had dominated the village power structures on the basis of their large holdings suddenly lost their vast landed assets. The prewar landlord class, the beneficiary of the "private ownership of landed wealth" that had been instituted during the Meiji period, was abolished. The ownership of agricultural land by industrial and commercial capital was also prohibited. This redistribution of landed wealth was intended to democratize the social relations within the agricultural communities, from the viewpoint of the GHQ. But we must also note that the policies restricting the landlords' rights had been institutionalized by the reformist bureaucrats during the war. The distribution of land to its actual cultivators, however, did not create the social conditions for a Western-style market economy and liberal politics. Generous agricultural subsidies and government price supports for rice discouraged the development of a capitalist market-oriented mentality among the farmers. From this perspective, the postwar land reforms almost turned the clock back to the communitarian notion of property that had prevailed during the Tokugawa period.

In the area of business regulation, the GHQ ordered the dissolution of the *zaibatsu*, because these conglomerates had a bad reputation as supporters of the Japanese military. They were under suspicion as reservoirs of undemocratic attitudes. The program of dissolution was mandated by the

GHQ's conviction that Japanese big business was the source of the militaristic ideology of the 1930s as well as monopolistic market behavior.
Whether prewar big business in Japan was monopolistic in its actual practices is still a subject of discussion. In terms of my brief historical overview,
it is clear that Japanese prewar big business was often opposed to the government interventions supported by the militarists. It was ironic that the
forced collaboration of the *zaibatsu* during the war gave the GHQ a reason
to dismantle them. From the viewpoint of property relationships, the forced
breakup of the *zaibatsu* further diffused and weakened the political power
and ideological legitimacy of Japanese property owners' exclusive control
over various forms of properties. By eliminating the antidemocratic authoritarian power structure without changing or weakening the institutional and
cultural structures of collaborative shared property relationships that the
wartime policy mix had created, the policies of the GHQ brought together
the raw materials for the subsequent development of Japanese capitalism.

To be sure, I am not saying that the organization of the postwar
Japanese economy was simply the product of initiatives on the part of government policy designers, who represented a new generation of elite national
bureaucrats. Unlike wartime interventions, government interference with
market activities during the postwar period remained largely indirect. In
other words, bureaucratic control is an important but partial legacy of the
war to postwar economic growth in Japan. Since the publication of the
influential work of Chalmers Johnson, *MITI and the Japanese Miracle*
(1982), postwar Japanese economic development is often regarded as a
typical success story of a bureaucratic state. More recent scholarship on
Japanese political economy, however, offers a more complex picture of
postwar development. The state bureaucrats are indeed influential actors
in Japan, but so are the large corporations and politicians. For example, the Japanese political scientist Inoguchi Takashi proposes the term
"bureaucratic-led, mass-inclusionary pluralism" in partial reconciliation of
the divergent views of other scholars.[11] In addition to the roles of the government bureaucracy and big business, mass participation in politics through
party politicians representing local interests has played a role in defining
the direction of state policies. These various local and industrial interest
groups, including farmers' organizations, were precisely the products of the
wartime and postwar redistribution processes; they insisted on protecting
their redistributive benefits in their property relationships in political bodies.
On the other hand, Kent Calder (1993) has underscored the role of the corporate managerial elite with the term "strategic capitalism." More recently,
Michael Gerlach (1992) has used the term "alliance capitalism" in order to
emphasize the structure of institutional arrangements that enmesh its
primary decision-making units in complex networks of cooperation and
competition. The outline that I am sketching belongs with these more
complex understandings of the Japanese political economy.

What I would like to emphasize is that this elaborate network of institutional arrangements that facilitated both collaboration and competition did not begin abruptly with the postwar period, nor can this arrangement be traced back to the economic policies of the Meiji period. The necessity of mobilization for war created a prototypical institutional arrangement within the Japanese postwar political economy. The wartime institutional reforms were the result of direct and forceful government interventions implemented *simultaneously* in a number of different socioeconomic areas. Once this system of renovations was established, however, it had its own institutional dynamism that evolved into the distinctive communitarian and collaborative managerial style of Japanese companies (Gerlach's "alliance capitalism").

Culturally, the image of the Japanese business corporation as a communal organization became even more entrenched during the economic boom of the 1960s. Otherwise put, the mechanisms that had served to mobilize popular patriotism and material resources during the war were used, with some modifications, to stimulate the loyalty of postwar workers and businessmen for the growth of their companies. This organizational development, however, had to take place within a complex network of legal and institutional fields that had arisen prior to market growth.

The wartime institutional mix also provided a platform for postwar social equity. While the effectiveness of the Japanese bureaucrats' strategic industrial policies has been widely acknowledged in the West, it is less well known that the bureaucrats worked even harder to alleviate the negative effects of rapid economic growth. To this end, the Japanese government has distributed large subsidies to underdeveloped regions as well as to inefficient or declining industries to offset the side effects of economic development. Scholars have rightly pointed to the continuity between the mind-set of the reformists of the prewar period and the postwar elite bureaucrats with their concern for social justice. At the same time, we must also note that the concern for distributive justice that was ideologically legitimated during the war had an even broader influence on Japanese political processes. Even the conservative politicians of the LDP (*Jiyû minshu tô*, or Liberal Democratic Party) following the war recognized that the egalitarian rhetoric of distributive justice was an important key to winning elections. The achievement of relative social equity was due not only to government leadership but also to private initiatives. The combination of government and company-sponsored welfare became a notable feature of the Japanese welfare system.

This review of the historical development of the Japanese state, market, and cultural identity indicates that the supposedly inscrutable Japanese system, based on collaboration, in actuality came together as a set of institutions at a specific point in time – during the crisis of total mobilization for war in the 1930s. The notion that the Japanese system is deeply embedded in ancient traditional culture is simply incorrect. And because this system has relatively recent roots, there is no guarantee that it will persist in its present form.

Recently, the bureaucratic strategic planning style of Japan's industrial policy has lost much of its early effectiveness. As was the case at the end of the Tokugawa period, market forces have expanded to a degree that the bureaucracy can no longer effectively guide. I predict that a major deregulation of Japanese financial markets is inevitable, and that this move will uproot the economic legacy of the wartime period. The management style of Japanese corporations is already undergoing significant changes. Japan has entered a new era in which the direction of future developments is unclear. We may ask whether the Japanese political economy will set aside the legacy of the wartime system. This question, in my opinion, is related to another important inquiry: evaluation of the postwar Japanese economic model in comparison with developing nations, as well as with the mature economies of the Western states.

We now witness many cases of rapid economic growth among newly industrialized countries whose systems of political economy differ significantly from that of Japan. The postwar Japanese experience, however, still holds a distinctive position in world history not simply because it achieved such spectacular economic success but also because it prevented the occurrence of pronounced economic stratification. At present, as was the case in the early Tokugawa period, Japan's political options are heavily influenced by the contingencies of the past, in particular with regard to the politics of moral sentiment and cultural identity. Wartime mobilization and subsequent political developments gave the Japanese a significant cultural legacy, a sense of community, and egalitarianism that has become very deeply ingrained in their modern cultural identity.

This egalitarian sentiment was well expressed by Naoto Kan, the former minister of health and welfare. When Kan founded a new party several years ago, he summarized the party's goal with a phrase that was reminiscent of old-style British utilitarianism while at the same time reversing the directional emphasis. Instead of promising the greatest happiness for the greatest number of people, Kan formulated his political goal as causing the *minimal* amount of *unhappiness* to the greatest number. It was a skillful summary of the popular ideology that has emerged in the wake of postwar Japanese economic development.

The moral sentiment that Kan expressed does not completely contradict the competitive ethos of possessive individualism, the basis of capitalist private ownership, but it does soften it significantly, and does not support an attitude of cut-throat competition in which the winner takes all. In that sense, it is almost diametrically opposed to the American version of unbridled capitalism that tends to reward only winners. The more egalitarian

Japanese ideal now constitutes a powerful collective cultural identity vested in the historically negotiated relationships between the Japanese state and individuals, as well as between corporations and employees.

This essay has highlighted some of the historical contingencies that Japan experienced in relation to war preparation, and how these contingencies affected the distinctive style of Japanese capitalism in terms of changing property relationships. To be sure, the institutional mechanisms of militarization that affect property relationships differ across societies and historical periods. The dimension of military mobilization and subsequent redistribution of possessive resources is only one of many complex factors that shaped the practice of capitalism in postwar Japan. On the other hand, without an adequate understanding of the effects of war and preparation for war through the mechanisms of mobilization and redistribution, it is difficult to trace the distinctive features in the emergence of the Japanese pattern of property relationships.

The perceptive reader may have noticed that the object of my inquiry in this chapter, namely the historical transformation of property relationships in Japan, is to clarify the fundamental significance of the challenge that Japan now faces. The recent new stage of globalization of the world economy made possible by instant and virtual monetary exchanges in cyberspace threatens the distinctiveness of Japanese property relationships. Now that the introduction of deregulation and a more competitive labor market are regarded as central to the revitalization of Japanese capitalism, the question arises as to whether the Japanese are ready to have their political economy move in an entirely new direction. This decision may require a cultural transformation of their communitarian egalitarianism, one that is intrinsically more far-reaching than the restructuring at the end of the Second World War. To realize the forced necessity of restructuring their entrenched property relationships, the Japanese media called the cyber-financial globalization "the second black ships" in recalling the image of Commodore Perry's steamships (1553–1554) that forced Tokugawa Japan to abandon its traditional policy of isolation. To be sure, it does not mean that Japan would move undoubtedly in the direction of American-style, stockholder-centered ownership of corporations. Whether Japan can successfully pass through a new phase of transformation in property relationships may determine the future course of its society.

Notes

1. I have discussed this history in detail in my *Taming of the Samurai* (1995).
2. An example of this line of analysis is John Brewer's *The Sinews of Power* (1985). In this work, Brewer examined the crucial role of the military in the political evolution of eighteenth-century Britain. The traditionally decentralized British

state underwent an astonishing degree of transformation in this period in order to carry the heavy financial burdens of the country's military involvements. As a result, Britain developed what Brewer terms a fiscal-military state – that is, a large and sophisticated bureaucracy to manage its system of taxation.

3. To be sure, war is not the only prime mover of state formation, nor is it invariably the major stimulus of the development of all modern states throughout the world. For example, a number of postcolonial states developed their administrative arms without significant investment in wars. Scholarly interest in the effects of military involvement on state formation, however, has shed new light on the fact that war sometimes has an irresistible impact on the reorganization of institutions and their administration.

4. The reader should note that I am not asserting here that the rise of economic developments was always solely related to the rise of the state that made such an institution economically viable. Note an important revisionist contribution of A. Greif that made clear the private institutions that reduced the cost of transaction. Medieval long-distance traders privately created an institution of enforcing contracts and trustworthy behavior through a mechanism of reputation. See Greif 1989, 1993.

5. I have used Macpherson's notion with modifications in order to apply it to a non-Western society. I have elsewhere described the medieval Japanese samurai's strong sense of sovereign autonomy and self-possession, based on their pride in feudal land ownership and military prowess, as "honorific individualism," an elitist feudal variant of "possessive individualism."

6. In his *Possessive Individualism* (1962), he analyzed the social process through which the conventional modern conception of property expanded its dominance at the expense of alternative definitions. On the other hand, although Macpherson's well-known theory of "possessive individualism" was presented in the course of analyzing the intellectual developments of the seventeenth century with regard to normative questions posed by an emerging commercial market society, he also criticized the narrowness of liberal political assumptions about property rights.

7. Macpherson, like other liberal political theorists, does not discuss the impact of military activity on property relations. It is true, of course, that changes in property relationships are not determined solely by preparations for and the prosecution of war. Moreover, the impact of war on property relationships does not fit the category of a one-dimensional causal association. But the patterns of property relationships in a given society cannot be understood only in terms of continuity.

8. The reasons for the oligarchy's concessions were complex and lie beyond the scope of this essay.

9. To begin with, Alexander Gerschenkron's model of the timing of industrialization is certainly applicable to the Meiji Restoration. As a so-called late developer, Meiji Japan attempted to speed up its industrialization with initiatives from the top down, in a manner analogous to Germany's race with Britain at the end of the nineteenth century. For example, the *introduction* of new industries and technologies was often initiated and supported by the government while the Meiji regime was also eager to build up modern institutional infrastructures for facilitating industrialization such as modern systems of transportation, education, and law.

10. The historical scholarship that emphasized the role of economic policies of wartime mobilization in the creation of postwar Japan rather than the aspects of discontinuity and renewal after 1945 include Takahide Nakamura, ed., *Senkan ki no nihon keizai bunseki* (Tokyo: Yamakawa shuppan, 1981); Takafusa Nakamura, *Senzenki Nihon keizai no bunseki* (Tokyo: Iwanami shoten, 1971); John W. Dower, *Japan in War and Peace* (New York: New Press, 1993); Tetsuji Okazaki, "Nihon ni okeru coporaito gabanansu no hatten-rekishiteki pâsupekutibu," *Kinyû kenkyû* 13, 13 (1994). More recently, a provocative essay by Noguchi Yukihiko in *Saraba Senji Keizai* (Tokyo: Toyo keizai, 1995) also sparked the debate on the wartime mobilization and postwar Japanese capitalism. For more on this debate, see Eiko Ikegami "Democracy in an Age of Cyber-Financial Globalization: Time, Space, and Embeddedness from an Asian Perspective," *Social Research* 66, 3. (1999): 888–914.

11. Takashi Inoguchi, *Gendai nihon seiji keizai no kôzu* (Tokyo: Tôyô keizai shinpᵀᴹsha, 1983). Also see Mark Ramseyer Rosenbluth and Frances McCall, *Japan's Political Market Place* (Cambridge, Mass.: Harvard University Press, 1993).

References

Blair, Margaret M., and Thomas Kochan, eds. 2000. *The New Relationship: Human Capital in the American Corporation.* Washington, D.C.: Brookings Institution Press.

Brewer, John. 1985. *The Sinews of Power: War, Money, and the English State, 1688–1783.* New York: Alfred A. Knopf.

Calder, Kent E. 1993. *Strategic Capitalism: Private Business and Public Purpose in Japanese Industrial Finance.* Princeton: Princeton University Press.

Downing, Brian. 1992. *The Military Revolution and Political Change: Origins of Democracy and Autocracy in Early Modern Europe.* Princeton: Princeton University Press.

Ertman, Thomas. 1997. *Birth of the Leviathan: Building States and Regimes in Medieval and Early Modern Europe.* Cambridge: Cambridge University Press.

Finer, Samuel. 1975. "State and Nation-Building in Europe: The Role of the Military," in Charles Tilly, ed., *The Formation of National States in Western Europe.* Princeton: Princeton University Press.

Gerlach, Michael L. 1992. *Alliance Capitalism: The Social Organzation of Japanese Business.* Berkeley: University of California Press.

Gerschenkron, Alexander. 1962. *Economic Backwardness in Historical Perspective.* Cambridge, Mass.: Belknap.

Greif, A. 1989. "Reputation and Coalitions in Early Trade: Evidence on Maghribi Traders," *Journal of Economic History* 49, 4: 857–882.

1993. "Contract Enforceability and Economic Institutions in Early Trade: The Maghribi Traders' Coalition," *American Economic Review* 83, 3: 525–548.

Ikegami, Eiko. 1995. *The Taming of the Samurai: Honorific Individualism and the Making of Modern Japan.* Cambridge, Mass.: Harvard University Press.

Johnson, Chalmers. 1982. *MITI and the Japanese Miracle: The Growth of Industrial Policy, 1925–1975.* Stanford: Stanford University Press.

Macpherson, C. B. 1962. *The Political Theory of Possessive Individual: Hobbes to Locke*. New York: Oxford University Press.

Mann, Michael. 1986. *The Sources of Social Power: A History of Power from the Beginning to A. D. 1760*. Cambridge: Cambridge University Press.

1988. *States, War, and Capitalism: Studies in Political Sociology*. Oxford: Blackwell.

North, Douglass. 1981. *Structure and Change in Economic History*. New York: Norton.

North, Douglass, and Robert Paul Thomas. 1973. *The Rise of the Western World: A New Economic History*. Cambridge: Cambridge University Press.

Tilly, Charles, ed. 1975. *The Formation of National States in Western Europe*. Princeton: Princeton University Press.

PART II

DECONSTRUCTING ARMED FORCES

From Militaries to Militias, Paramilitaries, Police, and Veterans

6

Send a Thief to Catch a Thief

State-Building and the Employment of Irregular Military Formations in Mid-Nineteenth-Century Greece

Achilles Batalas

The relation between war and state-building is a highly intricate phenomenon. Although war is not the sole justification for the emergence and development of the modern state, it has been acknowledged as one of the most important factors (Tilly 1992: 12, 14–15; Desch 1996: 241). One analytical avenue stresses that modern states are formed as state makers attempt to find ways of acquiring the necessary resources for military competition at a geopolitical level. In return, the difficulties encountered in building and maintaining an effective military force (social resistance, expense, organization, etc.) led to the creation of the modern centralized, bureaucratic state apparatus.

The main limitation of this approach is that it fails to account for the diversity of state-building processes and variations in outcome. Accordingly, Charles Tilly (1985) maintains that the development of Western European states was characterized by the variable interaction between state-making (elimination of internal competitors), war-making (elimination of external competitors), protection (elimination of the enemies of clients), and extraction (acquisition of the necessary resources to accomplish the former three).

This multilinear analytical model of state formation is based on the ideas that state protection is a revenue-generating affair, and that the process of state-building is a legitimate form of protection racket. States "themselves simulate, stimulate, or even fabricate threats of external war" (Tilly 1985: 171) in order to justify demands on the resources of private capital and the construction of larger and more powerful state institutions.

Explicit in this argument is the assumption that an effective state protection racket requires a monopoly of the means of coercion, not only the "centralization of administrative jurisdiction but also the demilitarization of regional power holders" (Barkey 1994: 4). States must acquire militaries that are capable of imposing and maintaining a monopoly of the means of coercion within the state's territory and "eliminating or neutralizing" competitor states. The former requirement, however, is of utmost significance:

"In the long run, it all came down to massive pacification and monopolization of the means of coercion" (Tilly 1985: 175).

Yet what transpires when state elites are unable to demilitarize regional elites and establish a monopoly of the means of coercion? First, state apparatuses that are unable to establish centralized administration and assert the all-important monopolization of coercive power will disintegrate. Second, when state elite's coercive efforts, aimed at the domestication of regional military elites, prove to be insufficient or impractical, for whatever reasons, they will resort to bargaining and co-optation. Moreover, the frameworks for the bargaining and co-optation processes are never universal and are based primarily on the unique sociopolitical environment and in the international context in which the state under study exists.

This chapter argues that during the mid-nineteenth century the modern Greek state's inability to impose a monopoly of the means of coercion led to what can be characterized as a case of "inverse racketeering": a situation in which the state becomes the client and not the supplier of protection against internal and external adversaries. On the one hand, the "racketeers" (i.e., bandits-irregulars) provided the state, via a patron-client relationship, with protection against themselves and other bandits-irregulars. In other words, bandits-irregulars directly and indirectly stimulated an internal threat. On the other hand, the bandits-irregulars were perceived and employed by the state as the primary means of war-making against the Ottoman Empire, albeit not successfully.

The case of mid-nineteenth-century Greek state-building is interesting in the following ways. First, it occurred within a non-Western European and noncolonial historical context. Although foreign involvement played an important role in the development of the state, direct and indirect interference was not based on a prior colonial relationship. Second, unlike most of the Western European cases where state builders did not emphatically visualize the pervasive bureaucratic and public authority of the modern state, Greek state-building occurred within a context in which state elites were explicitly aiming at the erection of a modern nation-state. This goal was influenced by two interrelated factors: timing and the social composition of the initial Greek state makers. On the one hand, many of the political aspirations of the Greeks were given concrete form by the Enlightenment and French Revolution. On the other hand, initial state-building was attempted by heterchthon Greeks and/or Western European elites. Third, it was during the period under consideration that the main characteristics of the Greek polity were patterned and/or institutionalized (and these characteristics diverged little in the succeeding decades): the establishment of Western European political institutions and their penetration by the traditional political practices of the local population; a predominantly agrarian economy with few advances in cultivation techniques, animal husbandry, industry and communication systems; the elaboration of

Greek national identity "as an organic whole in which Greek Orthodoxy, the ethnos [nation], and the state are a unity" (Pollis 1992: 171); the growth of a strong irredentism, termed the Megali Idea (Great Idea), which was to become the dominant political program of the state until the catastrophic expedition into Asia Minor in 1922; the influence exerted by the Great Powers in the external and internal affairs of the Greek nation-state; and the overt entanglement of the military in the political sphere.

Finally, an analysis of mid-nineteenth century Greek state-building can contribute to existing debates and theories concerning the relationship between armed forces, political development, and state-building endeavors in the following two ways. On the one hand, the Greek case accentuates the proposition that in order to comprehend better the diversity of state-building processes and variations in outcome, it is crucial to take into consideration not only regular, state-controlled forces but also the existence of irregular armed formations (i.e., formations that are not created and/or controlled by a centralized state). On the other hand, the case study also provides some valuable insights into the more contemporary phenomenon of the emergence and proliferation of numerous types of alternative armed forces. More specifically, although irregular armed forces may be deployed against the state institutions and agents, the Greek case gives rise to the general question, when and under what conditions do states employ alternative military forces, either alone or alongside regular ones?

Analytical Framework

Before proceeding with the case study, it is prudent to provide a basic conceptualization of the most important terms to be employed.[1] The first term that requires elaboration is a specific type of state: the nation-state. The nation-state is defined here as a political organization that attempts to exercise direct authority over a geographically bounded territory through centralized, differentiated, and autonomous structures (Weber 1968; Mann 1988; Tilly 1992); and "unite the people subjected to its rule by means of homogenization, creating a common culture, symbols, values, reviving traditions and myths of origin, and sometimes inventing them" (Guibernau 1996: 47).

The chapter is based on the assumption that state elites aim at erecting centralized and differentiated organizations with the monopoly of the means of coercion over a defined territory that requires extensive social engineering according to their own agendas. Three important caveats should be taken into consideration when reflecting on the conceptualization of states as social agents. First, states should not be perceived as anthropomorphic entities. States are not entirely organic rational units that confront situations by strategically appraising them with the intention of maximizing their interests and then act accordingly. Like other institutions, states are characterized by internal conflicts and divisions between individuals, groups, and bureaucracies.

Second, modern states are not omnipotent political organizations. In their attempts to restructure the indigenous society according to their own agendas, state elites are inevitably confronted with resistance from different classes and/or groups of the indigenous population. Struggles over a myriad of issues (national symbols, taxation, conscription, education, etc.) are processes of conflict, bargaining, and co-optation. The results of such struggles determine to a large extent the state's ability to successfully penetrate society. Accordingly, "popular resistance to war making and state making made a difference. When ordinary people resisted vigorously, authorities made concessions: guarantees of rights, representative institutions, courts of appeal. The concessions, in their turn, constrained the later paths of war making and state making" (Tilly 1985: 183).

Therefore, when analyzing state-building endeavors a dialectical approach should be emphasized: an approach that takes into consideration not only how state institutions and activities influence class and group activities, but also how indigenous structures influence state-building processes and levels of autonomous state power. As Skocpol has emphasized "studies of states alone are not to be substituted for concerns with classes or groups; nor are purely state-determinist arguments to be fashioned in the place of society-centered explanations" (1985: 20). The more general analytical point is that interest groups, social classes, and their representative organizations posses a variety of resources (capital, military power, technical skills, etc.) that enable them to negotiate with state elites, albeit on varying terms.

For Greece, this dialectical relationship produced a patrimonial nation-state (Mouzelis 1978; Tsoucalas 1978). One of the main characteristics of Greek society under Ottoman administration was the prevalence of clientelism: "a reciprocal personalized political relationship that involves economic or political favors from a notable or politician in return for a person's loyalty and support" (Kourvetaris and Dobratz 1987: 32–33).[2] It has been argued that despite the Kapodistrian and Bavarian attempts to erect a state based on modern Western European standards, social resistance to state centralization compelled the state to function within an identical political framework, which disabled its capacity to effectively implement policies (Mouzelis 1978: 17).

My contention is that, in the long run, state espousal of the prevailing patron-client relationship had a positive effect on state centralization and consolidation in that the state became the biggest patron in modern Greece. State patronage has been acknowledged as an important mechanism for early state builders. "The creation of reciprocal bonds with potential adversaries, reinforced by the inducement of a stake in the success of the emerging state apparatus, was an immensely useful method of eroding the unity of actors threatened by state-centralization" (Gould 1996: 401–402). Accordingly, Mouzelis writes that in mid-nineteenth century Greece "clientalism not only kept the peasantry, as a class, outside the sphere of active and autonomous politics, it also slowed down or actually prevented the political organization and the ideological coherence of the economically dominant classes" (1978: 17–16). The chapter focuses mainly on the military aspect of the patron-client relationship in mid-nineteenth-century Greece. It was within the wider patron-client relationship that the inverse racketeering relationship between state and bandits-irregulars was made possible.

The final caveat that should be taken into consideration is that no state can effectively impose and maintain a system of direct rule simply through the actions of a coercive state apparatus, although it does remain "the naked ultima ratio of state power" (Skocpol 1979: 215). In spite of the fact that the monopolization of the means of coercion is always the primary aim of state makers, the notion of the state as the ultimate source of authority is also created through ideological and cultural domination of various social classes and interest groups. Accordingly, emphasis must also be placed on the legitimacy dimension of state power.

The nation-state as a political institution seeks legitimacy as the primary political representative of the nation that it rules and may seek to create a nation as a means of establishing and/or reinforcing cohesion among its populace. In the case of modern Greece there occurred a process of state-led nationalism: "Rulers who spoke in a nation's name successfully demanded that citizens identify themselves with the nation and subordinate other interests to those of the state" (Tilly 1994: 133).[3] In other words, nationalism can be employed by state elites as a form of ideology to provide justification for state policies, and so that stability and conformity will be perpetuated through consensus and coercion (Glenn 1997: 52).

This does not imply that I am endorsing an outright conceptualization of nationalism as a simple, manipulatory, ideological device of state elites or other powerful groups-classes for identifying their interests with the interests of the entire society. Justification of state policies with nationalist rhetoric may occur at both a conscious and unconscious level. Even if nationalism is conceived primarily as an ideology of legitimation, it can, like other ideologies, be both enabling and constraining (Sewell 1994). More important, once mobilized national identities tend to become deeply embedded and independent of whatever elites have been responsible for constructing them and, therefore, they are not easily dismantled and/or reconceptualized.

In the case of modern Greece (1821–1922), the Megali Idea (Great Idea) – the unification of all Greeks within the Ottoman Empire into one Greek state – served as the primary ideological mechanism for justifying state centralization and consolidation and the creation of a homogenous indigenous population. However, the active pursuit and realization of the Great Idea became "an unquestioned precondition of political legitimacy"

(Kitromilides 1976: 16–17). In fact, the role of the Greek state as the nation's ultimate political expression was severely questioned in the last quarter of the nineteenth century, due to its inability to successfully incorporate the Greeks of the Ottoman Empire (Veremis 1990).

The final term that requires elaboration is the social phenomenon of banditry. This chapter breaks with other contemporary scholars (Skiotis 1975) in that it will not incorporate Hobsbawm's (1965, 1985) "social bandit" model. The reasons for this departure are basically two, both of crucial importance. First, Hobsbawm's analysis overemphasizes the positive connections between bandits and peasants. Greek bandits can be perceived neither as representatives nor defenders of the peasantry. In fact, banditry has a tendency to inhibit and repress peasant movements, either through the employment of terror tactics or "by carving out avenues of upward mobility which, like many other vertical bonds in peasant societies, tend to weaken class tensions" (Blok 1972: 499–500). Second, the line between legality and illegality for the Greek bandit was an extremely artificial one. Within both the Ottoman and early Greek state-building context, bandits constantly alternated between the roles of brigands (*klephts*) and state-employed guards (*armatoloi, gendarmarie*, national guards). Though the klephts-armatoloi constituted one of the provincial elites during Ottoman administration, their portrayal as a social class (i.e., whose constituent elements recognize a shared social position and common interests and who are organized for pursuing these interests) is misleading. As will be made evident here, despite espousing common military values, the klephts-armatoloi were by no means a highly unitary group that could overcome regional and personal familial rivalries. Accordingly, the bandit-irregular will be conceived as a "social type, a type clearly separate from his original birthplace in peasant society, fighting for some privilege and permanency in his own world" (Barkey 1994: 176).

Through the reexamination of two initial phases of Greek state-building – the Kapodistrian regime (1828–1831), and the Bavarian regency and monarchy (1833–1862) – it is argued that bandit-irregular formations played a fundamental role in the political trajectory of the modern Greek state. And that the state was compelled to employ alternative armed forces for state-making, war-making, and endeavors to extract resources because of (1) its inability to forcefully dissolve and nullify the previously mentioned group; (2) the indirect and direct influence of the Great Powers (i.e., France, Great Britain, and Russia); (3) the unavailability of extractable resources; and (4) the existence of a strong military tradition of irregular warfare.

Pre-Independence Greece: The Klephts and Armatoloi[4]

Two distinct groups of Greek elites emerged within the Ottoman Empire and can be distinguished on the basis of their types of connection to the

Ottoman state (Petropoulos 1968: 24; Koliopoulos 1987: 3).[5] First were those who were directly identified with Ottoman administration: the higher clergy of the Orthodox Church and the Phanariots (i.e., secular leaders who occupied important positions within the Ottoman state apparatus). The second group was less directly associated with the Porte, and was composed of three primary provincial elites: the landowning notable (i.e., primates) "who served as intermediaries between the local population and the central government" (Todorov 1995: 2);[6] the merchants and shipowners of the Aegean Islands; and "a fairly distinct military class, which was destined to play a very important role in the war of the 1820s, as well as in subsequent military events and political developments" (Koliopoulos 1987: 20).

This military class itself comprised two distinct but highly fluid groups: the klephts or brigands and armatoloi or militia men, who served the Ottoman Empire.[7] The klephts were basically men who resorted to brigandage for a variety of reasons: to pursue adventure, to avoid payment of taxes, to escape pursuit by the authorities, or as a result of family traditions and/or vendettas.[8] Although these two groups were distinct from the rest of non-Muslim society in that they "enjoyed military power and shared an ethos which exalted the military virtues and despised work on the soil" (Petropoulos 1968: 30), they were organized according to the wider patron-client relationships, albeit military ones. Individual captains secured their own men, resolved the amount of their compensation, and led them as their own, private armed bands. Less powerful and influential captains would contract their bands to more wealthy and powerful captains who "possessed considerable property [primarily land and flocks of sheep and goats]. They were as a rule men of substance. Property allowed them to provide armed employment and gave them the necessary prestige and power" (Koliopoulos 1987: 28).[9] Because the connection between the captain and the majority of his followers was based primarily on the appropriation and distribution of material rewards, these military groups were characterized by their inability to form enduring alliances. As a response to this rather loosely structured system, captains organized their bands around a small core of men whose loyalty was ensured through genealogical connection, marriage, adoption, *koumparia*, and fraternal friendships (Petropoulos 1968; Koliopoulos 1990: 75).[10]

The klephts were regarded by the Ottoman authorities as a serious enough threat to the establishment and maintenance of order that numerous injunctions were issued calling for vigorous measures to suppress their illegal activities (see Clogg 1976: 72–73). Incapable of holding the klephts in check, Ottoman authorities recruited local Christian irregular troops, the armatoloi, for maintaining law and order. In general, the armatoloi were former klephts who had been given amnesty in return for their assistance in curbing brigandage activity (Koliopoulos 1990: 27).

Armatoles were charged with the safety of the mountain passes, and the maintenance of law and order in the districts of their jurisdiction, the armatoliks.[11] . . . The
armatoliks, it seems, coincided with certain administrative units in areas were brigandage was prevalent. . . . Each armatolik was entrusted to a captain (kapitanos),
who was usually chosen from amongst the ablest and most dangerous outlaws and
received his authority directly from Turkish authorities in the presence of Christian
notables. . . . The captain once invested with formal authority, patrolled the armatolik, collected the special taxes the Christian subjects gave towards the salaries of
the armatoles under his command as well as state and other taxes, and did his best
to run the district as a family preserve, raising flocks and engaging in farming and
commerce. The position gradually became hereditary and was identified with a
number of local families. (Koliopoulos 1987: 27)[12]

In other words, the Ottoman Empire, operating within the larger societal
patron-client relationships, contracted the private armed forces of the most
powerful captains, whose loyalty was ensured as long as it could pay them.
The captains, in turn, paid the captains under their patronage who then
paid their men. As a result, the armatoloi were the men of their captains
rather than those of the Ottoman state (Petropoulos 1968: 74).

It cannot be overemphasized, however, that the distinction between an
armatolos and a klepht was a very narrow one. Armatolism often became
a racket when local landowners and peasants had to buy protection from
the pillaging with which the armatoloi threatened them. On the other hand,
as already noted, the armatoloi were customarily recruited from the klephts,
and returned to their ranks if persecuted by Ottoman authorities. The
change from armatolos to klepht, or klepht to armatolos was a normal
occurrence for the majority of these captains and their respective bands. In
fact, it is during Ottoman administration that the inverse racketeering relationship between state and the irregular military formations emerges:

[T]he existence and operation of the klephtic bands were necessary for the existence
and operation of the armatolic bands and indispensable for recruiting outlaws who
had proved their steel. While armatoles were officials in the service of the authorities and klephts were outlaws . . . in practice . . . the two elements often colluded
and merged; as the former were often engaged in the brigandage and extortion or
enjoined the ranks of the outlaws they sought to repress in order to increase their
bargaining power vis-à-vis the authorities. . . . It was a game that required guile, calculation, acceptance of the rules by everyone concerned, and carefully measured
defiance, and involved besides klephts and armatoles, a weak central authority
which was obliged to tolerate a measure of lawlessness, and a populace at whose
expense this lawlessness was practiced. (Koliopoulos 1987: 34)

In due time, some of the captains became so powerful that they were able
to prevent Ottoman troops from entering into their armatoliks, and, consequently, the Ottoman authorities sought to erode their rights. Accordingly, in 1637 and again in 1695 and 1704, the Porte attempted but failed
to abolish the armatoloi and replace them with Ottoman garrisons. The
institution itself was abolished in 1721. In 1787 Tepelini Ali was appointed

Dhervenci-Pasha and was more successful than any of his predecessors in bringing the armatoliks under control (Skiotis 1975). Despite these efforts, however, "by the time of the War of Independence, the captains of Rumely, Thessaly, Epirus, and southern Macedonia constituted a power military elite" (Koliopoulos 1987: 29).

The War of Independence, 1821–1827

The Greeks and non-Greeks who served in these armed formations, especially those from Rumely, provided the military backbone of the Greek revolt proclaimed by the Philiki Etairia in 1821.[13] As a result, the klephts-armatoloi provided this indispensable service for a society at war, and contrary to conventional Greek history, they participated in the conflict according to their own militaristic patron-client terms.

Only the coincidence of their personal or localist interests with those of the administration brought their activities in line with government orders. They served any regime which offered satisfactory military ranks and material gains. But when they thought it to be in their best interests they did not hesitate to abandon their military obligations or return to their pre-revolutionary kapakia with the Ottomans.[14] They would even accept to fight on the Ottoman side against the very revolution they had earlier supported. (Papageorgiou 1985: 26)

Despite their overall military ineffectiveness, the klephts-armatoloi were the only viable military force available to the different provisional governments of 1821–1827. Three attempts were made at establishing a regular army, and all three ended in failure. The main reasons for these failures were the overall unstable political situation, the lack of extractable resources, and, most important, the hostility of the primates and captains toward the formation of regular military units that would bolster the authority of the emerging nation-state (Papageorgiou 1986: 181).[15]

Due to their inability to establish regular army formations, the provincial governments were compelled to accept the armatolik institution and began confirming them under the title of military governor. In fact, "Rumeliots identified the position of military governor of a district with that of a captain of a pre-war armatolik" (Koliopoulos 1987: 44n12). Political independence was not a goal that was actually pursued by the captains. Adhering to the armatolik mentally captains wished to become agents of the emerging state and were more interested in village communities to tax.

In general, the War of Independence became for the captains of the klephts-armatoloi an opportunity for achieving greater economic and political power within their individual jurisdictions or armatoliks. The principal objective of the captains was the acquisition and/or expansion of their military jurisdictions and the consolidation of power within them, which was based on their ability to pay and feed as many armed men as possible. The larger their armed band, the greater the possible profits and the stronger their bargaining power vis-à-vis the state. Finally, because of the government's lack of funds and its administrative inability to mobilize the resources required to support the irregulars, conflicts between the captains "over the control of certain districts" (Koliopoulos 1987: 42–45) and altercations between the captains and other elements of the Greek leadership (primates, Westernized Greeks, Islanders) produced disastrous civil conflicts.

Thus the klephts-armatoloi immediately presented a severe twofold test to the authority and power of the emerging state institutions: (1) the establishment of a monopoly over the means of coercion via the elimination and/or reorganization of these irregulars into disciplined and loyal military formations, and (2) the much more complex problem of regionalism (i.e., the centrifugal tendencies of the indigenous elites). The problems presented by the irregulars were faced both by the first head of the Greek state, Ioannis Kapodistrias, and by the Bavarian regency and monarchy that succeeded him.

The Kapodistrian Period, 1828–1831

Independence was achieved by way of the Treaty of London of July 1827 when the Great Powers (i.e., France, Great Britain, and Russia) initiated a policy of "peaceful intervention" to secure Greek autonomy, and which culminated in the destruction of the Ottoman-Egyptian fleet at the Battle of Navarino (October 1827) by a combined fleet of the Great Powers. As concession to agreeing to the creation of an independent Greek state the Great Powers determined the borders of the state and its formal political structure (i.e., Greece was to be a hereditary monarchy whose ruler would be selected by the Great Powers but from outside of their own royal families).

In the meantime, Ioannis Kapodistrias, who had been elected president of the Greek National Assembly in April 1827, would remain in office until a suitable monarch could be found to assume the throne. Kapodistrias had two main political objectives: to create the foundations of a modern Western state structure and to attain the most favorable borders possible for the new state. The realization of the first objective revolved around an initial threefold plan: the consolidation of a strong and efficient state apparatus, the restoration and modernization of a war-ruined economy, and the creation of a regular army (Papageorgiou 1985: 23–24). Moreover, Kapodistrias required a disciplined and effective military for two main reasons: first, he faced the task of liberating the largest area of claimed territories from the Ottoman troops still occupying them and, second, the acknowledgment that the survival of his administration and programs would require strong military enforcement (Papageorgiou 1985: 22).

The major point that distinguishes the Kapodistrian regime from the Bavarian regency and monarchy is its nonirredentist policy. Kapodistrias believed that Greece had no chance of successfully expanding its frontiers, because of the prevailing international framework (Papageorgiou 1986: 203). In other words, the military was seen by the Kapodistrian regime primarily as a state-making mechanism (i.e., for the elimination of internal competitors).

However, due to the prevailing realities (Turko-Egyptian invasion, lack of state funds and the administrative apparatus for collecting such funds, no semblance whatsoever of a regular army, the power and influence of the provincial elites including the captains of the irregulars, etc.) and contrary to his own plans, Kapodistrias recognized that he was in no position to disband the irregular formations altogether and organize a regular army rooted in Western European military standards. The solution to the military problem adopted by the Kapodistrian administration was primarily one of co-optation: the integration of the irregulars "into semi-irregular formations and gradually transforming them into regular ones" (Papageorgiou 1985: 25), while at the same time endeavoring to form a regular army.

Kapodistrias's attempt at organizing the irregulars into semi-irregular units passed through two stages: the establishment of the *chiliarchies* (units of 1,000 men), followed by the creation of the light battalions. In both phases, the policy favored by the administration was one of co-opting the subordinate captains and followers of established captains. Kapodistrias sought to directly eliminate the powerful captain as the middleman and create a more direct dependence upon the state, while at the same time eliminating the possibility of these captains contracting large and powerful armed bands. What in essence transpired was a "reshuffling" of the hierarchy of the irregular captains by permitting less powerful and influential captains to rise at the expense of the more established and powerful captains (Koliopoulos 1987: 69–70).

Opposition to Kapodistrias's military policies, however, never really assumed any serious dimensions, for several reasons. First, though the ultimate aim of the military policies of Kapodistrias (i.e., the establishment of a state monopoly of coercion through the domestication and eventual elimination of the irregulars) was difficult to conceal, the irregulars, especially subordinate captains, could still perceive them as just another set of opportunities to be exploited in order to gain social mobility. Second, this impression was reinforced by the fact that, although the policies of the Kapodistrian regime may have posed a serious threat to a number of captains, on a more general level they never openly threatened the irregulars as a whole (Koliopoulos 1987: 73). For instance, the creation of semi-irregular and regular units was never perceived as a threat by the irregulars as a whole. On the one hand, the irregulars were "generally reluctant to enlist in these new units. . . . they disliked the discipline of a regular army unit . . . [and] their expectations of prompt and generous payment by the new regime had been dismally disappointed, as Kapodistrias and his government tried to limit the abuses in the remuneration of armed service"

(Koliopoulos 1987: 69). On the other hand, the newly created regular army, though loyal to Kapodistrias, was composed of only 3,500 troops and was in reality his personal armed force (Papageorgiou 1985: 33).[16] Moreover, Kapodistrias's energetic attempt at establishing a monopoly over the means of coercion within Greece proper was interrupted upon his assassination in 1831. Therefore, any plausible answers as to whether his regime could have established a monopoly over the means of coercion would be no more than idle speculation.

The military policies dictated by the Kapodistrian administration completely collapsed after his assassination. Though an act of personal vengeance, Kapodistrias's assassination can only be comprehended as the result of increasing opposition to his rule (Petropoulos 1968: 124–125). As for the indigenous and refugee irregulars of Rumely, they "went back into business and on their own terms soon after . . . and amidst the ensuing civil war" (Koliopoulos 1987: 74).

The Bavarian Regency and Monarchy, 1833–1862

In 1832 the Great Powers appointed Prince Otto, the seventeen-year-old son of King Ludwig I of Bavaria, to serve as the first sovereign of the Greek Kingdom. It is revealing of the dependent nature of the new state that Greeks were not an active party at the London Conference of 1832 between the Great Powers and Bavaria, which settled the terms under which Otto was to accept the throne and which placed Greece's sovereignty under the "guarantee" of the three Great Powers.

Otto arrived in Greece in January 1833, accompanied by a Council of Regents and 4,000 professional Bavarian troops.[17] On both theoretical and practical grounds the new state elites favored the construction of highly centralized and differentiated state institutions, which would neutralize the centrifugal tendencies of the provincial elites; and the creation of a strong national identity that would transcend the traditional loyalties of family, village, and Orthodox Church and provide a source of legitimation for state centralization and consolidation.

Both the regency and monarchy would face serious obstacles in their attempts to establish a Western-type nation-state. Bavarian state-making endeavors encountered strong resistance from almost all the elements of Greek society but especially from the local oligarchies – the clergy, the primates, and the captains of the irregular formations. Opposition to the Bavarian regency and monarchy took on a variety of forms: military revolts by both regular and irregular formations; uncoordinated and spontaneous outbursts of peasant violence; a failed attempt to assassinate the king's wife; the creation of conspiratorial organizations; and the emergence of rudimentary political parties, which had their roots in the period of the War of Independence.[18] If successful implementation of state policies required "a continuous supply of political entrepreneurs" (Tilly 1975: 40) to staff the new state institutions, then they would have to be trained or found abroad, for none was produced under Ottoman administration.[19] Moreover, Greece in 1833 had few if any extractable resources available: "Twelve years of war and civil war, a brutal military invasion and anarchy had left the country ruined physically, its economy in shambles, its population in misery" (McGrew 1985: 1).

Even the perceived legitimacy of the Greek state was highly qualified: With regard to polity, parliamentary constitutionalism based on popular sovereignty was combined uncomfortably with hereditary monarchy based on a foreign dynasty. Formal independence was qualified by an equally uncomfortable form of European protectorate exercised by three of the great powers. With regard to territorial and demographic definition, the state was confined to the southernmost tip of the Balkan peninsula in the heartland of what had constituted the ancient Greek homeland. (Petropoulos 1978: 165)

Almost inevitably, the aspiration to incorporate these Greeks into the nation-state became the predominant political and military program of the state for over a century, and served as the primary ideological mechanism for the creation of a homogeneous indigenous population and for justifying state policies.

State-Making and the Irregulars

The first concern of any state elite is the establishment and preservation of a monopoly over the means of coercion and the consequent pacification of society. Inevitably, in the state's effort to establish a monopoly over the means of coercion, the irregular military formations became the primary targets of the Bavarian regime. The state employed three main policies in order to combat the irregulars: the enactment of legislation, establishment of a professional and loyal military force (i.e., Bavarian recruits and a regular army loyal to the state), and the co-optation of the irregulars into various paramilitary units for the suppression of brigandage and/or the fulfillment of irredentist policies (Koliopoulos 1987).

From a legislative point of view, unlike the Kapodistrian administration, the Bavarian regency did not hesitate to order the irregulars to disband, and it prohibited the keeping and carrying of arms. In addition, the Western-based legal framework concerning brigandage and the overall question of the monopoly of the means of coercion specified that "public security was the exclusive responsibility of the central authority and its legally employed organs" (Koliopoulos 1987: 81). In other words, the state was officially abolishing the old Ottoman policy of "setting a thief to catch a thief" (McNeil 1982: 16), and consequently eliminating the armatolik institution and the social processes that perpetuated it.

Nevertheless, the state elites still had to deal with a large number of irregulars, who were anticipating some kind of state assistance, preferably employment. It must be kept in mind that most of the irregulars were accustomed to only one way of life – "paid military service in a band of comrades under a chief of their own choice" (Koliopoulos 1987: 78) – and considered civilian life, which in Greece translated into agricultural activities, as degrading. Moreover, after almost ten years of continuous armed conflict the lack of capital rendered agricultural settlement nearly impossible (Koliopoulos 1987: 78).

The foregoing circumstances compelled the Bavarian state elites initially to form two paramilitary units: a gendarmerie, an auxiliary branch of the regular army created ultimately for the maintenance of civic order throughout the kingdom but more immediately to garrison the towns for which there were insufficient Bavarian troops; and ten battalions of skirmishers (Petropoulos 1968: 79). "The incorporation of so many [1,200 posts] destitute irregulars and actual or potential outlaws in the new security force was a wise expedient which, moreover, followed the traditional practices and principles in combating lawlessness. The gendarmerie represented in more than one respect a compromise – the first of a series – of the new order with the old military regime" (Koliopoulos 1987: 79). By employing a substantial segment of the irregulars, the Bavarian regency aimed at shifting their loyalties from the captains to the nation-state. Despite the state's attempt, the majority of captains and their bands were neither incorporated into the paramilitary units or actually desired to be so incorporated.[20] Two options were left open to the foregoing captains and their bands: departure into Ottoman-held territories (i.e., Thessaly, Macedonia, and Epirus) where the armatolik institution still survived, or outright brigandage along the states' northern borders (van Boeschoten 1991: 23).

In the following decades, the state was unable to abolish or even curtail brigandage and would employ a variety of new and old mechanisms for confronting it: the deportation of the relations of brigands, with the aim of limiting their social base; communal responsibility of the municipalities for brigandage activity; and placing bounties on renowned brigands (Koliopoulos 1987). These legal measures would prove futile, however, because the state lacked the effective means of enforcing its decrees. Unlike the Kapodistrian administration, the Bavarian regime was, from the beginning, provided with 4,000 professional Bavarian troops to ensure the protection of the regime until an indigenous regular military loyal to the state could be constructed. Because Greece was under the protection of the Great Powers, the Bavarian troops became primarily a peace-keeping force aimed at restraining, and eventually eliminating, the strife between the irregulars and their claims upon the nation-state.

Nevertheless, the Bavarian mercenaries would prove to be largely ineffective when endeavoring to suppress the irregulars. On the one hand, the force was simply too small to undertake such an extensive mission and was therefore primarily relegated to garrisoning the strategic military installations throughout Greece proper. On the other hand, the Bavarian force proved unsuitable for defeating the guerrilla warfare tactics of the irregulars, as was made evident by the Mane Insurrection of 1834.[21] "The basic cause of the revolt was the regency's attempt to integrate all parts of Greece into a singly, unified state, and the specific measure that Mane resisted was one being applied to all Greece – the dismantling of towers, which were private homes traditionally fortified for self-defense.... In Mane, they represented the traditional way of life for the ruling warrior class" (Petropoulos 1968: 211). The Bavarian force that was sent to put down the revolt sustained many degrading defeats in the mountainous terrain of Mane. Owing to its military inability to compel the Maniats to dismantle the towers, the regency was forced to negotiate and reached the following compromise with the insurgents: limited dismantling of the towers for guarantees of Maniat autonomy, "monetary grants, the nonexecution of the monastic laws, and the organization of the Maniats into their own special organized military corps" (Petropoulos 1968: 210). In addition to making evident the weakness of the Bavarian military forces when dealing with irregular tactics, the Mane Insurrection validated revolt as a way of "extracting concessions from an apparently weak government" (Petropoulos 1968: 211).

Accordingly, in 1835–1836 bands of demobilized irregulars "sought to force the state to re-employ them" (Koliopoulos 1987: 11). It is within the context of the 1835–1836 revolt that the inverse racketeering relationship between the Greek state and the irregulars becomes apparent. Among the variety of causes attributable to the revolt:

It has also been maintained that disappointed captains like Grivas incited disobedience among the armed men of the region so as to force the government to ask for their services, allowing them to form bands of irregulars to suppress the outlaws and thus giving them the opportunity to employ their clients and strengthen their weakened position as influential patrons of their districts. (Koliopoulos 1987: 98)[22]

Although evidence is lacking as to whether disaffected captains actually instigated the revolt, ensuing events suggest that rebel captains acted within the framework of the traditional protection racket. Once again, the Bavarian forces were unable to put down the revolt; and the regency was compelled to make use of the indigenous military system "by offering the prospect of military employment to potential rebels" (Koliopoulos 1987: 98). On the one hand, the state offered appointments to the royal phalanx to most of the prominent insurgent leaders, "who were eager to abandon the rebels as soon as they received notice of their appointment" (Koliopoulos 1987: 89).[23] On the other hand, the state created the "National Guards," within which recruitment and payment of irregulars was the sole prerogative of individual captains.

The aftermath of the provocations and confrontations of 1835–6 was a further departure from principle with respect to the regular security forces and additional compromises by the central government with the traditional military element. The bands of irregulars formed in the first few months of 1836 were not dissolved after the collapse of the uprising, but were allowed to exist, not so much as a peace-keeping force but as an alternative and legitimate refuge for outlaws who might otherwise have taken up outright brigandage again. (Koliopoulos 1987: 102)[24]

Along Greece's northern frontiers the so-called border barons (Jenkins 1961: 5) emerged: powerful and influential captains who were practically independent of the nation-state. It must be accentuated, however, that the primary objective of border barons and most captains was not political independence but official state employment within the context of the arma-tolik system. Amnesty (i.e., a return to legality) and/or an armatolik was what most captains and irregulars sought (Koliopoulos 1979: 194). In the long run it was their desire and willingness to be employed by the state in this manner that rendered possible their domestication by the central authorities.

War-Making and the Irregulars

The "growth of domestically recruited standing armies [which] offered a strong stimulus to direct rule" (Koliopoulos 1987: 106) was effectively hindered in Greece during the period under consideration. With the departure of the majority of foreign mercenaries in 1837, the Bavarian regime attempted to lay the foundations of a regular indigenous army. This endeavor, however, encountered severe obstacles. First, the goal of the Bavarian regime to establish an army based on conscription foundered on peasant resistance. Second, the regular army would not achieve any legiti-macy within Greek society until the beginning of the twentieth century. This perception of illegitimacy was to a large extent connected with the illegiti-macy of the Bavarian regency and monarchy. One of the initial reasons for this perception is what Petropoulos (1968: 162) calls "Bavarianism – the policy of employing Bavarian nationals in the Greek state service." Bavarian control of the army rested on the Bavarian regulars but also on the fact that most key positions were held by Bavarians, even after the departure of the regulars.[25]

The issue of legitimacy also revolved around the inability of the regular military, as the armed force of the nation, to play a prominent role in the realization of the Megali Idea. The root of the Megali Idea has been a source of fiery debate and is beyond the scope of this chapter. In 1844, however, Kolettis articulated what has become known as a "classic" exposition of the Megali Idea by declaring that:

The Kingdom of Greece is not Greece. [Greece] constitutes only one part, the smallest and poorest part. A Greek is not only a man who lives in Ioannina, in

Thessalonike, in Serres, in Smyrna, in Trebizond, in Crete, in Samos and in any land associated with Greek history or the Greek race. . . . There are two main centers of Hellenism: Athens, the capital of the Greek kingdom, [and] "the City" [Constantinople], the dream and hope of all Greeks. (cited in Kitromilides 1976)

Foreign Intervention

The employment of the Greek irregular military forces for the realization of the Great Idea was to a large extent the result of the protectorate policies of the Great Powers, especially France and Britain, which had not only rele-gated the army to an internal peace-keeping force but also did not consent to the use of force for the fulfillment of Greek irredentist goals.[26] In con-junction with the Great Powers' disapproval of Greek irredentist policies, the ineptitude of the regular armed forces in dealing with the irregulars had buttressed the idea that the irregulars constituted the primary military arm of the nation-state. The Greek state elites would, therefore, turn to the irregulars and employ them for the realization of the Great Idea. State elites would "unofficially" direct brigand and irregular formations out of the kingdom's territories and into those of the Ottoman Empire to support irre-dentist rebellions. Thus, state elites "satisfied a potentially dangerous social element without burdening state finances, while creating the impression that Greek national aspirations were not being abandoned" (Koliopoulos 1987: 11).[27] It cannot be sufficiently sustained, however, that the Greek state employed the Great Idea, and the concept of the nation as solely mechanisms of legitimation and consolidation. The Greek state did go further than rhetorical assurances about territorial expansion. The Kolettis administra-tion (1844–1847), for example, perceived the irregulars as Greece's primary military force in an event of a Greek-Turkish war (Kofas 1980: 12).[28]

By September 1845, i.e. after a little more than a year of rule by Kolettis, the strength of the regular army had decreased by one third (from 3,546 to 2,388), while the number of the irregulars had been increased by more than one-third, from 1,890 to 2,962. Vacancies in the regular army units, which were created by expiration of terms of service and by desertions, were not filled on account of low conscription returns, while enlistment in the frontier guards and other less permanent irregular formations was encouraged. (Koliopoulos 1987: 123–124)

During his administration Kolettis instituted a governmental system that was to predominate until the removal of Otto in 1862. Patronage would become the main mechanism by which the Kolettis administration endeav-ored to remain in power.[29] Following the introduction of parliamentary government in 1844, many brigands took service under the Kolettis administration. The irregulars were employed as the main method of political intimidation and as a means of creating disorder on the northern frontier (Jenkins 1961: 6–7; Campbell and Sherrard 1968: 88).[30] Indeed,

"Kolettis, it appears, did succeed in directing considerable brigand activity towards the neighbouring Ottoman domains by harnessing brigandage more effectively than hitherto to irredentism" (Koliopoulos 1987: 122).

Nevertheless, considering that the Protecting Powers were unwilling to support Greek irredentist policies, Greek state elites searched for the right circumstances to assault the Ottoman Empire (Kofas 1980: 14). Three times during the period under study the Ottoman Empire became immersed in crises that appeared to have created the right conditions for Greek war-making (Jelavich and Jelavich 1979: 78). However, the outbreak of the Crimean War in 1853 appeared to the Greek state elites to have created the most favorable conditions.[31] The outbreak of hostilities had forced the withdrawal of Ottoman forces from Greece's northern frontiers and, most important, brought two of Greece's protectors (France and Britain) into open military conflict with the third (Russia). The Greek state promoted local insurrections in Macedonia, Thessaly, and Epirus, while irregular bands crossed into Ottoman territory. "The crossing of bands of armed men in particular eventually assumed such dimensions that the Turkish charge that the sultan's domains had been invaded by forces from Greece was not exaggerated. The bands from Greece, particularly following the outbreak of the rising in Radovisti and the adjacent districts did amount to an irregular army invading foreign territory" (Koliopoulos 1987: 143).[32] The attempt, however, to expand Greece's northern boundaries met with complete failure. By May 1854 the Ottoman Empire had effectively suppressed the insurrection, and most irregular bands had withdrawn behind Greek boarders. Nevertheless, the war-making activities of the Greek state brought about a strong reaction from the Western powers who occupied the port of Piraeus in retaliation. Otto was forced to renounce his alliance with Russia and appoint a government that was sympathetic to Western interests. The British-French occupation continued until February 1857 as a guarantee against the continued threat of brigandage and irrendentist activity. In addition to a number of other factors, the Bavarian monarchy's inability to successfully implement the Great Idea would slowly but surely undermine its political position and result in Otto's removal in 1862. What is more, the Great Powers refused to intervene on Otto's behalf because of his fervent espousal of the Great Idea. For example, in 1862 Otto rejected "a British offer to cede the Greek-populated Ionian islands to his kingdom on the condition that he refrain from aggressive action toward Turkey" (Couloumbis, Petropoulos, and Psomiades 1976: 26). "In so far as England and France were concerned Greek brigands were a Christian army when they crossed over to the Ottoman territory and that presented a threat to the peaceful coexistence of the two neighboring states and more importantly brigandage served to the Russian advantage under the present circumstances" (Kofas 1980: 101).[33]

To be sure, some scholars might see the participation of captains and irregulars, from Greece proper, in the events of 1854 as evidence of nationalist sentiment. And it is true that for brigands the active demonstration of nationalistic sentiments was not an entirely disinterested affair, but it also must be considered as connected to the prospect of favorable treatment by the state and/or with an amnesty (Koliopoulos 1979: 82).[34] Moreover, the predatory nature of the irregulars became evident when the insurrection degenerated into uncontrolled and indiscriminate depredation of the rural population (Koliopoulos 1979: 86–87; 1987: 148–150).

Unavailability of Extractable Resources

An additional factor that compelled the Greek state to employ irregular troops for state-making and war-making activities was the unavailability of extractable resources. Mouzelis designates the period 1830 to 1880 as one of "underdevelopment in a pre-capitalist context" (1978: 15). Before and after independence Greece was primarily an agrarian society based on subsistence farming and animal husbandry, with virtually no industry (except for handicrafts) or well-developed cities.[35] Almost entirely lacking indigenous concentrated capital, Greece's regional economic organization gave rise to a coercion-intensive path of political development in which state elites "in the absence of ready capital ... built massive apparatuses to squeeze resources from a reluctant citizenry" (Tilly 1992: 30).

An important qualification should be taken into consideration when reflecting upon the Greek state's method of resource mobilization. Contrary to the Western and Eastern European experiences, Greek state makers were not confronted with a class of large landowners. The regional economic organization of the Ottoman Empire did not contribute to the emergence of Greek landowners; and more than half of the arable land, including the most fertile areas, was "owned" by Ottoman Turks (McGrew 1976: 117).[36] More important, the War of Independence had created a situation where the state became the largest landowner "drawing power from its control of seventy percent of all cultivable land" (Veremis 1990: 20). From the outset, the ex-Ottoman lands were proclaimed "national lands" and came under the direct control of the state. In addition, the state directly controlled all the land that had not been officially granted by the Ottoman Empire (McGrew 1976: 115) and, via the subordination of the church to the state, all ecclesiastical properties within Greece proper. The state, in turn, impeded the development of a class of large landowners by refusing to sell by auction the "national estates" (Mouzelis 1978: 14).[37]

The Bavarian state builders were faced with the problem of erecting viable state institutions with a depleted state treasury and few extractable resources. First, after more than twelve years of constant fighting, Greece

was in a pitiable economic condition. The flourishing of small manufac-
turing enterprises in northern Greece and shipbuilding endeavors in
the Aegean Islands had been severely interrupted by the outbreak of the
War of Independence. The establishment of the state's official borders in
1827 and the subsequent upheavals along the northern border contributed
to the decline of animal husbandry. Moreover, most of the land was
naturally poor, only 25 percent being cultivatable (Jelavich and Jelavich
1977: 73).

The economic situation was made worse by the badly administered,
corrupt, and repressive system of revenue collection (Campbell and Sherrard
1968: 85). In fact, methods of taxation and tax farming were at times
so oppressive that many Greek peasants crossed the northern borders to
resettle in the Ottoman Empire. Moreover, the internal communications
and transportation infrastructure remained largely underdeveloped, directly
hindering the state's ability to appropriate resources and, in general,
penetrate society. For example, "between 1828 and 1852 road construction
did not exceed 168 kilometers, a state of affairs which could only hinder
the development of trade and the creation of a unified national market"
(Mouzelis 1978: 15). With the exception of the somewhat more developed
coastal plain of northern Peloponnese, the agricultural economy of
peasants aimed at little more than subsistence (Campbell and Sherrard
1968: 91).

Second, what private Greek capital remained was to a large extent
beyond the immediate grasp of the nation-state. High concentrations of
Greek capital were located primarily in the well-developed Ottoman and
European cities (Vienna, Venice, Ancona, Constantinople, Smyrna,
Thessaloniki, etc.) (Campbell and Sherrard 1968: 80). As Svoronos indi-
cates, "Constantinople and not Athens was the economic capital of Greece
throughout most of the 19th century" (cited in Kokosalakis 1995: 255).
Although diaspora entrepreneurs invested heavily in the kingdom, the
Greek state could neither directly control nor tax these manipulators of
capital (Jelavich and Jelavich 1977: 80).

In addition, the foreign debts incurred during and after the War of
Independence had to be paid.[38] In 1838 Greek finances were put under the
control of a French supervisor. Continually insisting on the payment of
interest on their loans, the powers pressed the Greek state to curtail its internal expenditures. In effect, this implied a drastic reduction of Greece's enormous military budget which absorbed about one-third of state revenues
(Jelavich and Jelavich 1977: 75; Kofas 1980: 19).

Greece's regular and irregular military forces were an enormous expense
for the state. The Bavarian troops were so costly that they "consumed
the greater part of the loan made to Greece by the Protecting Powers"
(Campbell and Sherrard 1968: 86), while the irregulars were paid 50
percent more than the regular indigenous troops (Koliopoulos 1987: 124).

This discrepancy indicates that state employment of irregular military formations was not pursued because of the latter's inexpensiveness. A more viable explanation for the employment of irregulars is the state's inability to impose and maintain a monopoly over the means of coercion. And that this inability is attributable to the lack of an effective standing army due to the lack of extractable resources. Patronage of a considerable part of the irregular forces and their employment in various irrendentist activities enabled the state, in the long run, to nullify this dangerous military elite.

Conclusions

Through an analysis of early nineteenth-century Greek state-building I have attempted to emphasize two general analytical and methodological points. First, the importance of taking into consideration irregular armed forces when investigating state- and war-making endeavors. As indicated by the case study, the irregulars played an essential role in establishing one of the main characteristics of the modern Greek state (i.e., its patrimonial character), a characteristic that was, in fact, contrary to the blueprints of the early state builders. The failure of the Greek state to impose and maintain a monopoly on the means of coercion led to an inverse racketeering relationship. Working within the context of the pre-Independence "armatolik mentality," the captains of the irregulars stimulated brigand activity so as to heighten their bargaining capacity vis-à-vis state elites concerning primarily issues of amnesty and state employment. In turn, the inability of the state's regular military forces to effectively curb brigandage compelled the state elites to employ irregulars for the task. Nevertheless, despite the absence of a monopoly of the means of coercion, the state was able to establish centralized, differentiated, and autonomous institutions by becoming the most powerful patron in Greek society.

Second, the case study indicates that state elites will utilize irregular troops when they are incapable of imposing and/or maintaining a monopoly over the means of coercion, when war-making activities are constrained by more powerful states, and when indigenous resources are not available for extraction; in addition, the possibility of employing irregular troops is reinforced when the native society displays an irregular military tradition.

An important caveat should be taken into consideration when reflecting upon the former propositions: I am not maintaining that irregular troops are necessarily more effective than standing armies as war-making and state-making mechanisms. In fact, the case study indicates that, especially for war-making activities, they are inadequate. Nevertheless, the employment of irregular troops by mid-nineteenth-century Greek state makers indicates that states have the *option* of employing such forces and that the employment of such forces does not necessarily hinder state centralization and consolidation processes.

Notes

1. Because state-building is characterized by different and complex processes that in the long run depend on particular circumstances, the subsequent conceptualizations should not be understood as an attempt to formulate objective features of the relevant terms but should be conceived as analytical tools for this particular case study, tools that may or may not fit other case studies.

2. A distinction should be made between contemporary Greek client-patron networks and those prevalent in the period under consideration. Mouzelis maintains that "[w]ith increasing urbanization and industrialization, clientalism not only underwent fundamental changes (such as a shift from the 'monopolistic' patronage of the local oligarchs to a more flexible, open 'party-oriented' clientalism), but it also became weakened as a mode of political integration (in the sense that the development of mass politics and the emergence of 'horizontal' organizations disrupt 'vertical' networks, especially in cities)" (1978: 209n28).

3. Three basic mechanisms were employed by the fledgling Greek state in its attempt at nation-building: a regular army based on the recruitment of citizens, a uniform education system, and a judiciary system (Kitromilides 1990: 36).

4. The following description and analysis is based primarily on the works of John Koliopoulos (1979, 1987, 1990), without which this chapter would have been a colossal undertaking.

5. As part of the Ottoman Empire, Greece was neither a political or administrative unit. In fact, the diverse populations of the Ottoman Empire were organized into religious communities or millets. Though the Ottomans labeled the Orthodox millet, millet-i Rum, or "Greek" millet, this category encompassed all Orthodox Christians in the empire (Bulgarians, Serbs, Romanians, etc.) (Clogg 1992: 10). Therefore the terms "Greece" and "Greeks" during the Ottoman period will be employed to indicate a distinct linguistic, religious, and cultural segment of the empire, without any extensive territorial and/or national identity. In addition, it should be kept in mind that the boundaries between the various ethnic communities of the millet were highly fluid "and a shift from one to another [occurred] without a change in those peoples' status vis-à-vis the Sublime Porte" (Roudomentof 1998: 32).

6. It should be noted that both Ottoman lords and Greek primates "derived their power and wealth more from administration, tax collection, and usury, than from the outright ownership of land or direct exploitation of land.... The extensive estates of powerful lords and archons [primates], therefore, consisted not of farms from which they would operate themselves, but rather of claims upon virtually every type of income which villagers produced, paid as rents, taxes, interest, and other exactions" (McGrew 1985: 38).

7. Scholars distinguish a third subgroup – called *kapoi* – composed of former klephts who were enlisted as bodyguards by the local Christian notables (Alexander 1966; Petropoulos 1968: 34; Skiotis 1975: 312; Papageorgiou 1968: 33–34). The kapoi will not be incorporated into the present discussion because this chapter is based on the premise that the klephts-armatoloi constituted, by way of arms, a provincial elite, something that the kapoi, in their capacity as bodyguards to primates, were not (Alexander 1966: 52; Petropoulos 1968: 33–34). The chapter, therefore, deals primarily with the irregular units of

Rumely, and captains, who for numerous reasons entered liberated Greece during and after the War of Independence.

8. Brigandage was prevalent in most of the Ottoman-controlled Balkans (i.e., the haibuts in Bulgaria, haiduks in Serbia, and haiduci in Romania) (Clogg 1973: 9).

9. Nikolaos Stornaris, for instance, controlled around 120 villages, of an average of seventy families. It has been maintained that he possessed 7,000 to 8,000 head of livestock, "while his family owned many times that number" (Koliopoulos 1987: 47). Therefore, Stornaris was able to maintain a band of 400 fighting men (Dakin 1972: 18–19).

10. *Koumparia* is "the relationship contracted between families of a bridegroom and his bestman or a man and his child's godfather. Confirmed by the church, it was regarded as binding as blood" (Petropoulos 1968: 58).

11. The exact origins of the armatolik institution remain obscure. It has been argued that the institution existed in Byzantine and Venetian Greece, which the Ottomans retained with some alterations (Alexander 1966: 17–27; Dakin 1972: 18). The first Ottoman armatolik seems to have been established during the reign of Sultan Murad II (Skiotis 1975: 312).

12. Rumely was divided between fourteen and eighteen armatoliks (Clogg 1973: 8).

13. The Philiki Etairia, or Friendly Society, was the secret organization that laid much of the organizational groundwork for the War of Independence.

14. *Kapakia* were the agreements made between the klephts/armatoloi and the Ottoman authorities based on a document of submission (Papageorgiou 1985: 26n18).

15. The primary driving force for the creation of a Western-type state and its corresponding institutions originated from a small group of Westernized and/or heterochthon Greeks. More specifically, what ensued during and after the War of Independence was a political conflict between "modernists" or "Westernizers" and the "traditionalists" (Petropoulos 1968; Mouzelis 1978; Diamandouros 1983). The "Westernizing" Greeks were primarily foreign-trained intelligentsia and diaspora middle class who aimed at the creation of a strong secular nation-state that would be able to limit and eventually eliminate regional fragmentation and the autonomy of the local elites. The "traditionalist" faction was comprised of the provincial elites (i.e., primates, clergy, captains, merchants) who simply wanted to replace their Ottoman over-lords without radically altering the prevailing political and economic structure, and who remained under the cultural hegemony of the Greek Orthodox Church.

16. The most distinguishing characteristic of this military force was its social composition: the rank and file came primarily from territories with no strong armatolik tradition, and the officers were either Philhellenes or heterochthons (Papageorgiou 1986: 208–209).

17. Because Otto was a minor at the time of this appointment, Greece was initially governed by a regency of three Bavarian ministers (Joseph von Armansperg, Major General Karl von Heideck, and George Ludwig von Maurer) and two advisers (Johann Greiner and Karl von Abel). Armansperg was appointed president of the regency, while the other members were given the task of centralizing and consolidating the different state branches. Heideck was charged with

the organization of the military; Maurer was concerned mainly with the legislative, ecclesiastical, and educational issues; the adviser Able was given jurisdiction over internal administration and foreign affairs; and Greiner, with economic matters. In time, the regency members would come into conflict with Armansperg achieving supremacy in 1834. Armansperg was replaced by Ignaz von Rudhart in 1837. In the same year Rudhart was forced to resign and the first Greek, Constantine Zographos, was appointed as prime minister (Petropoulos 1968).

18. Significantly, these political parties were known as the "English," "French," and "Russian," and their leaders retained close contacts with the ambassadors of the three Great Powers.

19. This deficiency was met with the establishment of the University of Athens in 1837.

20. In fact, the skirmisher units never took shape due to lack of recruits (Koliopoulos 1987: 80).

21. Under Ottoman administration, Mane was a semiautonomous community, "which performed no services for the Ottomans and [was] left unmolested except on the rare occasions when the Ottomans had sufficient forces in the area to compel the payment of the annual lump-sum tribute" (Skiotis 1975: 311).

22. Theodore Grivas was "a scion of an old armatolik family of western Rumeli whose members occupied senior positions during the revolution. A general during this period, he became a powerful political and military personality during the periods of the Capodistrias and Otho" (Papageorgiou 1985: 23n4).

23. The royal phalanx, which was nothing more than a state-sponsored pension system, aimed at pacifying captains that were considered dangerous to the security of the state (Petropoulos 1968: 240–241; Koliopoulos 1987: 80–81).

24. In 1838 the National Guard was incorporated into the frontier guards, "a new corps established to guard the border and keep the peace in the northern provinces" (Koliopoulos 1987: 102).

25. Bavarianism was eliminated by the constitution of 1843. In September 1843 a military coup d'etat forced Otto to agree to the formation of a constitution. In practice, however, the constitution guaranteed the king "such powers that if put to use, as they were, would in fact make him an absolute monarch" (Kofas 1980: 2).

26. In general, it has been maintained that the Great Powers were hostile to Greek expansionist policies for two main reasons: "The Greek question threatened a direct confrontation over the issue of the Ottoman Empire. It was the principal concern of the statesmen of Europe to avoid such a confrontation and to act with caution over any political rearrangements in the Near East which would alter the balance of power in the European community. Secondly, the interests of the Great Powers in the area were such that Britain and France, the natural maritime allies of the Greeks, generally favored Turkey over Greece in order to contain Russian expansion; and Russia preferred a militarily weak Greece for the protection of her primary interests in Constantinople and on the Danube" (Psomiades 1968: 18).

27. The Great Idea was not the only mechanism through which domestic issues were defused. "[S]ocial mobility through effectively controlled patronage or

taking to the mountains and resorting to brigandage, offered alternative ways of alleviating the destitution of the lower, especially rural social strata. Emigration . . . throughout the nineteenth century . . . provided the classical mechanism sustaining the conservative status quo by removing the demographic surpluses that could furnish the potential social bases of protest movements" (Kitromilides 1976: 16).

28. Both the Ottoman Empire and the Great Powers reproached the Greek state's inability and unwillingness to suppress brigandage activities in the northern frontiers. For instance, in the House of Lords, Lord Beaumont stated: "Not only had Athens become the scene of the deepest and strangest intrigues . . . but even beyond the internal affairs of Greece, beyond the frontiers, had that country already shown a total disrespect, not only for treaties, but for the common law of nations – for the common practice of international friendship; and set a defiance at the common laws of humanity, by establishing on the frontiers of Turkey an absolute system of Brigandage" (cited in Kofas 1980: 13).

29. In general, clients were secured and controlled through three primary means: by brides, promises, and violence (Campbell and Sherrard 1968: 87). Kolettis's patronage politics were continued after his death by Otto, albeit less successfully. The monarch's "patronage resources were nevertheless impressive, including appointments to the public service and positions of Demarch and alderman in the communes; appointments to the Senate for life at 20 [pounds] a month; the profitable operations of tax farming; commissions and decorations, and promotions in the army (there was one officer for every seven men and seventy generals in a force of 10,000); and the Phalanx" (ibid.); and the royal right of amnesty (Jenkins 1961: 9).

30. Kolettis governance was characterized by three overriding political objectives: "(1) The restoration of prestige to the Crown, (2) the permanent establishment of this Prime Ministership, and (3) the expansion of the country's boundaries" (Kofas 1980: 9). There is inadequate information as to the precise role played in Greek internal political events by the captains during the period under consideration. It appears, however, that captains within Greece proper became more dependent on state and party elites than during Ottoman rule (van Boeschoten 1991: 23).

31. The first two occurred in 1831–1833 and 1839–1840 when Egypt openly contested the Ottoman Empire's sovereignty (Jelavich and Jelavich 1977: 98).

32. The ranks of the irregulars were buttressed by regular army officers who resigned their commissions and formed bands of irregulars, and "escaped" prisoners. For instance, "the Chalcis prison was the first to be broken open by a non-commissioned officer, Leonidas Leotsakos . . . [who] took with him the prison guard and greater part of the prisoners, as well as the priest who was obliged to bless the arms. . . . The Leotsakos band crossed to Thessaly. . . . It is said that War Minister Skarlatos Soutsos was privy to the affair" (Koliopoulos 1987: 145).

33. It would be inaccurate to perceive foreign involvement in Greece within an entirely negative framework. Indeed, the existence of the protecting powers explains why the territorial integrity of the Greek state "remained unchallenged throughout the nineteenth century" (Couloumbis, Petropoulos, and Psomiades 1976: 21).

34. The captains in the Ottoman territory perceived "the events that led to the outbreak of open hostilities with the Turks in the light of the customary and time-honored pressure could be exerted on the authorities to make them less intransigent and agree to share power and the benefits from the exercise of power" (Koliopoulos 1987: 14).

35. For instance, "the major trading center and largest city, Patras, had less than 10,000 inhabitants. The bulk of the population was scattered in small villages, many of them in remote but secure mountain fastnesses" (McGrew 1976: 113).

36. In the Ottoman Empire, landownership is a highly complex phenomenon, and a fuller discussion of the topic is beyond the scope of the chapter. For our purposes it is enough to say that, in theory all land belonged to the Sultan, "but could be granted temporarily or permanently under a variety of legal formulae" (McGrew 1976: 113).

37. It was not until the annexation of Thessaly in 1881 that a large and influential landowning class would emerge. In an attempt to attract diaspora capital the Trikoupis administration supported the acquisition of Thessaly's large Ottoman estates by wealthy diaspora Greeks. These extensive landholding estates were eliminated by Venizelos's agrarian reforms in 1909.

38. The Treaty of London of 1832 stipulated a loan of 60 million francs by the Protecting Powers for which: "The sovereign of Greece and the Greek state shall be bound to appropriate to the payment of the interest and sinking fund of such installments of the loan as may have been raised under the guarantee of the three Courts, the first revenues of the state in such a manner that the actual receipts of the Greek treasury shall be devoted, first of all, to the payment of the said interest and sinking fund, and shall not be employed for any other purpose, until those payments on account of the installments of the loan raised under the guarantee of the three Courts, shall have been completely secured for that current year. The diplomatic representatives of the three Courts in Greece shall be especially charged to watch over the fulfillment of the last mentioned stipulations" (Article XII, cited in Kofas 1980: 3).

References

Alexander, John C. 1966. "The Klephtic Institution of the Morea and Its Destruction in 1806." M.A. Thesis, Columbia University.

Barkey, Karen. 1994. *Bandits and Bureaucrats: The Ottoman Route to State Centralization*. Ithaca: Cornell University Press.

Blok, Anton. 1972. "The Peasant and the Brigand: Social Banditry Reconsidered," *Comparative Studies in Society and History* 14, 4: 494–503.

Campbell, John, and Philip Sherrard. 1968. *Modern Greece*. New York: Praeger.

Clogg, Richard. 1973. "Aspects of the Movement for Greek Independence," in Richard Clogg, ed., *The Struggle for Greek Independence*, 1–40. London: Macmillan.

    1976. *The Movement for Greek Independence, 1770–1821: A Collection of Documents*. New York: Barnes and Noble.

    1992. *A Concise History of Greece*. Cambridge: Cambridge University Press.

Couloumbis, Theodore, John A. Petropoulos, and Harry J. Psomiades. 1976. *Foreign Interference in Greek Politics: A Historical Perspective.* New York: Pella.

Dakin, Douglas. 1972. *The Unification of Greece.* New York: St. Martin's Press.

Desch, Michael. 1996. "War and Strong States, Peace and Weak States?" *International Organization* 50, 2: 237–268.

Diamandouros, Nikiforos P. 1983. "Greek Political Culture in Transition: Historical Origins, Evolution, Current Trends," in Richard Clogg, ed., *Greece in the 1980s*, 42–69. New York: St. Martin's.

Glenn, John. 1997. "The Interregnum: The South's Security Dilemma," *Nations and Nationalism* 3, 1: 45–64.

Gould, Roger. 1996. "Patron-Client Ties, State Centralization, and the Whiskey Rebellion," *American Journal of Sociology* 102, 2: 400–429.

Guibernau, Montserrat. 1996. *Nationalisms: The Nation-State and Nationalism in the Twentieth Century.* Cambridge, Mass.: Blackwell.

Hobsbawm, Eric. 1965. *Primitive Rebels: Studies in Archaic Forms of Social Movements in the 19th and 20th Centuries.* New York: Norton.

1985. *Bandits.* Harmondsworth: Penguin.

Jelavich, Charles, and Barbara Jelavich. 1977. *The Establishment of the Balkan National States, 1804–1920.* Seattle: University of Washington Press.

Jenkins, Romilly James Heald. 1961. *The Dilessi Murders.* New York: Longmans, Green.

Kitromilides, Paschalis. 1976. "The Dialectic of Intolerance: Ideological Dimensions of Ethnic Conflict," *Journal of the Hellenic Diaspora* 6: 5–30.

1990. " 'Imagined Communities' and the Origins of the National Question in the Balkans," in Martin Blinkhorn and Thanos Veremis, eds., *Modern Greece: Nationalism and Nationality*, 22–36. Athens: Eliamep.

Kofas, Jon V. 1980. *International and Domestic Politics in General during the Crimean War.* New York: Columbia University Press.

Kokosalakis, Nikos. 1995. "Greek Orthodoxy and Modern Socio-Economic Changes," in R. Roberts, ed., *Religion and the Transformation of Capitalism: Comparative Approaches*, 248–265. New York: Routledge.

Koliopoulos, Giannes. 1979. Ληστεζ, Η Κεντρικη Ελλαδα στα μεσα του 19^{ου} αιωνα (Brigands: Central Greece during the mid-nineteenth century). Athens: Ermes.

1987. *Brigands with a Cause: Brigandage and Irredentism in Modern Greece, 1821–1912.* Oxford: Clarendon Press.

Koliopoulos, John. 1990. "Brigandage and Irredentism in Nineteenth Century Greece," in M. Blinkhorn and T. Veremis, eds., *Modern Greece: Nationalism and Nationality*, 67–102. Athens: Eliamep.

Kourvetaris, George A., and Betty A. Dobratz. 1987. *A Profile of Modern Greece: In Search of Identity.* Oxford: Clarendon Press.

Mann, Michael. 1988. "The Autonomous Power of the State: Its Origins, Mechanisms, and Results," in Michael Mann, ed., *States, War and Capitalism*, 1–32. Cambridge, Mass.: Blackwell.

McGrew, William W. 1976. "The Land Issue in the Greek War of Independence," in Nikiforos P. Diamandouros, James P. Anton, John A. Petropoulos, and Peter Topping, eds., *Hellenism and the First Greek War of Liberation (1821–1830): Continuity and Change*, 111–119. Thessaloniki: Institute for Balkan Studies.

1985. *Land and Revolution in Modern Greece, 1800–1881: The Transition in the Tenure and Exploitation of Land from Ottoman Rule to Independence.* Kent, Ohio: Kent State University Press.

McNeill, William. 1982. *The Pursuit of Power: Technology, Armed Force, and Society since AD 1000.* Chicago: University of Chicago Press.

Mouzelis, Nicos P. 1978. *Modern Greece: Facets of Underdevelopment.* New York: Holmes and Meier.

Papageorgiou, Stephanos P. 1985. "The Army as an Institution for Territorial Expansion and for Repression by the State: The Capodistrian Case," *Journal of the Hellenic Diaspora* 12, 4: 21–34.

1986. Η Στρατιωτικη Πολιτικη του Καποδιστρια (The military policy of Kapodistrias). Athens: Estia.

Petropoulos, John Anthony. 1968. *Politics and Statecraft in the Kingdom of Greece, 1833–1843.* Princeton: Princeton University Press.

1978. "The Modern Greek State and the Greek Past," in Speros Vryonis, ed., *The "Past" in Medieval and Modern Greek Culture*, 163–176. Malibu, Calif.: UNDENA Publications.

Pirounakis, Nicholas G. 1997. *The Greek Economy: Past, Present and Future.* New York: St. Martin's Press.

Pollis, Adamantia. 1992. "Greek National Identity: Religious Minorities, Rights, and European Norms," *Journal of Modern Greek Studies* 10, 2: 171–195.

Psomiades, Harry J. 1968. *The Eastern Question: The Last Phase: A Study of Greek-Turkish Diplomacy.* Thessaloniki: Institute of Balkan Studies.

Roudometof, Victor. 1998. "From Rum Millet to Greek Nation: Enlightenment, Secularization, and National Identity in Ottoman Balkan Society, 1453–1821," *Journal of Modern Greek Studies* 16: 11–48.

Sewell, William. 1994. "Ideologies and Social Revolutions: Reflections on the French Case," in T. Skocpol, ed., *Social Revolutions in the Modern World*, 169–198. Cambridge: Cambridge University Press.

Skiotis, Demetrios N. 1975. "Mountain Warriors and the Greek Revolution," in V. J. Parry and M. E. Yapp, eds., *War, Technology and Society in the Middle East*, 308–329. London: Oxford University Press.

Skocpol, Theda. 1979. *States and Social Revolutions: A Comparative Analysis of France, Russia, and China.* Cambridge: Cambridge University Press.

1985. "Bringing the State Back In: Strategies of Analysis in Current Research," in Peter Evans, Dietrich Rueschemeyer, and Theda Skocpol, eds., *Bringing the State Back In*, 3–37. Cambridge: Cambridge University Press.

Tatsios, Theodore George. 1984. *The Megali Idea and the Greek-Turkish War of 1897: The Impact of the Cretan Problem on Greek Irredentism, 1866–1897.* New York: Columbia University Press.

Tilly, Charles. 1975. "Reflections on the History of European State-Making," in Charles Tilly, ed., *The Formation of National States in Western Europe*, 3–83. Princeton: Princeton University Press.

1985. "War Making and State Making as Organized Crime," in Peter Evans, Dietrich Rueschemeyer, and Theda Skocpol, eds., *Bringing the State Back In*, 169–191. Cambridge: Cambridge University Press.

1992. *Coercion, Capital, and European States, AD 990–1992.* Cambridge, Mass.: Blackwell.

1994. "States and Nationalism in Europe, 1492–1992," *Theory and Society* 23, 1: 131–146.

Todorov, Varban N. 1995. *Greek Federalism during the Nineteenth Century: Ideas and Projects*. New York: Columbia University Press.

Tsoucalas, Constantine. 1978. "On the Problem of Political Clientelism in Greece in the Nineteenth Century," *Journal of the Hellenic Diaspora* 5, 2: 5–17.

van Boeschoten, Riki. 1991. *From Armatolik to People's Rule: Investigation into the Collective Memory of Rural Greece, 1750–1949*. Amsterdam: Adolf M. Hakkert.

Veremis, Thanos. 1990. "From the National State to the Stateless Nation," in Martin Blinkhorn and Thanos Veremis, eds., *Modern Greece: Nationalism and Nationality*, 9–22. Athens: ELIAMEP.

Weber, Max. 1968. *Economy and Society*. Vol. 1. Ed. G. Roth and C. Wittich. New York: Bedminster Press.

7

Reform and Reaction

Paramilitary Groups in Contemporary Colombia

Mauricio Romero

Paramilitary forces, or self-defense groups, have been associated in Colombia with drug trafficking and its conflict resolution techniques, with the counterinsurgency strategies of the armed forces and the tactics of the "dirty war" against the revolutionary guerrillas, with para-institutional forms of controlling social protest on the part of "mafia" capitalists, or with the growth of the large cattle ranches and the violent eviction of peasants from the land by large landowners (Medina 1990; Palacio and Rojas 1990; Uprimny and Vargas 1990; Reyes 1994). These were the interpretations put forward by academics, lawyers, human rights organizations, and left-wing sympathizers in the first publications on the subject during the 1980s and the beginning of the 1990s. Those initial perspectives relied on, among other sources, official reports of the prosecutor general's office or the Administrative Department of Security, DAS, in which members of the armed forces were linked to "vigilante groups."[1]

Along with these conceptions of the paramilitary phenomenon, another related to the lack of security for rural property owners, investors, and traders gained an audience during the second half of the 1990s and already had supporters in the cabinet by 1987.[2] This sector and its political allies preferred to call these groups self-defense groups, seeking legitimacy for what they considered to be the right of regional elites attacked by the different guerrilla groups to defend themselves.[3] So Fernando Botero, the first defense minister in Ernesto Samper's Liberal government (1994–1998) let it be understood in the cattlemen's congress of October 1994. This vision took shape in the proposal to create the security cooperatives CONVIVIR in 1995. These would be private surveillance organizations to bolster rural security and collect information, designed to foster cooperation between property-owning sectors and the armed forces in the work of maintaining public order.

That convergence between "society and armed forces" had long been sought by the military high command, given the distrust, and sometimes open hostility, of opposition sectors, social organizations, and the population itself toward the military institution in the regions with social and armed conflict. The denunciations of human rights violations made by groups of lawyers and social activists, mass media, and institutions of the judicial sector confirmed that feeling of insecurity evoked by the forces of public order. The measure on the CONVIVIR was finally revoked as the result of intense opposition from human rights groups, which argued that it ran the risk of legalizing groups of paid assassins and vigilantes. However, the initiative indicated the need to protect the rural proprietors from the increasing impact of the armed conflict. What was debatable was not the demand for security but the implicit delegation of justice in private hands.

That emphasis on security was also accompanied by a clear differentiation between self-defense and paramilitary groups. The distinction had been useful to separate the origins of these private armed groups: one organized for self-defense and the other composed of mercenaries and hired guns on salary to landowners or drug traffickers. Nevertheless, the distinction was losing its descriptive power by the mid-1990s as the different groups concurred, whether in idea or practice, with the security forces on how to solve the armed conflict. Without a doubt, the security forces have continued to be tied to the doctrines of the Cold War, without modernizing their conceptual framework to move beyond the dogma of the "enemy within," proper to the counterinsurgency wars. The necessary doctrinal renovation would resituate them in the new global context of democratization, and therefore would facilitate a negotiated solution to the armed conflict. The application of the principal of internal war by state institutions and its assimilation by private armed groups themselves created a playing field where different sectors came together. Within that arena the targets included not only competing politicians, social activists, and "plainclothes guerrillas" or "parasubversives," as the head of the paramilitary forces, Carlos Castaño, terms the guerrillas' support networks, but a wide spectrum of the civilian population that did not agree with paramilitary strategies and postulates on how to resolve the Colombian armed conflict. Thus, the ambiguity of the distinction has been used as camouflage for an expeditious and effective mechanism to fight not only the subversion but also attempts at reform and demands for democratization. Viewing the paramilitary groups only in the context of the right to self-defense has tended to reduce the phenomenon to a problem of supply and demand for security services, hiding its devastating effects on the political modernization initiated by President Belisario Betancur in 1982.

In this chapter we want to present a perspective that adds another dimension to the complexity of the paramilitary phenomenon, without ignoring the points of view just elucidated. The text seeks to emphasize an aspect that has received insufficient study: the context of political opening, decentralization, and peace negotiations with the guerrillas in which paramilitary

groups arose in the 1980s. The risks of a possible democratization provoked a negative reaction from regional elites affiliated with the Liberal and
Conservative parties, but mainly the first, related to the possible incorporation of former insurgents into different local political systems. With this
would come the inclusion of social groups that had been marginalized from
the public debate up to that point. The paramilitary itself can be analyzed
from a perspective of the fears and unease generated by the political inclusion of groups considered by the privileged sectors to be infiltrators. This
political opening brought local competition, extended the agenda of public
discussion to subjects of social justice and rights in general, and threatened
to remove from institutional power the traditional political networks and
interests, as well as extending the interpretive frameworks associated with
them.

The Political Equilibrium in Jeopardy and Reaction

This opening could be observed in the regions where the guerrilla movement and its legal political allies had significant support, such as Urabá and
the south of Córdoba, the lower Cauca and the middle Magdalena, and the
foothills of the eastern mountain range – indeed, the centers in which the
paramilitary nuclei grew up. These regions are largely dominated by networks related to the Liberal Party and with a tendency toward economies
based on large properties or concentration of landownership in few hands
(Cubides 1995). Those networks, besides perceiving the political risk, were
being courted at the same time by the emerging and powerful drug lords,
who were purchasing rural and urban properties in the zones with social
and armed conflict from the end of the 1970s onward (Romero 1995; Reyes
1997).

   In contrast, it is worth emphasizing the political evolution of the departments of Southwest Colombia (e.g., Nariño, Cauca, Tolima, Huila, and
Caquetá), in which the crisis of the Liberal and Conservative parties has
been profound. The leadership structures have tended to disintegrate, and
the paramilitary groups have had more difficulty consolidating their base,
an objective more easily attained in the aforementioned regions. The political vacuum is being occupied by new, nontraditional social and political
movements, with agendas closer to social democracy and multiculturalism,
as observed in the regional elections of October 2000. It is necessary to
underline the fact that these emergent networks in the Southwest have
managed to establish a progressive platform, condemning the use of violence and advocating a negotiated end to the armed conflict, without
renouncing greater democratization. Up to now these groups have not been
accused of supporting armed subversion, still the recourse of the traditional
politician to disqualify more democratic tendencies. They have been the
main target of the paramilitary groups, which faithfully apply the principle

of cutting the supply lines, meaning the relationship of the civilian population to the guerrillas. The result is a pattern of murder, disappearances,
forcible displacement, or the silencing of those who have sought reform and
greater participation in the structures of power. Meanwhile, the guerrillas
have responded to that "dirty war" by fortifying its military and intelligence apparatuses and by increasing kidnapping and extortion of wealthy
families of both urban and rural areas.

Thus, political opening and the peace negotiations, combined with the
decentralization and the election of mayors, jeopardized – or that was the
perception of the traditional leaders at least – the established political equilibrium in the regions where the guerrilla movement and its political allies
had acquired influence. But in addition, that same liberalization also offered
prospects for collective action on the part of the hitherto marginalized
groups and social sectors, an opening up of the limited system of electoral
representation and the overwhelming domination of the local and rural elites
in regional and national politics. The leaders and activists who headed the
mobilizations were the main victims of the resulting holocaust. It is true that
the guerrilla strategy of "combination of all forms of struggle" – electoral,
armed, and social – especially of the Revolutionary Armed Forces of
Colombia (FARC), contributed nothing productive to President Betancur's
1982 peace proposal. However, the counterinsurgency strategy had a still
more injurious effect on the possibilities for reconciliation by eliminating the
political movements that arose out of the peace accords with the guerrillas.
By annihilating the political arm of the strongest insurgent movement, the
FARC, and the regional movements of other leftist groups, the reaction
against the new movements ended all possibility of clipping the wings of the
"hawks" inside the guerrilla movement. It prevented those in favor of legal
forms of public participation from harvesting the benefits of a successful
political mobilization. That strategy also sent a signal from the authorities
that the use of violence as a means of resolving conflicts was legitimate. This
has been at the root of the human rights crisis that the country has been experiencing for the past two decades. Thus, through terror, the paramilitary
and its civilian and state collaborators began a career as decisive actors in
the possibilities of a negotiated peace.

Without being linked to the guerrilla movement, although some had
organic nexuses to it, many (landless peasants, indebted small holders,
exploited rural laborers, homeless urban dwellers and those living in neighborhoods that lacked most basic services, workers and unionists persecuted
for calling for labor rights and rights of free association) saw in the peace
negotiations the political opening and the decentralization an opportunity
to mobilize and to further the democratization of the country's social and
political relations. Something similar happened in the cases of the indigenous movement and the black communities looking for recognition of their
demands and multiculturalism; human rights and environmental activists

advocating respect for life, biodiversity, and sustainable development; and journalists broadening the attenuated local public spheres. In short, a diversity of groups, networks, and constituencies with proposals for greater social justice and pluralism became involved. These aspirations, without being revolutionary, had been supported by the different insurgent groups and ignored by the two main parties, Liberal and Conservative. Power sharing by these two parties consolidated a stable winning coalition at the local and national level, leaving radicals and communists without the possibilities of participating in even local or regional governments, not to mention national. Pushed to the margins and stigmatized, these groups, especially communists, took the road of armed insurgency and looked for the support of marginalized sectors, mostly peasants and poor dwellers, a support that should disappear as a result of the political process, and not through massacres, the paramilitary solution.

Political Modernization versus Restoration of Order

The central thesis of this chapter sustains that whereas the antecedents of the paramilitary groups lie in the retaliation of drug traffickers against guerrilla kidnapping and extortion in the early 1980s, they soon evolved toward an antisubversive project that relied on the complacence and collaboration of sectors of the armed forces (end of the 1980s and beginning of the 1990s). Finally around them coalesced a movement to restore the rural status quo, dating from the mid-1990s. Its aim is to neutralize any attempt at reform that would touch the structures of rural power and wealth. The established order has been disturbed by the attempts at political modernization and social reform led from the office of the president, especially under the conservative presidents Belisario Betancur (1982–1986) and the current president, Andrés Pastrana (1998–2002), implied by peace negotiations with the guerrillas.

In opposing the talks, regional elites have allied with sectors of the armed forces, local politicians, mostly Liberals, and the new landlords who originated as drug lords. Of significance is the fact that the growth of the paramilitary in recent years has been accompanied by an important recruitment of retired members of the armed forces. The core of the paramilitary's Calima Front in the Cauca Valley is made up of retired military personnel, as it proclaimed in the pamphlets announcing its appearance in Cali. The personal guard of the paramilitary chief, Carlos Castaño, also deserted from the ranks of the army's elite troops, according to Castaño's own reports.[4] However, it is possible that this powerful coalescence of such diverse sectors will lose force in the future as a result of Plan Colombia and the pressure of the United States to strengthen the legitimacy of the state – which also includes the armed forces. Those paramilitary and security forces alliances that arose in the face of a common enemy have been the target of Democratic senators in the U.S. Congress, an argument that will resurface when more external resources are needed. The warnings of the current U.S. ambassador Anne Patterson that she will cancel the visa to enter the United States of those found to be supporting or financing the paramilitary are an indication of pressure. Nevertheless, these pressures also can have a boomerang effect, as was demonstrated with the cashiering of 388 members of the armed forces at the end of 2000, some of them for human rights violations. The head of the paramilitary forces recruited approximately 50 troops, trained in all types of tactical warfare.[5]

Military discharges and condemnations of officers who through omission or commission aided the paramilitary can have a similar effect. An illustrative example is the case of the army general Jaime Alberto Uscátegui and the massacre of Mapiripán in 1997, in which more than forty-five peasants died despite the warnings of local authorities of the imminence of the attack. Nevertheless, everything depends on the development of a civilian-led policy and a policy of reconciliation. With vacillation and improvisation, it seems that President Pastrana insists on that direction. In particular, his defense minister, Luis Fernando Ramirez, responded to congressional critics who queried the official policy on the paramilitaries by indicating that the debate is hypocritical because it is confined itself to investigating members of the armed forces, without denouncing civilians and business leaders who endorse and support that practice. Such a charge, acknowledging the endorsement and support for private armies from the well-to-do sectors of civil society, had never before been heard in public from a high-level official, at least in the Liberal administrations that governed between 1986 and 1998.

The emphasis on security in the evaluation of the paramilitary phenomenon has been accompanied by other developments in the peace negotiations. A decade ago the discussion centered on the access to material resources and public recognition for excluded and dispossessed sectors; now the debate is focused on protection and security for affluent property owners affected by kidnapping and extortion. This change has been accompanied by numerical growth in the paramilitary organization, the tendency to weld different scattered groups into a single national organization, and an undeniable strategic and leadership capacity in its commander in chief, Carlos Castaño. He has managed to create an image of avenger and lawman opposed to the guerrilla abuses and kidnappings, guaranteeing explicitly the status quo and becoming the strategic opponent of those beyond the state organization. Castaño has revealed the absence of leadership and competence in the Colombian state, semiparalyzed by the prolonged crisis of the two major parties – if they can be called parties – and widespread corruption in the handling of public resources, accentuated by drug trafficking and the armed conflict.

Self-declared "representative of the middle class," the head of the self-defense groups has shown a deadly effectiveness in the counterinsurgency fight, assassinating those he considers a "guerrilla collaborator." In the process he not only has gained the support of those opposed to a possible peace process – cattle ranchers, large landowners, sectors of the armed forces, local power brokers, drug traffickers and others – but also arouses admiration in the urban public by combating kidnapping and extortion. Supposedly he also supports freedom, which, in his conception, is in no way a synonym for democracy. The head of the self-defense has followed to the letter the aphorism "In Colombia it is necessary to be rich or dangerous" to be heard by those with power (Salazar 1993).

In this counterinsurgency undertaking the paramilitary organizations have been successful in some regions, expelling the guerrillas from some areas without weakening them militarily, especially the FARC. In the process they are doing away with social and political movements trying to foster a democratization of the regional and national public life. This relation between the paramilitary and regional elites, and their reaction against the possibilities of democratization, are highlighted in this chapter. In order to substantiate the argument the chapter proceeds as follows. First, an assessment of collective action from the beginning of the 1982 peace negotiations and the pressure for a greater democratization is presented. Then the role of the armed forces in that process and its conception of "the enemy within" is discussed in relationship to the paramilitary's depictions of "guerilla collaborators" and "plainclothes guerrillas." Finally, the text recounts the development of the paramilitary groups during the 1990s, their growth during the Liberal governments, and the strengthening of the traditional political networks, particularly those that have flown the Liberal colors.

Collective Action, Peace Negotiations, and Democratization

As an outcome of the foreign debt crisis, the decade of the 1980s was baptized "the lost decade" in terms of economic development in Latin America. In Colombia the impact of that phenomenon did not require the structural adjustments demanded of most of the countries in the region. Nevertheless, in terms of political development and democratic governability, judging by the situation at the end of the 1980s, the results of almost a decade of peace negotiations were ambiguous, if not calamitous. *Al filo del caos* (On the edge of chaos) was the title of a book published by prestigious academics on the reality of the country as the new decade began (Leal and Zamosc 1990). With the exception of the constituent assembly called for in 1991, there was little to feel optimistic about. As one essayist expressed it after the promulgation of the new constitution, it needs a political agent, the collective will to put it into practice (Castellanos 1992).

In effect, the guarantees for the political opposition, one of the supposed results of the peace process, had for all practical purposes been erased by the annihilation, and silencing, of several of the more important opposition groups, and with this the possibilities for broader and more inclusive political movements. The antagonism to the peace process expressed by part of the military, a good part of the business elites, the rural landowners, and most of the hierarchy of the Catholic Church; the ambiguity of the two traditional parties; and an unfavorable international Cold War climate did not allow any progress toward reconciliation. The opposition by these groups and organizations created greater distrust and distance between the factions and polarized identities yet further.

The consolidation of drug trafficking and the purchase of rural and urban land in the regions in conflict were decisive factors for that polarization. The shared views of traffickers and the military about the necessity of a "political cleansing" to achieve pacification rather than employing a policy of reconciliation were decisive factors. The report of Attorney General Carlos Jiménez in 1983 and of the director of DAS in 1989 revealed the tip of the iceberg, not the shape of the whole. Likewise, the guerrillas' methods of generating income through kidnapping, extortion, and involuntary contributions laid the foundations for the discontent and polarization of rural proprietors, merchants, and shopkeepers and the subsequent consolidation of self-defense and paramilitary groups.

The period 1986–1993 was the most violent in the recent history of the country, precisely the period in which the largest number of political killings occurred and in which the first three elections of mayors took place. In effect, 15,958 politically motivated homicides and extrajudicial executions took place in those eight years, compared with 2,853 in the preceding eight years. In 1988 alone 2,738 cases occurred. Over the same period there were 1,379 disappearances, against 577 during the eight years prior to the period (Colombian Commission of Jurists 1997). During these years paramilitary groups financed by drug traffickers and rural elites, and supported by security forces, intensified a campaign of political cleansing directed against the left and began a career as decisive actors in the possibilities of a negotiated peace. Paradoxically, the decentralization, pushed as a way to promote democracy and local autonomy, polarized the armed conflict still further and has exposed those active in local politics to the threats of the paramilitary, the guerrillas, and the security forces.

In spite of the polarization on the subject of peace and the violence unleashed against groups and social actors opposed to bipartisanism, the period 1982–1990 was characterized by a significant popular mobilization. It comprised a diversity of responses to the structural changes in the economy, in the attitudes of the official elites, and in the state structure. Although the political violence reduced the possibilities of meeting, communicating, and demonstrating in public, the social organizations took advantage of the opportunities offered by the peace negotiations to make their voices heard. On many occasions these voices were manipulated by guerrilla groups in line with their strategic objectives; however, it also has to be recognized that the guerrilla groups were perhaps their only allies in their aims of social improvement. All in all, social organizations moved toward a greater pluralism and autonomy from both traditional parties, they questioned the authoritarianism of the guerrillas, and they achieved greater decision capacity.

This was clear in the trade-union arena. The creation of the Central Unitaria de Trabajadores or CUT (United Workers' Union) in 1986 was a landmark in the history of the country by moving beyond partisan trade unionism, promoting political and ideological pluralism. It also worked to form a common front in response to flexibilizing the labor market, technological changes in production, and a dramatic loss in the trade-union membership, which dropped from 15.9 percent affiliation in 1980, to 9.3 percent in 1984, and 6.2 percent in 1992 (Londoño 1993). The convergence in the CUT of Conservative trade unionism, much of the Liberal union movement, the union organized around the Communist Party, and the independents affiliated with other left-wing organizations indicated an encouraging degree of maturity in this social sector, or at least a sense of survival, for which it had not been known in the past. The formation of the CUT united under a single leadership nearly 65 percent of the unionized workers in the country. The consolidation of the process of unification, along with the political openness and peace, high-priority issues on the union agenda, also came accompanied by an increase in strike activity. In fact, between 1982 and 1990, 1,252 strikes were called, which represented an increase of 62 percent in relation to the previous period (Archila 2000). The years of greatest strike activity were 1985 and 1989, with 163 and 167 strikes respectively.

The civic and popular mobilization reached unprecedented heights in the 1980s, which demonstrated the opportunity sensed by different organizations and leaders. Without a doubt, the negotiations between government and the guerrillas opened spaces for the mobilization and expression of identities of resistance or radicalism in the regions, as well as demands for the recognition of rights and state investment. Between 1982 and 1990, 270 civic strikes were held (Archila 2000). According to Restrepo (1994), 163 municipalities served as the setting for the action between 1982 and 1986, and 298 municipalities between 1986 and 1989. The requests ranged from the provision of public services and support for peasant production, to defense of life and respect for human rights. Without hiding his enthusiasm, and also an exaggerated optimism, one of the leaders of the M-19 guerrilla movement declared sententiously that the "the sum of the Colombian revolution is the guerrilla movement plus the civic movement," recognizing the scope of the protest. Collective action in the countryside was also remarkable: 160 regional mobilizations between 1982 and 1990, 8 agrarian strikes between 1986 and 1990, 110 takeovers of public offices between 1982 and 1990, and 684 land invasions over the same period

(Salgado and Prada 2000; Archila, 2000). In the latter statistic the case of Urabá was outstanding.

Although collective action was also part of the guerrilla strategy of negotiation with the government, one should not scorn the capacity, autonomy, and opportunism of the organized social groups to push their agendas of greater state investment and greater democratization. The increase in protest was accompanied by various attempts at centralization and regional and national coordination: the Unitary Housing Congress in 1985, the communal congress in the same year that set up the National Commission of Communal Action Boards, the Second National Congress of Civic Movements and Popular Organizations held in 1986, and numerous local and regional meetings. With the growth of the guerrilla organizations over the decade – concretely the FARC, the M-19, the ELN, and the EPL – and the fight over control of the social organizations, an old debate resurfaced: whether the guerrillas acted to control state authoritarianism, or whether it exists as a result of guerrilla activities (Santos 1990). What is certain is that the greater pluralism within the social organizations won in this decade was crosscut by the polarization of the armed conflict and the attempts to subordinate them to a specific political project.

The indigenous movement also changed significantly in the 1980s. In 1982 the first National Meeting of Indigenous Peoples was held out of which the National Indigenous Peoples' Organization of Colombia (ONIC) was born. ONIC obtained official recognition and strengthened the hand of the Regional Indigenous Council of Cauca, CRIC. The Betancur government also accepted the indigenous councils as independent forms of political organization and the reserve as a territorial unit. This unleashed an unprecedented and accelerated process of ethnic and political affirmation. In part that process was expressed in the armed Movement Quintín Lame during the 1980s. The movement's leaders took advantage of the chance at reintegration into civilian life that was offered by the peace talks that closed the decade. The case of the Quintín is a unique experience of the successful reinsertion of the guerrillas and the social movement that supported it and a revealing example of electoral success. This was demonstrated by the election of Floro Tunubalá, the first indigenous governor in Colombia, who defeated a Liberal-Conservative alliance in Cauca in the elections of October 2000.

In the 1980s the pressure of the different armed movements and the disagreements with them contributed to reinforcing the cohesion of the different indigenous groups in the southwestern part of the country. They consolidated not only their organization, but also the independence and autonomy of the indigenous movement vis-à-vis the traditional parties and the armed actors. This also helped to strengthen the reserve system faced with the pressure of landowners and settlers, historical opponents for control of land. This cultural and ethnic affirmation was reflected in the constitutional guarantees of respect for their political and territorial autonomy, won in the 1991 constitution (Orjuela 1993). The recent electoral results recognize their persistence in the affirmation of rights routinely denied by the elites of Cauca, an affirmation that has still more merit because it was obtained through nonviolent means, despite the domination and persecution, sometimes violent, by these regional elites.

The subject of human rights was one of the most energizing for civil society during the 1980s. The way that political and military authorities have addressed this new issue since the 1970s, when it first became an area of public controversy, has exposed the official understanding about who is the subject of rights and who is not, and, therefore, what type of limits should the state acknowledge when the time comes to apply the law or to use coercion. The subject has been related to the state's handling of social protest, the opposition and political revolt, and whether these can be considered to be threats to national security or treason. Depending on where the different social sectors place the limit, the implications for the relations between authorities and citizenry are definitive.

One of the most hotly contested points during the 1980s was whether human rights comprised a legitimate public agenda, or whether they were only an instrument of armed subversion to discredit the troops. Although the subject has had a high priority on the international agenda on democratization since the 1980s, it is still viewed with suspicion in some political circles and with open misgivings by the military establishment. By the end of the 1980s there were approximately one hundred human rights groups and committees in different regions and municipalities of the country. These have gradually gained credibility at all levels, albeit only on the civilian side of the government. Confronted by the gravity of the violations and international pressures, the government inaugurated the Presidential Advisory Council on Human Rights at the end of the 1980s, recognizing the subject as a high-priority issue on the public agenda.

The mobilization by sectors described here gives some idea of the scope of the collective action advocating resources, reforms, and guarantees for the exercise of rights. Nevertheless, the regional contexts for the democratic *apertura* and negotiations between the central government and the guerrillas must be taken into account because they are critical to a correct appraisal of the social mobilization. The failure to consider the polarized regional contexts results in a failure to perceive the fear and intimidation of local elites by the new political situation. The violent response of these elites can only be understood by considering both the presence of new landowners associated with drug trafficking and the ideas held by the military high command about the peace process and political liberalization. The direct association of the demands for democratization, reform, and recognition with the armed insurgency, without recognizing the political nature of the situation, turned out to be fatal.

Democratization, the Armed Forces, and Military Autonomy

State transformation and the political *apertura* initiated at the beginning of the 1980s coincided with one of the most decisive moments of the Cold War and with the polarization born out of the Central American conflict. This context framed the opportunities that the changes offered in terms of the East-West dispute, emphasizing their ideological dimension. This happened to the detriment of calls for social justice, political recognition, and reforms from organized armed and unarmed actors. In this context, the Colombian military, molded and trained to fight the "enemy within," became a formidable opponent to the attempts at reconciliation and expansion of the political system initiated by President Belisario Betancur in 1982 (Leal 1994a, 1994b; Dávila 1998).

The tension between the executive branch and the military establishment, a situation that has occasionally reached the state of open confrontation between presidency and armed forces,[6] has been a constant up to now when peace talks between the insurgency and government are being discussed. The difference of opinion between these two has formed a "path dependency" that limits the peace initiatives and reduces the possibility of a political solution to the conflict.[7] This open rivalry, and sometimes subterranean dispute, over the handling of the problem of public order and the policy vis-à-vis the armed opposition has lasted nearly seventeen years, creating the context for the development of paramilitary and self-defense groups. The tension between the military and the presidency, and the resulting ambiguity in the military subordination-autonomy dichotomy[8] confronting the civilian government and its peace policies, has been the basis for the convergence at the regional level of the social and political sectors opposed to negotiation.

The struggle over autonomy-subordination between the presidency and armed forces, particularly the army, had unexpected effects at the subnational level. The military's opposition to the peace policies of the executive led the armed forces to seek support from the regional elites harassed by guerrilla fund-raising at their expense and distraught by the social mobilization. This was a fact during the beginning of the negotiations between government and guerrillas in the early 1980s. In fact, the sensation of betrayal felt by many generals and rural elites created a meeting place for these two groups (Behar 1985; Romero 2000).

Regional elites and the military agreed in their opposition to the Betancur government's peace policies, and since then that coincidence has defined the possibilities of attempts at reconciliation beyond simple demobilization and reintegration of the guerrillas, as demonstrated by the FARC and the ELN. That regional level convergence, added to the investment of drug traffickers in the purchase of rural estates and urban properties the length and breadth of the country, evolved toward the present-day paramilitary and self-defense phenomenon.

The functional alliance between regional elites, sectors of the armed forces, and drug traffickers against the guerrillas was further strengthened with the reforms of political and administrative decentralization begun in the mid-1980s. In effect the balance of local political power was threatened. As a result of the peace process, on the one hand, and of the new state structure that allowed the election of local-level leadership, on the other, there was a genuine possibility that former guerrillas or candidates from left-wing political fronts allied with the guerrillas – the Patriotic Union (UP), the Popular Front, and A Luchar (Fight!) – would win local elections. This would break the local and regional monopoly of the Liberal and Conservative parties.

This jeopardy brought the dispute over local political and bureaucratic power in the regions of guerrilla influence to a boil in 1988, 1990, and 1992, the years of the three first local elections. These electoral battles were unprecedented in Colombian history, because until 1988 the president named the governors of departments, and these subsequently appointed the mayors. To think that former guerrillas, their spokesmen, or the leaders of the traditional left parties would become powerful political leaders with the capacity to compete for local power worsened the intransigence of many years of resentment and hatred accumulated over the course of the irregular war.

While this process of radicalization and positioning of interests was taking place at the regional level, in which the armed forces found support and endorsement, at the national level the opposite was occurring. The greater protagonism of the military in the functioning of the political regime from the mid-1970s exposed the institution to scrutiny and criticism from national and international public opinion. Thus, from the start of the negotiations between the government and guerrillas in 1982, attempts to expand democracy and respect for civil and human rights were accompanied by a renewed interest on the part of the academy, intellectuals, factions of the two traditional parties, journalists, and the general public in the handling of public order and national security. Also, parts of the judiciary and civil society denounced the repeated violations of human rights and attacks directed against political opponents, left-wing activists, trade unionists, human rights defenders, and the population itself by the military, which also led to disciplinary and penal investigations.

The greater interference of the presidency in military and defense matters, as well as the public discussion on the scope of military jurisdiction, opened a debate on the military's jurisdiction and prerogatives. The country had lived under state-of-siege legislation in a practically uninterrupted fashion since the 1960s. That discussion was another facet of the intense pressures advocating democratization and affirming civil and human rights during the 1980s. These had been denied in practice through the policy on public order that dealt with social demands and, by extension, democracy on military terms during the National Front governments (1958–1974) and its formal and informal prolongation.

Attempts by the civilian side of the state to recover jurisdiction over the problem of public order and the defense of political and civil rights, an abridgment of military jurisdiction, were considered by the high command to be a reduction of instruments for the control of subversion. It also had the unexpected effect of reinforcing the regional alliances against subversion. "Attorney general syndrome" was what the military called the fear of possible legal consequences of "enforcing the Constitution." In the military environment it is commonly said that "we are in Cundinamarca [a department in the center of the country of which Bogota is the capital] and not in Dinamarca [Denmark]," in order to pressure for "war legislation" that could give them back the powers they lost a decade ago. In the opinion of the high command this would enable them to maintain public order. The absence of a legal status such as state of exception to protect military practices that ignore individual and collective rights has been the reason adduced by the Ministry of Defense to account for military inefficiency in combating the guerrillas. Thus indirectly to this is attributed the growth in demands for private security – that is, support for paramilitary groups.[9]

Tables 7.1 and 7.2 show important tendencies in military jurisdiction over different areas of public security, which indicate a conflicting demilitarization of these areas in favor of greater civil and democratic management.[10] This has been energetically resisted in the regions characterized by social mobilization and a guerrilla presence. The trying of civilians by military courts was one of the first prerogatives opposed by civil society and important groups of the judicial branch during the 1980s. It was finally prohibited in the 1991 constitution. The 1993 reform of the police granted the force greater independence from the military, but it continues to form part of the Defense Ministry.

The person responsible for this portfolio is a civilian appointed by the president since the early 1990s; prior to that it was the officer with the greatest seniority. Promotions are no longer the internal prerogative of the armed forces but are supervised by the executive branch and monitored by civil society, international nongovernmental organizations (NGOs), and even the government of the United States. An area in which there has been significant, but still insufficient, progress is that of the intelligence services, which still shows a strong military influence. The absence of extensive public discussion and congressional debate on the subjects of defense and security is nevertheless noteworthy, especially since the defense budget reached 3.6 percent of GDP in 1998, the highest in Latin America according to Semanario *La Nota* (June 1999).

A subject on which very little information exists, given its effects on military treatment of the general population, is that of foreign aid and training abroad, in this case by U.S. military advisers. This point is important

TABLE 7.1. *Change in Military Prerogatives in Colombia, 1974–2000*

Army Function	1974–1981	1982–1990	1991–1997	1998–2000
Coordination of the defense sector	High	High	Moderate	High-moderate
In the judicial system	High	High-moderate	Moderate	Moderate
Autonomy in disturbances and internal uprisings	High	High	High-moderate	High-moderate
In the political sphere	High	High	Moderate	Moderate-low
In the intelligence services	High	High	High-moderate	High-moderate
In promotion criteria	High	High	High-moderate	Moderate
In receiving foreign aid and training	Moderate	Moderate	Low	High
Control over economic activity	Military light industry, importation and domestic sale of arms and munitions	Military light industry, importation and domestic sale of arms and munitions	Military light industry, security services, importation and domestic sale of arms and munitions	Military light industry, security services, importation and domestic sale of arms and munitions

Sources: Torres 1986; Leal 1994a, 1994b; Reyes 1990; García-Peña 1995; Dávila 1998.

because the identity and internal cohesion of the armed forces in Latin America were constituted not only in relation to the domestic context, but greatly influenced by the international system, demonstrated during the East-West confrontation and the Cold War.

One of the prerogatives that has most polarized society is the concept of military jurisdiction, by which crimes committed by members of the armed forces are judged by military courts. This privilege, in the name of esprit de corps, has served to protect members of the military from administra-

TABLE 7.2. *Some Institutional Changes in the Defense Sector, 1974–2000*

	1974–1981	1982–1990	1991–1997	1998–2000
Congressional role in the defense sector	Low	Low	Low–moderate	Moderate
Level of defense minister	Highest-ranking officer	Highest-ranking officer	Civilian appointed by the president	Civilian appointed by the president
Military official member of the cabinet	Defense minister	Defense minister	None	None

Sources: Torres 1986; Reyes 1990; Leal 1994a, 1994b; García-Peña 1995; Dávila 1998.

tive and penal sanctions when they are accused of breaking the law. That tension between the military, on the one hand, and sectors of the judiciary and civil society, on the other, over the jurisdiction to judge the crimes committed by soldiers has been the terrain of a bitter dispute since the 1970s. This is accentuated when the accusations refer to human rights violations. The controls that the judicial sector has struggled to impose on the military during the 1980s have been considered by the high command as serious constraints to the fulfillment of their constitutional duty to maintain public order, especially during a period of armed confrontation.

This tension has had important operational consequences within the armed forces. It is frequently cited by the army as a factor generating low morale in the troops, as the factor responsible for their lack of effectiveness in combating the guerrillas despite increasing resources, and indirectly as an element favoring the development of paramilitary groups. In the most recent effort to recover the functions of the judicial police lost at the end of the 1980s, Defense Minister Luis Fernando Ramirez presented a package of reforms to "fortify the operational capacity" of the troops. The reform contemplated the extension of military jurisdiction in the area of public safety. The minister justified it by saying that "to the extent to which we strengthen the armed forces and the police with more legal tools to act, the fewer violations of human rights we will have in Colombia." Ramirez added that "what has happened is completely the inverse, we have been taking away their tools, their powers, their authority, with the result that we have encouraged them to sit with their arms crossed while vigilante justice comes into being."

As one would expect, the Ramirez proposal was received with enormous skepticism by the human rights NGOs, columnists and commentators, and opposition groups in Congress. The explanations that the new faculties would be closely supervised by the attorney general's office and the office of the prosecutor general were not convincing. It is important to point out that during the period 1991–1997, immediately following the conclusion of the Cold War, U.S. military aid and advice to the troops were at their lowest levels. This was the result of their record of human rights violations and the importance of this subject on the agenda of the Democratic government that replaced the Bush administration in 1992. It is also useful to remember that the beginning of this period coincides with the appointment of the first civilian defense minister in thirty-seven years and with greater interference from the executive branch in matters of security, financing, and organization of the armed forces. This was accompanied by a significant improvement in wages and social security for officers and a substantial increase in the budget, which reached 30 percent of the central government's annual budget. Paradoxically, these years – especially toward the end of the period – also coincided with one of the military's most serious institutional crises in recent decades and overlaps with the development and consolidation of paramilitary forces with a national scope and coverage.

Insofar as strong international and national leadership was missing, a reading of the situation suggests that significant sectors of the armed forces chose to continue to use the same outdated logic of fighting "the enemy within." They neither examined the new international agenda nor explored possibilities of reconciliation. Even more serious, they failed to examine the credentials of their fellow travelers on that antisubversive trip. A strong international leadership would have offered ideological, political, and ethical motivations to justify a mission in the conflictive and divided Colombian setting (the need formerly met by the Cold War). At the same time, they faced a loss of prerogatives to a domestic civilian authority that also failed to provide leadership. It would be worth examining the responsibility that Liberal administrations of the day bear for that absence of political leadership because the responsibility for leading the country through the period 1986–1998, precisely the period in which the paramilitary phenomenon developed, fell to that party.

Part of the origin of that military autonomy vis-à-vis the presidency can be located in the resistance of regional elites to the peace policies and, in general, to the elite's opposition to interventions coming from the center that entail social or political responsibilities – such as the abolition of large estates, respect for labor and political rights and freedoms, and property taxes on rural property. They also lent support to the hard-line policy favored by some sectors in the army (Romero 2000). Nevertheless the effects of the international East-West cleavage during the Cold War were also important. The beginning of the peace talks in 1982 paints a clear picture. Although the domestic conditions did not favor the initiative of President Betancur, the international situation was still worse. The Cold War was at its peak in the 1980s. In Central America, the Reagan administration openly supported the armed opposition to the Sandinista regime, and those counterattacking the revolutionary movements in El Salvador and Guatemala, while vehemently protecting its Caribbean backyard. President Reagan gave the name "freedom fighters" to the Nicaraguan "contra," a term that offered the hard-liners in the Colombian military a political and moral justification for its calls to landowners to take up their own defense. Groups within the armed forces needed to vindicate their violence against reformers and radicals, and thus to respond to the accusations of human rights violations. Lewis Tambs, U.S. ambassador to Colombia in the early 1980s, contributed to framing leftist rebels as common criminals by coining the term "narcoguerrilla," alluding to the role of the insurgents as middle-men between drug dealers and coca farmers.

The peace negotiations of the 1980s demonstrated the difficulties of creating a new political community and redefining the two-party system. The talks revealed the inflexible nature of the identities molded during the prolonged armed conflict conducted within a Cold War ideology. The situation of the armed forces during the 1980s reveals how their identities were forged in relation to both domestic and foreign actors, in this case the U.S. government. The asymmetry of the relations between the United States and a country like Colombia shows that not only the international policy of a small country but also its domestic policy is limited: a process of national reconciliation is simultaneously an internal and international affair. The obstacles to strengthening the Colombian state and its institutions by redefining the political community revealed the depth to which the interests, images, and representations favored by the National Front and the Cold War were interwoven into the Colombian political culture. That the armed forces, supported by regional elites and drug traffickers turned landowners confronted the President's peace policies reveals the intensity of the antagonism. Few anticipated the magnitude of the reaction.

The 1990s: The Paramilitary, Self-Defense, and Political Recognition

From the first groups of hired assassins who entered the service of drug traffickers in the mid-1980s to the national counterinsurgency organization of today, there have been many changes to the original intentions, their alliances, and the political protection received. From guarding the drug lords' new estates, they moved to cooperating with the army's security forces to eliminate civilians linked to left-wing movements or suspected of collaborating with subversives. Later they formed part of a broader project of reconstructing the rural order. In the regions they have managed to dominate, this approaches a corporatist political system, in some cases based on large holdings and agribusiness.

Although the proper term for them has been a subject of debate,[11] in this study paramilitaries are understood to be armed groups organized to carry out operations of political "cleansing" and military consolidation, prior to assuming territorial control of an area. "Self-defense" refers to the organized groupings who defend themselves from an aggressor and attempt to maintain control of a territory without expansionary pretensions. The chapter argues that the difference lies in the aggressive or defensive nature of the group. Although that analytical element was helpful in differentiating the origin of some self-defense groups that reacted to guerrilla authoritarianism and their methods of raising funds, it can be deceptive when examining the evolution of the conflict. This is even more true in fluid situations like the Colombian one, in which the polarization of the confrontation has tended to attenuate the initial differences between the two forces.

Today the United Self-Defense Groups of Colombia, or the AUC, are made up of six groups, of which the Peasant Self-Defense Groups of Córdoba and Urabá, ACCU, are the most important.[12] The ACCU is in the leadership and is the only group with a national presence. The general staff of the AUC is made up of a member of each of the six self-defense groups that compose it, although the ACCU has an additional representative. Each self-defense group is independent in its financing, expansion, or alliances, as long as it remains faithful to its counterinsurgency discourse. Although the regional origins of the different groups are very diverse, a hypothesis can be advanced on the confluence of four factors that made their emergence possible: regional elites ready to support politically and to finance the paramilitary apparatuses; military advice, or at least cooperation from sectors of this organization; leadership of groups or individuals linked to drug trafficking; and sufficient political and military pressure of the guerrillas, or its allies, to maintain such a diverse group united.

Two main groups can be identified from which the groups known today arose and evolved: the MAS and the self-defense groups organized by the XIV Brigade in the Middle Magdalena. The group Death to Kidnappers, or MAS, was set up by drug traffickers around 1981 (Castro 1996) with the objective of eliminating criminals or members of the guerrillas who had observed the conspicuous wealth of this group and decided to acquire a share through extortion or kidnapping. From birth the MAS was closely linked to security forces of the army and the police. This fact helps to explain how the initial objectives of the alliance were readily broadened to include a wider scope and coverage once the drug lords turned landlords and consolidated their economic power as important property owners and investors.

The second nucleus can be located in the organization, equipping, and training of self-defense groups by the XIV Brigade of the army in the Middle Magdalena during the early 1980s (Medina 1990). These armed groups, formed by farmers and rich landowners, had the original intention to protect themselves from the FARC, but they soon became controlled by the

Medellín cartel. Later they became the basis of the hired guns who eliminated candidates for public office and presidential hopefuls from the Patriotic Union and the Democratic Alliance M-19 (two leftist groups that were a product of the peace process of the eighties). They also killed judges, journalists, trade unionists, and all those who confronted the traffickers, such as Luis Carlos Galán, the Liberal presidential candidate who was viewed as a sure winner in the 1990 presidential race.

During the period 1991–1992 there was almost a year of cessation of hostilities, as a result of the discussions of the Constituent Assembly and the promulgation of a new constitution in 1991. An additional factor was that the M-19 Movement, the Popular Army of Liberation (EPL), and the Movement Quintín Lame laid down their arms (as did the Current of Socialist Renovation of the Army of National Liberation [ELN] in 1993). In turn, in the regions influenced by the demobilized guerrilla groups, the paramilitaries also began to disarm, at least partially. A significant case with effects at the national level was seen in the department of Córdova and the neighboring banana growing zone of Urabá. Here the EPL had its main area of influence, as did the Castaño family and its private army, with its older brother Fidel at the head. The demobilization of the EPL and its conversion to a legal movement – Hope, Peace, and Freedom – was followed by the announcement of Fidel Castaño of the distribution of nearly 16,000 hectares of its property to poor peasants or victims of the armed confrontation. As well, he announced the founding of FUNPAZCOR, Foundation for the Peace of Córdoba, that would be responsible for offering technical and financial advice to more than 2,500 beneficiary families.

In spite of the efforts and attempts to surpass the conflict that the political opening and the new institutional forms created in the 1991 constitution allowed in Córdoba during 1991–1992, the inertia of the war ended up prevailing once again (Romero 2000). The territory formerly held by the EPL was occupied by guerrilla organizations that had not participated in the peace process, the FARC in particular, which led to the reactivation of the Castaño's military apparatus in 1993. Now using the name ACCU, Peasant Self-Defense Groups of Córdoba and Urabá, the rearming and reorganization of this group included a broader and more organized social and political support. The new group had a more sophisticated discourse, in line with its intention to become a military-political apparatus similar to the guerrillas. By 1995 the group had already reaffirmed its role as a counterinsurgent force, gradually replacing the army's security forces. It mounted a radio-telephone communication network that in Córdoba alone allowed 950 cattle ranches in the region to be in continuous contact.[13]

This form of information and communication installed in the territories controlled by the ACCU served as a model for the CONVIVIR security cooperatives proposed by the Defense Minister Fernando Botero, with the enthusiastic support of the army, during the administration of President

Ernesto Samper (1994–1998).[14] It was made clear that the CONVIVIR primarily comprised civilian-led networks for gathering intelligence, working in coordination with the military to benefit the inhabitants of a specific region. However, the risk existed that this would end up legally authorizing the operations of paramilitary groups, given the impossible task that central authorities faced in monitoring these associations, the type of arms they carried, and the work they did. As criticism and denunciations mounted concerning the overlap between the paramilitary and the CONVIVIRs, the Constitutional Court declared these associations "unconstitutional and against the law," as reported in *Revista Alternativa*, no. 16, December 1997.

From its new beginnings in 1995, the military apparatus that had sprouted in Córdoba and Urabá, now called the ACCU, had promoted the unification of the different paramilitary and self-defense groups under the same command and using a common name. Carlos Castaño, brother of Fidel and now commander of the ACCU, managed to form a military-political front of national dimensions in 1997, called the United Self-Defense Groups of Colombia, AUC, which operates like an advanced anticommunist troop in "defense of private property and free enterprise." It also offers its model of security to landowners in other regions of the country affected by the guerrillas. It defines itself as a "defensive civil organization in arms,"[15] forced to assume its role in opposition to the extraction of resources by the subversive and their threats to life. They justified their political "cleansing" through the state's "abandonment" of its duty to ensure property rights. In the zones where it has managed to consolidate its control, it has moved toward less arbitrary forms of authority. However, the aggressive and expansionary character of ACCU activity causes them to continue to be thought of as a paramilitary group, a characterization that their leaders would like to avoid. They prefer to cultivate the image of a self-defense group, which is thought to be more advantageous for its project of rural restoration.

A surprising feature of the new stage initiated by the ACCU was its pretense of being a political-military organization, similar to that of the guerrillas, and the search for political recognition. Although its objective was not to confront the state but to buttress its "weaknesses," this evolution corresponds to a significant change in its composition. Although it seems paradoxical, the ACCU in its new incarnation absorbed some of the ex-combatants and political worker cadres of the old EPL and other leftist organizations. Since the 1970s they had maintained a serious and long-running confrontation with the FARC in the region. In general they critiqued the guerrilla methods of relating to peasant communities. Thus, in the mid-1990s the ACCU was an unusual alliance among traders and businessmen with links to drug trafficking, cattle ranchers and agricultural exporters, and ex–guerrilla fighters or old militants of the legal or revolutionary left. This was not possible without tensions; however, the coalition remains united in the face of a common enemy. Nevertheless, the role and the position of the group that came from the left in the hierarchy of the ACCU has not been clear, other than supplying military commanders and relating their experience with political and social work with the civilian population.

The new composition of the ACCU was marked by a certain distancing, at least in their discourse, from the army, traditional parties, and drug trafficking. The process of building up a military and political apparatus also strengthened internal solidarities. Another characteristic that flourished with the new composition was the start-up of productive, educational, and community development programs in the ACCU zones of influence. This work has increased its social base. No longer is it endorsed only by the affluent; its supporters now include people from lower-income groups who have benefited from the development programs. The years of the Samper government (1994–1998) can be considered an adjustment period for this unusual coalition. Two independent, but not contradictory, lines of action could be observed. The first related to the legalization of the CONVIVIRs and was pushed by the businessmen and ranchers, while the second was more interested in obtaining recognition of the self-defense groups as legitimate political actors, an effort led by the so-called ex-guerrillas and those with more counterinsurgent aims.

The very pressure exerted on the Samper administration by the government of the United States and the international human rights organizations to react to the obvious growth of the paramilitary phenomenon had cohesive effects. The solid social support that the ACCU received from landowners in Córdoba is testified to in the letter that seventy-five ranchers sent to the defense minister in January 1997. The letter was provoked by the persecution of Carlos Castaño and the public announcements offering 500 million pesos reward for information as to his whereabouts. The letter read, "Castaño took away our fear and taught us to fight against our enemy." This indicates the transformation of the political behavior of this social group, the support of central authority in this region of the country, and the solidity of local and regional loyalties, contrasted to national ties, that the ACCU has achieved.

Law, Democratization, and Armed Apparatuses

What the letter does not mention is that for Castaño the fundamental enemy has been the civilian population. He himself affirms it, "in war, the term unarmed civilian is relative. Two-thirds of the guerrillas are unarmed members who operate as civilians and collaborate with the guerrillas" (Castro 1996). This conception of the conflict has turned any individual that the self-defense groups consider suspect (a feat that is not difficult) into a "military objective." Another term coined in this peculiar way of understanding criticism and dissent is the "parasubversive," who can be anyone who disagrees with the AUC and its different components. A procession of intellectuals, university professors, journalists, simple human rights activists, and trade unionists has been exiled abroad or silenced by accusations of being a "parasubversive" – an increasingly frequent experience since 1998. To this must be added the two million people displaced by the conflict over the past six years and the human rights crisis that has been evident since the 1980s.

What continues to be troubling is the persistent relationship between sectors of the armed forces and the paramilitary observed in several regions of the country. Likewise, some of the ideological and operative accords between these two armed apparatuses, which want to defeat the FARC and ELN without establishing and holding a superior ethical and moral position, are causes for concern. Although the military has been one of the supporters of the fragmented two-party regime (questioned enough, by others), it has also become an institutional obstacle to the consolidation of democracy and a negotiated end to the conflict (Dávila 1998). In fact, recent events have to do with the retirement of three commanders between April and August 1999, accused of promoting paramilitary groups or allowing these groups to attack unarmed populations in two of the most crucial zones of guerrilla confrontation, with more than one hundred civilian casualties. They are General Rito Alejo del Río, commander of the XVII Brigade headquartered in Urabá; General Fernando Millán, commander of the V Brigade based in Bucaramanga; and General Alberto Bravo, Millán's successor in the same jurisdiction. Despite the reiterated announcements of the high command that this alliance is not an institutional policy, the periodic repetition of similar events suggests the conclusion that a tendency must exist inside the military that keeps this relationship alive and that along the way discredits the entire institution by showing the military violating the same law they claim to defend.

It is also necessary to recognize that part of the political conditions for the surprising advance of the paramilitary groups in the past two years started with the electoral boycott of the guerrillas, especially the ELN, during the municipal elections that ended 1997. This was clear in the south of the department of Bolívar, an area forming near the Middle Magdalena, the scene of an intense armed conflict, displacement, and massacres in recent years. The sabotage prevented very popular candidates from winning the races for mayor or opposed sizable groups of the population and the guerrilla, as occurred in Santa Rosa del Sur, Simití, and San Pablo – all in the south of Bolívar. Until recent years these were considered political bastions of the guerrillas. Today these municipalities are opposed to granting a demilitarized zone to the ELN, similar to the one the FARC hold in the south of the country. The guerrillas ignored not only decisions on electoral participation that whole communities had taken but also faced off against groups of the traditional elite from those municipalities. The guerrillas' enemies took advantage of these events to denounce their authoritarianism and to portray the arrival of the paramilitary as a chance at freedom. A similar feeling also arose following the exodus of about 5,000 peasants from the south of Bolivar toward Barrancabermeja (in the Middle Magdalena and where the main oil refinery of the country is located) at the end of 1999. They were protesting against the growing number of paramilitary groups in the region, the killing of several peasant leaders, and the inactivity of the authorities. However, the heavy-handed treatment of the marchers by the ELN during their stay in the urban center of Barrancabermeja also created discontent.

The case of the south of Bolivar shows that the new possibilities of participation offered by decentralization have shaken up the social organizations that benefited from the protection of the old system, allowing greater plurality and autonomy in its interior. However, it has also put into question the ways that the guerrilla movement exercises power. On the basis of guerrilla errors and authoritarianism, the paramilitary groups and their allies have managed to create a constituency for their project or points of their proposals, although the public may not agree with the terror of their methods. Although the use of violence against civilians suspected of helping the guerrillas, usually the poorest, has been a characteristic of paramilitary operations, it cannot be forgotten that concrete political and social groups have benefited from the effects of that terror, creating a powerful political base. It may be working quietly, but that does not mean that it is not maneuvering in the shadows.

In addition to the tension mentioned between the executive branch and the military over the definition of the peace policies, it is important to call attention to a new area of conflict between the military and another branch of the state that was strengthened by the 1991 constitution. This is the judicial branch, with the Office of the Prosecutor General at the top, and a series of instruments to defend the citizens from abuses of office on the part of state officials. This institutional strengthening was matched by a greater consciousness of the idea of rights and democratic demands coming from different social sectors, which has consolidated since the early 1990s. Nevertheless, this advance appears not to have been well understood by influential groups in the military establishment, aside from the police, a body that began its transformation in 1993 and continues the process today. In fact, perhaps the greatest concern of the army at the moment is the possibility that its members may be brought before the bench on charges of violating human rights. It is what a press commentator sympathetic to the armed forces described as "the state against the army," blaming the attorney general's office for a "war of laws" against the armed forces.[16]

At the heart of this new tension, this time not with the president's peace initiatives but with the enforcement of law and defense of the citizen by the prosecutor general, lies the conception of the conflict that still persists in the army, or at least within its security apparatuses. These groups still characterize those who do not accept their strategic postulates as "the enemy within." This is in harmony with the idea that the democratic struggle and the fight to reform the system, in the Colombian context of low-intensity warfare, is an "underground war." So says the general in active service, Adolph Clavijo, who considers that this war "is being directed and fought from the desks, from the political stage and with democratic universals, inside our own political, economic, legal, diplomatic and social institutions. The war has been deeply entrenched in the mass media to incline the balance in favor of this terrorist insurgency." In the breadth and vagueness of the previous line of argumentation, almost any activity could be fitted and made to appear as if it favored terrorism. Something similar happens to the AUC's incriminatory concept of "parasubversives."

It is known that the ACCU has become the refuge in the recent years of the military who have been "wallpapered," to use the colloquial term, or accused of violating human rights. The recent influx has been sufficient to generate friction within the coalition of the three sectors that compose the ACCU, in particular those identified as "ex-guerrillas," who have lost ground to the recent arrivals. In May 1999 Castaño acknowledged that thirteen army officers had joined the ACCU, not to break the law, but as a result of "the demoralization in the army." Castaño's head bodyguard, an army deserter, complains that "they want to put you up against the wall and smother you with paper day and night," at the same time as he rejects the control of civilian authorities.[17] This former army officer was a student at the School of the Americas, located at Fort Benning, Georgia. This school was famous for its counterinsurgency courses and its graduates' record of human rights violations, according to its opponents in the United States. In addition, the new AUC group in the Cauca Valley is made up of retired military, according to its own announcements.[18] Of 388 troops discharged, among other reasons for human rights violations at the end of year 2000, approximately 50 were recruited by Castaño.[19] The conclusion is that a broad spectrum of military in active service and retired members of the armed forces think that the military institution should be above the law, a special privilege of the job – or even a sector in which the end would justify any means.

Conclusions

The present work has examined the phenomenon of the paramilitary and self-defense forces from a different analytical framework than the one usually employed to address the subject. The context is that of the political modernization begun in 1982 with the peace negotiations between the government and leftist guerrillas, the political opening, and later the decentralization and the first election of mayors in 1987. The emphasis on the effects of the paramilitary on the possibilities of democratization initiated in 1982 aims to call attention to the extraordinary social mobilization for rights and democracy pushed by an impressive variety of regional, sectoral, and national actors over a twenty-year period from end of the 1970s. The almost exclusive attention directed to the guerrillas and the reaction to them have concealed those demands for justice and recognition. In their place appears a perspective in which armed actors have been almost the exclusive protagonists and, therefore, the ones around whom the peace negotiations have been centered. When examining the emergence of private armed groups with the opposite political orientation to that of the guerrilla, in a context of state transformation and change in the political equilibrium, this chapter attempts to locate them in a wider convergence of opposition to any reform that redistributes power and wealth in the rural sector. This would be a result of a successful negotiation with the insurgents. The chapter does not claim that this confluence has been the result of a plan defined beforehand by an upper echelon opposed to the peace talks and the possible reforms. Rather it is the outcome of different processes that were converging on the same point: to stop at any cost the redefinition of power and wealth that a successful incorporation of the guerrillas would bring to the regional political system in which they have – or had – influence.

The chapter discusses two well-defined periods in the origin and development of the paramilitary. First came the dispersed and uncoordinated appearance of different groups, prior to the 1991 constitution, which was partially a result of that great democratizing pressure to which those affected reacted violently but in a dispersed fashion. The second period, marked by coordination and expansion, began after 1992, when the failure of the negotiations with the largest guerrilla group, the FARC, led to an exacerbation of the armed conflict. This second period is characterized by the establishment of stages for the conquest of territories: first a period of military incursion, massacres, and "softening up" of possible civilian and social support for the guerrilla movement, with the purpose of isolating it and cutting any nexus with the population. Later comes a stage of consolidation, repopulation, and economic initiatives with the support of local elites. A third stage legitimizes the new order through state and private investments (CINEP-Justicia y Paz 1997). These three steps are what "paras" call "recovering territories for the established order," which is nothing other than the crudest form of *frentenacionalismo* as it functioned at its worst moments in the 1960s and 1970s, with its simplified public agenda of security and order. This is like taking a step backward of forty years in the slow and conflicting political modernization of the country, but now with rampant corruption and armed groups defending the interests of local elites.

The master key that triggered the different dynamics mentioned as promoting a convergence have been the efforts at political modernization led from the president's office through the peace negotiations. These attempts to redefine the political community, along with the political opening and decentralization, created opportunities for collective action by the different regional actors, but particularly for those in search of social justice and recognition. The tension between the executive and the military establishment with respect to the peace policy, and the convergence of regional elites and the most recalcitrant sectors of the armed forces to oppose the negotiations, created the space for the emergence of the paramilitary groups and, as an unintended consequence, the strengthening of their earliest promoters – the drug traffickers. From this it would be possible to conclude that the expansion of drug trafficking is a result of the failure of the peace negotiations, and not that its growth has exacerbated the armed conflict. The order of the sequence is critical, because the solutions proposed are deduced from it. Based on the first it could be argued that a successful peace process would lead to a solution for the eradication of illicit crops and drug trafficking. From the second it could be inferred that scaling up to a military solution would do away with drug trafficking, and thus peace would be achieved through the economic asphyxiation and military weakening of the guerrilla, but with little or no space for political reforms.

This work identifies three key actors in the reaction against political modernization: the drug traffickers; the economic elites and local politicians, largely rooted in the Liberal party; and sectors of the armed forces. Of the mentioned actors, the analysis gives the role of the armed forces and their conception of the armed conflict a greater explanatory weight in the trajectory that the democratization has followed in this country. The election of mayors and other electoral reforms in the late 1980s were expected to diminish violence. However, the failure of the peace negotiations and the possibility of redefining the political community produced an opposite effect. Local and regional politics became riskier than before and an arena of fierce and violent competition among the guerrillas, the paramilitaries, security forces, and local politicians. The reforms to improve political competition without peace, created the conditions for a visible state dissolution over the past decade in Colombia. Yet the work has also considered the explicit absence of civil leadership in the political sectors, in particular in the Liberal Party, the group that held the reins of power nationally, with parliamentary majorities during the years 1986 to 1998. The strategies derived from a Cold War ideology to solve the armed confrontation, whether by omission or commission, have turned the civilian population into the main target and, within this, the individual and collective agents who can – or could have – pushed a greater, and indispensable, democratic change in Colombia. To try to break the bonds between subversion and the general population by means of terror and assassination, without incorporating a political and reform process that demonstrates the value of change through nonviolent means, is to adopt the tactics of genocide, as in effect Castaño has done. The head of the AUC, in the name of freedom, may have isolated some territories from guerrilla violence, but at the cost of the possibilities of democratization and by sowing fear. Victims of the generals who led the coups in the Southern Cone in the 1970s know the argument well. And the outcome as well.

Notes

1. See the report of the Prosecutor General Carlos Jiménez Gómez, February 19, 1983, and the report on the paramilitary phenomenon prepared by the DAS under the direction of Police General Miguel Maza Márquez. Part of this report was published as "The Paramilitary Dossier" by the newsmagazine *Semana*, April 11–17, 1989.
2. See the report of the August 27, 1987, parliamentary debate (*El Tiempo*, August 28, 1987) in which the defense minister, General Rafael Samudio, and the minister of justice, Juan Manuel Arias, justified and supported the peasants' self-defense groups.
3. See Fernando Botero's speech to the cattlemen's congress in October 1994. Also it should be remembered that the term self-defense was what was used in the report on vigilante groups of the then Liberal minister of government Cesar Gaviria in 1987.
4. Interview with Carlos Castaño, *El Espectador*, May 18, 1999.
5. *El Espectador*, October 21, 2000.
6. The most recent example of this tension was the resignation of the defense minister, Rodrigo Lloreda, in May 1999 as a result of disagreements over the president's decision to grant an extension of the demilitarized zone for the FARC. This occurred only a few weeks after the president asked for the resignation of two generals accused of promoting paramilitary groups, a controversial decision in military circles. In solidarity with the outgoing minister, the majority of the upper ranks of the military threatened their resignation: seventeen generals, led by the commander of the army and more than a hundred colonels and majors as well as other officers and juniors. There were also rumors of possible movements of officers and soldiers under their command over to the paramilitary and self-defense groups (see the weekly newsmagazine, *Cambio*, no. 311, May 31–June 7, 1999).
7. This term refers to the trajectory followed by a social phenomenon, in which the decisions of those involved or earlier outcomes sketch a path or reduce the possible alternatives available to individual or collective actors. So the evolution of a specific phenomenon is determined by the variations within some foreseeable parameters. The peace negotiations begun in Colombia in 1982 are a good example. Each successive government has begun talks with the guerrillas, following the same board story: a first year of great expectations, followed by accusations from the armed forces that challenge the good faith of the

guerrillas, moving on to mutual accusations about the failure to keep their promises, and finally stagnation of the process. At least this has been the pattern with the FARC. The attempt at negotiation on the part of President Pastrana is the fifth since 1982.

8. This dichotomy is not exclusive. Rather it refers to a continuum through which there is continual movement, at times closer to one extreme than the other, depending on the conditions. So there are no situations of absolute autonomy or absolute subordination, only different combinations.

9. See *El Tiempo*'s coverage on August 18, 1999.

10. A distinction should be drawn between civil and civilian, because there are civilians who have a more militaristic solution to social and political problems than the military themselves. Likewise, there are military who think more in terms of the civil than many civilians.

11. Army officers consider that in the strict sense of the term the guerrillas are "paramilitaries," whereas the insurgent groups call the counterinsurgency forces and secret military operatives "paramilitaries." The groups considered to be paramilitaries by the mass media and the academics reject this term and call themselves "self-defence groups," while these reserve the word paramilitary for the army's security forces.

12. In addition to the ACCU, the Peasant Self-Defense Groups of the Western Plains, Cundinamarca, Casanare, Santander and southern Cesar, and the Middle Magdalena participate. Recently a new group in the Cauca Valley was created but it is not clear yet if it is an advance party of the ACCU or a group with an autonomous regional base and structure. According to the flyers distributed in Cali, this group is composed of retired military personnel.

13. According to the newsmagazine *Semana*, no. 669, February 28, 1995.

14. Botero was one of the first high-level officials to resign after having been accused, and later convicted, of receiving close to $6 million from the Cali cartel to finance the electoral campaign that culminated in the election of the Liberal candidate Ernesto Samper to the presidency.

15. According to a document of the AUC dated July 1997 in which it declares itself to be a political-military movement.

16. See the September 16, 1999, column of Plinio Apuleyo Mendoza "El Filo de la Navaja," which appears in the Bogota daily *El Espectador*. The quotation from General Clavijo appears in the same column dated September 30, 1999.

17. Interview with Carlos Castaño, *El Espectador*, May 18, 1999.

18. See note 12.

19. *El Espectador*, October 21, 2000.

References

Archila, Mauricio. 2000. "Luchas sociales del post-frente nacional (1975–1990)," *Controversia*, no. 176, CINEP, 12ff.

Behar, Olga. 1985. *Las guerras de la paz*. Bogatá: Editorial Planeta.

Castellanos, Camilo. 1992. "A la nueva república le falta el sujeto," in *Columbia: Análisis al futuro*, 9ff. Bogatá: CINEP.

Castro, Germán. 1996. "El libro que nunca pude escribir (Aproximación a Pablo Escobar)," in *En Secreto*, 141ff. Bogatá: Editorial Planeta.

CINEP-Justicia y Paz. 1997. "Una nueva etapa del paramilitarismo," *Noche y Niebla*, no. 3, CINEP, 41ff.

Comisión Colombiana de Juristas. 1997. *Colombia, Derechos Humanos y Derecho Humanitario: 1996*. Bogatá: Comisión Columbiana Jusistas.

Cubides, Fernando. 1995. "Los paramilitares como agentes organizados de violencia: Su dimensión territorial," in *Violencia y Desarrollo Municipal*, 147ff. Bogatá: Universidad Nacional-Centro de Estudios Sociales.

Dávila, Andrés. 1998. *El juego del poder: Historia, armas y votos*, 127ff. Bogatá: Ediciones UNIANDES-CEREC.

García-Peña, Daniel. 1995. "Light Weapons and Internal Conflict in Colombia," in Jeffrey Boutwell, Michael T. Klare, and Laura W. Reed, eds., *Lethal Commerce: The Global Trade in Small Arms and Light Weapons*, American Academy of Arts and Sciences.

González, Camilo. 1984. "Movimientos cívicos 1982–1984: Poder local y reorganización de la acción popular," *Controversia*, no. 121, CINEP, 47ff.

Leal, Francisco. 1994a. *El oficio de la guerra. La seguridad nacional en Colombia*. Bogatá: TM Editores-IEPRI.

1994b. "Defensa y seguridad nacional en Colombia, 1958–1993," in Francisco Leal and Juan Gabriel Tokatlian, eds., *Orden mundial y seguridad: Nuevos desafíos para Colombia y América Latina*, 131ff. Bogatá: TM Editores-IEPRI-SID.

Leal, Francisco, and León, Zamosc, eds. 1990. *Al filo del caos: Crisis política en la Colombia de los años 80*. Bogatá: TM Editores-IEPRI.

Londoño, Rocío. 1993. *Una visión de las organizaciones populares en Colombia*. Bogatá: Escuela de Liderazgo Democrático-Corporación S.o.S.-Viva la Ciudadanía.

Medina, Carlos. 1990. *Autodefensas, paramilitares y narcotráfico en Colombia*. Bogatá: Editorial Documentos Periodísticos.

Orjuela, Luis Javier. 1993. "Aspectos políticos del nuevo ordenamiento territorial," in John Dugas, ed., *La constitución de 1991: Un pacto político viable?*, 134ff. Bogatá: UNIANDES.

Palacio, Germán, and Fernando, Rojas. 1990. "Empresarios de la cocaína, parainstitucionalidad y flexibilidad del régimen político colombiano: Narcotráfico y contrainsurgencia," in Germán Palacio, ed., *La Irrupción del Paraestado: Ensayos sobre la crisis colombiana*, 69ff. Bogatá: ILSA-CEREC.

Restrepo, Luis Alberto. 1994. *El potencial democrático de los movimientos sociales y de la sociedad civil en Colombia*. Bogatá: Escuela de Liderazgo Democrático-Corporación S.o.S.-Viva la Ciudadanía.

Reyes, Alejandro. 1994. "Territorios de la Violencia en Colombia," in Renán Silva, ed., *Territorios, regiones, sociedades*, 111ff. Cali: Universidad del Valle-CEREC.

1997. "Compra de tierras por narcotraficantes," in *Drogas ilícitas en Colombia: Su impacto económico, político y social*, 279ff. Bogatá: Editorial Ariel-PNUD-Minjusticia.

Reyes Echandía, Alfonso. 1990. "Legislación y seguridad nacional en América Latina," in *El pensamiento militar latinoamericano: Democracia y seguridad nacional*, 58ff. Guadalajara: Centro de Estudios Militares General Carlos Prats, CEMCAP, Universidad de Guadalajara.

Romero, Mauricio. 1995. "Transformación rural, violencia política y narcotráfico en córdoba, 1953–1991," *Controversia*, no. 167, CINEP, 96ff.

———. 2000. "Changing Identities and Contested Settings: Regional Elites and the Paramilitaries in Contemporary Colombia," *International Journal of Politics, Culture and Society* 14, 1: 175ff.

Salazar, Alonso. 1993. *Mujeres de Fuego*, Medellín: Corporación Región.

Salgado, Carlos, and Esmeralda, Prada. 2000. *Campesinado y protesta social en Colombia, 1980–1995*. Bogotá: CINEP.

Santos, Boaventura de Souza. 1990. "Debate," in Germán Palacio, ed., *La irrupción del paraestado: Ensayos sobre la crisis colombiana*, 291. Bogatá: ILSA-CEREC.

Torres, Javier. 1986. "Military Government, Political Crisis, and Exceptional State: The Armed Forces of Colombia and the National Front, 1954–1974." Ph.D. dissertation, State University of New York, Buffalo.

Uprimny, Rodrigo, and Alfredo, Vargas. 1990. "La palabra y la sangre: Violencia, legalidad y guerra sucia," in Germán Palacio, ed., *La irrupción del paraestado: Ensayos sobre la crisis colombiana*, 105ff. Bogatá: ILSA-CEREC.

8

Policing the People, Building the State

The Police-Military Nexus in Argentina, 1880–1945

Laura Kalmanowiecki

Policing is a crucial instrument that reveals the relations between a state and its citizens. In Argentina, a modern police force did not develop until after the national state was established in 1880.[1] At that point, Buenos Aires was federalized and made the national capital. The Buenos Aires police became the police of the federal capital, directly subordinate to the president through the minister of the interior. Thus, the federal army and the police effectively consolidated the monopoly of legitimate violence, thereby putting an end to decades of factional struggles (Rouquié, 1985: 73). The result was the creation of bureaucratized forces distinct from the military that enjoyed state authority to coerce civilians and deliver them to judicial authorities.

This chapter focuses on the transformation and nationalization of policing in Argentina and its spread from Buenos Aires to the entire nation-state. This territorial shift resulted from the interplay of the national state's responses to contentious politics in Buenos Aires, and the need to protect the political order against perceived threats to national security. To achieve the internal pacification of the state effectively, police functions, increasingly seen in scientific terms, had to first share the definitions of politically destabilizing "enemies" and "threats." The centralization of the police mirrors the centralizing efforts of the modern nation-state (Reinke 1997: 103; Tilly 1975).

In Argentina, we see that greater state discretion and indiscretion went hand in hand with the expansion of police arrangements. Perceived political enemies became subject to an increasing range of centralized state competencies – including the means of repression, extraction, and coordination of information. Furthermore, as a result of the territorial expansion of police organization, police power was placed out of reach of civilian control. Repertoires of repression were cultivated to deal with criminality, political protest, and popular mobilization. Force was used arbitrarily against unprotected civilians increasing the accumulation of arbitrary means in the hands of the state. Finally, centralized control of the means of coercion within the state largely affected the extent and character of democratization, as described in the subsequent pages.

In order to shed some light on the models of police authority that prevailed in Argentina, I first explain some of the mechanisms that recurred in the history of policing in the European experience; then describe the establishment of direct executive control of the Buenos Aires City police starting in 1880; review the nationalization of policing; and, finally, show how the increased accumulation of powers led to increased arbitrariness. This accumulation of police powers affected civilian capacities of consultation and defense against an arbitrary state.

The Argentine experience with policing helps recast our understanding of the developmental processes of state formation in non-Western settings. The institutional distinctions between the war-making and policing capabilities of the state seem to be more complex than suggested by contemporary explanations of the European civilianization of governments and politics (Tilly 1985, 1990). The Argentine formation of an intensive surveillance apparatus aimed at enemies of the state in which both the police and the military are imbricated at the local, provincial, national, and even transnational levels suggests that we need to revisit the assumed distinction between protecting the state against internal or external threats respectively (Bayley 1975: 329). Indeed, functional distinctions between the police and the military become blurred in countries where, as Centeno suggests in this volume, less-intense war-making generates weaker states and the armed forces use their capacities in ways that largely affect the configuration of states and politics.

Policing and the European Nation-State

Professional policing is a creation of the modern state. The growth of policing goes hand in hand with the expansion of other branches of state administration (Tilly 1975; Bayley 1975, 1990). By the nineteenth century Europe experienced the civilianization of domestic politics. The police were entrusted with the maintenance of internal order, while military forces were directed against foreign threats. In Tilly's words, "although municipalities and rural jurisdictions had created their own small police forces long before, only during the nineteenth century did European states establish uniformed, salaried, bureaucratic police forces specialized in control of the civilian population. They thus freed their armies to concentrate on external conquest and international war" (Tilly 1990: 76).

Separation of police from the military in the Western historical experience generally signaled and promoted moves toward democracy and limitations on arbitrary state power. In Europe, state formation and consolidation corresponded to the adaptation of local societies to the dominant model of the state. The question of legitimization was at the heart of the construction of centralized police forces. Could police authority be legitimized by sheer force, or should it be based on consensus and negotiation with society? The nature of the relationship that bound states and citizens, rulers and ruled – authoritarian or contractarian – shaped the nature of police authority (Emsley and Weinberger 1991; Bayley 1975, 1990; Pizzorno 1991).

A distinction is commonly drawn between the Anglo-Saxon model of policing and the model of continental Europe. These models resulted from the configuration of state power. Decentralization of state power was intimately related to the bottom-up model; centralization of state power was intimately related to the top-down model. In general, European policing imitated the model of Paris, where policing began as part of the military. In France, policing was conceived as a responsibility of the central government, in a hierarchy down from the minister of the interior through the departmental prefects and their subordinates.[2] Imposed from above, authority was not negotiated with elected municipal bodies but was appointed by the ruler. The policeman was a military man and, like a soldier, was deployed as an instrument of central government (Emsley 1983: 30). A primary task of policing was surveillance to protect the security of the state.[3]

In contrast, the United States exemplifies the bottom-up model. Both the U.S. Constitution and popular and congressional antipathy toward centralized power shaped limits on the federal government's police powers (Theoharis 1997: 191). In the absence of a crown or central authority, control of the police oscillated between the city and state elective authorities. This stemmed from the belief that the state and local governments were responsible for law enforcement and that the constitutional system of countervailing powers should be preserved against any encroachment of the executive (ibid.). Federal authorities were not involved in the establishment of separate police forces in different cities. In this model, police authority was highly decentralized and remained that way. American policemen were directed by local government and accountable to their communities. Thus, from the beginning, policemen in a city such as New York represented municipal instead of national government, and its survival depended on closeness to the citizens and democratic government (Miller 1975: 85). The American police represented the "self-governing people," hostile to anything approaching a national standing army (Miller 1975: 95; Emsley 1983: 104). This model allowed for just a few highly specialized national police forces; local jurisdictions are central.[4]

In both London and New York, police authority rested on the voluntary compliance of most citizens (Miller 1975: 83). Indeed, the development of the New Metropolitan Police of London in 1829 went to great lengths to abide by the philosophical and political constraints against central authority upheld by the British. Robert Peel tried to avoid the pitfalls of military bodies like the gendarmerie, which the English feared and despised. According to Emsley, they would "rather lose their money to an English thief, than their liberty to a Lieutenant de Police" (Emsley 1983: 28). The bobbies were public employees with the primary duty to preserve public authority. Unlike continental Europe, they were servants of the people and not of the state. The metropolitan police was responsible to the home secretary (the Home Office was the closest equivalent to a continental Ministry of the Interior) but did not have centrally appointed agents in the provinces (Emsley 1997: 12). In Emsley's words, "provincial police forces were primarily supervised by, and responsible to, local authorities" (Emsley 1992: 122). Police and public order were the responsibility of local authorities, not of central government. However, this consensual model of police did not prevail in Ireland and the colonies of the British Empire, especially when British rule was threatened. Far from the ideal of the liberal model of consensual policing, policing under colonial rule could not help but be coercive; securing British authority against nationalists' threats was a top priority (Mazower 1997; Emsley 1997: 20; Killingway 1997). In this latter case "there were centralized, armed policemen, whose tasks, like those of gendarmes, guardias, and carabinieri, involved showing the flag" (Emsley 1992: 123).

Real or imagined threats that successive governments confronted had a major impact on the style of policing adopted by any given country. Even though it is difficult to generalize across the wide range of different political experiences (Zacks, Chapter 12 in this volume, makes this clear in her analysis of the role of *police municipales* in limiting centralized control in France), we could affirm that different policing regimes came to terms with the need to enforce codes of behavior, and to monitor and suppress threats to the security of the state (Emsley 1991; Bayley 1975).[5] Whether police authority concentrated on crime control or on political disorder, or some combination of each, depended upon the unique history of each country. The impact of social and economic transformations, wars, and revolutions spawned and shaped the forms and practices that states developed to deal with threats to public order (Mazower 1997), both real and imagined. The police shifted toward a proactive repression of persons, organizations, and events that could disturb public order, containing "militants and malcontents" (Tilly 1990: 115). Consequently, police powers were broadened and centralized. However, in most instances, efforts to centralize policing did not go without opposition by powerful municipal administrations, and the use of police powers was checked by magistrates, judges, parliament and public opinion (Mazower 1997).

Throughout the twentieth century policing acquired an ever increasing range of competencies. The particular style and method of policing adopted not only depended on the prevailing models of police authority but were also shaped by social and political development, challenges to the distribution of power in any given society, and the internal vulnerability of the state. The nature of the police was determined by the nature of the state, to be sure. However, the structure of the society, and the threats from groups making bids for power also had an impact (Bayley 1975: 378; Palmer 1988; Mosse 1975). It should be noted that there was no single progression in this process; the character of the police is a historical construction, centered around the state and in relationship with politics, justice, and the demands of the policed.

The Rise of Modern Police in Argentina

Generally speaking, policing in Argentina followed the French and continental type. Policing was a top-down, authoritarian construction. Unlike policemen in the Anglo-Saxon tradition, Argentine policemen perceived themselves to be at the service of neither the people nor the constitution. Simply put, the Argentine police were an instrument of central government against local challenges to state power. However, the centralization and territorial expansion of a "national" police force should not ignore the fact that the police force was developed to respond to local developments and their impact on Buenos Aires province.

In 1880 the triumph of federal troops under General Julio A. Roca over militia forces loyal to Governor Carlos Tejedor of Buenos Aires province marked the creation of a province-dominated political system. The province of Buenos Aires kept its police chief and moved its center of government to the city of La Plata, thirty miles from the capital. At the same time, the city of Buenos Aires was made the capital of the country and its preexisting police force was put under the jurisdiction of the federal government. A new chief of police, subordinate to the minister of the interior, was appointed (Maier 1996: 128; Rock 1987: 131).

To maintain his power base, General Julio Roca put policing under his direct control. This expansion of executive power was undertaken at the expense of local municipal power. According to José Nicolás Matienzo, it was impossible for the national executive power to relinquish the police in the hands of local councils or the municipality because "the resulting irresponsibility with respect to the exercise of police functions in that city would be so great that the population would soon call for a complete change of regime" (my translation, Matienzo 1926: 453). Ceding the control of the capital police to the municipality would have been tantamount to giving up control of Buenos Aires to political contenders. Argentine police were increasingly subject to centralization and presidential control rather than public negotiation and debates over individual liberties. Through the police, then, Roca oversaw the centralization of government, subordinating the provinces to his control.

Following the federalization of Buenos Aires, new laws determined provincial boundaries (Rock 1987: 155). The provinces chose their police powers in accordance with the federal character of the constitution in which the national state retained the right to limit their autonomy. New laws formalized legal administration in the national territories of La Pampa, Neuquén, Río Negro, Chubut, Santa Cruz, and Tierra del Fuego in the South and Southwest and, in the North, Misiones, Formosa, Chaco, and Los Andes (ibid.). Policing in those national territories was subordinated to the minister of the interior. In short, where each government of each province had its own police, the police of the capital (and national territories before they became provinces) were entrusted to the federal government.

In the decades that followed, the state secured the monopoly of violence. As the central government was consolidated, local powers and provincial autonomies were constrained. The 1880s paved the way for the oligarchic domination of power and the subjugation of federalist residues to the nationalization and centralization of power (Oszlak 1997: 128). In spite of the federalist principles proclaimed in the national constitution of 1853, the building of the Argentine state rested on the tutelage and dominance of Buenos Aires. Yet local, decentralized powers limited the power of definition of the police as it expanded throughout the national territory.

The Police Mandate

After 1880 the range of policing activities was narrowed, and the police acquired what would become its future organization.[6] At that point Argentina was in the process of becoming a dynamic capitalist society, organized around a dependent export sector. Increased European immigration remade the ethnic composition of the country. Economic growth, state-building, together with more vigorous central governments, brought about a need to adjust the police forces. In the early 1900s steps were further taken toward the establishment of a standardized career structure, uniform wages, and uniform conditions of service – all of which were instituted during the first half of this century (Blackwelder 1990; Gayol 1996; Kalmanowiecki 2000a: 198–201).

In countries that were undergoing rapid transformation and integration into the world market, such as Argentina, the ideals of a professionalized police were part of a more complex process of state intervention (Salvatore 1996; Salvatore and Aguirre 1996). The expansion of policing and state-building (e.g., education, building of a national army) were intimately connected. New developments in penitentiaries, criminology, and the professionalization of policing should be viewed as part of the complex nexus of institutions and disciplines devised to deal with the "dangerous classes." The international visibility of reforms in Buenos Aires – like the modernization of the Buenos Aires penitentiary – suggested that Buenos Aires would become the model of policing for South America.[7] Further, the development of asylums, "social hygiene," and the collaboration of police-men with reformers and doctors were part of a concern with the effects of rapid social change. The great transformation that resulted from immi-gration, the growth of industrial conflict, and the spread of anarchist ideas made such a collaboration the more important to prevent a widespread "epidemic" (Salessi 1995). The growth of Buenos Aires and its resulting political and social conflicts besieged the new capital police.

Colonel Falcón, appointed chief of police in 1906, set forth the frame-work of what constitutes the basic organization of the police (Fentanes 1955: 166). Before the tenure of Colonel Falcón, the Policía de la Capital was ruled by ad hoc presidential decrees, laws, police edicts, and ordinances (which perhaps were entirely useless in dealing with local urban problems), despite several attempts to provide the police institution with an organic code of rules and obligations (Mejías 1913: 32–38; Carracedo Nuñez 1928). Falcón divided the main activities of the police following a prin-ciple of hierarchical functional differentiation, with the chief of police at the top. He reorganized the preexisting sections and ascribed them to police divisions.[8] Although these police divisions and sections were frequently renamed, their personnel reallocated to different sections, and more spe-cialized branches created, this basic structure varied little until the creation of the Federal Police in 1943.[9]

In the thick of the growth and restructuring of the Police of the Capital lay the perception among propertied elites that Buenos Aires was a citadel under permanent threat by the "dangerous classes."[10] Indeed, fear of the dangerous classes was a common concern in the development of police forces in all the world major cities. Legislation was passed to crush any source of labor unrest, public demonstrations, and anarchism.[11] In sum, during the oligarchic pact that dominated Argentine politics until 1916, the mainstay of police structure and practices was the protection of the interests of the landed elites. Where assent to government domination was absent, obedience was promoted through the sheer force and "preventive police vigilance." Falcón masterminded the restructuring of the police in accordance with these principles.

How could the power of the Police of the Capital be centralized and imposed across the entire national domain? It was imperative to prepare the national state with the devices to deal with widespread social change and challenges to public order. Dominated by local governors, provincial police powers did not always follow national authorities but were rather influenced by local agendas, thus limiting the state's ability to carry out spe-cific tasks. Falcón feared that provincial police forces were concocted with anarchists constraining the state's ability to repress effectively local threats to the security of the state.[12] Provincial police powers limited the central state's power to define itself. Thus, for Falcón, the extension of police sur-veillance to the interior was an imperative; success would not be possible

unless the agents of coercion throughout the national territory agreed upon
who the enemies were, and how to deal with them (Memoria 1906/9:
152).[13]

According to the "Reglamento General" – a matrix of the police organization issued in 1885 – the police of the capital served a twofold purpose:
the protection of law and order and the security of the state (Rodríguez
1981: 63).[14] Thus, although the jurisdiction of the Policía de la Capital was
formally limited to the territory of the federal capital (the city of Buenos
Aires), it was already designated a statewide or national police de facto
when dealing with threats to the state. Further, Falcón's initiatives point to
a desire to infiltrate the entire territory of Argentina using the tools of collaboration and coercion in spite of limited technical means. Hence, police
functionaries came to believe that they were endowed with the right to intervene once a situation was defined as menacing – politically or socially –
wherever it occurred. Certainly, police claim to ubiquitous control was not
fully legitimated by the law.

Ironically, Colonel Falcón and his aide Alberto Lartigau were murdered
by an anarchist in 1909. These events, and the celebrations of the "Cente-
nario" of Buenos Aires, stimulated the reinforcement of the police and
a major increase in police personnel.[15] As early as 1914, the Buenos Aires
police department had already developed modern crime fighting functions,
including mobile patrols, crime labs, a detective branch, and new recruiting and training practices (Johnson 1990: 125; Rodriguez 1975a).

Changing definitions of "public disorder," "political threats," and potentially "dangerous sites" caused the police organization to adjust its territorial and bureaucratic repertoire. It also had to face new forms of collective
action that demanded from the oligarchic regime political openness (Hilda
Sábato 1991; Jorge Sábato 1991; Kalmanowiecki 1998, 2000a). During
that time police activity included control of the "dangerous classes," political demonstrations, and industrial disputes. Such work was seen as part
of the need to secure the common good in the face of rapid social change.
Political repression and the control of "deviant" behavior marked the police
"war against crime" (Guy 1991: 38). And when the police were unable to
contain strikes, the national government called in the army and the navy.
The use of force combined with inclusionary practices led eventually to the
opening of the oligarchic regime and to the triumph of the middle-class
Union Cívica Radical led by Hipólito Yrigoyen in 1916 (Collier and Collier
1991; Waisman 1989). Although the basic structure of the police organizations varied little in the following decades, the process of specialization
and professionalization within the police continued.

The political order created by the Radicals in 1916 did not survive the
economic crisis of 1930. The military coup, which immediately followed,
put an end to democratization in both politics and policing. President
Justo's conservative government proscribed Radical leaders and further

centralized the Capital Police, both in its territorial domain and bureaucratic procedures. Political policing became its mainstay. Thus, perceived threats to the security of the state – such as anarchism, communism, and radicalism – pushed the state further in the direction of ad hoc police federalization and the militarization of Argentine society and politics. But complete transformation did not occur for several decades, following World War II, the growth of labor, and the creation of the Federal Police in 1943–1944. With its creation, the process of police centralization initiated by Falcón was completed, giving the state a monopoly over the use of force. At that point, the police were so powerful that they became instrumental in checking the power of the military. With the establishment of Peronism in 1946, police had an expanded grip of the entire national boundaries.

Police and Repression

The following examination of the development of the Capital Police illustrates the growing capability of the national government to respond to perceived threats and enemies of incumbent regimes. The combination of increased police efficiency, extensive protection of police from civilian control, authoritarian national regimes, and attachment of police to the regime facilitated arbitrary state power. Force was used against unprotected civilians, who had no legal recourse.

The 1930 military coup that ousted President Hipólito Yrigoyen resulted in long-lasting changes in policing. Following the coup, and especially during the government of President Justo after 1932, an extensive information and surveillance service was mounted to monitor and repress the population. Political policing became the authorized business of the police: police practices such as monitoring, surveillance, infiltration, shadowing, vetting, and covert operations became a routine part of the secret police repertoire. These practices strongly limited the capacity of contestation and resistance of diverse actors. The use of arbitrary powers to deal with political threats also became part of the routine police repertoire when dealing with common criminals and those who defied the moral order.

Because the existing police organization seemed to be overwhelmed by the enlarged range of activities after the 1930 military coup, the police structure was refurbished to accomplish its new tasks: the repression of communism and radicalism. A special branch of the police intended to combat communism was created expeditiously. In addition to the creation of a new branch of the police, a major restructuring of the institution into prefectures was undertaken following the coup. Although this division of the police into prefectures was of short duration, the procedures devised by the police following the oligarchic restoration, especially by Chief of Police Luis J. García during Justo's government, left an imprint on the practices and organization of the police. Under President Justo police administrative practices were further rationalized and routinized, and anticipatory surveillance increased greatly. An intelligence network of surveillance and espionage was developed that transmuted the power of Buenos Aires throughout the national territory and also in its neighboring countries. This decade is marked by the creation of the means of repression, extraction, coordination, and information by state agents and its diversion to extra-legal action against putative enemies of the regime.

The Repression of Communism and Radicalism

Since its inception in 1931, the infamous Special Branch was characterized by secrecy and operated with impunity. Its origins are confusing due to the routine and surreptitious police practice of renaming branches without public notice. The agency grew at a formidable pace and remained active throughout the 1930s and 1940s.[16] The procedures of the Special Branch were then routinized and bureaucratized. These practices included the collection of ideological information about public employees, students, and new army draftees; international collaboration in the repression of communist suspects (*Libro Copiador de Notas*, Sección Especial, 1933–34: 295–447); and the monitoring of areas defined as trouble-prone, which included the use of torture and illegal raids. Such activity increased the state's capacity to act at the national level. Through the Special Branch, the Capital Police could collaborate with local provincial police in areas that were allegedly predisposed to communism. The capital police set up the model that other police forces should follow in political repression. In the provinces of Buenos Aires and Córdoba, for instance, local police forces were subordinated to the Special Branch and collaborated in their cen-tralizing efforts. The army also participated in this enterprise. In October 1933 in the province of Córdoba, the chief of Information Section of the Military Command, Major Rodolfo Luque introduced Cusell to archives containing abundant documentation of communists, classified by militant and organization.[17] Cusell credited Luque for his deep understanding of the "Bolshevik problem and the local situation" (Archivo Justo, box 54, docu-ment 12: 25–66). As the examples of Córdoba and Santa Fe demonstrate, the army provided parallel information to the national authorities. Because local policing was politicized by the interests of provincial authorities, the national government probably found army intelligence more trustworthy. This was also true for the national territories where presumably the army had a broader presence.[18] Thus, the army's physical presence throughout the country and loyalty to the national government drew the army into an arena that was de jure reserved to the police.

The practices inaugurated by the Special Branch can be traced through subsequent decades (Ciria 1985: 61). Its agents were known for the feroc-ity of the torture they inflicted upon their victims, and for their expertise in racketeering and in instigating actions that would end in police intervention. Some of them continued to practice their "trade" and train new recruits during Perón's presidency, in the 1940s and 1950s. They had a license to act with impunity.

The arrangements set up to deal with Radicals also illustrate the accumulation of police powers during this period; police practices became more centralized as they expanded from the location of the federal capital to the national territory. Following the coup, deposed Radicals resorted to armed insurrections with the help of civilians and military men loyal to *radicalismo* (the Radical Party also resorted to abstention, refusing to participate in fraudulent elections, as they had done prior to 1916) (Rouquié 1985: 266). Meanwhile, the government developed the capabilities to monitor, repress, and infiltrate these conspiracies, and policing was further expanded. A branch of the Investigative Division, Political Order, followed their leaders and tapped telephones (Police Dossier of Juan Carlos Vasquez, and Lieutenant Colonel Francisco and Roberto Bosch). Letters were intercepted (Archivo Justo, box 98, document 146). Each successive insurrection was crushed by the authorities, defeated by an efficient network of surveillance and infiltration.[19] The Argentine Maritime Police, the navy, and the army developed their own intelligence network, reporting the activities of the conspirators and collaborating with local police and the Investigative Division. These military intelligence operations and collaboration with the police were carried out through 1933, when the last Radical uprising took place, and continued thereafter until the end of Justo's presidency in 1938.[20] For example, in 1934 the army complained it lacked the personnel to infiltrate the activities of the exiles in Uruguay and suggested involvement through agents of the Investigative Division.[21] The army collaborated in policing in the provinces and national territories when facing the threat of communism and/or Radicalism. Furthermore, Argentine policing in the provinces involved the imbrication of local provincial police forces, the Capital Police, and also the army in the monitoring of local population.[22] Army reports of communism and radicalism often paved the way for federal interventions.[23] As I already pointed out, in the national territories, the army served as a parallel information service and was often viewed as more trustworthy than the local powers.

Finally, secret services developed, apparently as an outgrowth of the Political Order Branch of the Police of the Capital, although they could have emanated from the presidential secret service. They exchanged information with the army intelligence services and the Bureau of Posts and Telegraphs. They also intercepted telephone calls whose content was often reproduced to President Justo (Fraga 1993: 396). Again, the resources, geographical coverage, and capabilities of these secret services are remarkable, and largely escape the police mandate. These secret services could count on the resources and capabilities of the state to infiltrate and promote

conspiracies (Marx 1988). One such plot involved the framing of a prominent Radical politician, in need of money for his political campaign. Agent
O.1 met the Radical intermediary, Santiago Peralta, and offered him money
to establish gambling houses in the capital. When they needed to resched-
ule a second meeting with another person, Agent O.1 reported that "so as
not to make a false move and be introduced to a person who could recognize me as a police functionary, I did not arrange the hour of the interview,
but would do it the next day by telephone." An elaborate surveillance
network was set up with the assistance of the Bureau of Posts and the telephone company, allowing O.1 to do his job without being recognized.
Telegraphs and telephone conversations were intercepted across the country
to report to O.1 on the next meeting so as to avert any surprise. The agent
finally met the prominent politician, Vicente Gallo, who was without any
doubt guilty: "The fact that (Gallo) does not ask where the funds are
coming from, does not inquire, and commits his support is the most
palpable proof of his complicity. Otherwise, if it is an honorable enterprise, one talks about it."[24] The agent directly reported to Miguel Angel
Viancarlos, chief of the Investigative Division of the police.

The National-Local Conundrum

Even a superficial analysis of federal intervention in policing would suggest
a monumental undertaking. Within the scope of this chapter, we can only
touch upon the federal imposition of new forms of discipline, which were
dictated from the center of power to the periphery. As the following
citation illustrates, national interventions crystallized the instillation of national values throughout the territories: local police were a part of this
machinery.

Dr. Baldrich, minister of government (national intervention): "You have lied to me,
you are disloyal. . . . You have not followed my instructions."
Chief of police of the province of Catamarca, Comisario Juan A. Finochietto: "Don't
get nervous Mr. Minister . . ."
Dr. Baldrich (in nervous attitude, while striking the desk, lowering his voice): "I
have seen in the parade a North American flag!"
Chief Finochietto: "It is as well an American nation."
Dr. Baldrich: "No, it cannot be, because North America is our enemy, and it tried
to smash us." (Ministerio del Interior, 1944, Legajo 16, dossier 306)

The national intervention that followed the 1943 military coup entrusted
the intervenor to organize the celebration of a major patriotic feast, the
Dia de La Raza with a parade of schoolchildren. The altercation between
Dr. Baldrich and Comisario Juan A. Finochietto cost the latter his position
after thirty-four years of service in the Capital Police and Catamarca. The
local police chief, Finochieto, overlooked the presence of U.S. flags and thus

violated the nationalist principles of the national authorities (Ministerio del Interior, Legajo).[25] This example further illustrates the extent to which the Argentine military engaged in a broad scope of activities from repression to involvement in everyday forms of civic and moral education and domination and surveillance.

National forms of control and coordination ultimately overrode the local and regional powers. Apart from ad hoc interventions, in matters including not only anarchism but also important criminal investigations, local executive powers would defer to federal interventions (*intervención federal*) in matters that pertained to the provinces. The use of federal interventions after 1880 involved complex political alignments and protections or repression in conflicts originating within individual provinces (within the ruling elite and outside it).[26] Likewise, federal authorities could replace local authorities by appointed "commissioners" until new elections were held (Walter 1987: 38). Between 1912 and 1943 several provincial interventions by local governments were politically motivated (ibid.), as the example of Buenos Aires illustrates.

According to Richard Walter, policemen in the Buenos Aires province who were allied to caudillos were electoral powerbrokers appointed by local governments (Walter 1985: 37). They supervised elections, prepared reports on electoral campaigns, and were an essential source of information. As contemporary complaints suggest, the use of force for partisan and electoral aims was customary during both the oligarchic rule and the radical governments that followed.[27] During *radicalismo*, the politics of national intervention substituted comisarios for political aims replicating old regime practices.[28] For instance the intervention of José Luis Cantilo in the province of Buenos Aires was aimed at disarming the oligarchic machinery and weakening the nexus of comisario and intendente-caudillo.[29] Federal financial resources were used to keep the police stations under national oversight, thus weakening the power of local municipalities (Bartolucci and Taronchet 1994). Likewise, functionaries of the Capital Police were often appointed to handle interventions.

The Legacies of Cumulative Political Policing

We could think of the history of modern policing in Argentina as the cumulative organization of routines and repertoires for imposing top-down (i.e., state) controls on society. The Argentine historical trajectory of policing is marked by the centralizing tendencies of Buenos Aires. To be successful, the top-down model of centralizing control required police counterparts in the rest of the national territory who were willing to cooperate – to coordinate and exchange information and the means of coercion throughout the national territory. To be effective, local, provincial, and territorial policemen needed to advance the professionalization, and also standardization,

of their procedures and operations following the model established by
Buenos Aires. Most important, they needed to share certain basic values to
which specific groups posed a perceived threat to public order – criminals
and/or political criminals (Kalmanowiecki 2000b). The definition of public
order in Argentina had a political foundation. The centralizing force of
Buenos Aires expanded police arrangements to establish the means, routines, and rationale in the pursuit of enemies of the regime.

As I have shown, the military coup of 1930 catalyzed the reorganization
of the police into a violent and manipulative instrument of political repression. The police expanded its customary repertoire of repression to include
new targets. The apparent threat of anarchism and radical insurrection provided a justification for the enlarged scope of political policing. The police,
placed at the service of the new regime, became a highly politicized force
with more power to act arbitrarily throughout the territory. The Capital
Police, the navy, the army, and provincial police forces were diverted to
extralegal action against putative enemies of the regime.

The use of federal interventions also secured the dominance of the executive against other contenders and claimants for power. Indirect policing of
the interior – modeled on the Buenos Aires top-down model – would make
the inhabitants of the national territory, both immigrants and Creoles, into
Argentines. This was the case especially in territories with a large foreign
population, where it was difficult to recruit Argentine nationals in the police
force.

Furthermore, changes in police practices and organization resulted in the
accumulation and abuse of police power and placed it out of reach of civilian control. When the Federal Police was created in December 1943, its
commander was also the commander of the Police of the Capital. The Police
of the Capital was converted into the Federal Police. The Interior Division
(División Interior) was created, in charge of judicial and security tasks in
matters pertaining to federal jurisdiction in the provinces (Rodriguez 1981:
209). Whereas the 1943 decree gave the Federal Police jurisdiction only in
the national territories (i.e., not in the provinces), after 1944 its authority
was extended to the provinces and the federal capital. The creation of the
Federal Police in 1943–1944 crystallized (and gave a de jure character to)
the sort of policies of national intervention and control that were already
routine in the Capital Police. But the Federal Police had authorized direct
jurisdiction over the whole Argentine territory. Why did the creation of a
federal police take so long to happen?

I believe that the establishment of the Federal Police (through a presidential decree in December 1943, just a few months after the June 1943
military coup) only legitimated the long-standing practice of metropolitan
police intervention in municipal and local provincial matters, often in collaboration with other armed forces. But these interventions were now official. As the evidence suggests, the Capital Police had operated nationally

from Falcón to Castillo. As a chief of police acknowledged in an unpublished address, the police had, for many years, "cooperated with the army in national defense and with the minister of the interior, in antisectarian activities" (Bertollo 1950: 5–10). He further disclosed that the "information services" had been increasingly expanded, penetrating areas "not necessarily related to their existence but nonetheless . . . beneficial to the security of the state" (ibid., 8).

The nationalization of the Capital Police seems to have been a long-standing aspiration of police administrators. But the lack of uniformity of ideas and local politics strongly limited the power of state definition. Falcón had demonstrated that local politics made the repression of political crimes troublesome: criminals were "untouchables" once they had left the borders of the capital city. In the view of police administrators, only through the creation of a federal police on the model of the U.S. Federal Bureau of Investigation, the Chilean and Italian carabinieris, or the French gendarmerie could illegal activities be eradicated. Surely, the growth of labor and the impact of World War II and Cold War hostilities may have given more urgency to the federalization of policing.

The centralizing efforts started by Falcón were crystallized in the Federal Police in 1943–1944 and continued during the presidency of General Juan Domingo Perón. In fact, Perón's rise to power was initiated by his involvement in the 1943 military coup. He set in motion a political operation that led to the state co-opting the labor movement at the expense of labor autonomy (Collier and Collier 1991). Police action was instrumental in Perón's rise to power and in the maintenance of it.[30] With Perón, the police became the "pueblo," determined to fight against the armed forces to defend the "well-being" of the masses against the "selfishness of the Argentine oligarchy." As a corporation, the police organization had numerous advantages and prerogatives, such as a police code that gave police special legal status against civilian complaints (Memoria 1945: 407–500). Police personnel were completely removed from civilian jurisdiction, furthering police impunity (Código de Justicia Policial 1952; Comisión Nacional de Investigaciones 1958: 67). Under Perón, the police's cumulative powers increased on the basis of the preestablished, though arbitrary, foundations. The Investigative Division maintained its original structure; its targets were relocated according to the newly defined enemies of the state – students, intellectuals, and anti-Peronist labor among others. In 1944 the nationalization and bureaucratization of the national state manifested in a new agency, the Federal Coordination Division, entrusted with "international espionage" but which would eventually preempt some tasks of the Investigative Division (especially those pertaining to the Special Branch and political and social order). The establishment of a federal police structure had also created the conditions for a more systematic coordination of policing. This process was furthered in 1951 with the creation in the Ministry of the Interior of the

Federal Security Council (Consejo Federal de Seguridad), which coordinated the Federal Police with other national agencies, such as the National Constabulary and the Naval Prefecture. Finally, mounting opposition to Perón spurred new structures for extensive coordination of the means of surveillance, the Technical Advisory Board and the Commands.[31]

Again, although secrecy surrounds political policing in Argentina, the Special Branch was still in business after Colonel Juan Domingo Perón rose to power, and its arbitrary powers epitomized the abuses of state power. The accumulation of arbitrary means in the hands of the Federal Police and its insulation from civilian control made the police more dangerous and abusive. Perón was aware of the need of uniformity and rationalization of the state apparatus in matters of internal security. In a cabinet meeting in which he asserted the need to create a minister of politics to guide national politics, he was concerned about the need to "orient" and "direct" the politics of "communists, socialists, radicals, progressive democrats." In Perón's words, the minister of the interior could not "according with the law . . . interfere in politics. It has always done so, but it cannot, as I cannot myself. We need a special organism for that" (Archivo Secretariá de Asuntos Técnicos 1951). The Peronist government increased the centralization and nationalizing efforts of preexisting police institutions, new institutions that would target enemies of the regime were set up on the basis of preexisting arrangements.

The long accumulation of police powers by the Argentine police largely constrained the protection of the people from arbitrary action by rulers and governmental agents. The increased centralization of police powers implied a reduced competence of polity members to exercise controls and counterbalances against an organization that has been designed to spy and use arbitrary forces against those defined as enemies of the regime. In a spiraling logic, contested politics encouraged the centralization of powers in the hands of the police. As I have shown in this chapter, the military also directed its gaze inward, entangling its surveillance and its disciplinarian and civic and moral activities with those of the police. Rather than waging international battles, the army's battleground was fought internally, vexing the development of the Argentine state.

Notes

1. When referring to a "modern police force," I define the police as the "bureaucratic and hierarchical bodies employed by the state to maintain order and to prevent and detect crime" (Emsley 1991: 1). I am borrowing here Clive Emsley's broad definition of a state police – be it a national, county, or municipal authority – meaning that the employer is the state. In this sense, the modern bureaucratic policeman is not private but is an instrument of the state.

2. Emsley refers here to the administrative police. The *police judiciare* depended on the minister of justice (Emsley 1983: 3). The former was entrusted with combating crime and maintaining public order, and the latter was responsible for repressing criminal offenses, so despite being centralized they were also much more internally fragmented. The judicial police included functionaries in England or the United States who would also be recognized as policeman. Also Bayley 1975.

3. Similarly, policing in Prussia shared the broad French definition, and the powers of municipal authorities were limited by the powers of the state (Emsley 1983: 99).

4. However, municipal forces were overtly political institutions. Local control went hand in hand with a high participation of policemen in the electoral process. In any event, the democratic openness of the United States paved the way for public scrutiny of police behavior vis-à-vis top-down models of policing, and also in comparison to the model of the London Metropolitan Police that I describe later. The latter was more prone to closure from public scrutiny (Emsley 1992: 123–125). However, oversights and concerns against the encroachment of the state in the United States should not be exaggerated. The Federal Bureau of Investigation officials devised procedures that shielded them from public scrutiny in their monitoring of political activities violating their original mandate when the bureau was first conceived in 1908 as a special investigative agency of the Department of Justice. National security concerns engendered by the wars and intensified by the Cold War made possible its emergence as a permanent political agency. See Theoharis 1997.

5. The police could prevent order and detect crime, or it could police political demonstrations and industrial disputes, the most obvious examples of conflicting tasks. Even tough police action was enforcing the law; in enforcing these laws, the police enforced a dominant ideology (Emsley 1991: 2).

6. The Police of the Capital gave up areas of influence to the municipality in the administration of urban affairs, not without resistance given police ambitions for extensive control. See Kalmanowiecki 2000a; Gayol 1996; and Maier, Abregu, and Tiscornia 1996. It accused the municipality of invasion of jurisdictions. For police authorities, only the Capital Police had the necessary authority, through the use of coercion, to enforce norms. Typical functions under dispute were traffic control and the enforcement of ordinances regarding prostitution.

7. Positivist reformer Antonio Ballvé was the first career police professional appointed for the important position of general secretary during the tenure of Chief of Police Francisco J. Beazley (Rodriguez 1975: 6:209). Salvatore points out that it was Ballvé who brought the Buenos Aires penitentiary up to the "standards of the penitentiary ideal" between 1904 and 1914 (Salvatore 1996: 11).

8. The main component of the force was the Division Seguridad (Security Division), the uniformed police on street patrol distributed along the different precincts of the capital. It was in charge of public order, broadly defined. A second branch was the Division Investigaciones (Investigative Division). It consisted chiefly of the political and the criminal police (also called judicial police or detective force), operating in plain clothes. Other branches included the Administrative Division and the Judicial Division. Prisons, reformatories, and minor asylums belonged to the Judicial Division.

9. The reorganization of the police into prefectures upon the establishment of the military dictatorship in 1930 should be considered as an exception of short duration because in 1933 the previous structure was reestablished – although with a radically different degree of centralization, as I will show later.
10. On the citadel practice, see Ludtke 1989.
11. The 1902 Residency Law (Ley de Residencia) and the 1910 Social Defense Law (Ley de Defensa Social) gave the executive branch the tools to broaden the scope of police action to deal with the repression of anarchism (Walter 1977: 45–47).
12. Some voices openly contested Falcón's police reform as leading to the militarization of the police but were dismissed as being irresponsible and lacking an understanding of the need of order in society. See Rodriguez 1975a: 318, and also 1975b.
13. Efforts were undertaken at an international level for collaboration in the repression of anarchism and also the white slave trade.
14. Article 3 of the Reglamento of 1885 stated that these included "guarding against and repressing any plot, conspiracy, or subversive movement." In so doing it gave the Police of the Capital the power to intervene in matters that allegedly threatened the security of the state. See Fentanes 1979: 45.
15. Thus, police personnel were enlarged from 4,170 in 1907 to 5,372 in 1911 (Rodriguez 1981: 358–359, 184; Blackwelder 1990: 80). From the 1880s until World War I, the population of the city of Buenos Aires increased 250 percent, but the size of the police force increased only 20 percent (Blackwelder 1991: 80). Whereas in 1895 Buenos Aires had a population of 663,854, by 1915 it expanded to 1,563,082 (Johnson 1990: 120).
16. Comisario Federico Donadio ran the Special Branch for a year until Joaquín Cusell took over. Information about supposed communists was taken from 2,851 dossiers already available at the Social Order Section of the Investigative Division. Between 1932 and 1935 the number of dossiers almost tripled to 6,529, vividly illustrating the extraordinary momentum of the agency. See also Rouquié 1982 and Rodriguez Molas 1985: 94–100.
17. In the eyes of the "intelligence community," the large concentration of students in the province predisposed its population to communism, Archivo Justo, box 54, document 12, October 18, 1933, pp. 25–50.
18. Indeed the army was concerned by the fact that police personnel in border areas were not Argentines, putting the country at risk for espionage (Memorandum from Minister of War to Minister of Interior," secret dossier, Ministerio del interior 1928).
19. By date and leader the important insurrections were: February 1931, headed by Severo Toranzo; July 1931, led by Gregorio Pomar; January 1932, headed by Pomar, Atilio Cattáneo, and Benjamin Abalos; December 1932, directed by Cattáneo; and December 1933, conducted by Pomar and Roberto Bosch (Orona 1971: 139–162; Luna 1972: 90; Cattáneo 1959: 84–144).
20. Justo did not hide his hope for a second presidential mandate in 1943 (Privitellio 1997: 62) and until his death had access to confidential information.
21. Archivo Justo, box 98, document 33.
22. Before the elections for the renewal of members of the Chambers of Deputies and some legislatures in March 1934, President Justo appointed Brigadier

General Julio Costa of the Third Army Division as a military observer of the elections in the province of Santa Fe. In a confidential memorandum dated March 1, 1934, the Chief of the Eleventh Regiment in Rosario, Lieutenant Colonel Emilio Faccione, reported local police support of Radicals (Archivo Justo, box 46, document 28).

23. On March 13, 1934, Faccione wrote a six-page report that emphasized communist activity within the university. In his view, Santa Fe governor Luciano Molinas, together with the local police, was to be blamed for the spread of communism, anarchism, radicalism, and revolution. Therefore it was necessary to take action. The national government intervened in Santa Fe the following year. Luna considers that the Progressive Democratic governor was ousted because of Justo's need to prepare for the upcoming presidential elections. In his view, the Santa Fe intervention was one of the most arbitrary and unjustifiable acts of Justo's government. Luna 1972: 37–55.

24. Vicente Gallo belonged to the Alvearista sector of radicalism that opposed the personalism of Yrigoyen. Archivo Justo, box 100, documents 49 and 50, and box 49, document 216.

25. Federal intervention could also lead to arbitrary use of force. Juan Alvarez, a police officer from the national territory of Río Negro, narrates the extrajudicial powers used by a detachment entrusted with the elimination of "low-life elements" that were harassing local landowners. The arrested "vagrants and ne'er-do-wells" (*vagos y ociosos*) were concentrated in a cantonment were they were fed and "instructed in habits of honesty and hard work" and forced to work in the construction of public roads. Most of them were "illiterate, indigenous, or descendants of Chilean" (Alvarez 1940: 72). Alvarez was later accused of torture.

26. According to the constitution, the government could intervene to guarantee the republican form of government but did not specify what constituted a threat, leaving room for arbitrariness (Mustapic 1984: 98; Fleischman 1997: 159).

27. For instance, during communal elections in Posadas there were numerous complaints against the use of police violence against Yrigoyenistas (Ministerio del Interior, Legajo 16501, January 1, 1928). Similar complaints of local police abuses against *yrigoyenistas* surfaced in other areas of the country (Chaco-Charata, Neuquen, Ministerio del Interior, Legajo 57, expediente 31422). Also see Bartolucci and Taronchet 1994: 179–183.

28. According to David Rock, by 1880 the term caudillo lost its earlier connotation of regional or provincial leader and now referred to the political bosses who controlled elections on behalf of their elite patrons (Rock 1985: 129). Policemen were key pieces in this process.

29. After the intervention in 1918 Radicals dominated the two most decisive mechanisms of provincial political control: the police and local authorities (Walter 1987: 68).

30. In October 17, 1945, the police took Perón's side after a military movement attempted to oust him from power. Even before he was elected president, the police monitored elements among the armed officers who opposed his life-style and his suspected policies toward labor. In September 1945, the police frustrated a subversive movement by Artillery General Adolfo Espíndola (Rouquié 1982: 82). See also Potasch 1981: 387–388.

31. The Security Command was entrusted with the coordination of security, communications, and firefighters; the Political and Social Command was in charge of the security of the state; and, finally, the Interior Command was entrusted with extraordinary activities in the interior (Rodriguez 1981: 212).

References

Alvarez, Juan. 1940. *Policía Desamparada*. Viedma.
Archivo de la Policía Federal. Libro Copiador de Notas. Sección Especial. 1933–1934 and 1944–1945.
Archivo Justo. Boxes 45, 49, 54, 98, 46, 100.
Archivo Ministerio del Interior. 1908. Expediente 2054.
Archivo Secretaría de Asuntos Técnicos. 1951.
Bartolucci, Mónica, and Miguel Angel Taronchet. 1994. "Cambios y continuidades en las practices político-electorales en la provincia de Buenos Aires: 1913–1922," in Fernando Devoto and Marcelo P. Ferrari, eds., *La construcción de las democracies rioplatenses: Proyectos institucionales y prácticas políticas, 1900–1930*, 169–187. Buenos Aires: Editorial Biblos.
Bayley, David. 1975. "The Police and Political Development in Europe," in Charles Tilly, ed., *The Formation of National States in Western Europe*, 328–380. Princeton: Princeton University Press.
  1977. *The Police and Society*. New York: Sage.
  1990. *Patterns of Policing*. New Brunswick, N.J.: Rutgers University Press.
Bertollo, Arturo. 1950. "Las policías en sus misiones de seguridad civil de la nación." Unpublished manuscript.
Blackwelder, Julia. 1990. "Urbanization, Crime and Policing: Buenos Aires, 1880–1914," in Lyman L. Johnson, ed., *The Problem of Order in Changing Societies*, 65–87. Albuquerque: University of New Mexico Press.
Carracedo Nuñez, José. 1928. *Contribución al estudio y mejoramiento institucional de la polícia de la capital*. Buenos Aires: Talleres Gráficos de la Penitenciaría Nacional.
Cattáneo, Attilio. 1959. *Plan 1932: Las conspiraciones radicals contra el general Justo*. Buenos Aires: Procesos Ediciones.
Ciria, Alberto. 1985. *Partidos y poder en la Argentina moderna (1930–1946)*. Buenos Aires: Hyspamérica.
Collier, David, and Ruth B. Collier. 1991. *Shaping the Political Arena*. Princeton: Princeton University Press.
Comisión Nacional de Investigaciones. 1958. *Libro Negro de la Segunda Tiranía*. Buenos Aires: Integración.
Emsley, Clive. 1983. *Policing and Its Context*. London: Macmillan.
  1991. *The English Police: A Political and Social History*. London: Schoken Books.
  1992. "The English Bobby: An Indulgent Tradition," in Roy Porter, ed., *Myths of the English*. Cambridge: Polity Press.
  1997. "Introduction: Political Police and the European Nation-State in the Nineteenth Century," in Mark Mazower, ed., *The Policing of Politics in the Twentieth Century*, 1–25. Oxford: Berghahn Books.

Emsley, Clive, and Barbara Weinberger, eds. 1991. *Policing in Western Europe: Politics, Professionalism, and Public Order, 1850–1940.* New York: Greenwood Press.

Fentanes, Enrique. 1955. *Didáctica Policial.* Buenos Aires: Editorial Policial.

1979. *Compendio de ciencias de la Policía.* Buenos Aires: Editorial Policial.

Fleischman. 1997. "Civil Society and the State in Argentina: A Study of System Integration." Ph.D. dissertation, New School for Social Research.

Fraga, Rosendo. 1993. *El General Justo.* Buenos Aires: Emecé Editores.

Gayol, Sandra. 1996. "Sargentos, cabos y vigilantes: Perfil de un plantel inestable en el Buenos Aires de la Segunda Mitad del Siglo XIX," *Boletín Americanista* 36, 46: 133–151.

Guy, Donna. 1991. *Sex and Danger in Buenos Aires.* Lincoln: University of Nebraska Press.

Johnson, Lyman L. 1990. "Changing Arrest Patterns in Three Argentine Cities: Buenos Aires, Santa Fe, and Tucumán, 1900–1930," in Lyman L. Johnson, ed., *The Problems of Order in Changing Societies.* Albuquerque: University of New Mexico Press.

Kalmanowiecki, Laura. 1998. "Soldados ou missionarios domésticos?" *Estudos Históricos* 12, 22: 295–324.

2000a. "Police, Politics and Repression in Modern Argentina," in Ricardo Salvatore and Robert Buffinton, eds., *Reconstructing Criminality in Latin America*, 195–218. Wilmington, Del.: Scholarly Resources.

2000b. "Origins and Applications of Political Policing in Argentina," *Latin American Perspectives*, issue 111, vol. 27, 2: 36–56.

Killingway, David. 1997. "Securing the British Empire: Policing and Colonial Order, 1920–1960," in Mark Mazower, ed., *The Policing of Politics in the Twentieth Century*, 167–190. Oxford: Berghahn Books.

Ludtke, Alf. 1989. *Police and State in Prussia, 1815–1850.* Cambridge: Cambridge University Press.

Luna, Felix. 1972. *Las luchas populares en la década del 30.* Buenos Aires: Schapire Editor.

Maier, Julio Bernardo José. 1996. "Breve historia institucional de la Policía Argentina," in Peter Waldmann, ed., *Justicia en la calle. Ensayos sobre la policía en América Latina*, 127–137. Medellín: Biblioteca Jurídica.

Maier, Julio Bernardo José, Martín Abregu, and Sofía Tiscornia. 1996. "El papel de la policía en la Argentina y su situación actual," in Peter Waldmann, ed., *Justicia en la calle. Ensayos sobre la policía en América Latina*, 161–183. Medellín: Biblioteca Jurídica.

Marx, Gary. T. 1988. *Undercover Police Surveillance in America.* Berkeley: University of California Press.

Matienzo, Nicolás B. 1926. *Lecciones de derecho constitucional.* Buenos Aires.

Mazower, Mark. 1997. "Policing the Anti-Communist State in Greece, 1922–1927," in Mark Mazower, ed., *The Policing of Politics in the Twentieth Century*, 129–150. Oxford: Berghan Books.

Mejías, Laurentino. 1913. *La Policía por dentro.* Barcelona: Imprenta Viuda de Luis M. Tasso.

Memoria de la Policía Federal. 1904–1945.

Miller, Willbur R. 1975. "Police Authority in London and New York City, 1830–1870," *Journal of Social History* 8, 2: 81–101.

Ministerio del Interior. 1928. Memorandum from Minister of War to Minister of Interior, secret dossier.

    1928. Legajo 57, expediente 31422. National Territory of Chaco, Legajo 54, expediente 30210.

    1928. Legajo 16501, January 1 and 30.

    1944. Legajo 16, dossier 306.

    1952. Código de Justicia Policial. Buenos Aires. Buenos Aires: Imprenta del Congreso de la Nación.

Mosse, George L. 1975. *Police Forces in History*. London: Sage.

Mustapic, Ana María. 1984. "Conflictos institucionales en el primer gobierno radical," *Desarrollo Económico* 24, 93: 85–108.

Orona, Juan V. 1971. *La Revolución del 6 de setiembre*. Buenos Aires.

Oszlak, Oscar. 1997. *La formación del estado argentino, 1967–1970*. Buenos Aires: Editorial de Belgrano.

Palmer, Stanley H. 1988. *Police and Protest in England and Ireland, 1780–1850*. Cambridge: Cambridge University Press.

Pizzorno, Alessandro. 1991. "Police en Europe: Construction et developpement," in Jean Claude Monet, ed., *Police en Europe, Les cahiers de la sécurité intérieure*, 81–110. Paris: La Documentation française.

Police Dossier of Juan Carlos Vasquez and Lieutenant Colonel Francisco and Roberto Bosch, Division of Political Order.

Potash, Robert. 1981. *El ejército y la política en la Argentina, 1928–1948*. Buenos Aires: Editorial Sudamericana.

Privitellio, Lúcio. 1997. *Agustín Justo*. Mexico: Fondo de Cultural Económica.

Reinke, Herbert. 1997. "Policing Politics in Germany from Weimar to the Stasi," in Mark Mazower, ed., *The Politics of Policing in the Twentieth Century*, 91–106. Oxford: Berghahn Books.

Rock, David. 1985. *Argentina, 1516–1987: From Spanish Colonization to Alfonsín*. Berkeley: University of California Press.

Rodriguez, Adolfo Enrique. 1971. *Evolución Policial*. Junta de Estudios Históricos de San José de Flores.

    1975a. *Historia de la Policía Federal Argentina*. 8 Vols. Buenos Aires: Biblioteca Policial.

    1975b. El Coronel Falcón y la militarización de la policía," *Mundo Policial* 33: 26–57.

    1981. *Cuatrocientos años de policía en Buenos Aires*. Buenos Aires: Biblioteca Policial.

Rodriguez Molas, Ricardo. 1985. *Historia de la tortura y el orden represivo en la Argentina*. Buenos Aires: Eudeba.

Rouquié, Alain. 1985. *Poder militar y sociedad política en la Argentina*. Buenos Aires: Emecé.

Sábato, Hilda. 1991. "Citizenship, Political Participation and the Formation of the Public Sphere in Buenos Aires, 1850–1880s," *Past and Present* 136 (August): 139–163.

Sábato, Jorge. 1991. *La clase dominante en la Argentina moderna*. Buenos Aires: Cisea.

Salessi, Jorge. 1995. *Médicos, maleantes y maricas*. Buenos Aires: Beatriz Viterbo Editora.

Salvatore, Ricardo. 1996. "Penitentiaries, Visions of Class, and Export Economies: Brazil and Argentina Compared," in Ricardo Salvatore and Carlos Aguirre, *The Birth of the Penitentiary in Latin America: Essays on Criminology, Prison Reform and Social Control, 1830–1940*, 194–223. Texas: University of Texas Press.

Salvatore, Ricardo, and Carlos Aguirre. 1996. *The Birth of the Penitentiary in Latin America. Essays on Criminology, Prison Reform and Social Control, 1830–1940*. Texas: University of Texas Press.

Theoharis, Athan G. 1997. "Political Policing in the United States: The Evolution of the FBI, 1917–1956," in Mark Mazower, ed., *The Policing of Politics in the Twentieth Century*, 191–211. Oxford: Berghahn Books.

Tilly, Charles, ed. 1975. *The Formation of National States in Western Europe*. Princeton: Princeton University Press.

1985. "War Making and State Making as Organized Crime," in Peter Evans, Dietrich Rueschemeyer, and Theda Skocpol, eds., *Bringing the State Back In*, 169–191. Cambridge: Cambridge University Press, 1985.

1990. *Coercion, Capital and European States, AD 990–1992*. Cambridge, Mass.: Blackwell.

1997. "Democracy Is a Lake," in *Roads from Past Future*, 193–215. Oxford: Rowman & Littlefield.

Waisman, Carlos. 1989. "Argentina: Autarkic Industrialization and Illegitimacy," in Lary Diamond, Juan Linz, and Seymour Martin Lipset, eds., *Democracy in Developing Countries*. Boulder: Lynne Rienner.

Walter, Richard. 1977. *The Socialist Party of Argentina, 1890–1930*. Austin: University of Texas Press.

1987. *La provincia de Buenos Aires en la política Argentina, 1912–1943*. Buenos Aires: Emecé.

9

War-Making and U.S. State Formation

Mobilization, Demobilization, and the Inherent Ambiguities of Federalism

Susan M. Browne

U.S. political development presents a complicated problem; although war-making drove state-making, the process unfolded on two levels – local and "national." On the one hand, on the basis of the Declaration of Independence from England in 1776 each of the thirteen former British colonies constituted itself as a sovereign state; on the other hand, the states agreed to form an ad hoc confederation for the purpose of prosecuting the war for independence from Britain. It is not really accurate to refer to the Confederation as a "national" government. However, during the eight years that the Revolutionary War lasted many of those who served in the Continental Congress and in the Continental Army began to think in terms of a national state. Political struggles between those who sought to retain local control (localists) and those who wanted the individual states to form a national state (nationalists) placed control of the military front and center. Debates in the Continental Congress as well as in local state legislatures revolved around the issues of mobilization and demobilization of soldiers. How should the troops be mobilized – republican virtue and patriotism or the market? If the troops were to be paid, how much and who should pay them? Should the war be fought by local state militias or one large army? The problem of how to "get rid" of the army, as Alec Campbell puts it (in Chapter 4), surfaced in debates over whether officers should have a pension, one of the hottest political struggles.

Related to the questions about the military itself were the problems of how to pay for the war and the disposition of lands in the West. Each of these questions pitted localists against nationalists. Soldiers and officers during the Revolutionary War and veterans in the postwar period took an active part in the debates. On several occasions officers intervened directly in political affairs on behalf of their own interests, even to the point of threatening a coup d'etat. Moreover, officers and veterans of the Continental Army – the most professionalized soldiers – were most inclined to threaten civilian control. More important, their interventions as a political pressure group tipped the balance in struggles between nationalists and localists toward the formation of a national state.

Recognizing that military personnel and veterans played an important role in producing and "resolving" tensions between localists and nationalists not only helps us rethink and recast ideas about the larger patterns of U.S. state formation and political development. It also forces a rethinking of conventional wisdom about military subordination to civilian control and the formation of democratic states. In particular, Samuel Huntington's theory is especially in need of revision. In *The Soldier and the State*, Huntington argues that the officers in the U.S. armed forces are professionals with a "calling" to serve the public interest (1959: 9). He claims that their specialized training in the "management of violence" endows them with a professional ethos that places them on a par with doctors and lawyers. This, along with a conservative ideology that the military and a significant number of citizens and politicians share, would account for the military's subordination to civilian control in the U.S. case (Huntington 1959: 93). I argue that Huntington's thesis is incomplete at best and at worst is dangerously misleading, especially when applied to the U.S. case in early periods of national political development. The "professional ethos" of the military was not a free-floating, static cultural trait. Therefore, to the extent that it was dynamic and malleable, it must be the subject of sustained historical analysis. During the early period of U.S. state formation many people embraced the republican ideology of the virtuous citizen-soldier serving the public interest. Indeed, it was fear of a "professional" army that sparked many debates between localists and nationalists during the revolutionary period. How quickly the military discarded that ideology to defend its interests should give us pause. Once we recognize the importance of local-national struggles over control of the military and its finances, as well as the key role the military played in the political struggles, we begin to see that military subordination to civilian control may have been more tenuous than Huntington's model leads us to believe. We should also be leery of exporting the model to other countries seeking to "cage" their militaries.

The Military, Massachusetts Politics, and U.S. Politics

It is beyond the scope of this study to examine the national-local nexus for each of the thirteen states. Thus, I focus on one state, Massachusetts, while glancing only briefly in other directions. For several reasons, Massachusetts is a good case to start with in rethinking and recasting our ideas on how soldiers and veterans have shaped the tensions between local and national autonomy in U.S. politics. First, Boston was an important mercantile center involved in international trade. In the middle of the eighteenth century and especially after the Seven Years' War when Britain imposed measures designed to increase revenues and rationalize bureaucratic control over the colonies, Boston felt the weight of British intervention, and Whigs there were among the first and most vociferous organizers in the movement for independence. Second, during and after the Revolutionary War, officers from Massachusetts, especially General Henry Knox and General Rufus Putnam, were ardent nationalists who took an active role in organizing the officer corps into a political pressure group. Third, Massachusetts was the home of some of the most staunch localists who contested every attempt at both centralization and rationalization of the army and the Confederation's funding. Fourth, after the Revolutionary War, Massachusetts was a hotbed of political struggles over veterans' benefits, taxation to pay the war debt, and public land policy – struggles that culminated in Shays's Rebellion in 1786–1787. Thus, Massachusetts was a key state in the struggles between localists and nationalists, and the home of some of the conflict's key players – both military and civilian.

Massachusetts also makes a good focus for this study because in revising our understanding of how soldiers and veterans have shaped the process of state formation in the U.S. case, Shays's Rebellion is itself extremely important. In the struggles over local versus national control, Massachusetts refused to agree even to a reform of the Articles of Confederation. In late 1786, citizens, many of them former Continental Army officers, in the central and western part of the state, took up arms and began closing down courthouses in order to prevent the courts from enacting judgments on debt collection suits. The General Court, as Massachusetts's state legislature is called, declared the western counties in open rebellion against "the state." The rebellion caused such fear in the hearts of local elites that they finally agreed to participate in a national convention to reform the Articles. In part because of Shays's Rebellion, when the delegates finally met they were a more pliable group. That convention went beyond its original instructions, threw out the Articles, and instead made a new Constitution. When the Constitutional Convention ended and the new plan was submitted to the states for ratification, the framers insisted that specially elected assemblies rather than the local state legislatures should ratify the plan. The legality of the convention and the ratification procedure added yet another bone of contention between localists and nationalists. Had Shays's Rebellion not occurred, the United States might look very different today, not only because the Constitutional Convention might never have occurred but also because ongoing national-local tensions might not have been enshrined so firmly in U.S. politics. Furthermore, when we realize that veteran officers of the Continental Army led Shays's Rebellion, we begin to see just how central the military really was in the formation of the United States.

In this chapter I begin with a brief examination of class formation and structure in the former British North American colonies. I argue that freeholding farmers who composed the bulk of the military rank and file bargained from a stronger position than European peasants and were the key to victory in the Revolutionary War. Next I focus on three related debates in the Continental Congress: struggles over the military involving mobilization, pay, and demobilization; debt; and the disposition of the western lands and soldiers' land bounties. I show that the military played a key role in the political battles over local versus national control. Third, I turn to the Massachusetts political scene to show how national struggles played out in local struggles, particularly as evidenced in the struggle waged by Shays's rebels. I conclude with an overview of the role of veterans in the rebellion and in the formation of the United States as a national state.

Class Structure, Coercion, and Capital

The composition of the military forces that waged war with England in the struggle for independence was different from European armies. It was not an army of peasants, agricultural, or urban laborers. Rather, the bulk of the troops comprised young men who, in the normal course of their lives, could reasonably expect to own their own small farms or businesses. Although the relationship between war-making and state-making is well established, who does the actual fighting makes a difference. In *Coercion, Capital, and European States, AD 990–1992*, Charles Tilly presents a model to illustrate the dialectical, bargaining relationship between rulers of states and capitalists in cities. Cities are "containers of capital," which rulers tap for the funds to make war. Rulers, in their half of the bargain, pacify, protect, and expand territories (1990: 53). Colonies served a function similar to that of cities. However, the British North American colonies were initially a disappointment compared with the more lucrative British, Spanish, and French colonies to the south. No gold poured into the British economy from North America; tobacco, rice, indigo, lumber, and fisheries produced only modest revenues. The British crown granted large tracts of land to lords proprietors such as William Penn and Lord Baltimore, but no labor force habituated to agriculture presented itself, and thus staples production for export was only moderately profitable. In short, the North American colonies were poor containers of capital until well into the eighteenth century.

Faced with a chronic labor shortage, the planters offered generous terms (for the times) to those who came to North America as indentured servants. The process of class formation was different from the European experience. The lords proprietors had already enclosed large tracts of land. In order to attract people to develop it, they broke their tracts into smaller farms. We might say that in North America there was a "de-enclosure" movement. Second, because they had access to land, small farmers had a greater say, though a limited one, in political affairs. Third, because the colonies were such paltry containers of capital, the British government was less interested in their defense until the middle of the eighteenth century. Local militias of small farmers led by the local notable defended their settlements from Indian raids. Thus, the farmers were more apt to be armed citizens. By 1774, 75 percent of free white families owned a farm (Lebergott 1984: 30). We need to be careful about making broad generalizations about the thirteen British North American colonies since regional economies differed markedly in New England, the middle colonies, and the South. One thing, however, is fairly common to all – widespread landownership. Many analysts, Tocqueville among them, have noted the wide distribution of land, the smaller size of land holdings among white settlers, and the middle-class character of the early United States as compared with Europe (1969: 50–56). This was less so in the South.

Nor did urban areas – Philadelphia, New York, Boston, and Charleston – present much of a source of capital for Britain. Wealth was more highly concentrated in these areas, but it was not the old, accumulated, concentrated, liquid capital of the European financial institutions and markets (Hammond [1957] 1985: 4). Indeed, in 1766 the colonies were in debt to British merchants to the tune of over £4,450,000 (Egnal 1998: 13).

This brief sketch of the political economy of British North America shows that class structure was different from Europe: elites lacked access to liquid capital, they lacked coercive means, and these deficiencies prevented them from dominating each other and from dominating the small farmer. Thus, in mobilizing for war with Britain, the small farmer bargained with elites from a position of relative strength. This forces us to refocus Tilly's lens and consider more than the relationship between capitalists and rulers. The family farmer entered the political arena early in the process of forming the United States. Europe had rulers – kings and nobility – who exercised greater power over peasants and artisans dependent upon them. In British North America, elites governed rather than ruled. The stronger position of ordinary people, independent family farmers and artisans, resulted in what Jack P. Greene has dubbed a "negotiated authority," which was more contractual, based on the consent of both parties (1994: 44). It was a relationship of mutual interdependence rather than of dependence. British North America was predominantly a society of petite bourgeois agricultural producers.

This is not to say, however, that the local notable was not a powerful man. In lean years or in order to improve and expand their freeholds, farmers turned to the local "gentry" for credit because there were no formal financial institutions and cash was scarce (Anderson 1984: 30). The same was true for entrepreneurs who sought credit to start new businesses. It was a society of local, personal relationships (Wood 1991: 68–69).

Resistance to British measures to restrict colonial development and rationalize revenue extraction began in cities such as Boston and Philadelphia where merchants and artisans bore the brunt of the new measures. Virginia planters soon joined because British policies such as the Stamp Act raised the cost of shipping staples and disrupted their plans for developing lands to the west. Because freeholding farmers engaged in fewer transactions and used less cash, they were not affected nearly so much. If the colonies were to become independent from Britain, however, more than the mere acquiescence of the farmers was required; they had to be mobilized to participate in the movement. Europeans, as Alec Campbell pointed out, solved the problem of fielding large armies through the market. As we saw, because North American elites lacked access to liquid capital, a mercenary army was not an option. Boston Whigs came to realize that they would need to appeal to the farmers' "everyday experience," the things that interested them. Thus, Samuel Adams insisted that English ministers were corrupt men who threatened "to take away your barn and my house." John Adams argued that "considering the 'scarcity of money, we have reason to think the execution of that act [the Stamp Act] for a time would drain the country of its cash, strip multitudes of their property, and reduce them to absolute beggary'" (Kulikoff 1992: 134). Even so, the back country farmers were reluctant warriors. Most eligible males had some land or a reasonable expectation of obtaining enough land to be self-supporting eventually. Moreover, because British North America faced a chronic labor shortage and a huge development task, there was usually plenty of work in the rural areas to tide young men over until they inherited or earned enough to purchase a small farm. Nor was the offer of citizenship rights particularly compelling. White male suffrage requirements, although tied to landownership, were lower than in Europe so that small farmers already had citizenship rights. Robert Dahl observes, "The more that military superiority has depended on the capacity of a state for mobilizing large numbers of lightly armed foot soldiers, the greater have been the prospects for popular government" (1989: 245). In the case of the United States, the fact that the army was composed of freeholding farmers less dependent on a local landlord, with good prospects of a decent, even upwardly mobile civilian life and full citizenship rights, made the prospects for popular government very good indeed.

Soldiers' Pay and Professional Armies

After the flush of the first victories began to wear thin, maintaining the initial *rage militaire* became a problem. The farmers grew weary of war and wanted to return to their families, friends, and farms; the populace balked at the expense of supplying the army; the states began falling short of their enlistment quotas. Moreover, the local militias were no match for the better-trained and -equipped British army. George Washington complained bitterly about the militia: "'[T]hey come in you cannot tell where,' Washington wrote in exasperation, 'consume your provisions, exhaust your Stores, and leave you at last in a critical moment'" (Kohn 1975: 9). Washington and others believed that the United States required a better-trained and -disciplined army if the war was to be won. Localists in the Continental Congress and in the states immediately objected to a standing professional army, viewing it as the first step toward tyranny and insisting on the adequacy of the local militia. Advocates for the militia drew on an ideal based on their reading of the histories of Greek and Roman republics. In this view, once Rome developed a standing army, it began to rebel against the state and eventually led to a cycle of demagoguery, tyranny, and the demise of Rome. Many believed that the army should be like the Greek hoplites, free citizens defending their own lands. Washington rejected this fatalistic, cyclical reading of history and opted for a more pragmatic approach. He explained that "a Soldier reasoned with upon the goodness of the cause he is engaged in, and the inestimable rights he is contending for, hears you with patience, and acknowledges the truth of your observations, but adds, that it is of no more importance to him than others. . . . The few, therefore, who act on principle of disinterestedness, are, comparatively speaking, no more than a drop in the Ocean" (Royster 1979: 65). The republican ideal of virtuous citizen-soldiers defending their homes rested on a vision of volunteer, local militias rather than on a professional military ethos, as Huntington argues. The move to a more professional army, which Washington, Alexander Hamilton, Henry Knox, Robert Morris, and Gouveneur Morris advocated, was a move away from the localist, republican ideal.

As local militias began to suffer defeats at the hands of the British, the Continental Congress finally approved a plan to offer pay and land bounties to men who enlisted for the duration of the war. The plan, however, had to be approved by the individual states. Massachusetts refused to do so. Local states continued to offer their own enlistment bounties which competed with the Continental Army. At least some localists were willing to depart from the republican ideal of a volunteer citizen militia to the extent that they offered some pay to soldiers. The republican ideology provided a justification for retaining control of the army in the hands of local powerholders.

Funding the Debt

A second major political battle was how to supply the army. As we saw earlier, North America lacked the capital markets and financial institutions from which European governments drew to finance wars. Nor did the former colonies have the industrial capacity to manufacture the necessary war matériel. Guns, cannon, gunpowder, boots, clothing, blankets, and a myriad of other items could not be supplied in sufficient quantities. North America relied on the French and Dutch for manufactures and the funds to finance imports. Two competing schemes to finance the war developed. Again, the political struggle pitted localists and nationalists against each other.

Alexander Hamilton, Robert Morris, and Gouveneur Morris led a group in the Continental Congress favoring a funding scheme that involved tying the interests of the well-to-do to a central state. They would accomplish this by maintaining a running national debt and encouraging public creditors to speculate in that debt. The debt would never be paid; rather, creditors would collect interest. The plan provided a permanent funding mechanism for the Continental Congress independent of the states. Inducing people with money to invest in the government would also help to reduce the need to tax the people. In 1781 Hamilton argued, "A national debt, if not excessive, will be to us a blessing. It will be a powerful cement of our union" (Jensen 1950: 45). Hamilton's idea was not new. Indeed, Cotton Mather, a second-generation Puritan and an important leader in seventeenth-century Massachusetts, was one of the first to favor such a scheme, which involved issuing paper money (Newell 1998: 132). Mather's plan and later Hamilton's was to get wealthy men to invest and circulate rather than horde their money. Localists recognized that a central government with a funding mechanism independent from local state control was a direct challenge to local power. Thus the power of the purse became a second political struggle between nationalists and localists. Those favoring local funding schemes won out in the Continental Congress. They brought paper finance to an end and made the Continental Army dependent on supplies to be provided by individual states rather than a centralized supply system. Just as a decentralized militia proved to be ineffective in the field, so too a decentralized supply system proved inefficient in supplying the troops. Farmers held back supplies and balked at paying higher taxes. By the end of 1780 it looked as if the war would be lost as the British marched relentlessly northward, virtually unopposed by an ill-trained, ill-fed, and poorly equipped army composed of local militia units. The stresses of 1780 brought many nationalists back to the Continental Congress.

Western Lands

Throughout the colonial period land speculators and settlers pushed westward. Land development companies such as the Ohio Company in which Washington, the Lees, and other wealthy Virginia families owned a considerable interest, and the Wabash Company in which Benjamin Franklin was heavily involved, often established competing claims. Many land speculators were willing to uphold either local or national sovereignty provided they got their claims. Those who favored local control were often large landowners such as the Lees whose claims to western lands were safe in the local state. Richard Henry Lee, a staunch localist, feared that if the Continental Congress had an independent funding mechanism, the "monied interest" would gain ascendancy over the "landed interest." In order to keep the power of the purse in local hands, Lee was willing to cede territory claimed by Virginia to the Continental Congress to be sold in order to pay off the national debt and thus dissolve Hamilton's "cement." It should be kept in mind that the Lee family already had a secure claim to its western lands. Although Lee's words may seem to have an egalitarian ring to them, he was one of the wealthiest, largest landholders in Virginia. Lee was not talking about small family farmers when he spoke of the "landed interest." He meant large slaveholding plantation owners. Lee had nothing to lose in ceding Virginia's lands to the Continental Congress. Rather, it was a way to protect the power of local elites.

The Continental Army

Under the influence of "Baron" von Steuben, the Continental Army began to receive training in European-style drilling and combat. "The Massachusetts line during the war attained such discipline that Baron von Steuben 'admired' rather than 'inspected' it" (Pencak 1993: 130). The longer the war lasted, the higher the professional level of the army, and the more the soldiers and officers had invested in it.

Supply and pay shortages continued to plague the Continental Army because those who stayed at home resisted supply requisitions and higher taxes. It limped along – literally. An army of "lightly armed foot soldiers" is an understatement considering that many went without shoes and provided their own arms. From all accounts there was real hunger and sickness. Soldiers and officers alike began to feel increasingly isolated from civilians and perceived that those who had stayed behind were making money from the war while they, the soldiers, risked their lives and exhausted their own wealth (Royster 1979: 276). The men began to develop a consciousness of their interests as against those of civilians. Officers and soldiers alike began to engage in collective contentious behavior, although that which the rank and file exhibited was different from that of the officers.

Soldiers began to defy the harsh military discipline their commanding officers sought to impose. Mutiny and desertion rose as pay and rations failed to materialize. When the men deemed their enlistment period to be fulfilled, they deserted the line en masse (Neimeyer 1996: 146–153). The fact that the soldiers began to desert shows that they had secure places within their own communities and did not rely on service in the military as their only means of making a living. Rather, service in the military was a kind of "shortcut" to achieving the goal of independence sooner. In *A People's Army*, Fred Anderson argues that white males in New England went through a long period of dependence in which they worked on their fathers' farms and exchanged their labor with other farmers until their fathers retired or they had saved enough to buy a farm (1984: 32–35). Service in the military was a way for these young men to shorten the period of dependence and, with the promise of a land bounty, to assure themselves a larger farm than they might otherwise have acquired. In the case of immigrants, who, as John Patrick Neimeyer points out, composed a significant portion of the Continental Army, the situation was similar. If they served in the army, they could hasten the time when they would own their own farms. On the other hand, they could reasonably expect to become small farmers without service in the military. Soldiers in the Continental Army were in no sense a "proto-proletariat," as Neimeyer argues (1996: 19). Rather, they were young men who had not yet come into their own but who had a reasonable expectation of doing so (Anderson 1984: 38). Mutinies and high desertion rates show two things. First, it shows that the rank-and-file soldiers had alternatives to military service, and that if military service did not enhance their already reasonable life chances, they could afford to leave. Second, it shows that soldiers were capable of organizing themselves to press their demands.

Officers too exhibited a sense of their superior bargaining position and a willingness to act collectively in order to defend their interests. In their case this took the form of organizing collectively to intervene directly in politics even to the point of threatening a military coup. The first instance took place in 1782 when Continental Army officers from Massachusetts petitioned the Massachusetts General Court. The Continental Congress, in order to build an officer corps, had promised those who would stay for the duration of the war a land bounty and half pay for life. However, Congress could only recommend to the states; it could not make binding laws unless all the local states agreed. Massachusetts was one of the holdouts in approving the plan for the officers' benefits. General Henry Knox and General Rufus Putnam, both from Massachusetts and both "new men" who had come up through the ranks and made careers for themselves in the army, helped organize the officers and aided in writing the petition. General Putnam even wrote to Samuel Adams that if the General Court did not act upon the officers' petition, they could not be trusted with their arms. Despite this veiled threat to civilian authority, the "country dominated" House balked, although the mercantile dominated Senate was willing to go along. The General Court sent the officers away, but reassured them that the Continental Congress would take up the matter of officers' pay in early 1783. The officers dutifully returned to camp in Newburgh, New York, but began, again with Knox's assistance, to prepare their petition to Congress (Jensen 1950: 35). The new petition too contained a thinly veiled threat to civilian control.

Our distresses are now to a point. We have borne all that men can bear; our property is expended, our resources at an end, and our friends are wearied out and disgusted with our incessant applications. We therefore, seriously beg that a supply of money may be forwarded to the army as soon as possible. The uneasiness of the soldiers for want of pay, is great and dangerous; further experimentation on their patience may have fatal effects. (Cutler and Cutler 1888: 153)

The message is clear. Nor could it have come at a more opportune moment for nationalists such as Hamilton, the Morrises, and Knox who sought a tighter, permanent union and national control. They had developed another plan for funding the national debt. Their idea was to tie the interests of the army and those of the other public creditors together. This involved paying off the officers in a lump sum equivalent to five years' full pay rather than half pay for life as originally promised. The second part of the plan was an impost, a tax on imports, similar to one proposed in 1780. The impost, a relatively painless indirect tax, would have been used to pay interest on the debt accrued in paying the soldiers as well as the other public creditors. The plan became mired in political wrangling over whether the states or Congress would appoint collectors and other details, which again involved the issue of whether the power of the purse would remain under control of the local states or the national government. By using the very real threat of a military revolt, Hamilton hoped to scare Congress into approving the new funding scheme.

The army also submitted a second petition to the Continental Congress in 1783, this one with Washington's recommendation attached. The officers called on Congress to increase the land bounties offered in 1776 and 1780. Generals, originally promised 1,100 acres of land in the West according to the earlier plan, would get 2,400 acres in the new petition. Privates would receive a 500-acre increase. The petition offered Congress a way out of its funding dilemma by stipulating that the "associators" who settled in the West would accept provisions in lieu of back pay (Cutler and Cutler 1888: 156–157). The further advantage to nationalist interests was that veterans would help colonize the West, defending the newly opened territories from the Indians. A total of 288 officers signed the new petition, over half from Massachusetts, although New Jersey, New Hampshire, Connecticut, and Maryland were represented as well. Captain Luke Day, a future leader in Shays's Rebellion was among the signers (Cutler and Cutler 1888: 157–167).

Agitation over back pay and officers' benefits continued. It eventually culminated in the Newburgh Affair. As peace negotiations with England began and the war drew to a close, it was not lost on the officers that their political clout would diminish once the army demobilized. They might never collect their back pay, land bounties, and pensions. Hamilton and Robert Morris's plan to use the real grievances of the army as a political cudgel nearly backfired for it almost ended in a real coup attempt. One of Washington's rivals, General Horatio Gates, an appointee of the Lee-Adams localist clique, began planning to overthrow Washington and to take over leadership of the army. Hamilton had apparently clued Washington in on the plan to use the army to threaten Congress. However, it does not appear that either knew about Gates. One historian says that Gates's coup attempt was Robert Morris's doing (Kohn 1975: 37). It could be that Lee or a member of his clique actually put Gates up to a different plot. In their private letters the Lee-Adams group expressed dissatisfaction with Washington because they believed he had succumbed to Hamilton's flattery. They judged Washington to be weak and incompetent because of his moderation (Royster 1979: 179).

General Gates led a group of younger officers who had grown up in the military and were deeply disturbed at the thought of peace because it meant the end of their careers. Here again, we see that the most professional officers, those whose careers were at stake, were most likely to threaten civilian control. Gates's group circulated petitions among the officers. The petitions became known as the Newburgh Addresses. The first, written by Major John Armstrong Jr., one of Gates's aides, urged the officers to change the "meek language" and the "milk and water style" of their last petition to Congress. Armstrong also pointed out the country's ingratitude to the men who served in the army. The address urged the officers to refuse to lay down arms and to turn their swords against Congress if something were not done about their pay (Kohn 1975: 29–30). Washington, in the end, was able to defuse the situation and persuade the officers to remain subordinate to civilian control, but only barely. The Newburgh Affair left him deeply shaken. " 'The army,' Washington warned, 'is a dangerous instrument to play with. Its just claims should be settled and it should be disbanded without delay' " (Jensen 1950: 79).

The threat of a coup also left Congress deeply shaken. However, Hamilton and Morris's plan worked only superficially. The Congress voted the officers their five years' pay. The impost passed, but with such a jumble of compromises and concessions to local jealousies and state sovereignty that even Hamilton refused to vote for it. The tax was to be used only to pay the national debt, and thus would have dissolved Hamilton's national "cement." Moreover, enforcement was uncertain because the states were to appoint collectors (Kohn 1975: 33). However that may be, the nationalists made an inroad and laid a foundation for independent funding for Congress, and it was military intervention that tipped the balance.

Congress heeded Washington's advice to disband the army quickly but failed to address its just claims. Washington urged Robert Morris to obtain three months' pay for soldiers before discharging them, believing that the soldiers should not arrive home penniless. Morris used an intricate international funding scheme to obtain the money. However, Congress refused to delay disbanding the army until the funds arrived. In part, this was because the longer the army stayed together, the more pay the government would owe, and thus the greater the national debt (Royster 1979: 342). Fear of further outbursts from discontented officers and threats of mutiny from the rank and file also made it urgent to disband the army (Kohn 1975: 40). The men were released, officially on furlough, because British troops still remained on U.S. soil. Their pay did not arrive until nearly all had started for home (Royster 1979: 342). Thus Congress "got rid of the army" in an unceremonious way. Indeed, some soldiers resorted to begging as they made for their homes (Royster 1979: 352). The haste with which Congress disbanded the army left the matter of veterans' pay unsettled.

Demobilization, the Society of Cincinnati, and the Ohio Company

Knox also knew about the Newburgh Affair. Although his role is unclear, he was close to Washington and probably did not back Gates in his plan for a coup d'etat. On the other hand, we have seen that Knox played a key role in organizing the officers and helping them to petition Congress and the General Court. The fact that the army would lose its political influence once it demobilized was certainly not lost on him. In order to keep the officers together and maintain at least some of their power, he organized the Society of Cincinnati, a fraternal club for Continental Army officers. He clearly intended that the club would be a political pressure group. Washington was the president of the club. The organization caused quite a stir throughout the United States, especially in New England. Three attributes of the society were especially repugnant to New Englanders: the officers' fame, the badge they wore, and hereditary membership (Royster 1979: 356). Many viewed it as a first step toward a new aristocracy.

One of the interests Knox intended to protect was the army's land bounties. Knox and Putnam, along with a former chaplin, Manasseh Cutler, formed the Ohio Company to that end. It was a grand development scheme based on the petition the army had presented to Congress in 1783. Cutler shepherded the plan through Congress and finally got it approved in 1786. Things did not look so rosy for the veterans or the Ohio Company in Massachusetts, however.

Demobilization and Massachusetts Politics

When veterans returned to their homes in Massachusetts no heroes' welcome awaited them. On the contrary, civilians were suspicious of the Continentals, and the back country resisted paying veterans their settlements. Both civilians and Continental veterans claimed to be the upholders of republican virtue. Veterans' claims to moral superiority met with vilification. They received no special honors; celebrations of independence took the form of potluck dinners rather than military parades, and soldiers blended in with civilians. The attack on the Society of Cincinnati and resistance to officers' benefits was in part an effort of civilians to reclaim primacy in the revolutionary victory (Royster 1979: 357). Equally important, however, is the way that the General Court chose to pay veterans' benefits and the war debt.

So far, I have focused on debates in the Continental Congress between localists and nationalists over control of the military, control of government finance, and the disposition of western lands. Intuitively, we might think that local government would be more democratic, closer to the people. Tocqueville extolled New England for the excellence of its democratic local institutions. However that may be, there is evidence that local government in New England was not as democratic as Tocqueville thought. First, there is the matter of the local militia. Prior to the Revolutionary War, the local militias had been a school for social deference. "The militia, besides suppressing revolts, were also a means of forestalling them and of fostering consent to government, not by force but by instruction." Officers in the militia were chosen for social status rather than their military prowess (Morgan 1988: 169). There was no clear separation between civilian and military authority in the towns. Very often, the local notables and their family members were both politicians and military commanders. Continental Army officers who had risen in rank and gained experience organizing and commanding men showed less deference to local elites upon returning to civilian life (Morgan 1988: 305). Continental Army officers who organized and led Shays's Rebellion certainly exhibited a different attitude to authority. Second is the problem of patronage and multiple office-holding. Justices of the Peace also sat in the General Court; the men who made the laws also adjudicated disputes. There was no clear separation among branches of government. Although the Massachusetts Constitution of 1780 curtailed the practice on paper, the practice continued (Fairlie 1906: 33). Furthermore, the governor appointed the justices of the peace for all the counties and chose three of their number for the court of sessions (Tocqueville 1969: 76). This meant that local power holders depended upon patronage for appointment to public office. Third, as noted earlier, Massachusetts was still a place where credit depended on face-to-face relationships and personal standing in one's own small community. A relatively few important families dominated Massachusetts politics, while new men challenged local authority.

Politicians in Massachusetts fell roughly into four groups. Knox and Putnam exemplify the "new men" who entered the political arena. Knox had been a middling bookseller in Boston. He married into a wealthy Boston family and made a career in the Continental Army and the Confederation. Knox and Putnam were extreme nationalists. Others, less extreme, believed that some revision of the Articles of Confederation would be desirable if it would benefit commerce and the public creditors. James Bowdoin, John Hancock's successor as governor of Massachusetts, is a good example of this second group. A third group, of whom Theodore Sedgwick was the most outspoken, favored a "northern confederation" and wished to exclude the South from any political union. Sedgwick was intensely jealous of local rights. He lived in Stockbridge in Berkshire County on the far western side of Massachusetts where he was a scion of an old and powerful family. A fourth group, led by Elbridge Gerry and Samuel Adams, worried constantly about republican ideals and local rights, and rejected any proposal that seemed to threaten that ideal (East 1939: 366).

Localists in the latter two categories called the shots in Massachusetts politics. As we have seen, localists in the Continental Congress fought to keep the power of the purse in local hands by selling western lands to reduce the national debt, stipulating that the impost would be used only to pay off the national debt, and by disbanding the Continental Army in order to keep the national debt from growing. At war's end, it was determined that, based on population, each state would assume a portion of the national debt, and see to paying it off as the local assembly saw fit. On the face of it, this may seem to be the patriotic, democratic thing to do. Massachusetts led the way in paying off its portion. During the postwar depression, other states eased the burden on citizens by enacting tender laws, emitting paper money, and extending mortgages. Not so Massachusetts. In their haste to dissolve the "cement" of a national debt, localists in Massachusetts embarked on a massive revaluation of assets in the state. "The adoption of the new valuation opened the way to the assessment of the largest direct tax for specie the Commonwealth had ever laid" (Buel 1993: 53). The General Court turned a deaf ear to hard-pressed farmers, many of whom were veterans, for relief from the tax burden. To make matters worse the state found itself in a credit crunch, which caused an unprecedented number of lawsuits against debtors. In all, private debt stood at about $7 million, and the public debt was about the same. This amounted to about $200 on each head of a family at a time when most farmers hardly saw $50 in a year. Sheriffs began confiscating homesteads, farm animals, tools, and other assets and selling them at public auction to pay mortgages, debts, and taxes (Taylor 1953: 24). Captain Daniel Shays was prosecuted twice in 1784, once for a debt of twelve pounds and again for three pounds (Szatmary 1980: 66).

The situation of veterans in Massachusetts was made particularly acute by the vanguardism of localists in paying its portion of the national debt. One historian of the rebellion describes Captain Luke Day's conversion to rebellion: "The pittance he had received for his certificates had not sufficed to meet his obligations. In 1785 he had been put in debtors' prison. For two stifling months Day, a proud man, had endured the stinking confinement of Northhampton jail in the society of murderers, counterfeiters, and common thieves" (Starkey 1955: 27). "Now to be classed as criminals and outlaws because they [veterans] could not pay their debts was a humiliation which they refused to suffer" (Taylor 1953: 25). Soldiers had been paid in interest-bearing promissory notes. If they held the notes to maturity, they would collect the full amount plus interest. This they could not afford to do, and they sold their certificates to speculators for a small fraction of their value. Now public creditors in Massachusetts clamored for 6 percent interest on the notes and their retirement at face value. "After the war, ex-soldiers in Massachusetts wound up paying taxes to redeem those notes for the speculators, thereby paying twice for the privilege of receiving a small part of their army pay in cash" (Royster 1979: 298).

In short, wealthy local elites, jealous of their local power, sought to retain control of fiscal affairs within Massachusetts but sought to push the burden of their decision onto the veterans. They did so in order to maintain the public credit of the state. So long as public creditors received their interest payments on the debt, it mattered little to them how the debt was funded. This enabled localists in the General Court and in Congress to resist efforts to reform the Articles of Confederation. Moderate nationalists such as Bowdoin felt that the Articles were in need of reform. They were interested in establishing a uniform commercial code. To that end, in 1786 it was proposed that a convention would be held in Annapolis. Despite instructions from the General Court, the Massachusetts delegates to the Continental Congress snubbed the convention. Sedgwick was only too happy to see the Annapolis plan fall apart because he wanted nothing to do with the South and favored a regional alliance among the commercial states of the North. In the meantime John Jay had negotiated a treaty with Spain that favored mercantile shipping interests. In exchange for trading privileges in Spanish ports, the United States would cede navigation rights on the Mississippi. This was disastrous to speculators and developers in the West – the Ohio Company for one. Moreover, because of Jay's treaty with Spain, Kentucky was even talking about becoming a Spanish territory. The debates over the treaty nearly tore Congress apart, exacerbating sectional rivalries. Northern merchants were willing to sacrifice the West, while the South wanted no part of the treaty (McDonald 1979: 243–244).

In 1786 it looked as if the union might really break apart. What would become of the Ohio Company's land scheme? What would become of officers' benefits if left to the jurisdiction of Massachusetts? What little remnant was left of the army would disappear leaving the western frontier even more vulnerable to Indian attacks, the British to the north, and the French and Spanish to the south. It would also mean the end of Knox's career. Add to this the fact that several states were dragging their feet in repaying their portion of the war debt. Yet, the Annapolis Convention adjourned without acting to reform the Articles because no quorum was present. Hamilton and Madison, representing the nationalists at Annapolis, submitted a report to Congress stating that it was hopeless to address only commercial matters and continued to petition Congress for a constitutional convention to revise the Articles. Again Congress failed to act, with Massachusetts again being a major holdout. Congress referred the proposal to a committee of three, which referred it to a committee of thirteen, which Congress never appointed (McDonald 1979: 247). Congress reversed itself in early 1787, finally issuing a call for a convention to reform the Articles (Jensen 1950: 421).

Rethinking Shays's Rebellion

It could be that the timing of Shays's Rebellion and the failure of the Annapolis Convention are merely coincidental. Veterans and farmers in Massachusetts certainly had many problems, as we have seen. We have also seen, however, that Knox and Putnam organized soldiers to intervene in politics on other occasions. In the summer of 1786, as it became apparent that the Annapolis Convention would not act to give Congress additional powers, things in Massachusetts began to heat up. The citizens began taking up arms and closing down courts. The first court closing occurred in Northampton in the summer of 1786. About 1,500 armed farmers and veterans from nearby towns gathered, under Captain Luke Day, to request that the court not open. Some contingents marched with fife and drum in military style. The insurgents blocked the courthouse entrance, and Day presented the justices with a written statement asserting the people's right to protest unconstitutional acts of their government, and entreating the justices to adjourn until the "minds of the people can be obtained and the resolves of the convention can have an opportunity of having their grievances redressed by General Court." The sheriff realized he was powerless because the local militia formed a large part of the assembled men (Starkey 1955: 30).

Veterans of the Continental Army provided the leadership for the rebellion. Throughout Massachusetts during late 1786 and early 1787, former officers led the movement to close down the courts. There is some debate as to just how many Continental veterans were involved. One historian of the rebellion estimates that about one-third of the rebels had seen service in the Revolutionary War (Szatmary 1980: 65). William Pencak estimates that perhaps half the rebels had seen some service (Pencak 1993: 131). The names of fifty-six Massachusetts rebels sufficiently obnoxious to the General Court to be indicted for treason reveal that thirty-three, just under 60 percent, received a Revolutionary War pension, including a land bounty (*Index of War Pensions* 1966). Daniel Shays, Luke Day, Agrippa Wells, Adam Wheeler, Luke Drury, Reuben Dickinson, Oliver Parker, and Seth Murray, all leaders of the rebellion, had been captains. Although it may not be possible to generalize about the military service of all of the rebels, the leaders certainly were former Continental Army officers. We have seen that Massachusetts officers had organized, with Knox and Putnam's aid, to intervene in local and national politics on other occasions. We have also seen that Knox continued as a military figure in organizing the Society of the Cincinnati. In 1785 he became U.S. Secretary of War and was involved in political struggles to maintain a federal military, along with the national funding for it (Kohn 1975: 129).

Could Hamilton, Putnam, or Knox have used tactics similar to those they employed in the Newburgh Affair? Did they foment rebellion in Massachusetts in order to scare localists into cooperating with the drive to get more power for Congress and hold the union together? Knox advocated restraint in using the army to effect domestic political objectives; however, he also stated in a 1787 letter to General McDougall, an activist at Newburgh, that the army's endurance had limits. He hoped that the army would never be turned on any but the enemies of American liberty (East 1939: 381). It is also true that Shays had served under Rufus Putnam and that they knew one another (381). Mercy Otis Warren, who wrote one of the first histories of the Revolutionary War and was a member of an old, powerful Massachusetts family, certainly thought there was a nationalist-military conspiracy afoot. She wrote to John Adams in December 1786 that "Time will make curious disclosures, and you, Sir, will be astonished to find the incendiaries who have fomented the discontents among the miserable insurgents of the Massachusetts, in a class of men least suspected" (East 1939: 379).

Knox certainly made political capital from the rebellion in favor of the army and of more power for the Confederation. "On the strength of little more than his imagination," in one historian's words, "he shouted to all who would listen that a full-fledged rebellion was under way, that huge bands of armed men were about to seize the federal arsenal at Springfield, and that, for good measure, an Indian uprising was about to appear from somewhere" (McDonald 1979: 250). Knox made numerous reports to Washington, Congress, and every man of influence he knew. He consistently exaggerated the number of men involved and misreported their intentions, leading people to believe that the rebels intended to overthrow the government, install Shays as a military dictator, and redistribute all property – the exact "death cycle" of republican governments that localists feared. Knox began reporting that the federal arsenal at Springfield, Massachusetts, was the rebels' target before the rebels entered the town to close the court and after they had twice left Springfield without making a move toward the arsenal. Only federal troops could quell the disturbances (which had been going on in much the same way for fifteen years or more). Only a constitutional convention could check these "democratic excesses" and avert a national calamity (East 1939: 382). In their private letters, nationalists agreed that the rebellion was a golden opportunity for "increasing the dignity and energy of government" (East 1939: 383).

Putnam, Knox, and other nationalists also knew that the value of their securities and land bounty certificates would increase if a national government were formed. As early as 1784 Putnam wrote to Washington that if the government would receive military certificates for land in the Ohio country, their value would double. It should also be noted that Massachusetts had developed a local scheme to sell veterans land in the northern part of the state in order to assuage the "rage for migration," as well as to bring more money into the local state. Putnam had surveyed the land Massachusetts was offering to veterans and had determined that it was inferior to the lands in Ohio. The local plan competed with the Ohio Company's (Cutler and Cutler 1888: 175–176).

With the publicity the rebellion received, staunch localists and regionalists such as Sedgwick and Elbridge Gerry became ardent nationalists. They also began to think very highly of the Society of Cincinnati (East 1939: 389). Now they agreed to a convention to reform the Articles and make the federal government more powerful. As we saw at the beginning of this chapter, the Constitutional Convention went much further, and the United States ended up with a new Constitution that provided for a stronger federal government than it otherwise might have if not for military interventions into politics and the real and perceived threats to civilian government.

In contradistinction to Huntington's theory of military subordination, it was professionals, those with most at stake, who were most apt to be insubordinate in order to defend their interests. Those interests lay in establishing a national government. In Massachusetts the local government's policies actually threatened veterans' interests in back pay, benefits, land bounties, careers, and status. By imposing high taxes Massachusetts threatened the soldiers' assets and property, the loss of which meant jail, pauperization, dependence, and loss of citizenship rights. Veterans of the Continental Army had good reasons for casting their lot with nationalists.

After the War of 1812, the Mexican War, and the Civil War, the federal government continued to offer land bounties to veterans. Once the frontier closed in the late nineteenth century, veterans' benefits took a different form, but continued, as Alec Campbell shows in his essay (Chapter 4 in this volume), to be generous compared with veterans' benefits offered in other countries. The federal government's policy has made private property, education, and health care more accessible to veterans – all of which made for easier entry into the middle class for young males. Thus, the federal government has tied veterans' interests to itself from the beginning of its history and has mitigated possible class conflict. At the same time, because of localists' efforts to limit the size and expense of military forces, the United States had a small military throughout its early history.

References

Anderson, Fred. 1984. *A People's Army: Massachusetts Soldiers and Society in the Seven Years' War*. Chapel Hill: University of North Carolina Press.

Buel, Richard, Jr. 1993. "The Public Creditor Interest in Massachusetts Politics, 1780–86," in Robert A. Gross, ed., *In Debt to Shays: The Bicentennial of an Agrarian Rebellion*, 47–56. Charlottesville: University of Virginia Press.

Cutler, William Parker, and Julia Perkins Cutler. 1888. *Life, Journals and Correspondence of Rev. Manasseh Cutler, LL.D. by His Grandchildren*. Cincinnati: Robert Clarke.

Dahl, Robert A. 1989. *Democracy and Its Critics*. New Haven: Yale University Press.

East, Robert A. 1939. "The Massachusetts Conservatives in the Eighteenth Century," in Richard B. Morris, ed., *The Era of the American Revolution: Studies Inscribed to Evarts Boutell Greene* 349–391. New York: Columbia University Press.

Egnal, Marc. 1998. *New World Economies: The Growth of the Thirteen Colonies and Early Canada*. New York: Oxford University Press.

Fairlie, John A. 1906. *Local Town Government in Counties, Towns, and Villages*. New York: Century.

Greene, Jack P. 1994. *Negotiated Authorities: Essays in Colonial Political and Constitutional History*. Charlottesville: University of Virginia Press.

Hammond, Bray. [1957] 1985. *Banks and Banking in America: From the Revolution to the Civil War*. Princeton: Princeton University Press.

Huntington, Samuel P. 1959. *The Soldier and the State: The Theory and Politics of Civil Military Relations*. Cambridge, Mass.: Harvard University Press.

Index of Revolutionary War Pension Applications. 1966. Washington, D.C.: National Genealogical Society.

Jensen, Merrill. 1950. *The New Nation: A History of the United States during the Confederation, 1781–1789*. New York: Vintage Books.

Kohn, Richard H. 1975. *Eagle and Sword: The Federalists and the Military Establishment, 1783–1802*. New York: Free Press.

Kulikoff, Allan. 1992. *The Agrarian Origins of American Capitalism*. Charlottesville: University of Virginia Press.

Lebergott, Stanley. 1984. *The Americans: An Economic Record*. New York: W. W. Norton.

McDonald, Forrest. 1979. *E Pluribus Unum: The Formation of the American Republic, 1776–1790*. Indianapolis: Liberty Fund.

Morgan, Edmund S. 1988. *Inventing the People: The Rise of Popular Sovereignty in England and America*. New York: W. W. Norton.

Neimeyer, Charles Patrick. 1996. *America Goes to War: A Social History of the Continental Army*. New York: New York University Press.

Newell, Margaret Ellen. 1998. *From Dependency to Independence: Economic Revolution in Colonial New England*. Ithaca: Cornell University Press.

Pencak, William. 1993. " 'The Fine Theoretic Government of Massachusetts Is Prostrated to the Earth': The Response to Shays's Rebellion Reconsidered," in Robert Gross, ed., *In Debt to Shays: The Bicentennial of an Agrarian Rebellion*, 121–143. Charlottesville: University of Virginia Press.

Royster, Charles. 1979. *A Revolutionary People at War: The Continental Army and American Character, 1775–1783*. Chapel Hill: University of North Carolina Press.

Taylor, Carl C. 1953. *The Farmers' Movement: 1620–1920*. Westport, Conn.: Greenwood Press.

Starkey, Marion L. 1955. *A Little Rebellion*. New York: Knopf.

Szatmary, David P. 1980. *Shays' Rebellion: The Making of an Agrarian Insurrection*. Amherst, Mass.: University of Massachusetts Press.

Tilly, Charles. 1990. *Coercion, Capital, and European States, AD 990–1992*. Cambridge, Mass.: Blackwell.

Tocqueville, Alexis de. 1969. *Democracy in America*. New York: Harper.

Wood, Gordon S. 1991. *The Radicalism of the American Revolution*. New York: Vintage Books.

10

Politics Is Thicker Than Blood

Union and Confederate Veterans in the U.S. House of Representatives in the Late Nineteenth Century

Richard Franklin Bensel

The modern American state was born in the blood of the Civil War. In that respect, at least, the United States stands alongside many other nation-states (Bensel 1990: preface and chapter 1). But, unlike most civil wars in world history, the American conflict did not pit a professional military establishment against insurgent armies. Instead, the Confederate and Union mobilizations were composed of almost entirely new and volunteer units. They were also almost carbon copies of one another in terms of recruitment and organization; only the color of the uniforms and the design of the flags distinguished armed units on the field of battle. And, although the Civil War brought forth the modern American state, this birth almost produced twins. As it was, a stillborn Confederacy remained unburied for decades following Appomattox, while the Union, victorious in war, slowly evolved from a "northern" into an American or national state. In making this transformation, one of the first casualties was the Union Army which, after demobilization, once again became one of the smallest in the Western world.

The net result (and the basis for this chapter) was that the United States inherited two militaries after Appomattox, one Union and one Confederate. And, although the Union still possessed a small military establishment, in national politics the most influential factor was the hundreds of thousands of northern and southern veterans. As in the war, they faced off against one another in Congress; arrayed in competing parties and speaking with different accents, they nevertheless contested American state formation more or less as equals. The question is how much more or less that was.

Over 600,000 men died in the Civil War, more than in any other single conflict in American history (Long 1971: 710–712). Somewhere around three out of every four adult white males in the South enlisted in the Confederate Army. The North turned out just over half of all adult white males for the Union. The Union enrolled some 179,000 southern freedmen as well.

In total, over 2 million men fought, at one time or another, for the North and 750,000 did the same for the South (Long 1971: 704–706). Roughly one in five of the men in the Union Army died in the line of duty; the comparable figure for the Confederates was just over one in three. Many of the individual battles sported casualty lists that, in proportion to the effectives engaged, were almost as long. At Antietam on September 17, 1862, for example, the Confederate Army of Northern Virginia lost a third of its men either as killed, wounded, or missing in action. The ferocity of such engagements fixed political alignments in ways that endured long after the guns fell silent. This was obviously the case for those who were killed, but we are not here concerned with the passions and political commitments of the dead. Their politics stopped with the bullet or infectious diseases that laid them low. Instead, our attention centers on those who fought and survived – the more than 2 million men, both Union and Confederate veterans, who lived to participate in the politics of the postwar era.

There are several questions at issue. First and perhaps easiest to answer is how and to what extent veterans were politically mobilized in the postwar era. The second is how that mobilization affected recruitment into the major parties and, thus, alignments in national politics. The third is how and to what extent Confederate veterans, many of them having served as officers in the southern army, were reintegrated into national politics. This is not a very interesting question for Union veterans – after all, they were on the loyalist side of the war and thus their patriotic devotion to the interests of the federal government was never in doubt. But Confederate veterans had taken up arms against the government whose service they were now reentering as congressmen and senators. Although they had all taken new oaths of fealty to the victorious Union state, their pledges were, from where they stood, more than a little coerced by circumstances and policy. For these reasons, the reincorporation of former Confederate nationalists into the seat of government inevitably presented very difficult and delicate problems of policy and politics.

Finally, we can ask whether and how the policy priorities of Union and Confederate veterans, once in Congress, differed. Was, for example, the post-Appomattox era merely a continuation of the American Civil War by other means? Or, alternatively, was the period one in which military service, on either side, was merely incidental to policy alignments that arose out of other causes? A full answer to these questions would require much more attention than we can devote to them here. For the purposes of this article, we focus on the accommodation of Confederate veterans within the committee system of the House of Representatives between 1875 and 1895, the decades in which the greatest numbers of Confederate veterans served in the chamber. This analysis will suggest the policy priorities of these men, compared with those of Union veterans, as well as the limits placed on their influence.

Much of the stump rhetoric of national politics in the postwar era left no doubt both as to the importance of the Civil War as a symbolic watershed and a potential litmus test for voters in the North and South. A prominent example, widely cited and quoted by northern Republicans, appeared in an address delivered by Senator Wade Hampton in Staunton, Virginia, in July 1880. Hampton, who had risen to command of the cavalry wing of the Army of Northern Virginia late in the war and whose plantation had been burned by William Tecumseh Sherman's men in 1865, had been elected to the Senate from South Carolina in 1878. He was now addressing Staunton Democrats, from both the city and the surrounding Shenandoah Valley, on behalf of the Democratic presidential candidate, the former Union general Winfield Scott Hancock. Covering the speech for its readers, the Republican *Staunton Valley Virginian* reported the audience as the "largest political meeting ever held" in the city. The paper went on to say that the "Opera house was crowded with an audience variously estimated at from fifteen hundred to two thousand people.... Captain John H. Crawford was called to the chair, and Major Elder offered the resolutions, which were unanimously adopted. Captain Baumgardner, in his usually happy manner, then introduced" Hampton. From the context, it appears that all four officers were former Confederates.

Hampton opened his address with an allusion to his family's Virginia ancestry and to his service in the Confederate Army of Northern Virginia, which had often defended the Shenandoah Valley from Union invasion during the war. He then proceeded:

So it is that I am bound to you by bonds which death alone can sever.
So it is that I, like so many of the veterans of the Confederacy, am jealous of the honor and proud of the glorious heritage bequeathed to [Virginia] by her Lee and her Stonewall Jackson. Do not understand that I come here to dictate a policy to you, or to advise you what you must do; rather am I here to consult with you as a Democrat, as a man, and as a Southern soldier; as one who looks back to the time when he shared with you privations and suffering and defeat in the Army of Northern Virginia.

He concluded his speech with these words:

Consider what Lee and Jackson would do were they alive. These are the same principles for which they fought for four years. Remember the men who poured forth their life-blood on Virginia's soil, and do not abandon them now. Remember that upon your vote depends the success of the Democratic ticket.

Once in the hands of the Republican Party, this speech caused quite a commotion in the North. Hampton subsequently tried to disassociate himself from its sentiments by saying that he had not the "slightest recollection of having used the language" in this passage but leading Staunton Democrats, including the editor of the Democratic paper in the city, substantially corroborated the *Valley Virginian*'s account.[1]

The problem, of course, was that there was a natural asymmetry at work in the nation's politics. If Hampton had, instead, said that the Democrats were merely executing policies for which the Union Army of the Potomac had fought, northern Republicans would have had nothing but praise. In fact, such a speech would not have been noteworthy at all, both because such sentiments were the very stuff of northern politics and because southern Democrats could not have criticized a loyalist message without undercutting their northern colleagues. For that reason, Confederate sympathies were rarely uttered before audiences that could or would report them to the nation at large, whereas Union sentiment, especially when Republicans spoke, was usually combined with condemnations of southern rebels.[2] Intimately associated with southern whites and their movement to recapture state governments in the South, the national Democratic Party, even when nominating a former Union general such as Hancock, could not put its party's loyalty above challenge.[3]

During the 1880 campaign, for example, the Republicans first quoted the 1876 Democratic platform's plank on Union pensions: "That the soldiers and sailors of the Republic, and the widows and orphans of those who have fallen in battle, have a just claim upon the care, protection, and gratitude of their fellow citizens." While this plank was perfectly respectable, even from their emphatic Unionist perspective, the Republicans then juxtaposed the plank against a quotation taken from the *Okolona Southern States*, a Mississippi paper, without any attempt to demonstrate whether the latter passage was representative of Democratic feelings on federal pensions: "Let the Federal Brigadiers take back seats in the work of restoration. The Republic has no further use for the Lincoln hirelings. By the way, Yankees, don't it make you feel queer to think that we've defeated you fellows AFTER ALL and captured the capitol."[4] This was guilt by association, whether or not the southern quotation was accurate; from where the Republicans stood, treasonous resentment against Union veterans was only to be expected throughout the southern wing of the Democratic Party. Whether or not this resentment emerged into public discourse in just the way reported by the Okolona paper was a mere detail.[5]

In fact, as these passages suggest, party and pensions were the two most important mobilizing elements for veterans, at least in the North. The Democrats, for example, strongly opposed federal reconstruction of the South and thus supported an early return to regional power by white southerners. For this reason, the party succeeded in attracting almost all Confederate veterans into their ranks. For their part, the Republicans became the primary vehicle for Union veterans but their dominance within this group was far less complete than the Democratic stranglehold on Confederates. Still, the competing foundations of the party system turned the Republican and Democratic organizations into something like peacetime proxies for the armies that struggled through the Civil War. Because they represented the northern side of this division and thus could anticipate a natural majority in national politics, the Republicans were both strident and direct in their appeals to Union patriotism. The Democrats, needing a major fraction of the North to convert the party's strong position in the South into a national majority, was compelled to trim its Confederate-leaning sails. Carl Schurz, a Missouri Republican, summed up the Democratic dilemma when he said: "There is no heavier burden for a political party to bear, than to have appeared unpatriotic in war." For the Republicans, the situation made waving the "bloody shirt" politically irresistible as a way of simultaneously covering over internal party splits over policy, forcing the Democrats onto the defensive, and forging an electoral majority along sectional lines.[6]

With respect to veterans, the quest for ever more generous federal pensions for Union veterans gave birth and purpose to the Grand Army of the Republic (GAR), one of the largest voluntary organizations in the nation. In 1878, the GAR held a membership of only 30,000 but, as a consequence of its tireless campaigns for more generous pensions and benefits, the organization swelled to 409,000 by 1890 (Buck 1937: 237). Thereafter death harvested veterans faster than the GAR could replace them with new recruits and the organization began to decline. In the South, with no federal pension system to encourage their organization, the founding of a national group lagged behind the North by decades. In 1889, however, the United Confederate Veterans finally emerged as a counterpart to the GAR in the North. And, by 1896, there were United Confederate Veterans (UCV) posts in three out of every four counties in the former Confederate states (Ayers 1992: 334). By default, the United Confederate Veterans overwhelmingly supported Democrats throughout their native region; Republicans made little or no attempt to attract them to their party.

The position of the Grand Army of the Republic in the North, however, was more complicated. There both Democrats and Republicans supported military pensions for Union veterans and thus competed for the favor of the GAR. In this competition, individual Democrats could sometimes hold their own but the Republican Party, as an organization, had a clear advantage. One of the problems was that, as the pension rolls steadily increased and benefits became ever more generous, Union pensions could not be realistically favored without some program for raising the necessary revenue to pay for them. Between 1882 and 1900, for example, Union pensions never fell below 20 percent of all federal expenditures, peaking in 1893 at 41.6 percent. During this period the tariff was usually the largest single source of revenue, often providing over 50 percent of the federal total (U.S. Bureau of the Census 1975: 1106, 1114). Because the tariff protected northern industry from European competition and since northern industrial interests constituted one of the primary constituencies of the party, the Republicans constantly linked the two policies.[7] And, because Union pensions were generally more popular with the electorate than high tariffs, the party often justified the latter as necessary to pay for the former, rather than the other way around.[8] The Democrats, hobbled by their opposition to a protective tariff, were unable to make their competing offers to Union veterans believable in fiscal terms. For all these reasons, the Grand Army of the Republic, while officially nonpartisan, became in many ways the primary popular extension of the Republican party throughout the North.[9]

There was thus a substantial policy connection between the Republican Party, the protective tariff, and Union pensions that underlay recruitment of Union veterans into the party as candidates for federal office. While that connection was weaker for Democrats, the nomination of Union veterans still tended to neutralize some of the most effective criticisms of the party, particularly the charge that the northern wing was merely a stalking horse for the Confederate-leaning southern delegations. In the South, the Democrats tended to nominate Confederate veterans as a matter of course; in the complex sectional politics of the period, service in the Confederate Army was a guarantee of fidelity to southern interests in a period during which the South, in order to achieve any of its economic goals, was almost always compelled to yield primacy to its northern colleagues. In the analysis that follows, the focus is on recruitment of Union and Confederate veterans into the House of Representatives and their integration into the committee system.

Most of the politics that drove these electoral and committee patterns remains unknown for several reasons. With respect to committee assignments, for example, the Democratic leadership in Congress could not openly acknowledge the political liability that accompanied the almost universal tendency of southern districts to nominate and elect Confederate veterans as their representatives. To do so would have been to acquiesce in the Republican critique that branded the entire party as unpatriotic, at best, and openly disloyal, at worst. In addition, the distribution of committee assignments within both parties was bound up with internal contention for party leadership. Because the Speaker of the House of Representatives controlled the committee assignments of the majority party, manipulating them in order to both maintain control of the party and to alleviate hostility among his opponents, majority party assignments were often shaped by policy alignments and personal factions that had little to do with attitudes toward Confederate or Union veterans in the larger electorate (Seip 1983: 283–286). With respect to the minority party, the Speaker usually deferred to the minority leader, the unsuccessful candidate for his post. Thus, minority assignments reflected the internal factionalism of the opposition party as well. Although contests for party leadership were certainly public in many respects, they were not reported, either by the participants or by others, in the kind of detail that would now allow precise interpretation of motives. We are therefore limited to reporting patterns and suggesting interpretations in place of thick analytical descriptions.

In the early years of Reconstruction, Union veterans dominated southern delegations to the House by a wide margin (see Table 10.1) (Bensel 1990: 405–413). During this period, Union troops protected black voters in the South, many Confederate veterans were excluded from voting, and the Republican Party often recruited northern-born Union veterans as candidates for federal office.[10] As a result, over half of all southern congressmen in the 40th Congress had served in the Union Army during the Civil War, a remarkable statistic that substantially exceeded any comparable figure recorded in the North where, at the peak during the 50th and 51st Congresses, only 41.7 percent of all representatives had served with the Union (see Table 10.2). Former Confederates, albeit in small numbers, also began to arrive in the House during the 40th Congress. In succeeding Congresses, their presence rapidly expanded, both in absolute numbers and as a proportion of all southern representatives. In fact, the relative proportions of Union and Confederate veterans sent to Congress from the South between 1865 and 1881 serves as an excellent proxy for the waxing and waning of Reconstruction as a political project. Where Union veterans had outnumbered their Confederate counterparts by a margin of well over three to one in 1867, the Confederates were on top by almost thirty to one by 1879.[11] In the latter year, almost four out every five southerners elected to Congress had previously served in the Confederate Army. In fact, in every Congress but one between 1877 and 1893, the proportion of Confederates remained above 70 percent. Only a handful of these veterans were Republicans; almost all were Democrats.

The border states, those that had slave labor systems before the Civil War but had never seceded from the Union, presented a weaker version of the same pattern. There, too, Union veterans dominated the early postwar delegations with proportions that exceeded all northern experience, although the margin was narrower. The Union proportion also declined steadily until 1879, as it had in the South. Thereafter, however, the proportion of Union veterans tended to wax and wane in tandem with the national fortunes of the Republican Party. The 1894 Republican national landslide, in which the border states also participated, brought the percentage of Union veterans up to almost a quarter of all representatives. Democratic gains during Bryan's campaign in 1896 dropped the Union percentage down to under 11 percent once more. As in the South, the percentage of Confederate veterans in border state delegations peaked during the 46th and 47th Congresses when about a third of all border state representatives had fought for the South. In fact, in every Congress sworn in from 1877 to 1894 the number of former Confederates from the border states exceeded the number of Union veterans, a remarkable pattern in that more border state residents apparently served in the Union Army than in the Confederate.[12]

Only two Confederate veterans ever represented northern districts in the House between 1865 and 1900: William A. Harris, a Populist elected

TABLE 10.1. *Union and Confederate Veterans Representing Southern and Border State Districts, 1865–1900*

Congress (Years)	Southern Members			Border State Members		
	Percent Union Veterans	Percent Confederate Veterans	Total Number of Members	Percent Union Veterans	Percent Confederate Veterans	Total Number of Members
39th (1865–1867)	37.5	0.0	8	44.4	0.0	27
40th (1867–1869)	52.5	15.0	40	44.4	0.0	27
41st (1869–1871)	46.6	19.0	58	40.7	0.0	27
42nd (1871–1873)	25.9	39.7	58	25.9	7.4	27
43rd (1873–1875)	21.9	37.0	73	24.2	9.1	33
44th (1875–1877)	12.3	58.9	73	15.2	15.2	33
45th (1877–1879)	6.8	71.2	73	18.2	21.2	33
46th (1879–1881)	2.7	79.5	73	3.0	30.3	33
47th (1881–1883)	5.5	78.1	73	6.1	33.3	33
48th (1883–1885)	5.9	74.1	85	16.7	27.8	36
49th (1885–1887)	4.7	68.2	85	19.4	25.0	36
50th (1887–1889)	3.5	74.1	85	13.9	19.4	36
51st (1889–1891)	2.4	72.9	85	5.6	16.7	36
52nd (1891–1893)	0.0	72.9	85	5.6	22.2	36
53rd (1893–1895)	0.0	57.8	90	10.8	24.3	37
54th (1895–1897)	1.1	43.3	90	24.3	8.1	37
55th (1897–1899)	1.1	33.3	90	10.8	5.4	37
56th (1899–1901)	1.1	30.0	90	10.8	10.8	37

Note: For the purposes of this table, "South" is defined as the eleven former states of the Confederacy and "border states" include Delaware, Kentucky, Maryland, Missouri, and West Virginia.

TABLE 10.2. *Union and Confederate Veterans Representing Northern and All National Districts, 1865–1900*

Congress (Years)	Northern Members		All National Members		
	Percent Union Veterans	Total Number of Members	Percent Union Veterans	Percent Confederate Veterans	Total Number of Members
39th (1865–1867)	18.4	158	22.8	0.0	193
40th (1867–1869)	24.1	158	31.6	2.7	225
41st (1869–1871)	27.2	158	33.3	4.5	243
42nd (1871–1873)	23.4	158	24.3	10.3	243
43rd (1873–1875)	25.3	158	24.3	10.3	292
44th (1875–1877)	23.5	158	19.8	16.4	293
45th (1877–1879)	32.6	187	24.6	20.1	293
46th (1879–1881)	34.2	187	22.9	23.2	293
47th (1881–1883)	34.8	187	24.2	23.2	293
48th (1883–1885)	34.3	204	24.9	22.5	325
49th (1885–1887)	39.7	204	28.3	20.6	325
50th (1887–1889)	41.7	204	28.6	21.5	325
51st (1889–1891)	41.7	211	27.7	20.5	332
52nd (1891–1893)	32.7	211	21.4	21.4	332
53rd (1893–1895)	27.5	229	18.8	17.7	356
54th (1895–1897)	29.6	230	21.8	11.8	357
55th (1897–1899)	22.2	230	15.7	9.0	357
56th (1899–1901)	17.4	230	12.6	8.7	357

Note: For the purposes of this table, the North includes all districts not included in the South or border states. Because only two Confederate veterans were ever elected from northern districts, that column has been omitted from this table.

at large from Kansas to the 53rd Congress, and John R. Fellows, a Democrat elected from New York City to the 52nd Congress. Union veterans, on
the other hand, were much more common, usually comprising a quarter or
more of all northern representatives in the same period. Where the pattern
of Confederate service in the South peaked just as Reconstruction came to
a close and otherwise appeared to parallel the intensity of "redemption" as
a white Democratic campaign, the propensity of northern districts to elect
Union veterans followed the rise and decline of the Grand Army of the
Republic, rising slowly from the end of the Civil War to a peak in the 50th
and 51st Congresses and subsequently declining, along with the GAR membership, in later years. The difference is both striking and significant. Where
the southern pattern reflected a political impulse that strove to distinguish
sectional loyalty from northern hegemony, the northern tendency to favor
Union veterans can be traced to an interest group claim on federal largesse.
Put another way, whereas the election of Confederates from the South was
often an act of separatist defiance, the election of Unionists in the North
was frequently a conformist exercise in interest group claim-making.[13] The
latter appears to be the weaker impulse, in that the percentage of Union
veterans among northern congressmen was usually far lower than the
percentage of former Confederates among southerners.

   When the data from all three sections are combined, the national trends
in Union and Confederate service in the House show substantial divergence.
Union veterans arrive early in relatively large numbers, peaking during the
41st Congress, and then decline slowly over the years. The very high rates
of Union recruitment as Republican candidates in the southern and border
states during the early Reconstruction period bring up the northern trend,
and the later collapse of Republican strength in the same areas subsequently
depresses the national percentage, particularly in the Congresses held after
the Compromise of 1877. Without large numbers of Union veterans, the
South lacked the social base from which to claim a significant share of
federal pension benefits.[14] Without that social base, the Grand Army of the
Republic managed to establish only weak posts in the South. And many of
those camps quickly became embroiled in racism as white Union veterans
attempted to exclude black veterans from their own posts while also preventing the organization of separate, black branches (Dearing 1952:
412–419) As a result, the lure of federal pensions and the organizational
strength of the Grand Army of the Republic, so effectively combined in the
North, were largely absent from the South and most of the border states.
Union veterans thus became much less attractive as Republican candidates
for House seats, even where Republican candidates were viable competitors; in the southern wing of the Democratic Party, of course, Union
veterans were far beyond the pale. The Confederate pattern moved more
symmetrically, rising from nothing in the early years of Reconstruction,
peaking in the 46th and 47th Congresses, and then declining slowly until

TABLE 10.3. *Union and Confederate Veterans in the House of Representatives at the Beginning of the 51st Congress (1889–1891)*

Region and Party	Percentage of Membership Category			Total Number of Members
	Union Veterans	Confederate Veterans	Nonveterans	
South				
Democrats	0.0 (0)	78.9 (60)	21.1 (16)	76
Republicans	22.2 (2)	22.2 (2)	55.6 (5)	9
Border states				
Democrats	3.6 (1)	21.4 (6)	75.0 (21)	28
Republicans	12.5 (1)	0.0 (0)	87.5 (7)	8
North				
Democrats	17.5 (10)	0.0 (0)	82.5 (47)	57
Republicans	50.6 (78)	0.0 (0)	49.4 (76)	154
Nation				
Democrats	6.8 (11)	41.0 (66)	52.2 (84)	161
Republicans	47.4 (81)	1.2 (2)	51.5 (88)	171
ALL PARTIES	27.7 (92)	20.5 (68)	51.8 (172)	332

Note: For regional percentages that include all parties, see Tables 10.1 and 10.2. The numbers of members falling into each category are given in parentheses.

the 53rd Congress. At that point the downward slope accelerated until, by the turn of the century, former Confederate soldiers comprised fewer than one in every ten members of the House. Compared with Union veterans, the proportion of Confederates had two apices, one in the 52nd Congress when the percentages are identical and another in the 46th Congress when the number of Confederates actually exceeded Union veterans by a small margin.

These patterns overlapped with the major party alignment in interesting ways. For example, of the nine Republicans elected from the South to the 51st Congress, the party counted as many Confederate as Union veterans (see Table 10.3). In both instances, however, only two were elected. The southern wing of the Democratic Party boasted no Union veterans in its ranks, although former Confederates filled almost four out every five seats in its regional delegation. In all the nation's major regions, moreover, Union veterans constituted a greater proportion of the Republican members than of the Democrats. The reverse held for Confederate veterans, except in the North where no former Confederates held seats. As a result, the two parties resembled nothing so much as reincarnations of the battle formations that had fought some quarter of a century earlier. On the Democratic side of the House chamber, over 40 percent of the members had served the South;

on the Republican side, almost half had served the North. Although a handful of veterans strayed across party lines, the Republican caucus still held almost nine out of every ten (88.0 percent) of all former Union soldiers, while the monopoly of the Democratic caucus on Confederate soldiers was even more complete (97.1 percent). Even in the North, where many Union officers had belonged to the Democratic Party when the Civil War started, only 11 percent of all Union veterans elected to the 51st Congress claimed allegiance to that party.

With respect to the recruitment and election of Union veterans to Congress, the density of federal pension recipients played a key supportive role (see Table 10.4). We again take the 51st Congress, during which the GAR reached its peak membership as a national organization, as our example. In the southern and border states, where few Union pensioners resided, the pattern was weak but evident. In the North, it was much stronger. Union veterans in that region rose steadily with rising proportions of pension recipients in district populations, both as a percentage of Republican members as well as for all parties. Within the Democratic Party, however, there was no relationship between the density of Union pensioners and Union veterans within party ranks. Although Democrats were generally more successful in districts with few Union pensioners, the party appears to have been indifferent to the evident need to nominate Union veterans as candidates in those districts where pensioners resided much more thickly. The pattern for the nation as a whole more or less resembles that for the North, with the exception of an additional level in which federal pensioners comprised less than two-tenths of the district population. In that category, many districts contained fewer than one hundred pensioners within district populations of 150,000 or more. Not a single one of the sixty-five districts in this category, all of them in the former states of the Confederacy, elected a Union veteran to the House of Representatives in the 51st Congress. On the whole, the patterns strongly reflect the thick connection between the Grand Army of the Republic as an interest group claimant, the Republican Party as the agent servicing such claims, and federal pensions as the object of GAR attentions. The Democratic Party can be considered either unwilling or unable to compete with the Republicans in this role. For their part, Confederate veterans were so concentrated in southern districts with very few federal pensioners that the relationship between their recruitment as candidates for Congress and the density of pensioners was extremely steep and negative. Confederate veterans were not mobilized, at least primarily, in opposition to federal pensions; instead, their relative numbers reflected the underlying opposition of their constituencies to federal rule in any form.

We now turn our attention to how Civil War veterans were treated when committee assignments were awarded through their respective parties. We limit our analysis, for the most part, to the period between 1875 and 1895

TABLE 10.4. *Veterans as House Members and District Density of Union Pensioners: 51st Congress (1889–1891)*

Region	Union Pensioners as Percentage of District Population	Union or Confederate Veterans as Percentage of[a]		
		Republican Members	Democratic Members	All Members
South	<.2	0.0 (3)	0.0 (62)	0.0 (65)
	≥.2	33.3 (6)	0.0 (14)	10.0 (20)
Border states	<.7	0.0 (6)	5.6 (18)	4.2 (24)
	≥.7	50.0 (2)	0.0 (10)	7.7 (12)
North	.2–.3	37.5 (16)	13.3 (15)	25.8 (31)
	.4–.6	43.3 (30)	0.0 (13)	30.2 (43)
	.7–.8	44.0 (25)	50.0 (10)	45.7 (35)
	.9–1.1	52.8 (36)	33.3 (9)	48.9 (45)
	>1.1	61.7 (47)	0.0 (10)	50.9 (57)
Nation	<.2	0.0 (3)	0.0 (62)	0.0 (65)
	.2–.3	30.0 (20)	6.1 (33)	15.1 (53)
	.4–.6	40.0 (35)	3.7 (27)	24.2 (62)
	.7–.8	44.4 (27)	31.2 (16)	39.5 (43)
	.9–1.1	51.3 (39)	25.0 (12)	45.1 (51)
	>1.1	61.7 (47)	0.0 (11)	50.0 (58)
South	<.2	33.3 (3)	80.6 (62)	78.5 (65)
	≥.2	16.7 (6)	71.4 (14)	55.0 (20)
Border states	<.7	0.0 (6)	27.8 (18)	20.8 (24)
	≥.7	0.0 (2)	10.0 (10)	8.3 (12)
North[b]	—	—	—	—
Nation	<.2	33.3 (3)	80.6 (62)	78.5 (65)
	.2–.3	5.0 (20)	36.7 (33)	24.5 (53)
	≥.4	0.0 (148)	1.5 (66)	.5 (214)

Note: Pension recipients were measured as a percentage of the district population receiving benefits.
[a] Percentage of Union veterans given in top half of table, Confederate veterans in bottom half.
[b] No Confederate veterans elected.
Source: The data on recipients was taken from *Executive Documents of the House of Representatives for the First Session of the Fiftieth Congress*, Serial No. 2542 (Washington, D.C.: GPO, 1889), table 20, pp. 1090–1108.

when Confederate veterans comprised more than 15 percent of the total House membership. In no other years, either before or since, were they ever so numerous as in the Congresses that sat in this twenty-year period. With minor exceptions, the committee system in the House of Representatives was remarkably stable over this period; few new committees were established and even fewer were abolished. For that reason and because party control of the chamber was an important factor in determining the relative presence of Union and Confederate veterans on individual committees, the analysis focuses on only those committees that continuously existed throughout the two decades. Otherwise, the relative presence of veterans on individual panels might be influenced by whether they happened to exist in an atypical stretch of one-party control.[15] The Democrats organized the House during the 44th, 45th, 46th, 48th, 49th, 50th, 52nd, and 53rd Congresses (1875–1881, 1883–1889, 1891–1895). The Republicans controlled the House in the others (the 47th and 51st Congresses). Thus, for most of the period, Confederate veterans were in a favored position within the House committee system, with a friendly Speaker and panel memberships disproportionately weighted toward their party.

Former Confederates, however, do not appear to have turned these favorable factors into effective claims on committee assignments (see Table 10.5). The most important single panel in the House, for example, was the Rules Committee, which controlled the flow of major legislation to the floor of the chamber. The Speaker always chaired this committee, along with two close party colleagues, while the minority party placed its own party leaders on the other side of the committee list. Thus, the Rules Committee membership conflated both an important policy assignment with overall party leadership. As can be seen in Table 10.5, Confederates only succeeded in placing one veteran in every six appointments, one of the lowest such ratios within the entire committee system. To some extent, this reluctance to place Confederates in prominent leadership positions must have been due to northern public opinion; certainly the disproportionate favor shown Union veterans seems to point in that direction. Both the Democrats and the Republicans strongly favored Union veterans in the selection of party leaders, placing the Rules Committee almost at the top of the entire committee system (see Table 10.6). Aside from Rules, the most important panels in the House of Representatives were probably the Committees on Appropriations and Ways and Means. Appropriations controlled federal expenditures, a power that materially and sometimes qualitatively influenced a wide range of government policy. Confederates did slightly better than average in gaining assignments to this panel, even edging out Union veterans by a tiny margin. However, this was not a panel to which Civil War veterans who served either side were disproportionately assigned. The jurisdiction of the Ways and Means Committee covered the revenue-raising authority of the federal government. The panel thus dominated the tariff, which may have been the single most important policy dividing the major parties during this period. This power, in turn, made Ways and Means the most important legislative committee in the House during the late nineteenth century. While Union veterans did slightly better than Confederates

Standing Committee	Average Percentage of Confederate Veterans among		
	Total Committee Membership	Committee Republicans	Committee Democrats
Naval Affairs	31.2	3.7	52.6
Mississippi Levees	30.9	1.2	50.8
Indian Affairs	30.7	0.0	57.0
Agriculture	28.2	0.0	51.9
Post Office	25.9	0.0	45.9
Public Buildings	25.6	0.0	49.8
Patents	25.2	0.0	45.9
Railways and Canals	24.8	2.0	48.5
Pacific Railroad	24.6	0.0	38.6
Revision of the Laws	23.7	0.0	39.0
Manufactures	23.3	0.0	33.3
Territories	23.1	0.0	41.1
Elections	22.3	0.0	36.1
Appropriations	22.1	0.0	40.1
Claims	22.0	0.0	38.2
Judiciary	21.7	0.0	39.7
Pensions	21.6	1.2	36.7
War Claims	21.3	2.0	32.1
Ways and Means	21.2	0.0	34.4
Commerce	20.2	3.0	31.0
Foreign Affairs	20.0	1.2	34.1
Education and Labor	19.9	0.0	36.7
Mines and Mining	19.9	0.0	29.3
Private Land Claims	19.4	2.0	32.0
Militia	18.9	0.0	34.6
Banking and Currency	17.8	0.0	28.5
Military Affairs	16.8	0.0	31.4
Public Lands	16.5	0.0	28.7
Rules	16.0	0.0	28.3
District of Columbia	16.1	0.0	28.9
Coinage, Weights	15.9	0.0	25.8
Invalid Pensions	11.3	0.0	19.1

Notes: This table only includes standing committees appointed in every Congress from the 44th through the 53rd. From the 48th through the 53rd Congresses, there were two committees, one on Education and the other on Labor. The entries in the table represent the mean of the composition of these separate committees. Members of third parties are included in the total committee memberships but omitted from the major party figures. The Commerce Committee was named Interstate and Foreign Commerce in the 52nd and 53rd Congress. The Pensions Committee was named Revolutionary Pensions before the 47th Congress.

Sources: Information on the Civil War service of congressmen was taken from the *Biographical Directory of the American Congress, 1774–1971* (Washington, D.C.: GPO, 1971). Memberships of the committees was taken from the first edition of the *Congressional Directory* in which assignments appeared for each Congress.

TABLE 10.6. *House Committee Memberships Ranked by Percentage of Union Veterans, 1875–1895*

Standing Committee	Average Percentage of Union Veterans among		
	Total Committee Membership	Committee Republicans	Committee Democrats
Military Affairs	63.5	89.3	42.5
Rules	50.0	68.3	33.3
Invalid Pensions	43.8	62.4	32.7
Militia	31.7	61.0	10.0
Territories	30.6	60.0	6.6
Agriculture	29.4	54.1	8.4
Banking and Currency	26.3	38.7	17.2
Public Lands	25.9	49.6	8.6
Indian Affairs	25.8	47.9	8.4
Mississippi Levees	25.5	55.2	7.1
Private Land Claims	25.3	40.2	12.9
Education and Labor	24.0	45.1	7.5
Ways and Means	23.7	43.6	11.3
District of Columbia	23.5	39.4	13.4
Judiciary	23.4	44.9	7.5
Post Office	22.9	42.0	5.1
War Claims	22.5	48.1	8.6
Patents	22.3	43.8	4.9
Pensions	21.8	42.1	9.3
Claims	21.6	43.4	6.1
Appropriations	21.3	35.8	11.3
Elections	21.0	39.9	4.2
Manufactures	20.7	32.8	14.5
Pacific Railroad	20.2	46.0	2.5
Public Buildings	20.2	39.8	6.0
Naval Affairs	19.5	40.6	5.2
Railways and Canals	17.8	39.9	1.4
Revision of the Laws	17.4	43.0	2.5
Mines and Mining	15.7	23.7	7.7
Commerce	15.1	28.2	4.0
Coinage, Weights	14.0	19.4	7.4
Foreign Affairs	11.0	21.7	0.0

Note: See Table 10.5.
Sources: See Table 10.5.

in winning assignments to the panel, the pattern generally reflected, in both cases, the distribution of veterans within the House membership as a whole.

With respect to the remainder of the committee system, the relative importance of the separate panels had more to do with the individual characteristics of members' districts than with the general authority that the committees wielded. The Committee on Levees and Improvements of the Mississippi River, for example, ordinarily contained a large number of members from districts bordering the river, particularly along the banks below St. Louis where flooding was a chronic problem. Because the lower Mississippi valley was southern, a disproportionate share of the committee's membership was composed of Confederates. In fact, more than half of all Democratic assignments to the panel were Confederate veterans. As was also the case for the committee system as a whole, Republican assignments did not discriminate against Confederate veterans in their party – there were just very few Confederates in their ranks.[16] For that reason, whatever variation in Confederate proportions that appeared among the full committee memberships was almost entirely due to Democratic assignments. In this case, the heavy concentration of Confederate veterans on the Democratic side of the Mississippi Levees Committee placed the panel second on the overall list. With respect to Union veterans, the Republicans also heavily favored the committee. Aside from a few southern Republicans who had served in the Union Army, this concentration of Union veterans is partially explained by a general tendency for rural districts, in both the North and in the South, to disproportionately favor veterans as congressmen. Thus, Republican districts bordering the upper reaches of the Mississippi River, from which many committee members were drawn, tended to contain a higher percentage of Union veterans than more urbanized districts to the east, where the bulk of the party's congressional strength lay. This rural bias also accounts for the concentration of both Union and Confederate veterans on several other committees, among them Agriculture and the westward-oriented Territories and Indian Affairs. In all of these cases, the concentration of veterans was not directly related to the committee's jurisdiction, merely coincidental with the policy interests of the underlying districts.

An opposing tendency operated at the lower end of the committee spectrums, where urban districts were represented by comparatively few veterans. Because the South held comparatively few cities of any sort in the late nineteenth century, there was little opportunity for Confederate veterans to be elected from urbanized areas. In the North, however, large industrial cities elected many congressmen and a large proportion of those had not served in the Union Army. Many of the panels that attracted these urban congressmen thus contained few Civil War veterans, either Union or Confederate. Two of them were committees that dealt with matters undergirding the nation's financial system. The Banking and Currency Committee, for example, controlled legislation affecting the national bank system, both a major interest group in its own right and a major supporting actor in maintaining the international gold standard. Although Confederates on that panel were comparatively rare, the panel did attract northern Democrats who had served with the Union Army. Their presence pushed the Banking Committee up the ranks, in terms of Union members, beyond what the relatively low frequency of Republican appointments would have allowed. Assignments on the Committee on Coinage, Weights, and Measure, the other panel, were made to few veterans of either army. The Coinage Committee held jurisdiction over the mintage of silver dollars and was thus in a position to exercise that power in ways that could endanger the ability of the United States to maintain gold payments. Because, next to the tariff, the gold standard was the most divisive issue in American politics during this period, the committee's jurisdiction attracted a disproportionate number of members representing urban financial centers, as well as monetary insurgents. These tendencies, reflecting the distribution of strength over a policy more closely associated with industrialization than with issues arising directly out of the Civil War, reduced the proportion of veterans from both armies to what was, practically speaking, a bare minimum. The Committees on Commerce and Foreign Affairs exhibited somewhat parallel patterns arising out of similar situations. In fact, the Democratic Party never appointed a Union veteran to the latter during the entire twenty-year period.

Open discrimination against Confederates and favoring Union veterans was practiced for both parties with respect to the Committees on Military Affairs and Invalid Pensions. Military Affairs held jurisdiction over the United States Army, which, in the early years of the period, was still patrolling several regions of the South as part of Reconstruction. For that reason, southern Democrats yearned for assignment as a way of influencing federal policy toward their section. But the party leadership, reluctant to put former Confederates in a position to influence army policy in the South, kept veterans largely at bay. The problem for the Democrats was aggravated by the fact that the Military Affairs Committee also held jurisdiction over the United States Army, as an organization. And the idea of placing Confederate veterans in a position to influence, however indirectly, the careers and ambitions of federal officers who had served the Union during the Civil War must have appeared anathema to most northerners, even Democrats. As a result, less than a third of all Democratic assignments to the committee comprised Confederate veterans. In fact, that percentage was far smaller than the proportion of Union veterans that the Democrats appointed to the panel. Viewed more broadly, the Democrats appointed more Union veterans than Confederates to only three committees: Military Affairs, Rules, and Invalid Pensions. These were also the panels to which the Republicans appointed Union veterans with the greatest frequency. With respect to Military Affairs almost nine of every ten Republicans had served in the northern army during the Civil War. In many cases, these former soldiers were in a position not only to influence Reconstruction as that policy came to an end but could also promote the interests of the federal army, both as an organization and as a collective of Union officers with whom the veterans had previously served. There is little doubt that former Confederates were thus barred from Military Affairs because northern opinion would not have tolerated their presence in large numbers. And that hostility, in turn, arose out of continuing doubts as to the loyalty of Confederates to the government that had reimposed federal rule in the South.

As what must have been weak compensation, the Democratic Party appears to have granted Confederates easy entry onto the Committee on Naval Affairs. In fact, over half of all Democratic assignments on that panel were given to former Confederates, a proportion ten times as great as the mere 5 percent awarded to Democratic Union veterans. The distinction between the two services arose out of their respective relevance to the enforcement of federal policy in the South; where the army played a major role in garrisoning and patrolling the region, the navy was necessarily restricted to ports and even there could do little to carry out federal occupation policy. So Confederate veterans were, in effect, dumped onto the committee that had far less relation to their intensely held political and constituent interests than the one from which they were excluded.

A slightly different explanation can be proposed for the starkly contrasting patterns underlying assignments to the Committee on Invalid Pensions. This committee held jurisdiction over federal pensions for Union veterans, one of the largest items in the federal budget and, as has been described, an indispensable factor binding together the Republican Party and the Grand Army of the Republic. For that reason alone, it should come as no surprise that Union veterans in the Republican Party flocked to the panel in order to demonstrate both their party's and their individual fidelity to the pledges made during the preceding campaign. A disproportionate number of the small band of Union veterans who affiliated with the Democratic Party also found their way onto the committee as well, although one suspects that their purpose was more a matter of personal politics than party policy. Either way, the Committee on Invalid Pensions presented a more or less pure case of interest group representation on the Union side of the question. However, the committee was dead last when it came to Confederates; fewer than one of every eight members assigned to the panel had previously served in the southern army. Because Civil War pensions were such a large part of the federal budget, it is hard to believe that former Confederates were entirely indifferent to this committee's jurisdiction, even while ineligible for the benefits it controlled and distributed. Yet fewer than one in every five Democrats who served was a former Confederate. We can only assume that, in this case as in others, northern public opinion could not tolerate the notion that former Confederates could control or even influence the distribution of benefits to those who had loyally fought for the Union and, as a result, Democrats discriminated against Confederate veterans in making assignments to the panel.[17]

Conclusions

Confederate and Union veterans were major forces in American politics during the late nineteenth century but they generally responded to different impulses in their respective regions. In the South, Confederate service was generally a mark or guarantee of sectional loyalty, to be juxtaposed against an often vengeful northern hegemony. The election of a former Confederate to Congress symbolically described southern white attitudes toward reunion far more eloquently than any platform could have done but was otherwise largely devoid of policy content. The only claims that could be described as particular to Confederate veterans were ones that could not be allowed: revenge on Union officers who had served the North during the Civil War, separatist control of the Union Army where and when it was assigned police functions in the South, and influence over federal pensions to Union veterans. In control of the House of Representatives for most of the period between 1875 and 1895, the Democratic Party voluntarily discriminated against Confederate veterans in assignments to Committees on Military Affairs and Invalid Pensions in order to protect its northern wing from popular identification with the disloyal record of many of its southern members.[18] This concern also explains the favor shown Union veterans when recruiting party leaders in the period, a disposition that pushed the Rules Committee almost to the top of the Union list of committees and, correspondingly, almost to the bottom in terms of Confederate assignments.

In fact, the two major parties resembled nothing so much as encampments of the Civil War armies themselves, with almost all former Confederates falling out on the Democratic side of the chamber and the vast majority of Union veterans arrayed on the Republican side. On the Republican side, however, Union veterans participated in a much less ideological interest group politics in which pension benefits materially cemented a more or less open alliance between the Grand Army of the Republic and the Republican Party. With respect to the two sets of veterans, there was a certain asymmetry in many dimensions of American politics. Confederates, for example, had a much tighter hold on the political affections of their section than did Union veterans in the North. Once Reconstruction ended, the percentage of southern members who had served in the southern army was always higher, often much higher, than the proportion of northern members who had served as Union soldiers. This was despite the fact that Confederate service was nothing but a disability at the federal level; there was, for example, no federal pension bureau for Confederate veterans to influence through their official duties on or off the Committee on Invalid Pensions. In addition, Confederates appear to have been openly discriminated against in ways that responded to a potentially hostile northern public. But southern whites sent them to Congress in large numbers regardless. While much weaker, the northern propensity to elect Union veterans was much more understandable in policy terms.

Finally, one suspects that the politics that generated these large contingents of Union and Confederate veterans, one in the Republican Party and the other in the Democratic Party, tended to freeze alignments over some of the most important policy disputes of the period, while slighting others. Tariff protection, military pensions, and the steady resumption of political power by white Democrats in the South were all important issues with thick linkages to other conflicts over the pace, content, and site of industrialization, to take just one example. All three could be directly, even bluntly, addressed through the recruitment of veterans as congressional candidates. But other issues, such as whether the railroad system should be subjected to federal regulation, whether the gold standard should be replaced with silver or greenbacks, or whether civil service rules should apply to federal officials were not obviously connected to the Civil War, either symbolically or substantively. There were, of course, distinctively southern and northern answers to such questions but they were not answers under which the Confederate and Union armies had marched and ridden into battle. Still, veterans returned to Congress in such numbers that they appear to have remained effective candidates until old age and decrepitude forced them into retirement. Only then did a new generation of political talent, freed from some of the most indelible markings of what was the most bitterly fought war in American history, come to power.

Notes

1. Republican Congressional Committee 1880: 4–5. For general descriptions of the use of Civil War symbols and loyalty in Republican campaigns, see Hirshson 1968 and De Santis 1959.
2. Symbolic acts drew a wide line between blue and gray as well. From that perspective, the first years after the war were particularly bitter with the Confederate dead at Antietam left to rot in the fields while authorities debated whether they deserved burial in the battlefield cemetery, and Union soldiers, in the course of their official duties, preventing flowers from being laid on Confederate graves at Arlington on Memorial Day (Buck 1937: 15).
3. The national Democratic Party embraced southern white efforts to overturn Reconstruction by emphasizing the loyalty of former Confederates to the national government; ascribing violence against blacks in the South to a small minority of, from their perspective, understandably frustrated whites; and documenting at length the increasing indebtedness of the southern states under radical rule (Democratic National Committee 1876: 245–254, 741–746). Viewed as a debate between the two major parties, the issues underlying Reconstruction policy never squarely met. The Democrats stressed the alleged corruption and incompetence of radical rule under black suffrage; the Republicans cited the absence of any loyalist alternative to radical regimes in the South. Theoretically and practically, both contentions could be true at the same time.

4. The last portion of this quotation referred to the Democratic organization of the U.S. Congress (Republican Congressional Committee 1880: 119).

5. Official Republican rhetoric could be quite aggressive in trying to paint north-ern Democrats with the same brush used, with admitted effectiveness, on the southern wing of the party. "The plain truth of the matter [i.e., Democratic reluctance to enact generous pension bills for Union veterans] is that Democratic Congressmen have, as a rule, inherited a legacy of hate for the Union soldier, and while generally pretending to love him just before a Presidential election, the moment the election is over ... they would fling him aside like a piece of waste paper. It is the 'Confederate' and not the 'Union' soldier that they really love" (Republican National Committee 1884: 111).

6. Buck concluded that the "Republicans thus maneuvered, at least to their own satisfaction, the Democratic party with its millions of Americans into the cate-gory of enemies to the American state" (Buck 1937: 73–82).

7. On issues such as the tariff, southern Republicans were faced with a rather sharp choice between loyalty to the national party and fidelity to the interests of their constituents. Given their political dependence on the goodwill and protection of the party's northern wing, these southern Republicans still exhibited a remarkable willingness to defect from the party line on economic issues (Seip 1983: 6–8, 145–146, 273, 277). When the McKinley Tariff, which imposed heavily protectionist duties on most manufactured goods, came to the full House for a vote, only one Republican, Hamilton Coleman of Louisiana, defected. Stating that he opposed the bill because the sugar schedule would leave Louisiana producers unprotected, Coleman noted that he had been "a Confederate soldier, a private in Lee's army of Northern Virginia for nearly four years. During the month of May, twenty-seven years ago, I was a prisoner of war at Fort Delaware. When the Confederate battle-flag, endeared to me by the blood of kindred and comrades went down forever, twenty-five years ago, the war ended and the beautiful star representing fair Louisiana, my native State, was reset in that victorious union of the Stars and Stripes, that glorious emblem of our reunited country." But, having resumed loyalty to the "Stars and Stripes," he now served his state and nation in order "to protect the industries of the American people all along the line. From the lime in Maine to the sugar and rice in Louisiana; from the glass lamp-chimneys of New York and Pennsylvania to the wool of Ohio and Iowa and borax of California; also Michigan lumber and Wisconsin beer. [Laughter and applause] And now, fair play demands that you do not forsake the sugar interests of Louisiana, from which State I was elected a Republican member of Congress [Loud applause]" (*Congressional Record* 51:1: 5005–5006, May 20, 1890).

8. The party also attempted to make tariff protection a nationalist cause as well. For example, the Republican Congressional Committee denounced a free-trade resolution introduced in the House of Representatives as a measure sponsored "at the command of the English Cobden club and the Southern Brigadiers, and their purposes were very plain – to strike down the industries of the nation, and to impoverish all ranks and classes of our loyal people – all to open a market to the British trader, and to secure cheap products to their allies in war and peace, the Southern Brigadiers" (Republican Congressional Committee 1882: 196).

9. For an overview of the politics of the tariff and Union pensions, see Bensel 1984: 62–73, and 2000: chapter 7. On the close relationship between the GAR and the Republican Party, see Dearing 1952.

10. In the 40th Congress, 42 of the 45 southern congressmen were Republicans. Over half of these Republicans were northern men who had chosen to settle in the postwar South. Of the 122 Democrats the South sent to Congress from the 40th through the 45th Congress, almost "90 percent of the 122 Democrats were born in the slave states, and all but four were antebellum residents of the states they would represent during Reconstruction." In sharp contrast, 52 percent of the 129 Republicans who served from the South in the same period hailed from the North. Seip's analysis includes all eleven states of the Confederacy with the exception of Tennessee (1983: 2–3, 11).

11. In their desperate struggle with resurgent Democrats, southern Republicans were seriously handicapped by the refusal of the northern wing to provide financial support for their campaigns. In addition, northern Republicans all too readily accepted the Democratic description of their southern wing as an artificial creation of federal policy, corrupt, incompetent, and alien to the region. Once elected to Congress, however, the national party considered Republicans from the former Confederate states as "Southerners first and only secondarily as fellow party members" (Seip 1983: 110–111).

12. One admittedly rough estimate assigned Confederate sympathies during the Civil War to a little under 40 percent of border state white males of military age, the remainder assumed to be loyalist (Long 1971: 704). This estimate, however, probably overstates the percentage that actually entered Confederate service, in proportion to those in the Union Army. While the Union controlled the border states and thus could openly recruit in the region, the Confederates could only rely on volunteers who risked not only their own lives but the well-being of their families. In addition, because Union sentiment did not run very deep in the border states, the federal government promised border state enlistees that they would not have to serve outside of their states, a promise that effectively committed them only to garrison duty. Such an arrangement was obviously beyond the power of the Confederacy to grant to their own sympathizers. Everything else being equal, a Confederate enlistment from the border states usually represented a commitment to the southern cause that was somewhat greater than the average Union volunteer. As a result, there were probably more Confederate sympathizers in the postwar border state electorates, in proportion to Confederate veterans, than Union loyalists, in proportion to Union veterans.

13. Because these figures do not include civilian officials who served the national governments of the North and South during the Civil War, some of the most symbolically laden members are omitted. For example, the election of Alexander Stephens, the former vice president of the Confederacy, from Georgia and of John Reagan, the former confederate secretary of the Post Office, from Texas were obviously fraught with southern nationalist meaning and intent. More numerous was the election of former Confederate congressmen who, having served in Richmond, were now sent to the House of Representatives in Washington. Parallel elections in the North in which civilian officials who served the Union simply returned to Washington in the same

or a different capacity were comparatively unimportant. There would thus be some warrant for including the former Confederate officials and excluding the Unionists but this would have upset the symmetry of the analysis. As a result, both sets of officials were excluded.

14. For a national map displaying Union pensioners in 1887 as a percentage of county populations, see Bensel 1984: 68.

15. Although party majorities in the House of Representatives were sometimes narrow between 1875 and 1895, the controlling party always ensured dominance of the major committees and many of the minor ones by appointing disproportionately large majorities to their membership lists. Thus, during the 46th Congress, when the Democrats organized the chamber with a mere plurality of members in the House, the party ensured control of the Committee on Commerce by placing ten Democrats among its fifteen members, a two-to-one ratio. Most other committees, which usually ranged from eleven to fifteen in size, were given Democratic majorities of two or three members over the combined opposition (which, in itself, must have included some cooperating members or the Democrats could not have organized the chamber). Thus, in this Congress as in the others, the ruling party enjoyed extraordinary majorities on individual committees. As was demonstrated earlier in the text, almost all Confederates were Democrats and the large majority of Union veterans were Republicans. Thus, party control, combined with the tradition of appointing exaggerated party majorities to the individual committees, meant that the most important factor determining which set of veterans would be overrepresented in the committee system as a whole was which party elected the Speaker. By analyzing only those committees that existed throughout the entire period, this influence of chamber control by the major parties is, in effect, held constant.

16. Although the analysis here does not extend to assignment patterns for all southern members of the party, Seip concludes that Republican leaders regarded their southern brethren with studied indifference, if not open discrimination, in the latter part of the Reconstruction era. He also suggests that southern House members fared worse at the hands of their party than did senators (1983: 114–119). Treatment of southern Democrats by their party's leadership was much more friendly during the same period (1983: 116–117).

17. The Committee on Pensions, which held jurisdiction over all military pensions with the exception of those growing out of the Civil War, attracted almost as many Confederate and Union congressmen during this period.

18. This discrimination must have been somewhat consensual in that former Confederates were a major force in the Democratic caucus. In fact, in some years when the northern wing was weak and the party was in the minority, Confederate veterans constituted more than half the party's members.

References

Ayers, Edward L. 1992. *The Promise of the New South: Life after Reconstruction.* New York: Oxford University Press.

Bensel, Richard Franklin. 1984. *Sectionalism and American Political Development, 1880–1980.* Madison: University of Wisconsin Press.

1990. *Yankee Leviathan: The Origins of Central State Authority in America, 1859–1877*. Cambridge: Cambridge University Press.

2000. *The Political Economy of American Industrialization, 1877–1900*. Cambridge: Cambridge University Press.

Buck, Paul H. 1937. *The Road to Reunion, 1865–1900*. Boston: Little, Brown.

Dearing, Mary R. 1952. *Veterans in Politics: The Story of the G. A. R.* Baton Rouge: Louisiana State University Press.

Democratic National Committee. 1876. *The Campaign Text Book*. New York.

De Santis, Vincent P. 1959. *Republicans Face the Southern Question: The New Departure, 1877–1897*. New York: Greenwood.

Hirshson, Stanley P. 1968. *Farewell to the Bloody Shirt: Northern Republicans and the Southern Negro, 1877–1893*. Chicago: Quadrangle.

Long, E. B. 1971. *The Civil War Day by Day: An Almanac, 1861–1865*. New York: DaCapo.

Republican Congressional Committee. 1880. *Republican Campaign Text Book for 1880*. Washington, D.C.

1882. *Republican Campaign Text Book for 1882*. Washington, D.C.

Republican National Committee. 1884. *Republican Campaign Text Book for 1884*. Washington, D.C.

Seip, Terry L. 1983. *The South Returns to Congress: Men, Economic Measures, and Intersectional Relationships, 1868–1879*. Baton Rouge: Louisiana State University.

U.S. Bureau of the Census. 1975. *Historical Statistics of the United States*. Washington, D.C.

U.S. Congress, Senate. 1890. *Congressional Record*. Vol. 51.

PART III

NOT JUST THE NATION-STATE

Examining the Local, Regional, and International Nexus of Armed Force and State Formation

The *Police Municipale* and the Formation of the French State

Lizabeth Zack

The formation of the French national state is often characterized as a march toward centralization. Political histories recount the consolidation of a central authority and administration from the time of the Revolution and Napoleon (Skocpol 1979; Tilly 1992; Tocqueville 1955). Cultural histories focus on Parisian life and institutions or the gradual integration of provincial norms, languages, and customs into a broader French culture through school and the military during the Third Republic (E. Weber 1976). Analyses of citizenship follow an assimilationist ethos emanating from the Revolution (Brubaker 1992). Well established by now, this image of France as the central state par excellence sends us searching deep into the past for early clues – if need be, one can find central state institutions as far back as 1032 in Henri Ier's *Prevot de Paris* – and trains our eye to home in on the tendency for much of modern French life, including education, social welfare, even architectural innovation, gastronomy, and patterns of protest and revolution, to orient toward Paris. When it comes to the steady march of the French state, we conclude that all roads do, indeed, lead to Paris.

What is a central state par excellence? Max Weber defined the state as a human community that successfully claims a monopoly of the legitimate use of physical force within a given territory (Weber 1946: 78). A highly centralized state, we might assume from his definition, would establish an exceptional concentration of authority over the use of force, integrating agents and agencies of that force under one central command and controlling how and when they deploy it. In one sense, France achieved this in the early years of the French Revolution when revolutionaries placed the *maréchaussée* and private seigniorial armies of the Old Regime with the Gardes nationaux and the Gendarmerie nationale (Carrot 1992: 236; Tilly 1992). These military forces were mandated to protect *the* state and its people and, though modified in form and challenged in a variety of wars and political crises over time, they have remained in the hands of central state authority. Does the same conclusion hold if we extend the criteria to the broader range of coercive forces the French state has employed over time? These forces include the Police nationale, the Gendarmerie, a Paris Préfecture de police, the Police spéciale des chemins de fer, a Garde mobile for riots, a Garde champêtre, the Compagnie républicaines de sécurité, and local municipal police. They differ from the military in that they are utilized inside the state rather than to wage war outside of the state.[1] Despite the diversity of forces, it is easy to get the impression that the state monopolizes them as well. Many accounts focus on the powerful Paris police ministers of Louis XIV and Napoleon, Napoleon's tight vertical chain of command through the departmental prefects, and the extensive political surveillance all regimes have deployed since the seventeenth century (Bayley 1975; Roach and Thomaneck 1985; Stead 1983). In fact, a "French" model of policing, supposedly anchoring one end of the centralization spectrum, often provides a basis of comparison for other more decentralized police systems (Berlière 1996; Liang 1992; Meyzonnier 1994; Stead 1983).

This chapter examines the degree to which the French state has monopolized the police over time. Beginning with the assumption of centrality makes it difficult to answer this question. Focusing on existing central state institutions, the *effects* of policies *emanating from* Paris and the *intentions* of central state authorities, does not tell us about the reasons behind those policies or whether authorities were successful in carrying out their agendas. In this chapter, I conceive of the "police" as a set of institutions authorized by the state to use force to regulate social relations (Bayley 1975). But the term also comprises the broader set of relations and practices making up these institutions – the capacity to act; the chain of command; division of tasks and delegation of responsibilities, techniques, and procedures; philosophies; large-scale efforts; and everyday behavior, image, and reputation. The development of a police system over time is the product of ongoing negotiations between parties over these institutions, relations, and practices.[2] As a way of understanding the broader historical formation of the police in France, I focus on the relationship *between* two parties – the central state and the *police municipale* (the police forces operating in small and large cities around France) – in the nineteenth and twentieth centuries. Doing so reveals a variety of relations between these two parties: state-centered and local-centered, contentious and collaborative. Careful study of the relationship between the central state and the "provinces"[3] should also help clarify some of the conditions that made centralization both possible and difficult at different times. I examine the specific impetus to centralize city police forces in the 1890s and the *relative* success at doing so in subsequent decades. I argue that, ironically, measures of *decentralization* regarding the *police municipale* led to these changes in the broader state police apparatus. In the end, a clear-cut monopoly over the police on the part of the state is hard to identify.

Types of Relations between the Central State and the *Police Municipale*

Big and small towns gained some independence and communal powers between the eleventh and thirteenth centuries as kings sought to balance the power of the landed nobility (Stead 1983). One of those powers was the right to administer a local city police force, usually half military and half civilian in nature and overseen by the town *prévot* (Carrot 1992: 36, 54). This shifted later under absolutist regimes, especially under Louis XIV's strategy of state management, which was to move away from municipal independence and toward more uniform and centralized policing in urban areas.

For a brief moment in the French Revolution (1789–1790), the balance of power shifted again as municipalities regained the right to police the cities themselves.[4] On December 14, 1789, a *loi municipale* gave an elected municipality the power to "give inhabitants a good police" and the mayor the job of "chief of police" (Berlière 1996: 77).[5] This law instituted the modern French police as it charged them to protect the people, their goods, and public order – in essence, the society and state (Berlière 1996: 10, 11). Though brief, that municipal revolution constituted one type of relationship between the central state and the city police. Elected by local citizens *and* delegated the task of "chief of police," the mayor and his municipality had a wide capacity to manage and direct the city police. This *first* type of relationship can be considered quite localist in its direction and orientation.

A *second* type of central state–city police relation crystallized under Napoleon between 1800 and 1814.[6] Napoleon is often cited as the great centralizer of, well, most everything in the French state, and he did do a lot to bring the city police forces under central control. In 1800 Bonaparte instituted the system of departmental prefects through which he oversaw the city police forces now under *state-appointed* mayors (who remained the chiefs of police) and *commissaires*.[7] In the same year, he appointed Joseph Fouché the minister of police,[8] an office established under the Directory, and created the post of *préfet de police de Paris*, modeled on Louis XIV's idea of the Paris police chief.[9] But highly vertical chains of command can be deficient in funding and horizontal links. Waging war across Europe was expensive and Napoleon left the task of paying for local city police in part to the municipalities. Overall, the Napoleonic regime greatly narrowed the influence of local authorities over the city police and increased the central state capacities even if it did not sew up all the loopholes.

Napoleon III, Bonaparte's nephew, constructed a *third* type of central state-municipal police relationship.[10] In 1851 he put the Lyon city police force under the *direct* authority of the Rhone departmental prefect, its budget into the central administration, and decisions about personnel and recruiting in the hands of a prefect-supervised general secretary.[11] This process – known as *étatisation* – turned France's second city into a *"police d'état"* where central state authorities, acting as the chief of police, almost completely bypassed the mayor and city council.[12] This particular center-city relationship was the most state-centered thus far, but it was limited in scope being the only city like that other than Paris.[13]

Leaders of the Third Republic (1870–1940) opted to *étatiser* Marseille, the third city of France, in 1908, and a number of other cities in subsequent years. If, around 1851, no one had really imagined the *étatisation* for any city other than Paris, an impetus to monopolize those *polices municipales* emerged between the 1890s and 1941. In 1941, the Vichy regime integrated into the state the police forces of *all* cities of 10,000 or more inhabitants. This measure created a fourth type of state-city police relationship, one that was comprehensive and thoroughly state-centered. From here, the chapter focuses on the shift toward this type and attempts to explain why and how the French police system developed in this manner in the early part of the twentieth century. I examine a host of factors contributing to the need for central control in the 1890s, to the incorporation of Marseille in 1908 and to the eventual *étatisation* of other cities in subsequent decades.

Devolution of Power

Established in 1870, early Third Republic leaders set about to undo the monarchical and imperial authority and administration built up since the Revolution.[14] They intended to recapture the spirit of the Revolution by democratizing government and decentralizing authority to some degree. The outcome was a mixed bag when it came to the police. In many ways, Third Republic leaders in the early decades did centralize and modernize the police in an unprecedented fashion. In 1881 they extended the Sureté Générale to oversee all the police and made it autonomous from the prefects.[15] They further professionalized the police when they opened the first training school in 1883 and then set standard conditions of entry in 1889. They also sought to civilize the police when they appointed Louis Lépine as the prefect of police in Paris in 1893. This *préfet de la rue* adopted a new "maintenance of order" philosophy to policing the city of Paris, an approach that focused on *preventing* social unrest and limiting excessive violence (Berlière 1993: 7; 1996: 123). As well, Interior Minister Georges Clemenceau implemented reforms meant to improve coordination between forces and combat new kinds of crime, measures that helped Clemenceau earn the nickname of "top cop" in France at the turn of the century.[16]

Despite this steady drawing of a more modern and standard police under a single authority, Third Republic leaders also *reduced* their control over the *polices municipales*. In 1871 the Republic voted to reconstitute the municipalities. In 1882 the Goblet Law made the mayor an elected office in all cities except Paris, a move that reversed the nineteenth-century trend of state appointments. And another, the 1884 municipal law, returned the power to direct the city police to the elected mayor. Barring some exceptions, this meant that the mayor recruited personnel and gave them orders, and the city council managed the budgets.[17] The prefect retained some powers including the capacity to revoke recruits, to annul or suspend the mayors' decrees, and to substitute himself for a mayor who failed to provide safety, tranquillity, and public health (Berlière 1996; Tanguy 1987). These measures ushered in a *municipalisation* of the police.

Although a seemingly clear-cut devolution of power to the local, the laws actually reintroduced a jurisdictional ambiguity about who was in charge of the city police. The 1884 law, like the *loi municipale* of December 14, 1789, put the mayor "under the supervision" of the central state representative (the prefect) without ever clearly defining the boundaries of either's power (Berlière 1996). These new conditions – locally elected city officials and ill-defined limits of authority – fostered, at best, multiple interpretations of the law and confusion and, at worst, the basis for divided loyalties, rivalries, and conflicts between local and central state actors. A far cry from the picture of a unified central state, the French police could be seen as a piecemeal organization (Berlière 1996: 33).

This devolution of power to the municipality encouraged political competition and opposition to the state at the local level. The political culture in France was changing in important ways in the 1880s and 1890s. The republicanist Republicans – as opposed to the monarchist ones – were gaining a more secure hold on Parliament and the presidency, and the fundamental division between the monarchists and republicans gave way to differences among moderate, Opportunist, and Radical Republicans. The center-right Opportunists dominated government in the 1880s and 1890s, the Radicals after 1899. Other political movements were forming in France as well. A royalist or monarchist right had always participated in politics in France in the nineteenth century, but the Boulanger affair of 1889 left as a legacy the creation of a more populist and urban-based variety of right-wing movements. The number of elected municipalities that moved to the right increased in the late 1880s as a result of *boulangisme* and again in the late 1890s in the wake of the Dreyfus Affair, including Rennes and Paris (Wright 1981: 244).[18] Socialism also emerged at this time. Again, its roots were old, but it gained new organizational and political momentum in the 1880s and 1890s as the first socialist workers congress met in 1879, a French workers party formed, and socialist candidates won seats in the National Assembly in 1893, all culminating in the fusion of factions into the unified socialist party (SFIO) in 1905. Like the right, socialists developed a strong municipal base. Voting in municipal elections was one way for French workers to get back at a state that used the army and guns on them (Scott 1981: 230). In 1892 socialists won majorities in 23 city councils, including Toulon, Roubaix, Montluçon, and Narbonne. By 1896 they held majority in 150 municipalities and socialist mayors presided in Marseille, Lille, Dijon, Limoges, Roanne, and smaller towns (Scott 1981: 231). Having opened the municipalities as arenas of political competition, the Third Republic helped convert various organizations into popular, broad-based and locally rooted social movements that were sometimes hostile to tenets of moderate republicanism such as strong central control, laissez-faire economics, or anticlericalism. Central state authorities worried about these "red" or "right" municipalities and were suspicious of mayors in whose hands the tools of order rested (Berlière 1996: 118). Passage of a law in 1892 giving the prefect the *unlimited* right to suspend a mayor indicated early on the obstacles prefects ran into in trying to maintain order in their cities.

At times, this devolution of power served to paralyze state authorities in policing matters. Since it put some of those authorities under the influence of "dual powers," they were caught in the middle when the municipality parted ways politically from the central state (Berlière 1996; Tanguy 1987). The *commissaire de police* is one example. He was appointed and paid by the state, under the authority of the prefect, but he was supposed to "supervise" a city police *recruited, commanded,* and *paid for* by the mayor and municipality. Day-to-day working conditions depended on the city; larger policing matters on the state. The *commissaire* was compelled to divide his loyalty between these two authorities, something that was manageable when everyone got along. When the tugs from both sides were strong, however, he was forced to choose or to try to appease both. At times he was recalled. It was not uncommon for the government to use the *commissaire* appointments to weaken deliberately a hostile municipality in periods of political crisis, or to fire those who did not appear to be sure-bet instruments of power (Tanguy 1987).[19] The high turnover rate of *commissaires* in some cities, and the hope among them for short-term appointments hints at the tenuous hold the central state had on city police operations (Berlière 1996; Tanguy 1987).

At other times, the *commissaire* was thrust into conflict. For a long time, in the city of Rennes, the mayor and *commissaire* got along fine even though they were of different republican stripes – moderate and extreme. But when a rightist city council was elected in 1900, an intense conflict occurred between the *commissaire* and the majority of the city council (Tanguy 1987: 173).[20] The city council denied him some supplemental pay and called for the creation of a decentralized post to replace that of the *commissaire central* (Tanguy 1987). Eventually the mayor intervened to diffuse the tension, but the conflict, by jeopardizing the mission and career of the *commissaire*, put the fragile maintenance of order at risk in Rennes. In the previous year, the town had hosted the second trial of Captain Dreyfus, an event so threatening that it had prompted the mayor to hand over voluntarily the direction of the police to the prefect and the government to bring in a mass of troops (Tanguy 1987).[21]

The prefect, too, sometimes suffered the same logic as the middleman. The prefect was appointed by the state and charged with the general maintenance of order in the department, but he was also dependent on city authorities to help carry that out. Once elected, the mayor and city council had a lot of power to push a particular political agenda. In addition to doling out patronage jobs and city funds, the mayor, as chief of police, with the right to recruit and command, could calibrate protest by directing the police to repress it or to stand by and let it proceed. Understandably, a mayor hesitated to crush or repress the citizens who elected him. When that political agenda tended to the left or right, tensions rose between the city and prefect, especially during partisan events such as May 1 gatherings, funeral marches and commemorations, anti-Jewish protests, and strikes. Like the *commissaire*, the prefect could be strapped by hostile city officials or sent in by Parisian authorities to break them.[22] Prefects tried a variety of tactics to maintain order, including negotiation, pleading with the central government for help, and calling in the army from another area. In other cases, they had to take time to obtain approval for the dissolution of certain organizations or the revocation of a mayor, a move that exacerbated a contentious climate when the mayor was very popular. A prefect sometimes suffered the reprobation of both his Paris Ministers and the insults of local protesters. Only the most adept prefects managed to mediate effectively strong adversarial relations between central authorities and a city.[23] Across France, these situations where the city and state authorities conflicted had the potential to inhibit the carrying out of the main mission of the police – the maintenance of order.

And the maintenance of order was, well, a tall order in France in the decade between 1896 and 1906. In the late 1890s, both Dreyfusard and anti-Dreyfusard camps protested across the country in a variety of ways; mass action and some violence occurred in Paris, the western cities of Anger and Rennes, and in Algeria, then a part of France.[24] Plans to secularize the French nation provoked resistance from Catholics. In 1902 the government started limiting the place of the Catholic Church in the life of the nation, inventorying its property and dismissing clergy, and then instituted the official separation of church and state in 1905. Resistance to secularization appeared in the North and was especially strong in the Anjou (west); protest peaked in early 1906 and was quite serious in Paris.[25] Economic downturns, new modes of mass production and an expanding trade-union movement contributed to worker mobilizations. Smaller, localized strikes in the 1890s were followed by waves of larger ones in the early 1900s around the country. Miners struck in the Nord-Pas-de-Calais in 1902 and uprisings brewed in Nantes between 1904 and 1906. In 1906 industrial strikes broke out in the North around the cities of Lille, Roubaix, and Tourcoing, and in the Ile-de-France. May 1st Day celebrations in 1906 were well attended, particularly in Paris. The southern Languedoc region was the site of wine workers' strikes in 1904 and then the center of a huge wine growers mobilization in 1907. Concomitant with, and probably a result of, this social unrest was the widespread fear of crime that was developing both in Paris and the provinces around the turn of the century (Berlière 1996: 57).[26] Jurists, doctors, and criminologists obsessed over the repeat offender and recidivism, and numerous publications devoted to criminality appeared (Berlière 1993: 214; 1996: 41). Paris deputies complained regularly of crime in the capital and much parliamentary discourse fixated on the topic. The public expressed a strong fear of "roving criminal bands" and unrest. Together, these social conditions created a general climate of insecurity where just about everyone was under attack – Dreyfusards, Jews, socialists, capitalists, the minister of the interior, and, of course, the police.

Authorities responded in a variety of ways to these turn-of-the-century challenges to the maintenance of order. Regarding crime, government efforts were focused on developing a criminal science and precision techniques for identifying criminals, such as fingerprinting and photography. For smaller-scale threats, either political or criminal, the local police and elected officials were sometimes capable of solving cases and diffusing tensions but sometimes did nothing. When needed, they hired part-time *gardiens* or *gardes-champêtres* (Berlière 1996: 23). For public gatherings and protests that exceeded local capacities, however, the local police were overwhelmed or, in some cases, stood by and permitted them. So the central government often sent in the troops. It did so to stave off potential unrest, as was the case when Celestin Hennion was dispatched with a mass of troops from the Paris Prefecture to Rennes in 1899, during the second Dreyfus trial. The government sent troops to halt the industrial strikes in the north and the wine workers in the south. In Algiers, at the height of anti-Jewish rioting in 1898, troops were necessary to bring calm to the city.[27] In all these cases, as well as when Catholics resisted the reappropriation of church property, confrontations between citizens and the army occurred, sometimes violent and deadly.

Other common strategies for diffusing the power of these large mobilizations included arresting leaders, such as anti-Dreyfusard activists like Paul Deroulède and Jules Guérin (Bredin 1986: 394), and amnesty, a tactic that involved bringing in the troops, making arrests, then letting the detainees go (Tilly 1986: 366). Anticipating massive turnout for May 1st Day in 1906, Clemenceau and Paris prefect Lépine arrested the important CGT secretary, banned any parades and gatherings, then spread forces throughout the city (Tilly 1986: 316–317). Typical of the Lépine-style preventive policing, it resulted in some scuffles and lots of arrests rather than violent repression. As mentioned earlier, sometimes the government sent in new prefects or *commissaires* to break a municipality that permitted menacing protesters too much freedom. Mayors were fined, arrested, and suspended and their appointments revoked, as was the case in Narbonne, Montluçon, and Marseille in 1892, in Lille in 1896, and Algiers in 1898 (Scott 1981: 244). Over the years, the Paris Prefecture and central authorities continued to develop sophisticated and effective surveillance methods for tracking many political-social organizations (Berlière 1996; Tilly 1986).

These were containment strategies, short-term solutions. They worked fine for episodic events where a mass of troops could intimidate or strategically strike a mobilization. They also worked relatively well in Paris because of the large and resource-endowed police force of the Prefecture, the proximity of supplementary government troops, and the sophisticated tactics of Prefect Lépine. For a variety of reasons, however, these measures were limited outside of Paris and, in general, as long-term strategies for dealing with nationwide unrest and crime.

The *polices municipales* had structural and resource limitations. In the provinces, they continued to suffer from inadequate resources and personnel. The raised sensitivity to crime made the dearth of *police judiciare* (investigative police) in the provinces especially apparent (Berlière 1996: 58). Local police left large case loads untouched and state authorities had to regularly call on the Sureté Générale in Paris to send extra agents to help investigate criminal cases. *Gendarmes* in rural areas were used to dealing with sedentary populations; they did not adapt well to more mobile criminality (Berlière 1996: 56). In 1906, when Clemenceau took over the Interior Ministry, he declared the *police judiciare* "manifestly insufficient" (Berlière 1996: 58).

The plurality of policing services and their functional divisions inhibited coordination. When the Revolution granted cities the right to *a* decent police in 1789, it actually created hundreds of *different* police forces (Berlière 1996: 22). As one author put it, *the* police in France have always been a "plural" (Berlière 1996: 15). Over time, the state has continued to create new forces, such as the Police spéciale des chemins de fer, decreed by Napoleon III in 1855, when crisscrossing trains began rendering the sedentary Gendarmerie less effective. Functional divisions have always plagued this proliferating policing system. From the Middle Ages, two types of police forces developed, one to patrol rural areas and lines of communication (the Maréchaussée, now called the Gendarmerie) and another to monitor the cities and towns. This division persisted through the Third Republic and up to the present where the two forces operate under different ministries, the former under the military and the latter under the Interior Ministry. Agencies such as the Police spéciale des chemins de fer were created for and fulfill specialized functions. While these and other forces have fallen under the jurisdiction of the central authorities that created them, the state cultivated few horizontal links between them, conditions

that engendered problems of coordination, communication, and standardization of procedure, and caused rifts, conflicts, and rivalries to develop.
Under highly centralized regimes, such as Napoleon's, the improved coordination and communication between the central state and provinces were
sometimes offset by the countervailing problems between localities and
forces far from Paris.[28] Moreover, high turnover among intermediary officials such as prefects and commissioners made these deficiencies even
more apparent.[29] Common problems included getting the city police and
Gendarmerie to work together, deciding who would investigate criminal
cases, and personal rivalries.

   Though the Paris Prefecture of Police had advantages over the other cities
for managing crime and unrest, this institution posed another set of problems for the central state. In fact, conflating capital cities with the state
obscures important struggles *between* central state and city authorities and
the significance those struggles have for the larger picture of the French
police system. Starting with Louis XIV, state leaders believed Paris should
not escape central power and sought to put it in the service of protecting
the state (Berlière 1996: 31). He created the position of *lieutenant génén-
erale de police* in 1674; it was reinstituted under Napoleon, who established
the Paris Prefecture of Police in 1800. These leaders, and authorities since
them, have given the chief of the Paris police a unique combination of
powers – central and municipal, administrative and judiciary. Ironically, in
the interest of securing the state, they have made the Paris Prefecture of
Police into a very powerful "state within a state" (Berlière 1996: 33).[30] The
head – the Paris prefect – commanded a small army and was sometimes
capable of defying the ministers who appointed him. These insular qualities also made it susceptible to the influence of individuals closest to it; the
insularity isolated it from other *police municipale*. For example, improvements in policing techniques made in Paris never filtered to the provinces
(Stead 1983; Berlière 1996). The Paris Prefecture was also a divided institution. The prefect was named and paid by the minister of the interior, but
the Prefecture – its staff, budget, tasks, and the procedures of the force –
was a municipal institution, under the Paris city council.[31] This division
tested the temerity and loyalty of many prefects, especially when the elected
Paris municipal council and the central state were political opponents, as
was the case in the 1890s when the Paris council swung to the right under
a centrist Third Republic.[32] Rivalries existed between the different services
under the prefecture and among different categories of personnel. As one
author put it, the Paris Prefecture of Police was "one big divided family"
(Berlière 1996: 105).

   The Third Republic inherited all these conditions – shortage of resources,
functional divisions, poor coordination – and sometimes added to them.
This was the case with the Brigades regionales de police mobile which,
created in 1907 to aid the provinces in criminal investigation, exacerbated

existing rivalries and power struggles when it intervened at the local level (Berlière 1996: 64). As a result, it was difficult for the state to anticipate and manage widespread unrest and crime in a comprehensive way. These limitations were felt as late as the 1930s, when one general inspector wrote: "There is not one police in France . . . but *polices*, without liaisons between them . . . without coordination" (Berlière 1996: 33).

In addition to the structural limitations of the French police in handling large-scale and/or persistent local protest, there were both practical and political problems associated with calling in the troops. Many of the army officers, young and inexperienced recruits, were not used to dealing with civilian protests and the insults and rocks thrown at them. Sometimes the army and local police conflicted over instructions or failed to coordinate plans for handling unrest. Calling out, mobilizing, and coordinating army troops for long, drawn-out periods of protest over weeks or months was expensive and exhausting for prefects and army commanders. Moreover, Republican government officials did not want to be associated with earlier regimes that deployed the army regularly and in a severely repressive manner, as was the case in 1848 and 1871. In 1884 Waldeck-Rousseau wrote to the prefects asking that they avoid giving the impression of civil war and constant recourse to the army (Berlière 1996: 119).

The central government also risked greater reprobation from local citizens and exacerbation of unrest when it superseded local authorities, especially in the larger cities. It was relatively easy for the troops or gendarmes to intervene in a small city or town if the local police forces were too limited to handle large-scale threats and if the municipality voluntarily conceded authority. Bringing in the troops to quell protest that was supported by the municipality, or a *commissaire* to break up workers' meetings, could provoke larger demonstrations, attacks against the military and police commissioners, and even more contempt for central state authority. For example, prefect-authorized troops and the revocation of Mayor Régis served to radicalize the anti-Jewish movement in Algiers in the late 1890s. Socialists reelected revoked mayors in other cities. In general, none of these strategies solved the long-term and fundamental problem of having the *polices municipales* under the command of entrenched left-wing or right-wing municipalities hostile to the central state.

The March to Centralize?

Starting in the 1890s, people began to propose reforms in the French policing system, many of which were inspired by the idea of greater centralization as the key to improving it. As early as 1894 Prefect Leroux, who described the Rennes city police as insufficient and under too much local influence, called for the separation of city police from a security police (the former to help the mayor, the latter under direct control of the state).

In Algiers, prefects begged the central government to take the police out of the hands of the radical anti-Jewish city authorities and adopt the "Lyon model." In 1903 the Interior Ministry, in an effort to reduce the cost of sending agents from the Sureté générale to the provinces, proposed the formation of a mobile regional brigade (Berlière 1996: 55). In 1906, in an attempt to better facilitate the maintenance of order, Minister of the Interior Clemenceau embarked on a major structural reorganization of the French police, a strategy that departed fundamentally from the prevailing use of the troops and the scientific management of criminality and recidivism. In that same year, an old bill to integrate the Paris prefecture fully into the Ministry of Interior was revived.[33] And Clemenceau's right-hand man, Celestin Hennion, who was appointed director of the Sureté générale in 1907, lobbied to end the problem of "dual powers" and to put the *polices muncipales* in the hands of the central state. Even the municipal police agents began calling for *rattachement* to the Ministry of the Interior after attending a national conference in Versailles in 1907. Having compared themselves with their higher-paid Parisian counterparts, they hoped nationalization would increase their pay as well (Berlière 1996: 234). All these proposed measures reflected the tendency to see centralization as a solution for a variety of inadequacies and a necessity for the preservation of order.[34]

In 1907 Clemenceau successfully convinced Parliament to pass a variety of reforms. Parliament approved the creation of the Brigades régionales de police mobile to combat the new mobility of crime and criminals.[35] They also agreed to a number of new services for coordinating and rationalizing criminal investigation: the Controle général du service des recherches dans les départements for information on criminals, the Service d'archives as a central storehouse of files on criminals, the Service du recensement général et du contrôle des étrangers to track foreigners, the Service photographique to better identify criminals, the Bulletin hebdomadaire de police criminelle to diffuse information around the country. Clemenceau also requested a new directorship of the Sureté générale, to which he immediately appointed Celestin Hennion. Over the next year or so and after fierce debates, Clemenceau and Hennion also convinced Parliament to pay for these new positions and services. Playing on public fear of roving criminal bands, they had the police capture a motley group of bohemians, foreigners, and ex-soldiers known as the "Pépère caravan" and played it up in the press as evidence of the new ability to halt crime (Berlière 1996). And on March 8, 1908, without much debate, Parliament passed a law to *étatiser* the Marseille city police, to give the prefect of the Bouche-du-Rhône department the same direct powers the Rhône prefect had over the police of Lyon.

Why Marseille? Of all the city police forces that could possibly be made more adequate by increasing central control over the police, why did

Parliament agree to this relatively totalizing measure for Marseille? A simple answer is size and significance. Marseille was one of the three largest cities in France in terms of population (approximately 500,000), behind Paris (2.8 million) and about equal to Lyon (530,000). It also occupied a territory about three to four times that of Paris. Marseille, like Lyon, was a great commercial center and had a very active port; it benefited enormously from colonial commerce and provided a gateway to Algeria and other parts of Africa and the Mediterranean. In 1906 Marseille hosted the successful colonial exposition. Aside from Paris and Lyon, no other French city rivaled Marseille in size or significance.

Other factors no doubt helped inflate the significance of Marseille for France and the need to keep a central governing hand in its affairs. As mentioned, Clemenceau liked to play the crime card when arguing before Parliament. He painted a picture of Marseille with crime run amok – "on the Canabière, they steal and rob people in broad daylight" – and a city police force overburdened by unfinished criminal cases (of which there were supposedly 3,700) (Berlière 1996: 88). Yet insufficiency and inadequacy are relative terms, and the fact that plenty of other cities could have fit the picture makes these factors uncompelling on their own. On the other hand, it does seem reasonable to have granted the status of *police d'état* to a city comparable to Lyon in population, in the number of police personnel and in the ratio of agents to inhabitants.[36]

Another possible explanation for needing to secure Marseille was the large North African population in the city. Many of these North Africans, mostly from Algeria, were single men looking for work and a fair number had joined the striking dock workers in recent years, making them easily associated with crime and insecurity. If immigrants were a powerful rationale for increased police control, however, then why didn't the state *étatiser* Algiers, a city with a large native Arab-Berber population and tens of thousands of poor migrants from other southern European countries, years earlier when prefects begged the state to do so?[37]

Leftists argued that the *étatisation* of Marseille was a move to "knock out the socialists." As early as 1891 socialists in Marseille demonstrated their hostility to the central government by haranguing an entourage of government ministers, a posture that fell in step with a long tradition of resistance to Jacobin centralism (Busquet 1998: 370). Between 1892 and 1902 socialists dominated the city council and mayoralship through Dr. Siméon Flaissières. Tugs-o-war started immediately between the socialist municipality and the state, and erupted on May 1, 1893, when Prefect Deffès, under instructions from Interior Minister Dupuy, took control of the police, closed the Bourse du travail, and prohibited meetings. After fights broke out between police and protesters, arrests were made and the prefect revoked three of the mayor's assistants (Busquet 1998: 373). Workers in many industries, backed by different socialist and trade-union groups, went on strike throughout the late 1890s. In 1901 dock workers and marines shut down the port for a month and half. The minority in the city council, together with prefect Charles Lutaud, accused the municipality of encouraging the strikes and vowed to chase the socialists from office. After 1902 the socialists lost their electoral domination of the municipality to moderate republicans but they remained a vocal minority. Dock workers continued to agitate in the following years and other workers joined in as well. These events and the loud appeals of frustrated commercial elites gave state authorities good reason to see socialism as a threat in Marseille. Moreover, Edouard Vaillant's brand of socialism did more than just rile the workers; it saw *local power* as "a formidable fortress . . . against the bourgeois domination of central power" (Carrot 1992: 157; Scott 1981: 230). Permanently pulling the police out of the hands of the municipality could have been a measure of protection against and perhaps the most effective way to diffuse the power of this entrenched socialist force. Although none of these factors alone explain why Marseille was chosen, the hostile socialist forces in such a large and significant city together made it an easy target for Clemenceau's program of centralization.[38]

All those seeking greater central control over the *police municipale* – Clemenceau, prefects, agents, politicians, and some of the general public – finally saw the fruits of their labor. Was it the start of a trend? Had they ushered in a more comprehensive phase of centralization? Was the state finally capturing a monopoly on the means of coercion? Perhaps. As mentioned, the *étatisation* of Marseille was icing on the cake of a package of powerful reforms for restructuring the French police proposed by Clemenceau and Hennion. After Marseille, the state converted other large cities into *polices d'état*: Toulon and La Seyne in 1918; Nice in 1920; Strasbourg, Mulhouse, and Metz in 1925; Algiers in 1930; Seine-et-Oise/ Seine-et-Marne in 1935; Constantine, Bone, and the Algiers suburbs in 1936; Toulouse 1940. In 1933 a government decree brought all these *polices d'état* under a single authority – the Services des polices d'etat (Carrot 1992: 158). It certainly looked like absorption into the center.

From another vantage point, however, the creation of a *police d'état* in Marseille put in relief *again* the state's profound *lack* of a monopoly over the *police municipale*. Clemenceau and Hennion continued to call for a blanket *étatisation* of *all* large cities without success. In 1911 Hennion wanted to replace the de facto mayoral command with the rightful chief of police – the minister of the interior – and proposed to no avail the incorporation of all cities with more than 10,000 people (Berlière 1996: 24). In 1919 the government led an inquest into the inability of the municipalities to maintain order and security as a result of unrest associated with the war, strikes, and the Russian Revolution. In response, Clemenceau demanded a general reorganization of the rural and municipal police and an end to piecemeal *étatisation* (Carrot 1992). Without success, he and Minister of

Interior Steeg offered less ambitious plans – the *étatisation* of towns of 40,000 or more inhabitants. This failed as well. Moreover, the creation of *polices d'état* in some cities was not necessarily the result of systematic centralization. The state took over the Toulon police in 1918 because of the war and the need to protect the large naval base located there. In Toulon and Nice, the city requested it. Difficulties of coordinating 180 communes proved to be the reasoning behind centralizing the area of Seine-et-Oise/Seine-et-Marne. Even France's mobilization in World War I did not warrant or lay the groundwork for *étatisation* beyond a handful of cities. The vision of a centralized and unified municipal police system would have to wait until 1941, when the state – now the Vichy regime of occupied France – created a Police nationale and placed the police in all cities of 10,000 or more inhabitants into the hands of the interior minister. This policy would stick long after the war.

Why was a monopoly over the municipal police so difficult to achieve under the Third Republic? Like prior regimes, Third Republic leaders considered policing to be closely tied to governance and constituted a preoccupation *de premier plan* in France (Bayley 1975: 335; Tanguy 1987: 167). In 1923 Louis Marin, in a report on police reform, said: "if there's a service that must be a service of the state it is without contest the service of the police" (Berlière 1996: 234). Clemenceau, like Louis XIV, Napoleon, and Laval, sought to make the system of policing in France better serve *the* state. In addition to serving the state, the police and debates about how to organize, administer, and empower it, especially in key moments of regime transition, also *defined* the state. The *police municipale* was a particularly central tenet of those debates. For a long time, how to reform the Paris police was a central question about how to protect *the* state. The early constitution and meaning of the Third Republic rested in part on whether to keep the Napoleonic office of the Prefecture of Police of Paris. According to the prefect of Algiers in the 1890s, reforms of the city police would ultimately shape the larger relationship between France and Algeria, between European and African civilizations. Further evidence of the importance of controlling the *police municipale* was the fact that the Vichy regime, as one of its first measures, created the Police nationale and incorporated under it the police forces of all cities of 10,000 or more people. So, what prevented Clemenceau and other Third Republic advocates of greater central state control from carrying out their intentions with regard to the *police municipale*?

Despite the *desired* tight connection between state power and the police in France, certain conditions made it difficult for Third Republic authorities to monopolize the French policing system. In addition to the impediments mentioned already, such as poor coordination, functional divisions, and a shortage of resources, cost was a major barrier. The features necessary in their idea of a modern police – professionalism, unity, coordination, and standardization – were expensive to implement. Once police elites, meaning the Ministry of the Interior and Paris prefects, began shifting their strategies from reaction to prevention of crime and unrest, the costs increased as well. Obviously Clemenceau convinced Parliament to authorize and fund a broad range of new services and restructuring of the police, but reinventing Napoleon's tight vertical command over the provincial police would require enormous resources, including more intermediary state functionaries and other personnel, new networks of communication and surveillance, and uniform salaries and benefits. Perhaps Clemenceau and Hennion had reached the limits that citizens, politicians, and administrators were willing to pay for a more centralized system of police.

Additionally, the old tradition of passing some fiscal responsibilities to the cities might have created resistance to more centralized police budgets. Throughout the nineteenth century, the budgets were set and funds raised for the police at the municipal level, opening up those police forces to local influences. Local influences prevailed even under Napoleon, who appointed the mayors and prefects to oversee those local police, and in the case of Lyon, whose police force was incorporated under *direct* central control because its city council still had to raise one-third of the cost. The local fiscal influence endowed municipalities with power over the state-appointed *commissaries* and prefects to shape police personnel and loyalty, an advantage perhaps difficult to relinquish (Tanguy 1987).

The more difficult obstacle to overcome seemed to be the power of the cities, or at least the political and cultural distance that had been created between them and the state. The devolution of power to municipal governments in the early Third Republic created a bulwark of resistance to the central state. Not surprisingly, when crime, strikes, political protest, and hostile municipalities provided the impetus to reconsolidate power in the center, lots of resistance to state incorporation of city police came from mayors and municipalities of big cities, seeing that it would take away a central pillar of their power. The far left – including socialists like Vaillant – argued against increasing central authority over the police because it represented an imposition of bourgeois state power and the threat of a vast police state (Berlière 1996: 231; Scott 1981). Contrary to the ideas of Clemenceau and Hennion, Vaillant was in favor of the *municipalisation* of the police – of Marseille, Lyon, and Paris. Like the left, the right also sought to guard local domains of power, like the Paris city council did in 1900 when it demanded the dissolution of the Paris Prefecture and the return of the police to the municipality.[39] Together, these peripheral counterforces to central state power made more comprehensive centralization of the city police elusive.

Given this picture of the French *police municipale*, it is difficult to argue that the French state monopolized the means of coercion in the late nineteenth and early twentieth centuries. As key sites of struggles, cities and their *polices municipales* played an important role in defining the modern national police system in France and impeding centralized control of them. Local prerogatives and divided loyalties, rather than central and singular ones, often prevailed in the functioning of the police. Even if successive French state regimes had succeeded in designing a vertical and centralized police structure, other factors and conditions intervened to prevent the best of intentions from being carried out. Only in the Second World War when the Vichy regime adopted *étatisation* for the large city police forces did the French state come closer to monopolizing those means.

The Vichy policy stuck long after the war. The trend, however, is proving to be reversible. In 1987, one century after the 1884 *loi municipale*, a law ambiguously put order and security back "under the surveillance" of city agents. Municipalities contend the Police nationale cannot handle the difficulties of policing local communities, including crime and social unrest. Some cities are forming their own police forces to compensate. If centralizing local police was supposed to facilitate the maintenance of order in the past, *néomunicipalisation* of those same city police may be the way to achieve it in the present. If a close look at the *police municipale* in the past century challenges the idea of the history of the French state as a continual march toward centralization and France as the central state par excellence, this current trend may be the next chapter.

Notes

1. In France, the police and military do overlap to some degree. For example, the Gendarmerie – the rural police force – falls under the jurisdiction of the minister of war. That point will be touched on later in the chapter.
2. I think that state-building in general is a set of negotiations or struggles between parties both inside and outside the state. For example, war-making is an important condition of state-making as Charles Tilly has argued. For the purposes of this chapter, however, I focus on the internal state negotiations because I think they are more significant in the formation of the police in the nineteenth and early twentieth centuries.
3. I put the word "provinces" in quotes on purpose. It is a common term used by analysts of French history to refer to the outlying areas far from Paris – usually meant both geographically and culturally. However, I want it in general to refer to any "local" authority in the country delegated some responsibilities separate from those of the central state. Those "local" authorities include small towns, rural communes, departments, large cities, Algeria, and even Paris. This chapter focuses on larger cities – Paris as well as others such as Marseille and Lyon – with specific arguments to follow.
4. This was part of the municipal revolution characteristic of the early years of the Revolution.
5. To the cities went the police powers of "all that concerns the safety and right of way in the streets and public places" (Berlière 1996: 10).

6. Napoleon built on the centralizing tendencies of the later years of the Revolution and the Directory. In 1791 the state established the Commissaires de police in all big cities, elected every two years and at the disposition of the mayors. War with other European countries put pressure on the state to bolster direct central uniform rule, rule that could contain resistance and independent action (Tilly 1986: 109). In 1795 the Commissaire de police became appointed by municipality in towns of 5,000 inhabitants or more. In 1796 the Directory created the Ministere de la police general to oversee all police, and appointed Fouché in 1799. Under the Directory, the definition of the police was made more clear: "The Police is instituted to maintain public order, liberty, property, and individual safety. Its principal character is vigilance. Society is the object of its solicitude" (Carrot 1992: 105). This clarification marks the origins of the division of the police into judiciary and administrative.

7. This system included *commissaires particuliers de police municipale* and *commissaires généraux*, both appointed by the state. He even appointed *commissaires* for towns as small as 5,000.

8. Napoleon also continued Louis XIV's tradition of a *haute police*, or political police, a security strategy that focused on protecting *the* state and going after any threats to and enemies of it. Fouché was famous for carrying out these responsibilities, for his amazing surveillance of enemies of the state.

9. This office was retained under successive regimes including the Third Republic and is still in place today; the police prefect heads the capital city's police.

10. Some of the unity and centrality broke down when Napoleon was ousted from power. The Restoration monarchy sought a rupture with the *dictature napoléonienne* and proceeded to eliminate the Ministère de la police in 1818 and handed its functions over to the Interior Ministry (Carrot 1992: 132). Many of the *commissaires generaux* and *commissaires speciaux* disappeared at the same time.

11. At the time, the Lyon agglomeration had 240,000 people. There are different theories about why Lyon was incorporated: financial incapacity of the municipality and local political clientelism (Carrot 1992: 152); it was the second city of France at the time and a big industrial and commercial center where 60,000 people worked in the silk industry (many of whom were out of work, and production was paralyzed), a situation that posed a threat of disorder (Latta 1987: 61; Berlière 1996: 30); it had a reputation as a *ville rebelle* after the 1848 revolution (Latta 1987: 62); the administration of an agglomeration of communes was too complex (Berlière 1996: 30). In February 1848 workers and revolutionaries dominated the city's Comité executif; in June, a more conservative Comité replaced them. Parliament discussed conferring some power over the police to the prefect, which raised the problem of how to delimit and regulate that power. Finding it very confusing and difficult to separate out local and national powers, they opted to give total power to the state. The municipality consistently resisted the option of *étatisation* (Berlière 1996: 30).

12. Lyon, Paris, and other cities later on became known as *police d'état* (state police) and Lyon became known as the *modèle lyonnais*. Regarding the degree to which the state bypassed local authorities after *étatisation*, the mayors of the communes reserved their powers and responsibilities over the *collectivité locale* (public streets, lighting, fires, etc.) but that was all. Although integrated

into the national budget, the communes still had to pay one-third of the expenses of the police.

13. No other city except Paris came close to acquiring that structure and status; in fact, rarely had anyone envisaged making city police other than Paris into a *police d'état* (Carrot 1992: 152). Regarding scope, Lyon and Paris were the only cities at the time like this. In 1855 Napoleon issued a *loi municipale* that incorporated cities of 40,000 or more inhabitants but another law (1867) overrode it.

14. By "imperial" I am referring to Napoleons I and III, not the French colonial empire.

15. Napoleon III created the Sureté générale in 1854 and attached it to the Paris Prefecture of Police.

16. Clemenceau became *president du conseil* in 1907 (previously he was minister of the interior) (Berlière 1986).

17. The few exceptions: for cities of 40,000 or more, the central state reserved a *droit de regard* on the staff and budget of city police, and the prefect could only confirm recruits or revoke them; also the Rhone prefect was to remain in effect the chief of police of Lyon.

18. Action française founded in 1898 as a tool to fight the Dreyfusards, soon to be taken over by Charles Maurras.

19. For example, the government fired *commissaires* De La Chevardiere and Aigouy from their post in Rennes in the early 1900s.

20. Rennes is a large city in the Brittany region of northwest France. The city council was elected on the heels of the Dreyfus Affair and became a *bloc droit* for the first time in twenty years.

21. Similar stories abound for socialist municipalities. In Montluçon in 1893, for example, socialist mayor Dormoy repeatedly protected worker gatherings from the *commissaire de police* (Scott 1981: 238–239).

22. In Rennes, Edgar Le Bastard was mayor in the late 1880s. He was a republican but against the Opportunist government in power. He joined the boulangist movement (a leftist and populist version of it) with a deputy from Rennes, Le Hérissé. Le Bastard was very popular. The government sent a new *commissaire central*, Eugene Court, and replaced the prefect de Brancion with Leroux who was expected to "break" Le Bastard. Leroux revoked mayor Le Bastard who was subsequently reelected. Leroux also dissolved the city council, which was also reelected. The mayor's assistant M. Bebin, a Boulangist, also returned as the person in charge of the police. A battle between the court office and the Bebin office ensued with accusations of incompetence, monies denied, and the like. Finally, the government's mission was accomplished when Bebin relinquished responsibility of the police.

23. Although not a typical departmental prefect, Louis Lépine, the Paris prefect of police, successfully mediated between the minister of the interior and the Paris city council.

24. In Paris, street protests occurred in 1898. In Anjou, the Dreyfus Affair provoked in 1895 three days of large anti-Semitic demonstrations that involved priests and students. Between 1896 and 1901, Algeria, an official part of France, experienced mass protest, rioting, pillaging of Jewish neighborhoods, and the takeover of the Algiers municipality by anti-Jewish activists.

25. In 1902 demonstrations occurred in Angers to protest the dismissal of nuns; Gendarmerie brigades reinforced Angers gendarmes. In 1906–1907 Action française and Catholics occupied churches. Ile-de-France and Languedoc had some marginal resistance to laicization.

26. Whether and how much crime had increased is difficult to say for the same reasons it is today – it depends a lot on the nature of reporting. The number of crimes reported around the turn of the century had, indeed, increased several fold since the early nineteenth century. But techniques and statistics for reporting crime had also improved.

27. Throughout the years (1898–1901), the prefect constantly complained that the police stood by and watched as anti-Jewish protesters attacked stores, tramways, and people and insulted government officials.

28. Napoleon appointed prefects, commissaries, and mayors to directly oversee these police, a situation that changed only in 1882–1884 when elected municipalities regained control of their own police under the Third Republic.

29. There was an interesting exception in the Third Republic. Louis Lépine served as the Paris prefect of police from 1893 to 1897 and again from 1899 to 1913.

30. It is possible that Napoleon knew the perils of a vertical chain of command and created the Prefecture of Police and appointed Dubois to the post to counterbalance Fouché, whom Napoleon did not trust (Berlière 1996: 34). Also, the popular Louis Lépine (1893–1913) had strong influence under Clemenceau.

31. Another aspect of its originality, even distinguishing it from Lyon, was its funding. Its budget was voted by the Paris City Council and the state paid into its budget to compensate for its services.

32. Louis Lépine had an uncanny knack for currying the favor of a rightist, opposition Paris city council in the 1890s.

33. It seems that the Senate had approved it a long time ago, in 1888, but the Chamber of Deputies refused to approve it after four attempts.

34. For the most part, this chapter has focused on political conflicts between central state and municipal authorities. While neglected here, the role of other actors, especially economic elites, was important in shaping collective action and police action in cities. Commercial, industrial, and financial elites, acting in their interests to do business, took sides too. Sometimes they sided with Republican state authorities against contentious socialist, nationalist, or Catholic localities, other times not.

35. This Brigade later became the Gendarme mobile.

36. In 1907 Marseille had 855 agents, with 1 agent per 604 people; Lyon had 920 agents, with 1 agent per 575 people (Berlière 1996: 28). Plenty of other cities had much higher ratios, making the manpower shortage in them more problematic in some respects than in Marseille.

37. Prefects called for taking the Algiers police out of the hands of the mayor when he let anti-Jewish protestors have free reign in the city between 1898 and 1901.

38. Toulouse is another example of a city that became socialist in 1906 and had a long history of rebellion. It only had 150,000 people and was considered a backward, provincial city until after World War II.

39. Municipal control of the police remains a platform pillar of the right to this day in France.

References

Bayley, David. 1975. "The Police and Political Development in Europe," in Charles Tilly, ed., *The Formation of National States in Western Europe*, 328–379. Princeton: Princeton University Press.

Berlière, Jean-Marc. 1993. *Le Préfet Lépine aux origines de la police moderne*. Paris: Denoël.

1996. *Le monde des polices en France: XIXe–XXe siècles*. Paris: Editions Complexe.

Bredin, Jean-Denis. 1986. *The Affair: The Case of Alfred Dreyfus*. New York: George Braziller.

Brubaker, Rogers. 1992. *Citizenship and Nationhood in France and Germany*. Cambridge, Mass.: Harvard University Press.

Busquet, Raoul. 1998. *Histoire de Marseille*. Paris: Editions Robert Laffont.

Carrot, Georges. 1992. *Histoire de la police française*. Paris: Tallandier.

Cooper-Richet, Diana. 1987. "Le plan général de protection à l'épreuve de la grève des mineurs du Nord-Pas-de-Calais (september–november 1902)," in Philippe Vigier, ed., *Maintien de l'ordre et polices en France et en Europe au XIXe siècle*, 397–413. Paris: Créaphis.

Geslin, Claude. 1987. "L'administration et les syndicats ouvriers en Bretagne avant 1914," in Philippe Vigier, ed., *Maintien de l'ordre et polices en France et en Europe au XIXe siècle*, 361–382. Paris: Créaphis.

Latta, Claude. 1987. "Le maintien de l'ordre à Lyon (février–juillet 1848)," in Philippe Vigier, ed., *Maintien de l'ordre et polices en France et en Europe au XIXe siècle*, 61–85. Paris: Créaphis.

Liang, Hsi-Huey. 1992. *The Rise of Modern Police and the European State System from Metternich to the Second World War*. Cambridge: Cambridge University Press.

Meyzonnier, Patrice. 1994. *Les forces de police dans l'Union europeenne*. Paris: L'Harmattan.

Roach, John, and Jurgen Thomaneck, eds. 1985. *Police and Public Order in Europe*. London: Croom Helm.

Scott, Joan. 1981. "Mayors versus Police Chiefs: Socialist Municipalities Confront the French State," in John Merriman, ed., *French Cities in the Nineteenth Century*, 230–245. New York: Holmes & Meier.

Skocpol, Theda. 1979. *States and Social Revolutions: A Comparative Analysis of France, Russia, and China*. Cambridge: Cambridge University Press.

Stead, Philip. 1983. *The Police of France*. New York: Macmillan.

Tanguy, Jean-François. 1987. "Autorité de l'etat et libertés locales: Le commissaire central de Rennes face au maire et au préfet (1870–1914)," in Philippe Vigier, ed., *Maintien de l'ordre et polices en France et en Europe au XIXe siècle*, 167–182. Paris: Créaphis.

Tilly, Charles. 1986. *The Contentious French*. Cambridge, Mass.: Belknap Press.

1992. *Coercion, Capital and European States, AD 990–1992*. Cambridge, Mass.: Blackwell.

Tocqueville, Alexis de. 1955. *The Old Regime and the French Revolution*. Trans. Stuart Calbert. New York: Doubleday (Anchor Books).

Wakeman, Rosemary. 1997. *Modernizing the Provincial City: Toulouse, 1945–75.* Cambridge, Mass.: Harvard University Press.

Weber, Eugen. 1976. *Peasants into Frenchmen: The Modernization of Rural France, 1870–1914.* Stanford: Stanford University Press.

Weber, Max. 1946. *From Max Weber: Essays in Sociology.* Ed. H. H. Gerth and C. Wright Mills. New York: Oxford University Press.

Wright, Gordon. 1981. *France in Modern Times.* New York: W. W. Norton.

12

Domestic Militarization in a Transnational Perspective

Patriotic and Militaristic Youth Mobilization in France and Indochina, 1940–1945

Anne Raffin

Whereas state activities during wartime typically depend on the use of instruments of armed forces to destroy rival armies and to repress and control civilians and territories, a large part of the state's activities in France and Indochina during the Second World War was instead socially oriented, even civic-minded. Mirroring developments in the core, the colonial state in Indochina pursued a complex range of activities, from highly coercive ones to health and education policies, some supplemented with large elements of propaganda. This chapter focuses on the authorities' use of paramilitary and sporting youth organizations to build and channel conservative and patriotic feelings toward the Vichyist regime and its ideology (I define these youth groups as paramilitary because they were civic organizations that incorporated military cadres, military structures [often divided into divisions led by a "chief"], and military goals [i.e., regime defense, internal discipline]). In the case at hand, colonial authorities sought to build allegiance to the empire by militarizing and "patriotizing" youth attitudes through sports activities and paramilitary organizations. By militarism, I mean the material and ideological process by which segments of civil society become dependent on and subordinated to a set of militaristic beliefs, values, and institutions (Enloe 1983: 7–9; 1989: 139–140; Mann 1984: 25). In both cases the French administration operated only at the will of the occupiers; because the French state did not monopolize the means of violence in either location – due to the occupation of France by Germany and the stationing of Japanese troops in Indochina, creating two sets of hybrid powers – it redefined the roles of collaborators by devising new techniques to sustain its presence, such as youth corps. Thus this research examines state policy in recently defeated nations. Because more militarized and repressive options were limited by these circumstances, except against those directly challenging the hybrid powers, army personnel assumed unusually active roles in these educational and recreational organizations as a way, it is argued here, to control youngsters in an unstable political context.

How and why did the French state opt for a socially oriented approach to the mass mobilization of youth in France and Indochina? In analyzing such paramilitary activities as products of conditions in France and Indochina, we do not assume a clear distinction between national and colonial history, as is often the case. The French state-sponsored patriotism sought to shape the collective identities of the residents of both core and empire in a concurrent and transnational political process. In a concurrent reaction to the ongoing global war and to its own local insecurity, France responded to the national humiliation of the German invasion and occupation (1940–1944) while officials in Indochina sought to repel comparable Thai and Japanese challenges. The external policy served core domestic as well as imperial ends. The Vichy government of Marshal Pétain attempted to preserve its image as a great power during the occupation by defining the nation as incorporating not only France but also the empire (Ageron et al. 1990: 318–319).

War and armed struggle are often the key tools by which states mobilize and control people and goods when facing external dangers. In the case at hand, the French state sponsored patriotic and sporting organizations to combat internal threats. These policies would subsequently affect later patterns of state formation in both France and Indochina.

Socially Oriented Military Activities in the French Metropole

French Goals

The goals and methods of this initiative were driven by historical events. When the armistice of June 1940 ended the war in France and in the empire, more than half of the metropole was occupied by Germany. Marshal Philippe Pétain became chief of state on July 10, 1940, and the parliamentary regime of the Republic was replaced by his individual authority, as advised by ministers responsible to him. The so-called National Revolution was launched to reform not only political institutions, but also the nation and its collective identity, and the transition in ideology was summarized by the replacement of the motto "Liberty-Equality-Fraternity" with "Work-Family-Motherland." The new political context was driven in part by a sense of revenge, as the regime sought to capitalize on the defeat by scapegoating and punishing those it saw as responsible – democrats, Freemasons, Jews, and anticlerics. This conservative revolution was based therefore on "the politics of exclusion" (Paxton 1975).

Typical of defeated societies seeking to restore national greatness, the regime turned to youngsters in particular to save and remake a nation that had succumbed to "the cult of ease." Indeed, the Vichy regime was "obsessed by the idea, real or voluntarily exaggerated, of a physical and moral degeneracy of the French society, and especially of its youth" (Gay-Lescot 1990: 107). Nervous about their restlessness, the regime turned to youth organizations as a means to control youngsters outside of schools in "a healthy group experience" and properly guide them through the task of the rejuvenation of society (Paxton 1975: 160–161). The awesome defeat with the advancing of the German army on the French territory threw millions of people out on the streets. Many youngsters had lost their parents or were homeless; some who were unable to return to their homes formed begging or robbery gangs. This initiative was intended to train mentalities and behaviors not only to create disciplined, physically strong, and faithful citizens, but also to produce future elites for the new regime (Rousso 1990: 29).

These activities were viewed as noncoercive by French officials, and youngsters freely decided to join them; an exception was the Chantiers de jeunesse (youth construction sites), a compulsory service program for twenty-year-old males in unoccupied France and Algeria, formed to compensate for the repeal of the military draft with the armistice convention. According to the terms of the armistice, Germany allowed France to keep only those 100,000 troops needed to maintain order in the Unoccupied Zone of metropolitan France. Many preexisting cadres, temporarily retired, were reclassified, particularly into youth organizations (Bachelier 1992: 392–393). Indeed, military leadership in the metropole was animated by a certainty that the army's new role was to recapture and stimulate a lost morality within the nation. Officers would now become teachers. Part of the task was to counteract the negative influence of the Third Republic on youth, and officers in particular blamed the defeat on the prior regime's "fundamental hostility to the special values alleged to inhere in military life." The prejudices of antimilitarists, communists and left-wing teachers, it was argued, had undermined patriotism and weakened the will of boys and girls (Paxton 1966: 158–159, 171, 181).

After the turn of the century, Lieutenant Louis-Hubert Lyautey's ideas became very popular among professional officers who came to agree that they should aim their instruction not only at the body but also at the mind and spirit of each soldier (Lyautey 1891: 443–459). Because the defeat was explained from a moral and spiritual perspective – the Third Republic's replacement of the idea of leadership with notions of "ease and facility" – all cures had to be of the same vein (Paxton 1966: 190–191). One of the army's educational roles operated indirectly through the youth organization Chantiers de jeunesse and other affiliated organizations.

New Youth Organizations
The government of Vichy created the General Secretariat of Youth (Secrétariat Général à la Jeunesse or SGJ) in September 1940. Over time, it evolved from a relatively open and fluid ideology to one requiring formal membership through defined criteria. Particularly after June 1941, the Vichy regime demanded that these movements be hierarchically organized

and submit financial questions, programs, publications, and activities to state control (Coutrot 1972: 266, 278). In August 1940, civilian Chantiers de la jeunesse emerged to receive males in their twentieth year as conscripts for eight months in work camps located in the Unoccupied Zone and in Algeria. While this compulsory service program lacked military training, it was supervised throughout its existence almost entirely by army men. Its main goals were to mix all social classes, to teach moral and civic responsibility and military pride to youth, as well as to serve as an outlet for the unemployed due to a fear of social disorder (Paxton 1966: 202–213). The Chantiers de jeunesse were directly inspired by educational theories popular in the army, which posited that every aspect of life had to have educational significance, and promoted the belief in community life's positive effects. "The subordination of individual wills to corporate life" was pursued in a number of ways, including sporting competitions, outdoor work, and campfire ceremonies and discussion (Paxton 1966: 210). The day was filled with hard physical work, sports, civic and moral education, and leisure activities. Through all these activities, the purpose was "manly training," because through physical exertion was created a predisposition to moral development, and also direct moral training, effected through the "cult of honor" and through living together (Halls 1981: 286).

Love for and dedication to the motherland was fully cultivated up to the "departure ceremony" where an oath to continue serving echoed and reemphasized the promise to serve France that the recruits made upon joining the movement (Cointet-Labrousse 1987: 122; Christian Schlemmer, "Les mouvements de jeunesse en France," *Indochine*, no. 38, May 22, 1941, p. 7). Indeed, one of the books employed in the camps defined education's goals as the teaching of moral and patriotic beliefs (Paxton 1966: 188).

Because youth movements encompassed only one teenager out of seven in 1939, and thus largely represented the elite, Henry Dhavernas launched a private organization in July 1940 called Compagnons (Companions) to provide comparable opportunities initially for the unemployed youth segment of the unorganized masses while financially backed by the state (Halls 1995: 296). The goal of this association was to rally those French youngsters who were "avid for participating in the material and moral recovery of the country" by lending their support to the services assisting refugees and prisoners (Giolitto 1991: 505). Soon a "political" goal was added to their agenda: to gather youngsters to serve the National Revolution while developing their "taste for work and love for the homeland" (Giolitto 1991: 506). In 1941 "Colonel-on-Leave" Guillaume de Tournemire took over the organization (Paxton 1975: 163). Whereas the compulsory Chantiers de jeunesse targeted young men, the voluntary Compagnons was intended for adolescent boys, of fifteen to twenty, and sported outfits and rites influenced by the scouts. A strong emphasis was on manual work, civic service, secular humanism, cultural activities, physical fitness, and citizen attachment to the National Revolution (Comte 1992: 414; Cointet-Labrousse 1987: 123–124; Halls 1981: 269). Members made symbolic and dramatic patriotic gestures to stress their love to the motherland and its unity. In a common practice, a leader collected and honored "a bag containing soil from Alsace-Lorraine mixed with the ones of all the other provinces of France and the one of Algeria, of Tunisia" (Hervet 1965: 9). The gesture of gathering and combining soil was apparently a standardized political ritual that evoked the crucial role that the unity of the imperial nation played in the imagination of the members of this organization. The same ritual occurred during Pétain's visit for the second anniversary of this organization (Halls 1981: 276–277).

A network of "leadership schools" (*écoles des cadres*) emerged to train the elite among the youth and to supply chiefs for youth corps. Initially, part of the schools' staffs comprised officers on "armistice leave" (Halls 1981: 146). One of the key establishments was the *Ecole d'Uriage* (Uriage school) created by Major Pierre-Dominique Dunoyer de Segonzac, which aimed to offer a physical, intellectual, and moral training based on "lived experience" – rather than books – for any man who sought to perform tasks demanding responsibility and leadership. Again its rites drew from both the army and scouting. Financially backed by the state, Dunoyer's work carried a spirit of revenge against Germany (Paxton 1975: 165; Coutrot 1972: 268; Comte 1992: 415).

These new paramilitary organizations in the metropole, although socially oriented, were more militaristic in purpose than those in Indochina. Not only was the Chantiers de jeunesse viewed as a "substitute for conscription," General Maxime Weygand and other members of the General Staff hoped that youth movements could provide an analog to military service (Halls 1981: 133; 1995: 298). The militaristic style and training of the Compagnons and the Chantiers actually prompted the Germans to ban their presence in the Occupied Zone (Halls 1981: 141).

All these organizations promoted sports and physical education as a root method for the regeneration of the nation. They combined to create a larger educational program targeting the body itself, aiming at the virilization of probable elites, in an echo of the 1880s, where "a cult of sport and gymnastics" emerged as an answer to defeat at the hands of Prussia in 1870. Both periods' political cultures – the 1880s and the 1940s – explained defeat in terms of the "feebleness" and "limpness" of the population, thus predicating the need to reeducate the body (Muel-Dreyfus 1996: 284–285). At the same time, some Vichy officials viewed sport as a useful tool for diverting the young from politics altogether, because these corps provided great opportunities for youth who simply enjoyed sports and outdoor activities (Halls 1981: 190–191). Those organizations with military connections were part of a larger process of the rapid organization of the youth under the overarching "Youth of France." Other contemporary associations were Jeune France and Les Jeunes du Maréchal, for instance. Because they did not have military personnel or were not influenced by military ideas, I do not analyze them in this article. Nor do I examine profascist youth organizations whose ideological orientations moved away from the National Revolution's ideals (see Giolitto 1991: chap. 15).

The Transfer of the Vichy Youth Initiative to Indochina

The Military and Political Contexts

The armistice included no specific instructions regarding the size of the colonial force located outside of France and there was no German objection to military activities or military service in Southeast Asia. Because the defeat of June 1940 initially left the empire untouched, military chiefs in Indochina preferred to fight on, but Japanese claims over the colony and British regional policy made this option unrealistic (Hesse d'Alzon 1982: 85–86; Maurice Ducoroy, "Le chef vous parle . . . ," *Sports-Jeunesse d'Indochine*, no. 59, September 23, 1943, p. 3). Many administrators and military staff members quickly fell in with Pétain, including Admiral Jean Decoux, who was named governor general of Indochina in July 1940 (Coquery-Vidrovitch and Ageron 1991: 148–149). Conceived primarily as a policing force to maintain social order, the colonial legion was ill-prepared for invasion or war. These men in Indochina – fourteen metropolitan and twenty-eight indigenous battalions amounting to about 40,000 men within a total population of 25 million – tried to continue their assignments despite outdated and sparse equipment. Further, the French could not rely on the fighting potential of an indigenous population colored by strong nationalist movements contesting the colonial presence (De La Gorce 1988: 278).

The Japanese state regarded the defeat of June 1940 as an opportunity to expand its power over Indochina, whose wealth in rice and raw materials and whose strategic location were both targets of and means for its ambitious expansionism. Tokyo attacked the northern part of the colony on September 22, 1940; the immediate goal was to stop the shipment of provisions from Indochina to China. Earlier, the Japanese had objected to the transfer of military supplies by railroad from the port of Haiphong in Tonkin to the Chinese province of Yunnan (Hammer 1954: 14). Lacking a means to manage the area efficiently, Japan signed a series of agreements with France, including a particularly important one in July 1941, which provided mutual defense agreements and allowed Japanese troops to station themselves in the colony, which was then incorporated into the Japanese war economy. In return, the Japanese recognized French national sovereignty over this territory. This strange double-power reigned while Japan started to propagate the idea of "Asia for Asians" and the French responded by attempting to stimulate local and "imperial" patriotism (Héméry 1990: 77–78).

Taking advantage of France's weakened position, Thailand demanded the return of the Laotian and Cambodian territories it had ceded to France at the turn of the century. A conflict lasting from September 1940 to March 1941 led to the loss of parts of Cambodia and Laos to Thailand. (The name "Thailand" itself dates from January 1939, and is characteristic of the expansionist and nationalist pan-Thai policy of Pibul Songgram, who openly drew on the Japanese imperial example; see Decoux 1949: 123–147; Hammer 1954: 25). Seeing the Japanese attack on the Indochinese northern border as an opportunity, local communists of the border zone around Lang Son launched guerrilla activities to set up a revolutionary power, which would be subdued by late October 1940. Meanwhile, local communists in Cochinchina – the southern part of present day Vietnam – were benefiting from peasants' economic grievances and their opposition to conscription for military activity along the Cambodia-Thai border. Earlier on, high taxes, lower rice prices, and higher unemployment had translated into peasant protests. Uprisings in the Mekong Delta region emerged by the end of November 1940, leading to creation of revolutionary committees. With airplane bombings, the French harshly suppressed this opposition, killing thousands and arresting up to 6,000 people (Duiker 1981: 61–64; Ngo Van 1995: 282; Marr 1980: 141–142).

Unlike the case in Vietnam, the French defeat of June 1940 did not trigger any immediately serious rebellions against the colonial power in Cambodia and Laos. Whereas Vietnam acted like a sponge in absorbing foreign ideologies, Cambodia managed to keep "its political virginity" under the French protectorate (Lamant 1986: 190). Structural and cultural differences between the societies explained the lack of challenge to the French regime in Cambodia from 1936 to 1945 (Lamant 1986). Similarly, no Laotian groups seriously challenged French power in 1940. In Laos, fifty amateur students launched a coup attempt, which failed in July 1940. The initiators moved to Thailand, forming the Lao Pen Lao (Laos for Lao) movement (Stuart-Fox 1997: 55; Gunn 1988: 127). Still, in both of these colonies too, the war would stimulate nationalist sentiments and associations (Steinberg 1987: 328).

Youth Policies

In response to the external and internal challenges of Thai irredentists, Vietnamese revolutionaries, and Japanese occupiers and their claims of Asia for Asians and their support for noncommunist indigenous nationalist groups such as politicoreligious ones in Cochinchina, the French encouraged patriotic mobilization in Indochina as a countervailing policy (Hammer 1954: 30–33; Gunn 1988: 101–107). The goal was to incorporate youngsters into conservative political organizations that would encourage and channel existing patriotic feelings toward France, thus building faithful imperial subjects.

From 1940 to 1945 officials in Indochina built a youth initiative according to the French model, as ideas and techniques were borrowed from the metropole. Participation in youth organizations mushroomed in Indochina during these five years, gaining more than a million members in that short span (Hammer 1954: 32). The governor general of Indochina reported 600,000 members in February 1944 alone (Telegram, no. 783, agence FOM, box 272, file 451, Centre des Archives d'Outre-Mer, Aix-en-Provence [hereafter CAOM]). At the time, this represented 15 percent of the 4 million youth in Indochina (J. Sarlat, "Sports et jeunesse où en sommes-nous?," *Indochine*, no. 108, September 24, 1942, p. 2). The French sought to employ paramilitary youth organizations to promote patriotism – that is, the love of a people for its colonial country, for the colonial federation of Indochina (encompassing the colonies and protectorates of Tonkin, Annam, Cochinchina, Laos, and Cambodia), and for the French empire and the metropole – without furthering an elite-driven nationalist political program pursuing independence from external control (Huynh 1982: 26–34). It was a critical distinction for the French to draw, for many of their subjects abroad rejected the imperial model of the ruling nation-state and sought to replace it with one of their own making. The governor general of Indochina summarized the problem this way: "Although I actually encouraged specific 'patriotisms,' on the other hand I formally condemned all 'nationalisms' of all kinds, because they had a xenophobic and anti-French tendency, and received their orders from abroad" (Decoux 1949: 389).

Youth movements were first organized at the provincial level, within each colony, around a "local chief" and some provincial schools. At the federal level, a broad umbrella organization called Youth of French Empire (Jeunesse d'Empire Français) united existing movements such as the Scouts and various Christian and new secular groups, sporting leagues, "school youth groups" (*jeunesse scolaire*), and "local assemblies" (*sections de rassemblement*). The local assemblies were a means to control and organize youth who did not belong either to the school groups, sporting leagues, or to a specialized youth organization such as the Scouts (*Indochine*, no. 152, July 29, 1944, p. 13). At the level of each colony, there were important variations. Whereas the Cambodian local assemblies were usually organized around the pagoda, in Vietnam they were often centered on the village, where social life was concentrated. In June 1943 Cambodia provided approximately 15,500 youth members at local assemblies and 3,500 participants for a new youth movement called Yuvan. Created in 1941 and lead by King Norodom Sihanouk, they resembled Scouts in their khaki shorts, short-sleeved shirts, and forage caps. This movement, which drew its members from local assemblies, had specialized schools to train cadres capable of serving as the leaders of Cambodia under French supervision

TABLE 12.1. *Organizational Structure of Youth of French Empire in Indochina*

Specialized Movements		School Youth Groups	Sporting Organizations (Clubs)	Local Assemblies
Old Ones	New Ones			
Scouts	Young Campers			Target youth
Religious	Young Teams of Tonkin			who did not
groups	Youth of Annam			belong to any
	Young Laotians			of the three
	Yuvan			prior groups
Keep their	Physical education		Tournaments	Physical
own method	Choral singing		Competitions	education
and pedagogy	First-aid			Choral singing
	Supervised excursions			First-aid
				Supervised
				excursions

Source: No author, "L'organisation de la jeunesse en Indochine," *Le Nouveau Laos*, no. 15, August 1, 1943, p. 3.

(Vincent, Jean, "Rapport pout le livre vert," Phnom-Penh, 6/26/43, Résident Supérieur du Cambodge [hereafter RSC], reference 676, CAOM). The organization sought to enhance Cambodians' sense of national identity through the idealization of the Angkoran era but did so by organizing paramilitary youth groups along Vichy lines. For thousands of young Cambodians, this was their first membership in an extrafamilial group outside of the *sangha*, the Buddhist monastic order (Chandler 1983: 166).

Youth of French Empire, an exact analog to the metropole's Youth of France (Jeunesse de France), carried the same motto as the original: "United and Strong in Order to Serve." These organizations aimed to teach youngsters to obey instructions, to develop a spirit of social solidarity, and to foster harmony among ethnicities. These paramilitary corps were used to transcend key ethnic and linguistic differences within Indochina. They carried Vichy's focus on youth as the force that would make France stable and strong after the humiliating defeat of 1940. In addition, other youth movements were created after 1940, which varied somewhat in the different regions: Young Campers (Jeunes Campeurs) in Cochinchina, Young Teams (Jeunes Equipes) in Tonkin, Youth of Annam (Jeunes d'Annam), and Young Laotians (Jeunes Lao).

As Table 12.1 suggests, these new organizations offered an assortment of recreational activities, including physical education, singing, first-aid instruction, and excursions. Colonial leaders, on the one hand, saw these activities as social and cultural exercises to develop patriotic feelings for

France and to mold faithful subjects and citizens. As Navy Captain Maurice Ducoroy, head of Indochina's General Commissariat for Physical Education, Sport, and Youth, explained: "I desire to reach all the youth, French as well as Annamite, in the cities as well as in the countryside, to instill into them a sense of effort and work, and to fight against revolutionary or ultra-nationalist blind beliefs. I hope to reach this goal through youth camps, the teaching of morals, patriotic sessions, and sports" (quoted in "La tâche de renaissance parmi la jeunesse," *L'Annam Nouveau*, July 13, 1941, p. 4). Apart from this strategic use of recreational activities for political purposes, some French participants and leaders believed that they were assisting the population, and shared a racist belief that they could "improve" natives' well-being and potential by dragging them out of their "inertia" to prepare them for "the necessities and requirements of modern life," as Governor General Decoux put it regarding Cambodia (Letter from Governor General Jean Decoux, Hanoi, 12/11/44, HCI, box 240, CAOM).

Indigenous collaborators, through the propaganda press, supported these programs. Writer Le-Quang-Luat, for example, stressed how "a strictly intellectual culture makes only half men." Opponents to the regime on the other hand, perceived these efforts as harmful, because they diverted youngsters from the true causes such as national independence. The Indochinese Communist Party denounced supporters of both Decoux and Japan (Le-Quang-Luat, "La culture physique et nous," *L'Annam Nouveau*, August 10, 1941, p. 1; Marr 1980: 142). One article in the newspaper *Doc Lap* put out by Ho Chi Minh, in the spring of 1943, condemned Ducoroy's sports movement as a reactionary enterprise (Tønnesson 1991: 131). On the other hand, youth organizations provided a collection of adolescents, which could in turn be infiltrated. In this sense, the organizations inadvertently served to gather potential recruits into large groupings, which made recruitment appeals more efficient. They probably also helped to stimulate national patriotic feelings in a country like Laos, where regional identities were strongly developed. Marr argues that youth movements in Vietnam offered a peaceful political experience "in non-violent proselytizing and mobilization at a time when strikes, demonstrations or armed uprisings would have been suicidal" (Marr 1980: 137).

Military personnel played an important role within the youth movements at every level. At the institutional level, there were numerous navy officers such as Lieutenants Moreau and Vaziaga, who both helped build and manage the school that trained physical education monitors for youth movements in Phanthiet (Isoart 1982: 10; "Allocution prononcée par le moniteur-chef Petit à l'occasion du baptême de la promotion 'Lieutenant de Vaisseau Moreau' le 23 avril 1943," *Le Bulletin des Anciens Elèves de l'Ecole Supérieure d'Education Physique de l'Indochine*, no. 8, May 1943). Of the eighty-two students receiving diplomas at the Panthiet institute for physical education monitors in the fall of 1942, seventeen candidates were members of the armed forces, roughly evenly drawn from the navy and air force. Fifteen of these eighty-two men had French names, both first and family; eleven of these French candidates were from the armed forces ("Liste des élèves ayant obtenu le diplôme de moniteur d'éducation physique," *Bulletin des Anciens Elèves de l'Ecole Supérieure d'Education Physique de l'Indochine*, no. 5, November 1942, pp. 15–16). In a typical case, a Lieutenant Lafleur directed the Center of Physical Education in Tonkin (Centre local d'Education Physique or C.L.E.P.) in mid-1943, which provided physical and sports training for male and female youth group instructor candidates, male and female schoolteachers, and state employees (Note postale no. 6338/Cab, in Résidence Supérieur du Tonkin Nouveau fonds [hereafter RST NF], reference 6425, L.871(3), CAOM). The authorities issued decrees to relieve military personnel from their assignments to perform in youth movements, as in the December 1943 decree regarding Captain Noël Ilari's functions (Note no. 4306, RST NF, reference 6632, L.81.1, CAOM). This pattern was not unusual because, apart from North Africa and the French West Indies, military men were often the first practitioners of Occidental sports in the colonies (Hick 1992: 19). Further, the army played a key role in sport activities and especially in physical education due to the French practice of physical activities on military bases (see Spivak 1975). The practice of sport was a key component of youth organizations because sporting contests and practices were believed to develop the spirit of mutual aid and discipline and to build strong subjects and characters to replace the bookish and selfish students of the past. Thus, during colonization, military men played the predominant role as sport instructors for schoolteachers and pupils and led developments in civil sports in general.

Military personnel also appeared in vacation camps for children during the World War II period, such as the male Tam-Dao vacation camp in Tonkin, which received 285 Indochinese from the age of fourteen on; it was directed by Artillery Lieutenant Piquemal (Rapport sur les Camps de Vacances au Tonkin pendant l'été 1943, in RST NF, reference 6425, L871(2), CAOM). The regime offered camping and outdoor activities to promote virtue; for example, the Young Campers presented nature as offering a chance to test one's character. The group recommended "plunging [the youth] into a rough and sober [outdoor] life, to make it gain vigor and guts" ("Unis pour servir," *La Tribune Indochinoise*, July 7, 1941, pp. 1–2).

These militarized youth movements aimed at internal security by diverting indigenous youth from joining anti-French organizations and by teaching them to devote themselves to the imperial "motherland" of France. In the metropole, this service was performed by the Compagnons organization, which defended the regime by diverting youth from propaganda, encouraging them to join De Gaulle's troops, while the Chantiers de jeunesse provided a "form of national service" by January 1941 (Paxton

1975: 164). While both sets of paramilitary activities were relatively militaristic, in Indochina they were more recreational and sports-oriented projects. Yet, paradoxically, it was the Indochinese program that would contribute more directly to the militarization of that society.

The Impact of These Military Activities on State Development

In both cases, we could expect a limited legacy for these policies, because these paramilitary organizations were more voluntary than coercive in nature, and because the sponsoring regimes were short-lived. France returned to republican rule, while Indochina was fragmenting through wars of national liberation, which would incorporate some of the lessons of these youth movements through state formation. Although the programs varied according to local context, they did provide a general authoritarian model of state-building for the independent nations of Indochina. As Benedict Anderson's work suggests, an authoritarian model of nation formation was transmitted in "modular" form from France to Indochina (Anderson 1991). Yet, as Chatterjee points out, the natives appropriated and reshaped this module of nation formation according to their local needs (Chatterjee 1994). However socially oriented and noncoercive these activities were, they contributed to the later militarization of societies in Indochina.

France was fortunate to return to a democratic regime, which contributed to the disappearance of these youth corps. Army personnel returned to their barracks, and the majority of the officers claimed positions leading the republican French army. The Compagnons organization, invented in part to turn youngsters away from de Gaulle's influence, was no longer appropriate as the nation united and reconciled around him (Paxton 1975: 162). The French army, likewise, functioned again at full capacity and the Chantiers de jeunesse and its surrogate function as a "form of national service" became unnecessary. Compagnons was disbanded in 1944 because it was suspected of allying itself to the resistance movement against the Vichy regime and Germany; it also appeared to be a place for youth to evade its "obligatory service work" in German factories. Likewise, Chantiers de jeunesse was disbanded in 1944, as it interfered with this "service work" policy, which began in February 1943 with summons to whole age groups (Chauvière 1980: 31–32).

In fact, the only forms of paramilitary management of youth that was institutionalized in France were the programs governing "maladjusted youth," a term created and adopted by the Vichy administration by 1943. By 1940 and especially 1942, the institutions dealing with "misfit" children had consolidated and they would survive intact after 1945. World War II had caused a rise of juvenile delinquency due in part to the displacement of families, but also due to a more repressive policing system. In response, small host centers and host families appeared for youth. The life-style here was close to camp life, while the cadres in charge of them were often drawn from youngsters belonging to youth groups. Schools to train instructors followed, and the Vichy period marked the beginning of the institutionalization of child reeducation aimed at teaching discipline and proper behavior. The birth of these "moral technicians" clearly responded to Vichy's fear of youthful decadence. Even the short-lived Compagnons and Chantiers de jeunesse, which had combined Scouting with military practices, greatly influenced the youth centers managing these "maladjusted children" (Chauvière 1980).

As for Indochina, which remained an unstable environment of civil war, war, and contested forms of state-building, the taming of youth – that is the channeling of their potential for contesting authorities into supporting leaders and their causes – was crucial to the fate of a number of competing leaders, including Ho Chi Minh, Sihanouk, and Ngo Dinh Diem. In Vietnam, parts of these new youth movements would join Ho Chi Minh's troops. Tellingly, on the first page of a report written by Maurice Ducoroy attempting to legitimate his service as commissioner of youth and sports, a state employee scribbled that the youth "trained by Captain Ducoroy was really very disciplined, but they were against us" (Rapport du capitaine de Vaisseau Ducoroy, Saigon, 9/22/45, in Haut Commissariat d'Indochine [hereafter HCI], conspol 247, CAOM). A few months earlier, under the Japanese occupation and the new Tran Trong Kim's short-lived government, the youth minister's close associate, Ta Quang Buu, previously a scout chief, visited existing groups, especially Ducoroy's organizations and the Boy Scouts, pressing them to serve as disciplined examples for the building of a larger youth movement (the cabinet was created in April 1945 under the sponsorship of the Japanese authorities after the Japanese *coup de force* of March 9, 1945, which provoked the fall of the French colonial regime). In the imperial city of Hue, the new government launched the Frontline Youth (Tien Tuyen Thanh Nien) to serve as a school aiming to supply reserve officers for a future Vietnamese army; this group was often called the Phan Anh Youth, Phan Anh being the youth minister who served as a youth and sport cadre under Decoux's regime. At the same time, in the region of Cochinchina, the new Japanese Governor Minoda planned to transform Maurice Ducoroy's youth and sport network into "a regionwide paramilitary Vanguard Youth [Thanh Nien Tien Phong] organization," while drawing on Boy Scout methods, "and publicly exhorting members to 'reorganize society, improve the lives of our countrymen.'" ("The Vanguard Youth was permitted by the Japanese to be much more political in orientation, displaying its own flag [yellow with a red star], hanging banners across the street calling for 'National Liberation' [Giai Phong Dan Toc]"; see Marr 1997: 119, 133–135; Ngo Van 1995: 310, 314–315.) The Japanese-sponsored Vanguard Youth movement was led by Dr. Pham Ngoc Thach, a secret member of the Indochinese Communist Party [ICP] who

worked closely with Tran Van Giau, the chairman of the ICP leader in
Cochinchina. These two key actors were crucial in carrying the communist
revolution to Cochinchina. By the end of August 1945, the Vanguard Youth
was assimilated in the Viet Minh. Thus, the Youth Movement built in the
aftermath of the August Revolution of 1945 was modeled on Ducoroy's
Pétainist youth movement (Tønnesson 1991: 296, 341, 387).

Later, the anticommunist Ngo Dinh Diem, prime minister under Bao Dai
and later the head of the new Republic of South Vietnam from 1954 to
1963, also deployed a Vichy approach to its youth policy. Like the colonial
power it followed, this new regime did not have the full support of the Vietnamese population in its war against a communist insurgency. A National
Committee of Youth was constituted by this new regime in September 1954,
gathering representatives of youth movements who agreed on the need for
a centralized organism for the management of youth (V.P. no. 1300, file F
III 2 16, in HCI, SPCE 55, CAOM). For instance, the first graduating class
of youth cadres pledged an oath to the regime, promising "to be faithful to
the motherland and to serve the people," while a parade of all of the youth
organizations ended the ceremony. In his speech, Ngo Dinh Diem asked
them to "Rid yourself of all egoism, escape your isolation. . . . Live in
groups, cultivate the spirit of the team. Unite to create a powerful youth
movement. . . . Your strength, coming from your union, will only be dedicated to the service of the nation, to safeguarding liberty" (V.P. no. 1381,
file F III 274, in HCI, SPCE 55, CAOM).

Through these youth movements, cadres would teach the spirit of the
team to youth, which, through the practice of sport and camping, would
develop "a healthy and vigorous body, and . . . their virile qualities," as the
minister of work and youth, Dr. Nguyen Tang Nguyen, put it (V.P. no. 1381,
file F III 274, in HCI, SPCE 49, CAOM). The South Vietnamese situation
in 1954 was also similar to the French context during the German occupation in facing the problem of large numbers of dislocated youth wan-
dering about in the aftermath of the "debacle." The Southern Vietnamese
regime faced the arrival of "thousands of youngsters" from the North who
wanted to create a "Youth City" by establishing residence halls; here the
directors would teach 10,000 youngsters craft skills and find them jobs. The
youths would receive an intellectual, ideological, and physical education
and learn to live communally (V.P. no. 133, file F III 2 16, in HCI, SPCE
55, CAOM). Once again, Vietnam needed faithful youth's active participation in the building of a new state at a moment of extreme political uncertainty, where different forces competed for political control.

Cambodia had integrated youth most highly into state-sponsored youth
organizations (Rapport du capitaine de Vaisseau Ducoroy, Saigon, 9/22/45,
in HCI, conspol 247, CAOM). After the Japanese were defeated in 1945,
apart from Scouting organizations, "the movement sunk to oblivion"
(Martin 1994: 38). Perhaps the Cambodians' deference and love for their

king, and the organized enhancement of Cambodians' sense of national identity through the idealization of the Angkoran era, prevented it from becoming a space for contesting the colonial power. Still, according to Sihanouk's chronicle, in August 1945, following the Japanese surrender, 30,000 people participated in a national demonstration, among them various members of youth groups. At the same time an obscure antiroyalist coup occurred, "sponsored by some hotheaded members of Cambodian youth groups" (Chandler 1983: 172). In 1952 a wave of strikes hit the school system, where students held antimonarchic positions and criticized Sihanouk's dealings with France on independence. The king responded in 1953 by reconstituting the Yuvan, to be managed by the military and to organize for "military preparation." His cousin Prince Sirik Matak headed the project and contacted the prior chiefs of this movement to remove "the youth from pernicious political influences" (In Extrait du B.Q.R. no. 266/RG du 15/1/1953 du Cambodge; Formation de la jeunesse, NQ. 14 janvier 1953; both in HCI, SPCE 106, dossier F III 7, 10, Governement Cambodgien, Ministère de l'Education Nationale, CAOM). The Yuvan movement was perceived by Sihanouk as a tool for monarchic repression and absolutist state-building, inheriting the French rejection of political pluralism. "This asset [youth movements] was useful for King Sihanouk, who in 1953 easily remobilized the assemblages under the name of *chivapol* (active forces) to support him in his royal crusade for independence" (Martin 1994: 38).

In Laos, the organization of youth was relatively underdeveloped (Rapport du capitaine de Vaisseau Ducoroy, Saigon, 9/22/45, in HCI, conspol 247, CAOM). Instead, the colonial state invested its energy into stimulating the acceptance and validity of a common cultural Lao national heritage and identity and invited elite youngsters to join this project, the Lao Nhay (Lao Renovation Movement). It was initiated by the director of public education in Laos, Charles Rochet, and many youngsters participated. Yet sport was especially promoted because sporting groups offered a space for indoctrination against Thailand and in support of France (Stuart-Fox 1997: 55). Governor General Jean Decoux stated that he counted on "sports youth" activities to launch the Lao Nhay (Gunn 1988: 105).

A French political report of November 1945 asserted that the young Laotian elite – in particular, teaching personnel – had stayed faithful to France thanks to Rochet and the Lao Nhay movement (Note A/S de la situation politique du Laos, 11/17/45, file: "renseignements sur période libération," in HCI, reference 80, CAOM). On the other hand, according to one author, "The first generation of Laotian nationalists, whom the French had been grooming during the war, became anti-colonialists, formed the Lao Issara, and entered a temporary alliance with the Viet Minh. Some members of this generation made a lasting alliance with the Vietnamese communists

and formed the Pathet Lao movement [which would take power in 1975]"
(Ivarsson 1995: 13). Prince Phetsarath was a central actor in sponsoring,
presiding over, and assisting the many cultural and sporting events launched
by the wartime Lao Nhay movement and its quest of generating patriotism
and a sense of belonging to the same nation in an area of the world where
regionalism was strong. The Lao Issara (Free Laos), which arose during the
war to be led by Prince Phetsarath, took power after the Japanese surrender in August 1945; he entered exile in Thailand with the reappropriation
of Laos by France in April 1946. Some members of this Lao Issara government belonged to the colonial Lao Nhay movement and would later
serve in the core of the Lao independence movement arising in 1945–1946
(Stuart-Fox 1997: 63; Gunn 1988: 103). By March 1945, in the Lao cities
of Savannakhet and others along the Mekong River, which had important
Vietnamese communities and underground Indochinese Communist Party's
activities, Vietnamese youth involved in the Vichy youth program joined
the ICP, as in the Vietnamese case (Gunn 1988: 120).

Later, the Lao Issara broke up over the issue of what position to adopt
toward the Viet Minh. Some of them joined the Viet Minh's armed struggle under the name Pathet Lao. Laos's particular geopolitical situation, its
small size, and its recent creation meant that its elites looked favorably
on a "patron-client" relationship – either with France, Japan, Thailand, or
Vietnam. This strategy nonetheless spawned disputes among Laotians,
leading to numerous and competing, albeit minuscule, nationalist groups
emerging in provincial capitals by 1945, each trying to gain the support
and involvement of the youth (Adams 1970: 105).

Conclusions

The French armed forces played a critical internal social and political role
in France and Indochina during World War II. In both cases, the military
served as an engine of national renewal in a time of military defeat, and as
a safeguard against future subversion by enrolling youngsters into socially
oriented paramilitary activities. The cases also demonstrate how military
institutions respond to challenges to its power by reaching deeper into civil
society. The attempt to control youth resulted from a particular combination of external and international threats to the state. French officials
believed that only by correcting the internal weaknesses that had allowed
for invasion and defeat could the nation maintain its imperial status. Thus,
in an age of mass mobilization and under analogous emergency conditions,
French officials tried to orient the masses toward the Vichy regime and its
ideology. Youth in France and Indochina participated in transnational
behaviors (marching, chanting, youth camp activities) and discourses (the
need for disciplined leadership, the role of physical activity in moral development). Even though the colony was largely cut off from the metropole,

youth experiences in both settings were molded by the same fundamental knowledge and techniques, for youth was a potentially important collective force over which different political groups fiercely fought. Because they received physical, civic, and moral training to turn them into followers of Pétain's National Revolution, these groups could be reoriented toward other claims to represent the nation's interests by manipulating and channeling these patriotic feelings in other directions.

When the common paths of the two cases diverge, the eventual collapse and the consolidation of militarism in France and Indochina, respectively, serve as clear indicators of the political and social development of the nations studied. The new and more modest network of youth agencies and organizations in France suggests the receding influence of the military in a re-republicanized regime. In the nations of Vietnam, Laos, and Cambodia, on the other hand, the politicization of youth flowed in the opposite direction. The curious temporary comparability of these cases clarifies the political and national security factors driving both the creation and the consolidation or destruction of policies of societal militarization.

Better understanding of the legacy of these paramilitary and patriotic mobilizations in the 1940s provides scholars with additional insight into the larger puzzle of the evolution of many former French colonies toward undemocratic regimes. Very few former colonies have evolved toward stable democratic regimes. In 1987 one scholar of political development identified eleven states that emerged from colonial status to become stable democracies: Malaysia, Sri Lanka, Jamaica, Trinidad/Tobago, Papua New Guinea, Bahama Islands, Barbados, Botswana, Gambia, Mauritius, and Surinam (Weiner 1989: 21). None of them were under French control. Far from contesting the view that the French colonial state harshly and brutally repressed indigenous nationalists, this article offers an analysis of a less well known face of colonial control: the attempt to enforce order within nations through the socially oriented use of military forces via civic associations. War usually stimulates the development of a state's capacities to control the means of violence and to centralize further its other governing institutions (Tilly 1992). In the case at hand, the French state, sharing power with Germany and Japan, did not wield a monopoly of violent means and thus deployed the military toward the politically motivated "development" of youth. Although the French militarist youth activities dissolved at the end of World War II, Indochinese recreational and sporting youth activities continued to be a vitally important dimension of militarist state-building.

References

Adams, Nina S. 1970. "Patrons, Clients, and Revolutionaries: The Lao Search for Independence, 1945–1954," in Alfred McCoy and Nina S. Adams, eds., *Laos: War and Revolution*, 100–120. New York: Harper & Row.

Ageron, Charles-Robert, Catherine Coquery-Vidrovitch, Gilbert Meynier, and Jacques Thobie. 1990. *Histoire de la France coloniale, 1914–1990*. Paris: Armand Colin.

Anderson, Benedict. 1991. *Imagined Communities: Reflections on the Origin and Spread of Nationalism*. London: Verso.

Bachelier, Christian. 1992. "L'armée," in Jean-Pierre Azéma and François Bédarida, eds., *Le régime de Vichy et les français*, 389–408. Paris: Fayard.

Chandler, David. 1983. *A History of Cambodia*. Boulder: Westview.

Chatterjee, Partha. 1994. *The Nation and Its Fragments: Colonial and Postcolonial Histories*. Princeton: Princeton University Press.

Chauvière, Michel. 1980. *L'enfance inadaptée: L'héritage de Vichy*. Paris: Editions ouvrières.

Cointet-Labrousse, Michèle. 1987. *Vichy et le fascisme: Les hommes, les structures et les pouvoirs*. Brussels: Editions Complexe.

Comte, Bernard. 1992. "Les organisations de la jeunesse," in Jean-Pierre Azéma and François Bédarida, eds., *Le régime de Vichy et les Français*, 409–421. Paris: Fayard.

Coquery-Vidrovitch, Catherine, and Charles-Robert Ageron. 1991. *Histoire de la France colonial III – Le déclin*. Paris: Armand Colin.

Coutrot, Aline. 1972. "Quelques aspects de la politique de la jeunesse," in Fondation Nationale des Sciences Politiques, ed., *Le gouvernement de Vichy, 1940–1942*. Paris: Armand Colin.

Decoux, Jean. 1949. *A la barre de l'Indochine: Histoire de mon gouvernement général, 1940–1945*. Paris: Plon.

De La Gorce, Paul-Mairie. 1988. *L'empire ecartelé, 1936–1946*. Paris: Denoël.

Duiker, William J. 1981. *The Communist Road to Power in Vietnam*. Boulder: Westview.

Enloe, Cynthia. 1983. *Does Khaki Become You? Militarization of Women's Lives*. Boston: South End Press.

1989. "Beyond Steve Canyon and Rambo: Feminist Histories of Militarized Masculinity," in John Gillis, ed., *The Militarization of the Western World*, 119–140. New Brunswick: Rutgers University Press.

Gay-Lescot, Jean-Louis. 1990. "La politique sportive de Vichy," in Jean-Pierre Rioux, ed., *La vie culturelle sous Vichy*, 83–115. Brussels: Editions Complexe.

Giolitto, Pierre. 1991. *Histoire de la jeunesse sous Vichy*. Paris: Perrin.

Gunn, Geoffrey C. 1988. *Political Struggles in Laos, 1930–1945*. Bangkok: Duang Kamol.

Halls, W. D. 1981. *The Youth of Vichy France*. Oxford: Clarendon Press.

1995. *Politics, Society and Christianity in Vichy France*. Oxford: Berg.

Hammer, Ellen J. 1954. *The Struggle for Indochina, 1940–1955: Vietnam and the French Experience*. Stanford: Stanford University Press.

Héméry, Daniel. 1990. *Ho Chi Minh de l'Indochine au Vietnam*. Paris: Gallimard.

Hervet, Robert. 1965. *Les compagnons de France*. Paris: Editions France-Empire.

Hesse d'Alzon, Claude. 1982. "L'armée française d'Indochine pendant la seconde guerre mondiale – 1939–1945," in Paul Isoart, ed., *L'Indochine française, 1940–1945*, 85–89. Paris: PUF.

Hick, Daniel. 1992. *L'empire du sport*. Aix-en-Provence: AMARON.

Huynh Kim Khanh. 1982. *Vietnamese Communism, 1925–1945*. Ithaca: Cornell University Press.

Isoart, Paul, ed. 1982. *L'Indochine française, 1940–1945*. Paris: PUF.

Ivarsson, Søren. 1995. *The Quest for Balance in a Changing Laos*. Denmark: Nordic Institute of Asian Studies.

Lamant, Pierre L. 1986. "Le Cambodge et la décolonisation de l'Indochine: Les caractères particuliers du nationalisme Khmer de 1936 à 1945," in Institut d'Histoire du Temps Présent, ed., *Les chemins de la décolonisation de l'empire français, 1936–1956*. Paris: Les Editions du CNRS.

Lyautey, Louis-Hubert. 1891. "Du role social de l'officier," *Revue des deux mondes*, March 15.

Mann, Michael. 1984. "Capitalism and Militarism," in Martin Shaw, ed., *War, State and Society*, 25–46. New York: St. Martin's Press.

Marr, David G. 1980. "World War II and the Vietnamese Revolution," in Alfred W. McCoy, ed., *Southeast Asia under Japanese Occupation*, 125–158. New Haven: Yale University Press.

1997. *Vietnam 1945: The Quest for Power*. Berkeley: University of California Press.

Martin, Marie Alexandrine. 1994. *Cambodia: A Shattered Society*. Berkeley: University of California Press.

Muel-Dreyfus, Francine. 1996. *Vichy et l'éternel féminin*. Paris: Editions du Seuil.

Ngo Van. 1995. *Viêtnam, 1920–1945, révolution et contre-révolution sous la domination coloniale*. Paris: L'insomniaque.

Paxton, Robert O. 1966. *Parades and Politics at Vichy: The French Officer Corps under Marshal Pétain*. Princeton: Princeton University Press.

1975. *Vichy France: Old Guard and New Order, 1940–1944*. New York: W. W. Norton.

Rousso, Henri. 1990. "Vichy: Politique, idéologie et culture," in Jean-Pierre Rioux, ed., *La vie culturelle sous Vichy*, 19–39. Brussels: Editions Complexe.

Spivak, Marcel. 1975. *Les origines militaire de l'éducation physique en France (1774–1848)*. Vincennes: Château de Vincennes.

Steinberg, David Joel. 1987. *In Search of Southeast Asia: A Modern History*. Honolulu: University of Hawaii Press.

Stuart-Fox, Martin. 1997. *A History of Laos*. Cambridge: Cambridge University Press.

Tilly, Charles. 1992. *Coercion, Capital, and European States, AD 990–1992*. Oxford: Blackwell.

Tønnesson, Stein. 1991. *The Vietnamese Revolution of 1945: Roosevelt, Ho Chi Minh and de Gaulle in a World at War*. London: Sage.

Weiner, Myron. 1989. "The Indian Paradox: Violent Social Conflict and Democratic Politics," in Ashutosh Varshney, ed., *The Indian Paradox: Essays in Indian Politics*, 21–37. London: Sage.

13

The Changing Nature of Warfare and the Absence of State-Building in West Africa

William Reno

Accounts of war in Africa feature scenes of looting and banditry; greedy, self-interested warlords; and shadowy foreign business agents who profit from disorder. World attention to "conflict diamonds" – gems that warring groups mine and then trade for arms – has brought economic motives of warfare to a broader audience (UN 2000a). Yet mass-based protests of the kind that led to the January 2001 removal of Philippines president Estrada from power are notable in Africa for their relative absence. Even mass protests in October 2000 in Côte d'Ivoire to remove General Robert Guei from power, lauded in the international press as a sequel to the Serbian overthrow of Milosevic, upon closer examination reveal struggles for power and wealth among fairly narrow elite factions.

Looting for personal profit during warfare is not unique to contemporary Africa. What is new is the extent to which economic interests appear to predominate among armed groups, the great majority of which forgo ideologically motivated reform or efforts to mobilize mass-based followings. Most wars in Africa constitute a special category of conflict. They are the consequence first of the collapse of state institutions, often several years before the appearance of widespread fighting, then the collapse of centrally organized patronage-based political networks that use armed groups to enforce discipline. This method of rule exhibits a hostility to state institutions and systematically undermines basic public order and security for citizens. This generates substantial domestic criticism and support for systemic change. Yet this context explains the failure of opposition groups to build mass-based political movements or advertise clear ideological alternatives. Both corrupt rulers and their opponents appear insensitive to these elements of state-building as a means of gaining or consolidating power, despite the apparent long-term benefits seen elsewhere through history or the attractions that such a strategy might seem to have to those who want to maximize personal power, ultimately through building states.

This chapter considers many contemporary conflicts in Africa, but focuses on West African conflicts in Liberia, Sierra Leone, Guinea, and, to a growing degree, Côte d'Ivoire, and on civil violence and armed groups in Nigeria. These countries ought to be prime candidates for the emergence of political groups that present themselves as reformist ideological and programmatic alternatives to corrupt and violent politics. Even under the repressive rule of Sani Abacha (1994–1998), Larry Diamond wrote that "In Nigeria human rights organizations continued to research, publicize, expose, lobby, and organize, sometimes treading more carefully while still facing arrest and imprisonment" (1999: 238). Yet when armed and capable of opposing corrupt and violent officials, a Nigerian journalist reports that young men become "armed robbers who have formed a youth association." More unusual is his report that "The gang allegedly led by an influential chief in the community, brazenly and openly carry out its nefarious activities," which include preying on their own communities (Ikwunze 2000: 18).

These opposition groups signal the emergence of a social category associated with collapsing states and violent patronage networks. Although members view themselves as marginalized from, and opposed to, their rulers, they are often brought together by elites for elite interests, or by would-be patrons whose political goal is to join or replace those at the head of violent patronage networks. Rebellion in these terms is not the collective action that James Scott (1987), Eric Hobsbawm (2000), or Eric Wolf (1999) describe among social bandits usually associated with other marginalized or excluded groups amid corrupt and predatory regimes. Rather, once they join these groups, individuals end up seeking to gain as much utility as possible from existing political society, even if members join these groups for diverse ideological reasons. They and their backers – often from among the politicians they criticize – manipulate interstices of this system and proclaim no long-term allies or enemies. Their primary goal is to force their way into the social system from which they are excluded, not to overthrow it.

This chapter examines the internal structures and interactions of insurgencies to explain why these groups abjure state-building strategies. This context explains why some individuals or groups prevail over others, and why certain strategies are chosen over what appear to be more rational or attractive alternatives. This is not to say that easily available resources and short-term opportunities do not structure how insurgents organize themselves or behave. But it rejects the causality expressed in a recent World Bank report on Africa that "resources provide a convenient way to sustain 'justice-seeking' rebel movements and are easily lootable assets that can encourage 'loot-seeking' rebellion" (World Bank 2000b: 59). Although resources such as diamonds and gold play important roles in many African insurgencies, their predatory exploitation can be effects rather than causes of strategies described here.

The Intentional Destruction of State Institutions

Charles Tilly (1990) and Robert Jackson (1990) showed how Cold War–era support from superpower patrons and former colonial powers to rulers of internally weak states gave those rulers fewer incentives to build internal state administrative capacity or to mobilize citizens for nationwide projects. This did not preclude efforts on the part of rulers to articulate vague senses of nationalism, which during the Cold War usually found expression in domestic policies of economic self-sufficiency and diplomatic nonalignment. Ideally, these policies still contributed toward the country's economic prosperity in which an increasingly wealthy population would provide revenues to underwrite expanded and more effective government administration.

In fact, rulers faced growing threats from their own subordinates, complicating attempts to delegate authority to capable managers, lest they use their positions as bases to overthrow rulers. Sub-Saharan Africa's first coup occurred in 1963. As Table 13.1 shows, many African rulers during the 1970s and 1980s might anticipate that they could meet the same fate of the 72 percent of the continent's rulers leaving office in violent circumstances. This percentage fell to 41 percent after 1990, the end of the Cold War and rise of the practice of holding multiparty elections. Yet even after 1990, rulers faced considerable insecurity. In 2000, for example, six countries held elections for executive office. Two saw fairly uncontroversial defeats of incumbents (Senegal and Ghana). Oppositions boycotted elections in Sudan and Côte d'Ivoire. Côte d'Ivoire's reelected president fled amid mass protests. Tanzania's election (that returned the incumbent) generated riots in Zanzibar in 2001. Guinea-Bissau's main armed opposition leader died in violent circumstances after an election. Internal wars now pose a greater threat too. In 1999 and 2000, for example, Algeria, Angola, Burundi, Republic of Congo, Democratic Republic of Congo, Guinea-Bissau, Sierra Leone, Somalia and Sudan – nine of Africa's fifty-two states – harbored insurgents that challenged existing regimes (Sollenberg et al. 2000: 52–55). Six of these conflicts included elements of national armies and individuals who once served regimes they now oppose.

The immediate response from incumbent elites has been to undermine military command structures in order to create competing centers of coer-

TABLE 13.1. *Insecurity of African Rulers, before and after 1990*

Violent overthrow	53 (72%)	25 (41%)
Constitutional	13	16
Natural causes	7	2
Defeated in election	1	18
TOTAL TRANSFERS OF POWER	74	61

cive power. Liberian president Charles Taylor, for example, spent in 1999 an estimated 75 percent of Liberia's official budget on agencies primarily responsible for his personal security (*Jane's Defense Weekly* 2000). These agencies include an Anti-Terrorist Unit, Special Security Service, Joint Security Forces, National Bureau of Investigation, Counter Force, and Security Operations Division, along with the Armed Forces of Liberia. Prior to his election as president in 1997 Taylor's security details included less formalized agencies such as the female "Charlie's Angels" and a "Small Boys Unit" of child soldiers. This strategy leaves little to spend for social services, stymieing efforts among any state officials who might want to legitimate Taylor's regime through the provision of services to citizens. Likewise, Sierra Leonean presidents in the 1970s and 1980s encouraged ruling-party youth sections to arm themselves and fight on behalf of their political patrons. Nigerian presidents have exhibited similar behavior, encouraging disparate groups of supporters to exercise violence on their behalf while creating multiple security agencies.

Security for the ruler, therefore, has come to embody the opposite of the monopolization of coercion that Weber identifies as a cardinal feature of state-building (1947). This is a sensible precaution on the part of these rulers, however. Liberia's Taylor no doubt recalls his seven-year armed struggle that ended in his election as president. The prewar ruler, Samuel Doe, against whom Taylor began his struggle in 1989, executed his vice president in 1982 after an alleged coup attempt. In 1983 Doe's former minister of rural development (a future Taylor ally) attempted to overthrow Doe. In 1984 Doe accused another future Taylor ally of plotting against him. In 1985 Doe's deputy commander of the Executive Mansion Guard tried to assassinate him. Later in 1985 Doe's former military chief invaded Liberia with the aim of overthrowing Doe. Coup plotters in 1971 managed to enter the residence of Sierra Leone's president Siaka Stevens, one of Africa's few rulers to retire from office (in 1985). Sierra Leone's presidents are wise to be mindful of coup attempts (numbering at least three in 1996–1997), much less coups (in 1992 and 1996), and rebel invasions of the capital (1997–1998, 1999, and 2000). Nigeria's president Obasanjo (who became president in 1976 after his predecessor was assassinated in a failed coup attempt) rules a country that suffered coups in 1966 (twice), 1975, 1983, 1985, and 1993, and the mysterious sudden nocturnal demise of another in 1998, who, if popular opinion is to be believed, died of a heart attack in the arms of three specially selected acrobatic prostitutes and/or ingested extra-potent Viagra.

While providing greater short-term security for rulers, this strategy's long-term impact has been to distribute weapons and military expertise more widely in societies. These paramilitaries and local "action groups" that recruit from among unemployed urban youth become one of the few avenues of upward mobility for young people who suffer the consequences of declining state investment in infrastructure and economic development. Most African and a few post-Soviet "warlords" originate in this context of fragmented military organization and emerge once the centralizing authority of the president collapses.

Meanwhile, most rulers facing threats to their security take pains to buy the loyalty, or at least the compliance, of key groups in society, including armed groups. The most efficient way of doing this in the short run has been to use state assets and resources as patronage distributed at the personal discretion of the ruler. While effective at building power bases, this practice undermines long-term state capacity to provide services to the wider population. In this context, rulers find that effective bureaucrats pose a likely political threat. For example, the Sierra Leone president's Central Bank manager in 1980 echoed widespread societal complaints about the $100 million expense of an Organization of African Unity conference – equivalent to one year's total government spending. Soldiers killed the manager during his commute to his home during evening rush hour. Were the manager successful in pressing his criticisms or effective in executing his duties, he would stand in stark contrast to the record of incumbent elites and might find support among angry citizens.

The ruler's attentions to patronage and security siphon away expenditures from social services. This process is reflected in the collapse of state services, institutions, and infrastructure in several countries well before the outbreak of internal wars. By 1985, for example, Congo (former Zaire) had 12,000 miles of usable roads, down from 88,000 miles at independence in 1960 (Ayoade 1988: 106). Across the Zaire River in Congo-Brazzaville, agricultural services accounted for 2 percent of official expenditures in 1987, despite the fact that the great majority of the country's people supported themselves through farming (Radu and Sommerville 1989: 159). By the mid-1980s Sierra Leone's government ceased to provide regular salaries to teachers and health care workers. By 1989 electricity supplies in the capital became sporadic, the national radio transmitter failed, and the government television station stopped broadcasting two years earlier after the information minister sold the transmitter to a foreign businessman.

State shrinkage in most cases appears to have been the result of conscious choices on the part of hard-pressed rulers to divert state resources to patronage networks, where they could keep associates at bay, rather than use these resources for public services. Popular legitimacy would be slow to develop if citizens received aid from the state in their daily struggles for survival; certainly their support would be too little and too late to buffer the ruler from the ire of strongmen cut off from patronage payouts if this were to happen. Thus state spending on teachers, health care workers, or agricultural extension services wastes valuable political resources. Confirmation of this emerges in the ease with which many African rulers cut in government employment as a component of multilateral creditor-mandated reform programs. Former Zaire's top politicians in 1994, for example, proposed reducing formal (but fictitious) state employment from 600,000 to 50,000 as a means of appeasing the country's creditors (*Lettre du Continent* 1994). This was a rational decision in line with the decline of state spending on social services such as education and health, which had fallen from 17.5 percent of total state spending in 1972 to 2.1 percent in 1990 and zero by 1992 (World Bank 1992: 238; Banque du Zaire 1992: 14).

Thus rulers that rely on patronage to keep themselves in power may prefer to reduce the formal bureaucratic capacity of their states if this helps them to maintain their position at the center of a patronage network. The economic decline and growing poverty that accompanies the collapse of formal state services also generates political advantages insofar as shrinking economic opportunities force enterprising individuals to seek protection in the ruler's patronage network. Regimes heavily invested in patronage politics may even prefer to make citizens less secure, then sell protection in the form of access to state resources or other economic opportunities in exchange for support and loyalty much in the manner a racketeer sells protection. In Sierra Leone, for example, critics in Parliament warned that young "thugs" of the ruling party "under the cloak of the youth section of the All Peoples Congress intimidate the inhabitants and extort money" as part of the ruler's plan to force people to support his rule (Minute Paper, January 1969). Victims of predation and state collapse that followed patronage politics found incentives to demand inclusion into the system – "protection" – that many recognized as responsible for their unfortunate personal situations. This development, especially among young men, would have important implications for the organization of violence and, ultimately, of insurgencies in later years.

The collapse of formal state institutions and severe recessions of state revenues that accompanied patronage politics in many countries in Africa was not in and of itself a cause of conflict. Many rulers proved quite able to outlive their own states (as understood in a bureaucratic perspective). Table 13.2 illustrates the severity of formal bureaucratic recession affecting several African countries in the 1980s. Yet none of these states (at least not until late 1989 in Liberia) faced local insurgencies or mass uprisings. It has been noted that one reason may be that citizens of these states seek refuge in informal and clandestine markets to survive (MacGaffey 1991). Unfortunately for those attempting to weather official predations through withdrawal into informal markets, rulers followed to grab more resources and to manipulate these markets in place of state agencies to control people. Thus official figures that overstate the desperate situation of citizens likewise overstate the recession of patronage resources and strategies. This partly explains the seemingly strange survival of regimes that cannot call upon bureaucratic state capacity or effective militaries to survive. It also explains why mass-based revolutions remain very rare in Africa, despite the

328 *William Reno*

TABLE 13.2. *Bureaucratic State Shrinkage*

	Per capita GDP (1995 $US)		Domestic Revenues (%GDP)	
	1980	1990	1980	1990
Congo (Zaire)	620	210	27.2	11.8
Congo-Brazzaville	880	1,020	39.4	25.3
Liberia	620	410	28.3	13.9 [1989]
Sierra Leone	380	210	22.8	9.7
Nigeria	710	270	24.0	17.7
Cote d'Ivoire	1,140	780	28.9	19.5
Zambia	630	450	31.9	18.7

Sources: World Bank 2000a: 35, 194; Economist Intelligence Unit, individual country reports.

glaring shortcomings of many incumbent regimes, and helps explain why insurgents that do emerge organize themselves in the ways that they do.

These developments show that it is not simply that African rulers face short time horizons and high risk, and that this explains why they exploit opportunities for predation and enrichment now, rather than in an uncertain future, an explanation that some scholars use to account for a lack of interest in reform (Olson 1993; Nelson 1990). Some of Africa's most predatory presidents have ruled for lengthy periods; Mobutu ruled Zaire for thirty-three years, Kenya's Moi has ruled since 1982, Malawi's Banda lasted for thirty-three years, for example. Alternatively, countries with comparably high political instability since Africa's wave of independence in 1960 such as the Philippines, South Korea, and Thailand have regimes that are much more interested in building effective state institutions than is the case among their African colleagues. Rather, many African rulers respond to insecurity with the intentional destruction of state institutions in favor of basing political authority on the ability to control markets. They manipulate other people's access to resources created by those markets and divide opponents with the disorganization that multiple competing armed groups create.

Violent Commerce as an Alternative to State Institutions

Rulers' uses of violent informal structures in place of bureaucratic state institutions to control people is a second and more significant element of rule that develops in the context of collapsing state institutions and sources of formal revenue. These structures include controlling access to economic opportunities, especially clandestine ones, as the formal economy undergoes drastic shrinkage in tandem with the destruction of the bureaucratic state. Lacking strong state agencies, rulers try to control clandestine commerce, either to accumulate resources that they can use to finance political networks on their own, or distribute to associates who they invite to share in proceeds.

Rule through regulating all commercial opportunities also offers the advantage of enabling rulers to exploit conflicts – often long-standing but very local in focus – in communities over how resources should be divided. This ability to instigate local tensions and factional splits usually ends up militarizing commerce, which becomes insinuated more deeply in local matters such as succession crises among local rulers, land disputes, arguments over control of particular trades and resources, even family feuds and battles over local vendors' market territories. Disorder for such rulers plays an important role as a political instrument. It promotes disorganization and competition among potential opponents, leaving them to appeal to the personal favor of rulers to help them against rivals (Chabal and Daloz 1999). This manner of rule tolerates and even promotes the decentralization of violence via proxies and the intentional weakening of state agents' capacities to act. It also removes the ruler's need for a centralized, politically reliable military command that claims a monopoly on the exercise of coercion, a central feature of state-building strategies elsewhere in the world (Tilly 1990). It sacrifices these capabilities in exchange for a more comprehensive, intrusive, and immediate capacity to prevent people from organizing themselves.

These instrumental uses of violence and its incorporation of commercial concerns has been a long-term feature of Nigerian politics. Nobel laureate Wole Soyinka condemned the activities of secret "Kill-and-Go" paramilitary units in Nigeria in the late 1970s. In 1982, he observed that the real head of the president's party in the major city of Ife-Ife, an opposition stronghold, was "a psychopath who styled himself '007.'" A police officer reported to Soyinka that "I investigated this man ['007'] myself and I have given my superiors more than enough material to hang him for several murders and drug trafficking long before now," but for the fact that "007" was an associate of the country's president, often photographed in the company of high officials (1996: 67; see also Okanya 1999: 70–93).

A former high official in the military regime of Ibrahim Babangida (1985–1993), Oyeleye Oyediran identified strategic uses of violence to disorganize opposition and extend patronage beyond the confines of formal state institutions and resources. Oyediran, who served on a constitutional committee in the late 1980s, explained that the president created new states and local government areas to manipulate the institutional framework of government to centralize patronage, while simultaneously weakening formal state capacity. He explains how the dissolution and reconstitution of political units encouraged long-time local rivals to compete against each other for presidential favor and access to services of security forces for personal gain in a context of unpredictable and disruptive change. Federalism in this context enabled the president to centralize his personal power as creator of generalized insecurity and vender of individual security to local politicians (1997). This presidential capacity was extended to otherwise marginalized young men to whom arms were provided to promote this local strife and uncertainty (CLO 1996).

The regime of Sani Abacha (1993–1998) selectively applied violence to target alternative political leaderships. A Nigerian critic observed "anti-corruption measures" singled out the country's private business managers "to show that no civilian Nigerian leader is morally competent to bid for power" (Nwankwo 1996: 86). Meanwhile, the military ruler organized local militias styled as "tax consultants" to dispossess his political opponents forcibly. Other youths were recruited and armed in Lagos as part of "Operation Sweep," an "anticrime" force that functioned more as a counterinsurgency unit to seek out the regime's opponents. The Rivers State Task Force recruited soldiers returning from the Nigerian military expeditionary force in Liberia and Sierra Leone and attacked communities in southern Nigeria's oil-producing area that questioned the regime's allocation of oil revenues. The arrival of the Task Force emboldened some local politicians to ally with the task Force to settle neighborhood disputes with violence (CLO 1996). Average Nigerians might be excused for confusing their own country's security forces for brigands. So blurred had these distinctions become in the late 1990s that wayward security forces at Lagos's Murtala Mohammed airport ambushed passenger planes on the runway, culminating in the looting of a loaded Kenya Airways 737 on the tarmac (*Nation* 1999: 1).

Likewise, Sierra Leone's president Siaka Stevens in the 1970s and 1980s intervened in chieftaincy successions to create disputes where little dissention existed before. Stevens promised diamond mining licenses and exemption of prosecution for illicit mining to his preferred candidates, who would be expected to defend his political clique against local critics. For example, Stevens's choice for Gbense's chief, installed in 1971 over local objections, personally shot and injured a local dissident politician, then received a pardon (Minute Paper, 14 July 1982). More generally, this and other chiefs used groups of armed young men to fight political opponents in 1982, then again during the 1986 elections, which resulted in the deaths of more than 5,000 people (Turay 1987: 109). Employment of these youth as armed wings of a political faction also helped further integrate the violent skills and social organization of illicit diamond mining into the president's political network. Colonial officers long complained that illicit diamond mining attracted the "worst and toughest characters" and "undesirables" from outside Sierra Leone. A colonial officer reported in 1957 that illicit miners held a local police commander and "threatened to cut his throat" (Superintendent of Mines, 6 March 1957). These "tough characters" proved to be very able paramilitary fighters and could be incorporated into the president's political network, along with the proceeds of illicit mining that these youths actually carried out. This development also integrated into this violent political economy one of few economic opportunities available to young people without high-level connections or the means to get further education. Thus an arena in which young people had resisted the economic and political constraints of colonial rule was no longer a refuge, but instead a recruiting ground and an entry point for violent accumulation attached to Stevens's expanding patronage network.

Armed groups performed other duties for the president and his associates, including attacking Fourah Bay College students in 1977 when students called attention to the country's declining economic condition. This attack led to widespread looting of the capital by security forces, which introduced into Sierra Leone's language the term "Operation Pay Yourself." Noting the tendency of armed youth to combine their political work with looting, a local journalist described "reports of members of the Internal Security Unit capitalizing on their position to harass innocent traders at night, attempt assault on women and even go to the extent of store breaking" (*Daily Mail* [Freetown], 1977: 8).

Once States, Now Racketeers

The examples show applications of disorder as what economists term "negative externalities" that leave society as a whole worse off. This separates this strategy of rule from the provision of order that is a basic element of state-building. Contemporary rulers of collapsed states who rely on disorder to secure their hold on power cannot engage in "the pacification, cooptation, or elimination of fractious rivals" that Tilly regarded as central to the process of building governments out of what often had started as more private predatory organizations (1985: 175), nor are such rulers primarily concerned to extract protection rents from those who are not in a position to contribute to the ruler's disorganization of local groups.

These authorities who succeed collapsed states fail to fulfill Thomas Hobbes's minimalist definition of a sovereign as an authority that protects people whether they want it to or not – a basic, indivisible public good common to a public as opposed to private authority, regardless of how that authority is organized or styled (1996: 115–122). The ability of rulers to exercise coercion outside of a private commercial exchange in ways that protect at least some people is at the core of this relationship between ruler and subject that is a defining feature of contractarian notions of what distinguishes states from racketeers, syndicates, mafias, or other private businesses. Likewise, the strategy to disorganize all groups and to deny them unauthorized access to economic opportunities, even if they do not associate for any overt political purpose, greatly inhibits the creation of any substantial "civil society" or potential rival public authority that is autonomous from the interests of this sort of predatory ruler and from which people can assert their own contractarian relationships or press demands against this type of ruler.

The preceding examples of the political uses of private violence illustrate the extraordinarily difficult challenges any critic of patronage politics or state collapse would face. These examples show that rulers and other elites promote violence among young men who bear much of the brunt of state collapse and economic impoverishment. Their rebellion ends up getting incorporated into the strategies of junior partners in the collapsed state ruler's political network. This resembles the relationship that Karen Barkey describes for bandits and Ottoman rulers in the sixteenth and seventeenth centuries. There, as in many African collapsed states, "rebellion did not represent collective action in the conventional sense, since it did not attempt to destroy the social structure of society; it simply wanted to derive as much utility from society as possible. It manipulated the interstices of the system, having no proclaimed ally or enemy and no significant ideology" (1994: 176). Barkey makes the key point that rulers in league with violent commercial entrepreneurs – "bandits" – can strengthen rulers' hold on power since "'rebellions' were maneuvers for mobility within the system, not opposition to the system" (195), a strategy that Achilles Batalas describes in Chapter 6 in this volume, on state-bandit relations in nineteenth-century Greece.

This strategy depends on a ruler's capacity to control access to resources among his associates. This task becomes more difficult as rulers are forced to permit allied strongmen to exploit clandestine markets in place of dwindling state assets and diminishing prerogatives of office. Successful associates also gain commercial experience of their own, often developing their own overseas commercial contacts. The increasingly violent character of exploiting resources and local conflicts give strongmen additional military experience and coercive skills. Sudden external shocks, such as the ruler's loss of Cold War–era superpower diplomatic and military support helped shift this balance of power in favor of strongmen in Liberia and Somalia, although Mobutu's survival in Congo (Zaire) until 1997 with little aid from overseas and the success of the Sierra Leone's government in attracting foreign support show that the end of the Cold War was not a determining factor in all conflicts. Instead, primary causes of internal war are found in the internal nature of patronage and the consolidation of strongmen's military and commercial positions.

Armed groups associated with once loyal agents of presidents, key politicians, and paramilitary commanders have fought most of Africa's internal wars since 1990. These men find that they can grab resources more efficiently without the ruler's assent, or fear that others among them are poised to defect from centralized patronage networks, so they rush to get a lead on their rivals. Nearly all "warlords" in Somalia, Congo (Zaire), Republic of Congo, and Liberia held high positions in former governments, and developed important commercial connections as part of old patronage networks. Congo-Brazzaville's Ninjas, a major force in 1992 and 1997 battles, backed Bernard Kolélas, mayor of Brazzaville and close associate of a former prime minister. Rival Zoulous backed Professor Pascal Lissouba, also a former prime minister and victorious presidential candidate in 1992 (Kounzilat, 1998). Southern Somalia's General Mohamed Said Hersi ("Morgan") played a leading role in destroying the city of Hargeisa in 1988 at the bidding of former Somali president Siad Barre (1970–1991). Mohamed Farah Aideed, was once the trusted defense minister and private business partner of the Somali president and was responsible for formal and clandestine arms purchases prior to the start of the war in 1991. Hussein Mohamed Aideed, Aideed Senior's son who now controls much of Mogadishu, was once a U.S. soldier.

Liberia's warlord-turned-president, Charles Taylor, ran the state procurement agency for President Samuel K. Doe in the early 1980s. Jean-Pierre Bemba, whose Mouvement pour la Liberation du Congo (MLC) occupies substantial parts of north-central Congo, is the son of a former minister under both Mobutu and Kabila Senior who emerged in the 1980s as Mobutu's major local business partner. One of the founders of the Rassemblement Congolaise pour la Démocratie (RCD), active in eastern Congo, is a former prime minister under Mobutu. The prevalence of titles such as "Doctor" and "Professor" underscores the elite origins of the leadership of most insurgencies. Professor Wamba dia Wamba's faction of the RCD competes with that of Dr. Emile Ilunga. Dr. George Boley's Liberian Peace Council managed to occupy the eastern third of Liberia for several years in the mid 1990s.

Chechnya's experience, throughout the 1990s an area also ruled more through business networks and other personal ties than through bureaucratic state institutions, suggests that political fragmentation produces similar outcomes in other effectively stateless regions where previous rulers manipulated local factions to divide and co-opt opposition. Dzhokhar Dudayev, the first president of Chechnya, left his position as a major general commanding a wing of Soviet nuclear bombers in Estonia. He received financial backing from Yaragi Mamadayev, the head of Chechnya's biggest state construction company until 1990, in his bid for power. Prior to the first Chechen war (1994–1996), Dudayev recruited followers from among young men released from jails as Soviet, then Russian, power collapsed. His successor, Ruslan Khasbulatov, who allied himself with Russian forces, rose to prominence with the backing of Sulieman Khosa, a leading Moscow gangster who was concerned that Chechnya remain in Russia, along with its clandestine trading opportunities that extremely weak and personalized government bureaucracies permitted. A major military figure, Shamil Basayev, who later fought Russian forces, gained military experience when

Russian politicians recruited him as a proxy in 1992–1993 to fight on behalf of Abkhaz separatists in Georgia Republic (Lieven, 1999).

These commercial and military connections that developed within non-bureaucratic, patronage-based prewar regimes were valuable resources for strongmen who want to fight their own ways into power. The dominance of these groups has a decisive impact on the nature of insurgencies in collapsed states, especially in marginalizing other individuals and groups who prefer to pursue more conventional, more overtly ideological, and mass-mobilizing insurgency strategies. The latter, however, usually lack the commercial ties, experience, and capacity to accumulate resources of their rivals who are better connected to global business networks.

No Mobilizing Ideology, No Liberated Zones

It would seem sensible amid state collapse for insurgent leaders, even if they have personal and professional ties to old regimes, to recruit followers with reformist appeals and to condemn the violent, corrupt rulers they seek to topple. In fact, Africa's Cold War insurgents often styled themselves as reformist governments-in-waiting. The African National Congress, Southwest African People's Liberation Organization, the Zimbabwean African People's Union, and others projected ideological images to attract followers, and experimented with building their own administrations in zones that they controlled (Clapham 1996: 222–226). While these groups often adopted the ideological frameworks of foreign governments that gave them aid, they also confronted Africa's most bureaucratized and strongest state institutions. Most leaders in these insurgencies held no previous office in administrations that they fought, nor could they cash in on benefits of membership in informal political networks associated with those rulers. Most important, they confronted states that used bureaucracies to battle opponents, not invasion of clandestine markets. Likewise, apartheid states generally used ground-level political intelligence to co-opt and coerce local leaders to promote passivity, rather than creating more disorder by pitting them against one another with informal intrusions in family and business affairs.

In contrast, Sierra Leone's Revolutionary United Front (RUF) and those factions within Sierra Leone's army and government that occasionally side with it, the National Patriotic Front of Liberia (NPFL), Uganda's Alliance of Democratic Forces (ADF), and many others fighting in Congo, Guinea, and elsewhere do not advertise a concrete, broad ideological alternative to local people among whom they fight. These groups show little or no real evidence of civil or military administration, even when they exercise control over significant chunks of territory over many years.

Yet groups do emerge as political alternatives to corrupt rulers and the dwindling capacities of their governments, as cases from Nigeria illustrate.

Armed citizens' groups such as Neighbourhood Watch, Ijaw Youth Congress, Egbesu Boys, and the Anambra State Vigilante Service Committee (Bakassi Boys) have battled police and military units that they believe collude with criminal gangs that prey upon their communities. "Residents of Aba prefer Bakassi Boys to the police because of their 'jungle' (immediate) justice unlike the judicial procedure which takes a long time and may result in the guilty getting freedom. . . . They prefer the Bakassi Boys to the police on the premise that they do not collect bribes to free criminals" (*Sunday Punch* [Lagos], 2000: 15). Bakassi Boys occasionally attack politicians who have local reputations for corruption, and even kill some of them. Some politicians acknowledge their own unpopularity, despite the installation of a civilian regime in 1999. The legislative head of a major party even confessed: "Majority of us cannot go home. You drive your NASS (National Assembly) car on the streets and people shout 'thief, thief' " (Onyeacholem 2000: 18).

These groups, constituted mainly of unemployed and underemployed young men, at first glance appear to be good candidates to become popular insurgencies, especially in places where these youth often receive official scorn as marijuana-smoking agents of violence and social disorder. Eric Wolf observed (of rural revolutionaries) that marginalization from centers of political and economic power give peasant revolutionaries "fields of leverage" that translate into social autonomy and independent resources to organize actions against their oppressors (Wolf 1999: 290). The solidarities, resources, and popular support of these groups in Nigeria, as with many throughout Africa where regimes are oppressive or perform miserably, ought to reward resistance movements that place high priorities on mobilizing, protecting, and ultimately taxing populations.

Closer examination of "fields of leverage" in the context of Nigerian patronage politics, however, reveals numerous informal linkages between groups like Bakassi Boys and the political class they criticize. These linkages reinforce economic components of political relationships in the same way that centralized patronage-based authority in Nigeria integrates commerce and violence into political networks. The social origins of Bakassi Boys highlight this linkage. A journalist observed that "a good number of these boys were also used for some of the dirty jobs carried out during the Abacha rein of terror, and they are all moving about freely, ready for the highest bidder to engage their services" (Agekameh 2000: 25). The demobilization of paramilitaries and security agencies formed under former president Sani Abacha's security advisor, Ismalia Gwarzo, also contributes military skills and weaponry to this group.

Crime fighting and criticism of corruption secures for Bakassi Boys a local political patron in Governor Chimaroke Mbadinuju of Anambra State, who is often at odds with Nigeria's new president. The governor skillfully integrates anticorruption rhetoric into his justification for Bakassi

Boys' attacks on his local political opponents and to underwrite his own place in Nigeria's political establishment:

They came to me and said that they had been looking for this man [legislator] . . . and that they had gone to his house to catch him because he committed criminal offenses and I said no matter how highly placed a person is, anyone who is suspected of being an armed robber, we will bring him out and test him so they [Bakassi Boys] tested him [legislator] as they normally test everybody and he didn't meet up with the test. (Onwubiko 2000: 11)

The governor of Abia State also supports Bakassi Boys. This governor noted that a murdered rival "made confessional statements acknowledging his misdeeds before he was killed" (Akparanta 2000: 17).

Co-optation into a local factional battle promotes personal aggrandizement over ideological commitment among members. The dead Abia politician's personal property served to reward Bakassi Boys for services on behalf of the governor. Bakassi Boys also intervene in disputes between market vendor associations and truck hauler unions, each of which is aligned with a particular politician. These groups approach Bakassi Boys with their own payoffs to influence their economic fortunes and to curry favor with local political patrons. These rewards undermine Bakassi Boys' group solidarity: "The leadership of the group was soon embroiled in a bitter tussle over who would take ownership of the sleek silver colour Mercedez Benz car" that belonged to the politician (Akparanta 2000: 17). This ties what otherwise would be social bandits in Wolf's terms to the interests of the elite they criticize.

Would-be revolutionaries in this context are creations of the collapsed state, whether as former paramilitary members or, more indirectly, as those who suffer consequences of misrule and the collapse of the formal economy. These youth have few viable economic alternatives but to organize to force their own incorporation into this system of rule on better personal terms. This action presents a serious collective action problem for potential revolutionaries and reformers, because they must contend with associates who fear that if they do not find a politician who will give them access to loot, others will get goods – and guns – before them. Wolf's "field of leverage" for ideologues becomes extremely narrow in this context. Scholars of Sierra Leone's insurgency observe that "armed marginals" act on their own behalf as centralized patronage networks break down, much as Bakassi Boys do in Nigeria. As in Nigeria, the protests and social deviance of these youth remain attached to a political class that uses the violence of these youth to claim their own positions among competing factions (Abdullah and Muana 1998; Kandeh 1996, 1999).

The continuing connection in Sierra Leone between youth violence, insurgency, and patronage politics appears in local notions of "bush rebels" and "town rebels." A Freetown journalist describes "bush rebels" as "made up of young and old people (including children) all under the influence of hard drugs and always shabbily dressed." His description of "town rebels" is:

They are in constant help and communication with bush rebels. They are always neatly dressed and so are not easily identified. They live in towns, just next door to you. . . . They work for the established government. They work in offices close to the seat of the President. They are present in all spheres of work. Private businesses as well. Even in the churches and mosques. They are always neatly dressed in coats and ties. This class of rebels are responsible for the ugly state (and pleasant state) you are today. . . . With just a signature they robbed your country of billions. They give you right when you are wrong and wrong when you are right. (Nasralla 1999: 2)

Mutual interests of politicians, soldiers, and rebels appeared soon after RUF's 1991 invasion from Liberia. Then-president Joseph Momoh rapidly doubled to 6,000 the army that his coup-wary predecessor had kept small. Momoh's foreign minister later reported that recruits consisted "mostly of drifters, rural and urban unemployed, a fair number of hooligans and drug addicts and thieves" (quoted in Gberie 1997: 153). After a coup in April 1992, the country's new military rulers (who had been previously junior officers in their twenties) expanded the army to 14,000 soldiers, and also drew heavily among unemployed youth and those with experience in armed gangs. In this context, "there developed," wrote Arthur Abraham (a former government minister) "an extraordinary identity of interests between NPRC [regime] and RUF [rebels]." As senior officers helped themselves to diamonds and war supplies, less well connected soldiers did the same for themselves. "This" continued Abraham, "was responsible for the rise of the sobel phenomenon, i.e., government soldiers become rebels by night" (1997: 103). This relationship culminated in the eight-month joint rule of RUF rebels and the Sierra Leone army until a Nigerian expeditionary force expelled it from the capital in February 1998.

Then head of RUF, Sierra Leone army corporal Foday Sankoh, explained his own motives for battling Sierra Leone's government:

Den say lef RUF lef for mine diamond. Why den nor bin tell Jamil or Shaki dat when APC bin de power? Una mine ya! We na RUF believe in wealth, arms en power na de people den hand. . . . We nor de lef we diamond or we gun gie nobody. AND we go get de POWER jis nor! [They ask why RUF mines diamonds. Why didn't they ask Jamil (a presidential business partner) or Shaki (former president) that when the APC was in power? We mine! We in RUF believe in wealth, arms and power in the hands of the people. . . . We're not going to give up diamonds or our guns to anybody. And this is how we will get POWER]. (*For di People* 2000: 3)

Sankoh's analysis of the sources of power in Sierra Leone accurately focuses on the violent commercial networks in diamond fields that former presidents used to sustain their patronage networks. Capturing state agencies or mobilizing populations does little to advance conquest of these resources, except insofar as external recognition of sovereignty reduces the risk premium of selling diamonds overseas or eases the task of finding foreign investors to help mine more efficiently.

The use of soldiers in weakly institutionalized, patronage-based armies in other countries generates sobels there too. The intervention of the Ugandan Peoples Defense Force (UPDF) in Congo since 1998 brings local complaints of banditry. A trader riding a taxi "claims and insists that robbers were rogue members of the UPDF and most of the other passengers agree with her" (Bisiika 2000: 23). These and other suspicions that senior officers in the UPDF loot Congo's resources further blur lines between the military and rebels. It also renders dangerous for Uganda international pressure on Uganda's president Museveni to repatriate this expeditionary force, spreading sobels on the Sierra Leone model.

Why do ideological critics of this behavior that most Africans regard as inappropriate and predatory not appear at the helm of mass-based movements? Africans do not appear to be significantly different from other people in condemning misrule. Yet their insurgencies appear no match for the task of creating new political authority or reforming states that already exist.

Economic Motives over Ideology

Ideological critics do express alternatives to corruption and play roles in the formation of many contemporary insurgencies in Africa. In Liberia, for example, Elmer Johnson emerged in the first months of the NPFL challenge to President Doe as an able, charismatic, and successful young military commander. Using his skills as a former U.S. Marine, he mobilized multiethnic groups of fighters. A local rumor held that NPFL head Charles Taylor felt that this leader threatened his position. Johnson was later shot under mysterious circumstances. Likewise, several Sierra Leone university students fled to Libya in the 1980s for ideological and military training, along with individuals who returned when RUF invaded Sierra Leone. These students disappeared very early in the conflict (Abdullah and Muana 1998: 179).

The internal context of state collapse in which strongmen appropriate or create violent groups to serve shared material interests offers little room for ideological insurgents to take time and resources to build support through administering liberated zones and mobilizing populations. Especially when the field is crowded with contending armed groups, the ideological insurgent is at a serious military disadvantage. This is especially true when contenders are from among well-armed militias and private armies that characterize the violent politics of patronage politics in collapsed states.

Former Yugoslavia shows important parallels to state collapse and protest and their relation to private violence in Africa. Armed gangs, usually under the leadership of men who provided clandestine services for the old regime, recruited followers from among economically marginalized youth. One gang leader, Zeljko Raznajatovic (Arkan), robbed banks in Western Europe. Arkan escaped from prison in Belgium, the Netherlands, and Germany, and evaded arrest in Sweden and Italy. Such was Arkan's ability to escape that he was suspected of having ties to Yugoslavia's secret service. He returned to Belgrade in 1986 (where he was not arrested) to found the official fan club of Belgrade's Red Star soccer team, which he named Delije (Warriors). By November 1990 Arkan and his followers, now "Tigers," worked with Serb authorities to destabilize Croatia. Moving to Slavonia to fight in the siege of Vukovar, Arkan built a corporation (Erdut) out of loot he acquired there. He further consolidated his cultural ties to youth with his 1995 marriage to Ceca, a glamorous "turbo-folk" music star.

The Yugoslav army found that these groups' "primary motive was not fighting against the enemy but robbery of private property and inhuman treatment of Croatian civilians" (UN Commission of Experts 1994: para. 100). As among Bakassi Boys, Yugoslav groups often presented themselves as protectors of a particular community and punishers of corrupt politicians (and, like African counterparts, taking names like "Ninjas" and "Dragons") (Maas 1996: 21–22).

V. P. Gagnon makes the important observation that this violent opportunism results in "political homogenization" that suppresses less violent and more programmatic political protest, and pressures otherwise passive individuals to seek protection from armed groups (1994–1995). This occurs where government officials use armed proxies to fight factional battles, create conflict between communities, and disorganize opponents, leaving local people to flee or make deals with local protectors (who are often those who cause disorder). Violence then offers enterprising local politicians and strongmen means to integrate themselves into larger patronage networks. The consequence of growing confrontation between rival political networks is that those with the most well-developed commercial contacts from service to the previous regime are likely to be the best-armed and therefore most successful insurgents – and also the most wary of popular political programs. The best skills to have as an insurgent in this context are ease with extreme violence to intimidate rival claimants to these commercial opportunities, and openness to potential followers who are at least in part motivated by economic gain.

Thus the most typical followers of these insurgents are young men (and occasionally women) who use warfare as an opportunity to improve their economic circumstances. Many agree with Sankoh that having a gun and an alliance with a local strongman is the best way to remedy their marginal status, thereby joining their economic and political interests. A Nigerian officer observing warfare in Liberia noted that fighters were eager to sack the town that the Nigerians guarded. "From discussions with them, it was quite clear that most of them believed that Buchanan was their prize for several years of combat. They planned to utilize their fortune they made in Buchanan to start off business or advance their education after the war" (Nass 2000: 166). Economic motives are compatible with the use of force to settle scores, dispossess corrupt politicians, and serve political ambitions of patrons, all motives for fighting that attract influential and wealthy backers. A Nigerian reporter observed this fusion of interests in Bakassi Boys: "Warlords may be used to eliminate creditors, opponents, rivals, enemies or just persons who are not liked by others" (Ezeife 2000: 12).

These followers may have other grievances and criticisms that could have become instrumental in motivating them to act in other contexts. They may hate corrupt government in general, recognize that insurgency will not bring development and peace, and condemn petty tyrannies of local officials. But they may conclude that it is safer to be associated with those with guns rather than be a victim of the same. This context reinforces nonideological elements of warfare among other fighters too. A refugee from Liberia's war described the impact of youthful fighters on others as "a condition in which fear of death and humiliation puts the genuine adults and achievers into their shells. The vacuum is then filled by the young ones who become dare devils, not caring about death or any related end. For them, chance (and not age, valuable time and energy) creates material wealth" (Nagbe 1996: 53).

International Society Privileges Nonideological Insurgencies

Opportunities present in the global economy play a major role in strategies that insurgents use to support themselves, as noted at the start of this chapter. The presence of these opportunities, however, does not explain why some insurgents exploit them while others do not. We see that the organization of insurgency plays a greater role in shaping how particular groups exploit economic opportunities. No group can impose a monopoly on predation where patronage-based political systems cannot centralize the exercise of violence in a single hierarchy and, later, when rival syndicates compete with one another for loot. Even when one group dominates a territory, we see that in a context in which leaders are hostile to bureaucratic institutions and delegation of authority, none can organize violence entirely for themselves. Because they cannot discipline their own fighters and rely instead on integrating armed groups into their own political network, leaders of gangs (whether they are presidents or warlords) cannot exercise stable control over territory or eliminate other thieves from their domain.

Thus warring groups, and even those who prevail over their opponents, have an incentive to take everything from local inhabitants, effectively imposing a 100 percent "tax" rate on their victims. A consequence is that it is unlikely that the "stationary bandit" that Olson describes (2000: 11–12) will replace collapsed states and fragmented patronage networks to monopolize predation. The absence of this monopoly over coercion fails to give these predators an encompassing interest in the people and territory he controls such that he has an incentive to increase the well-being of inhabitants. Absent these incentives, the warlord neither becomes an autocrat nor does he provide public goods.

Yet much literature on conflict resolution still proposes that negotiated settlements to wars provide gang leaders with stability such that they may change their perspective on these matters (Weiss and Collins 2000). The 1995 Abuja Accords in Liberia, the 1999 Lomé agreement in Sierra Leone, and discussions at the time of writing to settle conflicts in southern former Somalia and in Congo prescribe coalition governments, international monitoring, and limited enforcement, alongside institutional structures that provide predictability in the division of loot to encourage leaders of warring groups to develop interests in the prosperity of their victims. In 1997, for example, Liberian citizens made the sensible calculation in an internationally mediated election that it was best to elect the warlord most successful at predation and violence as president, even though many who voted for him were also his victims (Harris 1999). Under the slogan "he killed my ma, he killed my pa, but I'll vote for him for president," voters showed their preference for a bandit who settles down and extracts loot year to year to bandits who rob sporadically but thoroughly. Likewise, foreign diplomats mediating the 1999 Lomé agreement included RUF head Foday Sankoh in a coalition government as head of a diamond resource commission to encourage him to shift his loyalty to this institution. Sankoh was to develop an interest in exploiting diamonds that would be compatible with increasing productivity in the mining sector to maximize the revenue of the agency under his command.

In fact, international interventions in these conflicts tend to reinforce incentives for war leaders to maximize their predations, even if they secure international recognition as members, or even head, of a government. This outcome recalls the earlier point about the material rewards that accrue to recognized leaders of areas of anarchy in the context of global order. In Liberia, for example, Taylor was able to attract International Monetary Fund (IMF) interest. IMF visitors told his agents that minimal payments of $50,000 against arrears of $3.1 billion might give his government access to more cash (IMF 2000). IMF motives for negotiating with Taylor appeared to lie in regularizing Liberia's token arrears payments so as to qualify Liberia for the Highly Indebted Poor Country Initiative program to write down uncollectable debt in an orderly fashion. Meanwhile, Taylor's sovereign status gave him access to bilateral aid of $159 million in 1997–1999 (IMF 2000: 12), while he reportedly spent 75 percent of internally generated revenues on his personal security and invited foreign firms to exploit natural resources for his private benefit.

While talking to IMF officials, Taylor allegedly used Liberia's sovereign prerogatives to shield his commercial dealings with RUF insurgents in Sierra Leone, to trade with them, and to give military support to them (UN 2000b). Taylor appears to be aware of the nature of his support for Sierra Leone insurgents, earlier reportedly threatening President Momoh that he would "do a RENAMO" on Sierra Leone, referring to a Mozambican insurgency's destruction of infrastructure and state institutions after Momoh refused to give him a base to launch his attack on Doe. Sankoh in 1999 used his official position as diamond commissioner to organize private diamond-selling trips to South Africa. He used the cover of anticipated elections to import dump trucks, explaining "I want to be adequately prepared for full-fledged campaigning" (Kamara 2000: 1).

Multilateral agencies such as the UN and regional intervention forces appear most anxious to preserve the external form of the state intact, rather than to recognize these areas of conflict as stateless zones. As with the case of the IMF, this recognition would disrupt orderly operation within the organization, even if the "state" cannot fulfill basic obligations. The absence of sovereignty complicates commercial, diplomatic, and military norms that are predicated on the exchanges with recognized interlocutors. War leaders who obtain recognition of sovereignty therefore can behave as free riders, using these norms to shield their essentially private transactions. Alternately, military intervention forces and diplomats argue that they must negotiate with these groups because they have guns and are capable of spreading disorder (Aboagye 1999).

In contrast, groups that grow out of popular efforts to defend communities against predators, religious movements that seek reform, or other citizens groups that protest against war have a more difficult time attracting attentions of diplomats. Government officials-turned-warlords usually speak a European language and wear Western suits. Home guard leaders and indigenous leaders without connections to a ruling elite class may speak only indigenous languages, dress in unconventional manners (in diplomatic terms), and, most important, do not possess the guns and commercial wherewithal to disrupt agreements if not included in them. Such disadvantages render these groups unable to build on contractarian relations with members and undermine fundamental attempts to build public authorities in Africa's more disorderly places.

References

Abdullah, Ibrahim, and Patrick Muana. 1998. "The Revolutionary United Front of Sierra Leone," in Christopher Clapham, ed., *African Guerrillas*, 172–194. Oxford: James Currey.

Aboagye, Festus. 1999. *ECOMOG: A Sub-Regional Experience in Conflict Resolution, Management and Peacekeeping in Liberia*. Accra: Sedco.

Abraham, Arthur. 1997. "War and Transition to Peace: A Study in State Conspiracy in Perpetuating Armed Conflict," *Africa Development* 22: 3–4.

Agekameh, Dele. 2000. "War of the Killer Gangs," *Tell*, June 12, 19–27.

Akparanta, Ben. 2000. "We Assist Society – Bakassi Boys," *Guardian* (Lagos), July 22, 17.

Ayoade, John. 1988. "States without Citizens," in Donald Rothchild and Naomi Chazan, eds., *The Precarious Balance: State and Society in Africa*, 100–118. Boulder: Westview.

Banque du Zaire. 1992. *Rapport annuel*. Kinshasa: Mimeo.

Barkey, Karen. 1994. *Bandits and Bureaucrats: The Ottoman Route to State Centralization*. Ithaca: Cornell University Press.

Bisiika, Asuman. 2000. "UPDF Tense as Mai Mai 'restore Congolese Pride," *Monitor* (Kampala), January 21, 23–25.

Chabal, Patrick, and Jean-Pascal Daloz. 1999. *Africa Works: Disorder as a Political Instrument*. Bloomington: Indiana University Press.

Civil Liberties Organisation (CLO). 1996. *Ogoni Trials and Travails*. Lagos: CLO.

Clapham, Christopher. 1996. *Africa and the International System: The Politics of State Survival*. Cambridge: Cambridge University Press.

Daily Mail (Freetown, Sierra Leone). 1977. "Halt Deteriorating Situation," February 3, 8.

Diamond, Larry. 1999. *Developing Democracy: Toward Consolidation*. Baltimore: Johns Hopkins University Press.

Ezeife, Chukwemeka. 2000. "Bakassi, Police and Politicians," *Punch* (Lagos), August 5, 12.

For di People. 2000. "What Foday Sankoh Really Said in Makeni," February 1, 3.

Gagnon, V. P. 1994–1995. "Ethnic Nationalism and International Conflict: The Case of Serbia," *International Security* 19, 3: 125–152.

Gberie, Lansana. 1997. "The May 25 Coup d'Etat in Sierra Leone: A Militariat Revolt?" *Africa Development* 22: 3–4.

Harris, David. 1999. "From 'Warlord' to 'Democratic' President: How Charles Taylor Won the 1997 Liberian Elections," *Journal of Modern African Studies* 37, 3: 431–455.

Hobbes, Thomas. 1996. *Leviathan*. New York: Oxford University Press.

Hobsbawm, Eric. 2000. *Peasant Wars of the Twentieth Century*. Norman: University of Oklahoma Press.

Ikwunze, Chris. 2000. "Ngugo Town: A Community Under Siege," *Weekend Vanguard* (Lagos), September 9.

International Monetary Fund. 2000. *Staff Report for the 1999 Article IV Consultation and Staff Monitored Program*. Washington, D.C.: IMF, February 14.

Jackson, Robert. 1990. *Quasi-States: Sovereignty, International Relations and the Third World*. Cambridge: Cambridge University Press.

Jane's Defense Weekly. 2000. "Liberia Allocates 40m for Army," March 8.

Kamara, Augustus. 2000. "Sankoh's Vehicles Arrive at Quay," *Pool* (Freetown), April 5, 1.

Kandeh, Jimmy. 1996. "What Does the Militariat Do When It Rules? Military Regimes: The Gambia, Sierra Leone and Liberia," *Review of African Political Economy* 23, 69: 387–404.

 1999. "Ransoming the State: Elite Origins of Subaltern Terror in Sierra Leone," *Review of African Political Economy* 26, 81: 349–366.

Kounzilat, Alain. 1998. *Ninjas, Cobras et Zoulous: Les guerres congolaises*. Paris: Editions ICES.

Lettre du Continent. 1994. "Bemba haut de GAMM," December 22.

Lieven, Anatol. 1999. *Chechnya: Tombstone of Russian Power*. New Haven: Yale University Press.

Maas, Peter. 1996. *Love Thy Neighbor: A Story of War*. New York: Alfred A. Knopf.

MacGaffey, Janet. 1991. "A New Approach to Evaluating Economic Reality," in Janet MacGaffey, ed., *The Real Economy of Zaire*, 7–25. Philadelphia: University of Pennsylvania Press.

Minute Paper. 1969. Government of Sierra Leone, Cabinet Deliberations, July 3.

 1982. Sierra Leone Government, Cabinet Deliberations, July 14.

Nagbe, Moses. 1996. *Bulk Challenge: The Story of 4,000 Liberians in Search of Refuge*. Cape Coast: Champion Publishers.

Nasralla, As. 1999. "Types of Rebels." *For di People* (Freetown), February 5, 2.

Nass, Major I. A. 2000. *A Study in Internal Conflicts: The Liberian Crisis and the West African Peace Initiative*. Enugu: Fourth Dimension Publishers.

Nation. 1999. "Bandits Hijack Aircraft," *Nation* (Nairobi), January 15, 1.

Nelson, Joan. 1990. "Conclusion," in Joan Nelson, ed., *Economic Crisis and Policy Choice*, 321–362. Princeton: Princeton University Press.

Nwankwo, Arthur. 1996. *Nigerians as Outsiders*. Enugu: Fourth Dimension Publishing.

Okanya, Dan Osy. 1999. *Political Violence in Nigeria: The Experience under the Second Republic*. Enugu: Auto – Century Publishers.

Olson, Mancur. 1993. "Dictatorship, Democracy and Development," *American Political Science Review* 87, 3: 567–576.

 2000. *Power and Prosperity: Outgrowing Communist and Capitalist Dictatorships*. New York: Basic Books.

Onwubiko, Emmanuel. 2000. "Why Obasanjo Unbanned Bakassi Boys, by Mbadinuju," *Guardian*, August 30, 11–12.

Onyeacholem, Godwin. 2000. "This House Stinks," *Tell* (Lagos), September 4, 14–20.

Oyediran, Oyeleye. 1997. "The Reorganization of Local Government," in Larry Diamond, Anthony Kirk-Greene, and Oyeleye Oyediran, eds., *Transition without End: Nigerian Politics and Civil Society under Babangida*, 193–212. Boulder: Lynne Rienner.

Radu, Michael, and Keith Sommerville. 1989. "People's Republic of Congo," in Chris Allen, Michael Radu, Keith Sommerville, and Joan Baxter, *Benin, The Congo, Burkina Faso*, 145–236. London: Pinter Publishers.

Scott, James. 1987. *Weapons of the Weak: Everyday Forms of Peasant Resistance*. New Haven: Yale University Press.

Sollenberg, Margareta, Staffan Angman, Ylva Blondel, and Andres Jato. 2000. "Major Armed Conflicts, 1999," in SIPRI Yearbook 2000, *Armaments,*

Disarmament and International Security, 50–58. New York: Oxford University Press.

Soyinka, Wole. 1996. *The Open Sore of a Continent*. New York: Oxford University Press.

Sunday Punch (Lagos). 2000. "How OPC, Bakassi Boys Operate," July 22, 15–16.

Superintendent of Mines. 1957. Letter of the Superintendent of Mines, Government of Sierra Leone, to the Chief Inspector of Mines, March 6. Photocopy, State Archives, Freetown.

Tilly, Charles. 1985. "War Making and State Making as Organized Crime," in Peter Evans, Dietrich Rueschemeyer, and Theda Skocpol, eds., *Bringing the State Back In*, 169–191. Cambridge: Cambridge University Press.

1990. *Coercion, Capital and European States, AD 990–1992*. Cambridge, Mass.: Blackwell.

Turay, Edward. 1987. *The Sierra Leone Army: A Century of History*. London: Macmillan.

United Nations, Security Council. 2000a. *Final Report of the Panel of Experts on Violations of Security Council Sanctions against UNITA*. New York: UN, March 10.

2000b. *Fourth Report of the Secretary General on the United Nations Mission in Sierra Leone*. New York: UN, May 19.

2000c. *Report of the Panel of Experts Appointed Pursuant to UN Security Council Resolution 1306 (2000), Paragraph 19 in Relation to Sierra Leone*. New York: UN, December 20.

United Nations Commission of Experts. 1994. *Final Report of the United Nations Commission of Experts Established Pursuant to Security Council Resolution 780 (1992, Annex III.A, Special Forces)*. New York: UN, December 28.

Weber, Max. 1947. *Theory of Social and Economic Organization*. New York: Free Press.

Weiss, Thomas, and Cindy Collins. 2000. *Humanitarian Challenges and Intervention: World Politics and the Dilemmas of Help*. Boulder: Westview.

Wolf, Eric. 1999. *Peasant Wars of the Twentieth Century*. Norman: Oklahoma University Press.

World Bank. 1992. *World Development Report*. New York: Oxford University Press.

2000a. *African Development Indicators*. Washington, D.C.: World Bank.

2000b. *Can Africa Claim the 21st Century?* Washington, D.C.: World Bank.

14

The Ghost of Vietnam

America Confronts the New World Disorder

Ian Roxborough

The United States military has never been comfortable with irregular and unconventional warfare. Its defining moment was the conventional clash of arms in the Second World War, and during the Cold War, nuclear deterrence aside, it prepared itself for conventional war with the Soviets in Europe. Military planners envisaged a great clash of armor and tactical air in the Fulda Gap where Soviet forces were expected to attack into the North German Plain. In this optic, Vietnam was a distraction and an aberration. Yet Vietnam proved a traumatic experience for the U.S. military, particularly the army, and its shadow continues to hang over America's military as it enters the twenty-first century. The great lesson of Vietnam for the U.S. military was a refusal to ever again fight a limited war against irregular forces. After the Vietnam War the U.S. military increasingly came to develop a new way of war – what I call standoff precision strike warfare – which exploits high technology to produce rapid, decisive victory in conventional combat. The Gulf War was the most obvious example of this new way of war.

Yet irregular forces and unconventional war will not go away. In the post–Cold War period, the U.S. military has been faced with increased demands for dealing with irregular warfare in the Balkans, Somalia, Haiti, and elsewhere. It has responded by trying to avoid another "quagmire." There has been intense internal debate about how the U.S. military should respond to the demands of "peace operations."

The attacks on the World Trade Center and the Pentagon on September 11, 2001, revealed a new face of irregular warfare. At issue now is whether the U.S. military, configured to fight a high-tech conventional war, will adapt to the demands of irregular warfare in the new world disorder that is emerging from the ashes of the Cold War.

This chapter discusses the response by the U.S. military to the challenge of irregular warfare, beginning with Vietnam, through the development of a new American "way of war" in the decade following the end of the Cold

War, and ends with some speculations about the challenges implied by a possible "global war against terrorism."

The specter of terrorism not only raised questions about military doctrine and force structure, it also opened the Pandora's box of the role of the military in domestic policing, and at the very least suggested the need for a reorganization of the institutions of national security. This would necessarily entail a redefinition of civil-military relations. At the time of writing (November 2001) the United States was possibly on the brink of changes in its national security system as far-reaching as those that had occurred between the end of the Second World War and the freezing of the Cold War in 1947–1948.

The contemporary U.S. military is as thoroughly enmeshed in its larger society as any other military, and cannot be properly understood except by placing it in that larger context. Evolving military operations and doctrine have implications for the role of the military in society and for the relationship between the military forces and their civilian masters. As Samuel Huntington (1957) has argued, the issue of civil-military relations is one of the relation of the expert to the politician. In a political system designed to provide checks and balances, this relationship is a complex and fragile one, constantly in the process of redefinition.

To understand both the underlying tensions in American civil-military relations and the emerging American "way of war" it is necessary to understand the cultural and institutional dynamics that make the military an integral part of the society and, at the same time, set it apart from, and at odds with, civilian society. In the aftermath of the war in Vietnam, and accelerating during the Clinton presidency, many observers noted with some alarm the emergence or widening of a "gap" between the military and civilian society. While in part this gap was the result of the dynamics of the nation's culture wars, it also had roots in military doctrine and in the tensions generated by a military that was uncomfortable with its new role in the post–Cold War world.

The evidence for a widening gap notwithstanding, this chapter argues that the real danger lies not in increasing tensions between the military and civilians, but in the acceptance on both sides of a set of assumptions about the proper use of military force that may lead to a foreclosing of America's strategic options. The issue, in other words, is not the alienation of the military from civilian society, or whether the military is subordinate to elected civilian leadership, but whether civilian and military elites collude with each other to narrow the range of strategic options open to the United States. While any crisis of civil-military relations that the United States is likely to face will be manageable, there is much that ought to trouble us about widely shared assumptions about the proper use of military force by the United States.

This chapter argues that the new American way of war reflects changes in America's role in the world and has implications for the kind of military establishment and the kind of civil-military relations that are likely to exist in the future. There are subtle changes in the world views of both civilian and military elites, and these are likely to foreclose options in terms of reform of the American state and its role in the world. Despite the announcement of a new "global war on terrorism" in the wake of the September 11 attacks, there is considerable continuity in American military doctrine, which could pose serious problems of mismatch between strategic aims and operational doctrine in America's efforts to deal with the new face of irregular warfare.

The Long Shadow of Vietnam

Any assessment of the modern American military must start with Vietnam. Of all the factors at work, this is probably both the most important and the least understood by civilians. For the American military, particularly for the army, the Vietnam War was a disaster. It was a disaster not because the war was lost by the United States but because the war severely stressed the military as an institution. Discipline broke down, drug use and racial tensions were rampant, careerism and cynicism abounded, the military felt abused and misunderstood. At the end of the war the U.S. military was morally adrift and without a clear sense of identity and mission. It took a decade for the military to recover. In the process a number of beliefs about the reasons for the U.S. failure in Vietnam crystallized in the course of intense debates among the officer corps. These beliefs were to have profound effects on both military doctrine and on civil-military relations.

In the short run the military recovered from the trauma of Vietnam by consciously refocusing on what it had always believed to be its primary mission: major conventional war with the Soviet Union. In the navy this led to the development of a highly offensive strategy of using attack submarines to seek out Soviet nuclear missile submarines in the seas close to the Soviet Union. Made public in the mid-1980s, the "Maritime Strategy" threatened to tip the nuclear balance in America's favor. The Reagan years also saw an expansion in the size of the navy. In the army the end of the draft led to an effort to create a more professional force. To meet the threat of large numbers of Soviet forces on the central front, the army developed an aggressive doctrine of air-land battle, emphasizing rapid and deep penetration by armored forces. A National Training Center was created in the California desert to simulate the clash of large armored forces. The air force moved away from its previous concern with strategic nuclear deterrence to active participation in the deep battle with the Soviets. The revamping of War College curricula and the intense discussion of Clausewitz that occurred at roughly the same time provided intellectual underpinning to these efforts. The Reagan buildup and then the triumphant execution of the Gulf War provided the culminating point of this regeneration of the

American military. In short, the military returned to an emphasis on "warfighting" as its raison d'être, contrasting this both with the limited low-intensity conflict of Vietnam and the deterrent posture of nuclear conflict.

In institutional terms, the emphasis on "warfighting" was successful. One consequence, however, was the accentuation of one part of military rhetoric at the expense of another. As Morris Janowitz argued, the modern military must blend the warrior ethos with the skills of a bureaucratic manager (Janowitz 1960). These two orientations exist in tension, and creating the right balance is no easy task. In the aftermath of Vietnam the institutional changes in the military were accompanied by a disparagement of the managerial orientation (usually associated with Secretary of Defense Robert McNamara and the cult of budgetary planning) and an emphasis on the central task of warfighting.[1]

The attitude to unconventional war implied by the new emphasis on warfighting was not entirely consistent. On the one hand, the office of the deputy secretary for special operations (low intensity conflict) was created in the office of the secretary of defense, and an independent Special Operations Command, with its own budget line, was established, both in 1987. And the operations during the Reagan years against guerrillas in El Salvador and against the Sandinista regime in Nicaragua were largely fought by Special Forces assisting indigenous forces in the conduct of, in the one case, counterinsurgency and, in the other, unconventional war. Special Forces advising local forces was the way to deal with "communism" in Central America in the 1980s and was, as far as the United States was concerned, largely successful.

Yet at the same time Special Forces was a small minority within the military as a whole and was largely sidelined from the central debates. Unsure of its future, Special Forces had a tension-filled, ambivalent relationship with mainstream conventional forces. Whether Special Forces' distinctly minor role in the U.S. military will change in the aftermath of the Afghan campaign remains to be seen.

For the U.S. military as a whole, there were more pressing concerns than the role of Special Forces. The collapse of the Soviet Union generated a serious case of goal deprivation for the U.S. military. For more than forty years it had prepared itself to fight the Soviet adversary: what was it to do now that peace had broken out?

As it turned out, the answer came swiftly, courtesy of Saddam Hussein. The Gulf War enabled the military to argue that the world was still a dangerous place. With remarkable agility, the U.S. military switched its focus from conflict with the Soviet Union to the containment of "rogue states." With the Gulf War as the template, American military planning focused on the need to plan for two major regional conflicts, with Iraq and North Korea as the illustrative examples for force-sizing purposes. Future military operations were to be conducted in a similar mold: halt the enemy, deploy forces, and strike with overwhelming force to achieve rapid and decisive victory. Warfighting, not peace-keeping or other missions, was to be the defining characteristic of America's military machine. There was thus a considerable measure of continuity in U.S. military doctrine and force structure as the Cold War transitioned into the amorphous security environment of the new world disorder.

The Emergence of the No-Casualty Constraint

Vietnam had another impact on the American military. Postmortems by the military produced something of a stab-in-the-back legend. There developed a belief among some in the military that the Vietnam War was unpopular in part because the political leadership had failed to rally Congress and the American people around the cause. By failing to declare war and mobilize the American population, the political leadership had done the military a disservice. In the future, military leaders were determined that military force would only be used when there was a clear mandate from Congress, rather than simply at presidential discretion (Summers 1982). The leadership of the armed forces also came in for its share of retrospective criticism. The Joint Chiefs of Staff (JCS) was accused of moral cowardice in not standing up to President Johnson and demanding to fight the war without "one hand tied behind their backs" (McMaster 1997). What might be seen by some as the proper subordination of military officers to their civilian masters was seen by military critics as moral weakness and a failure to properly exercise the military's duty to provide sound military advice. Clearly the emerging role for the chairman of the JCS was to prevent civilian political leaders from leading the military into conflicts that it could not manage.

The postmortems on Vietnam had clear implications for the future use of American military forces. Most importantly, by the 1990s, men – like Colin Powell and Norman Schwartzkopf – who had served in Vietnam as field-grade officers had risen to top positions. They had seen their troops killed in the "bad war" in Vietnam. They had lived through the collapse of morale in the army in the immediate aftermath of that war. As a result, they were as concerned as the peaceniks that there be "no more Vietnams," though what they meant by this was altogether different. Now senior generals, these officers were intensely reluctant to risk their troops unless it was absolutely necessary.

In the aftermath of the Vietnam War the top leaders of the military determined that they would never again allow themselves to be pushed into a war that they could not win and that would produce an institutional trauma similar to that of Vietnam. The army was reorganized so that it could no longer go to war without calling up the Reserves. Secretary of Defense Weinberger enunciated a set of six criteria that should be met before American troops were committed to action (Daggett and Serafino 1995). Key points were clear objectives, clear civilian support, and an exit strategy. As chairman of the JCS, Colin Powell added his amendments to the Weinberger doctrine, calling for the use of overwhelming force if troops were committed. Codified as the Weinberger-Powell doctrine, the top leadership of the American military came to believe that if a decision was made to use military force, there should be no half measures. There was to be no incrementalism or fuzziness: once the politicians had been forced to define a clear end state and exit strategy, the U.S. military would go in with overwhelming force, achieve decisive victory, and leave. The unstated assumption was that, at least as far as the methods of war were concerned, America would no longer wage war with limited resources. But although the application of violence was to be overwhelming, the war itself would be limited in both duration and objectives. Military operations would be swift and decisive. Overwhelming force would result in fewer American casualties and precision munitions would mean that civilian casualties and collateral damage could be minimized in a way that was quite different from the total wars of the twentieth century. The American people should be rallied around the effort, political leaders should provide the military with clear and unambiguous objectives, and then leave the conduct of the war to them. Moreover, overwhelming force should be applied to achieve decisive victory, and the troops should come home after a short and victorious campaign.

In this light, the Gulf War of 1990–1991 was the "good war." Fought exactly as the military wished, it did not put the nightmare of Vietnam to rest as many commentators believed but rather reinforced the lessons drawn from that conflict. Indeed, to the dismay of many top officers who saw their hands being tied behind their backs in an unanticipated manner, the mantra of force protection and "no casualties" was consolidated as a core component of the new American "way of war."

Among both military and civilian political elites, the issue of the "no-casualty constraint" has now become an important "social fact." There is a general assumption today that the American public will not support military operations if American troops die. The withdrawal of troops from Somalia after eighteen Rangers were killed in a firefight is often cited as evidence of this "no-casualty" constraint. It is further argued that the impressive success of the Gulf War has led the American public to believe that modern war can be sanitized. Distinguished military strategist Edward Luttwak even elaborated a theory that purports to explain why modern society produces a "post-heroic military" that cannot be allowed to accept casualties (Luttwak 1995). There is, however, not much in the way of solid sociological evidence to support these propositions. John Mueller argues that public support for military operations is an inverse log function of casualties (Mueller 1973). This implies that a reasonably large number of casualties will be accepted before there are major calls to end the war. James Burk has also argued, though from a somewhat different perspective, that the public will accept casualties if convinced that the price is worth paying (Burk 1999). The weight of evidence about the opinions of the American public gives little credibility to the "no-casualty" constraint. However, true or false, there is now a generalized belief among policy makers in the existence of the "no-casualty" constraint, and this belief has taken on a life of its own (Feaver 2000). American military operations in Panama, the Gulf, Bosnia, Kosovo, and Afghanistan all seemed to provide evidence that "no casualty" operations were possible as well as desirable.

And it is not only casualties among American troops that is seen to matter. The increasing use of precision munitions suggested that civilian casualties might be a thing of the past. This seemed to fuel a concern among liberal sectors of the public that avoiding the death and wounding of "innocent civilians" was a reasonable and realistic expectation. This seems to have influenced policy makers during the Gulf War and the Kosovo operation, and there was a clear – if decidedly minority – public concern to limit civilian deaths in the Afghan campaign. The point here is not the desirability of avoiding civilian casualties: everyone, including top military officers, is agreed upon this. The question is whether public opinion on this matter will so constrain military operations that certain kinds of strategy are effectively precluded.

Can Policy and Military Operations Be Neatly Separated?

Reflecting on the Vietnam War, American military officers came overwhelmingly to believe that the war was lost because of misguided civilian constraints on the proper use of military force. As articulated by Harry Summers and others, this view held that the conflict in Vietnam was primarily a conventional military conflict with North Vietnam. The application of sudden, overwhelming force would have won the war. Instead, the political leadership pursued a policy of incrementalism and sending "messages." The war was lost because the civilian political leaders would not allow the military forces to do their job (Johnson 1997). In this view, micromanagement of military operations from the White House had imposed unnecessary and counterproductive constraints on American strategy. The gradual buildup of troops in the south, and the gradual and measured escalation of the bombing of North Vietnam had made it impossible to deliver a "knockout" blow against the enemy early in the war. Never again would the top leadership of the military allow this kind of incrementalism to occur.

This interpretation of the Vietnam War is hard to sustain. That war contained elements of both irregular guerrilla war and conventional war between the military forces of North Vietnam, South Vietnam, and the United States. Ignoring the important irregular side of the war, for all intents and purposes, the U.S. military chose to conduct the war along conventional lines (Krepinevich 1986) and many postwar interpretations of the conflict stressed its conventional nature.

Along with the notion that Vietnam was a conventional conflict went the view that the civilian leadership had been responsible for losing the war by tying the military's hands behind its back. This view is based on the notion that the appropriate role for civilian political leaders is to decide whether to go to war. Once war is declared, the military – as technical specialists – should be left to conduct the war.

This sharp distinction between political goals and technical means was articulated early in the twentieth century. Led first by General Helmuth von Moltke and then by Erich Ludendorf, the German High Command in the First World War argued that once the fighting started, the politicians should leave the conduct of the war to the professionals. This "Moltkean" view of civil-military relations is widely held in the United States.[2] It assumes that politics and military operations are distinct and separate spheres. It makes it easy for military officers to be "technical experts" and "nonpolitical," and to know where their responsibilities begin and end. It implies that civilian political leaders should also be aware of the limits of their responsibilities. In the liberal world view, war is not an extension of policy, but rather results from the breakdown of diplomacy. War and peace are quite distinct and separate spheres. Not surprisingly, such a view of peace and war tends to produce demands for total victory. The "problem" that caused the war should be "solved" once and for all. This is unrealistic: many of the problems arising between states are due to clashes of interest that are likely to endure for long periods and are, hence, not soluble in any direct or "technical" manner. This "Moltkean" view, with its sharp distinctions between war and peace, and between military operations and political reconstruction, runs the risk of producing policy that fails to integrate optimally the various elements of national power, leading to a certain level of incoherence in the conduct of foreign policy.

The "Moltkean" separation of military and political spheres is not the only way to conceptualize the relationship between war and politics. It can be argued, for example, that war is a subset of politics. War is an extension of politics by other means. This view (the "Clausewitzian" view) sees all military operations as political in purpose. The boundaries between war and peace are permeable. In both war and peace, the aims of the state are political. It follows from the Clausewitzian view of war that civilian direction of military operations is entirely appropriate. In the Clausewitzian view there could be no sharp boundary separating politics from military concerns. All military operations are inherently political. The "Clausewitzian" subsumption[3] of military operations by political ends poses real difficulties for military officers in terms of deciding where their responsibilities begin and end.[4] If civilian politicians are to involve themselves with the conduct of military operations, should military officers then concern themselves with policy-making? What right do they have to do this when they are not elected officials? There are tensions here that make American military officers uncomfortable. However, these tensions are inherent in reality and must be managed. The way to do this is to bring about a greater integration of top military and civilian leadership, rather than by attempting to draw clear lines of demarcation between diplomacy, "politics," or policy on the one hand, and "technical," "military" matters on the other. The top leadership of the military (including the operational commanders in the theater) must be more involved with civilian policy debates, and top civilian leaders must be more intimately involved in all aspects of military operations. Lyndon Johnson was right to closely supervise the selection of targets to be bombed in Vietnam. That war was not lost because of civilian "meddling" but because entirely inappropriate methods were applied to what were, in any case, poorly defined and unrealistic strategic goals. The solution to the "politicization" of the conduct of military operations by civilian leaders is to accept that war is politics.

But this was not the lesson that the U.S. military drew from Vietnam. The lesson was simple: don't do it again. Never again fight a limited war. A corollary was a version of a stab-in-the-back legend, whereby civilian meddling and restraints on the conduct of military operations produced defeat. Both of these came together in a Moltkean separation of policy and military operations.

The real turning point in civil-military relations came when the Weinberger-Powell doctrine of overwhelming force was accepted with little or no debate by civilian political elites. This was a historic abdication of civilian control over military operations. Powell was strongly opposed to committing American troops to long drawn-out, messy conflicts with poorly articulated goals and unclear strategies for winning and withdrawing. While many of the Weinberger-Powell prescriptions made a lot of sense, they ruled out American intervention in many forms of low-intensity conflict. That was a political decision and should not have been preempted by the military. It assumed that America could simply choose which wars it wished to fight and walk away from others. While this might be true in some sense, the wisdom of being unprepared to fight certain kinds of wars and allowing the military to make that decision was quite debatable. The military leaders had come round to the view of "no more Vietnams," meaning that they were not about to let civilian politicians send them into a messy fight that they didn't like, and the civilians went along with this. This was a failure on the part of civilian elites and meant that the military had, in effect, exercised an important agenda-setting power to exclude some uses of military force from serious consideration.

As Deborah Avant has noted, the alternative lesson of Vietnam is that the military was unprepared to fight that kind of low-intensity conflict and should therefore get its house in order and prepare to fight such wars (Avant

1994). Civilian political leaders should, in principle, have the option to engage in such conflicts. There may well be messy, low-intensity conflicts in which the United States does want to intervene. Bosnia and Somalia are obvious instances. The genocide in Rwanda and Burundi was a conflict in which the United States ought perhaps to have intervened. Exactly how military force might be applied in these kinds of conflicts is a complicated question; but that is no reason to rule it out of consideration entirely.

Nor was the demand that political leaders present the military with clearly defined aims and an exit strategy entirely unproblematic. In general it is a truism to say that one should know what it is one is fighting for. But there is much about war that cannot be predicted. To put limits beforehand on war is not always possible. Wars may change their character for unforeseen reasons, war aims may need to be modified, strategies (including exit strategies) may need to change. War is an uncertain enterprise.[5]

While one can sympathize with the military commander who is frustrated by the political leader who gives him vague guidance, the fact is that political leaders often have multiple, poorly defined, contradictory, and shifting goals. This is the nature of politics, not a set of individual failings on the part of civilian politicians. Politics is about reconciling divergences and responding to poorly articulated demands. To ask state managers to clearly define the goal of a military operation is entirely reasonable; to expect them always to deliver the goods is unrealistic. Political leaders will often view military operations, at least in part, in terms of their impact on domestic politics. To expect them to do otherwise is wishful thinking. One can reasonably ask for clarity and candor in the setting of strategic goals, but even this is unrealistic. The skills that enable politicians to be successful do not generally include analytic clarity and a careful regard for the truth.

Another complication must be mentioned. Policy is made not by a single individual but by a complex process. The president responds to multiple political pressures: Congress, lobbies, the public, his advisers. And the governmental machine is a vast and complex bureaucracy that may not always facilitate the formulation of coherent, rational policy (Allison 1971). While not desirable, the output of policy in a polity as complex as that of the United States may well be poorly defined and at times incoherent. Military commanders have to learn to live with this. That this can be a very frustrating experience is well attested to in General Wesley Clark's memoirs of his position leading the NATO campaign in Kosovo in 1999 (Clark 2001).

The Moltkean paradigm of civil-military relations that had developed after Vietnam was given a seal of approval in the Gulf. As a result, the maintenance of working civil-military relations in the decade following the end of the Cold War depended on a general acceptance of a set of conceptually unsound dichotomies: between "political" and "military" tasks and objectives, between "war" and "peace," between "external" threats and

enemies and "internal" or domestic sources of disorder, and between the
military and the society in which it is embedded and the state of which it is
a core component.

These elements of the Weinberger-Powell doctrine for the conduct of
limited war had come under stress in the decade following the end of the
Cold War. They, nevertheless, had seemed to define military policy for the
post–Cold War period. Once the Afghan campaign began in 2001, however,
the Weinberger-Powell rules were consigned to the dustbin. The United
States committed troops without an exit strategy and with no expectation
of a short war. While the goals for the campaign in Afghanistan seemed
reasonably limited to the destruction of Al Qaeda and the Taliban regime,
the goals of the larger war against international terrorism were sweeping and
poorly defined. (And even in terms of the campaign in Afghanistan itself,
the politics of war termination and reconstruction were dealt with, as was
perhaps inevitable, in an entirely ad hoc manner.)

It is conceivable that there will be a greater awareness of the need to integrate political and military considerations in the aftermath of the September
11 attack, if only because a "global war on terrorism" will require much
higher levels of interagency coordination than has been the case in the past.
We can expect some blurring of the cultural distinctions that have been so
important to everyone: acts of war versus acts of crime, military versus political, war versus peace. These distinctions were always cultural constructs;
they will increasingly be seen to be inadequate, and we can expect efforts
to deal with the semantic confusion engendered by their use. It is possible,
though unlikely, that the Moltkean dualism will increasingly be discarded in
favor of a more subtle analysis of the relationship between war and politics.
Logical though it might be, the Clausewitzian approach is also fraught with
danger. The antimonies of war versus peace and political versus military
served a useful purpose: they sought ultimately to establish civilian direction
of military policy. Albeit with limited success, these distinctions provided
danger markers that were more or less clear to all concerned. They served
to sound the alarm when a clear imbalance in civil-military relations was
occurring. Handled without any great degree of subtlety or judgment, the
Clausewitzian subsumption of military operations to political goals runs
the risk of overly politicizing the military as an institution.

The New American Way of War and Its Implications

The evolving orthodoxy in American military thinking can be summarized
with the terms precision strike, dominant battlespace knowledge, systems
integration, force protection, and expeditionary warfare. The Gulf War
provided the exemplar and template for this doctrine, much of which had
been articulated in the 1980s, and which drew on deep historical roots. This
notion of war may be termed "standoff precision strike warfare."

In standoff precision strike warfare large platforms (aircraft carriers, cruisers and destroyers, manned bombers, tanks) continue to be central to military operations. War will be fought with missiles, precision-guided munitions (smart bombs), and space-based assets. All these weapons and platforms will be brought together, through advanced computing, into a "system of systems." The use of satellites and a variety of sensors, together with advanced computing, will give U.S. forces "dominant battlespace knowledge" or "information dominance." Together with the capability for precision strikes, information dominance will mean that U.S. forces can target the enemy with a hitherto unprecedented level of certainty. Wars will be conducted in the form of limited "expeditions." The evolving doctrine does not contemplate lengthy wars or wars with major powers.[6] The United States will generally deploy its forces directly from the continental United States, conduct the requisite military operations, and then withdraw. In recent years the American military has reorganized in ways that will improve its ability to strike rapidly anywhere in the globe.

This is a technicist view of warfare. It seeks information superiority in order to control the enemy. It downplays to an extreme the notion that warfare is a process of strategic interaction between two antagonists. The idea that one has to adapt to unexpected moves by the adversary finds expression only in vaguely expressed concerns about "asymmetric response." This strategic assessment puts a premium on rapid, unexpected strikes by U.S. forces, usually from outside the enemy's range. Air and missile strikes are the obvious weapon of choice in such circumstances. Instead of seeing war as a contest, the American military sees it as a form of punitive action. The only uncertainty in this view of warfare is exactly what part of the enemy system one should strike in order to achieve the desired effect. Warfare is reduced to an exercise in targeting.

The new American way of war suggests a routine and regular resort to (or threat of) air or missile strikes against adversaries in order to induce compliance with U.S. wishes. Prevailing assumptions will be that the U.S. public is strongly averse to casualties, and so ground conflict will be avoided if possible.[7] The Afghan campaign is likely to reinforce this orientation, given the success of Special Operations Forces in directing airpower and in assisting the Northern Alliance to roll back the Taliban forces. The need to work with local (and perhaps irregular) forces was a lesson learned in Nicaragua and El Salvador in the 1980s and applied to equal effect in Afghanistan. The military will focus on targeting enemy leadership and there will be little sustained effort to understand the enemy's society, culture, or political system. Public attention to these foreign policy crises will only develop in the period immediately prior to the use of military force. After the usual "rally effect" public interest in foreign policy issues will return to its normal low level. The standard and deeply American assumption that the problems are simple and can be solved in a brief period of time will continue to dominate strategy. But precisely because many problems in international relations are not amenable to quick and neat solutions, there is likely to be a mismatch between the goals of policy and the military instruments used. The evolution of military doctrine will have foreclosed many strategic options.

At the level of military operations there is considerable continuity from the invasion of Panama via the Kosovo operation to the Afghan campaign. In these operations air power and minimal use of ground forces have combined to produce rapid victory (Desert Storm is a partial exception in that it involved the buildup and employment of large ground forces). There is a confluence of tactical, operational, and political aspects of military actions. The weapons themselves are "smart": they can be fired and then left to do the rest on their own. At the operational level, this is an expeditionary form of warfare. U.S. military forces move into a region, strike, and then withdraw. There will be no permanent military presence of any size. There might be regularly stationed air and naval assets, but these can be shifted elsewhere with little notice. At the political level, the attention of the public will be episodic. War will have some aspects of political spectacle (Baudrillard 1995). The principal difficulty will reside in the need to garrison trouble spots with peace-keepers. The experience to date has been that Europeans and other non-U.S. forces have contributed the bulk of peace-keeping forces. Nevertheless, public perceptions in the United States are that the United States is contributing too much in the way of peace-keeping troops, and military leaders constantly complain about the negative impact of increased operational tempo, particularly the dissatisfaction expressed by many personnel who are separated from their families during peace-keeping deployments. The long-term trend will surely be toward a form of imperial intervention in which U.S. strikes against recalcitrant trouble-makers become routinized and no longer worthy of extended media attention. The political correlate of standoff precision strike operations will be "fire-and-forget warfare."

Policy makers will be under some pressure to strike at identified enemies in order to be seen to be "doing something." On the other hand, their inability to resolve permanently the crises they will face will mean that problems won't go away. They will have to manage problems rather than seek their definitive solution. This will apply to international terrorism and to other kinds of challenges to U.S. hegemony. Even a generally inattentive public will begin to get restless. We may well see increased public frustration as strikes on "rogue" regimes and terrorists fail to "solve" the problems in a definitive manner. There are likely to be mounting calls to "get the job done, once and for all" by a public unable to appreciate strategic complexity and constraints. These sentiments will find their supporters in the policy-making elites, as the calls during the Afghan campaign to "finish the job" in Iraq suggest. Yet the general reluctance to commit ground troops or to support a protracted military operation will produce precisely the conditions that will nourish continuing political frustration in the United States.

The lessons of the Afghan campaign are likely to be somewhat ambiguous. On the one hand, it appears to provide further validation for this new American way of war. It demonstrated the ability of the United States to conduct military operations on short notice thousands of miles away from its bases. But such a conclusion might well prove premature. The United States did not employ large numbers of ground troops in the Afghan campaign. Had this been necessary, we would have been better able to judge the ability of the United States to deploy large numbers of ground troops to an environment with poor infrastructure halfway across the globe. The army's interim brigades equipped with light armored vehicles instead of seventy-ton Abrams tanks were, in 2001, still some years from becoming a battlefield reality. Until they came on line, there would be severe logistical limits to the ground elements of America's expeditionary forces. The U.S. military was clear about the kind of expeditionary operations for which it needed to prepare; whether it had entirely made the transition from the armor-heavy formations of the Cold War was, however, another matter.

A second lesson of the Afghan campaign is likely to be that Special Operations Forces in combination with local irregular forces can operate effectively to meet the challenge of unconventional warfare. There are likely to be calls to expand Special Operations Forces and place greater reliance on them in the future. But there is a considerable bias against Special Forces. Low-intensity conflict and guerrilla warfare have never been attractive to the mainstream army and are unlikely ever to become so. Vietnam is not something the conventional military wishes to return to, and the general thrust of military planning since Vietnam has been to focus on high-tech conventional warfare. Nor is there much of a constituency for low-intensity conflict among the public. It is only among civilian strategists and policy makers that the utility of this form of warfare is appreciated. Whether this will change in the aftermath of the Afghan campaign remains to be seen. Certainly the notion that the campaign would be conducted by Special Operations Forces in concert with local forces suggests that a return to unconventional warfare cannot be discounted. However, the quick success of the Afghan operation, and the central role played by airpower, will probably mean that there will be little serious discussion of unconventional operations in the American military. The hold of the technicist view of war is far too strong for that.

The new American way of war is designed primarily to deal with external and relatively conventional threats. Both the push toward an expeditionary posture and the efforts to erect a national missile defense focus on traditional kinds of external enemies: states. But in the years prior to the attack on the Pentagon and the World Trade Center, there had also been concern to protect America against a novel threat: terrorists armed with weapons of mass destruction[8] intent on causing major damage in the American homeland. This new concern became actualized in 2001. It has the potential to fuse with a long-standing undercurrent in military thinking that places the military in a guardian role vis-à-vis civilians. It raises the possibility of a highly politicized military operating within the United States, with all the concerns about rule of law and civil liberties that follow. To evaluate this scenario, we need to turn to a discussion of the current state of civil-military relations in the United States.

Politicization

In the decade after the collapse of the Berlin Wall, close observers of the U.S. military began to worry about an increasing "gap" between civilians and the military. Recent survey research shows, for example, that approximately four-fifths of senior officers in the United States military identify themselves as supporters of the Republican Party. This is new, surprising, and worrying. Readers of this volume are, no doubt, accustomed to thinking of military elites as profoundly conservative in orientation. But within a broadly conservative world view, American military officers have traditionally upheld an explicit ideology of nonpartisanship, of strict neutrality in political affairs. The finding that military officers are openly Republican ought to come as a surprise, and it should concern us.

Until recently, most military officers in the United States held to an ideology that they were not politically partisan in an overt manner, whatever their personal feelings might be. This belief enabled them to accept civilian direction even though this might run counter to the beliefs of individual officers. The notion of apolitical nonpartisanship as an integral part of what it meant to be a professional officer was highly functional. This nonpartisan stance has disappeared. Political scientist Ole Holsti recently analyzed data on the political attitudes of military officers. He used a survey mailed to samples of approximately 4,000 opinion leaders at four-year intervals from 1976 to 1996. For all but one of those years, a sample of between 115 and 177 top military leaders was included.[9] This survey enabled Holsti to compare systematically the political attitudes of military elites with civilian elites. His key finding is that the party identification of military officers has changed markedly over the twenty-year period. In 1976, 46 percent of military officers considered themselves political "independents," compared with 31 percent of civilian elites. Members of the military were somewhat more likely than civilians to identify themselves as Republicans that year, with 33 percent of the officers so identifying themselves, compared with 25 percent of civilians. Democrats were weakly represented among the military, with only 12 percent identifying themselves that way, compared with 42 percent of civilian leaders who said they were Democrats. Thus, in 1976, there were substantial differences between military and civilian leaders in party identification, with the largest group in the military being nonpartisan, and a marked Republican bias. By 1996 this already wide gap had increased. In that year, the percentage of officers identifying themselves as independents had dropped to 22 percent. (Civilian leaders identifying as independents also dropped, though less dramatically, from 31 percent to 22 percent.) Identification with the Democrats among the military, never very high, dropped further, from 12 percent to 7 percent, while for civilian leaders Democratic identification remained roughly constant. The military, officers who were strongly Republican in 1976 (33 percent), increased their identification with that party by 1996 to a staggering 67 percent. During the same time period, civilian elite identification with the Republicans also rose, but only from 25 percent to 34 percent. To summarize, there have been three changes: the officer corps has ceased to espouse the ideology of nonpartisan political neutrality, the number of openly Republican officers has risen, and this trend does not mirror any similar trend among civilian elites (Holsti 1998–1999: 11). These are dramatic findings. They were repeated in a specifically designed survey administered by the Triangle Institute for Security Studies in 1998. The results of that second survey generally support Holsti's earlier findings (Holsti 2001).

Holsti is cautious in drawing implications from these findings. The data from the survey show no clear trends with regard to social attitudes or the use of force. This may be due to the fact that the survey was not designed to gather data on such things. Nevertheless, this increased partisanship is disturbing, although its implications are far from clear. When things are routine, there is no particular reason to assume that a politically self-identified military means trouble. Other mechanisms must come into play to translate the fact of a highly partisan officer corps into disobedience to civilian leadership.

There are hints that, although military officers explicitly adhere to professional values of subordination to civilian authority, in practice a significant minority among them might be willing to subvert the expressed intentions of the civilian leadership. The Triangle Institute survey asked respondents "if civilian leaders order the military to do something that it opposes, military leaders will seek ways to avoid carrying out the order all the time, most of the time, some of the time, rarely, never, or no opinion." The "correct" answer, of course, is "rarely or never," and more than two-thirds of military officers gave this as their answer. But as Paul Gronke and Peter Feaver note, "nearly one fifth of elite military officers expect the military to try to avoid orders from civilians some of the time, and a not insignificant 5 percent think the military will do so most or all of the time" (Gronke and Feaver 2001: 156).

The Alienation Issue

Not only are American military officers increasingly identified with the Republican Party, they are also uneasy with the culture and values of civilian society. The civil-military gap, in this view, is one of values. Tom Ricks, defense correspondent for the *Washington Post*, has analyzed this gap in a number of publications. In one of his books, he followed a platoon of U.S. Marine recruits through eleven weeks of boot-camp training on Parris Island in 1995. What the Marine Corps offers these young men is a sense of discipline. Through a series of grueling experiences which break down their previous identities and rebuild them as marines, the Marine Corps instills a sense of pride and self-discipline in them. When they return home from boot camp they become aware of just how different they have become. As he says, "I was stunned to see, when they went home for postgraduate leave, how alienated they felt from their own lives. At various times, each of these new marines seemed to experience a moment of private loathing for public America. They were repulsed by the physical unfitness of civilians, by the uncouth behavior they witnessed, and by what they saw as pervasive selfishness and consumerism" (Ricks 1997b: 66).

Ricks argues that "in a society that seems to have trouble transmitting values, the Marines stand out as a successful and healthy institution that unabashedly teaches values to the Beavises and Buttheads of America. . . . But over the last thirty years, as American culture has grown more fragmented, individualistic and consumerist, the Marines have grown more withdrawn. . . . Today's Marines give off a strong sense of disdain for the very society they protect" (Ricks 1997a: 20–22).

One might be inclined to dismiss Ricks's evidence as exaggerated: the reactions of young men fresh from boot camp are not likely to be the primary determinant of relations between military personnel and civilians. That there is more to it than this is suggested by the survey data. Top military officers as well as recruits fresh from boot camp not only have negative attitudes toward civilian society, but also believe that the military holds a higher moral standard. The Triangle Institute survey shows that "neither the elite military nor active reservists hold contemporary civilian culture in very high regard. . . . civilian culture is viewed as, materialistic, self-indulgent, undisciplined, and dishonest . . . and disloyal" (Holsti 2001: 57). Well over two-thirds of those in the military subsamples believe that "the military could help American society become more moral" (Holsti 2001: 53).

Ricks also looks briefly at some writings by military officers. He argues that their analysis of American society and their suggestions for increasing the role of the military in domestic police activities are a symptom of the growing alienation among the military. Ricks mentions a novel by retired Marine Corps Major Gene Duncan, with the title *Clint McQuade USMC: the New Beginning* (1990). He says that the novel "shows part of the military talking to itself when it doesn't think it is being overheard" (Ricks 1997a: 284–285). The novel portrays a Marine superhero who takes it on himself to punish the "bad guys," here identified as corrupt politicians and drug traffickers. What is most startling about the book is the premise articulated by the eponymous hero that American society is largely composed of sheep, wolves, and lions. The vast majority, the sheep, "graze around, living for today.... They are shallow beings ... they are selfish by nature." The wolves (crooked businessmen, drug dealers, labor unions, the American Medical Association, crooked politicians, etc.) prey on them. Then come the elite of lions. The lions are the good guys who protect the sheep. Duncan's off-duty marines are lions who protect the sheep – and they do so without regard to due process. When they find a bad guy, they kill him. It's that simple (Duncan 1990: 129–130). The conceptual structure of the three groups – sheep, wolves, and lions – is elitist. The large number of groups that fall into the bad-guy category reflects the right-wing populist orientation of the author. And the solution to the problem – a totally unauthorized hit squad of marines and ex-marines going around assassinating the bad guys and thereby solving America's problems – would be laughable were it not so dangerous. The novel is not, of course, official Marine Corps policy; nor is it necessarily representative of thinking in Marine Corps circles. These views are almost certainly only held by a minority of military officers. And there is some evidence that higher-ranking officers are more likely – at least in public – to have more moderate, pragmatic approaches to politics (Dowd 2001). But if even a minority of officers adhere to this sort of world view, there is a need for vigilance. It reveals a world view that sees civilians as qualitatively different from, and inferior to, their uniformed guardians.

There is another way to interpret the claim that the gap between the military and civilians has increased. In this view it is not the military that has changed but the civilians. Many officers express concern that the American public has somehow lost touch with the military and no longer really understands military concerns and issues. The end of the draft, and the declining number of congressmen who have had military experience are sometimes cited as causes of the widening incomprehension between the military and civilians. It should be noted that there is some ambivalence about this gap between the military and the civilian society it is pledged to support. On the one hand, the American military is proud to "represent" its nation and frequently invokes the notion of "citizen-soldier" as a key criterion defining what it means to be a serving military officer. On the other hand, the military is now a professional, all-volunteer force and has its own professional ethos. Not surprisingly, many officers believe that the military should hold to a higher moral standard than the rest of society.[10] They also believe that it does.[11] The effect of this claim about higher moral standards is to emphasize the alienation of the military from a morally inferior civilian society and to align the military in the nation's culture wars.

A distinct but related belief is that the military is not appreciated by the rest of society. This is usually expressed by saying that while those in the military are prepared to "make the ultimate sacrifice" and give up their lives for their country, civilian policy makers may thoughtlessly send them in harm's way without adequate preparation and/or for no very good reason. There are two observations that should be made. First, most civilians *are*, indeed, profoundly ignorant of, and disinterested in, military matters. This reflects the insulation of most of our lives from questions of war and peace. These are issues that for many years have been of only marginal relevance to the majority of Americans. Second, serving in the military is more than "just another job." For large numbers of officers there is an element of "calling" in the profession. This sense of calling and duty is constantly stressed, in innumerable ways, throughout the officer's career. A central part of the ideology that underpins the officer's sense of calling is the notion that he is prepared to risk his life for his country (i.e., for the bunch of ungrateful, lazy, hedonistic civilian slobs he is defending). This sense of honor is central to the professional officer. It is reinforced by rituals and symbolic acts, such as the conferring of medals, parades, saluting. Unsurprisingly, a perceived failure on the part of civilians to accord due honor and worth to the military is deeply troubling to them. Nor is it easy for the military to understand the seeming lack of patriotism among American youth. When the campaign in Afghanistan began in October 2001, many in the military were puzzled by the failure of America's youth to flock to the colors. There was discussion of instituting some form of national service, largely to instill appropriate values in America's youth.

The military sense of being separate from the rest of America is reinforced by several aspects of its life-style. With the exception of Washington, D.C. (itself often intensely disliked by officers who want to "get back to the troops"), most military bases are located in small towns and rural areas. Many officers live in neat, ordered communities on base. Because military families move around so frequently, there are extensive community support systems which make the on-base community resemble our mythical image of small-town America.[12] Conservatives, both within the military and in society more generally, are likely to yearn for a mythical past. U.S. military officers are likely to believe that the "true" America is one of small towns. That is certainly their experience. They are likely to believe that America is about "families" because that is their experience. They are likely to believe in the importance of religion because, even in a society that is much more religious than other industrialized countries, military officers are likely to be at least, if not more, religious than the rest of society. Military officers are less likely to belong to evangelical churches than the general public, possibly because they are recruited from Catholic groups to a considerable degree (Holsti 2001: 23). However, qualitative research suggests that evangelical Christianity has been spreading in military circles at least as fast as in America as a whole, and possibly faster (Loveland 1996). The Triangle Institute survey found that military officers were more likely to believe that the Bible is the "inspired word of God, true, and to be taken word for word" than was the case with civilian elites (Holsti 2001: 85). All of these factors work to produce a tendency to hold views about morality and politics that are at the conservative end of the spectrum. One must endorse Ricks's claim that there is a growing gap between civilians and the military.

Just as the military often feels that there are moral problems with civilian society, so also do civilians, particularly liberals, often feel that there is much to be concerned about in the social and cultural values of the military. Social relations in the American military have long been a matter of interest to civilians. Racial integration within the military was a political issue. The role of women in the military has, in more recent years, become an important point of political debate. And when Bill Clinton became president in 1993, one of his first acts was to attempt to improve the status of gays and lesbians in the military. This generated considerable opposition in the military and led to acts of incivility to President Clinton by uniformed military personnel. Whatever civilians might think about the reasonableness or otherwise of military opposition to equal treatment for gays and lesbians in the military, many military personnel feel that an unnecessary liberal social experiment is being foisted on them.

Does this matter? What does it matter what the cultural values of the military are, so long as it does its duty? While it is hard to deny that taxpayers have, in principle, the right to concern themselves with social relations in an institution which they fund, there is much to be said for caution and moderation in such intervention. Institutional sectors do have distinct cultures, and well-meaning social intervention may have unintended consequences. Making the personal political (which has been an important part of the feminist agenda) works in both directions. Conservatives also can make their personal values (such as opposition to abortion) part of the political agenda. The defense of "family values" by the military can thereby become a political issue. Although it is difficult to imagine how a liberal president could have avoided some action on the issue of gays and lesbians in the military, introducing the current culture wars into this particular arena was bound to trigger off a sequence of reactions.

The rise of moral politics is an important form of political discourse in the contemporary United States.[13] The effect has been to politicize personal morality. The coincidence of the rise in cultural politics with the increasing political alienation among large segments of American society has created a situation in which it is not surprising that a vast cultural gap has emerged between the military and civilians. Given the increasing polarization of American society as a whole, this entails the risk that the increasingly politicized military will be enlisted in the causes of the civilian cultural conservatives. America has a highly professional military. Most officers are committed to service to the nation (CSIS 2000). But they feel estranged from a civilian culture that many of them despise; they believe that their values are superior and that civilians could learn from them; a significant minority among them contemplate disobeying orders from civilian superiors; the majority are partisans of the Republican Party; and they generally distrust their elected leaders.

Waging Peace

In an atmosphere of distrust of civilian leadership and distaste for the values of much of civilian society, the military were tasked to undertake a series of relatively novel missions. The end of the Cold War brought with it an unexpected and unprecedented demand for the military to act as a global policeman and social worker. These "nontraditional" missions were initially greeted with some dismay by the armed forces. The traditional, conventional role of the military as "warfighters" was seen to be in jeopardy. However, as it became obvious that peace operations were here to stay, both the army and the Marine Corps became increasingly eager to define these as an integral part of their mission. The elusive concept of "nation-building" began to reappear, reawakened from its post-Vietnam hibernation.

The idea is that soldiers, more or less equipped as they are now, would engage in a variety of low-intensity constabulary duties in "failed states." Advances in technology for "warfighting," while welcome, are not centrally important. While there are debates about the extent to which space-based intelligence, surveillance and reconnaissance, airpower, and heavy army units can assist constabulary forces, the basic image remains one of "boots on the ground." It is a manpower-intensive concept. Military force will be applied in relatively well known ways to achieve fairly limited objectives. Despite a few efforts by doctrine writers, there is little connection between the practice of peace operations and the evolving doctrine for the conduct of modern warfare.[14]

The Marine Corps quickly adopted peace operations as an integral part of its mission. The image of the "three-block war" captured the new reality: marines on one city block might be engaged in a firefight, while marines on the next block might be separating hostile local forces, and marines a block further away might be helping with medical attention and assisting in restoring civilian government. This image of the three-block war stressed the complexity of peace operations and suggested that there was a seamless border between conventional applications of military force and less conventional roles of peace enforcement and humanitarian assistance.

But while there was some adaptation to peace operations, they also raised serious concerns in the military leadership. For the military leadership, the danger of peace operations is two fold. First peace operations distract from the core mission of warfighting. They lead to wear and tear on both equipment and troops, resulting in considerable stress and dissatisfaction (CSIS 2000). Second, military leaders worry that these peace operations will slip into warfighting of the wrong kind. What was supposed to be a humanitarian aid mission to Somalia slipped into urban warfare of a very destructive kind. Humanitarian operations demonstrated an alarming propensity to drift into conflict with irregular forces (Bowden 1999). Here the shadow of slipping into the Vietnam quagmire hangs heavy over military leaders.

As parts of the electorate brought increasing pressure on President Clinton to get involved in the Bosnian conflict, JCS Chairman Colin Powell strongly resisted commitment of American troops (Halberstam 2001). When U.S. military involvement became politically unavoidable, the first response was to rely on airpower in order to keep some distance and reduce casualties. Then recourse was had to training and equipping the Croatian army through semiofficial means. Finally, when the Dayton Accords meant the presence of U.S. ground troops, the army responded in a way that deserves comment. One might have thought that large numbers of light infantry engaged in widespread patrolling would be the preferred action. Instead, what was uppermost on the mind of the army leadership was to avoid involvement in a messy low-intensity conflict that might resemble Vietnam. It solved the problem by sending an armored division to Bosnia and hunkering down in its camps. It was with great reluctance that the U.S. military gradually began to conduct patrols and to arrest suspected war criminals.

The subsequent operations in Kosovo followed a similar pattern. There was intense pressure to intervene to prevent the killing and expulsion of large parts of the population of the province of Kosovo. This time the United States and NATO acted more swiftly. But, as in the earlier operations in Bosnia, a central concern of the United States was force protection. Air attacks were to be carried out from high altitude to avoid Serbian air defenses, even at the risk of increased casualties among civilians. More to the point, intervention by ground forces was initially ruled out in public statements by President Clinton, and when ground forces did begin to deploy for operations in Kosovo, they moved with ponderous slowness toward the theater of operations. If General Wesley Clark is to be believed, the Joint Chiefs of Staff was anything but supportive of a vigorous campaign to achieve victory (Clark 2001). In the end, the air campaign brought the submission of Milosevic to NATO demands before ground combat began. Once again air power had shown (or seemed to show) that it could deliver a casualty-free victory. But what the Kosovo campaign also underscored was that peace operations were to be conducted with more attention to force protection than to the central political objectives that had brought about the intervention in the first place.

The Role Expansion Argument

Picking up on dissatisfactions with peace operations, Charles Dunlap, a colonel in the legal section of the Air Force, wrote his "American Military Coup of 2012" as his National War College dissertation in 1992 (Dunlap 1992–1993). It has been widely commented on, and he has continued to publish similar pieces. As I read it, it is an argument against the efforts to expand military roles in the aftermath of the Cold War. Such role expansion, Dunlap argues, may well politicize the military, leading to disagreeable results. It is a warning cry, intended to prevent a deterioration in civil-military relations.

Dunlap's thesis is in the form of a letter from Prisoner 222305759 to a friend who had been at the National War College with him in 1992. The letter is written shortly after the seizure of power by General Brutus, who has instituted a military dictatorship in the United States. The author of the letter has been imprisoned for opposing the coup and is awaiting execution. In his letter the author chronicles the events that led to a military coup. His principal argument is that the American military came to take on a whole range of missions that were more properly performed by civilian agencies. As "Americans became exasperated with democracy" and became increasingly politically apathetic, they continued to have great confidence in the military as an institution. With massive social problems, soaring crime, and a general societal malaise, Americans increasingly turned to the military to help out. The military came to take on policing of urban areas and helped out in health care and education. Military involvement in the drug war and the passage of the Military Co-operation with Civilian Law Enforcement Agencies Act of 1981, was a "historic change of policy" that brought the military into police work. The military also came to be tasked with environmental cleanup, running essential air and sea transport, and rebuilding infrastructure. Outside of the United States, humanitarian and nation-building missions proliferated. This process of role expansion directly reduced military training for combat with "an authentic military opponent. . . . People in the military no longer considered themselves warriors." As a result, when U.S. forces confronted the Iranians in the Second Gulf War of 2010 they produced a "wretched performance." The military responded by blaming "inept civilian leadership" for its defeat.

Dunlap's narrative continues by noting that throughout this period the military had been increasingly drawn from the Service Academies, rather than ROTC, and the officer corps was increasingly becoming a narrow elite tied together with close personal bonds. Cloistered living in the "islands of tranquillity" that were military bases furthered the gap between the military and the rest of society. Involvement in an increasingly wide range of nontraditional domestic missions led directly to the politicization of the officer corps. The continuing trend toward unification of the armed services reduced the "checks and balances" built in to the system of separate services.

According to Dunlap, the confluence of these factors, all of which were visible in 1992, produced a situation where a military coup was possible. His prescription for preventing such a situation is a return to a focus on warfighting. Where possible, the goal should be to reduce the isolation of the officer corps and "foster a citizen-soldier attitude among the full-time professional soldiers" (Dunlap 1992–1993: 23).

Dunlap's work has been widely read among the military. It speaks to real concerns and anxieties. How is it to be evaluated? The fact that it has been widely read is a good sign: it shows that military officers are concerned about the state of civil-military relations. This is all to the good, and the more soldiers worry about this sort of thing the safer democracy will be. It is, however, the reassertion of a view of war as something quite distinct from peace, a distinction that, as this chapter argues, is generally untenable.

Dunlap is right to be concerned about the politicization of the officer corps but wrong about the causes of this. Does politicization arise from involvement with "civilian" tasks? Does civil action produce politicization? Possibly, but the evidence for that is weak. Rather than involvement in "nontraditional" missions, military institutions become politicized when they are regarded as "arbiters" or "moderators" by civilian elites (Stepan 1971); when they have a strong corporate identity, which is in conflict with the values and actions of civilian elites; and when defeat in war produces institutional trauma and this is displaced onto political leaders through a "stab-in-the-back" legend. These factors can give rise to the development of doctrines that advocate a more active role for the military in domestic affairs or lay great claims to military autonomy from civilian direction, and they can reinforce attitudes of moral supremacy.

The first factor, the military acting as moderators between contending civilian elites, seems quite unlikely as a scenario for the United States in the foreseeable future. Whether it arises as an issue depends on whether American politics becomes polarized and whether the contending parties no longer feel that matters can be resolved in mutually acceptable constitutional ways. The second factor, corporate identity in conflict with the values of civilian elites, is happening, and is something to be concerned about, but it is not in itself a sufficient cause of a crisis in civil-military relations. The third factor, the stab-in-the-back ideology, is the one to really worry about. This would set the military as an institution against civilian elites. (Interestingly, although Dunlap mentions defeat in the Second Gulf War and attributes the blame to the civilian leadership as a reason for the military coup of 2012, he hardly discusses this. It simply serves as the trigger that explodes the other factors.)

Dunlap is also right to focus on civilian alienation from the political system, together with a sense that societal problems are large and insoluble, as factors contributing to the possibility of a military coup. But he underestimates the importance of this relative to changes in the military, and his argument is based on a linear extrapolation from 1992 that things will go from bad to worse. That might have been a plausible prognosis in 1992; but economic activity is cyclical and the trend in crime rates is not always uniformly upward. A similar linear extrapolation made eight years later would have come to entirely different conclusions. Prognostications about the future are notoriously difficult and are frequently influenced by tendencies to extrapolate short-term trends.

Dunlap's arguments about the need to train for warfighting and the need for a military self-image as warriors require discussion. The argument that peace operations have a negative impact on readiness for war is, as we have seen, very much a mainstream position. The top leadership of the military (particularly the army) is ambivalent about peace operations. Initially, the army leadership was loath to get heavily involved in peace operations. According to traditional views, reinforced by the post-Vietnam regeneration of the armed forces, the primary mission of the army was to fight and win America's wars. All else was secondary: either a "lesser included case," or a distraction. However, in the face of declining budgets and increasing demand from civilians for intervention in humanitarian and peace operations, the army came to embrace these missions and began to rewrite doctrine accordingly. This shift, however, continued to generate concern about reduced training, increased operational tempo, strains on families caused by frequent and prolonged operations overseas, and retention difficulties. However, it is by no means clear that these very real problems could not be solved by such normal managerial expedients as raising pay and making assignments more predictable and less onerous. With the advent of the Bush presidency in 2001, there was some expectation that the government would seek to reduce operational tempo, though there could be little certainty about how likely success would be. The attack of September 11 made all such prognostications quite problematic. If anything, it was likely that non-traditional roles for the military, and particularly the Army National Guard, would increase. The attack, most importantly, was a reminder that the problem of irregular warfare would not go away.

The Mantle of Imperialism and the Image of the Other

In 1997 the commandant of the Marine Corps, General Charles Krulak, gave a speech to the National Press Club. He began with this story: "In 9 A.D., Roman Proconsul Quinctilius Varus crossed into Germany to bring recalcitrant barbarian tribes to suppression. . . . On a hot August morning, the two sides joined battle in the Teutoberg Forest. . . . By nightfall, Varus had lost the eagles of three legions and was conducting a desperate rear-guard action to save his remaining forces. During the withdrawal, Varus could be heard muttering under his breath . . . 'Ne Cras, Ne Cras' – 'Not like Yesterday.'" Krulak went on to analyze the reason for the Roman defeat at the hands of the barbarians. He argued that it resulted from the ability of the Germanic tribes to neutralize the advanced technology of the Romans by luring "the Roman heavy cavalry into marshes where their mobility and shock power were rendered useless. They led the Roman bowmen into the forest where the trees negated the effectiveness of their arrows." An underdeveloped people had defeated the imperial power by an asymmetric response, rendering its advanced technology useless. The Romans' mistake was to assume that nothing would change. Krulak then went on to make the point that the United States was in danger of repeating this mistake. He argued that "our enemies will not allow us to fight the Son of Desert Storm, but will try to draw us into the stepchild of Chechnya." The United States needed to prepare now to meet this eventuality (Krulak 1997).

Krulak presents himself as a realistic thinker: here is the future of warfare; it will be dirty, prolonged, and political; we cannot avoid it; let us therefore prepare for it realistically. In this view, advanced technology is welcome, but overreliance on technology runs the risk that purely technical solutions will be sought to what are human problems, and technological hubris will lead the United States into another Teutoberg Forest.

Krulak's point is the need to prepare for an asymmetrical response by one's adversaries. He could have used any one of a number of historical cases to illustrate his point. The fact that he chose the Roman Empire and felt no need to distance himself from some possible implications of this particular example is perhaps worthy of comment. Intentionally or otherwise, Krulak sees future conflict as one of the imperial civilization against the barbarians.

Implicit in Krulak's historical analogy is the assumption of the imperial role. This is a sensitive point in American foreign policy. Despite much talk of the "unipolar moment" and the emergence of the United States as the world's sole superpower, there is at the same time a reluctance to take on the burden of being the world's policeman. This tension in the American body politic is unlikely to be resolved in the near future. The military have reacted to the changed security environment by stressing their "expeditionary" capabilities. They are no longer primarily forward deployed to meet a Soviet threat or in a posture of active nuclear deterrence. Rather, they expect to be called to respond to crises around the globe. This is, in fact, the entire raison d'être of the Marine Corps, and is one reason why Fourth Generation theories hold such an attraction for Marine Corps theorists. But an "expeditionary" orientation has also been adopted by the air force and the navy (and to a lesser extent, the army.) However, while the air force and the navy now see themselves as "expeditionary," they intend to prosecute high-intensity, high-technology, standoff strikes. The marines, on the other hand, are committed to putting troops on the ground and to the messy business of combat with relatively light forces.[15] The army began to shift from its love affair with heavy tanks when General Erik Shinseki became chief of staff in 1999 and promoted the interim brigades based on light armored vehicles as an alternative.

The Roman analogy has further implications for military operations. The Roman response to troublemaking by barbarians, subordinate groups, and rival power centers was draconian. Punitive expeditions were the means of enforcing Roman rule in the hinterlands. Providing the Romans had the military capacity, the legions would be dispatched, the tribes would be subdued, their lands would be laid waste, captives and slaves would be taken. The modern analogy is the air-missile strike against "rogue" states. Exemplary punishment is aimed at containing "rogues" and deterring potential imitators. The central difference, of course, is that while the Romans were primarily exponents of engineering and siege warfare, the preferred American way of war stresses rapid, decisive operations. And, whereas the Romans were inclined to inflict summary punishment on recalcitrant tribes, the exponents of standoff precision strike warfare are inclined to target only the leadership.

Krulak's speech was an alarm call, aimed to shock a complacent military out of its fascination with a high-tech "revolution in military affairs." Implicitly, by the choice of historical example, it accepted America's hegemonic role in the post–Cold War world as the strategic reality. The implication was that this strategic role would not be well served by a military doctrine of standoff precision strike warfare. Something else would be needed.

Asymmetry: Irregular Warfare Returns to the Agenda

The official view of future war leans heavily in the direction of what I have termed standoff precision strike warfare. In a culture that is technologically minded, this is hardly surprising. In this view, the application of precision strikes through information superiority and densely networked systems is the new American way of war. As a means of conducting military operations it has two possible vulnerabilities: asymmetric responses, and mismatch between political goals and military instruments.

By the mid-1990s, American defense planners had come to appreciate that future adversaries might choose not to pit weakness against strength by attempting to fight modern U.S. forces on their own terms. Instead, they are likely to probe for weak points in the American way of war, developing an "asymmetrical" response to U.S. military power. The term "asymmetrical" came to represent a wide gamut of unconventional and irregular challenges to the high-tech, conventional forces of the American military. Future adversaries might, for example, attempt to take out U.S. satellites, thereby rendering the U.S. military blind, deaf, and dumb. They might launch a cyber attack on the American economy. Or they might use relatively low-technology weapons such as naval mines to hinder the deployment of American forces. Alternatively, adversaries might attempt to impose casualties on U.S. forces and/or civilians[16] by, for example, the use of weapons of mass destruction either on deploying forces or on targets in the United States itself, or perhaps by using terrain to bring U.S. troops to the killing fields.

As the American military reflected on the lessons of the Gulf War, the term "asymmetry" began to creep into discussions of military operations. In 1997 the prestigious blue-ribbon National Defense Panel highlighted the possibility of asymmetrical attack (National Defense Panel 1997). By 1998 it was common to hear comment to the effect that because the U.S. was so dominant militarily, adversaries would avoid a head-to-head confrontation of military forces and instead seek to challenge the United States in an asymmetric manner (U.S. Army War College 1998). Asymmetric warfare was not the same thing as unconventional or guerrilla warfare by irregular forces, although it could include this. It initially referred primarily to the use of novel weapons and tactics by adversary states to negate the technological advantages of the United States.

As in a game of chess, U.S. military planners found themselves attempting to think through a series of moves and countermoves. Initially, in line with the notion that the adversary would be a state contesting the employment of conventional U.S. military forces, the standard response was to emphasize force protection measures. But as the debate continued, the U.S. military increasingly paid attention to possible attacks by nonstate actors of various kinds and to attacks on the U.S. homeland. Beginning in the late 1990s, more and more attention was devoted to homeland defense. When the attack on the World Trade Center and the Pentagon occurred on September 11, 2001, the mental preparation on the part of responsible civilian and military planners had to a considerable extent already been done. Although the precise modality and timing were unknown, that there might very well be an attack of this kind came as no surprise to those who had thought about the issue. In 1998 Madeline Albright, secretary of state during the Clinton administration, argued that "terrorism is the war of the future" (Albright 1998). Policy makers were sufficiently concerned to set up a blue-ribbon congressional commission to review American security strategy for the post–Cold War world. The deliberations of the United States Commission on National Security/21st Century, popularly known as the Hart-Rudman Commission, reinforced the concern with catastrophic terrorism. In its 1999 report, the commission stated that the greatest danger that would face the United States in the twenty-first century would be the threat of a terrorist attack on the American homeland using weapons of mass destruction which would result in thousands of civilian casualties (U.S. Commission on National Security/21st Century 1999).

Fourth Generation Warfare

Standoff precision strike warfare had been challenged by the irregular warfare associated with peace and humanitarian operations. It was now challenged by the specter of international terrorism. While for some military strategists all that was required were a few modifications to the basic doctrine, for others a fundamental rethinking of the nature of modern warfare was called for.

As the Cold War began to wind down, a number of thinkers associated with the Marine Corps began to argue that the character of warfare was about to undergo a radical transformation. This change, however, would not be the "revolution in military affairs" envisaged by the mainstream of the U.S. military. Indeed, in many ways it would be its polar opposite. They called their theory "Fourth Generation Warfare."

Like many attempts to conceptualize changing forms of warfare, Fourth Generation theorists use the device of a series of stages or generations of warfare. They are: (1) the age of gunpowder and the smoothbore musket; (2) the age of rifled muskets, barbed wire, and machine guns; (3) the age of infiltration tactics and blitzkrieg; and (4) the emerging fourth generation of warfare in which terrorism and widespread violent protest will threaten to undermine Western ways of waging war (Bunker 1994).

The Fourth Generation theorists have a view of future war that is quite distinct from both the technicist orthodoxy of the mainstream military and from the constabulary notion that the primary mission for America's military was peace enforcement and humanitarian assistance. Fourth Generation thinkers emphasize the role of a small elite of warriors. The idea is that small units of highly trained, self-reliant warriors will wreak havoc among the enemy. America's enemies will be motivated by hatred and envy. They will live in societies unable to adjust to modernity. Ethnic micronationalism, religious fundamentalism, and terrorism will be the hallmarks of this enemy. According to Fourth Generation theorists, to fight Jihad, the United States will have to develop a warrior culture in its armed forces. Failure to do so will result in defeat.

This prognosis is based on a generally pessimistic observation about the forces of primordialism in the contemporary world. The themes combine a pessimistic view of human nature as prone toward irrational hatred and violence, together with an extrapolation of present levels of ethnic and religious conflict into a future in which nonstate actors become central. The more intellectually respectable authorities are Samuel Huntington (1996), Robert Kaplan (1996), Benjamin Barber (1995), and Martin van Creveld (1991). This line of thinking is at present a distinct minority view within the modern military. In stark contrast to "realist" views of international relations, this view argues that future conflicts will be primordial in nature. They will pit one civilization against another. Religious fundamentalism and ethnic hatred will be the forms this takes. Future war will be a clash of Western civilization against barbarism.

As the global hegemon, it is generally held that the United States must act to preserve the current world order. This will inevitably mean tensions and clashes with enemies. For Fourth Generation thinkers this implies a clash between (Western) civilization and the barbarians.

The best-known exponent of this view is William Lind. He and his coauthors argue that there is a possibility that the U.S. military might, at some not-too-distant point, be engaged in military operations within the United States against certain civilian groups (Lind et al. 1989, 1994).[17] Lind et al. argue that "Three central ideas shape . . . the emerging fourth generation: the nation-state's loss of its monopoly on war; the return to a world of cultures in conflict; and "multiculturalism" in the United States, which is to say "the abandonment of Judeo-Christian, Western culture and values here at home" (Lind et al. 1994: 34). They go on to argue that "starting in the mid-1960s, we have thrown away the values, morals, and standards that define traditional Western culture. In part, this has been driven by cultural radicals . . . [who] have successfully pushed an agenda of moral relativism, militant secularism, and sexual and social 'liberation.' This agenda has slowly codified into a new ideology, usually known as 'multiculturalism' or 'political correctness,' that is in essence Marxism translated from economic into social and cultural terms" (Lind et al. 1994: 37). The result will be the United States will come apart at the seams and turn on itself in a series of messy internal conflicts. In this scenario, the role of the military is to deal with the internal danger to the Republic before it gets too far out of hand.

Such a trend would, of course, pose a grave danger to civil-military relations in this country. Military operations against domestic enemies would have the likely result of politicizing the armed forces, with incalculable consequences for civil-military relations. It should be emphasized that the line of thinking behind it is, at least at the moment, a minority view within the armed forces. In the immediate aftermath of the September 11 attacks, the U.S. military was extremely cautious about doing more than provide aid to the civil power. At most, the Army National Guard – a force that answered directly to the state governors – might be tasked with central homeland defense functions. The vast bulk of military thinking remained focused on external enemies and on standoff precision strike capabilities.

Yet Fourth Generation views of future war are attractive to many. They fit with widely held Manichaean world views, both in the military and in American society as a whole. They exalt a warrior image that is deeply appealing to at least some sections of the military. Fourth Generation thinkers point to the very real possibility that future conflicts might pit vastly different societies against each other. In such circumstances the U.S. could not count on an enemy being obliging enough to fight the way

Americans have been organized and trained to fight. In the wake of the September 11 attacks, the notion that the United States finds itself embroiled in a "clash of civilizations" with militant Islam as its adversary may well come to seem like a good explanation of the current security environment.

If Fourth Generation views were ever to become dominant in the U.S. military, we would need to worry about an impending crisis in civil-military relations. At their extreme, Fourth Generation views suggest that the military will have to be used in a routine manner to control sources of disorder within the borders of the United States. They suggest that the military play a role in policing domestic cultural "disorder." The salience of homeland defense issues in the wake of the attack on the Pentagon and the World Trade Center has the potential to reinvigorate Fourth Generation theories and similar views.

But Fourth Generation views are also deeply unpopular with the mainstream military for the same reasons that they are attractive to light infantry types. The warrior image exalted by Fourth Generation thinkers is distinct from the "warfighter" image that dominates orthodox military thinking. When the mainstream military talks about "warriors" and "warfighters," what it has in mind are disciplined soldiers in highly structured units. Initiative is rewarded, but the primary values are those that enable a well-oiled machine to run efficiently. The emphasis remains on conventional forces and conventional warfare, not on the sort of irregular warfare and irregular forces suggested by Fourth Generation thinkers. Only certain groups within the military (Special Operations Forces and Marines) have an institutional interest in Fourth Generation warfare: for the mainstream military, it is not the kind of war it wants to fight. Nor is the Fourth Generation image of the American soldier, despite the popularity of Rambo movies, entirely acceptable to the electorate. Although it does not mind the heroics, it does object to the casualties and to the messy, long-term commitments implied by Fourth Generation warfare. For these reasons, this vision of future war is still a minority view within the U.S. military. Although it speaks to anxieties about moral decay and cultural conflict, it is a "down and dirty" form of warfare. And that makes it very unattractive to a military and a public whose heritage is one of increased reliance on technology.

There is, however, a scenario in which Fourth Generation theories of war might rise in popularity. If political elites managed to define the security environment as one dominated by a struggle against international terrorism, then views of war as a clash of civilization (Western) against barbarism (Islamic fundamentalism) would become more attractive. If the struggle against international terrorism were to be defined publicly as a new Cold War, as a protracted struggle requiring massive military mobilization, then we might see a rise in the popularity of views associated with Fourth Generation theory.

Global War on Terrorism?

In the wake of the September 11 attack, the fears about terrorist attacks causing mass casualties in the American homeland, fears expressed by top political leaders as well as by obscure military strategists, seem remarkably prescient. If the United States is now engaged in a global war against terrorism, then – as the Hart-Rudman Commission argued – we are at a moment of redefinition of the global security environment not unlike the years immediately following the end of the Second World War. Just as it took a few years for the contours of the Cold War to become defined, and for the institutional framework of national security to be reconfigured, so today we can expect a brief period of uncertainty while the body politic absorbs the lessons of September 11 and adjusts to the new security environment. If this analogy with the Cold War is correct, then we are on the verge of a new, protracted conflict the end of which is not in sight. The new war will produce major transformations in the structure of military forces, and in how they relate to civilian government. It will lead to broader transformations of politics, both domestic and global. But is this diagnosis correct? Is the United States now committed to a lengthy global war against terrorism? We cannot be certain.

If the security agenda becomes defined as a prolonged, highly militarized struggle against international terrorism and Jihad, then civil-military relations might well become a major issue. War is unpredictable. There are several dangers. The collapse of the Pakistani or Saudi Arabian governments could well prove to be seriously destabilizing on a global scale. Nor is it entirely clear that the strategy of denying terrorists sanctuary by attacking states that support them will prove entirely effective. Although state sponsorship certainly is a great help to terrorists, they can operate in all sorts of environments, even in the United States itself. The exigencies of energy policy, coalition-building, and logistical support have produced an alliance between the United States and two states that financed and supported the Taliban: Saudi Arabia and Pakistan. In this case, the United States may be failing to address more fundamental bases of terrorism, such as support for the religious schools and fundamentalist movements that fuel the fire of politicoreligious martyrdom. To this extent, the United States is currently engaged in an alliance of convenience with countries that might well be its real enemies. Just as in the Cold War, the pragmatics of coalition-building and geopolitics lead to U.S. support for unsavory dictatorships that are both vulnerable to overthrow (the case of Iran in 1979 comes to mind) and are, in the long run, allies of dubious worth.

In November 2001 President George W. Bush suggested that a linkage be made between the global war against terrorism and a serious American effort against regimes deemed to be proliferators of weapons of mass destruction. The ideological mechanism for this was a broadening of the notion of "terrorism." Implicitly it involved a revival of the notion of "rogue states." After several years as the slogan of choice for military strategists, this term was officially declared passé in 2000 and replaced by the more neutral "states of concern." The concept, if perhaps not the phrase, may well be revived. American strategy will then focus on a global campaign to persuade such rogues to mend their ways; failing that, they can expect attacks by the U.S. military. Iraq is, of course, the most likely target, and calls to deal with "unfinished business" were being uttered in the fall of 2001.

The announcement by President Bush in his State of the Union address in January 2002 that the United States was engaged in a war with an "axis of evil" (Iran, Iraq, and North Korea) appeared to cement a rhetorical linkage between the states formerly known as "rogues" and the new global war against terrorism. This rhetoric papered over the real strategic differences between a struggle against a global terrorist movement and concerns about potentially dangerous medium-sized states, and simultaneously provided an ideological connection to the Cold War rhetoric of "evil empire." From "evil empire" to "axis of evil" American strategy seemed to have come full circle.

Yet this sort of global war may not materialize. The Afghan campaign could conceivably be merely one more of the short campaigns that have been fought by the United States since the end of the Cold War. The linkage between the Afghan campaign and a revived pressure on Iraq might prove politically difficult to sustain. Moreover, rather than a general acceptance that the world has now entered a new world war, the situation of strategic indefinition may well continue. Prior to September 11, 2001, Pentagon strategists worried about a wide range of security threats, and these security concerns might well resurface at some point. There is also a concern about a future threat from a near-peer competitor such as China or a revived Russia. The strategic realignment of China and Russia with the U.S. war on terrorism in the aftermath of the September 11 attacks might prove short-lived. At the time of writing (February 2002) it is impossible to say which, if any, of these diverse threat scenarios would emerge as the axis around which a coherent strategic vision is articulated.

Conclusions

What are the implications of changes in the international security environment for state and society in America? We cannot at this stage be entirely sure. There are four central questions: (1) How will America define its enemies? (2) Will the doctrine of standoff precision strike warfare work? (3) What will be the implications for civil-military relations in the United States? (4) What restructuring of the institutions of national security (and of American politics in general) will occur?

The definition of the strategic situation was still in February 2002 a matter for debate. Consensus had not yet crystallized on the idea that the United States was committed to a new world war, a prolonged struggle against "global terrorism," "militant Islam," "rogue states," or whatever. Indeed, the very identity of the enemy was still in some doubt. How these questions would be answered would largely determine the nature of the transformation that might occur in the United States in the first decades of the twenty-first century.

If the United States embarked on a series of military campaigns, would standoff precision strike warfare work? This new American way of war had been designed for the use of expeditionary force by a global hegemon. It aimed to target the enemy leadership and required neither an analysis of the enemy society nor attention to the social origins of conflict. Averse to casualties, this high-tech mode of war saw "boots on the ground" as only the last option. Faced with unconventional warfare and irregular forces, standoff precision strike warfare was likely to encounter, at some point or other, military reverses and generate political frustration.

Although this new American way of war has been dominant in official circles, it has not gone unchallenged. It is possible that the next few years will see substantial amendments to the current doctrinal orthodoxy. Theories deriving from Fourth Generation concepts may be increasingly influential. This could set the stage for a crisis in civil-military relations.

Since Vietnam the military has successfully exercised an agenda-setting power so that some options are no longer available as real choices. It is a foolish arrangement, which gives the military too much discretion in the development of doctrine, forces, and weapons for future operations.

A politicized military that comes to accept a "stab-in-the-back" legend that its troubles are the fault of unwanted civilian meddling is a recipe for a crisis in civil-military relations. As the Holsti data suggest, the politicization has already occurred. The alienation and apartness are there. There is a deep cultural confrontation and incomprehension between the conservative military and the liberal sections of American civilian society. What is missing is the "wretched performance" of the U.S. military in some future conflict (Dunlap 1992–1993: 12). If the United States fails to win decisive victory at little cost, there might well be a reaction that would take the form of an increased distrust by the military of the elected civilian leadership.

The electorate and the civilian political elite have the military they deserve. They have abdicated many issues concerning the conduct of military operations to the uniformed military. Left to its own preferences and its own reading of the political environment, the military has opted for a doctrine that effectively forecloses America's strategic options. Standoff precision strike warfare is at present America's only military response to the challenges of irregular warfare. This cannot be a desirable state of affairs.

Even in the Afghan campaign very few American ground troops were employed. Special Operating Forces played an important role and conducted a number of different kinds of operations. However, Special Operations performed (initially at least) largely as the eyes and ears of the air force, as an adjunct to precision targeting. This means that the military is not simply an instrument of policy but itself set the limits of policy. The point here is not that the military should simply do whatever civilian leaders tell it. This is a civilian version of the Moltkean view of the separation of policy (civilian) from the technical tasks of the military. The only sensible form of civil-military relations is for there to be detailed and realistic discussions between top civilian and military elites. However, the military must remember that it is subordinate to the elected representatives of the people, and that potentially all military operations have policy consequences. What this means in practice is that civilian political elites must be intimately involved in the planning of military operations, and that military commanders must constantly discuss with civilian political leaders the policy implications of intended courses of action. Civilian leaders must be better educated about military operations, in order that they can exercise proper control. Military officers must be better educated politically so that they can discuss the political ramifications of military operations more directly with their civilian bosses. How the obvious dangers of a Clausewitzian approach would be dealt with remains an open question.

The real danger is that military and civilian elites, together with the mass publics, have become complicit in a new style of warfare, fire-and-forget warfare, that may in the long run be both brutal and ineffective. New technology enables U.S. policy makers to play an active role in "disciplining" rogues and barbarians; the promise is that with high-tech weapons the no-casualty constraint can be overcome, making this form of warfare politically palatable to the American electorate. Bashing the barbarians may be well suited to a new imperial mantle for the United States; but that does not make it the wisest way forward, or one that most effectively pursues America's strategic interests. Particularly if the United States finds itself engaged in a protracted war against global terrorism, it will need to reexamine its preference for standoff precision strike warfare in favor of more "political" and unconventional forms of war. The Moltkean separations of peace and war, and of war and politics, will need to be abandoned in favor of a Clausewitzian fusion. While the needs of global conflict may compel these changes, the implications of this for civil-military relations in the United States are fraught with peril. Embarking on a protracted struggle to refashion the current disorderly world into one that is more to Americans' tastes can only increase these dangers.

In the fall 2001 there was no shortage of commentators urging the United States to commit itself to a new world war. If such a crystallization were to occur, then everything would point to a massive transformation of the institutional apparatus of national security, much as occurred in the early years of the Cold War.

If an ideological crystallization of this kind were to happen, if there were to be a new version of the "Long Telegram" or NSC-68 (which some commentators have called for), then we would be well advised to concern ourselves with unanticipated long-term consequences. It will be remembered that the Cold War brought forth concerns about a "garrison state" and a "military-industrial complex." It led to the creation of the National Security Council, the CIA, NATO, and to a redefinition of the Joint Chiefs of Staff and the military apparatus more generally. It also brought forth McCarthyism and the search for spies and traitors. The Cold War produced decades of anxiety and conformism. The crystallization of a new prolonged struggle would almost certainly generate similar preoccupations and efforts at institutional reform. It would lead to a major transformation of both American society and the American state similar in scale to those that accompanied the beginning of the Cold War. The pressures to change domestic policing and the administration of justice could have wide-ranging repercussions. Immigration policy might change. Depending on how internal enemies might come to be defined, all sorts of transformations in American politics are possible. And just as in 1948 no one could accurately foresee how the Cold War would end, embarking on a protracted struggle against "global terrorism" or "militant Islam" would be a leap into the dark.

Notes

1. The widespread dislike of McNamara is worthy of comment. McNamara's goals were unobjectionable: to bring the vast and unwieldy Pentagon bureaucracy under civilian control and to ensure that decisions about defense acquisition were made rationally. The evaluation and planning techniques he brought with him from the Ford Motor Company were, in principle, quite appropriate. The general approach of unemotional, technical rationality, however, ran against the deeply held value orientations of the warrior ethos and challenged the exclusive claim to professional knowledge put forward by the military. For their part, civilian publics vented much of their anger and frustration over the course of the Vietnam War on McNamara, often unjustly.
2. Moltke, chief of staff of the German Imperial Army, believed that once war started, the civilian leaders of the state should step aside and allow the military to conduct the war without interference. See Hughes 1993 for a discussion of Moltke's views.
3. Of course, Clausewitz also argues that military operations have a logic of their own (Clausewitz 1976). I do not believe this contradicts the notion that war is an essentially political act.
4. It cannot be said that Clausewitz ever satisfactorily solved this tension. He believed that the integration of politics and military issues worked best when the head of state was also the key military strategist and decision maker. But

in modern complex states, and particularly so in democracies, this is unlikely. The resolution of the tension is not to be found in organizational reshaping, important though that might be, but in the acceptance on the part of both military and civilian decision makers that there is no clearcut boundary between "politics" and "military operations."

5. Again, Clausewitz was unable to resolve this tension. On the one hand he constantly stressed the uncertainties involved in war; on the other hand, he made it clear that the first duty of a statesman when embarking on war was to determine the nature of the war and act accordingly. Foresight is necessary, but it cannot rule out unanticipated events.

6. A minority current within the military argues for the need to prepare now to respond to the possible reemergence of a peer competitor (or near-peer) in the next twenty years or so. This would mean preparation for a quite different kind of war. For the present, the presumed enemy is a medium-sized "rogue" state such as Iraq or North Korea.

7. Whether such assumptions are correct or not is not the central issue. As long as policy makers believe the assumptions to be correct, they will act on that basis.

8. Neither of the terms, "terrorist" and "weapons of mass destruction," is entirely satisfactory, and they are used here only because of their familiarity. "Terrorist" implies something about the intentions of the perpetrator: to strike terror into his or her victims. Whether this is always the intent when there is a mass casualty attack on civilians is open to question. Similarly, "weapons of mass destruction" suggests that it is something inherent in the weapon itself that is of concern. Because civilian airliners can be used to kill large numbers of people, a focus on the "weapons" is misplaced.

9. Holsti's military sample consists of officers undertaking a year of study at the National War College. These officers are lieutenant colonels or colonels (or their navy equivalents) and have been tapped as likely to do well in their careers. (The National War College is more prestigious than the other service war colleges.) My judgment is that Holsti is correct in designating his sample as "elite," although it might be strictly more accurate to view the sample as a potential or future elite.

10. This is not a new concern. Janowitz (1960) discusses it.

11. In light of the numerous cases of sexual "misconduct" in the military, this is remarkable and worthy of reflection.

12. The standard of housing on military bases often leaves much to be desired, and wages and benefits for many enlisted personnel are so low that families rely on food stamps. Nevertheless, children of military families do better at school than one would expect from a comparable group, largely, one imagines, because of the tightness of community and family structures.

13. Of course, there have been other moments when moral politics has been important. And there is a sense in which all politics is "moral." Nevertheless, my view is that the 1980s saw, in the sex, gender, and reproduction debates, an important change in American politics.

14. The role of new military technologies in peace operations continues to be debated. The air force and navy argue that air power can play an effective role in peace operations and might, in at least some circumstances, obviate the need for boots on the ground.

15. The army occupies a difficult, intermediate position. It, too, sees itself as an expeditionary force, but because it is committed to heavy mechanized and armored forces, it requires a long buildup time before it is ready to deliver the knockout punch. This puts it at a major disadvantage vis-à-vis the other services in the debates about future war.
16. And/or on allies and third parties.
17. The *Marine Corps Gazette*, November 2001, reflecting on the meaning of the September 11 attack on the World Trade Center and the Pentagon, saw fit to reprint these articles.

References

Albright, Madeline. 1998. *New York Times*, August 21.

Allison, Graham. 1971. *Essence of Decision*. New York: HarperCollins.

Avant, Deborah. 1994. *Political Institutions and Military Change*. Ithaca: Cornell University Press.

Barber, Benjamin. 1995. *Jihad vs. McWorld*. New York: Times Books.

Baudrillard, Jean. 1995. *The Gulf War Did Not Take Place*. Bloomington: Indiana University Press.

Bowden, Mark. 1999. *Black Hawk Down*. New York: Penguin Books.

Bunker, Robert. 1994. "The Transition to Fourth Epoch War," *Marine Corps Gazette* 78, 9: 20–32.

Burk, James. 1999. "Public Support for Peacekeeping in Lebanon and Somalia: Assessing the Casualties Hypothesis," *Political Science Quarterly* 114, 1: 53–78.

Clark, Wesley. 2001. *Waging Modern War*. New York: Perseus Books.

Clausewitz, Carl. [1832] 1976. *On War*. Princeton: Princeton University Press.

Center for Strategic and International Studies (CSIS). 2000. *American Military Culture in the Twenty-First Century*. Washington, D.C.

Daggett, S., and N. Serafino. 1995. "The Use of Force: Key Statements by Weinberger, Shultz, Aspin, Bush, Powell, Albright, and Perry," *CRS Report for Congress*, December, no. 94–805F, 1–55.

Dowd, James. 2001. "Connected to Society: The Political Beliefs of U.S. Army Generals," *Armed Forces and Society* 27, 3: 343–372.

Duncan, Gene. 1990. *Clint McQuade USMC: The New Beginning*. Blountstown, Fl.: Privately published.

Dunlap, Charles. 1992–1993. "The Origins of the American Military Coup of 2012," *Parameters* 22: 2–20.

Feaver, Peter. 2000. "The Public's Expectations of National Security," in Max Manwaring ed., . . . *To Insure Domestic Tranquility, Provide for the Common Defense* . . . , 63–74. Carlisle, Pa.: Strategic Studies Institute.

Gronke, Paul, and Peter Feaver. 2001. "Uncertain Confidence: Civilian and Military Attitudes about Civil-Military Relations," in Peter Feaver and Richard Kohn, eds., *Soldiers and Civilians: The Civil-Military Gap and American National Security*, 129–161. Cambridge, Mass.: MIT Press.

Halberstam, David. 2001. *War in a Time of Peace*. New York: Scribner.

Holsti, Ole R. 1998–1999. "A Widening Gap between the U.S. Military and Civilian Society? Some Evidence, 1976–1996," *International Security* 23, 3: 5–42.

2001. "Of Chasms and Convergences: Attitudes and Beliefs of Civilians and Military Elites at the Start of a New Millenium," in Peter Feaver and Richard Kohn, eds., *Soldiers and Civilians: The Civil-Military Gap and American National Security*, 15–99. Cambridge, Mass.: MIT Press.

Hughes, Daniel, ed. 1993. *Moltke on the Art of War: Selected Writings*. Novato, Calif.: Presidio Press.

Huntington, Samuel. 1957. *The Soldier and the State*. Cambridge, Mass.: Harvard University Press.

1996. *The Clash of Civilizations and the Remaking of World Order*. New York: Simon and Schuster.

Janowitz, Morris. 1960. *The Professional Soldier*. New York: Free Press.

Johnson, David E. 1997. "Modern U.S. Civil-Military Relations: Wielding the Terrible Swift Sword," *McNair Paper*, no. 57, July, 1–106.

Kaplan, Robert. 1996. *The Ends of the Earth*. New York: Random House.

Krepinevich, Andrew. 1986. *The Army and Vietnam*. Baltimore: Johns Hopkins University Press.

Krulak, Charles. 1997. "Draft Remarks for the National Press Club." October 10. Washington, D.C.

Lind, William, et al. 1989. "The Changing Face of War: Into the Fourth Generation," *Marine Corps Gazette* 73, 10: 22–26.

1994. "Fourth Generation Warfare: Another Look," *Marine Corps Gazette* 78, 12: 34–37.

Loveland, Anne C. 1996. *American Evangelicals and the U.S. Military, 1942–1993*. Baton Rouge: Louisiana State University Press.

Luttwak, Edward. 1995. "Toward Post-Heroic Warfare," *Foreign Affairs* 74, 3: 109–122.

McMaster, H. R. 1997. *Dereliction of Duty: Lyndon Johnson, Robert McNamara, the Joint Chiefs of Staff, and the Lies that Led to Vietnam*. New York: Harper Collins.

Mueller, John. 1973. *War, Presidents and Public Opinion*. New York: John Wiley.

National Defense Panel. 1997. *Transforming Defense: National Security in the 21st Century*. Arlington, Va.

Ricks, Thomas. 1997a. *Making the Corps*. New York: Scribner.

1997b. "The Widening Gap between the Military and Society." *Atlantic Monthly*, July, 66–78.

Stepan, Alfred. 1971. *The Military in Politics: Changing Patterns in Brazil*. Princeton: Princeton University Press.

Summers, Harry. 1982. *On Strategy: A Critical Analysis of the Vietnam War*. Novato, Calif.: Presidio Press.

U.S. Army War College. 1998. "Challenging the United States Symmetrically and Asymmetrically: Can America be Defeated?" Carlisle, Pa.

U.S. Commission on National Security/21st Century. 1999. *New World Coming*. Washington, D.C.

van Creveld, Martin. 1991. *The Transformation of War*. New York: Free Press.

CONCLUSION

15

Armed Forces, Coercive Monopolies, and Changing Patterns of State Formation and Violence

Anthony W. Pereira

Violence and coercion have always been key elements in human affairs, but their specific forms and the meanings attached to them have changed constantly and are changing still. In particular, societies have always contested the distinction between "legitimate," state-sanctioned violence and coercion and its "illegitimate" counterparts, between war and peace and war-making and policing, between military and civilian, between insurrection or political violence and crime, and between legal and illegal violence, and have drawn the boundaries between these categories differently at different times. In making sense of all these distinctions, it might seem at first that little of general value can be said, except that coercion and violence form part of the interactive networks that hold large-scale societies together, as well as drive them apart (sometimes irrevocably), and that the capacity to assemble and deploy armed forces is an essential attribute of the state, without which it disappears.

However, existing models of state formation offer more than this. The classic works of Otto Hintze and Max Weber, as well as the work of contemporary scholars such as Michael Mann and Charles Tilly, offer a highly suggestive analysis of European state formation, a "stylized fact" that consists of the following assertions. First, "war made the state and the state made war" – states survived, defeated other states and incorporated their territory, grew and prospered by mobilizing the resources, weaponry, and men to fight wars. The institutional apparatus of the modern state grew out of this war-making function, as cycles of extraction and coercion succeeded one another. Second, in order to mobilize the resources and men for war, the rulers of states had to offer inducements to subjects who gradually acquired the rights of modern citizenship, including those of equality before the law, universal suffrage, and parliamentary representation, as well as (in some cases) universal education and the social rights of the welfare state. Third, in developing its "warfighting" capacity, the state gradually developed a near monopoly on legitimate violence, disarming its civilian population and gradually accumulating an overwhelming superiority of force vis-à-vis social actors. Fourth, military power was gradually "caged" by civilian institutions, and the state's coercive forces came to be divided between specialists in fighting external wars (the military) and uniformed but civilian forces responsible for domestic order (the police).

The chapters in this volume suggest that such a model of state formation is useful but incomplete. Their revisionist histories show that as an explanation of the past, the model needs to be questioned, refined, and even refuted in places. They also suggest that it is not universally applicable in all its details, nor can the trajectory it describes simply be extrapolated into the future, because contemporary changes in the international political economy and the use of force may be making some of its assumptions obsolete. In particular, the work of this volume's authors suggests and supports the following propositions, usually explicitly, and sometimes implicitly. Where appropriate, I have indicated the authors who make these points in parentheses, without trying to be exhaustive:

1. The near monopoly of legitimate coercion attained by northwestern European states in the nineteenth century was never attained by many states in "developing" countries (Batalas, Reno, Romero) or in other "developed" countries such as the United States (Browne, Campbell).
2. The complexity of the state's efforts to monopolize coercive force has been underappreciated. Such near monopolies as have been achieved are the result of the activities of various armed forces, some of them "alternative" or irregular, whose coordination has been difficult and which variously compete, cooperate, clash over jurisdictions, and often became part of political conflicts between local and national forces, regional powers, class organizations, ethnic groups, and other political actors. On closer inspection, state capacity to centralize coercive control appears to be the result of intricate, contingent, inter- and intrainstitutional political bargains that are frequently renegotiated (Zack, Kalmanowiecki, Raffin).
3. The state's attainment of a near monopoly of legitimate force is not permanent. Instead, it is temporary and reversible. The end of the Cold War, economic globalization, and the spread of cheap, light weapons are making the state's monopoly on legitimate violence increasingly tenuous, most dramatically in the Middle East, Central Asia, and Africa, but everywhere else, even in northwestern Europe itself.
4. The neat division between specialists in external warfare (the military) and internal control (the police) that characterized much of northwestern Europe did not occur in many countries outside this region, where militaries have substantial internal roles and often control police forces (Kalmanowiecki). Such overlapping functions

can also be seen in some northwestern European countries such as France, where for many years the Gendarmerie was controlled by the military (Zack).

5. The evolution of military forces in northwestern Europe from armies based on personal service, to contractor-supplied mercenary forces, to massive, conscript-based standing armies financed internally by the state (as described by Charles Tilly in this volume) did not occur everywhere. In many countries today, members of armed forces who are personally loyal to their leaders (often on the basis of kinship, ethnicity, religion, or some other tie), or who have been privately contracted as mercenaries, security specialists, or paramilitary forces are important wielders of coercion within their territories. Most wars since World War II have involved irregular forces – armed forces that have not been controlled by a centralized, national state, whether they are called guerrillas, bandits, terrorists, or something else (Batalas, Reno, Romero) – on at least one side.

6. While mobilizing people for war and making them soldiers has been a major challenge for states, so has demobilizing those soldiers after war, and retaining their political loyalty once they become veterans. The politics of military demobilization have had a major impact on state formation and, in particular, the creation of welfare institutions in modern states (Bensel, Campbell, Browne).

7. In northwestern Europe, war had an impact on the institutional configuration of states, establishing the revenue-collecting and coercion-wielding bureaucracies that constitute the state's "spine," as well as inducing the creation of citizenship rights that form the basis of modern democracy. Outside of northwestern Europe, while similar causal mechanisms seem to have been at work, less-intense war-making resulted in much smaller levels of taxation and conscription, creating states that were weaker, less able to monopolize the means of coercion and reorganize society, and provided less certain and less universal guarantees of citizenship rights (Batalas, Centeno, Reno).

8. Different types of capitalist organization produce different types of armies and, in turn, important features of actually existing capitalisms can be traced back to different kinds of war mobilization (Bensel, Ikegami). While capital is obviously essential for war, war-making also affects patterns of economic organization and the ideologies justifying them, especially as those concern distributive justice and the nature of the "national interest" and the nation.

9. Military service, and participation in organized violence and coercion in general, has traditionally been seen as an essentially, even quintessentially masculine activity (Raffin). However, the contemporary deployment of armed forces may, to some extent, be breaking down traditional gender roles, and increasingly involving women

in combat roles. This may be particularly true of the long-distance, high-technology, precision-bombing warfare developed by the armed forces of the United States, which are less reliant on a macho "warrior mentality" than it is on the techniques of bureaucratic management and the manipulation of sophisticated communications equipment, aircraft, bombs, and missiles (Roxborough).

10. Military "professionalism," long considered to be a guarantee of civilian control over militaries, is based on an artificial distinction between "military" and "political" considerations that obfuscates rather than clarifies the military's political role. In fact, highly "professional" militaries, under certain circumstances, may attempt coups d'etat and make similar interventions in politics, as well as forbid certain strategic options in ways that diminish genuine civilian control (Browne, Roxborough).

These points are complicated responses to large bodies of literature, and each deserves the more detailed attentions the authors in this volume have devoted to them. Each challenges, clarifies, or extends some element of the standard model of the role of armed forces in state formation derived from the historical experience of northwest Europe. This exercise is valuable because unreflective and indiscriminate use of the model has created two problems for the understanding of contemporary patterns of coercion and violence. First, there may be a false, teleological sense of security among scholars about the relative ease, inevitability and unilinearity with which the state's near monopolization of coercion was achieved in northwestern Europe (and to a lesser extent, the United States). Closer inspection of the historical record reveals the many failures, false starts, and confusions surrounding the process; state managers' frequent reliance on alternative, irregular, hard-to-control grass-roots wielders of violence to impose their vision of order; and the often large and oscillating "gray area" between legal and illegal, legitimate and illegitimate uses of force, as well as the groups (usually men) using such force.

Second, recent history allows us to perceive how exceptional and perhaps temporary the northwestern European experience is. In many developing countries, irregular armed forces are as or even more important than uniformed, state-financed soldiers and policemen using standard equipment and subject to centralized command and control. Around the world, political outcomes have been shaped by these irregular forces, such as guerrillas in Chiapas (Mexico), Colombia, Sri Lanka, Afghanistan, and many countries in Africa; death squads in Central America; vigilante groups, private security guards, and organized criminals in violent megacities such as Moscow, Mexico City, São Paulo, and Johannesburg; separatist forces in Chechnya in Russia, Kashmir in India, and Kosovo in Yugoslavia; Israeli settler organizations on the West Bank; paramilitary units, whether loyalist or irredentist, with more or less contact with official militaries, in northern Ireland, East Timor, and Colombia; heavily armed narcotraffickers in Russia, Eastern Europe, the Middle East, East Asia, and Latin America; terrorist factions of all creeds and identities, size and lethality. The relationship of these forces to states is highly variable, while others, such as special police-military intelligence, assault, antikidnapping, bodyguard, or SWAT units, *are* merely more specialized or secretive branches of larger, more public armed forces of the state. Although the idiosyncrasies of these armed forces are almost infinite, what their existence suggests is that the standard, teleological trajectory of state centralization of the means of violence is not being repeated in "developing" countries nor is its presumed end point being maintained. The armed forces of the present in much of the world look more like the Europe of the Middle Ages than they do of Europe in the nineteenth century. If the future comes to resemble the past, that will probably be the distant, rather than the recent past, in that states will increasingly compete with nonstate armed forces for the political power that can be obtained from the threat or use of violence.

New and Old War

In his provocative book *On Future War* (1991) Martin van Creveld suggests that we may be witnessing the end of an era of "Clausewitzian" warfare, based on the distinction between government, army, and people. In an apocalyptic final chapter and postscript, van Creveld argues that "Clausewitzian" war involved large standing armies controlled in a centralized fashion by national states, which fought other states for territory in clearly demarcated battlefields. This kind of war solidified dichotomies that came to be taken for granted, such as military-civilian and combatant-noncombatant. However, in recent years these dichotomies have been undermined, the nature of war has been changing, and the strategic doctrines developed by Clausewitz and his contemporaries may soon become as obsolete as the bow and arrow.

After examining the approximately 160 armed conflicts in the world from 1945 to 1990,[1] van Creveld characterizes roughly three-quarters of them as "low intensity conflicts." That is, they have taken place largely in "developing" countries; have not relied mainly on high-technology weapons cherished by militaries of the richest countries; and, most important, rarely involve regular armies on both sides, instead often pitting a regular army against guerrillas, terrorists, and even civilians (van Creveld 1991: 20). Furthermore, in comparing the performance of regular armies against irregular ones, van Creveld arrives at the conclusion that "modern" armies are relatively ineffectual; in his words, "modern regular forces are all but useless for fighting what is fast becoming the dominant form of war in our age" (van Creveld 1991: 29).[2]

Recent changes in global economics may reinforce the tendencies identified by van Creveld. Analysts of economic "globalization" – the "growing
relative weight of transactions and organizational connections that cross
national boundaries" (Evans 1997: 65) – argue that it has reduced the
potential economic gain from the seizure of territory, further diminishing
the importance of traditional, "Clausewitzian" armed forces. As one author
puts it, "access to capital and technology depends on strategic alliances with
those who control global production networks, rather than on the control
of any piece of territory" (Evans 1997: 66). Or, in Susan Strange's words,
"the nature of the competition between states has fundamentally changed
. . . in the past states competed for control over territory and the wealth-
creating resources within territories, whether natural or man-created. Now
they are increasingly competing for market shares in the world economy"
(Strange 1995: 55). Furthermore, "globalization" has reduced transportation and communications costs, accelerating the transnational movement of
people, information, and goods, and making the selective application of
lethal violence by small groups easier to administer. To the extent that this
shift has occurred, the potential advantages of conventional, large-scale
armed forces with heavy weaponry have diminished, or at least been altered.

If, for van Creveld, "old" war will be replaced by the "new," what will
the new look like? He answers, in effect, that the new form of warfare is
already here. This new form is pervasive but of low intensity. Large set-
piece conflicts between uniformed armies on battlefields – the hallmarks of
the "Clausewitzian" era – are likely to be increasingly replaced by shadowy,
intermittent confrontations between a bewildering array of small, well-
equipped, mobile armed forces, some organized by states and some not.
States will lose any ability to claim a monopoly of violence, due to the
pervasiveness of powerful, light, cheap arms and sophisticated networks of
communication between combatants and their supporters. The resulting
wide variety of armed forces, many held together by ties of ethnicity, religion, language, or other types of what Charles Tilly in this volume calls
"embedded" identities, will confront one another in everyday settings: fields
and schools, villages and barracks, markets and apartment buildings, airports and roads. The separation between battlefields and ordinary life, war
and peace will break down. Society as a whole will be increasingly organized to maximize "security," with barriers and checkpoints where guards
force individuals to produce identification, armed defenders patrol the
perimeters of important facilities, and preparation for an outbreak of conflict is permanent. If the possibility of what Miguel Centeno in this volume
calls "total" war will diminish, "everyday" coercion and conflict that affects
everyone – civilian and military, women and children as well as men – will
become commonplace. The line between armed insurrection and crime,
between warfare and policing, will disappear. The worst fear of the late
twentieth century – nuclear Armageddon triggered by superpower con-

frontation – will be replaced by a new fear of armed anarchy, as coercive power is deconcentrated and states' attempts to provide "security" to their citizens look increasingly tenuous.

Van Creveld's hypothesis seems prophetic. Published ten years before the September 11, 2001, terrorist attacks in the United States, and the subsequent "war on terrorism" launched by the U.S. government, his vision has at least been partially realized in the contemporary world. However, van Creveld may have been too quick to dismiss the value of conventional armed forces. Ian Roxborough, in Chapter 14 in this book, suggests several reasons why traditional war-making, involving large-scale, sophisticated weaponry controlled by states, will continue to be politically expedient and militarily effective under certain circumstances, even if the importance of irregular, nonstate armed forces in warfare is increasing. If these reasons are accepted, one is forced to question some of van Creveld's assumptions, and the dichotomy upon which his book is based. To what extent was the Clausewitzian paradigm ever really dominant? Haven't irregular armed forces always been a feature of war-making? Perhaps even at the height of the "Clausewitzian" era in Europe, the armed forces that could fight wars according to Clausewitz's dictums were the exceptions rather than the rule, and could be effectively challenged by irregular armies such as the Cuban guerrillas who fought the Spanish in the Cuban Ten Years War (1868–1878) or the Boers who fought the British in South Africa in the First Boer War (1880–1881).[3] And aren't regular armed forces still useful? The leaders of the United States, for example, have continued to use conventional forces (the air force, and to a lesser extent, the navy) to bomb their adversaries. In the United Nations operation against Iraq in Operation Desert Storm in 1991, in the NATO war against Yugoslavia in 1999, and in the war against the Taliban and AI Qaeda in Afghanistan in 2001–2002, the U.S. government seems to have concluded that such bombing campaigns work and should be tried again.

These wars have not been thoroughly Clausewitzian. For example, they have involved a minimal role for the U.S. Army's "ground troops." They have also involved the crucial deployment of irregular forces incited and supported by the U.S. – Kurdish resistance fighters in Iraq during Desert Storm, the KLA in Kosovo during the war against Yugoslavia, and Northern Alliance fighters and various Pashtun militias in Afghanistan. But they are also not exactly the kind of war-making that van Creveld has in mind when he describes "future war."[4] They are perhaps best described as conflicts involving a combination of conventional and irregular methods and forces, or a hybrid of what van Creveld identifies as old and new wars. The U.S. war in Afghanistan in 2001–2002 is perhaps the best illustration of this combination. The United States used sophisticated technology to conduct its bombing, including a higher percentage of "smart" or precision-guided bombs than were used in the Gulf War, and a variety of manned

and unmanned aircraft. Special forces were deployed on the ground to identify targets and guide the bombing. All of these technologies and personnel
were coordinated in a centralized fashion by the U.S. military. Yet the bulk
of the fighting was done by ethnically based irregular forces commanded
by warlords who were not in control of a state, and the battles tended to
be small-scale encounters among and around civilians in villages and towns.

It therefore seems more plausible that twenty-first century war, at least
so far, has reconfigured elements of conventional and irregular warfare,
rather then moved decisively from one to the other. But if it fails to convince wholly, van Creveld's argument alerts us to the possibility, reinforced
by the chapters in this book, that we need to rethink the connection between
new and old wars, society and armed forces, policing and war-making, civilian and military, law and force. In particular, it suggests that what war is
lies partly in the eye of the beholder, and that what armed forces do goes
well beyond most people's definition of war-making.[5]

The Varieties of Coercive Experience

It is a central contention of this volume that armed forces do much more
than make war. Furthermore, the various activities of armed forces that do
not include war have often had important consequences for the institutional
configuration of states, and the nature of state-society relations more generally. These activities include policing, civic and moral education, "nation-
building," legislating, interpreting and enforcing law, economic planning
and development, and spying and surveillance. Regular as well as "alternative" armed forces have engaged in them.

It would be inappropriate here to attempt an exhaustive review of such
activities. What might be useful, on the other hand, is to mention one aspect
of armed forces that tends to be neglected, and that is the relationship of
organized violence to the law. Whether internationally through the laws
of war, or domestically through systems of military justice, armed forces
have often been concerned that their actions conform to some prevailing,
accepted notions of legality. Systems of military justice, in particular, have
become objects of conflict in the modern world, as some civilians seek to
institutionally "cage" military power and reduce the power and prerogatives of military officers, while others utilize military justice to deal with
political enemies. U.S. President Bush's November 13, 2001, emergency
order creating special military tribunals to try noncitizens accused of terrorism is a striking example of the latter, one whose constitutionality and
consistency with U.S. legal traditions was questioned. Similarly, the U.S.
military's opposition to the creation of an International Criminal Court,
and the ambiguous legal status of detainees captured in Afghanistan and
held by the U.S. military in 2002, point to the significance of the legal
dimension in the application of coercion.

However, this volume's chapters do not cover this topic. Instead, we merely point to the military's role in judicial systems; the views of military leaders of the proper conduct of war and the armed forces' rightful place in domestic politics and the allocation of internal military missions; and the connection or disjunction between views of citizenship developed in society and those that become prevalent within the (sometimes rather insulated) corporate environment of armed forces as all being worthy of future research. They are vitally important in ongoing struggles to achieve peace, democratize state-society relations, and make citizenship rights a living reality for the millions of people who do not enjoy them in the modern world (Foweraker and Landman 1997). Some work in this direction has been done (see Loveman 1999 and Schirmer 1998), but this is just the beginning of what could become an expanding research agenda.

Despite this lacuna, the contributors to this volume do much to expand our awareness of the rich variety in the origins, activities, and impacts of armed forces and, in particular, their influence on state formation. In addition to the general propositions summarized earlier, the chapters in this volume make important contributions to our understanding of the concrete political influence of armed forces at specific historical moments. Taken together, these insights can contribute to the development of a new perspective on the role of armed forces in state formation.

Charles Tilly calls for just such an enterprise in his sweeping survey of the role of armed forces in the creation of distinctive political regimes in Europe since 1650. He distinguishes between coercion-intensive paths of state formation, in which large landowners retained control over armies recruited from a dependent peasantry, and capital-intensive paths, in which sovereigns borrowed from urban merchants to pay for mercenary and then conscripted armies. He argues that state capacity has generally been higher at intermediate levels of coercion, capital, and what he calls connection (linkages between social actors), rather than in states with large amounts of one without the others. Tilly points out the mutually constitutive nature of coercive force and state-making – the organization of coercion is "a feature of regimes but also part of each regime's immediate environment."

Miguel Centeno's contribution follows directly from Tilly's efforts, by applying Tilly's European model to the states of Latin America. While Centeno does find similar causal mechanisms at work in both regions, he concludes that the model does not apply in toto to Latin America, due to the limited nature of wars in that region. Centeno contrasts European "total wars" of the nineteenth and twentieth centuries (characterized by widespread civilian and military mobilization for the war effort, heavy propaganda and ideological indoctrination by the state, and huge amounts of death and destruction) to the more limited wars in Latin America in the same period. Limited wars were preferred by Latin American elites, who feared the social consequences of full-scale mobilization of their subaltern populations. Centeno argues that this preference for limited wars is self-perpetuating, because once it was entrenched, Latin American states seemed to lack the "cultural repertoires" (including a unifying ideology and practices and symbols evoking past national sacrifices and honor) for mass mobilization and total wars. He also implicitly suggests that there might be a connection between patterns of war-making and the state's ability to concentrate coercive force. Where wars have been limited, as in Latin America, states have generally not challenged the wide dispersion of the means of violence within society. Total wars, on the other hand, furnish the state with at least the possibility of acquiring a much greater concentration of coercive force, and such near monopolies were attained by many European states.

Centeno's piece seems to suggest a paradox: if (in U.S. Civil War General Sherman's words) "war is hell," less war is not necessarily heaven. Total war in Europe culminated in regimes characterized by universal citizenship, democracy, and extensive welfare provisions, whereas limited war in Latin America led to intermittently authoritarian and inegalitarian regimes in which citizenship rights and welfare provision were only partially and tenuously granted by the state. The message here seems to be that total war, while devastating in its immediate consequences (think of the "lost generation" in Europe after World War I), may have had considerable positive political effects compared with more limited wars. In matters of war, more may be better for citizenship than less. Such a notion disturbs conventional wisdom about democracy, which values democratic regimes in part because they can peacefully resolve conflicts and do not entail the violence and repression of authoritarianism. If this is true, but democracy has historically been built in the aftermath of incredibly violent total wars, then democracy's claim to moral superiority over authoritarianism would seem to be undermined.[6]

Alec Campbell pursues a different question in his chapter, about how the managers of states confront the dilemma of demobilizing large armies after war's end, and dealing with the inherent danger to political leaders and the dominant class posed by potentially disgruntled veterans. (Such a danger arose often in the Roman Empire, as is shown in Plutarch's *Lives*.) Campbell sees this dilemma not in purely military terms but as one involving essential questions about the distribution of resources in the political economy and class relations. Whereas veterans of losing armies after World War I were major actors in the creation of revolution and fascism in Russia, Italy, and Germany, veterans in Britain, France, and the United States generally supported the status quo, in part because they were "bought off" with substantial welfare benefits that were nowhere more abundant than in the United States. The American Legion in the United States eventually included one of every four men who served in World War I, and its activity contributed to the creation of a distinctive veterans-based welfare state in the United States, one that was less universalistic than its European counterparts.

Like Campbell, Eiko Ikegami assesses the impact of armed forces on political economy, in this case in post–World War II Japan. Ikegami argues that Japan's distinctive capitalism in this period, characterized by an emphasis on egalitarianism and distributive justice, does not spring from inherent attributes of Japanese society but instead can be traced back to specific compromises made between rulers and ruled during mobilization for war, beginning in the 1930s, as well as reforms carried out during the U.S. occupation of Japan after the war. Ikegami is right to conclude that the "Japanese way" of capitalism is now being dismantled by the pressures of economic globalization, and that Japan is moving closer to a U.S.-style liberalism in which differences in rewards for economic "winners" and "losers" are widening and solidaristic claims to entitlements such as job security and basic welfare are being marginalized.

While Japanese capitalism after World War II was distinctive, so was the pacifism of its state, a legacy of the U.S. occupation. It will be interesting to observe whether or not this pacifism, like the "Japanese way" of capitalism, is eroded by the pressures of the modern world. Much was made of the fact that in 1993, Japanese troops were involved overseas for the first time since World War II, when they went as peace-keepers for the United Nations operation in Cambodia (UNTAC). Will Japanese forces be deployed overseas again in post–Cold War Asia?

Achilles Batalas shifts our attention to another era and region when he shows how the mid-nineteenth-century Greek state represents the inverse of what Charles Tilly calls "racketeering." Instead of the state operating a "protection racket," with its armed forces as the "muscle", it became a client rather than a supplier of protection. Unable to build their own armed forces directly, Greek leaders paid brigands to fight the forces of the Ottoman Empire and pursue the "Great Idea" of Greek independence. The Ottomans did much the same thing themselves, creating a confusing situation in the hills and mountains of what is now Greece, in which many armed "captains" switched sides more than once, fighting for the Greeks, then the Ottomans, and (perhaps always) for themselves, using their control over armed men to extract concessions from travelers, villagers, and politicians needing their "protection."[7] Because of its long reliance on such armed forces, the Greek state developed a particularly patrimonial style of rule.

Mauricio Romero describes a contemporary reality that is perhaps even more complicated and fluid than that of mid-nineteenth century Greece. The de facto partition of Colombia between the regular armed forces, nominally leftist guerrillas (principally the FARC and the ELN), and paramilitary units under the umbrella of the AUC (Autodefensas Unidas de Colombia) is a relatively extreme example of a state's loss of monopolistic control over coercion. Over 1 million people have been internally displaced as a result of fighting between these forces, and Colombia has one of the highest homicide rates, and the highest kidnapping rate, in the world. The ambiguous relationship between the paramilitaries and the armed forces was revealed in the peace negotiations of 1998–1999, when the FARC demanded – and the government consented to – the removal of several high-ranking army officers suspected of having close ties to the paramilitaries.

Romero argues that the Colombian conflict cannot be explained primarily in ethnic or religious terms, unlike many other conflicts around the world, nor can it be reduced to a purely class conflict. Instead, Romero argues that regional elites develop strong claims to the right to self-defense from guerrilla groups, claims that are reinforced by continued failures on the part of the national state to provide security and protection to those elites. Whatever the initial origins of this multiparty conflict, Colombia has witnessed a spiraling escalation of violence, in which increased guerrilla, paramilitary, and narcotrafficker activity further undermines state efforts to secure a coercive monopoly, and society drifts toward a Hobbesian war of "each against all," in which kidnapping and homicide become commonplace. Judges are assassinated, the court system breaks down, and the state's legal apparatus becomes almost irrelevant to the conflict. Peace negotiations may achieve a truce, but enduring peace may take a long time, due to the multiplicity of relatively autonomous armed forces in the country, and the creation of regional traditions of self-defense that go back decades, including "La Violencia" of the 1950s. Furthermore, the implementation of the U.S.-funded "Plan Colombia" in 2001 promises to escalate, rather than reduce, the level of violence in the country.

However, even the bloodiest civil wars do eventually end, as Richard Bensel's chapter on the United States reminds us. When they do, the war tends to leave a strong imprint on subsequent politics. If for Clausewitz, war was "politics by other means," then peacetime politics in the post–Civil War United States was "war by other means." As Bensel writes, "the two major parties [the Republicans and Democrats] resembled nothing so much as encampments of the Civil War armies themselves." Two million soldiers survived the war, and the two parties elected veterans to Congress in great numbers. The meaning of the election of a veteran was not symmetrical; in the defeated South, it tended to reflect a separatist defiance of northern hegemony, or at least regional pride and loyalty; in the North, Bensel argues, it had more to do with claims on federal largesse, specifically, the payment of veterans' benefits. The Democratic Party, carefully trying to build support on a national basis, tended not to place its Confederate veterans in key committees in the House of Representatives, for fear of alienating public opinion in the North. Perhaps in these acts of self-limitation, the seeds of a new political consensus in which the wounds of war were made relatively unimportant – something that was probably not achieved until Roosevelt's New Deal – were planted.

Laura Kalmanowiecki shifts the focus of the volume to another political system marked by deep divisions and the legacy of violence – Argentina between 1880 and 1945. Consistent with the claims of this volume, Kalmanowiecki includes the police in her examination of armed forces and, specifically, the tensions, connections, and cooperation between the police and the military. She argues that the Argentine police's adoption of a political role in this period, in which they monitored the statements and activities of opponents of the government, and the centralization of many police functions at the national level, created the institutional structure and orientation that was later used to such deadly repressive effect in the "dirty war" of the late 1970s.

Picking up a theme begun by Alec Campbell, Susan Browne confirms the importance of demobilization to state formation in the eighteenth-century United States. She suggests that Samuel P. Huntington's influential argument in *The Soldier and the State* (1959) that the "professionalization" of armed forces makes them more willing to submit to civilian political control is historically contingent and sometimes misleading. In her case, it was actually the officers and veterans of the Continental Army, the most "professional" of the soldiers who fought in the war for independence (rather than non-professional, local militias) who most threatened civilian control after the war's end. Focusing on Shays's Rebellion (1786–1787) in Massachusetts, she shows how veterans' grievances about the losses they incurred while fighting and the draconian manner in which local political elites enforced the veterans' debt obligations led to the uprising. Advocates of a strong national state and a professional standing army then seized upon Shays's Rebellion, using it to argue against (and eventually defeat) advocates of states' rights and an army composed of republican citizen-soldiers. Once again, the aftermath of war and arguments surrounding demobilization, and not just war-making itself, decisively influenced state formation.

Lizabeth Zack turns her attention to the centralized state par excellence – France – and argues that even there, the state's monopoly of coercive force was nowhere near monolithic. In the nineteenth century the French state required municipalities to pay for part of the costs of the police, opening the door to some degree of local control over these forces. The Gendarmerie, or rural police, controlled by the military, competed to some extent with the urban police, under the control of the Ministry of the Interior. The railroad police added to this picture of divided loyalties, overlapping jurisdictions, and the struggle between local and national control. Even Paris, often considered part and parcel of the national center, had considerable autonomy from national ministers in deploying its police force.

The systematic centralization of the police force was attempted but not achieved during the Third Republic. Only with the creation of the Vichy regime in 1941 was a national police force for cities of 10,000 people or more established. While managers of the national state wanted central

control of police forces because of their fear of strikes, crime, political
protest, and recalcitrant local authorities, such central control was in practice difficult to achieve even in France, because of both the costs of central
control and the continued interest of local power holders in retaining their
own control over the police. Even where central control was achieved, it
proved reversible: some cities in France have recently established their own
municipal police forces because, they argue, the national police are not
effective. It seems, concludes Zack, "that we can start writing the next
chapter on the ever elusive monopoly of the means of coercion."

The Vichy regime exercised semisovereignty over not just France itself
but the French colonies of Indochina, a situation that Anne Raffin examines. Comparing the Vichy regime's promotion of paramilitary and sporting youth groups in both France and Indochina, Raffin shows how the same
impulse – to inculcate conservative and patriotic feelings in youth, and
channel these toward support of the regime – led to different political
outcomes. In France, the influence of these groups proved to be rather
ephemeral, as the postwar regime demilitarized the state and restored a
republican ideology that had little need for the "virilizing" and patriotic
activities of the youth groups. In the countries that formed out of French
Indochina, however (Cambodia, Laos, and Vietnam), postwar political
leaders reconfigured Vichyist recreational and sporting groups for youth
into pillars of support for their own militaristic projects. These groups and
their activities were thus part of two very different paths of state
formation.

William Reno also identifies distinctive paths of state formation in his
contribution to this book. Like Miguel Centeno, whose chapter was discussed earlier, Reno takes Charles Tilly's analysis of Europe as his point of
departure. Reno concedes Tilly's point, made in the final chapter of
Coercion, Capital, and European States (1992), that the international
alliances of the Cold War enabled the rulers of West African states to fend
off external threats. However, he adds that those rulers mainly feared coups,
insurrections, and other internal threats to their personal safety rather than
foreign invasion. Because their own militaries were the prime suspects for
attempted coups, they divided their militaries and built patronage networks
to ensure political loyalty. Strongmen within patronage networks recruited
military personnel and marginalized youths for "muscle," eventually splitting the state's coercive forces into essentially private, rival armies. These
private armies took over several West African countries in the 1980s and
1990s. For Reno, unlike for Tilly, the end of the Cold War was not a pivotal
event for West Africa. Warlordism and the collapse of the state in the region
were primarily internal phenomena, developing over a considerable period
of time and only indirectly linked to other, more global transformations.

This account, like the one about Latin America offered by Miguel
Centeno, therefore questions the applicability of some aspects of the

European experience to states in the postcolonial world. Largely due to the different relationships between classes and ethnic groups in Latin America and West Africa, state formation in these two regions did not result in the "virtuous circle" found in Europe, where war-making led the state to demand revenue and soldiers from its citizens, who in turn extracted rights to representation and citizenship from the state. In contrast, war-making did not lead to mass democracies and the welfare state in Latin America or West Africa, but rather weak states presiding over segmented societies in the first case, and collapsed states and warlordism in the second. Such findings demand that we turn our attention back to Europe itself and the way that postcolonial states are analyzed. Perhaps we should no longer be asking why state formation in postcolonial countries does not match the stylized facts of the large European countries, but why European state formation itself appears to be so unique and nonreproducible in the "developing" world.

Ian Roxborough rounds out this volume with an incisive analysis of civil-military relations in the contemporary United States. Roxborough argues that the greatest danger to civil-military relations is not dissensus between military and civilian values but a stifling consensus that has foreclosed strategic options that should remain open to the United States. While Roxborough acknowledges that a gap between military and civilian values and political orientations has developed, he argues that this will only cause problems for civilian political control over the military if the military whole-heartedly adopts so-called Fourth Generation strategic doctrine (a doctrine based on a view of war not unlike that of Martin van Creveld) as its vision of future war. Such doctrines are not mainstream and are likely to remain marginal in the short term, because the Bush administration's massive increase in military spending in 2002–2003 effectively foreclosed a fundamental reform of the armed forces. Instead, a preference for "standoff precision strike" or "fire-and-forget" warfare is dominant among the officer corps.

Such warfare, used to devastating effect in the Gulf War, Yugoslavia, and Afghanistan, is troubling for many reasons. First, as Roxborough persuasively argues, in trying to solve complex political problems by applying overwhelming force, it will often be politically ineffective. There is likely to be a mismatch between the military instruments used in such conflicts and the political goals for which they are used, so that massive destruction and casualties will produce relatively minor shifts in the political situation on the ground, thus returning political leaders to the need for the negotiation of complicated political settlements, often made much more difficult by the prior devastation. For example, it is unclear to what extent the U.S. campaign in Afghanistan has reduced its citizens' vulnerability to terrorist attacks, or whether such a war can in fact achieve such a goal, given the clandestine, decentralized, and transnational nature of terrorist networks.

There is another problematic aspect of such warfare, hinted at by Roxborough. The U.S. military seems to have learned from Vietnam that it should only be committed when it has overwhelming superiority, and its deployment in the Gulf War – and again in Yugoslavia and Afghanistan – seems to have convinced many that U.S. military power can be effectively used with only a minimal loss of life on its side. Consequently, there is a serious danger that the massive bombing that is part of fire-and-forget warfare could be conducted for relatively trivial reasons, because it is almost costless for U.S. politicians worried only about domestic constitutents.[8] As Roxborough writes, today's strikes against "rogue" or uncooperative states by the United States are comparable with Rome's expeditions against rebellious parts of its empire: they are punitive and exemplary, designed to keep other states in line.

Such warfare is morally troubling.[9] If war does have ennobling qualities, and many claim that it does, one of the most important of those involve soldiers' willingness to die for their cause, to make "the ultimate sacrifice" for what they and their brothers in arms believe. Providing a reason for soldiers to fight has always been an important role for military officers, and belief in the rightness of a cause has often contributed to numerically or technologically inferior forces outperforming objectively superior forces in battle. However, high-tech precision bombing can be conducted without the moral seriousness of more traditional forms of warfare, because invulnerability to large-scale casualties is almost guaranteed as long as "ground troops" are not deployed or only deployed after enemy forces have been virtually destroyed.[10] In the country conducting the bombing, war becomes one more in a plethora of televised sporting events. In 1991 and 1999, while the entire infrastructures of recalcitrant countries (Iraq and Yugoslavia) were laid to waste, the mass public of the United States was barely aware that it was at war, and certainly not intensely involved in discussions about the soundness of the policies that had led to the bombing.[11] Such warfare seems potentially corrupting to the country that engages in it; if moral reasons are insufficient, it might also be added that continued bombing of a variety of enemies in this fashion could sow the seeds for future acts of terrorism similar to those that took place in the United States on September 11, 2001.[12]

Roxborough persuasively argues that the emergence of this style of warfare is due to a "Moltkean" bargain between civilian politicians and military leaders, in which civilians retain the right to decide whether to go to war but subsequently cede to the military all important decisions about the war's conduct once the war begins. Even though President Harry S. Truman defied such a division of labor when he dismissed General Douglas MacArthur during the Korean War (MacArthur argued for just such discretion, advocated by Moltke, to prosecute the war on his terms without interference from civilian politicians), it has reappeared in the wake of the military's debacle in Vietnam and now seems firmly entrenched in Washington.

The solution, for Roxborough, lies in dissolving the presumed distinction between "military" and "political" decisions (like Susan Browne, he finds the Huntingtonian distinction artificial and unconvincing) and forcing political and military leaders to collectively and searchingly discuss the proper use of U.S. military force. The military's a priori veto of any use of force that does not conform to the "Powell Doctrine" (there should be an overwhelming superiority of force on the U.S. side before troops are committed, as well as clear objectives, strong civilian support, and a predefined exit strategy) should be rejected, for as long as it is accepted, genuine civilian control of the military does not exist. Unless this occurs, the United States is likely to possess armed forces that are very strange indeed, and perhaps unprecedented in history: the most expensive, technologically sophisticated military in the world, overwhelmingly ahead of all its potential adversaries, but one that will not be used in most situations if more than a handful of its troops might be killed.

Goodbye to All That?

The authors of this volume have attempted to chart changes in the composition, activity, and conflicts of armed forces, adducing the causes of specific outbreaks of violence, and the role of armed force in the creation of different kinds of states. In order to do this effectively, they have broadened the focus of traditional civil-military relations and looked beyond uniformed, conventional forces specializing in the external defense of a national state. It is significant that of the twelve chapters presented here, only four of them (those by Tilly, Centeno, Ikegami, and Roxborough) focus primarily on regular armed forces. The rest deal almost exclusively either with the police (Kalmanowiecki and Zack), or irregular forces such as paramilitary groups, guerrillas, and brigands (Batalas, Romero, Raffin), and even groups that derive their power from the past use of arms and are not usually thought of as armed forces at all – veterans (Campbell, Bensel, and Browne). These case studies, spanning four continents and a 600-year period between the sixteenth and twenty-first centuries, alert us to the fact that irregular armed forces often shape the trajectory of states as much as, and sometimes more than, their conventional counterparts. Such forces are also particularly important in the development of states outside Europe, and may become increasingly significant everywhere.

The study of armed forces and state formation is not simply a clinical exercise. It reveals the violence and brutality embedded in many human interactions, and engenders in many of us the understandable hope for perpetual peace. Nevertheless, there are good reasons to believe that coercion and violence will remain an intrinsic, important, and unavoidable aspect of human affairs. Peace and voluntary cooperation between people will always be difficult; never, in specific instances, impossible; and probably always unattainable in universal terms. Therefore, studying armed forces and their role in politics and state formation in an analytical fashion, without glorifying fighting and war, should continue to be an important intellectual activity for a long time to come. The challenge, which has only been begun by the authors of this volume, is to chart changes in the composition, activity, and conflicts of armed forces, adducing the causes of specific outbreaks of violence, and the role of armed force in the creation of different kinds of states. A better knowledge of various uses of coercion in the past should lead us to a clearer understanding of the world's present political condition, because, as Miguel Centeno argues in this volume, we are how we fight, and what we choose to fight about is a good indicator of our deepest values, fears, and aspirations. In addition, such studies might help illuminate and even shape possible global futures, helping the most violent excesses of armed forces to be curbed, and the outbreak or at least the continuation of the most damaging wars prevented. The twentieth century was the most violent in human history, with two world wars, the dropping of the atom bomb, and scores of lesser but equally destructive and bloody conflicts. There is no intrinsic reason why the twenty-first century must repeat that tragic pattern.

Notes

1. The total number of wars since 1945 is higher than this, as van Creveld's book was published in 1991. Since then, there have been wars between, for example, a U.S.-led alliance and Iraq (1991); the Russian military and Chechen separatists (1994–present); Peru and Ecuador (1995); India and Pakistan (1999); Ethiopia and Eritrea (1999); NATO and Yugoslavia (1999); and the U.S. and Taliban and Al Qaeda forces in Afghanistan (2001–2002), as well as multiple "internal" conflicts, including those in Afghanistan, Angola, Sudan, Liberia, Sierra Leone, Guinea-Bissau, Congo, the Republic of Congo, Somalia, Colombia, East Timor, Georgia, Sri Lanka, India, southern Lebanon, and Chiapas in Mexico, many of these ongoing.
2. For similar conclusions, see Alexander 1999.
3. From Kohn 1987: 57, 459. Although Clausewitz (born in 1780) died in 1831, his influence was perhaps at its height from the period between the Franco-Prussian War of 1870–1871 and World War I of 1914–1918. Ibid., 165–166.
4. For example, it could be argued that NATO's bombing of Yugoslavia in 1999 achieved its political aims partly because the irregular Albanian guerrilla organization, the Kosovan Liberation Army, engaged Serbian troops and induced the Serbian leadership to concentrate its forces, where they became more vulnerable targets for bombing. Consequently, the action is not such a clear triumph of what Ian Roxborough in this volume calls "standoff precision strike warfare" but rather represents a combination of it with guerrilla warfare. This

combination of high-tech bombing by conventional forces and irregular, proxy "ground troops" appeared again in the U.S. war in Afghanistan in 2001–2002.

5. Van Creveld also writes persuasively about the causes of war, asserting that war is not solely a means to an end but is also valued in itself by many people; war "is life written large" and "alone permits and demands the commitment of *all* man's faculties, the highest as well as the lowest" (van Creveld 1991: 226–227). Therefore, "eternal peace is a dream. Given the price that we would have to pay, perhaps it is not even a beautiful dream" (van Creveld 1991: 221). The author then comes close to glorifying war by asserting that it can give its participants "joy, freedom, happiness, even delirium and ecstasy" (van Creveld 1991: 227). This sits rather uneasily with the book's dedication to his children, "may they never have to fight."

6. In a different way, Barrington Moore attempted to show the role of violence in the formation of modern democracies such as Britain and France (focusing not on their involvement in total wars, but on their revolutions of the seventeenth and eighteenth centuries respectively), thus undercutting liberals' condemnation of twentieth-century communist revolutions as morally inferior to Western paths of state formation.

7. These fluid relations between "bandits" and enforcers of law and order also existed in late nineteenth- and early twentieth-century Mexico, as described by Vanderwood 1981.

8. This criticism does not apply to the U.S. war in Afghanistan, which was a response to an attack more serious than that of the Japanese on Pearl Harbor in 1941. Even in the case of the Afghan war, however, the U.S. military's style of warfare may impose serious constraints on the eventual political effectiveness of armed action and raises moral questions about the casualties of bombing, even when those casualties were killed or wounded unintentionally.

9. The moral ambiguity of this form of warfare is exacerbated by the fact that conscription was eliminated after the Vietnam War, and the enlisted personnel in the military are drawn overwhelmingly from the ranks of the poor and ethnic minorities.

10. The very use of the term "ground troops," a fairly recent neologism to denote the infantry, reveals the primacy of the air war and the new doctrine of "fire-and-forget" warfare.

11. In the Yugoslav war, NATO forces bombed Yugoslavia for seventy-eight days from March 24 to June 9, 1999 without losing one of their personnel. The bombing, dubbed Operation Allied Force by its planners, reached the level of 250 sorties a day at its peak. This killed an estimated 2,000 civilians, while 10,000 Serbian soldiers and policemen were thought to have been killed or wounded. In addition, the damage to factories, refineries, power plants, railroads, airports, bridges, roads, and other infrastructure was estimated at $100 million, without taking into account houses and the environmental cost of such destruction. (Some of this data are from "OTAN-Yugoslavia Firmaron Pacto de Paz para Kosovo," *El Mercurio* [Santiago, Chile], June 10, 1999, A1 and A10.) The bombing probably also greatly accelerated the outflow of refugees from Kosovo, although this is disputed.

12. I am not here arguing that NATO's 1999 war against Yugoslavia was undertaken for trivial reasons. Quite the contrary, the justification for the war was

that Serbian forces in the Yugoslav province of Kosovo were undertaking ethnic cleansing on a scale not seen since World War II. However, the rhetoric about these human rights abuses was exaggerated, as when commentators made the comparison between the holocaust and the treatment of the Kosovar Albanians. While the war was undertaken in the name of a morally substantial cause, the apparently low cost (in terms of lives lost among the aggressive party's forces) of such endeavors, combined with the ubiquity of human rights abuses in whose name such wars could be waged, raises the specter of an almost limitless series of punitive strikes against enemies. Perhaps the August 1998 bombing of a Sudanese pharmaceutical factory by the United States (whose justification, that the factory was making chemical weapons, was never proved) is a better example of the danger of the trivialization and banalization of this kind of warfare.

References

Alexander, John B. 1999. *Future War*. New York: St. Martin's.

Bayley, David H. 1985. *Patterns of Policing: A Comparative International Analysis*. New Brunswick: Rutgers University Press.

Desch, Michael. 1996. "War and Strong States, Peace and Weak States?" *International Organization* 50, 2: 237–268.

Diamond, Larry, and Marc F. Plattner. 1996. *Civil-Military Relations and Democracy*. Baltimore: Johns Hopkins University Press.

Evans, Peter. 1997. "The Eclipse of the State? Reflections on Stateness in an Era of Globalization," *World Politics* 50 (October): 62–87.

Foweraker, Joe, and Todd Landman. 1997. *Citizenship Rights and Social Movements: A Comparative and Statistical Analysis*. Oxford: Oxford University Press.

Kohn, George C. 1987. *Dictionary of Wars*. Garden City, N.Y.: Anchor Books.

Leys, Colin. 1996. "The Crisis in 'Development Theory,'" *New Political Economy* 1, 1: 41–58.

Loveman, Brian. 1993. *The Constitution of Tyranny: Regimes of Exception in Spanish America*. Pittsburgh: University of Pittsburgh Press.

1999. *For La Patria: Politics and the Armed Forces in Latin America*. Wilmington, Del.: Scholarly Resources.

Mann, Michael. 1997. "Has Globalization Ended the Rise and Rise of the Nation State?" *Review of International Political Economy* 4, 3: 472–496.

Moore, Barrington. 1966. *Social Origins of Dictatorship and Democracy*. Boston: Beacon Press.

Pereira, Anthony. 1998a. "Persecution and Farce: The Origins and Transformation of Brazil's Political Trials, 1964–79," *Latin American Research Review* 33, 1: 43–66.

1998b. "O Monstro Algemado? Violência do Estado e Repressão Legal no Brasil, 1964–1997," in Jorge Zaverucha, ed. *Democracia e Instituições Políticas Brasileiras no Final do Século Vinte*, 13–61. Recife: Bargaço.

Przeworski, Adam, and Fernando Limongi. 1997. "Modernization: Theories and Facts," *World Politics* 49 (January): 155–183.

Ricks, Thomas. 1997. *Making the Corps*. New York: Scribner.

Schirmer, Jennifer. 1998. *The Guatemalan Military Project: A Violence Called Democracy.* Philadelphia: University of Pennsylvania Press.

Sennett, Richard. 1997. "The New Capitalism," *Social Research* 64, 2: 161–180.

Strange, Susan. 1995. "The Defective State," *Daedalus* 124, 2: 55–72.

Tilly, Charles. 1992. *Coercion, Capital, and European States, AD 990–1992.* Cambridge, Mass.: Blackwell.

van Creveld, Martin. 1991. *On Future War.* London: Brassey's.

Vanderwood, Paul J. 1981. *Disorder and Progress: Bandits, Police, and Mexican Development.* Lincoln: University of Nebraska Press.

Zakaria, Fareed. 1997. "The Rise of Illiberal Democracy," *Foreign Affairs* 76, 6: 22–43.

Index

absolutist state, 99
ACCU, *see* Colombia, paramilitaries
ACLU (American Civil Liberties Union),
110
Acuña, Carlos, 11
Adams, John, 237, 249
Adams, Nina, 318
Adams, Samuel, 237, 241, 246
Afghan campaign, 346, 349, 351, 356,
357–359, 378, 380
Afghanistan, 351, 356, 357–359 390, 393,
394, 401, 402, 404 n. 1
Afghanistan War, 28, 393, 401, 402
Africa, 85, 388, 390, 393, 400, 401;
see also Algeria; Burundi; Liberia;
Nigeria; Rwanda; Sierra Leone;
Somalia
warlords in, 322–342, 394
West Africa, 400, 401
Ageron, Charles-Robert, 304
Aguero, Felipe, 11
Al Qaeda, 393, 404 n. 1
Albright, Madeline, 373
Alexander, John Christos, 170 n. 7,
171 n. 11
Algeria, 293, 295
Algiers, 288, 291–294
American Civil War, *see* United States, Civil
War
American exceptionalism, 111
American Legion, 109–110, 111–113, 396
American way of war, 347, 351, 356–360,
379
anarchism, 215–217, 222
Anderson, Benedict, 90, 314

Annapolis convention, 247, 248
anticolonialism, 303, 309
anticommunism, 111
antiradicalism, 109–110, 111
Arato, Andrew, 17
Arendt, Hannah, 15
Argentina, 85, 87, 92, 94
anarchism in, 215–217, 222
armed forces, 94, 210, 219, 222–223
dirty war, 399
police forces, 209–224, 399
armed forces, 3, 4, 387–395, 397, 398,
399, 403, 404; *see also* army; irregular
armed forces; soldiers
armed citizens' groups, 178, 198, 245
private armed groups, 329–331, 334–
339
reconceptualization of, 7–9, 28–29
Armstrong, Major John, Jr., 243
army, 4; *see also* armed forces; soldiers
in France, 305, 391, 393
in Indochina, 308
intelligence, 218–219
in Japan, 129–132
standing army, 129, 238, 399
supply, 238, 239, 240
U.S. Army, 348, 350, 351, 367, 398, 399
Asia, 391, 397; *see also* Cambodia; China;
Japan; Laos; North Korea; North
Vietnam; Thailand; Vietnam
Articles of Confederation, 234, 245, 247,
250
asymmetric response, 352, 371–373
AUC (Autodefensas Unidas de Colombia),
397; *see also* Colombia; paramilitaries

409